The South Bend Blue Sox

The South Bend Blue Sox

*A History of the All-American Girls
Professional Baseball League Team
and Its Players, 1943–1954*

JIM SARGENT and
ROBERT M. GORMAN

Forewords by Betsy Jochum, Sue Kidd and Jean Faut

McFarland & Company, Inc., Publishers
Jefferson, North Carolina, and London

LIBRARY OF CONGRESS CATALOGUING-IN-PUBLICATION DATA

Sargent, Jim, 1941–
The South Bend Blue Sox : a history of the all-American girls professional baseball league team and its players, 1943–1954 / Jim Sargent and Robert M. Gorman ; forwords by Betsy Jochum, Sue Kidd and Jean Faut.
p.   cm.

Includes bibliographical references and index.

ISBN 978-0-7864-4647-6
softcover : acid free paper ∞

1. South Bend Blue Sox (Baseball team)—History. 2. All-American Girls Professional Baseball League. 3. Baseball for women—United States—History. 4. Women baseball players—United States—History. 5. Baseball—Indiana—South Bend—History. I. Gorman, Robert M., 1949–
GV875.S62S37 2012   796.357'640977289—dc23   2011042981

British Library cataloguing data are available

© 2012 Jim Sargent and Robert M. Gorman. All rights reserved

No part of this book may be reproduced or transmitted in any form or by any means, electronic or mechanical, including photocopying or recording, or by any information storage and retrieval system, without permission in writing from the publisher.

On the cover: The 1949 South Bend Blue Sox (back row, left to right) Bonnie Baker, Jeep Stoll, Jean Faut, Shoo-Shoo Wirth, Rita Briggs, Shirley Stovroff, Helen Filarski, Betty Whiting, and Betty Wagoner; (front row) chaperone Marge Stefani, Lil Faralla, Norma Metrolis, Josephine Hasham, Marge Callaghan, Dolly Niemiec, Jaynie Krick, Dolores Mueller, Lou Arnold, and manager Dave Bancroft (Louise Pettus Archives and Special Collections, Winthrop University)

Manufactured in the United States of America

McFarland & Company, Inc., Publishers
Box 611, Jefferson, North Carolina 28640
www.mcfarlandpub.com

To the remarkable women who made the league come alive and who became heroines to countless baseball fans. Your example lives on.

Table of Contents

Forewords by Three South Bend Blue Sox (Betsy Jochum, Sue Kidd, Jean Faut)   1
Preface   5
Introduction   9

1. The Blue Sox and the All-American League: 1943   11
2. South Bend's Second Winning Season: 1944   31
3. The Last Wartime Season: 1945   52
4. Making the Playoffs in the First Postwar Season: 1946   72
5. Havana Adventure, Sidearm Pitching, and the Playoffs Again: 1947   94
6. Overhand Pitching and the Ten-Team League: 1948   117
7. The Blue Sox and the Peaches Win the Pennant: 1949   137
8. The League Crisis and Fifth Place: 1950   157
9. South Bend Wins the Shaughnessy Championship: 1951   177
10. Champions Again — The Beautiful Dozen: 1952   200
11. The Blue Sox and the League Struggle: 1953   220
12. The Blue Sox and the Final Innings: 1954   239

Appendix: South Bend Roster, 1943–1954   261
Chapter Notes   263
Bibliography   285
Index   287

Forewords by Three South Bend Blue Sox

Betsy Jochum, 1943–1948

I was one of the original people who tried out and played in our league the first year. In 1943, P.K. Wrigley sent a scout to Cincinnati to hold tryouts for his professional league for women. We were sent to Wrigley Field in Chicago for the final trials. We stayed at the Belmont Hotel, all expenses paid. I was selected to play on the South Bend team. Needless to say, it was the thrill of a lifetime to actually try out on Wrigley Field!

In 1947, the entire league had spring training in Havana, Cuba. That was my first plane trip, a beautiful trip flying over the ocean. We practiced and played in the Gran Stadium. We received more publicity than the Brooklyn Dodgers, who trained earlier in Havana. I remember Grantland Rice, well known at that time for his movie shorts that were often played after feature films in theaters all over the United States. He took pictures of all the teams coming down a huge staircase in front of the University of Havana. While there, we enjoyed many huge stacked ham sandwiches at Sloppy Joe's. We also enjoyed the best coconut ice cream and fresh fruit that was sold by street vendors. The taxicab rides to the ball park every day were wild. Beeping your horn first at the intersection gave you the right of way!

We finally got our own chartered bus in 1946. No air conditioning, but it was better than riding those trains and lugging your own suitcase from one train to another on our wartime road trips. Who could forget our barnstorming trips throughout the South after spring training? Ride the bus, play ball, ride the bus, play again, every day for a week before returning to the Midwest.

In 1983, I donated my uniform, spikes, cap, and glove to the Smithsonian Museum in Washington, DC. Later, in October of 2004, I received an invitation to be part of the grand opening of the exhibition of "Sports, Breaking Records, Breaking Barriers," and 450 people attended. It was the highlight of my life to be there in that huge rotunda with the images reflecting on the ceiling, seeing the old-fashioned popcorn carts and cotton candy stands that were scattered along the walls. Elite stars like Bill Russell were there. He gave a very inspiring speech to everyone. It was the first time I saw the display of my uniform and some nice remarks in print about my baseball career. They gave each of us a small book filled with pictures of all the stars, old and new, and their donations—and me too, with my Blue Sox uniform. I was on the same page with the Harlem Globetrotters and Billie Jean King.

What a thrill, "Sockum Jochum" in with all the well-known sports figures! After the grand opening, the exhibition was sent on a two-year tour all over the nation. In 2005 and 2006, I went to the showing in Grand Rapids, Michigan, at the Gerald Ford Museum and marveled again at the display with some of our ballplayers. What fun that was!

In 1988, there was the unforgettable opening of our display at the National Baseball Hall of Fame in Cooperstown, New York, and the commemoration of our league and the roster of everyone who played in the AAGPBL. Later, another memorable moment took place in Cooperstown when the Hall of Fame unveiled a statue of a player, no one in particular, outside in the courtyard. It was quite impressive to be there and see the ceremony.

In 1992, I went to Evansville, Indiana, to see the movie, *A League of Their Own,* being filmed and produced by Penny Marshall. I met all the stars, and they were very gracious toward us. It was very interesting to watch the movie being made and see the styles of dress from that era. Men and women actually wore hats to our games. The men wore straw hats or felt hats, but no baseball caps. Old cars from that time were parked outside of the ballpark. Red, white, and blue banners were draped all over the park. It was really something to see how the movie people went back to the 1940s. We waited in line for hours early one morning to be part of the costumed people in the stands, but they ran out of costumes by the time our line reached the entrance. We watched the filming, out of view of the cameras, and we ate in the tented food area, along with the stars.

I would also like to say we had the best "true blue" fans in South Bend. They had an outstanding group of people, the Ushers Club, who worked at all of our games. We also had the most faithful fans who sat behind our dugout and watched us play and slide in the cinders at home plate. At our new field in 1946, Playland Park, there was a car racetrack — a cinder track. Home plate was in the cinder area, and it was pretty "Ouchy" to slide in that stuff with our short skirts. In spite of that, I liked our uniforms.

Our AAGPBL archive is very well preserved at South Bend's Center for History, which has many displays of our league in our own special space. The University of Notre Dame also has some of our memorabilia stored in the Special Collections Department. I often get requests and questions from students who write papers or make displays of our league and enter them into national or state contests. Thanks to *A League of Their Own,* our history became known throughout the nation.

We had the big 50th AAGPBL Reunion in South Bend in 1993. Our committee planned for two years for the event. We came up with the idea of selling watches with our logo on the face, and we made a little money for our Players Association. The Marriott, with the beautiful glass-enclosed atrium, ran out of rooms for us, so some of the guests had to stay at the Holiday Inn down the street. We had 436 people attend our South Bend Reunion. That was a labor of love and gave us such a feeling of well-being to see everyone having a good time together again.

I made many new friends at our AAGPBL Reunions. We have lots of talented members of the Players Association who, bless their hearts, are helping us preserve our legacy. That is important to all of us. We don't want to be forgotten.

How often could the daughter of immigrant parents have all these wonderful experiences and meet so many people from all walks of life, and win silver dollars with my birth date on them for hitting doubles, triples, and home runs? Well, mostly doubles! We proudly formed our "V for Victory" before the games when they played the National Anthem.

I had the time of my life playing in this very unique league of our own. I was getting paid to play a game I loved. It was a lot of work and tiring, especially when you came home to South Bend early in the morning, maybe 5 am, and played that same evening. But I wouldn't trade the experience for anything. If I could, I would do it all over again. The mind is willing, but the body isn't!

You might say that we were pioneers in our field of dreams. I hope we helped make a change in women's sports opportunities. Back in the 1940s, there weren't too many avenues for women. We were among the few fortunate ones.

With much gratitude, I would like to thank the authors of this book for their hours and hours of research and for writing a history about the Blue Sox. They tell of the women's experiences on and off the playing field, and they give an exceptional insight into what it was like to play in our league. I would like to encourage anyone who is interested in women's sports history to read this book and realize what it was like for women to play a professional team sport during the 1940s and 1950s.

Sue Kidd, 1949–1954

As a kid growing up, I played baseball every chance I could. In a small community it was the main recreation. My father managed the team from Choctaw, and as I reached age 12 and up, Dad would sometimes let me play against weaker teams. I always thought I would play pro men's baseball.

In high school in 1949, when I was 15, my guidance counselor got me out of class one day to show me an article in *Life* magazine about the girls' professional baseball league. That was my first knowledge of girls actually playing professionally in their own league.

Later that year in June, two teams came to Little Rock and played two night games. They offered tryouts before the first night game, and my folks took me to try out. Before the night was over, I had signed a contract, and we drove back home to get my clothes ready so that I could leave with the teams after the second night game.

For a 15-year-old traveling without my parents, it was somewhat scary, but exciting, and we were assured that the girls were well-chaperoned. This was the beginning of six of the happiest years of my life. I played on the Sallies' touring team, and we played in some 25 states that summer, seeing sights I could never have imagined, like Yankee Stadium!

In 1950, I went into the main league, played a few weeks with the Peoria Redwings, and I was traded to the South Bend Blue Sox, where I played most of my career, until the league folded at the end of 1954.

Getting to play baseball, and being paid for playing, was the greatest. It opened many doors for me, helping me make the greatest of friends for life. After I finished high school, and grew a little older, I was able to stay in South Bend to get a job and play basketball several more winters through the 1960–1961 season. At that time, I had to keep a promise I made to my dad, that that I would stop playing and go to college.

I could go on about what getting to play in the All-American Girls Baseball League meant to me, and still does. For example, getting to be a small part in the making of the movie *A League of Their Own*, when more people became friends. The movie gave me more opportunities to meet people and do things, and get to talk about it. Although I do not like to speak in public, I have done so many times.

I will forever be grateful, thankful to God for giving me this opportunity, for having parents and family who encouraged and made sure I had the chance when the teams came to our state playing exhibition games.

I shall always be very thankful for the friends I've met, for their support and help for a very backward, bashful, 15-year-old from the hills of Arkansas, over the years, even after the league ended. There was still encouragement to go to college, to become a teacher and a coach from several old AAGPBL friends, and eventually I did accomplish both goals.

I should mention that the icing on the cake was getting to play for the Blue Sox with great players that won league championships in 1951 and 1952. What could be a greater experience!

Last, but certainly not least, it has been wonderful to communicate with Jim Sargent and Bob Gorman, researchers and writers of this great book, which follows the South Bend Blue Sox through all 12 seasons the league was in existence. This is another experience I never would have had except for the interest these two men took in the league and its history. I am thankful for their interest and to know that my name will be mentioned in some chapters of this book.

Jean Faut, 1946–1953

"I love the game of baseball!"

Growing up during the Great Depression, you did not have many choices of what to do in the summer. You played ball, went swimming, read books, or worked at home. We lived off the land. We had a truck, and my father was a hunter and a fisherman. My mother sewed at a local factory.

I was born and raised in the small town of East Greenville, Pennsylvania, and I was the fourth of six children. If I was not helping my mother, it seemed like I always had a ball in my hand, a baseball or a basketball.

Our town of 1,700 people had a men's semiprofessional baseball team in the East Penn League. Every evening they practiced a couple of blocks from my home. At the age of 14, I was there practicing with them. They taught me how to pitch, but usually I was shagging fly balls during batting practice. I did play in a couple of exhibition games with them.

The United States of America entered World War II when I was a senior in high school. Everybody ended up with a war-related job. I worked at a nearby factory that made trousers for men's uniforms.

One day in 1946, I got a phone call from a scout in the All-American Girls Professional Baseball League asking me if I would like to try out. The league planned to expand to eight franchises and was looking for 500 rookies to report for tryouts at Pascagoula, Mississippi, at an abandoned Navy base that had ball fields. It took me two seconds to say, "Yes!" That was the best phone call I have ever received in my life.

The league sent me a train ticket to Pascagoula. After two weeks of playing baseball daily in the hot sun, I was chosen by the South Bend Blue Sox. I spent eight seasons with the Blue Sox, as you will learn by reading this book. I loved all the traveling and playing all the games.

I have never regretted my decision to play professional baseball. I made many friends all over the country, and I enjoyed having many interesting employment opportunities. Also, I enjoy giving speeches about our league. I have received hundreds of autograph requests. Mostly, I thank God for keeping me safe and giving me the strength and talent to be a success. Those eight years of baseball were the most enjoyable times of my life.

I very sincerely want to thank the two baseball historians, Jim Sargent and Bob Gorman, for telling the story of this memorable time in baseball history.

"I still love the game of baseball!"

Preface

Women played professional baseball in the United States at a time when baseball was the national pastime, the sport most widely attended, enjoyed, and revered by the majority of Americans. Women were able to play pro ball as a result of World War II, when females benefited from a variety of opportunities previously reserved for males.

Baseball is a team sport, and this book was a team effort. We wrote a history of one organization, the South Bend Blue Sox, and featured many of the women who competed on that ball club in the All-American Girls Professional Baseball League or, as it was renamed in 1951, the American Girls Baseball League. The *South Bend Tribune* preferred a shorter but more descriptive name, the Girls' Pro League. In any event, we tried to name every player who played even one game in the pastel blue uniform of South Bend's greatest baseball team.

This book details women playing baseball during the 1940s and the early 1950s, and since we are revisiting the standards of those bygone decades, we sometimes refer to the players as "girls," because that term was then widely used to talk about females playing pro sports. In other words, you didn't sit in a ballpark in one of the many league cities and hear spectators yell, "Look at those female athletes!" Actually, the players usually called each other "kids," even though most were skilled ballplayers in their teens or their twenties.

To understand better the history of the Blue Sox and the All-American League, we examined a number of sources, particularly the *South Bend Tribune*, but also other newspapers like the *Rockford Register-Republic*, the *Racine Journal-Times*, the *Kenosha Evening News*, the *Grand Rapids Press*, the *Fort Wayne Journal-Gazette*, and more. We also perused a variety of books that have been written about the league and about women's baseball, and Bob conducted the bulk of the newspaper research. The printed sources are documented in the notes for each chapter.

Regarding newspapers of the era, the reader should know that sportswriters usually had to meet a deadline and often took little or no time to verify information. Therefore, newspaper stories from different papers about the same event may conflict in names or details. Also, editors or writers were not interested in publishing "inside" information during those years. Anyone familiar with journalistic writing prior to the 1960s knows that longtime sportswriters often knew a good deal about players' private lives, but mostly they kept it to themselves. Finally, many former players have indicated that statements they made to reporters appeared in print in a different or garbled form. Thus, readers should be aware that we have attempted to filter through as many contemporary published sources as possible to get at the truth of the matter.

In addition to published sources, we researched materials in the archives that contain holdings for All-American teams and the league, notably the Center for History in South Bend, Indiana, the Joyce Sports Collection of the Hesburgh Libraries of the University of Notre Dame, and the National Baseball Hall of Fame's Library, and again, all such materials are cited in the notes.

When engaged in research and writing, the historian's best friends are archivists and librarians, because they know their collections better than anyone else. While many of them helped our quest, we particularly want to thank George Rugg, curator of the Special Collections Department of the Hesburgh Libraries at Notre Dame; Scott Shuler and Kristen Madden of the Center for History in South Bend; Tim Wiles, Freddy Berowski, and the research staff at the Baseball Hall of Fame Library; Alex Forist at the Grand Rapids (Michigan) Museum; Gordon Olson, now retired, and Larry Halverson at the Grand Rapids Public Library; Jean Town at the Hackley Library in Muskegon, Michigan; Mark Okkonen, an expert on baseball in Muskegon; and Deb Stephenson at the Carnegie-Stout Library in Dubuque.

To our home libraries we owe a special debt. At the Brown Library of Virginia Western Community College, Jim received unfailing assistance from Judy Weller, Faith Janney, and Lynn Hurt, all of whom helped acquire newspapers, articles, or books on interlibrary loan. In Bob's case, Ann Thomas and Jean Wells of the interlibrary loan department at the Dacus Library, Winthrop University, went above and beyond in securing microfilm copies of the *South Bend Tribune* as well as other essential books and articles. Most of the photos used in our book came from the Lib Mahon and Jean Faut Collections held by the Louise Pettus Archives and Special Collections at Winthrop University. Gina White and Andy Johnston were most gracious in allowing us to use these unique resources. Indeed, this project would not have been possible without the assistance of all these dedicated professionals.

In addition, we have benefited from interviews, letters, and e-mails with a number of former All-Americans, but most recently with Jean Faut, Betsy Jochum, and Sue Kidd, because we chose them to represent the three periods of the league. Betsy began playing in the league's inaugural season, and her career bridged the circuit's first stage, going from underhand to sidearm to the first year of overhand pitching in 1948. Jean's career began in 1946, when sidearm pitching appeared, and peaked during the overhand years after 1947. Sue's career was more typical of younger women who played during the 1950s.

During the past several years, the following former players and related persons, listed in alphabetical order, also sent letters or e-mails or were interviewed, mostly by Jim:

Lou Arnold; Chris Ballingall; Wimp Baumgartner; Erma Bergmann; Ruth Born; Wilma Briggs; Dottie (Wiltse) Collins; Mina Costin, the daughter of Jim Costin and a writer for the *Tribune* during the war years; Marge (Villa) Cryan; Jo D'Angelo; Lee (Surkowski) Delmonico; Alice (Pollitt) Deschaine; Anne (Surkowski) Deyotte; Marilyn (Jones) Doxey; Tiby Eisen; Gloria (Cordes) Elliott; Mary (Holda) Elrod; Lil Faralla; Betty Francis; Mary Lou (Graham) Hamilton; Katie Horstman; Marion Hosbein; Fran Janssen; Edie (Perlick) Keating; Vivian Kellogg; Arlene Kotil; Sophie Kurys; Jeneane (Descombes) Lesko; Marie Mahoney; Helen Nordquist; Carolyn Odell, a bat girl during the mid–1940s; Mary (Froning) O'Meara; June Peppas; Pinky Pirok; Mary Pratt; Ellen (Ahrndt) Proefrock; Maxine (Kline) Randall; Beans Risinger; Jenny Romatowski; Lucella (MacLean) Ross; Janet Rumsey; Betty (McFadden) Rusynyk; Doris Sams; Dottie Schroeder; Janet (Wiley) Sears; Helen "Gig" Smith, who first told Jim about the league 16 years ago; Helen (Filarski) Steffes; Betty Trezza; Inez Voyce; Joyce (Hill) Westerman; Dolly (Brumfield) White; Karl Winsch; Mary (Nesbitt) Wisham; and Lois Youngen. Some former players and league personnel provided more information than others, but we appreciate all who were willing to share their memories.

In addition, former professional ballplayers, male or female, like to remember their experiences as largely great and glorious. Stated differently, athletes, like the rest of us, prefer to tell stories about the best times and their most exciting experiences. Former All-Americans, all part of an elite sorority, are frequently reluctant to criticize a teammate or an opponent, no matter how many years have passed. However, when the more outspoken among them did reveal sensitive or personal information, they sometimes did so with the stipulation that they not be quoted directly.

As a result, we have been careful not to quote material that a former player did not want in print. Given that parameter, many individuals provided firsthand information that, taken together with other available resources, offered valuable insights into the lives and times of a league, a team, a player, or an event. Also, when two or more sources who did not know each other still remembered an incident in similar fashion, we concluded the information was worthwhile for use in the book. We have tried our best to assemble useful information and document those sources.

Last but not least, several friends have read the manuscript and offered useful suggestions, and two have read the entire manuscript. Jan Finkel, one of the top editors on SABR's Bio-Project and a retired professor of American literature, offered his valuable experience and suggestions to help correct factual and other errors, and David Hillman, retired as the director of VWCC's library, offered a variety of useful corrections and comments. Also, Jackie Sargent, Jim's sister-in-law and a retired high school American history teacher, commented on several of the early chapters. Merrie Fidler, who has published the best history of the league, and Lily Rhodes Novicki, an adjunct history professor at VWCC, also offered useful insights for several chapters. Our wives, Betty Sargent and Jane Gorman, have lived with this project for more than four years. Betty and Jane have patiently listened so long about the league and the players that they have developed a special expertise of their own, and we thank them.

In fact, we thank all of those who helped us in larger or smaller ways, but any mistakes in the manuscript or the information provided are our responsibility alone.

Our goal was to place the South Bend Blue Sox and the league into the historical perspective of the times. When readers look at the richness of the experiences and the uniqueness of the people involved, we hope they will share our wonder at the accomplishments of the talented heroines of the All-American League. For without these remarkable women, this history of the Blue Sox would not have been possible. So take your favorite seat in the ballpark, and think back to a different time, the so-called golden age of baseball when girls had their own league. The home plate umpire is ready to call, "Play ball!"

Introduction

For more than 600 of the finest female athletes in the United States and Canada, it was a dream come true. For ball fans in the upper Midwest, it was an opportunity to see women professionally play a sport that had until 1943 been the exclusive domain of men. For young girls growing up in World War II and the immediate postwar era, it served as a shining example of how independent-minded women could achieve and prosper in a male-dominated world.

While the All-American Girls Professional Baseball League, as it is known today (the name varied over the league's history), lasted for just a brief moment in time before fading from the nation's memory for decades, it had an impact far beyond the sport of baseball. Indeed, it was a direct challenge to the sexism and the powerful gender barriers that, up until that time, had limited women's opportunities and confined them mostly to subservient roles. Interestingly, few of the women who played in the league saw themselves as social revolutionaries. They simply wanted to play the sport they loved, and get paid to do it to boot. But revolutionaries they were, for never before had women been afforded the opportunity to challenge existing stereotypes on so public a stage.

At one time, baseball was viewed as a sport that was "too strenuous" for women. In 1931, for example, Commissioner Kenesaw Mountain Landis voided the contract that the Class AA Chattanooga Lookouts had extended 17-year-old pitcher Jackie Mitchell on those baseless grounds. The All-American League exploded this sexist canard. While the league started as a modified form of softball, it evolved steadily toward the type of baseball played by men. And the women on the field were every bit as tough and competitive as their male counterparts. They played with a singular determination to win. They fought hard, even with each other. Bench-clearing brawls were not uncommon and umpires were sometimes the victims of physical assaults when disputed calls turned into confrontations. The players ran with abandon, they dove for catches heedless of potential injury, and they slid wearing short skirts, which often resulted in painful "strawberries" on their legs and thighs. Any fan expecting to see a lady-like powder-puff style of play was in for quite a surprise.

The league began in 1943 as the All-American Girls Soft Ball League. It was the brainchild of Philip K. Wrigley, chewing gum magnate and owner of the Chicago Cubs. Wrigley responded in businesslike fashion to the serious concern that Major League Baseball might suspend operations during World War II due to the loss of players to the military. Fearing that their parks would remain empty during the war years, Wrigley and his cohorts organized the league as a way to fill what otherwise would have been empty seats. Women's softball was very popular at the time, they reasoned, so a female pro league that was a hybrid of men's baseball and women's softball should attract fans by the score. They decided that the mid-size cities of the upper Midwest offered the best venues for this endeavor.

There were four teams in that inaugural year: the South Bend Blue Sox, the Rockford Peaches, the Kenosha Comets, and the Racine Belles. Before long, Softball was dropped from the league's name in favor of Baseball. This change was made partly to distinguish the new league from traditional women's softball and partly because pressure was already building to move more toward baseball. The league was popular from the beginning, so much so that by 1948 there were ten teams spread throughout the states of Illinois, Indiana, Michigan, and Wisconsin. At the same time, the game continued to evolve. The ball became smaller and livelier, underhand pitching was abandoned in favor of baseball's overhand style, and the base path and pitching distances were lengthened. As the league began its slow decline in the late 1940s, it took on even more of the trappings of men's baseball, so that by the middle of 1954, the league's last year, the women's game was virtually indistinguishable from men's baseball.

Only two of the teams that began in the 1943 season were still in existence in 1954: the Rockford Peaches and the South Bend Blue Sox. What follows is a history of the league as seen through the experiences of the South Bend franchise, its management and players. Many wonderful women wore the Sox colors. They exemplified the best of their generation in terms of both athletic ability and strength of character. For most, playing ball in South Bend was the first time away from their families of origin. For some, joining the league went against the wishes of their parents, their spouses, or their boyfriends. It was no small feat for these young women (some of them still teenagers) to leave the world they knew to enter an entirely different environment. As intimidating as it may have been at first, nearly all of these women now look back at this time as one of the greatest thrills of their lives. And whether they realized it at the time or not, they were trailblazers who helped pave the way toward greater freedom of choice for the generations of women that followed. The All-Americans were, in every sense of the word, heroines.

• 1 •

The Blue Sox and the All-American League: 1943

"There you have Miss America, 1943. No, she's not a bathing beauty — she's a softball player, and a darn good one, too."— Mina Costin, May 28, 1943[1]

Origins of the All-American Girls Soft Ball League

Once upon a time in America, girls played professional baseball. The unique circuit immortalized by the 1992 movie, *A League of Their Own*, resulted from talented women undertaking nontraditional roles and occupations due to the manpower needs of World War II. When girls such as Betsy Jochum, 20 years old, from Cincinnati, Jean Faut, 16, of East Greenville, Pennsylvania, and Sue Kidd, an eight-year-old in Choctaw, Arkansas, read reports of the destruction inflicted by Japanese naval and air forces at Pearl Harbor on December 7, 1941, they had no idea the war later would offer each of them — as well as hundreds of other young women — the opportunity of a lifetime. The 1942 baseball season saw every major league club and most minor league teams lose players to the war. Before the conflict ended in August 1945, the US armed forces numbered almost 16 million men and women. Organized baseball also enlisted, declaring that the game reflected America's values. "Trotting out capital letters in plenty," wrote historian William Mead, "The Game gloried in its role as The National Pastime, one of the Institutions American Boys were Fighting to Preserve."[2]

President Franklin Roosevelt, like the majority of his countrymen, was a baseball fan. On January 15, 1942, in an oft-quoted letter written to Kenesaw Landis, the Commissioner of Major League Baseball, FDR approved keeping the game going. The home front was gearing up for war, people were working longer hours, and workers needed recreation to take their minds off the war and off their work. The President also encouraged playing more night games in order to benefit war workers on the day shifts.[3] The public agreed, according to a survey by the American Institute of Public Opinion. The Gallup Poll reported that 59 percent of Americans surveyed wanted baseball to continue, 28 percent favored stopping it for the duration, and 13 percent were undecided.[4]

Blessed with the President's support, baseball owners like Philip Wrigley proceeded with the 1942 season, but questions remained. Surely the manpower drain would decrease the quality of athletes available to play for Wrigley's Cubs and other ball clubs. At the bottom of the Great Depression in 1933, total attendance in the major leagues hit an all-time season low of about six million, but for 1940, attendance climbed to nearly ten million. In 1941, despite Joe DiMaggio's 56-game hitting streak and Ted Williams' .406 season, paid admissions slipped to about 9.6 million. In 1942, the war affected baseball, and 8.5 million fans walked through the turnstiles, a decline of nearly one million.[5] The loss of more spectators seemed inevitable for 1943.

Wrigley thought about the wartime changes. Based on material from Ken Beirn in the federal Office of War Information, the Cubs' owner believed the real crunch in manpower would occur in 1943. Given the possibility of Wrigley Field sitting empty while a large number of women's softball leagues were playing a fast-paced game in and around Chicago. the gum magnate devised a plan at once simple and breathtaking. Why not draw from the large talent base of hundreds of thousands of skilled female softball players across the US and Canada to create a professional league to substitute for the men's game throughout the war's duration?[6]

During the fall of 1942, Wrigley authorized Arthur E. Meyerhoff, his main advertising agent, team attorney Paul Harper, and chief scout Jimmy Hamilton to devise a preliminary plan to create what became the All-American Girls Soft Ball League, a loop that could be launched in 1943. Meyerhoff, Harper, and Hamilton were assisted by Cubs general manager Jimmy Gallagher, among others, and Wrigley agreed to invest $100,000, a princely sum in the 1940s. Each of four cities would have to pledge $22,500 to host a team, and Wrigley would match that amount. An innovative sportsman whose business profits after taxes reached $8 million in 1940, he had the interest, the means, and the personnel to create a regional social experiment — and he did. The league's articles of incorporation were filed in February 1943.[7]

Wrigley's associates, thinking of baseball, devised a league of modified fast-pitch softball for women, but with key differences. First, the All-American Girls Soft Ball League would operate on a nonprofit basis and be supervised by three trustees, namely, Wrigley, Harper, and Branch Rickey, the general manager of the Brooklyn Dodgers. Second, the league would hold tryouts, select the best candidates, and allocate players to teams. Third, players would sign contracts with the league, not teams. Also, Wrigley and his staff would recruit former big leaguers as managers, boosting the league's fan appeal. On the field, the circuit would use underhand pitching and the 12-inch circumference ball used in softball, but hit it with Louisville Slugger baseball bats. The rules were revised to use nine players, not softball's ten; to allow base runners to lead off and steal; to set the base paths at 65 feet, not 60, and the pitching distance at 40 feet, not 35; and to let pitchers start with one foot on the pitching rubber, not both.[8]

The league was an ongoing social experiment. The name changed over the years, and so did the rules and the game on the diamond. As author Barbara Gregorich explained, Wrigley and his associates used their beliefs — and the beliefs of most Americans — about baseball being a masculine pastime, not a gender-neutral one, where good women ballplayers had to balance their athletic skills with behavior that society considered feminine.[9] The idea worked: a game graced with "skill and femininity" following the basic concepts of baseball while pointing the way toward baseball. Historian Susan M. Cahn concluded that Wrigley and Meyerhoff had good instincts: "In this way the league would try to establish itself as a cut above women's softball, avoiding its mannish image and reputation for rougher, tougher players with less audience appeal."[10]

Betsy Jochum — Classic Softball Player

Because of her talent and skill in softball, Betsy Jochum was one of more than a dozen female athletes invited to a tryout on Saturday, April 18, 1943, at Turkey Ridge Field on

Cincinnati's Eastern Avenue. Scout Jack Sheehan, director of the Cubs' farm system and organizer of many All-American tryouts across the Midwest, watched the girls hit, run and slide under chilly conditions. Afterward, Sheehan selected six girls, including Jochum, an outfielder; Dorothy Kamenshek, a first sacker; and catcher Marion Wohlwender. Sheehan asked them to attend final tryouts at Wrigley Field in mid–May.[11] Excited, Jochum signed and mailed back her contract.[12]

Women like Jochum read about the All-American League when the *Cincinnati Enquirer*— along with many other newspapers around the country — carried a story explaining the "Girls' League." League president Ken Sells said the women would sign contracts like those of the Actors Equity Association, meaning players had an option for renewal, but they were not bound to one team in perpetuity by a "reserve clause."[13] However, as later events would show, having the All-Americans contract with the league instead of a team had the same result: players were not free agents, so they had little bargaining power over salaries and trades. Still, the loop needed to market the game to fans. Explained Sells: "We're going to rewrite the rules entirely, cut the number of players on a team from ten to nine and dress the girls in swank outfits either of the type worn by ice skaters or women tennis players. They'll come in pastel shades for our teams."[14]

On Sunday, May 16, when Jochum and the other prospects rode the streamliner *James Whitcomb Riley* to Chicago for tryouts at Wrigley Field, Betsy reflected on the good fortune leading to her once-in-a-lifetime opportunity. Born and raised in Cincinnati along with her older brother Nick and her younger sister Frances, she grew up in a working-class family with her parents' newly-learned American values. At age eight or nine, she started playing ball.

A classic personification of the league's athlete, Jochum was modest, bright, and talented. She studied at Hughes High and played the sports available to girls. After graduation in 1939, she attended business school and learned to use the comptometer, a calculating machine. Jochum came of age in the Great Depression, when jobs were hard to find. She also loved to play ball, so she combined her passion for sports with a job, working and playing on the H.H. Meyer softball team.[15] Betsy was playing semipro ball and earning $16 a week when Jack Sheehan offered a contract for $50 per week to join the new girls' league. Like many young women with her skills, she jumped at the chance to be a professional ballplayer.

From Chicago to South Bend

Baseball was not integrated before 1947, and founders of the All-American League adhered to the accepted social norms of the era.[16] Jochum and more than 200 other white softball stars from 26 states and five Canadian provinces arrived in Chicago, checked into the Belmont Hotel, and walked three blocks to Wrigley Field for the tryouts that began on Friday, May 17. The competition was intense because just 60 players would be chosen for the four teams to be located in Racine and Kenosha, Wisconsin; South Bend, Indiana; and Rockford, Illinois. League officials could use Wrigley's facilities because the Cubs left for an "Eastern swing," starting in Cincinnati on May 7 and ending on May 23. But rainy weather limited the outdoor workouts, forcing the girls to do most batting and fielding drills under the stands.[17]

The players also attended two-hour evening sessions at the Belmont for the "Charm

School" hosted by Helena Rubenstein, owner of a chain of popular beauty salons. Girls received loose-leaf binders, titled "Notes of a Star to Be." The charm school plan, dreamed up by Meyerhoff, allowed Rubenstein's staff to show ballplayers how to sit, eat, arise properly, apply make-up, and display good manners. According to the guide, "The All American girl is truly all American in every respect — a fine specimen of physical fitness, neat, cultured and attractive, adept at the arts, often capable at dancing, swimming, drawing, writing, homemaking and career work."[18]

Appearances were important. Wrigley and Meyerhoff wanted female athletes to display beauty, femininity, and grace combined with intelligence, athleticism, and skill. They believed the league could not win public support without projecting an "All-American girl" image. Teams planned to use chaperones to enforce rules, and players were given conduct guidelines, including wearing feminine attire when not engaged in practices and games; avoiding smoking and drinking in public; and letting chaperones approve of social engagements, living quarters, and eating places. Newspaper and magazine stories called the girls' circuit the "Glamour League," and it was.[19]

On Tuesday, May 25, after ten days of workouts, president Ken Sells, managers Josh Billings, Johnny Gottselig, Eddie Stumpf, and Bert Niehoff, and other officials met in an office at Wrigley Field to allocate ballplayers. The pilots did not yet know the identity of their own teams, so they could not load up with talent.[20] At the Belmont on Wednesday morning, players saw the names of 60 finalists and their teams. For some, seeing their names posted meant a dream come true. Sophie Kurys, an infielder from Flint, Michigan, who became one of the league's top stars, reflected in 1996 about the thrill of seeing her name on the chalkboard, but she added, "Racine? God, where's Racine?" Like many others, she had never heard of Racine.[21]

Regardless, people in the four league cities welcomed the new diamond stars later that day. In South Bend, Mayor Jesse L. Pavey and other officials rolled out the red carpet at city hall for Bert Niehoff, the Denver native, former National League second baseman, and manager of the Blue Sox. They also greeted chaperone Rose Virginia Way and the 15 players arriving from Chicago on the old South Shore Elevated, or El. After the ceremony, civic leaders and the girls enjoyed a luncheon. Later, players were escorted to homes where they would room, and they learned about their new outfits. Jochum, whose uniform is displayed at the Smithsonian, explained that the outfit was powder blue, and that the cap, belt, satin shorts, and socks were royal blue.[22]

League officials had created the design: a pastel-colored, one-piece, flared-skirt uniform with contrasting cap, satin shorts, knee-

Blue Sox Original Insignia — This insignia, with gold letters and gold background in the center, and royal blue background for the letters and the emblem in the center, appeared on the front of Blue Sox uniforms from the inaugural season of 1943 through the 1950 season (courtesy of the Louise Pettus Archives and Special Collections, Winthrop University).

length stirrup socks, and belt. The Kenosha Comets wore a light green uniform with caps, shorts, socks, and belt of dark green. The Racine Belles sported a light yellow outfit, with brown caps, shorts, socks, and belt, and the Rockford Peaches had a peach, or tan-colored, uniform with red caps, shorts, socks, and belt.[23] Each team had the city's name and seal — such as the City of South Bend, Indiana — on the front of the uniform. Few players liked the uniform. Hemlines "went up and up," observed Lucille Moore, later South Bend's chaperone. Sliding in skirts left abrasions on players' legs, so some girls would not slide.

For most male spectators, good-looking, shapely women attired in short-skirted uniforms playing hardball embodied a built-in sex appeal, and the league liked that. "For obvious reasons," commented sportswriter William Cullen Fay, "Bonnie Baker provokes more wolf whistles than, say, Ernie (Schnozz) Lombardi."[24] For the pioneering women of the All-American League, the short-sleeved, one-piece, skirted uniforms were just one more obstacle they lived with in order to pursue their dream of playing professional ball.[25]

The Blue Sox practiced for the rest of the week before launching the regular season on Sunday, May 30, when they hosted the Rockford Peaches for a 4:30 game at Bendix Field. The late game was to be played under the lights at nine o'clock, but fans could see both games for the price of one ticket. The five-game series included a doubleheader on Monday, Memorial Day, and a solo game on Tuesday. Under league rules, the first game of a twin bill was scheduled for seven innings, but the late game would last the full nine frames. Racine's Belles were arriving Wednesday for three games, and afterward, the Blue Sox would leave for an 11-day road trip.

The *South Bend Tribune* printed the team's official roster. The four pitchers were Margaret Berger, 20 years old, from Homestead, Florida; Muriel Coben, 22, from Saskatoon, Saskatchewan; Betty McFadden, who was 18, from Savanna, Illinois, and Doris "Dodie" Barr, 21, of Winnipeg, Manitoba. Both catchers came from Canada: Mary "Bonnie" Baker, 24, from Regina, Saskatchewan, and Lucella MacLean, 22, from Lloydminster, Alberta. The infielders were Johanna Hageman, a 24-year-old from Chicago; Margaret "Marge" Stefani, 25, of Detroit; Lois Florreich, 16, from St. Louis, Missouri; Dorothy "Dottie" Schroeder, the youngest on the team at 15, from Sadorus, Illinois; and Mary Holda, 28 and the team's oldest player, from Mansfield, Ohio. Beside Jochum, the outfielders were Ellen Tronnier, 15, from Cudahy, Wisconsin; Josephine "Jo" D'Angelo, 18, of Chicago;[26] and Geraldine Shafranis, from Chicago.[27] Barr was the team's only southpaw, batting and throwing left-handed.

Wrigley's public relations machine was running in high gear, and most newspapers, realizing that the new girls' sport would add value to hometown social life, backed it. In South Bend, Mina Costin, the daughter of *Tribune* sports editor Jim Costin, asserted that the "All-American girls" not only had athletic ability but that they also had brains and beauty. The teenager, who identified with the women, wrote, "Time was when girl softball players were thought of as brawny, tough-looking and acting babes who couldn't do anything but heave a ball and swing a bat. But the members of South Bend's girls' team are ladies, in appearance and character, without exception."

For example, Mina described Margaret "Sunny" (because of her tan) Berger, "a small, sun-tanned, blue-eyed blonde who looks like a college coed." She finished a degree at a laboratory technicians' school in Chicago, after studying at Florida State and Tulane universities. Skilled at horseback riding and tennis, Berger pitched for softball clubs that competed on the national level for six years, most recently with Chicago's Garden City team. "There you have Miss America, 1943. No, she's not a bathing beauty — she's a softball player, and a darn good one, too."[28]

Opening the 1943 Season

In the league's inaugural twin bill, South Bend won twice, edging Rockford, 4–3, in the 13-inning first game and winning the second tilt, 12–9. In cool weather, a small crowd of 700 paid to see the afternoon game, but 900 showed up for the contest under the lights. The All-American League, like the majors, gloried in displaying patriotic images, for instance using red and blue lettering on printed schedules with the reminder, "Buy War Bonds."[29] Introducing what became the loop's usual pregame ceremony to salute the nation's fighting forces, players marched into the park and formed two lines starting at home plate, the Blue Sox, the home team, stood along the third base line and the Peaches, the visitors, on the first base line. They formed a "V" for victory, the flag was raised, and a band played the "Star-Spangled Banner." Afterward, the home team entertained fans by playing recorded music over the public address system, including favorites like "Canadian Sunset," a song recognizing players from Canada, and "The White Cliffs of Dover." During the game, the team's broadcaster called plays over the PA.

The 4:30 game was the circuit's first-ever contest, because Kenosha's day game at Racine was rained out. Berger battled Rockford's Marjorie Peters, and the Blue Sox won in

Original Blue Sox—This picture, taken near mid-season in 1943, shows South Bend's team after a few personnel changes. The Blue Sox pictured in the front row (left to right) are Bonnie Baker, Mary Holda, Jo D'Angelo, Sunny Berger, and Rose Virginia Way, chaperone. In the middle row (left to right) are Ruth Born, Lois Florreich, Lucella MacLean, Bert Niehoff, manager, Doris Barr, and Kay Bennett. In the top row are (left to right) Betty McFadden, Mabel Holle, Dottie Schroeder, Jo Hageman, Betsy Jochum, and Marge Stefani (courtesy of Betsy Jochum).

the 13th, 4–3, when Florreich slugged an RBI double down the left field line. Berger, a windmiller, fanned 11 batters, and the Peaches collected six of eight hits and scored three runs in the first five innings. In the second, Peters singled home the first run in league history.

"The story of the South Bend team's 12–9 victory last night," concluded Jim Costin, "is wrapped up in a succession of bases on balls, wild pitches, balks, stolen bases, base-hits, and errors." The Blue Sox swiped 21 bases, mainly because Olive Little had not yet learned to hold the runners close, and fiery catcher Helen Nelson had a sore arm. Little, the 26-year-old fastball ace from Popular Point, Manitoba, who used the figure-eight delivery favored by most Canadians, wild-pitched a few runs home. For South Bend, Barr relieved Coben in the eighth. The Sox, aided by ten walks, scored 12 runs on nine hits.[30] In the end, the opening day games were sloppy. The girls were talented, but they were learning to play together as a team under the different rules of a unique league. For pitchers, they had to learn to hold runners on base, which was not the case in softball. Regardless of age, they were all "rookies."

After Sunday's long day of pro ball, both teams made valiant efforts in Monday's Memorial Day doubleheader, despite little rest between games — a circumstance that would occur all season. As the league planned, the teams were slated to play almost every day from Memorial Day through Labor Day, and rainouts meant that successive doubleheaders were not unusual. On Monday, South Bend claimed the seven-inning opener, 11–5, behind the four-hit pitching of Barr, but Rockford won the nightcap, 12–10, thanks to a 15-hit attack and an unassisted game-ending double play in the ninth.[31] Betty McFadden, the Sox' hurler in the late game, took the loss. McFadden, incidentally, was invited to Wrigley Field after performing well at a tryout in her hometown of Savanna, Illinois. The right-hander hoped to play first or third base. Instead, league officials insisted that she pitch. Betty made a strong effort, but she had never pitched softball.[32]

Leading the loop with a 3–1 ledger, the South Benders, practicing every day, returned to Bendix Field's dusty clay diamond on Tuesday evening (almost all games were played under the lights) and played better ball. Still, the home team lost a pitchers' duel, 2–1, when Marge Peters, the right-hander from Greenfield, Wisconsin, spaced four hits, and Berger, who yielded seven. lost on an unearned run.[33] The Blue Sox hosted three games against Racine, beginning Wednesday night at 8:30, the usual time the umpires called "Play ball!" Facing Annabelle Thompson, the home team grabbed a 1–0 lead in the second inning when Florreich boomed a solo home run to left field. South Bend scored another run, but Thompson prevailed, and Coben, a figure-eight hurler, lost a seven-hitter, 3–2. Also, Jean Wilson, from Rochester, New York, was signed for the roster spot vacated by Shafranis (who left the loop after the first twin bill).[34] On Thursday, the yellow-uniformed visitors won, 9–3, as Chattanooga lefty Mary Nesbitt permitted seven hits. Again Barr was wild, issuing seven walks, and five of those who walked came around to score.[35]

On Friday night, the Blue Sox hit well and defeated the Belles, 9–3. Berger led her team with a fine performance, and the right-handed batter also drove home two runs with a pair of singles, as South Bend out-hit Racine, ten to eight. When the two teams, tired but feeling good, walked off Bendix's field after the one hour and 28 minute contest (most games were played in less than two hours), Racine led the circuit with a 3–2 record, South Bend and Rockford were tied for second at 4–4, and 2–3 Kenosha was fourth. The Sox were "quite chipper," reported the *South Bend Tribune*, as they boarded the South Shore for their first late-night rail odyssey.[36]

Wartime Life in South Bend

War manufacturing in 1943 boosted the four medium-sized cities that represented the All-American League, notably South Bend. The St. Joseph's River flows northward through Indiana to Lake Michigan, passing through South Bend — so named because of its location on the river. The diverse roots of the town began decades before it was founded in 1831. French priests visited the area in the 1660s, and by 1686 French missionaries from Canada had established a mission called St. Joseph's. Notre Dame, a small Catholic college for men located northeast of South Bend, was destined to become a famous center of higher education and a pillar of the community. In the 1850s, St. Joseph's County saw the arrival of hundreds of immigrants of Scotch-Irish and Pennsylvania Dutch descent. In the last third of the 19th century, the city and the county received Polish, Irish, Belgian, Hungarian, Italian, and Jewish immigrants, and after the turn of the century, African Americans, Greeks, and Italians came looking for jobs in local factories. During the Great War, the city's industrial production boomed.

Throughout the 1920s, the nation experienced economic prosperity, and so did South Bend. Later, during the Great Depression, most people suffered economically and psychologically. Growth declined, notably in the industrial sector. The census of 1940 showed South Bend's population was 101,268, a decline of 3,000 since 1930. World War II loomed on the horizon, the US government and the nation were in a preparedness mode, and South Bend had defense contracts worth nearly $13 million, more than any other city in Indiana. After the Japanese bombed Pearl Harbor, Studebaker, the local automaker that started producing horse-drawn wagons in the 1850s, converted to heavy trucks, truck engines, airplane engines, and an amphibious military vehicle called the Weasel. Bendix Aviation worked on secret government projects, including gyroscopes, bombsights, and turrets for B-17 and B-24 bombers. Agriculture was essential for the war effort, and the Oliver Farm Equipment Company, a firm that started making iron plows before the Civil War, made tractors and farm implements. South Bend was booming when the All-Americans stepped off the train from Chicago in late May 1943.[37]

The Blue Sox made a stir during the league's first week, and the women who departed from Union Station after the first home stand were embarking on a grand adventure. In South Bend, they roomed in private homes within walking distance of Bendix Field. The ballpark could seat more than 2,000, but it was located on the west side of town, meaning that many fans had to ride a city bus to get there. According to team members, the families housing them provided excellent support, including cooking and laundry privileges. South Bend offered the same recreation and entertainment found in most cities. On an off night, or on the road, players could see a motion picture, the favored entertainment of the 1940s. On the weekend of Memorial Day, folks paid between 15 and 30 cents and chose from two dozen features, but most people had already seen the Academy Award-winning *Casablanca*, starring Humphrey Bogart and Ingrid Bergman.[38]

Radio flourished during the war, but people received most of their information from newspapers. Stories in the *South Bend Tribune* ranged from war news to local politics to women's events to the sports pages. Typically, the movie section ran an eye-catching ad announcing each day's local contest of the All-American League. The display featured a silhouette of a female hitter with her bat cocked and her left leg lifted as she prepared to swing. The model was Edie Perlick of the Racine Belles.[39] The ad, updated daily all summer, appeared in the newspapers of league cities, listing the visiting team, the game date, and the ticket prices — currently 65 cents for adults and 35 cents for children — for a chance to see "American's Greatest Girl Softball Players!"⁴⁰

"What I do remember," Betsy Jochum recalled about South Bend during the war years, "everyone treated us royally. Wherever we went, we were always welcome. I don't remember anyone ever booing us in South Bend or any other town. When we played at Bendix Field on the west side of South Bend — the home of the former Bendix Brakes men's softball team, I lived in the upstairs part of a house owned by a Scottish lady named McAdams with Dottie Schroeder, 'Jo' Hageman, and Lucella 'Frenchy' MacLean. We used to eat breakfast and lunch, always the best hamburgers, at a restaurant down the street called the Black Cat.

"We walked to and from the ballpark for our games and practices. When we were in South Bend on a Sunday, we would walk down Lincoln Way West to eat around noon downtown at the Philadelphia, a restaurant and candy store. We walked all the way back, around 45 minutes one way.... Dan Clark, one of the best Blue Sox presidents, owned Clark's Lunch Room downtown. The visiting teams would sometimes eat there.... Another memory — you would see a lot of Studebaker cars, since they were manufactured there.... I liked Studebaker's 'Starlite Coupe,' which came out later, with the round bullet nose and the wrap-around rear window."⁴¹

Betsy Jochum — One of South Bend's stars from the first Blue Sox team. This picture shows Betsy in 1943 in the kind of promotional glamour pose the league snapped of players during the early years (courtesy of Betsy Jochum).

Rookies Become Professionals

Early on Saturday, June 5, the Blue Sox stepped off the train in Rockford, and, taking their bags, rode taxis to the Faust Hotel. They caught a few hours sleep (hard to do sitting up on a train's day coaches during the war years), walked to the ballpark, took batting and fielding practice, came back to the hotel for a meal, rested in the afternoon, and returned to the facility on 15th Avenue, Beyer Stadium, later dubbed the "Peach Orchard."⁴² Beginning at 7:30, the teams played the city's first-ever women's professional softball game. Rockford, located along the Rock River on the plains of northern Illinois 90 miles west of Chicago, was a thriving industrial center. Many of the city's more than 100,000 residents worked in factories specializing in metal products like hardware, machine tools, machinery, and automotive parts.⁴³

Rain was expected in Rockford on Saturday, but instead, the Peaches' home opener was a fast-paced game played in a chilly breeze. Coben, controlling her good fastball, won her first game, 5–2, with late relief from Berger. Rockford's Eddie Stumpf used his second-best hurler, Marge Peters. Coben no-hit the Peaches for five innings, first surrendering a run in the sixth, and the Blue Sox broke a 2–2 tie by scoring two runs in the eighth and adding one more in the ninth.[44]

The teams were scheduled for a doubleheader on Sunday, June 6, but rain washed out the league's schedule. On Monday night, Rockford and South Bend split a twin bill. Behind Olive Little's two-hitter, the Peaches squeaked to a 5–4 victory over McFadden in the seven-inning opener. Sparked by Barr's hurling in the nightcap, the visitors pounded out a 12–2 victory, starting with five runs in the second off Josephine Skokan.[45] The triumph kept South Bend in first place with a 6–5 record, but rainy, chilly spring weather cancelled the series finale on Tuesday. After packing, the Sox continued their first excursion, riding the day coach to Chicago, carrying their suitcases to another track, and boarding the North Shore El for Racine.[46]

Racine was an industrial city of 67,000 located 30 miles south of Milwaukee on the banks of the Root River and the shore of Lake Michigan. The port, called the "Belle City of the Lake," welcomed the new women's professional teams.[47] Many of the Belles recalled loving to play ball at home. Limestone-walled Horlick Field included nice showers and locker rooms. Kids and adults waited outside the doors to get autographs before walking home or catching a city bus. Unlike other cities where few restaurants stayed open at night, the Belles and visiting players could walk across the street to the Bright Spot Café. Featuring signed pictures of Racine players, the eatery was open after games so that players could buy sandwiches and sodas.

On Wednesday, June 9, Berger faced Gloria Marks, the Los Angeles glamour girl, and the Blue Sox won in 12 innings, 5–3. Slender lefty Mary Nesbitt relieved Marks in the ninth, but Nesbitt lost when the visitors scored twice in the 12th.[48] One night later, South Bend dumped the local favorites, 10–3. Coben gave up ten hits, but the Blue Sox reached Anna Thompson for 15 safe blows, four by Jean Wilson and three each by Jochum and Stefani. Wilson, the right fielder, enjoyed a career day with two singles, a double, and a triple.[49] In a twin bill on Friday, the blue-uniformed visitors split, losing the opener, 10–5, after the Belles exploded for nine runs against McFadden in the third. In the late tilt, Barr spaced eight hits, fanned seven, and issued four passes, but the Blue Sox won, 5–2, connecting with Nesbitt's slants for three runs in the ninth to overcome a 2–1 deficit. Afterward, the happy South Benders showered, packed and boarded North Shore, laughing, singing, and talking ball on the way home.[50]

On June 12, a windy Saturday evening at Bendix Field before an enthusiastic crowd of 1,000, the Blue Sox slugged out a 9–4 victory over the Peaches. Jim Costin, praising the teams for exciting, fast-paced ball, wrote, "The games had everything: fine pitching, spectacular defensive work, a long home run, hustle, noise, and of course manager Eddie Stumpf's frequent disagreements with the umpires." The opener was played in one hour and 11 minutes and the nine-inning late game took an hour and six minutes. Said Costin, "The girls hurry things along and don't do any loafing, another feature of their games which is catching on rapidly with the South Bend fans."[51]

After nearly a month, the All-Americans were playing the game well and using the same strategies as major league teams. Most managers were former big leaguers, so the women's style of pro ball should have been no surprise. They played "small ball," looking for walks, base hits, stolen bases, and bunts, anything to keep a rally going or to score a run. Sometimes players hit home runs, but the ballparks were built for men's teams, so the fences were too far away to be cleared by even a well-hit 12-inch softball. Still, as fans later said, they attended at first for the novelty or the sex appeal, because the women in their skirted uniforms were attractive, to be sure, but most returned to the ballpark because they liked the first-rate ball played by All-Americans.[52]

Growing in Popularity

By the middle of 1943, the All-American League was growing in popularity throughout the circuit's four cities. For example, Kenosha, Wisconsin, an industrial center located on Lake Michigan ten miles south of Racine, boasted a population of 50,000; the loop's smallest city was home to the Comets.[53] Appealing to readers, the *Kenosha Evening News* published several stories about local heroines, stories that rivaled the coverage given to major leaguers. Sports editor Eddie McKenna, writing about the game at Kenosha's Lakefront Stadium on Tuesday, June 15, described the Blue Sox jumping to a 5–0 lead in the first frame and hanging on for a 6–5 victory. The Comets tied the game with a four-run fifth, but the visitors won on Stefani's RBI triple in the ninth. McKenna's story also pictured the Comets' infield: third baseman Ann Harnett of Chicago, the first player signed by the league and one of the designers of the circuit's uniforms; Mary Lou Lester of Nashville, at second base; Irene Ruhnke of Chicago, the shortstop; and Janice O'Hara from Beardstown, Illinois, at first base.[54]

South Bend won four of the six contests, splitting a doubleheader on Wednesday, winning on Thursday, and dividing another twin bill on Friday night. On Friday, a crowd of 1,326, a big turnout on a special "night" for employees of Cooper, Inc., saw Helen Nicol fire a four-hitter and win, 3–1. Due to "constant bickering" by players with the umpires, the games dragged on until the "nightmarish" hour of 11 o'clock. Coben, scattering five hits, lost the opener when Kenosha scored twice in the second, and Nicol protected the lead. In the late game, Barr lost her control in the seventh, and after McFadden walked two batters, Berger, with her quick delivery, good fastball, sharp curve, and change-up, preserved a 7–4 victory. The Blue Sox scored three runs in the first and never trailed, thanks to Jochum's leadoff triple, Stefani's fly, an error on a grounder by MacLean, Hageman's RBI double, Baker's walk, Barr's single, and D'Angelo's grounder. Afterward, South Bend held first place with a 16–9 ledger, Kenosha was second with an 11–11 record, Racine was third at 9–12, and 9–14 Rockford was last.[55]

On Saturday, June 19, returning to their homes away from home and the now-familiar clay infield at Bendix, the All-Americans, wearing the powder blue outfits, dumped the visiting Belles, 19–6, thanks mainly to Racine recruit Martha Walker walking 20 batters in seven and a third innings.[56] In Sunday's doubleheader, 1,100 spectators saw a good show. Riding McFadden's seven-hit hurling and errorless support, the local heroines won the short opener, 6–2. The Belles, however, bounced back to win the late tilt when ace Mary Nesbitt threw shutout ball until the ninth, when she walked the bases full and gave up two runs. Barr, again too wild, surrendered 11 hits and 11 walks, and South Bend's record slipped to 18–10.[57]

The defeat touched off a streak of inconsistent outings, as the Blue Sox lost six of nine games, including the next three to Racine. On Thursday, June 24, Kenosha won, 10–3, on Lee Harney's nifty hurling and some timely hitting. The defeat dropped South Bend to second place, as Racine won twice from Rockford, making seven straight victories for the suddenly surging Belles. Further, when Pauline "Pinky" Pirok (pronounced pie-rock) was thrown out stealing in the fourth, she spiked shortstop Dottie Schroeder, who made the play but suffered a gash to her leg that required several stitches.[58] South Bend chaperone Rose Way cleaned and bandaged the cut, but Schroeder was lost to the team for ten days.

Female chaperones had multiple functions, Betsy Jochum recalled, and they "did an excellent job of counseling, checking out housing, hotels, part-time nurse to treat injured players on the field, and being our friend."[59] Also, the chaperones served partly as the dressing room link between male managers and female players. "Our managers never came in the locker room," recollected Lucella (MacLean) Ross, "and if they did, it was only after the chaperones said they could."[60] The locker room leadership, therefore, usually came from players with strong personalities.

Wrapping Up the Season's First Half

The league's first All-Star break occurred on Thursday, July 1, 1943. Held at Wrigley Field, the program included free admission in order to support the Chicago area's recruiting drive for the Women's Auxiliary Army Corps, an organization that President Roosevelt converted into a regular branch of the armed forces by signing a new law on July 3. As a result, American women were recruited, and soon they were serving in England with the Eighth Air force, working as switchboard operators, clerks, typists, secretaries, motor pool drivers, and also cryptographers or photo interpreters. Across the US, people read about women actively participating in the war effort, and they often took jobs normally worked by men.[61]

Newspapers prepared for the All-American exhibition by inviting fans to submit an All-Star lineup, a common practice in major league cities before baseball's annual All-Star game. For example, Kenosha readers were urged to complete a lineup, mail it to the *Evening News*, or take it to the Comets' office in the National Bank Building by June 29, along with a stamped self-addressed envelope. Each person who sent a list of starters received a free ticket to a Comets' game.[62] League officials used the ballots to pick two teams: 15 players from Racine and Kenosha, and 15 from South Bend and Rockford. Slated as the first night game in the history of Wrigley Field, the event began with a tilt between softball teams representing the WAACs at Fort Sheridan and at Camp Grant, and the Sheridan girls won, 11–5.[63]

The All-Americans played an interesting if one-sided game, and the Wisconsinites blanked the Indiana-Illinois team, 16–0. Jo D'Angelo rapped her team's first hit, a single in the seventh inning (she went 1-for-4), and the Peaches' Olive Little beat out an infield single in the ninth. Helen Nicol and Lee Harney, both of Kenosha, as well as Racine's Gloria Marks hurled for the Wisconsin squad. Sunny Berger and Dodie Barr joined Little and Marge Peters on the mound for the Indiana-Illinois girls. Bonnie Baker and the Peaches' Dorothy Green split catching duties, and the Belles' Irene Hickson and the Comets' Helen Westerman caught for the opponents. Racine's Sophie Kurys collected three singles, and the flashy fielding of Kenosha's Shirley Jameson excited the crowd. The Sox provided eight All-Stars: Berger, Barr, Baker, D'Angelo, Jochum, Hageman, Stefani, and Florreich. Jochum, who didn't get a hit in two at-bats, remembered the evening's patriotic features as more memorable than the contest.[64]

On Friday, July 2, after traveling to Racine, the Blue Sox fell to the streaking Belles, 4–3, as Barr walked nine and lost a four-hitter, 4–3. The victory lifted 21–16 Racine into first place by four percentage points, leaving South Bend second at 22–17.[65] Returning on Saturday, the home team belted the visitors, 13–8. Right-hander Joanne "Jo" Winter was more effective than Coben, who, with shaky control, yielded 12 hits, walked four, and watched her teammates commit eight errors, several during the Belles' winning six-run eighth inning.[66]

Tired and down, the Blue Sox rode the night train to Rockford for a doubleheader on Sunday, the Fourth of July. The blue-uniformed visitors split the two games, but rain washed out twin bills on Monday and Tuesday. For two days the Blue Sox lounged around the Faust Hotel. The weather cleared on Wednesday, 1,500 fans showed up on "Berry Melin Night," and the Peaches won, 8–6. Berger, Bert Niehoff's ace, relieved Barr in the eighth, but gave up three runs and lost. On the trip home, the Sox players talked about how they started the trip a few percentage points out of first, but trailed Racine by three and a half games for the league's first-half honors.[67]

At Bendix Field for a home stand against Kenosha starting on Thursday, July 8, South Bend won a pair of single games before the teams were idled by rain for the Saturday night contest. On Sunday evening, under a threatening sky, Kenosha won the ten-inning opener, 1–0, as Nicol fired a three-hit shutout, but the home team rallied for three runs in the ninth to win the late game, 6–5. Disappointed spectators were moving toward the exits in the late tilt as the Comets led, 5–3. Suddenly, with two outs, Baker singled past third base, and Stefani hit a one-hopper to Kay Bennett, the Regina right-hander, who threw wildly to first, and the runners moved up. Hageman singled off Bennett's glove, scoring Baker, and when second baseman Mary Lou Lester threw away a grounder, Stefani scored for a 5–5 tie. Hageman walked, and MacLean, who took over Marjorie Hood's place in right field, hit an RBI single, and McFadden preserved the win.

The split left South Bend in second place with a 26–21 mark, but Racine, winning 20 of its last 23 games, clinched the first-half title with a 34–20 record. The second half of the 108-game schedule was set to open on Friday, July 16. "Attendance is picking up all over the circuit," reported the *Tribune*, "particularly in South Bend, and it now looks like Phil Wrigley's belief that the sports public would go for the girls' game when properly presented is a clickeroo."[68]

Winding down, South Bend journeyed to Kenosha and split two straight twin bills on Monday and Tuesday. On Wednesday, the weary South Benders, after riding most of the night to Rockford, lost both ends of their fourth doubleheader in four days. In the finale at Rockford on Thursday, July 15, the Blue Sox fell to the Peaches, 7–0. Fifteen-player teams found it tough to handle the grind of back-to-back doubleheaders, let alone South Bend's eight games in four days. Rockford's Marge Peters threw a four-hit shutout that kept the visitors in a slump, and Barr suffered another poor outing. Again, the tired Hoosierites faced a long train ride, but they were encouraged, because the second half opened on Friday at Bendix Field's friendly confines.[69]

According to first-half statistics, Helen Nicol of Kenosha topped the league's 19 hurlers with a record of 12–6 and a 1.76 ERA. Sunny Berger ranked second with her 13–3 ledger and 2.13 ERA. Other Blue Sox included Dodie Barr, placing fifth with a 7–6 mark and an ERA of 3.08; Ruth Born, a rookie underhander who joined the team but lost her debut in the opener of the doubleheader at Kenosha on July 12,[70] was 12th at 1–2 and 3.86; Muriel Coben was 3–8 and 4.53; and Betty McFadden owned a 4–7 mark with a 5.22 ERA. In batting, Rockford's Terrie Davis led the regulars with a .372 average. Barr averaged .266, and Bonnie Baker hit .265, finishing 12th and 13th, respectively. Overall, South Bend ranked third in hitting with a team average of .228. Racine led the league by averaging .257, Rockford was second with a .251 mark, and Kenosha was last at .222.[71]

Further, the league announced a three-team trade: South Bend sent Muriel Coben and outfielder Marjorie Hood to the Peaches, Rockford shifted right-hander Clara Cook and infielder Ethel McCreary to the Comets, and Kenosha moved Canadian Kay Bennett and flychaser Mabel Holle to the Blue Sox.[72] The league was trying to make the teams more competitive and create a more interesting second-half pennant race, so league-leading Racine was not involved.

Overall, South Bend ranked second in a four-team start-up league that did not exist three months earlier. The women wearing the powder blue uniforms were gelling as a team. As part of that process, the more mature players, including Baker, 24 years old, Stefani, 25, Hageman, also 25, and Jochum, 22, emerged as role models and team leaders, both on and off the diamond. Niehoff, the former big leaguer, was dealing with managing women, but by mid-season, he was relying mainly on input from Baker and Stefani.[73] At the same time, the team's chemistry, the intangible factor called camaraderie, was developing.

Starting All Over

Reflecting on the learning curve for All-Americans, Jim Costin found the overall play improved, thanks to coaching by the managers. For example, hardly any infielders, except Stefani, at first looked to get the lead runner out. Instead, they usually tried to retire the batter, but now most of the girls were looking to start double plays, cut the runner off at the plate, and more. Costin, enthusiastic about the league, credited the managers: "The spectacular plays that featured the South Bend-Racine series which ended last night were due, in large part to the girls' added confidence after receiving such splendid coaching from their managers."[74]

The managers were schooling their protégés in finer points of baseball, like teaching batters to lay down good bunts; instructing infielders to make plays cutting off the lead runner; having outfielders throw the ball ahead of the runners; stressing how pitchers should work away from a hitter's strength; and encouraging players to learn all the rules of the game. As amateurs, the women used most of these tactics, but they improved markedly as pros because they practiced the fundamentals and played the game *daily*. "They were very serious," recalled Betty (McFadden) Rusynyk. "You had to be on your toes and hustling."[75] More important, Betsy Jochum emphasized that the women were talented professionals, so they improved for one main reason: they practiced and played seven days a week, not just two or three times weekly.[76]

Despite the team's increasing experience, South Bend started the season's second half with mixed success, posting a 6–6 mark in the first 12 contests. In a roster note of August 1, the Sox released right-hander Betty McFadden and replaced her with Bea Chester, an infielder from Brooklyn, New York. McFadden, who had a 4–8 record at the time, was frustrated by having to pitch without ever getting a chance to play first or third base.[77]

Playing at Kenosha for first place on Saturday, August 7, Barr and Berger combined to outlast Nicol in 17 innings, 10–8. Barr, with good control, yielded seven hits before departing with two outs in the tenth, after the home team scored for an 8–8 tie. Finally, in the 17th, Jochum and Stefani singled, Baker sacrificed, Florreich was passed, Berger hit a two-run single, and Sunny retired the Comets in the bottom of the tenth for the win.[78]

Returning to Lakefront Stadium on Sunday evening, South Bend, boosted by the team's two first-rate catchers, completed a sweep of the four games by winning a doubleheader. Bennett, the onetime Comet curveballer, tossed a three-hitter and won the opener, 3–0. In the late tilt, Berger replaced Born, the 17-year-old from Bay City, Michigan, in the sixth with Kenosha ahead, 6–5. Sunny twirled six innings and won, 9–5. Her teammates tied the score with one run in the ninth and won with four more in the 12th. When the tired Sox boarded the South Shore, they owned first place with a 16–9 mark, leaving the disappointed Comets second at 14–12.[79]

A big reason for South Bend's success was the team's two catchers, Bonnie Baker and Lucella MacLean. No other All-American team could match the talent and skill of the two Canadian receivers. After the Wrigley Field tryouts, the league allocated each team two catchers, four pitchers, seven infielders and outfielders, and two utility players — making a total of fifteen.[80]

Mary Baker became famous in South Bend partly because she portrayed the league's glamour image: good looks, charm, and sex appeal, combined with good athletic skills. Born in Regina the year after the Great War ended, Mary George grew up in an athletic family with four brothers and four sisters, and all nine became catchers. Later known as Bonnie, Baker (her married name) was poised in front of the camera, thanks to her good looks, warm smile, and modeling experience. Sportswriter Tom Hawthorne called her the "face of the league," but she was also an intense competitor blessed with fine all-around skills. A fast runner, she stole 506 bases in her career, including 94 in 1946 when she was an All-Star. A timely hitter with a discerning eye at the plate who fanned just six times as a rookie, Baker batted .235 lifetime. The 5'5" brunette was 24 when the women's pro circuit began,[81] and in South Bend, she quickly became friends with Marge Stefani, a take-charge, domineering, mother-hen personality who was 25. Baker and Stefani soon became Bert Niehoff's favorites.

Unfortunately for South Bend, Baker, playing the first half of a twin bill at home against Racine on Thursday, August 12, was hit by a foul tip in the first inning. Afterward, doctors learned she suffered a broken fourth finger on her throwing hand. Bonnie was out for the season. At the time, Jim Costin thought the loss was a serious blow to the Sox.[82]

Mary "Bonnie" Baker — The photogenic star catcher from Regina, Saskatchewan, circa 1943 (courtesy of the Louise Pettus Archives and Special Collections, Winthrop University).

The other Canadian catcher, Lucella MacLean, the Alberta star, also attended the try-outs in Chicago. MacLean, complete with dark brown hair, beaming smile, and outgoing personality, was blessed with all-around athletic ability. At age 15 in 1936, she started playing "fastball" (fast-pitch softball) with Lloydminster's Nationals. She was the team's regular receiver in 1937, and the Nationals won the Estey Trophy four straight times. After the Second World War began, the military called, and MacLean, 19, wanted to be a nurse, but the Saskatoon, Saskatchewan, Pats offered her a job. In September 1940, Lucella moved to Saskatoon and worked as a clerk-cashier for the taxi company. A 5'2" athlete who could call games well, throw hard, and swing a good bat, she starred for the Pats. She learned about the All-American League because a scout offered Muriel Coben, her friend and battery mate, a contract. For South Bend in 1943, MacLean hit .206, but Baker swung a better bat, averaging .250, before she was injured.[83]

The Blue Sox not only had two fine catchers but they also started stellar performers at every position. Jo Hageman covered first base nicely. Marge Stefani, a good clutch hitter, and youthful shortstop Dottie Schroeder formed a good double-play combination. Lois Florreich displayed a strong but erratic arm at third base, but like MacLean, she could also play the outfield. Betsy Jochum anchored the outer gardens from her slot in left field, and she led the loop's regulars in hitting in the season's second half, averaging .273 overall. Speedy Jo D'Angelo, a fine contact hitter who struck out just three times in 1943, ranged over center field.[84] The Blue Sox acquired help for right field when they traded for Mabel Holle from Kenosha. Led by the mound work of ace Sunny Berger and the sometimes wild Dodie Barr, as well as good performances from Ruth Born and Kay Bennett, the South Benders chased the elusive vision of a championship.

All-Americans Are Regular Girls

Starting on Friday, July 30, when they hosted the Comets at Bendix Field, the Blue Sox capitalized on five Kenosha errors to score five unearned runs and win 6–4, even though Barr surrendered three runs in the ninth.[85] After that "gift" victory, Niehoff's charges put everything together for a hot streak until mid–August, winning six in a row, losing twice, and winning five straight. The last victory in the string came over Rockford in the first game of a twin bill on Friday, August 13, but the Peaches won the nightcap. On Saturday, the never-say-die Blue Sox bounced back to whack the Peaches, 8–1. Born squared her record at 2–2, Jochum was the circuit's top hitter with a .306 mark, and the victory, coupled with Racine's win over Kenosha, gave the Blue Sox (22–11) a three-game league bulge over the second-place Comets (19–14).[86] The local heroines, even without Baker, seemed to be on their way to winning the pennant.

During South Bend's final home stand in mid–August, the *Tribune* ran a series of stories to illustrate how the All-Americans lived away from the ballpark. "The girls who make up the Blue Sox softball team are just like any other girls you would come across right here in South Bend," claimed Mina Costin, a big Sox fan herself who was serving as an intern with the newspaper. For example, four players lived with Mrs. Harriet Ludwig on Lincoln Way West, not far from Bendix Field. Harriet worked at Bendix Aviation at night, but she was a second mother to the players by day, and three of her four grown children served in the armed forces. Barr, Bennett, Baker, and Stefani liked "Mom" and spent most of their free time at the Ludwig home.

The women usually arose around ten o'clock each morning, ate breakfast, and walked to the team's practice, returning home for lunch and relaxing in the afternoon, until it was time to go to the ballpark and don their uniforms. Stefani liked reading murder mysteries, and Bennett liked writing letters to family and friends. Baker and Barr enjoyed yard work, usually while chatting with "heroine worshipers," the teenage boys who lived nearby and liked the Blue Sox. The boys arrived on their bikes, hung around, and liked running errands for the players, perhaps going to the drug store for Coca-Colas (Baker's favorite). Bonnie planned to resume her modeling job in the offseason, and all four women hoped to return to South Bend and play pro ball in 1944.[87]

Four more players, all from the Midwest, lived at the home of Mrs. Thomas McAdams on nearby Goodland Avenue: Betsy Jochum, Jo Hageman, Dottie Schroeder, and, later, Mabel Holle. Unlike their stay-at-home teammates, these girls enjoyed exploring South Bend, borrowing bikes to ride, walking, or taking the bus. They called the game their "favorite indoor sport." After pay days, they would eat together at a good restaurant, see a movie, or go shopping. Like the others, they ate two regular meals, breakfast and lunch, but night games caused them to eat a late dinner, and if a complete meal was not available, they usually had a sandwich and a soda or a beer.[88]

Four more Blue Sox lived on North Meade Street with the Arnold Bauer family: Rose Way, the chaperone, Lois Florreich, Sunny Berger and Jo D'Angelo. As a highlight, Bauer, a Bendix worker in his early thirties, and his wife Nadine hosted buffet dinners, complete with meats, side dishes, coffee, and sodas after the games on Saturday nights. They invited players, team personnel, including Bert Niehoff, and even visiting players. Naturally the girls who lived there remained enthusiastic about the friendly and generous couple, and they viewed Arnold as the team's best fan. Indeed, the Bauers created more camaraderie, good cheer, and once-in-a-lifetime experiences with parties and get-togethers than anyone else in South Bend.[89]

The final group included Bea Chester, Lucella MacLean, Mary Holda, and Ruth Born. Chester and MacLean lived at the home of Mrs. Betty Makielski on Eclipse Place, and Holda and Born lived with Mrs. Randall Hunt on North Meade, near the Bauers. Like the others, these girls favored the daytime attire of shorts, blouses, slacks, or bathing suits. Also, they agreed, "playing ball in the All-American League is more like a vacation than earning a living."[90]

Regardless of age, these women were ballplayers and friends, and they shared much about their lives away from the ballpark. Holda, a reserve infielder, was homesick for her family in Mansfield, Ohio. As a result, she helped fill time by ironing shirts for the elderly Niehoff.[91]

The personal lives of All-Americans illustrated at once the adventure and the difficulty of playing pro ball. The girls lived in the homes of supportive families, but they were sharing rooms away from their own homes, thus missing their family and friends. In the league cities, they mainly knew each other and their "adopted" families. On the road, they relied on each other and the friends they made on other teams. Fame is fleeting, but good memories linger in the mind. Later, players often remembered their camaraderie more than events on the diamond. Ruth Born, the teenage Michigan rookie, said she could not remember much about the games, but "It was wonderful doing what you loved to do and getting paid for it."[92]

The bustle of wartime life continued to swirl around the players, even as the Allied Army drove into Italy's capital of Rome,[93] and the league changed its name in mid-season.

To emphasize the circuit's innovations, including allowing hurlers to start with just one foot on the pitching rubber and base runners to lead off and steal, loop officials asked newspapers to use the more descriptive name, "All-American Girls Base Ball League." Papers such as the *Tribune*, when printing standings, used the shorter, and perhaps more accurate, Girls' Pro League.[94] In 1943, the game was modified softball, but the league was already promoting a baseball image.

Finishing Second Again

Praising Jochum in mid–August, the *Tribune's* Jim Costin credited her with a "hitting rampage." Betsy's average after two weeks in August was .328, the best Blue Sox mark all season. Further, South Bend owned the best team average at .231, trailed by Racine at .221. Other good-hitting South Benders were Barr at .313 (she was 10-for-32), Stefani at .287, Bennett at .250 (she was 3-for-12), and Baker at .250. The remaining averages were lower: Berger at .200, Holle at .196, Hageman at .193, Schroeder at .184, Chester at .182, D'Angelo at .179, and MacLean at .147.[95]

The relatively low batting averages reflected the quality of the league's pitching and the size of the 12-inch "deadball," rather than a lack of skills by the hitters. As of August 11, the circuit's statistics for 59 players showed the top 30 were averaging .200 or above, and the other 29 were hitting .199 or less. However, the best 20 hitters ranged from Racine's Charlotte Smith at .440 (11-for-25) through Sophie Kurys at .238 (25-for-105). Except for the injured Edie Perlick at .315 (she was 17-for-54), Jochum was the only regular position player hitting above .300. Nevertheless, once the loop's strong-armed underhand hurlers adjusted to the mound distance of 40 feet, the base paths of 65 feet, and the runners leading off and preparing to steal, they were tougher to hit.

At the very time Mina Costin was describing how All-Americans lived, South Bend was hosting a critical series with Kenosha. The Blue Sox had won 17 of 22 games since losing to the Comets on July 30, but facing pennant pressure, they found winning elusive in the season's final two weeks. At Bendix Field on Tuesday, August 17, 2,000 shivering fans saw Lee Harney defeat Barr, 3–1, as Dodie spaced six hits but also issued seven walks. When the Belles defeated the Peaches, the Sox saw their league lead shrink to two games.[96]

At Bendix on Wednesday, South Bend fell again, 5–2, when Bennett, the pitcher, committed a surprising six errors in eight fielding chances, allowing the first two Comet runs. Berger took over in the eighth and pitched well until the 11th, when Kenosha scored three unearned runs on two singles, a walk, an error, and Nicol's fly, leaving the disappointed Blue Sox with a one-game margin.[97] On Thursday, the valiant Berger matched the stalwart Nicol for nine frames, but in the tenth, sloppy fielding by the local favorites ruined Sunny's effort and led to a 2–0 defeat, a result that tied the two teams with 23–15 records. "Not a runner should have reached first base on Berger in that [tenth] inning," lamented Jim Costin, "yet two of them scored and beat her."[98]

South Bend, minus the injured Baker, was still a team of professionals that kept battling back. Embarking on the final 13-game trip, the Sox won four straight games at Rockford. But on Tuesday, August 24, the blue-clad visitors fell to the Peaches, 5–2, when southpaw Mary Pratt, pitching tough with runners aboard, outlasted Barr, despite the ten-hit attack by the Blue Sox. Elsewhere, Kenosha defeated Racine and again tied South Bend for first place with a 27–17 mark.[99] Riding the night train to Kenosha, the Blue Sox arrived, slept, and, during two straight rainouts, hung around the Hotel Dayton, chatting, playing cards, reading, and writing letters.

On Friday at Lakefront Stadium, the Comets swept a twin bill by scores of 9–0 and 8–1. Harney and Nicol pitched brilliantly, but Barr was wild in the opener, Berger gave up eight hits in the nightcap, and Kenosha took a two-game lead over South Bend.[100]

The Blue Sox persevered, beating the Comets on Saturday, August 28, but the teams split two games on Sunday. Kenosha won the opener, 1–0, as Nicol, who topped the league with her 33–8 record, spaced three hits, but South Bend won the nightcap with a 15-hit barrage, 12–1. Berger, who won 25 games, hurled both contests, an unusual feat for even a great softball pitcher. Afterward, Kenosha (30–19) still had a one-game lead over South Bend (29–20).[101]

Facing five games against the Belles, who were always tough at Horlick Field, the travelers fell short. On Monday night, the Blue Sox lost, but Kenosha also fell to Rockford.[102] On Tuesday, the blue-uniformed visitors divided a twin bill with Racine, but the Comets and the Peaches also split. South Bend lost Tuesday's opener, 7–2, against Californian Gloria Marks, who outpitched a tired Berger. Rallying once more, the Blue Sox won the late game, 8–3, behind Bennett's slow stuff, a 13-hit attack, and Berger's stout relief in the last two innings.[103]

The season came down to the final day: South Bend needed to sweep Racine, while Kenosha needed one win at Rockford. The Comets slipped by the Peaches, 1–0, behind Nicol, but at Horlick, a crowd of 1,784 saw Bennett last only one and a third innings. Born relieved her, but Clara Schillace's three-run homer in a four-run sixth won it for the Belles, 6–3. In the end, Racine and Kenosha swept their respective doubleheaders, but it didn't matter to the dispirited Sox. All they could do was shower, change, console each other, and ride the train home.[104]

Maybe Next Year

The Blue Sox arrived in South Bend early on Saturday morning, and the women began packing to return to their own homes. In a footnote to the season, the *Tribune* reported: "The manager had no alibis to offer for the disastrous slump encountered by his players which saw them slough away a three-game lead in the final two weeks of the campaign to lose the pennant eventually by three games." In fact, the South Benders lost 12 of their final 19 contests.[105]

The team had good news, notably that Betsy Jochum won the second-half batting crown with a .295 mark. Terrie Davis, Rockford's shortstop, won the first half title with a .372 mark, but in the second half, she was second to Jochum at .282. Overall, Racine paced the circuit with a team average of .236, South Bend placed second at .222, Kenosha third at .219, and Rockford last at .191.[106] For the Blue Sox, however, the season's end was anticlimatic. The local heroines won neither a first nor a second-half pennant, even though they led the loop for more than half the split campaign. Still, the players knew the league would return in 1944.

Despite being a blip on the national sporting scene, the league's historic 1943 season ended when Racine swept Kenosha in three games of the best-of-five Scholarship Series. Mary Nesbitt was Racine's pitching star, winning the first and third games, while a tired Helen Nicol lost two of Kenosha's three games. Later, each Belle earned $228.31 as the winners' share of the gate receipts, and each Comet received the losers' share of $146.32.[107]

The Second World War was still raging, but for the more than 60 exceptional women who played the All-American League's speeded-up game of professional softball in 1943, at a time when baseball was considered by most people to be America's national game, it was largely a happy and memorable summer. "We were a close bunch," reflected Lucella (MacLean) Ross. "We loved the game. We played it very hard." The Alberta star recalled that the girls often had fun together after a contest. "We went for a meal, and we ate at a place where we could dance a little. It was very nice. But everything was ball."[108] Indeed, after returning to their homes in several states and Canada, the All-Americans could not help but keep telling stories about their new teammates and friends as well as the diamond events that were indelibly etched into their memories. More important, most of them were already looking forward to next summer.

• 2 •

South Bend's Second Winning Season: 1944

"Attendance in the four [All-American League] cities represented in 1943 is surprising.... The gals play harder than men, put their heart and soul in it, cry when they lose"— Harry Grayson, Newspaper Enterprise Association, July 14, 1944[1]

The Blue Sox Return

The *South Bend Tribune's* Jim Costin, following news about the Blue Sox securing local support and the funding needed to return the team to the All-American Girls Professional Ball League,[2] often dubbed the Girls' Pro League, named star outfielder Betsy Jochum as one of last year's players anxiously awaiting word of the team's survival. "Practically all the girls," Costin said in his column on April 8, 1944, "have written to friends here saying they want to return and play in this city, which was rated the best for sportsmanship by all the girls on all the teams." Jochum had already signed her 1944 contract; she would earn $65 per week, a $15 raise.[3]

The league was returning, but the structure had changed. For the inaugural season, Philip Wrigley, Arthur Meyerhoff, and other All-American officials operated the four-team circuit as a trusteeship, giving each team $22,500 and requiring them to contribute a matching amount. For 1944, the league granted franchises to the original four cities for $25,000 and required a minimum of $50,000 in capital to operate each franchise. In return, teams paid the franchise fee plus three cents per each charged admission, up to 90,000. Each franchise would select a board of directors to oversee the team, and the manager and chaperone would report to the board.[4]

The Blue Sox needed financial support, but in late February, two local businesses backed the team and caused the club's stock, listed at $250 per unit, to sell well. On April 12, 50 subscribers met downtown at the Odd Fellows Building and picked last year's president, Al McGann, to head the board. The eight directors rehired manager Bert Niehoff, who led the team to second-place finishes in each half of the 1943 season. For 1944, the league featured the four original clubs, South Bend, Racine, Kenosha, and Rockford, plus new franchises in Milwaukee and Minneapolis.[5]

League officials continued preparing for the new season. On April 16, Ken Sells, serving his second year as president, announced the circuit would follow a 120-game schedule, up from 108 games in 1943. South Bend was scheduled to open on the road on May 27, and the first home game was on Wednesday, May 30, Memorial Day. The teams again played doubleheaders on holidays and Sundays. Milwaukee and Minneapolis, the new franchises, would play games at local American Association ballparks. The four original teams kept their same uniform colors: light blue for the Sox, peach for the Peaches, yellow for the Belles, and lime green for the Comets. Milwaukee's Chicks would wear a gray uniform outfit featuring black stirrup over-the-calf socks, a red belt, and their red-billed black cap had a patch with a black M inside a yellow circle. The Minneapolis Millerettes would wear a pink uniform set off by dark red socks, belt, and cap, and the cap's patch had a gray-colored M inside of a pink circle.[6]

Also, South Bend workmen were building three rows of box seats (120 total) to surround the clay-surfaced diamond at Bendix Field, again the team's home park. Ticket prices in the grandstand were $1.00 for adults and 55 cents for children, and bleacher tickets cost 74 cents for adults and 35 cents for children. Tickets for the prized box seats were selling for $1.55.[7]

On May 15, 120 women, lodged at the Hotel Peru, reported to Washington Park in Peru, Illinois, 90 miles southwest of Chicago. League officials, including the six managers, would select 90 players for the 15-person rosters of the six teams. With players working out in chilly weather, the training routine featured chalk talks and calisthenics as well as instruction in hitting, pitching, sliding, and infield and outfield play. Interesting stories emerged from the camp, including one about Max Carey, Milwaukee's manager, ten-time National League stolen base leader, and master of the "fall-away," or hook slide. The girls were expected to slide into bases wearing thigh-length uniforms, satin shorts, and long socks, but previously they had not been taught to do so. Carey and Niehoff, another expert base runner in his heyday, were teaching players how to slide properly in a special sliding pit. Niehoff, wrote Jim Costin, must be relieved, because aggressive runners like Lois Florreich preferred hitting opponents with a "jarring body block," rather than sliding and risking cuts and abrasions.[8]

At the allocation meeting on May 24, the Blue Sox received the new maximum of 16 players, and most were returning from the 1943 squad. The experienced players were Bonnie Baker and Lucella MacLean, the catchers; right-handers Sunny Berger and Kay Bennett and lefty Dodie Barr; second baseman Marge Stefani, third baseman Lois Florreich, shortstop Dottie Schroeder, and first baseman Jo Hageman. The outfielders were Betsy Jochum, Jo D'Angelo, and Mabel Holle, but Holle was released a few days later, ending her All-American career.

South Bend also added five new players:

- Lena "Lee" Surkowski, 18 years old, an outfielder from Moose Jaw, Saskatchewan
- Vickie Panos, 24, a left-handed batting flychaser from Edmonton, Alberta, wife of a Canadian Air Force bomber pilot serving in Europe (Vickie had a two-year-old child, making her one of the league's two mothers — and the other was Rockford's Terrie Davis)
- Charlotte Armstrong, 19, a right-hander from Phoenix, Arizona
- Rose Gacioch, 28, a third baseman-outfielder from Wheeling, West Virginia
- Ellen Ahrndt, 21, a utility player from Racine

Finally, Helen Moore, from West Allis, Wisconsin, was the new coach-chaperone, replacing Rose Virginia Way, whom the team's directors deemed "too young."[9]

A Winning Start

On Thursday, May 25, the Blue Sox looked for living quarters in private homes, and on Friday morning they practiced at Bendix Field. Afterward, the players boarded the South Shore Elevated, or El, headed for Milwaukee. After arriving, riding taxis to the Ambassador Hotel, and registering, the players walked to the ballpark to prepare for a four-game series against the expansion Chicks. The circuit's first game of 1944 began at three o'clock on Saturday, May 27, on the diamond in front of the wooden grandstand at Borchert Field, longtime home of the Double-A Milwaukee Brewers. The All-Americans who took the field played by the same rules and essentially the same distances that the league adopted in 1943.

As Lavonne "Pepper" Paire of Minneapolis later expressed it, "We were playing a game that was a cross between softball and baseball."[10] Pitching, the signature feature of softball, was underhand, and the distance from the mound to home plate was still 40 feet. The ball's size was again 12 inches in circumference, but reduced to 11.5 inches at mid-season. The base paths started at 65 feet, but the distance was increased to 68 feet, also at mid-season — changes designed to improve hitting in a pitcher-dominated league.[11]

Sunny Berger, South Bend's ace, dueled 5'8" Connie Wisniewski, but Wisniewski, a rookie, was hurt by nine errors. After a see-saw battle, the Blue Sox won in ten innings, 5–4, when Stefani walked, advanced on a grounder, and scored on Baker's single. Berger retired the side in the last of the tenth, and the powder blue-clad visitors enjoyed another winning start. However, in what soon became a financial problem for the Chicks, the game drew only 700 fans.[12]

South Bend played three more games in Milwaukee, winning a twin bill on Sunday and losing a Monday afternoon "Ladies Day" game, an attraction that meant women paid only the federal tax on tickets. The Sunday contests drew an attendance of 1,470, double the number that saw the franchise's first game on Saturday. In the seven-inning opener, the league's usual doubleheader format, Dodie Barr and Kay Bennett, two of the circuit's original pitchers, combined to no-hit and beat the Chicks, 9–3. They lost a shutout by issuing nine passes, and their teammates committed three errors. Panos paced South Bend, collecting two out of five hits. In the nine-inning nightcap, the Blue Sox won, 13–0, behind Charlotte Armstrong's stellar hurling. The visitors raked three pitchers for 17 hits. Panos, Jochum, Gacioch, and Schroeder, who blasted a two-run homer, rapped three hits apiece. The sweep left South Bend in first place with a 3–0 record, followed by Racine and Rockford at 2–1.[13]

On Monday afternoon, the Chicks, derided as the "Schnitts," or "Little Beers," by the *Milwaukee Journal*, prevailed in 12 innings, 7–6. The Blue Sox, led by Stefani's 4-for-5 performance, outhit Milwaukee, 13 to nine, but Wisniewski, a fastballing windmiller, hurled the entire game. In the 12th, Barr, who worked the last six innings and yielded nine walks, two hits, and three runs, fired a wild pitch that allowed Thelma "Tiby" Eisen to score the winning run.[14]

Later, the Blue Sox rode the North Shore electric train to Chicago and, after switching, the South Shore El the rest of the way. Wartime travel regulations were still in effect. Due to the seating needs of military personnel, who traveled free, the All-Americans had to take available seats on day coaches, and on occasion they sat on suitcases in the aisle. Back in South Bend, the girls carried their luggage to homes where they roomed. Comfortable again, the Sox prepared to launch a 17-day home stand with a Memorial Day twin bill on Tuesday, May 30.[15]

Long Home Stand

The defending champion Racine Belles arrived on the holiday and practiced at Bendix Field. On Tuesday night (again, most games were played in the evening), Berger and South Bend won the short opener, 1–0, but Racine and right-hander Dorothy "Blondie" Ortman won the nine-inning nightcap, 3–0. Despite rain for two hours, a near-capacity crowd of 2,252 waited until the delayed first game started at 7:45. The local favorites won the game on Berger's two-hitter and Gacioch's first-inning RBI single. In the late tilt, Jochum doubled in the first, but Ortman pitched shutout ball. The Belles, scoring once in the second, won with two unearned runs off Armstrong in the seventh. Afterward, the teams were tied for first with 4–2 ledgers.[16]

On Wednesday, the Blue Sox took the league lead with an 8–5 victory, thanks to Bennett's five-hitter. Jo Winter, pitching due to an injury to Mary Nesbitt, the ace southpaw from Chattanooga, gave up ten walks and eight hits, the big blows being two-run singles by Baker and Stefani in the five-run sixth inning. On Thursday, the Blue Sox defeated the Belles for the third time, 3–1. Racine's Jane Jacobs permitted only five hits, but when the first three South Benders were safe on errors in the opening frame, two runs scored—the first on a wild throw and the second on Gacioch's single. Berger scattered six hits, but the yellow-uniformed visitors spoiled her shutout bid with an unearned run in the ninth.[17]

Milwaukee arrived at Bendix Field on Friday to face South Bend, an experienced team off to a good start. Against the youthful, talented Chicks, the Blue Sox won three out of four, taking the opener on Friday, losing on Saturday night, and sweeping the Sabbath doubleheader. On Sunday, more than 2,300 enthusiastic fans saw Armstrong fire a three-hitter to win the opener, 6–0, and Berger, showing her good stuff, spaced six hits to win the nightcap, 4–3. The Sox now led the loop with a 9–3 record, followed by the expansion Millerettes at 7–5.[18]

The South Benders, however, received a rude jolt from visiting Minneapolis on Monday. Only 475 customers shivered through a windy evening with temperatures in the low 50s to see what the *Tribune*'s astute Jim Costin called "one of the most exciting games played yet by the girls." The Millerettes broke a 1–1 tie in the sixth inning, hitting six singles and scoring five runs off Bennett, the Regina curveballer. Barr took over in the seventh and yielded a final run. The home team scored four runs in the eighth, but rookie Marguerite Jones held on for the 7–5 win.[19]

South Bend was scheduled to finish the two-game set with Minneapolis on Tuesday, June 6, but news of "Operation Overlord," the Allies' D-Day invasion of France, caused the league to postpone all games. United States forces assaulted two beaches, British-Canadian troops hit three more in the Normandy area on the southwestern coast of France, and President Roosevelt led the nation in prayer over the radio.[20] Such events affected the home front, including sports. D-Day was a critical turning point in the World War, and the Allied victory was now a matter of time.[21]

Six days later at Bendix Field, on Monday, June 12, after South Bend made a variety of mental errors, including "aimless" baserunning and throwing to the wrong bases, and lost to Milwaukee, 5–2, Bert Niehoff started a team "shakeup" by releasing Vickie Panos, who did not play that night, saying that Lee Surkowski was "more valuable to the team."[22] When Niehoff made the decision, he made a major mistake. Panos, who signed with Milwaukee and came back to haunt her former team more than once, finished her combined season by playing 111 games and hitting .263, the sixth-best mark in the league and higher than any Blue Sox player, except for Jochum.

Winning on the Road

South Bend and Racine were tied for first place with identical 13–10 records after the Blue Sox lost their fifth of seven games on Thursday, June 15, this time to Rockford, 4–0. Packing and departing from Union Station on the South Shore, changing trains in Chicago, and riding the North Shore to Kenosha, the Blue Sox arrived at the Dayton Hotel in the early hours of Friday.[23]

Playing Friday evening with a revamped lineup at Kenosha's stadium with its concrete grandstand facing Lake Michigan, the Blue Sox whipped the Comets, 8–1, and launched a ten-game winning streak. Niehoff took Gacioch out of the lineup because she was batting 4-for-46, and shifted Florreich from center field to third base, where Lois played in 1943. Surkowski was sent to right field, and D'Angelo, an excellent contact hitter who had played mostly center field, moved back to the middle. Later, D'Angelo was released and Gacioch took over in right. Tonight, riding Armstrong's six-hitter, the Sox scored three runs in the first, added two more in the second inning, and won easily, 8–1. South Bend remained tied for first with Racine, after the Belles defeated the Chicks in 15 innings.[24]

Blue Sox in Racine — South Bend took an afternoon break before an evening game with the Racine Belles in 1944. Pictured at Horlick Field in July 1944 are, in the front (seated, left to right), Sunny Berger, Mary Lou Lester, Kay Bennett, and Lee Surkowski. Kneeling in the middle row are Marge Stefani, Lois Florreich, Doris Barr, Dottie Schroeder, Bonnie Baker, and Rose Gacioch. Standing in the back row are Bert Niehoff, manager, Betsy Jochum, Jo Hageman, Charlotte Armstrong, Loretta Dwojak, and Helen Moore, chaperone (courtesy of Betsy Jochum).

In Saturday's game, South Bend took over first place by outlasting Kenosha in 13 innings, 2–1, and elsewhere, Milwaukee beat Racine. Berger pitched the first seven innings, allowing a run in the second, and Bennett took over in the eighth. The Blue Sox scored the game-winner in the 13th when the hustling D'Angelo, sliding into second on a bouncer to center, was ruled safe when shortstop Pinky Pirok dropped the ball. MacLean, playing first base, singled to left field, and D'Angelo held at third. Jo's big lead induced catcher Lucille Colacito to throw, the ball sailed into left field, D'Angelo scored, and Bennett retired the Comets for the victory.[25]

The vagaries of Midwestern weather surfaced on Sunday, raining out the doubleheader scheduled in Kenosha. South Bend still owned the top spot when Racine split a twin bill with the Millerettes before 3,000 folks, the biggest crowd yet to see All-Americans play in Minnesota.[26]

The Blue Sox continued the winning ways in Minneapolis. Arriving on Pullman sleeping cars early on Monday, June 19, the visitors practiced at Nicollet Park, the venerable 8,500-seat home of the Millers of the Double-A American Association — and now also home to the Millerettes. Manager Bubber Jonnard started Winnipeg right-hander Audrey Haine, but South Bend rapped five hits, featuring Baker's triple, and counted seven runs in the first frame. Armstrong allowed five hits, and Annabelle "Lefty" Lee, the knuckleballing rookie from North Hollywood, California, thereafter pitched shutout ball, but the visitors won, 7–1.[27]

On Tuesday, the Blue Sox won their fourth straight, 7–1, by the same method: riding good pitching, this time by Berger, and one big inning. Haine pitched well until the sixth, when she walked five batters, hit another, and yielded five runs to break the 1–1 tie.[28] The blue-clad visitors swept the set on Wednesday, 8–7, by overcoming a 5–4 deficit in the seventh with a four-run burst. The game's highlight came when Jochum torched a Dottie Wiltse fastball for the first home run in a women's game at Nicollet Park, and South Bend improved to an 18–10 record.[29]

Life on the road continued as the Blue Sox rode the train to Rockford, arriving early on Thursday. Following a few hours of sleep at the Hotel Faust, the visitors practiced at mid-day, rested, took care of laundry at the hotel, and returned to Beyer Stadium, located a mile from downtown Rockford. Lefty Amy Applegren twirled a three-hitter, but the Blue Sox struck quickly, scoring three runs in the first inning. Armstrong, showing her blazing speed, won an eight-hit shutout, 3–0, for the sixth straight Sox victory.[30] After winning on Friday and Saturday, South Bend led the loop with a 21–10 mark and Kenosha was second at 16–13, but Racine (16–17), Milwaukee (13–16), Minneapolis (13–18), and Rockford (11–18) had losing records.[31]

On Sunday, June 25, South Bend, having arrived overnight in Minneapolis, took a doubleheader from the Millerettes, winning the club's tenth straight game and breaking the old All-American record of eight straight wins set by Racine in 1943. In both games, the Blue Sox followed their recent pattern of jumping off to a big lead, scoring three runs in the first inning to win the opener, 3–1, and building up a 6–1 edge in the first three innings to win the nightcap, 9–3.[32] However, the Indiana club's win streak ended on a bad hop. On Monday night, Minneapolis halted the visitors, 2–1, thanks to two errors by the normally reliable Schroeder. Instead of a scoreless tie, the visitors trailed 2–0 in the ninth when Jochum slammed a Wiltse slant to deep left-center field, recording the longest home run hit by a woman at Nicollet Park. Elsewhere, Kenosha (17–15) lost to Milwaukee, leaving the Comets five games behind 23–11 South Bend.[33]

The New Blue Sox

When South Bend's 1944 season began, manager Bert Niehoff welcomed five new players, including third baseman-outfielder Rosie Gacioch. Her father died before she was born in Wheeling, West Virginia, in 1915, and her mother Anna remarried around the time the U.S. intervened in the Great War. The youngest of four children, she was raised by her mom and her stepfather. Surrounded by poverty, Gacioch, sturdy and aggressive, plugged her energy into swimming and playing games like baseball. Her mother died when she was 16, and Rosie lied about her age to work at Wheeling Corrugated, where her father had worked. The plant's president obtained her a tryout with the All Star Ranger Girls, a barnstorming team of "Bloomer Girls" (often featuring seven women plus a male pitcher and catcher). But the Great Depression curtailed traveling, and the Bloomer Girls died out. Switching to fast-pitch softball, Rosie traveled and played against all-star squads. Strong and talented at 5'6" and 130 pounds, she earned up to $50 for a weekend of games. When World War II began, she returned to the factory in Wheeling.

One day during lunch in early 1944, Gacioch, an unpolished but ambitrous southerner, saw a newspaper story about the All-American League. After trying out at nearby Pulaski Park, she received an invitation to the league's spring camp, where she made the league and was allocated to South Bend. A good hitter and fielder, she loved the game, and Niehoff began playing her at third base.[34] Later, Gacioch praised the manager, recalling that he taught them a great deal about fundamentals. At one point, Niehoff switched her to right field. Strong-armed Rosie recalled, "After Bert taught me how to play the outfield better, I made the second baseman get closer to the infield. I could throw players out from the outfield."[35] Later, Gacioch became one of the league's best players with Rockford, but in 1944 she hit only .161 for the Sox.

Two Canadian outfielders also joined the Blue Sox. Vickie Panos, a left-handed batter from Moose Jaw, Saskatchewan, was married and had one child. The 5'3" Panos, displaying good speed and agility, started in center field because Florreich, who shared the position with D'Angelo in 1943, was not out of high school until mid–June. Panos enjoyed several multi-hit games, beginning with five safe blows in a twin bill against Milwaukee on Sunday, May 28. When Florreich returned, Niehoff saw her as the better fielder and hitter. After a 5–2 loss to the Chicks at Bendix Field on June 12, Niehoff released Panos, and the Canadian speedster finished 1944 with the Chicks. Overall, she stole 141 bases in 115 games while averaging a solid .263. Despite her hitting heroics, Panos, perhaps because of her husband, did not return in 1945.[36]

Lena (or Lee) Surkowski was another Saskatchewan star who came to South Bend, and she roomed with the Arnold Bauer family. Recalling her experiences, Surkowski said she used to play softball during the summer and ice hockey in the winter. Lee liked skating, but she loved fast-pitch softball, or fastball, as folks living on the Canadian prairies called the game. She and her older sister Anne, who joined the Blue Sox in 1945, starred for the semipro Moose Jaw Royals. The Royals won provincial titles in 1942 and 1943, thanks partly to the hurling of Olive Little, later a heroine for the Rockford Peaches.[37] A league scout made Lee an offer in 1943, but she was not ready to leave her home and job. After another good season, the fleet flychaser received a contract for 1944. At age 19, she leaped at the wartime adventure.

At spring training in Illinois, Surkowski, a right-handed batter, enjoyed the beauty and behavior tips the women learned at the charm school directed by Frances McCune of the Ruth Tiffany School. An attractive 5'5" brunette with dark eyes and wavy hair, Surkowski made the league and was allocated to the Blue Sox, but she was homesick for weeks. Only later did she bond with other players. As the ritual of practices, games, and life with roommates in town and on the road continued, she adjusted, proving herself a timely hitter and

Rookies in 1944 — Lee Surkowski (left), from Moose Jaw, Saskatchewan, and Ellen Ahrndt, from Racine, pose before a practice in the spring of 1944 (courtesy of Ellen (Ahrndt) Proefrock).

a fast base runner. In mid–June, the assertive Surkowski, blessed with a strong arm, played center field in place of the departed Panos. Years later, Lee's favorite memory was her two-homer game of July 8, 1944.[38]

Another newcomer was Charlotte Armstrong. She was born in Dallas, and her parents moved to Phoenix when she was two years old. Charlotte grew up playing sandlot baseball, and former National Leaguer Hank Lieber, a Phoenix resident, befriended the young right-hander and taught her to pitch. In 1939, at age 13, she began hurling for the Phoenix Cantaloupe Queens, a semipro team that toured many states and played at such sites as Madison Square Garden. A quiet, pleasant person, the 5'7" brunette threw a moving fastball second to none. When the windmiller had her usual sharp control, she was as tough to hit as any pitcher. A talented athlete who enjoyed painting, Armstrong—who liked making funny faces in the dugout to loosen players up—joined Berger, Bennett, and Barr as mainstays of the pitching rotation.[39]

The Blue Sox also received infielder Ellen Ahrndt. Born on a farm outside of Racine, she grew up in a working class family with one older brother, an avid ballplayer, and five sisters. At William Horlick High, where she graduated in 1941, Ahrndt played basketball and tennis. At 13, she played on a softball team managed by her brother. After the war started, the team disbanded, and Ahrndt began playing for the Dumore Company squad. Dumore, where two sisters also worked and played ball, manufactured electric heaters and engines, and the company's squad competed against teams from nearby towns. Once hired, Ellen became a regular at second base. A league scout saw the 5'4" infielder play in the city tournament in 1943, and she was invited to the 1944 spring camp. Twenty-one years old during the tryouts, she made the league and was sent to South Bend, where she and Lee Surkowski lived with the Bauers.

On Sunday, September 27, 1944, the *Milwaukee Journal* ran Ahrndt's photo in the section called "This Week," and friends discovered that she had played in the All-American League. Speaking in a 2007 interview, Ellen, nicknamed Babe by her teammates, was released after a month, but she remembered going to see her Blue Sox teammates when they arrived for games in Racine, Kenosha, or Milwaukee. Though she was a rookie, most of the players were friendly, notably Jochum, MacLean, Hageman, and Schroeder, who "took her under their wings." Ahrndt felt honored by the privilege of playing part of a season in the All-American League. As she said later, "All of those girls played in the league because they loved it."[40]

Ups and Downs

Ready to start a new winning streak, the Blue Sox arrived at the Belle City of the Lakes early in the morning on Tuesday, June 27, checked in at the Hotel Racine, and prepared for a game at Horlick Field. Steady Kay Bennett pitched and, relying on her rising fastball and slow curve, won a three-hitter, 5–0. Before the game, Ellen Ahrndt, the reserve infielder from Racine, enjoyed a memorable moment, receiving a bouquet of roses and a $50 war bond from friends at Dumore's on "Babe Ahrndt Night." A crowd of 2,378, the largest in circuit history to date, paid to see South Bend and Racine. Ahrndt, who started at second base, walked in her only at-bat. Niehoff, lacking confidence in the older rookie, removed her and sent in Stefani—who played 116 games at second base—to pinch-run.[41]

As a result, Ahrndt spent most of her special "night" on the bench, realizing she would never get a chance to play in place of one of the manager's favorites. Recalling those events, Ellen wrote, "Needless to say, I was devastated and humiliated. I guess I was glad to be released after that."[42]

Following the game, the South Benders traveled to nearby Milwaukee, registered at the Ambassador Hotel early on Wednesday morning, and moved through the daily on-the-road pregame ritual. At Borchert Field that night, the Blue Sox fell in 12 innings to the Chicks and Connie Wisniewski's four-hitter, 2–1. The home team reached Armstrong for 13 hits, three by former teammate Vickie Panos, who played especially hard.[43] Thursday's result was worse, as Milwaukee managed four hits off Berger and Barr, but won, 6–3, on eight South Bend errors.[44]

On June 30, following a late-night train trip, sleep, and practice at the friendly confines of Bendix Field on Friday afternoon, the Blue Sox met the Comets that evening in the first of a four-game series. A noisy crowd of 1,784 fans enjoyed a typical 7:15 preliminary event, on this occasion pitting local policemen against the firemen. In the main contest, Bennett outlasted Lee Harney, 5–2. The Comets scored in the sixth on Ann Harnett's RBI single, and in the home sixth, Jochum, happy about the pregame presentation of a pair of $25 war bonds for the two homers she slugged on the last trip, was hit on the foot, advanced to third on two grounders, and scored on Baker's fly. In the seventh, batting with two outs and the bases loaded, Betsy lined a two-run single to center, and Stefani added a two-run single. The victory upped South Bend's record to 25–15 and increased the club's lead over Kenosha to four and a half games.

After the game, Bert Niehoff released Ellen Ahrndt, bringing her brief All-American career to an end.[45] The next day, the manager signed infielder Mary Lou Lester, a former Tennessee state champion in golf and tennis who had averaged .201 for Kenosha in 1943.[46]

Fighting for the First Half Title

South Bend, however, dropped the remaining three games of the set to Kenosha, reducing the club's lead over the second-place Comets to one and a half games. Packing again, the Blue Sox traveled to Rockford and won three out of four contests, journeyed to Kenosha and lost two out of three, and returned to Rockford for a doubleheader on Sunday, July 9. Lounging at the hotel, with the season's first half slated to end in a week, the Sox, having held or tied for first place since opening day, talked about winning the title — the dream that eluded them in 1943.

In the lid-lifter against the Peaches, Berger's two-hit effort ended in a 3–0 loss when she yielded a pair of runs in the third on a walk, an error, and a two-run triple by Irene Ruhnke, while Applegren blanked the visitors on three hits. In the nightcap, the fastballing Armstrong, backed by three double plays, won, 3–1.[47] On Monday, South Bend fell to Rockford, 4–3, thanks to an interference call allowing the winning run to score. Bennett spaced nine hits, but in the bottom of the tenth with the score tied at 3–3, Dottie Kamenshek, who singled and took third on a bunt and a steal, stole home. Charley Ullenberg, the home plate umpire, allowed Kamenshek's run, ruling that Baker interfered with the batter's swing during the steal attempt. Elsewhere, Kenosha (31–20) defeated Minneapolis, and South Bend dropped into second place with a 30–21 mark.

Also, Niehoff cut Jo D'Angelo, the Chicago native who was an original member of the Blue Sox and a fan favorite. Jo showed occasional power with a two-homer game earlier in

1944, but she was averaging .149 and had lost her position in center to hard-hitting Lee Surkowski.[48]

On July 11, the same day that President Roosevelt publicly confirmed his willingness to run for a fourth term,[49] the Blue Sox arrived home in South Bend. On a rainy Tuesday, they beat Racine, 9–1. Berger not only tossed a neat one-hitter but she rapped three singles and retired the Belles in the top of the fifth just ahead of the rain. However, Kenosha's game at Rockford was rained out.[50] On Wednesday, South Bend topped Racine, 3–0, on Armstrong's two-hitter, and Florreich led the way with a triple and a double for two of her team's six hits. Also, Kenosha split two games with Rockford, leaving the Sox and the Comets tied for first place with records of 32–21.[51]

Disappointed Again

In the torrid race for the first-half title, South Bend looked forward to five games at Racine, two being make-ups of rainouts, and Kenosha faced a five-game road trip to Rockford. As the Blue Sox rode the South Shore late Wednesday night, they knew it was a critical time.

Racine, however, played tougher under pressure. At Horlick Field on Thursday, July 13, the Blue Sox, suffering the "first place shakes," committed five costly errors, ruining Berger's six-hit hurling and handing the Belles a 7–5 triumph. Meanwhile, Kenosha divided a doubleheader with Rockford and moved half a game ahead of South Bend.[52] On Friday, the visitors suffered their most frustrating defeat, 10–9, after grabbing a 9–8 edge in the top of the tenth when Schroeder walked, stole second and third, and scored on Florreich's single. In Racine's tenth, a tired Berger, pitching in relief, took the defeat, allowing a base hit, a walk, and a double steal before weak-hitting Anna Hutchison grounded a two-run single past shortstop to win the battle.[53]

The resilient South Benders won on Saturday, 8–4, boosted by Baker's four hits. Armstrong limited the Belles to five hits, and four errors accounted for Racine's runs, but the visitors from Indiana piled up 13 thefts to match their 13 hits. Also, Kenosha improved to 34–23 by defeating fifth-place Rockford.[54] However, South Bend, playing a Sunday afternoon twin bill reminiscent of the team's season-ending double loss to Racine in 1943, suffered two devastating defeats, losing the opener, 3–2, and the late tilt, 5–4.

The Blue Sox, who once won ten straight times and led the Comets by five games, virtually reversed their early success and finished the season's first half with a 10–25 mark. Against Racine on the final Sunday, South Bend stranded seven runners in the first game as Berger, who yielded six safeties, lost her third straight, and Winter, the right-hander who led the loop with 23 losses, scattered six hits. In the late game, Nesbitt tossed a six-hitter to outlast Armstrong, who gave up just four hits—but two were homers. Eleanor "Ellie" Dapkus, the Chicago slugger who led the loop in home runs in 1943 with ten, hit a three-run blast to make the score 5–3 in the sixth, after two Blue Sox errors extended the inning. Elsewhere, Kenosha topped Rockford, 2–0 and 3–1.[55]

One day later, Jim Costin quoted Bert Niehoff, who, shortly before the season began, predicted that his team would get off to a fast start, as they did in 1943, but other clubs would catch up and South Bend would lose out in the end. "We have several players on our team," Niehoff said "who simply don't have the ability to play in this league, but they've sent them back to us again this year and we'll have to get along as best we can with what we have." Niehoff named no names, but he hurt player morale. Costin defended him, pointing out Niehoff won seven pennants in years in the high minor leagues, including one with Double-A Jersey City in 1939.[56]

In retrospect, South Bend's failure to win in the clutch was faced by all other All-American teams. Each squad, barring injuries, had only 16 players, including four pitchers, so managers used a set lineup that varied, except for injuries, only with a new pitcher each day. Furthermore, the success of former major and minor league pilots in managing *men* did not necessarily transfer to managing *women*. Still, the manager's job was teaching fundamentals, devising strategy, coaching the games, and nurturing camaraderie on his team. Niehoff, an intimidating presence because of his age, 60, and his status as a former big leaguer in the "man's world" of the era, needed to maintain influence and respect among all his players, and not favor a few.

If he had an Achilles heel, Niehoff slighted the intangible but important factor of team spirit by playing favorites. South Bend had cliques, a situation that undermined camaraderie. Even among professionals, the feeling of unity was important during a long season, particularly during the grind of road trips, hotel living, and closely-contested games. Niehoff needed to exert more influence and maintain his independence. For chaperones during his tenure, the Blue Sox had youthful Rose Virginia Way in 1943 and Helen Moore in 1944. Given the values of the era, female chaperones would not attempt to influence male managers about how to treat players. As a result, the strongest personalities on the team exerted the most influence on the pilot. In other words, Niehoff let Baker and Stefani sway his thinking. Normally during practices, most of the girls shagged flies while others were batting. Baker and Stefani took their turns hitting, and often retired to the locker room to enjoy a Coke and a smoke. When they did, the manager let it happen.[57]

"We never discussed it," remembered Ellen (Ahrndt) Proefrock, "but we all knew I'm sure from the beginning that Marge and Bonnie had some kind of hold on him, because he did whatever they would say."[58]

Launching the Second Half

On Tuesday, July 18, after spending an off day in Chicago, the Blue Sox and three other All-American clubs again displayed their patriotism by playing in a wartime charity twin bill that attracted a crowd of 16,000, with proceeds going to the Red Cross. Actor Victor Mature, now serving the Navy as Chief Boatswain's Mate, and the Navy's Pier Band opened the evening's entertainment. In the first game, Bennett and MacLean formed the battery against Milwaukee, and the Chicks pounded out a 20–11 victory. In the second contest, limited to three and a half innings because both teams needed to catch a train, Kenosha and Racine played to a 6-all tie. Afterward, South Bend's club arrived home in the wee hours of Wednesday morning.[59]

According to statistics issued by the league office on July 18, Faye Dancer, the Los Angeles outfielder starring for Minneapolis, won the first half batting title with an average of .313. Betsy Jochum, known for her good eye at the plate and her quick bat, finished at .303. Ann Harnett, the brunette third sacker who was the first player to sign with the league in 1943, led in three departments: 34 RBI, 83 total bases, and six triples. Jochum led in total hits with 69, and the Millerettes' Pepper Paire hit the most doubles, seven. Kenosha's Helen Nicol, the Alberta ace, led the pitchers in winning percentage with a 9–4 record, and Mary Nesbitt, Racine's southpaw knuckleballer, ranked second with a 12–6 mark.[60]

The league also announced the resignation of Jack Kloza as manager of the Peaches. Kloza, a former Milwaukee Brewer who began with Rockford in the spring of 1944, gave no reason for leaving, but local sportswriters said he was disappointed when the circuit did not send any new players to help his fifth-place team. In 1943, the Peaches finished fourth (last) in both halves of the season, and they had improved little in 1944. Jim Costin faulted the circuit for discounting the wishes of local officials representing each team. In Kloza's case, he agreed to send Terrie Davis, a fine hitter, to Milwaukee, and he was promised a player of comparable ability. That player never arrived. After the switch, however, Rockford posted an 11–14 record while Milwaukee, managed by the influential Max Carey, improved to 17–8.[61]

On Wednesday, South Bend opened the race for the championship on a sour note, losing at Bendix Field to Rockford, 6–4. The loss revealed several weaknesses, but the big problem was three critical errors committed by Stefani, costing Armstrong a four-hit shutout. Rockford, with Bill Allington as the new manager, won with a four-run fifth inning. There were no other errors, but, observed Costin, the "continued inability of Catcher Baker to throw out base stealers hurt the home cause again." When the night ended, Rockford, Milwaukee, and Racine had 1–0 records, while South Bend, Kenosha, and Minneapolis started the second half with a loss.[62]

After a day of cold rain washed out Thursday's schedule, the Blue Sox met the Peaches in a doubleheader at Bendix on Friday night.[63] The make-up twin bill gave fans their money's worth as each team won a well-played squeaker. The Peaches took the opener, 2–0, but the Blue Sox prevailed in the second game, 1–0. "Both games abounded in spectacular stops, throws and catches," commented Costin, "and both were as brilliantly pitched as any league games ever seen here." The first game lasted 13 innings, and Bennett scattered four singles, but Applegren, who also spaced four hits, retired the Blue Sox in their 13th after Rockford scored on a single, a sacrifice, an infield out, and Dodie Nelson's bouncer to the mound. In the late tilt, Berger, permitting a single to Kamenshek, outdueled Marguerite Jones, who allowed two hits.[64]

Berger's skillful pitching launched South Bend on an eight-game winning streak, the first six at home. On Saturday, the Blue Sox rode Armstrong's stellar outing to another 1–0 victory. The game was decided in the fourth when Jochum singled, advanced on a steal and a grounder, and scored when Loretta Dwojak, a rookie who began with the Millerettes, singled.[65] On Sunday, the Blue Sox returned to the dusty diamond at Bendix and swept the evening's twin bill against Kenosha. Bennett won the 13-inning opener, 3–2, when Stefani singled, stole second, and scored on Gacioch's single off reliever Mary Pratt. In the late tilt, South Bend won, 7–2, when Barr walked four straight in the first inning, but Armstrong relieved her and saved the game.[66] The Blue Sox won their fifth and sixth straight over the Comets, one featuring Berger's two-hitter[67] and another highlighted by Barr's two-hitter. Niehoff had worked with Barr, changing her delivery. The wins improved South Bend to 6–2 and preserved a first-place tie with Racine.[68]

Fighting for First Place

The Blue Sox, already packed, boarded the South Shore, rode for part of the night, changed to the North Shore in Chicago, and arrived at the Hotel Dayton in Kenosha early on Wednesday, July 26. Accustomed to late-night travel, the South Benders practiced at

Lakefront Stadium in the afternoon, rested, and returned that evening to win, 4–2, marking their seventh straight — and fifth in a row from the Comets. The victory gave them first place when Racine fell to Milwaukee. The Comets, facing injuries, including Helen Nicol with a sore arm, competed with 11 players. Armstrong outpitched little Mary Pratt, the visitors' scoring began with Florreich's two-run homer to center in the third, and Charlotte protected the growing lead.[69]

Rain in the Midwest washed out the schedule on Thursday, and the Blue Sox, after hanging around the hotel, rode the day train to Rockford to open a two-game set on Friday night. After reading reports about their skimpy batting averages, many of the players were pleased to be on top of the standings. The *Chicago Tribune* reported that South Bend had the circuit's lowest team average, .172, while fifth-place Minneapolis was leading with a hefty .230. Milwaukee's Merle "Pat" Keagle led hitters with her .387 mark, followed by teammate Tiby Eisen at .344. In other words, the Blue Sox were winning with good pitching. The only two Sox hitters averaging more than .200 were Rosie Gacioch at .250 (she was 7-for-28) and Betsy Jochum at .235 (8-for-34). Again, the league's statistics illustrated the All-American was a pitcher's circuit, despite efforts to speed up the game and give hitters a better chance to make games more exciting.[70]

At Rockford's Beyer Stadium on Friday night, South Bend won its eighth in a row, 2–0, based on steady six-hit pitching from Berger as well as three double plays, the most unusual being Jochum's running catch in left and her bullseye throw to Schroeder to double a runner off second base. The Peaches' Betty Luna, a versatile hurler from Los Angeles, gave up just five hits, but she was hurt by five errors. Afterward, the Sox held first place with an 8–2 mark.[71]

Occasionally South Bend's pitching faltered. On Saturday, July 29, Rockford snapped the visitors' eight-game success streak with a 5–0 victory. Carolyn Morris, the Phoenix beauty, tossed a three-hitter, but Armstrong surrendered four runs in the first inning without a ball leaving the infield.[72] Returning to South Bend on Sunday for a twin bill with the Millerettes, the Blue Sox split the doubleheader and won three of six in the Minneapolis series. In the finale on Thursday, Berger hurled a four-hitter for a 2–1 triumph.[73] The win launched South Bend on a five-game win skein, the last four against Racine. The Belles, helped by six errors, finally won, 7–4, in the second half of a doubleheader on Monday, August 7. Still, Milwaukee improved to 14–8 by beating Kenosha, cutting South Bend's league lead to one game.[74] Suddenly the Blue Sox lost four home contests in a row, two to Racine and a pair to Milwaukee.

Three of those losses were close, tense affairs, but at Bendix on Thursday, August 10, the Blue Sox, on another hot evening, bounced back to edge the Chicks, 1–0. Armstrong faced the seemingly tireless Wisniewski, but Charlotte's hurling received a boost from great plays by Gacioch. In the fifth, Jochum singled to center, stole second, took third on a groundout, and scored when Gacioch legged out a perfect bunt down the first base line. The West Virginian saved the lead in the sixth when Milwaukee had the sacks full with one out and Whiting flied to right field. Gacioch made the catch and fired a strike to Baker at the plate, with the throw beating Pat Keagle by so much that she turned to go back to third. Baker tagged Keagle, who swung an elbow and knocked the ball out of Bonnie's mitt, finishing the swing by clipping her on the chin. Umpire Rob Kober called Keagle out for unnecessary roughness, Baker went after Keagle, and players from both teams pulled them apart. Normally mild-mannered Bert Niehoff protested the "gashouse" tactics of the Chicks, but Milwaukee's Max Carey argued Keagle was safe on the dropped ball.

Arriving at the Ballpark — Dressed for travel by train in 1944, Blue Sox players pose outside Rockford's Beyer Stadium. They are (left to right) Lucella MacLean, Betsy Jochum, Dottie Schroeder, Helen Moore, chaperone, Lee Surkowski, and Rose Gacioch (courtesy of Betsy Jochum).

After the verbal spat, the game resumed. In the ninth, Gacioch, in right field, saved the victory by throwing out Emily Stevenson at first base, after the Chick catcher hit what looked like a single. The strong-armed Gacioch turned the same trick against Whiting in the eighth, and in fact, Rosie had recorded two assists in Wednesday's game. The Blue Sox improved to 16–10, one game behind the 17–9 Chicks, and the teams rode late trains to their four-game set in Milwaukee.[75]

For the Blue Sox, the remainder of August continued to be a series of streaks and tight games. Playing at Milwaukee's Borchert Field, South Bend divided four games, losing the finale, the second game of a twin bill, 9–0, due to Armstrong's unusual wildness, a lack of hitting, and five errors. Afterward, the Chicks, with a 19–11 record, held onto a one-game league lead over the Blue Sox (18–12).[76] South Bend's road trip continued with two wins in three games at Racine, followed by three losses in five tries to the green-clad Comets at Kenosha. South Bend's odyssey was capped by Berger's disappointing 2–1 loss to the Comets on Saturday, August 19, when she gave up a 1–0 lead on Janice O'Hara's bases-loaded double in the ninth. Elsewhere, red-hot Milwaukee (26–11) beat Rockford, boosting the Chicks' loop lead to four and a half games.[77]

Playing as Professionals

Despite any off-the-field problems, the Blue Sox kept making stellar efforts on the half dozen All-American diamonds where they performed, often with touches of brilliance. Upon returning to Bendix Field on August 20, the local heroines swept the Sunday evening twin bill over the last-place Millerettes. Bennett pitched a three-hitter and won the first game, 2–0, as the Blue Sox, who managed two hits, bunted home one run in the second and another in the fourth. In the late game, Armstrong battled Winnipeg's Audrey Haine and won, 6–5, in a contest marred by many "errors of commission and omission." The home team collected eight hits, three by Jochum and two each by Gacioch and Baker, and the visitors picked up six. South Bend improved to 24–16, but Milwaukee (28–11) remained four and a half games ahead by beating Racine twice.[78]

Facing the Millerettes on August 21, designated Ladies Day, South Bend's standard at-home attraction on Mondays in 1944, Berger and Wiltse hooked up in a 12-inning battle before the Blue Sox lost, 2–1, to the "orphans," so called because the league designated Minneapolis a road team after the club lost the use of Nicollet Park in mid-July.[79] The travelers, adorned in their bubble-gum pink uniforms, won in the 12th, starting with Helen Callaghan's infield single. When she took off for second, Baker's throw caromed off her back into left field, and Callaghan scored when Jochum's throw to third bounced into the Sox' dugout. Coupled with Milwaukee's 11th straight win, the loss left South Bend (24–17) five and a half games out of first place.[80]

Just as their hopes for a second half title were fading, the Blue Sox won four straight—the first three against the Millerettes. Bennett pitched well to earn a 1–0 victory in a well-played contest on Tuesday,[81] and Armstrong overcame shoddy fielding before 600 shivering fans to prevail on Wednesday, 6–4, a score inflated by nine errors. Neither catcher, Bonnie Baker nor Ruth Lessing, looked sharp as the teams stole 25 bases, 16 by the Blue Sox.[82]

The local heroines returned to Bendix on Thursday for the 8:30 call to "Play Ball!" On yet another cold night, they won their fifth out of six games as Bennett pitched out of turn to defeat Wiltse, the Minneapolis curveballer, 3–1. A "Merchants Night" crowd of 1,400 enjoyed the well-played game, but the Blue Sox failed to gain on the league-leading Chicks, who rocked the Belles, 15–2. The two-team race for the playoffs was coming down to the final days.[83]

By mid–August, Niehoff continued to use the same lineup, but his team batted a league-worst .193 for the season. Milwaukee topped the loop with an average of .207, 14 points higher than South Bend. Again, considering that pitchers dominated the league during the underhand years, Niehoff hoped his hurlers would keep performing well. His daily lineup card usually showed:

Florreich, 3B — Lois, only 17 years old but in her second season, proved quick and agile with a strong, if erratic, arm. In 99 games, however, the Missouri speedster had trouble hitting the league's best pitchers, averaging .178, well below her 1943 mark of .231. Leading off, Lois drew 54 walks and stole 113 bases, but struck out a team-high 50 times. Still, she could hit with power, slugging four doubles, six triples, and one home run, and producing 25 RBI.

Jochum, LF — Betsy kept proving her value to the team, ranking among the loop's hitting leaders for the entire season. Playing 112 games and usually batting in the second slot, she totaled a league-best 128 hits, drew 40 walks, stole 127 bases, scored a team-high 72 runs, slammed five doubles, one triple, and two home runs, and contributed 23 RBI.

Stefani, 2B — Marge, an experienced and mature player like Baker and Jochum, was a good second baseman. In 116 games, all at second base, she hit .218, down 31 points from her 1943 mark. Batting third, Marge walked a team-best 66 times, made 83 thefts, scored 57 runs, belted four doubles and five triples, and produced a team-best 46 RBI.

Gacioch, RF — Rosie, seemingly an odd choice for the cleanup spot because of her low batting average, was a versatile player, covering third base or the outfield and displaying a strong, accurate arm. In 98 games, she hit only .161, drawing 25 walks, stealing 27 times, and scoring 29 times, while adding two doubles and two triples. More important, Gacioch was best under pressure, delivering timely hits with runners in scoring position, which she proved by knocking in 37 runs.

Surkowski, CF — Enjoying a strong rookie season, the Moose Jaw star replaced Jo D'Angelo in the outer gardens by the end of June. Fleet, talented, and sure-handed, Lee made a number of great catches in center field. Playing 100 games and hitting in the fifth slot, she averaged .212, walked 36 times, stole 37 bases, tallied 32 runs, and cracked the most extra-base hits on the team, seven doubles, four triples, and three homers, and she came through with 24 RBI.

Ready to Play — Posed just before an evening game in mid–1944, these Blue Sox regulars are (left to right) Charlotte Armstrong, Sunny Berger, and Lee Surkowski (courtesy of Lucella (MacLean) Ross).

Baker, C — Considering her batting prowess, Niehoff might have listed Baker higher than sixth in the order, except she toiled behind the plate and had to remove catcher's equipment before she could bat. Already experiencing problems throwing to second base after the base paths were lengthened from 65 to 68 feet at mid-season, the Regina model caught 109 games and swung a good bat, averaging .236, second best on the team behind Jochum. Baker also drew 49 walks, stole 92 bases, scored 48 runs, belted one double and four triples, and drove home 20 runners.

Hageman, 1B — Managers like a good run-producer at first base, but the Blue Sox also ended up with a steady fielder. Playing 116 games, Jo averaged just .142, the lowest mark among Sox regulars, but like Gacioch, she was a timely hitter. Hageman drew 52 walks, pulled off 23 thefts, scored 24 times, hit two doubles, and led the team with 39 RBI.

Schroeder, SS — The youthful Dottie, still only 16, played a slick shortstop, moving like a gazelle around the left side of the infield — her trademark twin ponytails flying — and making good plays. However, Schroeder's hitting slipped from .188 in 1943 to .180. Like all the girls, she contributed in other important ways with 58 walks, 70 swiped bases, and 50 runs. Showing occasional power with one double, two triples, and one home run, she also batted in 24 runs

Beyond the regulars, Niehoff had few choices. South Bend's best reserve was Lucella MacLean. The equal of Baker as a receiver, Lucella, however, injured her right (throwing) arm sliding into second base in mid-season, and, taking daily treatments at the hospital, she was unable to play for several weeks. MacLean finally appeared in a game at Kenosha late in the season,[84] but overall, she played in 31 contests, 15 as the catcher, batted 66 times, and hit .197. Niehoff also had Loretta Dwojak, acquired from Minneapolis. A 5'5" outfielder, Dwojak played 63 games, often replacing Gacioch in right field. The Chicago native hit .201, walking 18 times, making 18 thefts, scoring 19 runs, and contributing 19 RBI, good figures for a recruit. Mary Lou Lester, from Nashville, was Niehoff's last reserve. A 5' 3½" infielder acquired from Kenosha who enjoyed a solid season in 1943, Lester played 18 games in 1944, but failed to hit safely. Pitchers sometimes served as pinch-hitters, but none averaged more than Armstrong's .133. Barr, who hit a substantial .269 in 1943, fell to just .127. Berger, a timely hitter who averaged .195 in her first season, batted only .110. Finally, Bennett plunged from her .208 mark in 1943 to only .051.[85]

When it came to hitting in 1944, South Bend's bottom line was simple: only Jochum hit better than she did in her rookie season, and only Jochum failed to see her average dip in the second half. On the other hand, Niehoff released Vickie Panos in mid–June. The Canadian outfielder batted .263 and became a first-rate contributor for Milwaukee. Niehoff also released Jo D'Angelo, another speedy flychaser who was a good contact hitter with a knack for getting on base, and he dumped Ellen Ahrndt, who, given a chance, might have proven better than Lester, who was hitless in 26 at-bats. After the season, Jim Costin concluded that South Bend needed "one or two real hitters" for 1945,[86] but he forgot the batters Niehoff dropped, notably Panos.

Fighting Spirit

Playing at Milwaukee on Friday, August 25, the Blue Sox won, 5–1, in a game notable for two flare-ups — both ignited by the spirited Surkowski. Berger pitched well, scattering seven hits, but Jo Kabick, the Michigan right-hander, allowed nine hits and walked four. Stefani rapped three hits, but Surkowski, with two safe blows, provided the big highlight after the Sox scored twice in the sixth for a 3–1 lead. Surkowski, resenting rough-house play by Keagle and Dorothy "Mickey" Maguire, gave both a verbal "dressing down" for sliding hard into Schroeder at second base.

Fireworks erupted in the ninth after Surkowski slugged a two-run triple to left center for a 5–1 lead. On the next pitch, Baker missed a squeeze, and Surkowski was caught in a rundown. When third baseman Doris Tetzlaff tagged her out, Lee slipped to the ground. The incident would have ended, because Tetzlaff was helping Surkowski to her feet, but the aggressive Alma "Gabby" Ziegler, the sparkplug second sacker, went after Surkowski. Lee knocked Gabby down, players from both teams ran onto the field, and Niehoff, coaching at third base, separated the women. Umpires Al Gembler and Jack Rice didn't eject either player, ruling Ziegler went after trouble and got it. After the game, Milwaukee players rushed the normally mild-mannered Surkowski, but the Moose Jaw star was "taking on all comers when Bert [Niehoff] arrived on the scene."

The upshot of the night's activities was that, first, a special detail of Milwaukee police was requested for Saturday night's game, and second, the Blue Sox, improving their record to 28–17, moved within two games of the Chicks. Ironically, only 89 cash customers saw the game which, like too many others at Borchert Field, was played in front of thousands of empty seats.[87]

Before Saturday night's contest, Niehoff and Carey met with players on both teams and spelled out their conduct as professionals, emphasizing that the girls needed to compete hard but with "good sportsmanship and fair play." There were no further scuffles. Instead, the game featured Wisniewski's one-hit 3–1 victory. Armstrong permitted seven hits, but the Chicks bunched three safeties, two bunts and Wisniewski's double, for a 2–0 lead they never lost. When the evening ended, Milwaukee, with a 31–15 mark, led South Bend (28–18) by three games.

Ironically, the *Tribune's* phones rang constantly Saturday and Sunday with requests for news from the Milwaukee "battlefront"! Fans liked the fighting spirit suddenly shown by the Sox, notably Surkowski. Although a "mild mannered lady-like youngster" off the field, she was defending her teammates. Accusing Milwaukee of playing rough-house ball, Jim Costin pointed out that Surkowski and Baker in particular were taking on the tough Chicks "at their own game."[88]

Whether Surkowski acted on the spur of the moment, or whether she was trying to fire up her teammates is unknown, but nevertheless, the Blue Sox soon fell apart. On Sunday, August 27, the team returned home for a twin bill against Rockford, but the league's games were washed out by a Midwestern storm.[89] Milwaukee arrived for a critical series on a drizzly Monday, and that evening, Wisniewski, the rubber-armed Polish fireballer, won a two-hitter, 3–0. A small crowd of 800 saw the Chicks manage just three hits off Berger, but they scored one run with a batter who should have been out on a pop fly and two more with hitters who were trapped off base but escaped. The win gave 32–15 Milwaukee a four-game league lead,[90] and the loss, South Bend's second straight, became another bad night in a frustrating seven-game losing streak.

The slide continued on Tuesday before an "Elks' Family Night" audience of 2,300, the largest South Bend turnout to date, when Chicks rookie Jo Kabick won a two-hitter, 2–0. Kabick, en route to a 26–19 season, walked five, hit one, and made an error — giving the home team several opportunities, but to no avail.[91] On Wednesday night, Milwaukee won, 4–0, in ten innings, making it four straight losses in which the slumping Blue Sox collected a total of nine hits and one run. Wisniewski pitched tough and so did Berger, but Sunny received "disheartening" support, as Baker singled twice and Jochum and Surkowski each singled, but with no runners aboard. In the top of the tenth, the visitors scored four runs, ignited by the good-hitting Wisniewski's two-run blooper to left. The Chicks, improving to 34–15, took a six-game lead with 11 games left, crushing the South Benders' fading dreams for a second-half title.[92]

Facing first-half champion Kenosha for the season's last two games at Bendix, South Bend lost both. On Thursday, the Blue Sox reached Pratt for seven hits, but Barr's wildness — she walked nine — overshadowed the home team's improved hitting, and Kenosha won, 3–2.[93] On Friday night, Gertrude "Lefty" Ganote, normally a first sacker, tossed a shutout and won, 2–0. "But the clutch hits were missing, as usual," commented Jim Costin.[94]

During the past week, the faltering Blue Sox had scored just three runs in 54 innings of play. South Bend's record of 28–23 left the club seven and a half games behind Milwaukee. As they boarded a late train for three games at Racine and the final four games at Rockford, the light blue-clad All-Americans were playing for pride.

Winding Down a Disappointing Season

The Allied war effort in Europe, notably across France, was going well by September,[95] but South Bend was winding down a season once full of hope and promise. At Racine on Saturday night, September 2, the Belles won in ten innings, 2–1.[96] Still, the Blue Sox, proud professionals, showed their mettle again in Sunday's twin bill when they snapped the seven-game losing streak with two extra-inning victories. Bennett's steady hurling won the short opener, 6–4, and Armstrong's fine performance won the nightcap, 2–1. In the first game, Racine almost won on stolen bases, swiping 16 off Bennett's "slow-ball hurling." But South Bend broke a 3–3 tie in the top of the seventh with three runs. In the nightcap, the Blue Sox broke a 1–1 tie in the tenth, scoring the game-winner on Florreich's single, two thefts, and Hageman's crucial squeeze, giving Armstrong, who retired the Belles in the bottom of the inning, the victory.[97]

Traveling to Rockford, the Blue Sox played another doubleheader on Monday night, winning the opener, 2–0, behind Berger's five-hitter, and losing the nightcap, 9–3, as Barr gave up eight hits. The split clinched second place for South Bend, a small consolation for the players. Still, Rockford's fans proved their enthusiasm when 3,265 paid to see the contests, making a total of more than 75,000 who saw the Peaches play in 1944.[98] On Tuesday, South Bend suffered another painful defeat, 2–1, losing on Dorothy "Snookie" Harrell's RBI triple in the ninth.[99]

The *Tribune's* Jim Costin labeled the Blue Sox "Always A Bridesmaid," because they had finished second in four straight half-seasons.[100] On Wednesday, the final night of the regular season, South Bend played poorly, but Carolyn Morris, Rockford's ace, fired her second no-hitter and won, 9–0. The Blue Sox posted a second half record of 31–27, and the third place Peaches finished at 29–28.[101] Later, the league's campaign ended when Milwaukee beat first-half winner Kenosha in a best-of-seven playoff, winning the finale, 3–0, on Wisniewski's three-hitter.[102]

The Blue Sox rode one more pair of trains home early on Thursday morning. After packing and resting much of the day, Bert Niehoff and his players were guests of the team's board of directors for a "Farewell Dinner" at the South Bend Country Club. Featured speaker Jim Costin observed that the Blue Sox had compiled the best two-year record of the original All-American teams, going a combined 122–102 in 1943 and 1944. He concluded by saying that everyone hoped the directors could announce "one or two real hitters had been corralled for the '45 season."[103]

South Bend's hitters and pitchers ranked on opposite ends of the league's spectrum. Betsy Jochum led the league in 1944 with an overall .296 average, but South Bend finished last in hitting as a team at .193 (and .180 for the second half). Based on ERA, the Blue Sox placed three hurlers in the top five. Kenosha's Helen Nicol again led in earned run average, fashioning an ERA of 0.93 and a record of 17–11. Charlotte Armstrong ranked second with marks of 1.51 and 21–15, Sunny Berger was third at 1.57 and 21–17, the Millerettes' Dottie Wiltse was fourth at 1.88 and 20–16, and Kay Bennett was fifth at 2.04 and 14–9. Dodie

Barr posted a 2.98 ERA with an 8–11 mark, but she issued 141 walks, a figure exceeded by just three other pitchers.[104]

Also, the league's managers were polled for a postseason All-Star team. Four women won the first-place choice of all six pilots: Rockford's Dottie Kamenshek, first base; Helen Callaghan of Minneapolis, an outfielder; Pat Keagle of Milwaukee, another flychaser; and Milwaukee's Mickey Maguire as catcher. Sunny Berger was one of four pitchers named by all six managers, and the others were Milwaukee's Connie Wisniewski, Kenosha's Helen Nicol, and Minneapolis' Dottie Wiltse. Also, Bonnie Baker was chosen by four pilots as the backup to Maguire. The remaining All-Stars were Milwaukee's Gabby Ziegler, second base; Kenosha's Ann Harnett, third base; Milwaukee's Terrie Davis, shortstop; Minneapolis' Faye Dancer, outfielder; and Kenosha's Shirley Jameson, utility outfielder. Some of the voters liked Jochum, but in the end, she was outpolled by Dancer and Jameson.[105]

In retrospect, the All-American League fielded six good teams and established a stronger presence in 1944, and Philip Wrigley's financial backing assured the league's return in 1945. Furthermore, the Blue Sox, despite certain problems, fielded a very good club with a strong core of talented professionals playing a sped-up hybrid of fast-pitch softball and baseball. Indeed, the game looked "much like regulation baseball," George Berkowitz claimed in his nationally syndicated story that included three pictures, one captioned, "Shortstop Ellen Ahrndt corrals a hot line drive."[106] Overall, for many of the players who completed the second season, the Girls' Pro League had a more permanent feeling. Many players believed already that the circuit would renew itself each spring and that they could go on playing for pay and living their diamond dreams through endless summers.

• 3 •

The Last Wartime Season: 1945

"The Blue Sox will be stronger this year than in the past two years, in the opinion of Marty McManus, the team's manager, but, then, he adds, the whole league will be stronger and the fans in the league's six cities will see the best brand of girls' baseball they have ever seen"—*South Bend Tribune*, May 22, 1945[1]

The League Evolves

The All-American Girls Professional Ball League,[2] as the circuit was known in 1944, evolved further down the road toward baseball, rather than the sped-up fast-pitch softball that existed for the first two seasons. In November 1944, the league switched from the Trustee Administration started by Philip Wrigley and his associates to a more decentralized setup, the Management Corporation. The new structure permitted team officials to run their activities under the control of the league's president and the board of directors, a group that included team presidents, or their representatives. As a result, teams supervised the adoption of rules and regulations, including schedules and the changing direction of the game on the field. Still, the Management Corporation, or Management, took care of all phases of the league's promotion and advertising, recruiting players and managers, hiring umpires, creating the schedule, and handling day-to-day business. Arthur Meyerhoff, head of Wrigley's advertising firm, had worked with the circuit from day one. He purchased Wrigley's interests after the 1944 season and ran the well-organized league on a profit-making basis, but the teams were nonprofit civic organizations.

Men again operated women's teams in a "league of their own," but given the culture of the 1940s, male management was not questioned.[3] The schedule, however, was a source of irritation with most teams, and South Bend's officials were as unhappy as anyone. For the second straight year, the Blue Sox were forced to end their 1944 season with a long road trip, and, partly as a result, many folks, notably directors, believed the schedule caused the team to finish in second place. Regarding personnel, Meyerhoff's proposals allowed the four original teams to retain up to ten players from the current rosters. Furthermore, the Charm School was dropped, and the two-week spring training was slated for one week in a central camp, and a week of exhibitions that showed fans the girls' game.[4]

Meyerhoff, like Wrigley, envisioned the league moving toward baseball because fans knew and loved the national pastime. For 1945, the league's schedule adopted the name All-American Girls Professional Baseball League,[5] but the game was the same. The circuit again used the big ball measuring 11.5 inches in circumference, the base paths remained at 68 feet, and underhand pitching, softball's trademark, was continued, but the pitching distance was lengthened from 40 to 42 feet at mid-season. As usual, pitchers were forced to adjust their motions to succeed, and the league continued to be a historic work in progress.[6] Still, as *Life* magazine phrased it on June 4, 1945, "Girls' professional ball is something less than regulation professional baseball, something more than softball." The story featured six pictures of players, and the large lead photo showed Bonnie Baker smiling through her softball catcher's mask. The story and picture helped make the photogenic Baker part of the league's glamour image.[7]

Al McGann, president of the Blue Sox, announced that Marty McManus was hired as manager. McManus replaced Bert Niehoff, who, in early 1945, left to manage Chattanooga of the Class A Southern Association.[8] McManus had led Kenosha to the league's first half title in 1944, but the Comets fell to the Milwaukee Chicks in the championship playoffs. Once a star infielder for the St. Louis Browns and the Detroit Tigers, McManus piloted the Boston Red Sox in 1932 and 1933.[9]

In addition, the league's spring training was slated for a Chicago ballpark. Similar to the first two training camps, more than 100 top female athletes from all over the United States and Canada were invited to work out with circuit personnel from May 9 to 16.[10]

The league's allocation board picked six 16-player teams on Wednesday, May 16, and the regular season began a week later with Racine hosting Rockford, Kenosha at South Bend, and Grand Rapids (the Milwaukee franchise in 1944) at Fort Wayne (which was formerly in Minneapolis). The biggest change was having teams play one season, not a first and second half. After Labor Day, the top four clubs would meet in semifinal and championship rounds of Shaughnessy Playoffs: first versus third place, second versus fourth, and winner versus winner.[11]

In addition, the six teams held tryouts on the last Sunday of April to allow local talent a chance for a trip to the league's camp. Bill "Wamby" Wambsganss, Fort Wayne's manager, supervised tryouts in Fort Wayne and in South Bend, after Marty McManus was called home to St. Louis due to his daughter's illness. Wamby chose three recruits of the 17 who worked out. Two made the cut at Waveland Park and played briefly for the Blue Sox: Dorothea Downs, a South Bend native who played first base for the Bendix plant, and Doris Marsh, an Elkhart pitcher.[12]

Additionally, South Bend's enlarged board (now with an unwieldy 25 directors, instead of eight) decided the team would again play home games at Bendix Field, although the larger Playland Park was considered, partly because Bendix was located out on the city's west side.

The team's last two holdouts soon signed. The *South Bend Tribune* announced that Bonnie Baker, who was demanding a big pay increase, agreed to undisclosed terms on May 5 with Max Carey, the league's new president. Betsy Jochum, the loop's top hitter in 1944, had rejected two small raises. Four days later, however, she traveled to Chicago and inked her contract.[13]

Jochum's holdout illustrated the circumstances faced by All-Americans — and all professional ballplayers. In organized baseball, the teams owned the players' contracts. The standard contract included a reserve clause legally binding, or reserving, a player to the contracting team until retirement or an owner-related action like a trade. Even stars as famous as Stan Musial of the St. Louis Cardinals had to sign for salaries lower than they would have earned as free agents.[14]

Jochum's experience with Max Carey, who managed Milwaukee in 1944, was similar. Despite the fact that the All-American League used personal services contracts binding players to the circuit, not to a team,[15] the league's ownership of contracts and allocation of players had the same effect as baseball's reserve clause: it held salaries down. When Betsy asked for a raise based on her standout 1944 season, Carey, citing lack of funds, claimed the loop paid more money than did men's Class B, C, and D leagues, and more than "quite a few of the major league players, and you can check on that" (an impossibility — baseball salaries were not published). Carey, in condescending fashion, said Jochum needed to learn more about "playing this game, especially from the fielding and base-running standpoints." He offered her $5 per week more.[16]

Years later, Jochum, a first-rate hitter, an excellent defensive outfielder, and a fine base runner, called Carey's letter an "insult." In 1943, she played 101 games (injuries forced her to miss seven contests), stole 66 bases, batted .273 overall, and won the second-half title with her .295 average. In 1944, the Cincinnati star played 112 games, stole a remarkable 127 bases, and led the league with her .296 average. No All-American gave a better overall performance. Betsy refused a contract for $75. She was still holding out in mid–April, so Carey wrote again, claiming just one outfielder (the newspapers identified her as Faye Dancer) was "getting a trifle more than you are, and she came in on an original three-year contract, so that you really are getting more."[17]

However, as South Benders like Jochum and Jean Faut later learned, the league set a salary maximum, but certain players were favored and paid more "under the table."[18] The bottom line remained the same: men ran the Girls' Pro League, and they used their experience in men's baseball to justify the often second-class treatment given to female players. Meanwhile, South Bend drew a paid attendance of 49,294 in 1944, third best in the league, and generated $35,000 in revenue, but operated at a loss of more than $13,000. Naturally the businessmen who ran teams like the Blue Sox were concerned with keeping costs like salaries as low as possible.[19]

The Blue Sox in 1945

The day Jochum signed, May 9, the league launched spring camp in the chilly winds at Waveland Park, located a few miles off Lake Michigan on Chicago's north side.[20] Since a new rule allowed each team to retain up to ten of the 15 players on the 1944 roster, the league would have about 30 veteran players, along with the rookies, to allocate to new clubs. The camp began with Max Carey, aided by the managers, directing two days of batting and fielding practice for 100 prospects, all of whom roomed at the Allerton Hotel. The six teams, each with up to 20 players, began playing games at Waveland's three diamonds. If the weather was too cold, players moved to nearby gyms for indoor conditioning drills.[21]

On May 16, the allocation board assigned players to the teams. South Bend received eight veterans from the 1944 club, including pitchers Doris Barr and Charlotte Armstrong, catcher Bonnie Baker, infielders Dorothy Schroeder, Lois Florreich, and Marge Stefani, and outfielders Lee Surkowski and Betsy Jochum. The ball club's allocation representative, however, allowed Rose Gacioch to be reallocated, and Rockford acquired her. Later, Gacioch recalled that certain Blue Sox officials and players disliked her southern manner of speaking.[22]

As of opening day, the new Blue Sox were:

- Nalda Bird, the five-foot Los Angeles southpaw who looked to be an excellent prospect

- Betty Luna, a 5'5" right-hander who posted a 12–13 record for Rockford in 1944
- Dolores Klosowski, who was the regular first baseman for the Chicks in 1944, until a back injury forced her out of the lineup
- Gertrude Ganote, or Lefty, the Comets' first sacker and sometime hurler who batted .133 in 1944, but led the league's first basemen in fielding with a .988 average in 86 games
- Anne Surkowski, elder sister of Lee, a fleet flychaser who was expected to replace Gacioch, South Bend's strong-armed third sacker and right fielder
- Elizabeth "Lib" Mahon, a second baseman who played for Minneapolis and Kenosha in 1944
- Kay Sopkovic, a 5'5" rookie designated as a catcher,[23] from Youngstown, Ohio
- Darlene Mickelsen, a reserve outfielder who played briefly for the Comets in 1943

After playing a pair of exhibitions over the weekend, the Blue Sox arrived in South Bend on Tuesday, May 22, practiced, and received a day off on Wednesday. As in previous seasons, the women were assigned to rooms with a private family in neighborhoods within walking distance of Bendix Field. Returning players often stayed with the families they knew the previous summer. However, the game times had changed. To accommodate war workers leaving for the 11 o'clock night shift at the Bendix plant, games would begin at eight o'clock, not 8:30, and Sunday evening doubleheaders would start at seven, not 7:15.[24]

Marty McManus, with his blue eyes, black hair, and occasionally fiery temperament, treated players with respect. Talking to the *Tribune*, Marty offered positive comments about the players, notably pitchers Betty Luna and Nalda Bird. He gave up Jo Hageman (Kenosha obtained her) to get "speed and more power" at first base, saying either Ganote from the Comets or Milwaukee's Klosowski would play, depending on which one hit the best. Recognizing the girls' game had improved greatly over last year's level and that other teams were also finding first-rate players, he concluded, "We've got a better team, but it's going to be tougher to win, too."[25]

Detailing McManus' experience in the majors and the minor leagues, Jim Costin, implying autonomy was not always the case with the Blue Sox, observed, "If he is given a free rein in running the team as his ability and experience dictate, supporters of the club are in for a fine season of interesting entertainment."[26] Regardless, the new pilot found his hands full trying to meld together so many new players into a veteran-led squad that could develop into an excellent team.

The Third Season

Before the Blue Sox and the Comets launched the league's third season at Bendix Field on Wednesday, May 23, the teams took their batting and fielding practice. Afterward, the Post 50 American Legion band paraded around the outfield, entertaining the crowd with popular tunes. Fans also enjoyed the wartime patriotic ceremony featuring players lined up in the usual "V" for victory formation along the base lines, after which the crowd recited the Pledge of Allegiance with a spotlight highlighting the American flag — a ritual led by the acting mayor, Ken Dempsey.

After the pregame fun, South Bend lost to Kenosha in ten innings, 5–3. The Blue Sox looked like world-beaters for eight innings, opening with the season's first run by Jochum, who singled and later scored on Florreich's fly to center. In the ninth, the lime green-uniformed visitors tied the game at 3–3 on a walk, a passed ball, a grounder, two singles, Anne Surkowski's two-base error on the second hit, and an infield out. The Comets won in the tenth when Shirley Jameson walked, advanced on a bunt, and Kay Shinen was safe on Schroeder's wild throw. Nervous, Anne Surkowski, who was not used to night games, dropped Audrey Wagner's pop fly, and Jameson scored. After a walk, Betty Fabac bounced to Luna, who threw home to start a double play, but Baker fired the relay into right field, Wagner scored, and Helen Fox retired the home team for the win.[27]

On a rainy, chilly Thursday night, the Blue Sox torched the Comets, 12–2, behind the two-hit hurling of Nalda Bird, the team's new California girl. Schroeder, normally one of the league's best gloves, made four errors, and her three miscues in the first frame gave Kenosha two runs. Thereafter, Bird dominated, showing good speed and a nifty curve, and she added two singles to the 12-hit attack.[28] On Friday, heavy rain cancelled a third game with the Comets.[29]

On Saturday, the two teams returned to Bendix and, at the starting time of eight o'clock, the umpires called "Play ball!" Working in chilly conditions, Luna spaced six hits, and, thanks to 11 safe blows and good defense, she blanked Kenosha, 8–0. Lee Surkowski turned in two great running catches in center, and Jochum made a pair of fine catches in left. The win lifted the 2–1 Blue Sox into second place, half a game behind the Fort Wayne Daisies (3–1).[30]

The next day, South Bend was scheduled to meet last year's All-American League champions, the former Milwaukee Chicks, now playing in Grand Rapids, Michigan. Instead, rain cancelled the league's three-game schedule, and the Chicks journeyed back to Grand Rapids. The Blue Sox left by train on Monday for a Tuesday night tilt in Michigan's "Furniture City." as observed by the *Tribune's* Jim Costin, Lib Mahon, who replaced the inexperienced Anne Surkowski in right field, was leading the Sox in batting at .625, Betsy Jochum, last year's batting champ, was averaging .418, and Marge Stefani, a dependable run producer, topped the team with six RBI.[31]

The Blue Sox arrived in Grand Rapids on Tuesday, May 29, stayed at the Hotel Rowe, and prepared for the usual night contest. In 1945, the last wartime season, Grand Rapids, the center of the state's furniture industry, was a well-to-do city located along the Grand River, 30 miles east of Lake Michigan. First settled in 1826 by French-Canadian fur traders, Grand Rapids soon had a large element of thrifty Dutch settlers with traditional Christian values. The area became a center for cabinet-making in the 1840s and furniture manufacturing within a decade. By 1900, the city had more than 50 furniture factories, and churches dotted the landscape. By 1920, Michigan cities such as Flint, Saginaw, Jackson, Lansing, and Grand Rapids also manufactured auto parts. During World War II, many of the state's cities boomed with federal contracts, because auto makers and parts manufacturers converted to wartime production. Grand Rapids, with a population of 175,000, was no exception. The factories of Michigan's second largest city built gliders, gunstocks, parachutes, and bullet molds, where they once turned out beds, dressers, dining tables, and chairs. In 1945, the Chicks were welcomed by a large working-class fan base.[32]

At South High Field, the teams met on a gridiron set up for women's pro ball. Surrounded by stands and buildings, the oblong ballpark had a long left field but a short right field bounded by the Dexter Lock Factory. The stands seemed close enough for fans to touch the players, and folks seated behind first base liked to shake hands with Chicks who hit "short porch" home runs.[33]

In the first away series, South Bend lost two of three contests. On Tuesday, facing rain blown by a chilly wind, Connie Wisniewski, the tall fastballer who led her team to the 1944 All-American title with a 23–10 record, blanked the Blue Sox, 8–0. Wisniewski, with her fastball popping, gave up singles to Mahon and Barr, who took over in the fifth for Bird, after Nalda had yielded five runs on six hits and four walks. On Wednesday, in the seven-inning opener of a doubleheader, Grand Rapids won in 16 innings, 2–1, when Tiby Eisen belted a home run over Jochum's head. In the nightcap, limited to seven frames due to the late start, Bird took revenge by winning a two-hitter, 5–0. Over 4,000 fans saw the games, South Bend (now 3–3) fell to third place, and Fort Wayne (5–3) held first place by splitting a twin bill with second-place Rockford.[34]

Taking the 120-mile train trip home, the Blue Sox received a day off when the weather remained cold. However, they learned about the kind of behind-scenes maneuvering that increasingly led to discord between the league and the teams, when Jim Costin published the story of Max Carey's aborted attempt to shift Charlotte Armstrong to Racine. After the star right-hander arrived in Chicago en route to South Bend, the loop's president, acting on his own, ordered her to report to the Belles. The switch failed when the Blue Sox' board revolted against the idea, and Armstrong refused to go, saying she would sign with the "Chicago League." The Phoenix hurler had that option, because officials of the girls' league in the Windy City, upon hearing about her situation, sent a scout to offer her a higher salary. Armstrong stayed in South Bend only after being assured by Howard Feaser, president of the local board, and Carey, who backed off, that she played for the Sox. "It looks like the South Bend club's directors," concluded Costin, "will have to keep on their toes at all times to see that none of this city's star players are moved out to other teams."[35]

In fact, the Chicago League, or the National Girls Softball League (the name was changed to Baseball in 1946), began in 1944 with four teams in Chicago or suburbs such as Des Plaines, Rockola, and Forest Park. Businesses sponsored the teams and gave selected players jobs. Teams like the Admiral Music Maids, the Rockola Chicks, and the Match Corporation Queens played four or more games a week. The league paid competitive salaries, which is why players like Armstrong threatened to "jump" the All-American League (Charlotte did play in Chicago in 1946), and others like former South Bender Lucella MacLean did leave the nation's best-known Girls' Pro League in 1945. In fact, the Chicago League actually played fast-pitch softball with underhand pitching, and players like MacLean disliked how the All-American game was moving closer to baseball. The NGBL posed an ongoing threat to the talent pool of the All-American League in the late 1940s, and players as famous as Racine's Sophie Kurys and Jo Winter, Grand Rapids' Connie Wisniewski, and Armstrong later played in the Windy City.[36]

Enduring cold, wet weather for the twin bill at Bendix on Friday, June 1, the Blue Sox swept the visiting Daisies, who sported pink uniforms (some called the color "purplish-rose,"[37] or orchid) with dark red accessories and caps.[38] In the opener, Armstrong scattered four hits and topped Lefty Lee, 2–1. The home team scored both runs in the third when, with two outs, Ganote and Baker singled, and Jochum slammed a three-bagger. In the nightcap, 646 shivering customers saw their favorites play well as Bird, who allowed three hits, beat Dottie Wiltse in ten frames, 4–3. Other games were rained out, so South Bend took first place with a 5–4 mark, followed by Rockford at 4–3 and Fort Wayne at 5–5.[39]

Rain and cool temperatures caused cancellation of Saturday's Fort Wayne game. On Sunday, the temperature dropped to the low 40s, and management, fearing another poor turnout, chose not to play. Elsewhere, Rockford won twice from Kenosha, Grand Rapids took two from Racine, and South Bend (5–3) slipped to second place, while Rockford, now 6–3, took over the league's top spot.[40]

Road Trips, Personnel Changes, and Injuries

On Tuesday, June 5, the Blue Sox made another trip on the old South Shore Elevated to Chicago, making the usual switch of trains, and taking the newer North Shore to Racine. Doris Barr, however, remained at home, because the club asked waivers on her, despite Marty McManus' objections. The popular Winnipeg lefty had made one relief appearance, yielding five runs, four hits, and five walks in four frames. Jim Costin wrote, "Barr has a world of stuff on the ball, but her peculiar 'stiff-arm' delivery seems to cause her to release the ball in such a manner that she rarely knows where it's going." Utility player Darlene Mickelsen was also placed on waivers.[41]

Beginning that night at limestone-walled Horlick Field, South Bend split a four-game series with Racine, losing the first two contests and winning the last two. In the fourth game on Friday night, South Bend played well and won, 9–3, beating Jo Winter on what the *Tribune* called "murderous hitting," exploding in the sixth for seven runs and an 8–3 lead. Luna prevailed, after throwing away three runs on a bases-loaded pickoff attempt. Also, Kenosha topped Fort Wayne, and Rockford defeated Grand Rapids, so the 7–5 Blue Sox rose to second place behind the 8–5 Chicks.[42]

Traveling again, the South Benders arrived in Fort Wayne on Saturday, hoping to succeed on the Daisies' home field, but rain wiped out the visiting team's sixth game to date.[43] Reflecting on those long road trips, Betsy Jochum observed, "Our travel itinerary was very demanding, but when you love what you are doing, it doesn't matter too much — you endure."[44]

Fort Wayne, located 110 miles southeast of South Bend and near the confluence of the St. Joseph, the St. Mary's, and the Maumee rivers, was a prosperous industrial city with a number of factories converted to war production. The fort, named after General Anthony Wayne, was the last of several built on that site in 1794. Fort Wayne was the center for Indian trade and commerce in the northeast region of Indiana, known as Indian Territory before statehood was conferred in 1816. The fur trade brought pioneers to the region, and construction of the Wabash and Erie Canal fostered growth in the 1830s. After tracks were laid in the mid–1850s, the Pennsylvania Railroad became the region's dominant business. Following the Civil War, the city witnessed the growth of industries such as the Bass Foundry and Wayne Knitting Mills. The population exceeded 114,000 by 1930. Unlike most cities, Fort Wayne grew during the Great Depression. With railroads, Essex Wire, Zollner Piston, Central Soya, and other businesses thriving during World War II, Fort Wayne became the ideal host for an All-American team.[45]

The Daisies' home games were slated for North High Field. As a result, the school's gridiron was marked off as a baseball diamond, with home plate in the southwest end of the oblong area. The field had a seating capacity of 4,000, and light poles were installed to allow for night games, but the playing surface, after years of football, was hard and rough, a fact the Sox soon learned. Only one locker room was available, so the league told visiting teams to shower and dress at their hotel, often the Hotel Anthony. Such were the facilities and conditions often available to the loop's women, who were willing to overlook such obstacles because they loved the game.[46]

Rain washed out the Fort Wayne game on June 9,[47] but in Sunday's doubleheader (Saturday's rainout would be made up later) at the wet field, the Blue Sox kicked away each game with a bad inning—and, worse, lost three players to injuries in the nightcap. In the short lid-lifter, Luna was trailing in the sixth, 2–1, when the Blue Sox committed three errors, opening the door to five runs and a 7–1 loss to Dottie Wiltse and her sharp-breaking

Elizabeth "Lib" Mahon — South Bend's longtime outfielder, Mahon is shown in 1946. She had injured her knee and had to wear an Ace bandage or a brace to play in 1945 (courtesy of the Louise Pettus Archives and Special Collections, Winthrop University).

curve. In the nightcap, Bird took a 3–1 lead into the fifth before her teammates blew up, making four errors that led to eight runs. Fort Wayne collected eight hits and scored four more times for a score of 13–6. South Bend rapped eight hits but could not overcome seven errors.

The blue-uniformed travelers also suffered critical injuries. Florreich was shaken by a bad hop when fielding a grounder at third, and Stefani took over her post. Mahon and Luna, who subbed for Lib at second base (Mahon moved from the outfield when Stefani went to third base), were both hurt sliding into second. Mahon tore a ligament in her left knee and was lost for 30 days, and Luna sprained her ankle, an injury that sidelined her for ten days. Both injuries proved costly to South Bend, and all resulted from the "poor condition of the infield" at North High's field.[48]

On Monday, the Blue Sox lost their third in a row due to sloppy fielding, the team's nemesis in 1945. Armstrong allowed one run in six innings, but endured an error-filled, seven-run seventh and lost, 8–2. Schroeder rapped three singles, and Lee Surkowski, who was 2-for-4 and scored twice, was shifted to third base after the youthful Florreich, an erratic infielder, made five of nine Sox errors. South Bend slipped to a 7–8 ledger. Elsewhere, Grand Rapids blanked Racine and Kenosha beat Rockford, leaving the Chicks and the Daisies tied for first place with 11–6 marks.[49]

Fighting for First

By mid–June, the South Benders, 16 when all felt healthy, were fighting to overcome injuries and maintain a grip on first place. No games were scheduled for Tuesday, June 12, but the Blue Sox rode the rails to Racine where they won two games in four days, with rain or wet grounds cancelling two more contests. On Wednesday at Horlick, McManus started Florreich in center, Lee Surkowski at third, Ganote in right, and Klosowski at first base, and he pitched Bird.

Nalda came through with a two-hitter and the Blue Sox won, 4–0, rapping four hits but winning on six throwing errors by Racine third sacker Madeline "Maddy" English.[50] Thursday's tilt was rained out, and on Friday, South Bend won, 2–1, as rain shortened the game to five frames. The Belles scored once on Baker's wild throw in the first inning, and the visitors scored twice in the fourth on singles by Jochum and Surkowski and two errors.[51] Rain cancelled the final game, but Grand Rapids (13–7) defeated Rockford and Fort Wayne (12–8) beat Kenosha, dropping the Blue Sox (9–8) into third place as they returned home to host Rockford for a Sunday day-night twin bill.[52]

Injuries continued to plague South Bend. At Bendix Field, Mahon (knee) and Luna (ankle) were still out, but their teammates persevered, winning a rainy three o'clock game over Rockford, 3–2. Bird pitched well, but she was carried from the field in the seventh after aggravating a charley horse while running out a grounder. Armstrong preserved the lead but lost the nightcap, 3–0, when Carolyn Morris hurled a four-hit shutout.[53] On Monday, "Ladies Night," McManus had to start Ganote on the mound. The Louisville left-hander (the league had few southpaw pitchers) threw an assortment of breaking balls, allowing eight hits, four in Rockford's two-run eighth. Still, Ganote won easily, 12–2, when the home team pounded out a league-record 19 hits, paced by Jochum's four safeties. South Bend native Dorothea Downs played right field (she was 0-for-4) in her first-ever game, Surkowski moved back to center field and ripped three hits, Florreich returned to third base and added two safeties, and Ganote went 2-for-5.[54] On Tuesday, the Sox lost to the Peaches, 6–3, as Ganote moved from right field to the mound for the last two innings, but lost when she surrendered three runs in the 11th. However, Surkowski twice failed to slide into third base, or the Sox would have won in nine frames.[55]

Following the Rockford series, the South Benders boarded the first of two Els and arrived at Kenosha early on Wednesday, June 20, for a four-game set with the last-place Comets. The blue-clad visitors won all four games, with the finale being the nightcap of a twin bill on Friday. Bird, sore-legged, gave her second superb performance in two days, as strong underhanders could do, tossing a four-hitter for a 2–0 victory. The double wins, coupled with Fort Wayne's victory over Grand Rapids, moved South Bend (15–10) into the league lead by seven percentage points.[56]

Neither team had a game on Saturday, so the Blue Sox remained in Kenosha at the Hotel Dayton. Wherever All-American ball was the topic of conversation, people were talking about Nalda Bird. The owner of two shutout victories in two straight games, the gutsy Bird talked McManus into letting her pitch the second night, despite her painful leg, and the Sox regained first place. "Quite a gal, that little 'Birdie,'" added the *Tribune*.[57]

Despite Bird's highlights, South Bend was still facing injuries, and McManus was working to improve the team. Bucking pressure from club officials, including Howard Feaser, McManus, a newcomer to backdoor politicking by board members who understood finances more than baseball, agreed to release Darlene Mickelsen because she failed to meet "league standards."[58] Still, the pilot was opposed to putting Dodie Barr on waivers because, regardless of her frequent wild streaks, she was a versatile player who showed good hitting ability, and he wanted to make an outfielder out of her.[59] McManus, a longtime baseball man, recognized athletic talent when he saw it, a statement that could hardly be made about the businessmen on the Blue Sox board.

After the overnight train trip to Illinois, South Bend won one of three games at Rockford. On Tuesday, June 26, the Blue Sox salvaged the series finale, 6–2, drawing five straight walks that led to three runs in the second inning. Armstrong, the healthiest Sox hurler, spaced five hits and never gave up the lead.[60] Returning home to face Grand Rapids, South Bend again lost two out of three. After being stifled on Wednesday, 11–1, by Connie Wisniewski, the loop's best pitcher,[61] the resilient Sox bounced back on Thursday, winning, 4–2, behind Luna's three-hitter.[62]

On Friday at Bendix, the fastballing Wisniewski blanked the home team, 5–0, as Grand Rapids scored four unearned runs in the first inning. Armstrong lost mainly because of two costly errors each by Florreich and Schroeder. Nearly 1,700 fans saw the game of "missed chances," and the Sox fell to fourth place with a 17–14 record. Elsewhere, Fort Wayne (21–15) beat Rockford, staying a game and a half off the loop-best pace set by 22–13 Grand Rapids.[63]

McManus Shakes Up the Sox

Immediately after the second loss in three days, McManus, displeased with his team's performance, particularly on defense, and needing to assert his independence as South Bend's field boss, made a trade with the Comets. The Blue Sox sent their two youngest players, light-hitting but good-fielding shortstop Dottie Schroeder and hard-hitting but inconsistent-fielding third baseman Lois Florreich, to Kenosha for shortstop Pinky Pirok and Phyllis "Sugar" Koehn, a versatile outfielder who could play third base (and, it turned out, could pitch). McManus hoped to boost the Blue Sox in hitting and fielding. In the previous season, Pirok hit .233 with 38 RBI, but Schroeder, her counterpart at shortstop, batted just .180 and added 24 RBI. Koehn averaged .213 with 42 RBI over 114 games in 1944, and Florreich hit .178 with 35 RBI in 99 contests. McManus, who piloted the Comets into the 1944 playoff championship, knew Pirok and Koehn, and he figured that they added experience, hitting, and "spirit and aggressiveness."[64]

However, trades in pro sports are unsettling. Many South Bend fans criticized the deal, hating to see two favorites leave town, and some of the players wondered who might be swapped next.

Actually, the trade was the visible tip of a problem within the South Bend ball club. According to the notes of Harold Dailey, a dentist who joined the board of directors in 1945 and became the team's president in late 1947, Clarence Livengood, credit manager of the *Tribune* and the ball club's treasurer, was one of the businessmen-turned-baseball "experts" who interfered in the field management of the team. For example, Livengood, representing the team at the spring allocation meeting, agreed to shift Rose Gacioch to Rockford because "she used poor English." Later, with the season in full swing, board president Howard Feaser overruled McManus and ordered Doris Barr listed on waivers and returned to the league. In the greatest irony of the season, Barr ended up with Racine, where, after improving her control, she produced a 20–8 record and helped her new team edge South Bend for the fourth and final playoff spot. To address such concerns, the board met on June 30 and resolved to give McManus "full charge of running the team."[65]

The upshot of McManus' vote of confidence, although short-lived, was the Kenosha deal. The team's behind-the-scenes leadership struggle did not help on-field performance, because the players realized the manager could be overruled on baseball decisions. Indeed, the board kept meddling in the business of the capable McManus, who resented the interference and, finally, resigned at the season's end. Later, in 1948, Dailey either started or passed on a rumor that MacManus' problems stemmed from drinking, and author Lois Browne repeated that claim.[66] However, the women who played for the spirited, temperamental manager in 1945 and 1948 never saw him any way but sober. Betsy Jochum, who starred for the club's first three pilots, remembered McManus as having a sense of humor. "It was more fun and [we] learned more from Marty."[67]

At Bendix on Saturday, June 30, with the four players in new uniforms all performing well, Kenosha's Helen Fox won a pitchers' duel, 2–1, tossing a three-hit gem, while Bird hurled a four-hitter. Florreich, stationed in center field, starred for the Comets, getting one hit, scoring both runs, and stealing four bases. Also, Schroeder forced in Kenosha's winning run in the sixth with a bases-loaded walk, but her error led to an unearned Sox run in the fourth. For the home team, Pirok scored once, after she doubled in the ninth. Koehn singled home Pirok, and in the bottom of the ninth, Sugar made a bid to tie the game with a shot toward first base, but former South Bender Jo Hageman smothered it for the putout. Pirok took third on the play, but Schroeder threw out Jochum to end the tilt. Around the league, Rockford beat Grand Rapids, the Fort Wayne-Racine game was rained out, and the standings stayed the same. Grand Rapids, at 22–14, held first place, and Rockford and Fort Wayne were tied for second with 21–15 marks. South Bend, with a revamped lineup, remained fourth at 17–15, followed by Racine (13–22) and Kenosha (12–25).[68]

For a time, South Bend did play better ball, winning a Sunday evening twin bill from Kenosha. On Monday, Bird, with her sore leg improved, no-hit the Comets for five innings and won, 7–2, thanks to fine defense and timely hitting. The Sox tallied two runs in the second, three more in the fifth, and another pair in the seventh, moving into third place with a 20–15 ledger.[69]

The league had no games scheduled for Tuesday, but with a record Bendix crowd of 2,585 enjoying Wednesday's Fourth of July doubleheader, the Blue Sox split two games with Grand Rapids that offered a virtual microcosm of their season. Luna pitched tough but lost the opener to right-hander Jo Kabick, 3–1, due to two unearned runs — the albatross of South Bend's year. Bird, however, won a thrilling battle with Wisniewski in the nightcap, 1–0, when Pirok blasted a triple to center field in the ninth. Pinky kept running when the throw bounced past third sacker Doris Tetzlaff, who recovered it and fired home a second late, but missed the sliding Pirok. Wisniewski spaced four hits, two by Jochum, but until Pirok's triple in the ninth, Connie was in control. Bird yielded a single and a walk, but retired the last 16 hitters to earn the win.[70]

South Bend never occupied first place again in 1945. Instead, the Blue Sox spent the rest of the season fighting for fourth place, the final playoff spot. Foreshadowing the home team's struggle, Grand Rapids won shutouts at Bendix on Thursday and Friday, July 5–6, and both losses came on errors. As a result, South Bend slipped to fourth with a 21–18 record. Also, Rockford, after Carolyn Morris hurled the All-American's second perfect game, a 4–0 victory over Fort Wayne, held the league lead with a 27–16 ledger.[71] For the Blue Sox, the big trade mainly allowed McManus to acquire two new regulars that he trusted in the field and at the plate.

More New Sox

One of South Bend's best new players in 1945 was Elizabeth "Lib" Mahon, a native of Greenville, South Carolina, and a 1942 graduate of Winthrop College (now Winthrop University). The 5'7" brunette was a natural all-around athlete who grew up playing sandlot ball with other kids and, later, fast-pitch softball in a mill league. In May 1944, Lib was working in the Greenville Post Office when she and teammate Viola "Tommie" Thompson, from Anderson, South Carolina, received contracts to attend the All-American League's spring camp in Peru, Illinois. Making the loop, Lib was sent to expansion Minneapolis. Usually a shortstop or third baseman, she hurt her arm on the first day of spring training and never again threw as well. After three weeks, McManus, Kenosha's manager, traded infielder Anna Meyer for Mahon. Playing 107 games overall, Mahon spent the rest of the season at second base for the Comets, averaging .211 with 38 RBI and three home runs. Bright, outspoken, and friendly, Mahon was a solid right-handed hitter with the clutch ability to drive home runners who were in scoring position.[72]

Nalda Bird, or Birdie, the five-foot southpaw from Los Angeles, also made a strong contribution to the Blue Sox, at least until July. A talented, hard-throwing brunette who was 17, she began playing ball in LA at the age of ten. The next year she joined a semi-pro team, becoming a fine pitcher by the time she graduated from high school. A good pianist and singer, Nalda composed a version of the league's "Victory Song," termed "The All-American Girl" by the *South Bend Tribune* in May 1945.[73] Pepper Paire later recalled writing her version of the song late in the 1944 season when she was out with a broken collarbone.[74] In any event, Bird, a right-handed batter, was a good hitter, and she could play the outfield. Birdie, however, played just one year, because she married after the season. A modest person, she later remarked, "When I was on I pitched well — when off, I couldn't throw a strike even if I handed the ball to the catcher." Fortunately for the Sox, Bird flew high for the first half of 1945.[75]

South Bend also acquired Anne Surkowski, the sister of Lee. At age 21, Anne, a 5'3" brunette who had smiling eyes and long, curly hair, was two years older than Lee. Both threw and batted right, both showed good speed in the outfield, and both could fly on the base paths, but Lee performed better under pressure. The sisters starred for the Royal Theater's team in their home town, Moose Jaw, a Saskatchewan city of 35,000. Lee came to the All-American League in 1944, but Anne played that summer for the Royals. During the '44 season, Anne's team won the Western Canadian Championship and played in the world tournament in Detroit.

In 1991, when the All-American League was inducted as a *team* into the Saskatchewan Baseball Hall of Fame (25 women from the province played in the loop), Anne said the Blue Sox "traveled first-class. They didn't want you looking 'butchy.' We had a chaperone with the team. And we had a type of skirt, like a jumper but it was a flared skirt. We couldn't have them more than six inches above the knee. There were a lot of rules." Reflecting on the greatest times of their lives, Anne observed, "You wonder whether marriage measures up to ball. It's one sport for another." Recalled Lee, "It's something that happens only once in a lifetime."[76]

South Bend also acquired right-hander Betty Luna, who, like Bird, hailed from Los Angeles. A good hitter, Luna averaged .250 in 42 games, clubbing seven doubles, two triples, and one home run, and driving home three runs. The talented 18-year-old, with hazel eyes and sandy-brown hair, was the youngest of 11 children. She learned to pitch from her father Walter, also known as "Tex" (the family moved from Dallas when she was nine), but she could play any position. In 1945, Betty, strong and athletic at 5'5", was the top Sox hitter, followed by Mahon, who batted .246. Further, Luna was the team's best hurler as measured by earned run average. She fashioned a 14–15 record (no Blue Sox hurler had a winning mark in 1945) and a 1.53 ERA in 30 games. Without the quiet, friendly, talented Luna, South Bend fielded a weaker team.[77]

Pinky Pirok, who took over at shortstop after the Kenosha trade, had a tough act to follow in replacing the popular Schroeder, but she gave it her best. Pirok, who grew up in Chicago, started her six-year league career as a shortstop for the Comets in 1943. A streak hitter, she enjoyed a highlight evening against the Blue Sox on August 17, 1944, when she went 4-for-5 and led Kenosha to a 10–0 victory. In that memorable game, she hit two singles, a double, and a triple, and batted in three runs. In 1945, however, Pinky batted only .163, contributing five doubles, two triples, and 18 RBI in 106 games. On the diamond, the 5'2" infielder didn't match Schroeder (Dottie fielded .883 with 51 miscues in 94 games). Pirok, who suffered an ankle injury, fielded just .754, committing 49 errors and ranking ninth (last) among shortstops. Despite the injury, she reached base often, drawing 48 walks, stealing 27 bases, and scoring 37 runs. For her career, the fiery infielder averaged .208 with 262 runs scored, contributing 127 RBI in 559 games from 1943 to 1948.[78]

Phyllis Koehn (pronounced cane) also helped South Bend in many ways. Not quite 21 when she began with the Comets in 1943, Koehn, who grew up in Madison, Wisconsin, but later lived in Chicago, was another of the fine athletes who graced the All-American uniform in the 1940s. She began as an underhand pitcher, but because of her bat, she also played the infield and outfield. She enjoyed an eight-year pro career, almost half with the Comets and the rest with the Blue Sox. Because the overhand motion hurt her arm, she quit pitching after the league shifted to baseball in 1948. Earlier, a sportswriter called her "Sugar Cane," and the nickname stuck. In 1945, McManus wanted her for third base, and he traded Florreich to acquire Koehn. The 5'5" right-hander batted .233, third best among South Bend's regulars. Only Mahon (.246) and Jochum (.237) enjoyed better seasons. Sugar, playing 115 games, showed occasional power with five doubles, three triples, and a homer, producing a team-high 43 RBI. Described as a quiet, nice person, Koehn helped make the Sox a playoff contender.[79]

Even though the South Bend-Kenosha swap made no major difference for either team, McManus continued fitting his many talented women into the changing mosaic of the up-and-down Blue Sox. Despite good seasons from stellar athletes like Baker, Stefani, and Jochum, McManus, a good teacher of baseball skills, never saw his team gel. The Blue Sox lacked the fortuitous combination of players, the sparkplug leader, and the deeply-felt camaraderie needed to transform a good team into a great one.

Injuries Hurt

July was an unusual month. Continuing the home stand at Bendix Field, the Blue Sox beat the Comets three straight, but, after splitting their Fourth of July twin bill with the Chicks, the local favorites dropped the next two games to Grand Rapids. Facing Racine in two straight series, the Blue Sox won two out of three at Horlick Field and, back at Bendix, they won three straight.

On Wednesday, July 11, in the third game of the four-game home set with the Belles, the Blue Sox "walked" by Dodie Barr, 6–0, scoring six times in the seventh on Surkowski's bunt single, base hits by Pirok and Koehn, four walks (Barr passed eight altogether), a wild pitch, and an error. The home team totaled seven hits, and Luna, scattering six safeties, received fine defensive support. The win kept 26–19 South Bend in second place, two games behind league-leading Rockford (30–19).

Coincidentally, just when it looked as though McManus had turned the Blue Sox into a pennant contender, the league made a change to help the hitters. Starting with games of July 14, Max Carey announced that the pitcher's mound would be shifted from 40 to 42 feet from home plate. The plan

Margaret "Marge" Stefani — One of South Bend's original players and a stellar second baseman, circa 1945 (courtesy of the Louise Pettus Archives and Special Collections, Winthrop University).

was designed to give batters a split-second longer against the circuit's fastball hurlers. In women's softball, the pitching distance was 35 feet, and in men's softball, the length was 43 feet. The league's base paths remained at 68 feet as the game evolved further toward baseball.[80]

Carey, meanwhile, removed Charley Stis as Racine's manager and shifted him to a role scouting for the league, and the president took over the Belles for one night. Carey, the master of "small ball," guided Racine to a 2–1 victory over South Bend. Bird allowed only two hits, but she was wild again, and walks figured in both of the Belles' runs. The Blue Sox tied the contest at 1–1 in the second when Jochum was safe on an error, stole second, and scored on Mahon's single to center. The yellow-uniformed visitors won in the sixth, when with two outs, Ellie Dapkus walked and stole second, Edie Perlick walked, and when Dapkus broke for third, Baker threw the ball away. The loss dropped 26–20 South Bend to third place and kicked off a four-game losing string.[81]

The weather, bad breaks, and injuries combined to hurt the Blue Sox as the summer proceeded. Rain halted the finale against Racine, and South Bend, traveling to Fort Wayne, saw the first game of the series washed out. At that point, the Blue Sox were leading the league in hitting with a .221 average, almost 30 points above Rockford's second-place mark of .193. However, the South Benders were last in fielding with a .935 clip, well below Fort Wayne, the loop leaders at .951. Rockford's Dottie Kamenshek was the top hitter, averaging .292, but Marge Stefani was second at .270. Lib Mahon and Betsy Jochum were batting .250, with Lefty Ganote at .236, Lee Surkowski at .230, and Baker and Bird both at .224. Still, Betty Luna's .216 figure made her the only other South Bender above .200. Lois Florreich, out with an ankle injury, paced the league in RBI with 21, but Stefani, Pinky Pirok, and Sugar Koehn led the Sox with 18 RBI each.[82]

When the weather cleared in Fort Wayne, the Blue Sox lost three in a row, and the finale was a disappointing 7–3 defeat. On Monday, July 16, on the rough surface of North High Field, Bird, working on the new 42-foot hurling distance, was spinning a no-hitter when she gave up a single in the seventh frame. Along with her own error, she added five walks, giving up three runs in the seventh and four more in the eighth. Still, South Bend lost a pair of scores when two girls refused to slide, and another who wouldn't slide was tagged out at third. Pirok twisted her ankle sliding into second base, received medical treatment, and limped through the game. "If some of the other Blue Sox had about half of Pirok's spirit," Jim Costin observed, "they'd be giving some evidence of trying to earn their money and making a determined effort to win ball games."[83]

Returning by train to South Bend, the Blue Sox hosted the first-place Peaches and split a four-game set, winning the finale, 8–4. Armstrong scattered eight hits and walked two, but her teammates ripped rookie Alva Jo "Tex" Fischer for ten hits, two by Stefani. Still, the Blue Sox gave away all four runs on errors, the team's Achilles heel.[84]

If Marty McManus thought he was already dealing with problems on and off the field, the bottom dropped out during South Bend's next road trip. The Blue Sox lost all nine games, four at Kenosha and five at Rockford, partly because three regulars, Stefani (knee), Mahon (knee), and Pirok (ankle), sat out with injuries. Bird lost three times, including the finale, a 3–1 setback. For that game against the Peaches, McManus again juggled his lineup, listing Anne Surkowski in right, Ganote at first base, Baker catching, Koehn playing third, Lee Surkowski playing center and batting clean-up, Luna in left, Jochum playing second base, Bird, the pitcher, batting eighth, and rookie shortstop Lou Stone batting ninth. The visitors scored when the slow-moving Ganote tripled to the wall in right-center, and she scored when Baker's grounder was booted. Amy Applegren, however, permitted only six other hits and remained in control. Afterward, Rockford (41–27) remained in first place and South Bend (28–34) was mired in fourth.[85]

On July 29, Luna finally broke South Bend's losing streak in Sunday's Bendix doubleheader against visiting Fort Wayne. The California blond with the good breaking stuff hurled a five-hitter to top the Daisies, 1–0, thanks to Koehn's long triple in the first frame that scored the courageous Pirok, who drew a two-out walk and hobbled around the bases on the blast. In the late tilt, the local favorites fell, 3–1, when Armstrong saw her six-hitter marred by errors, including her own wild throw in the opening inning that allowed Helen Callaghan, who scratched a single off Stefani's glove, to score all the way from first base. McManus returned Stefani, Mahon, and Pirok to the lineup, but they were slowed by their injuries.[86]

The league had no contests scheduled for Monday, but South Bend and Fort Wayne would play Game Three on Tuesday, with Chet Grant, Notre Dame's colorful assistant football coach, set to take over the team for a few days. McManus left Monday afternoon for St. Louis to see his son, Marty, Junior, a Marine who had fought through campaigns on Saipan, Iwo Jima, and Okinawa in the Pacific. Grant, George Gipp's quarterback on the Fighting Irish Eleven of 1920, wrote sports stories for the *Tribune* and later served as Notre Dame's backfield coach.[87] By no coincidence, Grant, although never a baseball man, was hired to pilot the Blue Sox in 1946.

In Grant's debut on Tuesday, July 31, a downpour washed out Wiltse versus Bird in the bottom of the second inning.[88] At Bendix one night later, the Blue Sox, playing flawless defense, won twice. Bird, mastering the 42-foot distance, walked three but beat curveballing Dottie Wiltse in the short opener, 4–2. In the nine-inning late tilt, Luna beat knuckleballing Lefty Lee, 3–0, as Jochum and Koehn led an eight-hit attack with two apiece. The *Tribune* said Grant managed the Sox in "a faultless manner, and they played heads-up ball throughout the evening."[89]

Grant's "Luck of the Irish" did not last. The Blue Sox traveled to Fort Wayne and, handcuffed by Daisy pitching, lost four straight, scoring a total of one run in the first three games. On Sunday evening, South Bend, winless for the season in Fort Wayne, lost, 5–3. Audrey Haine won a four-hitter, despite walking 11, a splurge that led to South Bend's three-run eighth. Wiltse finished up, blanking the Sox in the ninth, and Armstrong, who gave up five walks and nine hits, took another tough defeat. The loss dropped 31–39 South Bend into fifth place for the first time. Riding home on the late train, the Blue Sox pondered facing first-place Grand Rapids.[90]

As the league's tension-filled pennant chase continued, World War II ended a few days after the U.S. exploded an atomic bomb over the Japanese city of Hiroshima on August 6. Summer moved into fall, and newspapers, magazines, and the radio reported on postwar conditions, including labor strikes, the rising cost of living, and how soldiers and sailors were adjusting to home life.[91]

Fighting for Fourth Place

The All-American League succeeded beyond all expectations by the end of the Second World War. In 1943, the four-team circuit played games witnessed by 176,000 fans. Expanding to six teams in 1944, the league drew a total of 259,000 paid, and the same six clubs attracted more than 450,000 in 1945. As a result, Max Carey and his associates were planning an eight-team league for 1946, with Peoria, Illinois, and Muskegon, Michigan, selected for new franchises.

Carey, a former ballplayer with the usual social values of his era, said the league appealed to all members of the family, regardless of sex or age. "The 'first timers,' upon viewing the game, invariably express amazement at the ability of the girls. Skeptics become dyed-in-the-wool fans." The circuit featured, Max wrote, baseball played by good-looking "All-American" women wearing fluted uniform dresses who played with skill and passion and, he could have added, sex appeal. Still, the Blue Sox ranked fifth in attendance in 1945, drawing a total of 49,223 paid. Only last place Kenosha (41–69), a much smaller city, attracted fewer fans: 38,841.[92]

After a three-game win streak against Kenosha at Bendix Field ended on August 12, South Bend managed to win back-to-back games only three more times in 1945. Following a trip to Grand Rapids, where they lost three straight, and a journey to Racine, where they won three out of four, the Blue Sox took the short ride to Kenosha late on Friday, August 17, and dropped two out of three to the last place Comets. For example, on Saturday, Birdie displayed virtually none of her good stuff, and Kenosha reached her for eight hits, six walks, and nine runs in the first four frames, winning, 13–0.[93] In Sunday's twin bill, South Bend lost the opener, 3–0, but won the late game, 4–2, gaining a game on the Belles, who lost twice to the Chicks.[94]

Journeying around the south end of Lake Michigan to Grand Rapids, the Blue Sox began a five-game set with the second-place Chicks on Monday, August 20. The travelers lost that game and divided a twin bill on Tuesday. Due to an unusual turn of events, South Bend was short-handed, because McManus sent Betty Luna and Nalda Bird back to South Bend for undisclosed reasons. In Wednesday night's doubleheader, the manager pitched Koehn in the opener, but Wisniewski won her 30th game, 7–2, with a three-hitter. In the nightcap, Armstrong spaced three hits and yielded a run, but won, 2–1, on Jochum's two-run triple in the top of the ninth.

South Bend, with a 43–50 mark and a three-game lead over the Belles, made yet another late-night trip home for five games against fifth-place Racine. Talking and wondering about their departed teammates, the Sox knew the last playoff spot was on the line.[95]

Finishing Short-Handed

At Bendix Field on Thursday, August 23, the Blue Sox, learning Luna and Bird — the team's two California hurlers — were suspended for what the *Tribune* called their "unfortunate defection" (the league termed their behavior "insubordination"), played the team's third straight twin bill, and lost both games. In the first Racine tilt, Armstrong pitched for the third straight day, but Mary (Nesbitt) Crews won, 3–0. In the nightcap, McManus had to use Lefty Ganote to pitch the entire game, and the Belles won, 8–4, racking up seven hits and drawing 12 walks. Afterward, the Sox owned a 43–52 record and held a one-game edge over the fifth-place 43–54 Belles.[96]

On a chilly Friday night, the spirited Blue Sox, short on pitching and playing their fourth doubleheader in four nights — and fifth twin bill in six nights — beat Racine twice. More than 1,600 fans saw Koehn make her home debut and outlast Barr, 4–3, because Dodie walked 14 batters, forcing home the winning run with a walk in the seventh. In the

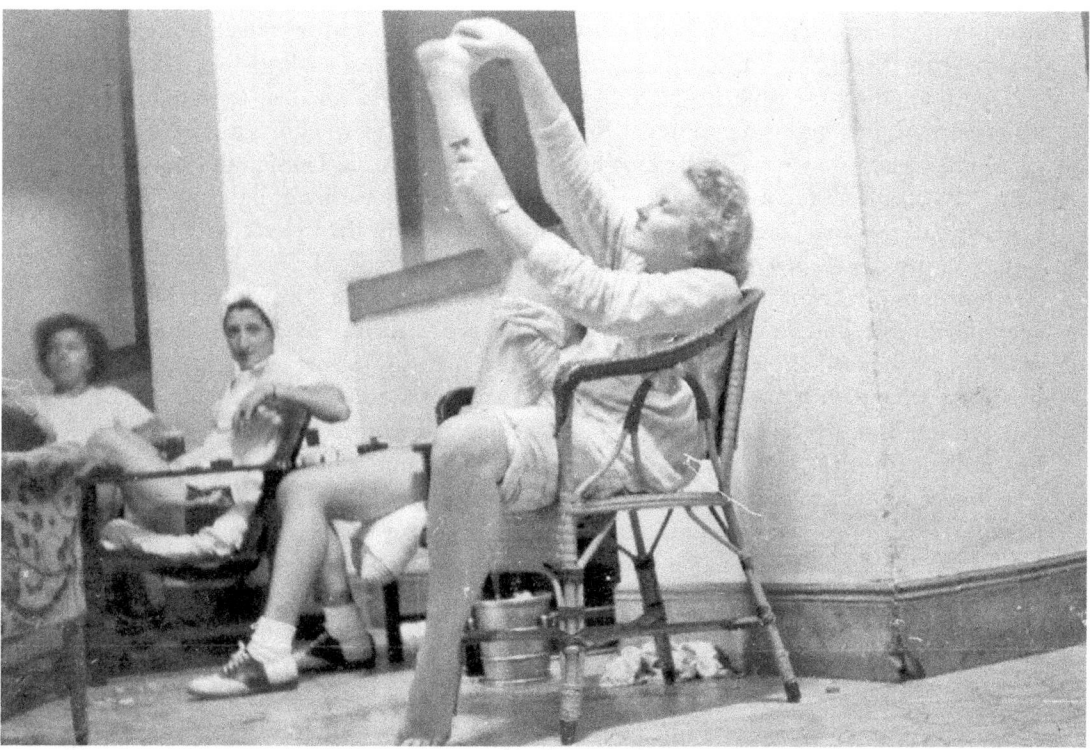

Baseball Is Not for Sissies — Marge Stefani, seated on left with a towel wrapped around her head, watches as Faye Dancer shaves her legs at the hotel before a game, circa 1945 (courtesy of the Louise Pettus Archives and Special Collections, Winthrop University).

late contest, Armstrong scattered eight hits and won, 7–2, as Jochum led a 12-hit assault on Winter with two singles and, in the seventh, a bases-loaded triple that gave the Sox a 7–1 lead. Later, Bird and Luna appealed the suspensions to Max Carey, but he upheld the manager, meaning the two women were gone for the season. Also, South Bend (45–52) now held a three-game bulge over Racine (43–56).[97]

The Blue Sox kept proving their persistence as professionals. In "Overcoming Adversity," Jim Costin called South Bend's "excellent" chance of making the playoffs a tribute both to McManus' managerial skills and to the fighting spirit of the players, who battled long odds all summer. Following injuries to Florreich (later traded), Mahon, Luna, Bird, and Pirok, the team at times had one regular pitcher, Armstrong. When Ganote was out for two weeks with a twisted knee, Stefani played every infield position. Also, Baker, who recently sustained a bad cut over her left eye when she hit the stands at Grand Rapids chasing a pop foul, had caught all 98 games to date. Moreover, Koehn and Ganote were helping out by pitching.

Costin concluded, "Practically every girl is solidly backing manager Marty McManus in his drastic action of fining and suspending Bird and Luna, even though their absence might deprive the team of a spot in the playoffs." Regardless, the fact that the manager had to take such drastic action revealed the iceberg of internal problems, although details about the women's misconduct were never revealed. Still, seldom-used Anne Surkowski later termed McManus her "champion," because he involved Anne by using her to coach at first base.

Betsy Jochum remembered McManus as the most respected and best liked Sox manager of her six years.[98]

At that point, the Blue Sox faced five games at home with the Daisies; a rainout make-up in Fort Wayne; and three games at Rockford. Their best two efforts came on August 30 at Bendix, when they excited the fans by taking two from the Daisies and moving into a tie for fourth place. On a Thursday evening punctuated by flashes of lightning, Armstrong gave an "iron woman" performance and won twice, taking the opener with a two-hitter, 2–0. A noisy crowd of 1,400 cheered as the Blue Sox scored twice in the fourth off Lefty Lee, bunching Baker's single, a bunt by Betty "Moe" Trezza (on "loan" from Fort Wayne), Mahon's double, and an error by Faye Dancer. In the late tilt, newly-signed Irene Headin, from Saskatchewan, showed a good fastball but a bad case of nerves. Armstrong relieved her in the second with the Sox behind, 1–0, and proceeded to win, 3–2, thanks to Jochum's run-scoring bunt in the eighth. Racine (49–57) beat Rockford, leaving South Bend (48–56) tied for fourth.[99] Headin never played in another game.

In yet another twin bill on Friday, the Blue Sox lost a crusher, 1–0, and, in the season's toughest break, *tied* the five-inning late game, 1–1. A crowd of 1,992, South Bend's third largest of 1945, saw Koehn match Wiltse for six innings, but Penny O'Brian's RBI single in the seventh scored the game's only run. In the nightcap, with the Sox trailing 1–0 in the fourth, Baker walked and advanced on Ganote's bunt. Bonnie overran the second base, but when Vivian Kellogg threw the ball away, Baker scored for a 1–1 tie. "The storm which was threatening to break," wrote Costin, "came in the sixth and washed the season away." The Racine-Rockford contest was rained out, so the 48–57 Sox were in fifth place, half a game behind the 49–57 Belles.[100] In the end, the tie cost South Bend the playoffs, because on Saturday, the Blue Sox and the Belles both lost, and there was no time left in the season for South Bend to make up the possible win lost by Friday's tie.[101]

Arriving early on Sunday, September 2, in Rockford for a three-game series, the Blue Sox lost the most critical contest of the season, 4–0. Amy Applegren, cheered by a raucous audience of 2,898, yielded a double to Koehn, who also spun a six-hitter, and two singles to Pirok. Elsewhere, Racine, riding fine hurling by Dodie Barr, won the team's biggest game, blanking Fort Wayne, 7–0, and lifting the Belles (50–58) one and a half games above South Bend, now at 48–59.[102]

On Monday, Labor Day, the Blue Sox confronted the same must-win situation they faced at the end of 1943 and 1944: they needed to win twice for a shot at the playoffs. Instead, South Bend fell short as Rockford won the opener, 9–2. McManus had little choice but to use the weary Armstrong against Tex Fischer, who posted a 4–7 mark in 1945. In the seventh, Rockford, bunching six hits and taking advantage of errors by Pirok and Armstrong, scored six times to go ahead, 6–2, and Fischer protected the lead. The seven-inning nightcap turned into "horseplay," because the playoff race was over and the managers scrambled their lineups. The Blue Sox, fueled by pride, won, 10–3, on Ganote's pitching, eight hits, and seven Peaches errors.[103]

For South Bend, the often exciting, often frustrating season ended with a disappointing finish similar to 1943 and 1944. The *Tribune*'s Jim Costin criticized the league for sending the Blue Sox several (unnamed) players who "did not measure up to professional caliber." Bonnie Baker, however, caught all 110 games, indicating that she had no adequate backup. Despite the pressing need for new players after injuries began piling up in mid–June, the league provided no help.[104]

In addition, the Blue Sox lost important players who could not be replaced: Sunny

Berger left to pitch in the Chicago League; team officials allowed Rose Gacioch to be allocated to Rockford, where she played 105 games and hit .211 with 44 RBI; and the club released Doris Barr, who went 20–8 for Racine and helped lift the Belles into the playoffs. In the end, McManus frustrated for much of the summer by the board's meddling and by injuries that kept him juggling too few good players, resigned.[105]

For the All-American League, the third successful season was over, but team batting averages as well as the hurlers' earned run figures indicated the circuit was still dominated by pitchers. By mid-season, when he ordered lengthening of the base paths, Max Carey knew that changes were needed to help the hitters as well as appeal to a growing fan base.

After the final wartime season, Carey and other league officials were planning to expand to eight teams for 1946.[106] By any measure, the Girls' Pro League was thriving in the Midwest. Asked shortly after Christmas about the upcoming season, Dottie Schroeder wrote to a youthful friend, "Well, that's about all I've been thinking and talking about too."[107] Hope springs eternal in the diamond sport, and most of the experienced players were already dreaming about baseball next year.

• 4 •

Making the Playoffs in the First Postwar Season: 1946

"The finest managerial job in the girls' pro league during the last season was done by Chet Grant, who brought the Blue Sox home in third place and just missed by one game getting them into second place"—Jim Costin, September 4, 1946[1]

The Postwar Era

Boosted by a new manager, D.C. "Chet" Grant, a virtually new roster, and several good rookies, notably third baseman Jean Faut and shortstop Senaida Wirth, the South Bend Blue Sox, after finishing fifth of six teams in 1945, spent much of the 1946 season contending for second place in the expanded eight-team All-American Girls Baseball League. According to loop president Max Carey, the circuit's paid attendance grew from 259,000 in 1944 to over 450,000 in 1945. By the time the 1946 season ended, more than 750,000 had paid to see the eight teams play that year. Therefore, the players as well as the fans in many Midwestern cities believed the Girls' Pro League, as the *South Bend Tribune* usually called it, was here to stay.

Several league records were broken, Carey wrote, by "the spirited and often amazing play of the girl athletes." Twelve new batting marks and nine new pitching records were set. For example, Racine's rookie right-handed sidearmer Anna Hutchison hurled a no-hitter, and she set another record by appearing in 51 games. The Belles' Jo Winter, the right-hander with three straight losing ledgers, learned the slingshot motion from Phoenix softball hurler Nolly Trujillo. Now a winner, Winter hurled six straight shutouts for one record, pitched 63 consecutive scoreless innings for another, and tied Connie Wisniewski of Grand Rapids for victories with 33. Rockford's Dottie Kamenshek led all hitters with a .316 mark, and South Bend's Lib Mahon set the RBI standard with 72. Furthermore, the All-American had grown from a wartime start-up circuit with four teams to a prospering eight-team postwar league that not only boosted community pride but also promoted youth recreation activities, including girls' baseball.[2] For example, the South Bend Recreation Department's "Bobby Sox League" featured 12 teams by 1947.[3]

The Second World War ended in August 1945, and a new age dawned in America. The postwar decade, however, turned out to be a troubled era, as reflected by the many political, economic, and social adjustments. After President Roosevelt died on April 12, 1945, Vice President Harry Truman rose to the Presidency. Roughly 12 million Americans, including two-thirds of males between the ages of 18 and 35, remained in the armed services.

The 1946 film, *The Best Years of Our Lives,* offered a sensitive portrayal of adjustments faced by veterans, including restoring family relationships, finding jobs, dissolving often-hasty wartime marriages (the divorce rate doubled in 1945), and living with disabilities.[4]

Spring Training at Pascagoula

By April 1, 1946, the Blue Sox had signed last year's outfield and infield, but no pitchers. Betsy Jochum, Lee Surkowski, and Lib Mahon, the left, center, and right fielders, respectively, rejoined the team. The club also signed first baseman Lefty Ganote, but she got married and left the league[5]; Marge Stefani, the second sacker; Sugar Koehn, a third baseman and outfielder who could also pitch; and Betty Trezza, a reserve infielder loaned from Fort Wayne who finished the 1945 season with South Bend. Club officials said they hoped Regina catcher Bonnie Baker would return, and that seemed likely. The *Tribune* reported that since hurlers Charlotte Armstrong and Nalda Bird "either jumped the team or quit the league," the Sox needed a new pitching staff.[6]

Three days later, Max Carey and his staff met in South Bend with team officials to discuss 1946 rule changes as well as new players, notably pitchers for the Blue Sox. Among other innovations, Carey said the roster would increase from 16 in 1945 to 18 (the maximum of 15 in 1943 was raised to 16 in 1944); each team would carry five pitchers, including two rookies; and after spring camp, the eight teams would pair off and play exhibitions while traveling to their home cities.[7]

The historic All-American League continued evolving toward baseball. The changes for 1946 included reducing the ball's size from 11.5 to 11 inches in circumference; moving the pitcher's mound back from 42 to 43 feet; and increasing the base paths from 68 to 70 feet,[8] despite Harold Dailey's later mistaken claim that base paths were set at 72 feet in 1946.[9] Furthermore, to limit stolen bases, the league allowed a "half-balk" move to make it harder for runners to read a pitcher's delivery. More importantly, Carey wrote in 1947, the "pitching rules were relaxed sufficiently to allow for a limited side-arm pitch from an underhanded delivery with certain restrictions...."[10]

Necessity, however, is the mother of invention, not vice versa. Teams that needed hurlers converted hard-throwing position players into pitchers by having them drop their arm motion down and throwing sidearm. Racine's Anna Hutchison, who began as a catcher, recalled being the first sidearmer in 1946,[11] and Joyce (Hill) Westerman, then a catcher, confirmed the switch.[12] Jean Faut, who never played softball but pitched in a few semipro baseball exhibitions, used the new style. She said pitching sidearm meant her delivery could not be above the shoulder, an often-used motion for a third baseman, and the league's umpires, hired to official baseball, not softball, allowed it.[13] In a maneuver typical for the season, Muskegon's Erma Bergmann recollected that manager Buzz Boyle converted her from a third baseman to a sidearm pitcher.[14]

The changes began in the spring camp at Pascagoula, Mississippi. Located on the Gulf of Mexico 20 miles east of Biloxi, Pascagoula was a fishing port of 5,000 before World War II. Because of the city's waterfront, the federal government allocated wartime contracts, boosting the business of the Ingalls Ship Yards and bringing about the construction of a housing project for workers. The U.S. also expanded the Navy Station on the Singing River, adding another economic stimulus. Later a city of more than 30,000, Pascagoula offered its now unused facilities to the league. On paper, spring training in a warm southern city looked good.[15]

Nearly 200 women participated in the Pascagoula camp that was arranged by Arthur Meyerhoff's staff. Starting Thursday, April 25, the camp, led by Max Carey and the managers, featured two weeks of intensive drills lasting from 9:30 to 3:30 daily. Veterans came the second week, and everyone attended nightly meetings to learn fundamentals of the game. Carey sent each girl a schedule of activities and the league's rules of conduct.[16] Jean Faut arrived to play *baseball*, as the league advertised, and she recalled being surprised to see underhand pitching. The players stayed in dirty barracks where wartime shipyard workers lived. The insect-infested facility was soon dubbed "Cockroach Haven," but the weather was sunny and warm, unlike the chilly Midwestern spring camps. Hustling during the conditioning drills and practices, the prospects dreamed of making the eight 18-person rosters.

On Saturday, May 4, they enjoyed a day off, and the loop's allocation board, with a director from each club, met at the Edgewater Gulf Hotel in Biloxi and assigned players to teams. "They are chosen for their looks as much as their long hits," reported *Newsweek*. "And the public likes it."[17]

After Saturday's allocation, South Bend had 12 new players. Of the five pitchers, Koehn, an underhander, was the only holdover. New hurlers included lefty Tommie Thompson, the onetime cotton mill athletic director from South Carolina who pitched two years for the Chicks; Jane Jacobs, the Cuyahoga Falls, Ohio, right-hander who spent two seasons with Racine (she was later sent to Peoria); and rookie Mona Denton of Denver, a right-hander who would enjoy little success in the league (she was 1–11 over two seasons). The team received three catchers: right-handed batting Dorothy "Dottie" Naum of Dearborn, Michigan; Joyce Hill, the former Kenosha receiver; and Syracuse's Kathryn Beare, a right-handed hitter who, after Baker returned, was sent to Fort Wayne. The outfielders were Jochum, Lee Surkowski, and Mahon, whose left knee was improved after her ligament injury in 1945, plus slender Daisy Junor, the Regina native. At third base, the Sox received Jean Faut, a right-handed hitter who began pitching sidearm in late July. The shortstops were fourth-year veteran Pinky Pirok, who soon jumped to Chicago's National Girls Baseball League,[18] and rookie Senaida "Shoo-Shoo" Wirth, a five-foot speedster from Tampa. At second base, the Sox had the intimidating Marge Stefani, who, with Baker, dominated the younger players. Two rookie first sackers were left-handed Inez Voyce, from Seymour, Iowa, and Amy Shuman of Mohrsville, Pennsylvania, but Shuman's boyfriend was unhappy about his girlfriend playing pro ball, and she soon returned home.[19]

The league paired South Bend with Grand Rapids for a 12-game exhibition tour. The teams traveled first to Knoxville, Tennessee (where Doris Sams learned about the league), then to Macon (Georgia), Anderson (South Carolina), and Birmingham and Gadsden (Alabama), before a final two-game set at Bosse Field in Evansville, Indiana, on the weekend of May 18–19. That Sunday before an Evansville crowd of 3,000, Grand Rapids, riding a combined four-hitter by Alice "Al" Haylett and Jo Kabick, won the final exhibition, 7–1. Later, the teams left for home, but managers Chet Grant and Johnny Rawlings traveled to Chicago for a reallocation meeting.[20]

A Star Is Born

Jean Faut, gifted with both natural ability and feminine grace, rose from a working class family in a small town in eastern Pennsylvania to lasting fame as one of the great stars of the All-American League. Her hometown, East Greenville, a borough with about 1,500 people, was located about 40 miles northwest of Philadelphia. Now 21, the second oldest daughter of Robert and Eva Faut, Jean grew up reading about sports and playing ball with two sisters and three brothers. She was an exceptionally talented female athlete living in a man's world. In high school, Jean thrilled to the competitive excitement of field hockey, basketball, and track, the three sports that girls usually played in the 1940s. She never played softball. Her favorite sport was baseball, and she watched guys compete in the East Penn Semiprofessional League, because the East Greenville Cubs played in a nearby ballpark. Seeing her interest, Snucks Reifinger, the second baseman, taught her the basics of pitching. As a teen, Faut often pitched batting practice and, later, she hurled in a few exhibition games.

An attractive young woman with sandy blond hair and blue eyes, the 5'4" Faut, who spoke with a trace of Pennsylvania Dutch accent, was bright, energetic, and modest. Her strong arms and wrists and sharp mind helped her as a ballplayer. Later, in the All-American League, she memorized pitching patterns to each batter. Jean, a pro ballplayer in a time period before athletes engaged in weight training, later explained: "I had to do chores, like chopping wood. At a meeting in Delaware last year, I told these athletes. 'You girls are lucky. You can get in shape by pumping iron. I had to chop wood to get my strong wrists.' I think they thought I was lying!"

After graduating from East Greenville High in 1942, Faut worked in nearby Pennsburg at a factory making trousers for officers' uniforms, earning $25 to $30 per week. Occasionally she worked out with the East Greenville Cubs. Faut never heard about the All-American League until Charles Shuler, a scout from Allentown, saw her pitch batting practice. After calling, he sent her a ticket to Pascagoula. Excited by the thought of living her baseball dream, Faut packed her gear and rode the train to the league's camp. The managers, notably Chet Grant, saw her strong arm, fine fielding prowess, and good hitting ability, and the rest, as they say, is history.[21]

The First Postwar Season

When the Blue Sox arrived at chilly South Bend on Monday, May 20, prospects for the postwar season of 1946 looked better. First, Betty Luna, the stellar right-hander from Los Angeles who was suspended by manager Marty McManus late in the 1945 season, traveled to Chicago on Sunday, and Max Carey reinstated her. The league also sent South Bend rookie hurler Frances Sloan of Miami, Florida, and reallocated right-hander Jane Jacobs to Peoria. Inez Voyce, the Iowa lefty soon to be discharged from the WAVES, was expected to be a good first baseman. The team's two original players from the 1943 Blue Sox were Jochum and Stefani, and Marge's injured knee was now better. Faut, reported the *Tribune*, "owns one of the strongest throwing arms in the league and is a good hitter as well." Outfielder Lee Surkowski injured her ankle and played little in exhibitions, but Saskatchewan rookie Daisy Junor was playing well in her place.[22]

The Blue Sox departed on the bus chartered through South Bend's White Star Lines. Women's teams no longer traveled by rail, and the same bus and driver would be used for the entire season. Jochum recalled that the bus was a big relief compared to the trains: "We could wear our shorts on the bus when it was hot. No more dragging your suitcase to the next train." The teams needed buses, Betsy added, "even if it meant traveling most of the night and arriving home early in the morning and playing that night. Much nicer than South Shore and North Shore trains."[23]

Riding the Bus — Starting in 1946, the end of gas rationing meant that All-American teams traveled by bus. The Blue Sox, wearing casual clothes for traveling instead of the more formal attire they were required to wear when they rode trains during World War II, get ready to board their chartered White Star Line Bus after a stop at the farm of Joyce Hill's uncle, George Clausen. Pictured are (back row, left to right) Senaida "Shoo Shoo" Wirth, Dottie Naum, Marie Kruckel, Lib Mahon, Inez Voyce, and Lillian Luckey. In the center row are Chet Grant, manager, Jenny Romatowski, Lucille Moore, chaperone, Betty Luna, Betsy Jochum, Daisy Junor, Jean Faut (partially hidden), and Mike Moore, Lucille's husband. Kneeling in the front are the bus driver, Mona Denton, and Joyce Hill, holding her nephew, James Mentink. Incidentally, if any of the players left the bus during a road trip, they had to put on a skirt, usually a wrap-around garment, over their shorts (courtesy of the Louise Pettus Archives and Special Collections, Winthrop University).

Traveling to Fort Wayne, South Bend split the four-game series. On Wednesday night at Dwenger Park, the Blue Sox, who lodged at the Hotel Anthony, outlasted the Daisies, 6–5, in 12 innings before more than 2,500 fans. After one out in the 12th, Naum walked and, when Dottie Collins threw a wild pitch for ball four, Naum advanced all the way to second base and, moments later, stole third. After a pop out, Wirth beat out a roller, and Naum scored. Thompson retired the Daisies, and the visitors won their first-ever game in Fort Wayne. Faut paced the 13-hit attack with four safeties, and Jochum added three.[24] On Thursday night (again the league played night games), the Blue Sox won, 6–0, behind Luna's three-hitter. The game's feature play came in the ninth when Wirth, after snagging Marge Pieper's low drive, tossed to second, and Stefani fired to first for a triple play to seal the victory.[25] On Friday, the Daisies won, 7–3, thanks to a seven-run sixth when Koehn walked five and gave up two-run singles to Faye Dancer and Helen Callaghan.[26] On Saturday, Thompson hurt her cause with three errors, notably her miscue in the eighth, when the Daisies broke a 2–2 tie to win, 4–2.

Jim Costin praised the Blue Sox for their aggressive play, saying Grant had his players running the bases, taking an extra base when possible, and sliding "into a base head first,

Ace Rookie — Jean Faut, batting second in South Bend's order, beats out a bunt in the first inning for the first hit of her eight-year All-American Girls Baseball League career. On May 22, 1946, at Fort Wayne's Dwenger Park, the Blue Sox prevailed over the Daisies, 6–5, scoring an unearned run in the 12th inning. Faut, the third baseman, collected four of South Bend's 13 hits in her debut. Fort Wayne's first baseman, stretching to catch the ball, is Vivian Kellogg (number 17). In the background (left to right) are Fort Wayne catcher Kate Vonderau, third baseman Marge Callaghan, who made the play, pitcher Dottie Wiltse Collins, and South Bend manager Chet Grant, who is coaching near third base (courtesy of the Louise Pettus Archives and Special Collections, Winthrop University).

feet first, any way to get there." The club's all-out style put pressure on opponents and often drew hurried throws that led to extra runs. Costin, long since a die-hard Sox backer, added, "you'll probably agree that it makes for a highly interesting and entertaining exhibition."[27]

Welcome to Playland Park

On May 26, a nice Sunday evening, South Bend won the home opening day attendance award when 5,328 folks paid their way into spacious Playland Park — designed to serve also as an amusement park with an oval track for the popular sport of auto racing. One thousand were sitting in the concrete grandstand with wooden seats behind home plate two hours before the 8:30 starting time. Fans later filled the right and center field bleachers and the temporary seats flanking the grandstand. A wall of automobiles parked several deep ringed the outfield. The all-dirt infield was laid out inside the cinder racetrack, but the batting area — a long walk from the dugouts — was on the cinders, and the clubhouse with the home team's locker room sat on top of the hill behind the grandstand. The Ushers Club, headed by Playland's owner Pete Redden, was made up of men and women who greeted fans, sold tickets and scorecards, and seated people.

Grand Rapids ruined the fun by winning, 7–0, as Jo Kabick, the Detroit right-hander, hurled a five-hitter. Wirth led the Blue Sox with two singles, but Luna, the starter, was wild, walking five while spacing five hits. Three Chicks that drew walks scored, and Luna's bad throws allowed two more runs.[28] Before a Monday crowd of 1,383, Koehn pitched well, but the home team lost, 4–1, when Stefani, usually reliable, made two big errors, notably her miss of a bases-loaded grounder in the sixth that let three runs score.[29] On Tuesday, South Bend lost in ten innings, 5–4, when right-hander Connie Wisniewski, facing Luna in the tenth, singled and later scored on Twila "Twi" Shively's single. Wirth and Voyce led

Playland Park — This aerial photo is looking north at the Playland Park complex circa 1946. The picture shows the cinder-surfaced auto racetrack running through the home plate area, the infield was hard dirt, and the outfield was grass. The picture also shows the concrete grandstand behind the home plate area and, on the hill behind the grandstand, the press boxes. Behind them and to the right is the team's rectangular-shaped clubhouse (courtesy of the Louise Pettus Archives and Special Collections, Winthrop University).

the nine-hit attack with two each, and Jochum's first inning homer was called a ground rule double when it bounced into the left field bleachers.[30] On Wednesday, Kabick, backed by Teeny Petras' bases-loaded triple, handed Luna and the Blue Sox a 7–3 defeat. The local favorites, now with a 2–6 record, scored on Mahon's single and an error in the first, on Voyce's homer in the second, and on Jochum's RBI single in the sixth.[31]

On Memorial Day, South Bend, entertaining 4,676 fans, the club's second largest crowd, snapped the string of six straight losses with a sweep of visiting Kenosha, 11–0 and 13–9. Bonnie Baker, who arrived on Wednesday, returned to action (she went 1-for-4) in the seven-inning opener, but Jim Costin raved about Wirth, who had five hits in the twin bill. Shoo-Shoo was a great crowd pleaser, and her "spectacular fielding and sparkling base running won her round after round of applause." Luna blanked the Comets on four hits, and trailing 5–0 in the second inning of the nightcap, the Sox rallied by combing Lee Harney and Janet Anderson for 15 hits, three by Wirth, although Koehn allowed 13 hits herself.[32]

After a rainout on Friday, South Bend defeated Kenosha on Saturday evening, 6–5. Mona Denton made her home debut, pitching well for seven innings, but Thompson recorded the win. A cold night, tough on women wearing uniforms with flared skirts that barely covered their thighs, limited attendance to 788 and forced cancellation of the loop's other games. South Bend improved to 5–6 and moved into fourth place, 11 percentage points ahead of 4–5 Peoria.[33]

The Blue Sox Improve

Riding the bus to Grand Rapids for a four-game set, the Blue Sox found the undefeated Chicks tough to beat. On Sunday evening, June 2, at South High Field, Grand Rapids swept a twin bill, and on Monday the Chicks won again. But on Tuesday night, 3,000 local fans wondered how their favorites had won 13 straight, because Grant's South Benders exploded for eight runs and a 9–4 lead in the fifth, and they went on to rout the league leaders, 17–5.[34] After the all-night bus trip around Lake Michigan, the Blue Sox arrived at Kenosha's Hotel Dayton on Wednesday morning, rested, practiced at mid-day, took a break, and returned to Lakefront Stadium by 5:30. The *Kenosha Evening News* called it a "free hitting, wild scoring, and loosely played game," as each team made six errors, but Kenosha won, 8–7.[35]

Regrouping, Grant's forces, using a rotation of Thompson, Luna, and Koehn, plus spot starters Lillian Luckey, a right-hander from Niles, Michigan, and Mona Denton, won the next three games against Kenosha. In Saturday's finale, Luckey beat the Comets, 6–5. Nervous, she walked 11 and gave up seven hits, but Voyce and Jochum each drove in two runs. When the night ended, Grand Rapids (16–2) and Rockford (10–7) remained the league's top two teams, and South Bend, at 9–10, held fifth place, half a game behind improving Racine (8–8).[36]

Yet another bus trip brought the Blue Sox home for a doubleheader with Rockford, and South Bend fans learned that "pint-sized" Senaida Wirth was leading All-American hitters with a .386 mark. Shoo-Shoo, the nickname fans in Birmingham, Alabama, gave her on the tour,[37] was 17-for-44 with six RBI over eleven games. South Bend led the loop with a .248 mark, followed by Rockford at .236 and Grand Rapids at .225. Lib Mahon, averaging .316, ranked second for the Sox, and Betsy Jochum was third at .275. Other solid hitters included Marge Stefani, .237; Jean Faut, .214; Joyce Hill (later loaned to Fort Wayne); .208, and Inez Voyce, .200.[38]

On June 9, South Bend swept Rockford in the Sunday night doubleheader at Playland Park by twice beating Chicago model Carolyn Morris, the Peaches' pretty ace, 4–1 in the opener and 5–2 in the nightcap. Thompson led the Blue Sox to the first win, spacing five hits. Dottie Kamenshek, stealing second, spiked Wirth, and a doctor used four sutures to close cuts around her left knee. Marie Kruckel, a utility player from the Bronx, New York, took over for the Sox at shortstop, but went hitless. In the late tilt, Koehn held the 1945 All-American Champions to four hits and two runs.[39] On Monday, Rockford topped South Bend, 10–4, thanks partly to the home team's old nemesis, sloppy play. Denton surrendered nine of the Peaches' ten hits in the first six innings, and tossing in six errors, the Blue Sox fell behind, 7–0. Outfielder Rose Gacioch pitched for Olive Little, who returned to Canada on business. Using her "sidearm-underarm" delivery, the right-hander from West Virginia gave up seven hits and won her second game (Rose was 2–2 in 1946).[40]

Monday's game had consequences around the league. Following the example of Racine's Anna Hutchison, Rose Gacioch and her slants further moved the circuit toward authorizing the sidearm delivery in 1947, a change that foreshadowed overhand pitching in 1948.

Other managers followed suit. In South Bend, Tuesday's final Rockford game was rained out in the first inning, and Fort Wayne arrived on Wednesday, but cold and rainy weather cancelled that night's game. On a chilly Thursday at Playland, the Daisies' Bill Wambsganss, "hearing about that Gacioch business," started hard-throwing Faye Dancer, and the Daisies won, 5–3, scoring four unearned runs off Luna. Regardless of weather, the league was booming, and the latest crowd, numbering 2,254, raised South Bend's attendance to 23,556, nearly half the team's 1945 total.[41]

On June 14, with fans also excited about a big promotion, the Blue Sox won a Friday evening twin bill while hosting 19 South Bend and Mishawaka auto dealers. The dealerships purchased 1,500 tickets for their employees and, after the games, displayed the new 1946 models on Playland's racetrack. The home team rocked the Daisies, sporting their eye-catching orchid (a blue-red hue) uniforms with red accessories and caps,[42] blasting Dottie Collins for six runs in the first, keyed by Stefani's bases-loaded triple, as Thompson coasted to an 8–1 win. In the late tilt, Koehn and Lee Harney dueled for 11 innings, but the Sox won when Mahon walked, stole second, advanced on a sacrifice, and scored on Faut's bunt.[43] On Saturday, with the auto show continuing and over 2,000 fans on hand, Stefani paced a 7–4 victory, walking twice, rapping two hits, scoring four runs, and batting in two more. Afterward, South Bend ranked third at 14–12, but Grand Rapids (20–5) held a big lead on second-place Rockford (13–10).[44]

Immediately after the game, the South Benders boarded the bus for Rockford and, as often happened on bus trips, spent much of the night playing cards, chatting, singing the "Victory Song," or trying to sleep. In the short opener of Sunday's twin bill at Beyer Stadium, a throng of 3,570 saw the blue-uniformed visitors, fueled by Jochum's fourth-inning RBI single, win Luna's three-hit shutout, 1–0. In the nightcap, the home team won a slugfest, 10–6, as rookie Dottie Moon, from Belleville, Michigan, pitched well, and the Peaches reached Thompson and Koehn for 12 hits.[45] The series with the Peaches was cut short when Monday night's game and Tuesday's make-up twin bill were rained out. In the interim, the Sox acquired utility infielder Jenny Romatowski, while Frances Sloan, yet to pitch in a game, was sent to Grand Rapids.[46]

Back at Playland Park on Wednesday night, June 19, South Bend hosted seventh-place

Peoria and won four straight. In the finale on Saturday, the Blue Sox won, 4–3, and Luckey, who matched Jacobs' five-hitter, contributed an RBI single in the ninth — winning her own game and drawing a big round of applause from more than 2,000 happy fans. The victory moved 19–13 South Bend into second place, two and a half games ahead of the Peaches (15–14).[47]

Afterward, South Bend announced that Lee Surkowski was loaned to Rockford on a two-day recall. Surkowski, a reserve behind Daisy Junor, last appeared in a South Bend uniform on June 14 when the Sox topped Fort Wayne, 5–3, and Lee, who was 1-for-4, played center, and Jochum subbed at first for the ailing Voyce. As it transpired, Surkowski finished the season with Rockford.[48]

Two New League Cities

Reinvigorated, the Blue Sox rode the bus to Peoria, where they stayed at the Hotel Jefferson and prepared to meet the Redwings in a Sunday twin bill. Peoria, the first European settlement in Illinois, was located on the west shore of Peoria Lake, part of the Illinois River and 170 miles southwest of Chicago. The name Peoria came from the Native American tribe that settled the region. French explorers, including La Salle, canoed through the area in the 1660s, and a settlement grew among villages of the Illini tribes. As a result of the 1763 treaty ending the French and Indian War, Britain acquired the territory, and during the War of 1812, American soldiers entered the region. Fort Clark was built in 1813, and the fort became a town as settlers arrived and farmed the area.

Renamed Peoria, the city grew. River steamboats arrived in 1830, and the railroad brought prosperity by the 1850s. In 1882, local leaders built the Grand Opera House, the "Jewel of Peoria." When Vaudeville appeared in the early 1900s, the Illinois city was often the last stop before a show hit New York's Broadway — thus, the phrase, "Will it play in Peoria?" Since the 1830s, industries had spread along the banks of the Illinois, including milling, meat-packing, casting foundries, coopers, cabinetmakers, distilleries, and, later, earth-moving and farm machinery manufacturers. The Holt Manufacturing Company, founded in 1909, expanded into Caterpillar, Inc. Peoria was also known as the "Whiskey Capital of the World," and distilleries brought more wealth. At the end of World War II, because of the diverse cultural, social, and economic environment and a population exceeding 100,000, Peoria was known as the quintessential Midwestern city.[49]

At Peoria Stadium on Sunday evening, June 23, the Blue Sox split a twin bill with the expansion Redwings, outfitted in maroon-trimmed white uniforms (they wore gray on the road) and maroon caps. The visitors won the short opener behind Thompson's five-hitter, 8–5, but Peoria won the late game, 10–4. Enjoying the new electric scoreboard, 4,000 fans were buzzing about the teams' fine play, notably glove work by Peoria's first baseman Jean Cione and left fielder Mary Wood. In the nightcap, Koehn lost her control in the sixth, walking five batters, hitting two, and yielding two hits and six runs, but Lefty Lee, the little California knuckleballer, won a four-hitter.[50] South Bend came back on Monday as Koehn, helped by fine defense, won a three-hitter, 3–1.[51] Two days later, the blue-clad visitors reached Betty Tucker for 11 safeties to back Luna, who spaced six hits and won, 10–4. Winning three out of four and seven of the last eight from Peoria, the surging Sox, now 22–14, were four games behind first-place Grand Rapids (26–10).[52]

After the game, the South Benders embarked on yet another late-night trip, this time more than 300 miles to Muskegon, a thriving industrial center in Michigan. The medium-sized city was a few miles away from the east shore of Lake Michigan and 40 miles northwest of Grand Rapids. Muskegon, a name derived from the Ottawa term Masquigon, meaning "marshy river," or swamp, was populated by Native Americans for hundreds of years before Father Marquette journeyed by canoe through the area in 1675. French-Canadian fur traders lived in the region, and by 1800 a trading post was established at nearby Duck Lake. Settlement of Muskegon County began in 1837 when the first sawmill was built on the southeastern shore of Muskegon Lake. The local lumber industry peaked in the mid–1880s, as nearly 50 sawmills surrounded the lake and a similar number of mills lined the shores of nearby White Lake.

When the lumber business played out toward the end of the 19th century, Muskegon's leaders worked to attract new industries. Before the Great War, major businesses included Shaw-Walker, Brunswick, Campbell, Continental Motors, and Central Paper. The Great Depression of the 1930s hurt economic growth, but when federal contracts flowed in during World War II, Muskegon boomed, producing tank engines, landing craft, and other war-related products. The wartime need for manpower brought in large numbers of Mexican-Americans, Appalachian whites, and Southern blacks. When the Lassies of the All-American League arrived in 1946, Muskegon was a healthy Midwestern community with a diverse population of nearly 100,000.[53]

The Blue Sox and the Lassies seemed evenly matched. On Thursday night, June 26, at Muskegon's Marsh Field, an old minor league park set up for the girls' game, the Lassies, sporting their home white uniforms — they wore mustard yellow for away games — and green caps, defeated the visitors, 8–3.[54] Seventh place Muskegon won again on Thursday night, but South Bend won on Friday. The Blue Sox squared the series on Saturday when Luna twirled a five-hitter and won 4–1. Afterward, the standings showed Grand Rapids in first place with a 24–11 mark, South Bend was second at 24–16, and Racine third at 22–16.[55]

Later that night, the Blue Sox and the Lassies journeyed on their respective buses 125 miles to South Bend, where the travelers lodged at the Oliver Hotel. Both teams followed the usual ritual of morning practices, late lunches, and resting — the local favorites at the homes where they roomed and the visitors at the hotel. The Blue Sox, playing good ball by the time they made the first Muskegon trip, won three of four, splitting Sunday's twin bill and winning the next two contests. At Playland on Tuesday before 1,493 fans, Koehn pitched a 4–2 triumph, as her teammates managed only three hits but drew nine walks, scoring once in the third, adding two more runs in the sixth, and clinching the win with one run in the seventh. The loop scheduled no games for July 3, and South Bend now 27–17, prepared to host third-place Racine (26–16) on the holiday.[56]

Before a league record crowd of 6,745 on Thursday, July 4, the standings remained the same as South Bend won the short opener, 9–5, but Racine took the late game, 5–4. The gates at Playland opened at five o'clock, and within two hours the grandstand and bleacher seats were filled. The air buzzed with excitement as fans flowed into special bleachers (borrowed from Notre Dame) behind the wire fences in center and right field, and sat on the ground from behind first base on around to left field. Luna won the opener after the local favorites, trailing 4–1, rallied for four runs in the fifth and four more in the sixth — featuring the Californian's own bases-loaded triple. In the nightcap, Luckey was wild and ineffective, and Koehn relieved her for the last two and two-thirds innings, but Racine already led, 5–4, and Dodie Barr preserved the lead. When the action ended at 11:22 pm, the 27–17 Belles held a one game lead over the 28–18 Sox.[57]

On Friday night, Racine's Jo Winter, her slingshot stuff working, spaced three hits for a 7–0 win. According to Jim Costin, the Blue Sox played their worst game, but "lenient scoring" limited their errors to seven, and Thompson was raked for 11 hits.[58] On Saturday, behind Luna's two-hit shutout, the home team took an 8–0 triumph. Wirth led the 11-hit assault with three safeties, and Mahon, Stefani, and Junor added two each. The win left the Sox (29–19) a game behind the second-place Belles (28–18), but Grand Rapids paced the Girls' Pro League with a 33–14 mark.[59]

The Blue Sox in Mid-1946

Baseball requires more than talent. Good players, male or female, have natural ability, especially excellent hand-eye coordination, as shown in the finely honed skills needed for batting, throwing, fielding, running, and adapting quickly to game situations. Such skills are improved by practice — and the Sox usually practiced daily from around ten o'clock until noon or so.

Also, players have to adjust to feeling the exhilaration of good plays and big wins and the frustrations of bad plays and tough losses on the diamond, where an athlete's talent, skill, and experience are displayed day after day. The best players come through under game pressure, whether at bat or in the field, and the girls seemed to have the poise and grace, Chet Grant concluded, needed to recover quickly from bad plays or "nightmare innings."[60]

Additionally, professional players who last even part of a season must survive the rigors of life on the road, staying in hotels, and playing in ballparks filled with often hostile fans. Based on the usual lineup in 1946, South Bend fielded a very good team, but not a great one. Incidentally, characteristic of prevailing attitudes, newspaper and magazine articles usually described the players, many in their teens and others in their twenties, as "girls." Furthermore, All-Americans were excited about playing the game as professionals, and regardless of age, most of them referred to their teammates as "kids."[61]

The Blue Sox had a handful of talented and experienced players, notably Bonnie Baker at catcher, Betsy Jochum in center field, Marge Stefani at second base, and Betty Luna and Phyllis Koehn on the mound. The team also boasted four stellar rookies: Jean Faut at third base, Inez Voyce at first base, Shoo-Shoo Wirth at shortstop, and Daisy Junor in left field. However, the fact that four rookies were regulars showed that the Sox lacked experience. South Bend had good talent, and Grant, a gentleman and a serious manager, worked well with veterans and rookies.

Grant, later curator for the sports collections at the Notre Dame's Hesburgh Library, was a football man with coaching experience. He played pro baseball (aspiring to play football at Notre Dame, he used an assumed name) in the old Michigan State League in 1912 and 1913. He also "pinch-managed" the Blue Sox for a week in 1945 when Marty McManus took a short leave. In his memoir, Grant, who was a 5'7" 138-pound quarterback for Notre Dame under Coach Knute Rockne in 1920 and 1921, recalled that the team's talent ranged from the naïveté of rookies to the savoir faire of veterans. And women did something men would not — slide on bare legs!

Grant explained that male managers were viewed by the fans, and likely by many players, as a "necessary evil," but most men, when they saw the women play, marveled at their ability to perform so well on the ball field. The male ballplayer had an edge in running speed and throwing strength as well as in batting power, but with the All-Americans, their "masculine skill and feminine grace cast the spell."[62] Grant knew athletes, and he led the Blue Sox to a third-place finish in 1946, after they missed taking fourth place on the last day of the 1945 season.

The strong-minded Baker was an important player for the South Benders. A fixture behind the plate, the fourth-year standout turned 28 in mid-season when she was tied for the league lead in hitting with Rockford's Naomi "Sally" Meier. Both were averaging .308.[63] Grant later said that Baker was "wooed out of retirement by a salary hike to $100 a week," and, if she played well, Harold Dailey, a board member, secretly promised her a cash bonus.[64]

Newspaper stories indicated the Regina star might not return in 1946, but Baker was holding out for more money. On December 1, 1945, writing to a young admirer in South Bend, Bonnie expressed satisfaction with Playland Park as the team's new home for 1946, adding, "we should make more money next season. It will seem so strange living over on the other side of town, but that way we'll get better acquainted with So[uth] Bend."[65]

A skilled athlete, Baker thrilled to the excitement as well as the glamour of the All-American League. Thanks to her good looks, charm, and skill at posing, she was photographed often enough to be the face of the Blue Sox, and maybe the entire circuit. She made a big hit with the team's directors, especially Dailey.[66] After returning on Memorial Day, Bonnie again proved her value. She made the postseason All-Star team by averaging .286, tying her for second in the league with Racine's Sophie Kurys, voted Player of the Year. Rockford's Dottie Kamenshek led the hitters at .316, making her the only All-American to bat more than .300 in 1946.[67]

Lib Mahon, who paced the loop with 72 RBI, placed second to Baker on the Blue Sox by hitting .276, ranking Lib sixth among the league's regulars. Even with her left knee often wrapped by an ace bandage, she proved a major asset to the team. In addition to her solid fielding and her skill in producing runs, Mahon was a stable influence on new players and often showed them the ropes. An independent-minded woman, she was, like Baker, a formidable presence in the dugout and the locker room. Most of these women lived with families near Playland Park, and, despite differing personalities, managed to live reasonably well together, both on the road and in their South Bend homes. Mahon, 26, was not a favorite of male club officials or managers, partly because she insisted on fair treatment for female athletes and top dollar salary for her efforts. No matter: Lib said what she thought, but she also gave the game her best shot.[68]

Betsy Jochum, a fourth-year Blue Sox star, was one of the league's best all-around athletes. Strong, agile, and speedy, she was blessed with the natural instincts to excel at any position. A strong but reserved individual, Jochum, 25, let her actions on the field speak for her. She won the league's second-half batting title in 1943 with a .295 mark, and she won the overall batting championship in 1944 by averaging .296. Her hitting slipped to .237 in 1945, but Betsy ranked third on her team. Further, she performed well in clutch situations. If the manager needed her to bunt, hit-and-run, steal a base, or deliver a big hit, she often came through, averaging .246 for six seasons. In 1946, she batted .250 with seven doubles, seven triples, two home runs, 43 RBI, and 73 stolen bases. Jochum was the ultimate team player, and her career was a classic example of the "All-American" girl playing softball and gradually adapting — along with the league — to baseball.[69]

South Bend's two returning pitchers were Betty Luna and Sugar Koehn. Luna, a 19-year-old right-handed batter and pitcher who was born in Dallas, Texas, but grew up in Los Angeles, was another blond star who matched the loop's ideal of masculine skill and feminine grace. In addition, Betty, a 5'5" third-year veteran who began her career with Rockford in 1944, could play the outfield and, if necessary, third base, making her a useful team member. A timely hitter, she averaged .250 in 1945. On the mound, she improved her underhand motion and her control, fashioning a 14–15 mark with a team-best 1.53 ERA, and she pitched a no-hitter against Grand Rapids on August 6. However, Marty McManus suspended her for undisclosed reasons late in the 1945 season. Reinstated in 1946, Luna led the Sox hurlers with a 23–13 ledger. In 48 games, she also batted .207, adding a double, three triples, and 12 RBI.[70]

Koehn, a right-handed batter who began pitching in late 1945 when the Blue Sox needed hurlers, began in 1943 as a utility player for Kenosha, where she spent her first two seasons. On June 30, 1945, McManus, the former Comet pilot, engineered South Bend's trade of Lois Florreich and Dottie Schroder to Kenosha for Pinky Pirok and Koehn. Pirok was slowed by injuries later that season, but the versatile Koehn, who stood 5'5" and could play any position, made a big contribution to South Bend's fight for fourth place. Born and raised in Marshfield, Wisconsin, Phyllis moved with her family to Madison in 1938. Like many girls, she grew up playing ball with her brother and his friends. She played semipro softball for the Kennedy Dairy in 1939 and 1940, and for Red Dot Potato Chips in 1941 and 1942. In 1943, Phyllis wrote to the league and received a tryout at Wrigley Field, and she made it. She signed for $60 a week, doubling her secretary's salary with Red Dot. In addition to her 2–4 record in 1945, the curly-haired star hit .233, delivering several clutch hits during July and August. Twenty-three in 1946, Koehn ranked second on the team in wins with a 22–15 record. A steady underhand pitcher, her hitting fell to .159, but she added five doubles, a triple and 14 RBI.[71]

South Bend acquired some exceptional rookies in 1946, and besides Faut, one of the best recruits was Inez "Lefty" Voyce, soon a popular star. Tall and strong at 5'6" and 145 pounds, the 21-year-old Iowa native played ball with her brothers and other boys. Seymour High did not have softball for girls, but she played guard on the basketball team for four years. After graduating in 1941, Inez spent two years at a business college, the American Institute of Commerce. Her first job was as a $15-per-week secretary in a local garage. Her father, a coal mine superintendent, moved to California for his health in 1941, and her mother followed two years later. In November 1943, Voyce moved to Santa Monica to join her parents. The Post Office hired her for Christmas, and she remained, working in the money order department until joining the Navy in 1944. On a trip to Chicago to visit her sister in August 1944, she saw a Cubs game. Inez also inquired at the All-American League's office, and she received a tryout in Los Angeles. After looking good, she received a contract to go to Pascagoula, where she made the cut. Her contract paid her $65 per week in 1946. The league's perks included $3.50 a day for meals, which Voyce remembered as a detail compared to being "paid to play baseball!"[72]

Voyce covered first base for South Bend and averaged .210, the team's sixth-best mark, including a double, three triples, 12 stolen bases, and 12 RBI. She kept improving and became a stellar All-American. Traded to Grand Rapids in 1947, Lefty spent seven seasons with the Chicks. A good clutch hitter, she compiled a lifetime total of 422 RBI, ranking second on the league's all-time run-producing list behind Dottie Schroder, who had 431 RBI in 12 years. Voyce was agile, skilled, and savvy, a dependable hitter as well as a consistent, often acrobatic, fielder. Some called her "The Hook," because she seemed to get her glove on every throw.[73]

Another good rookie was Regina's Daisy Junor. By June, the Canadian softball star held down the left field slot once occupied by the fleet Jochum, who was shifted to center field during the spring tour when Lee Surkowski, later loaned to Rockford, hurt her ankle. Described as a good flychaser with blazing speed on the bases, the slender Junor, who stood 5'6", threw and batted right-handed. In 1943 in Regina, her team won the title for the Western Canada Softball League. Daisy, then 24, had just married Dave Junor, so she turned down an All-American contract. After the war, she took the offer, made the circuit at Pascagoula, and went to South Bend. Junor, however, struggled trying to hit pro pitching, batting a career-best .186 in 1946. Still, she collected 60 hits, drew 21 walks, stole 35 bases, and scored 30 runs.[74]

Talking about her career in 1996, Junor explained that the women took the game seriously, with practice sessions almost every morning and games under the lights at night. The travel was tough, as road trips occurred every other week. "We were living out of a suitcase most of the time," she recounted. "I always said, 'Gee, it'd be good to have some home-made mashed potatoes.'" Since road games ended between nine and ten or eleven o'clock, the only places usually open were cocktail lounges and bars, and the girls would get a steak and a beer and hurry to the hotel to make curfew. Chet Grant and Lucille Moore were usually waiting in the hotel lobby. "As soon as the chaperone and the manager went to bed," Junor said, "the girls would get together and pick up the phone and order beer and play poker. And sometimes we'd play until two or three in the morning, and the stakes were always pretty high."[75]

While Junor had fond memories of life with the Blue Sox, including on the road, her late-night experiences were not shared by all the players.[76] Jean Faut remembered rooming in the Kahn home along with Marie Kruckel, another rookie. Partway through the 1946 season, Baker, Stefani, and Mahon invited the pair to share an apartment they were renting. Kruckel agreed, and made the move. "I figured living with them would mean drinking and card-playing," Faut recalled, "so I stayed in the home. I came to South Bend to play ball."[77]

Rookie Senaida Wirth made a big splash at shortstop. Her slick fielding, speed on the bases, youthful good looks, and bubbly personality appealed to everyone. Known as Shoo-Shoo by fans and friends, the five-foot Latina grew up in Tampa speaking fluent Spanish and English (her mother was Cuban-born). She skittered all over the infield making plays. Hitting the league's pitchers like a seasoned veteran, Wirth was averaging more than .330 in July, but she finished with a .245 mark, including four doubles and a triple. She ran well, until a spiking injury slowed her, but she stole 89 bases and produced 27 RBI. Looking younger than her 19 years, she received her nickname from Dinah Shore's "Shoo-Fly Pie and Apple-Pan Dowdy," one of the year's most popular songs. Along with Baker, Wirth was voted to the league's All-Star team.[78]

Equally important, Wirth and other All-Americans became role models and heroines, notably for young girls. Author Sue Macy quoted a letter written by a South Bend mother in the spring of 1947. Her three-year-old daughter Karen saw Wirth play in 1946. The mom hoped to meet the shortstop: "We have heard nothing but 'Shoo Shoo,' since she calls you on her play telephone as if you were really there.... She throws the ball and says she's playing ball with Shoo Shoo."[79]

The teams also had bat girls, one for the home team and another for the visitors. Carolyn Odell, a Niles, Michigan, native who grew up in South Bend, began seeing league games in 1943 with her father, a doctor. In 1944, Carolyn often walked to Bendix Field in the morning and watched the Blue Sox practice. The bat girl was board member Al McGann's daughter, and, on occasion, Carolyn subbed for her. In 1945, following her ninth grade year, Odell served as bat girl, often for opposing teams. In 1946, business manager Joe Boland, the Notre Dame announcer, asked her to return. Carolyn treasured the time she spent at practices and games for two more years.

After graduating from South Bend Central in 1948, Odell left to attend Stephens College in Columbia, Missouri, later graduating from the University of Missouri. While at college, she lost touch with her beloved Blue Sox. Years later, Odell still cherished the memories and friendships, and she kept the players' letters in the original envelopes — more than 80 from 1946 alone.

The All-Americans were Carolyn's heroines. Like boys who admired masculine heroes and saved baseball cards, she loved taking snapshots of players, writing letters, usually with pictures enclosed, and receiving the often heartfelt replies. If Odell's experience was any example, the league played a big part in the lives of countless Midwestern girls in the 1940s.[80]

Bat Girl — Muskegon player Dorothy "Dot" Montgomery (left) poses with South Bend's visitors' bat girl, Carolyn Odell, at Playland Park in 1946. Odell enjoyed exchanging letters and pictures with many of the players she met (courtesy of Carolyn Odell).

Winning, and Losing, in July

July and August were roller-coaster months for South Bend. As fate would have it, the Blue Sox were not able to mount another good winning streak until early August. For example, Chet Grant's charges, hosting Kenosha, swept a doubleheader on Sunday, July 21, by scores of 10–4 and 4–3, playing before a vocal crowd of 3,546 and setting a league attendance mark for one week with 18,758 paid. Koehn won the opener when her teammates teed off for 12 hits and ten runs against Theresa Kobuszewski and Jo Kabick. In the nightcap, Wirth served as both goat and heroine, failing to run hard and score the winning run in the tenth when Baker beat out a slow roller down the third base line, but, in the 12th, rapping her fourth single and scoring the winning run after Voyce and Junor singled. Shoo-Shoo goofed in the tenth, but when Grant screamed at her, the crowd booed him.[81]

Wirth, on second base with the potential winning run in the tenth, raced around third on an infield roller, and Grant thought the Sox won when he saw the throw pop out of the

Let Them Eat Candy — Enjoying an afternoon away from the ballpark in 1946, three Blue Sox players are eating cotton candy. Pictured (left to right) are Lillian Luckey, Mona Denton, and Betty Luna (courtesy of the Louise Pettus Archives and Special Collections, Winthrop University).

first baseman's glove. When the crowd roared, he turned and saw Shoo-Shoo, 20 feet short of home plate, trotting. She figured the third out was routine, but alerted by screaming fans, she headed back to third base. After a dive for the bag, she was called out. Wirth charged the umpire, but Grant retorted, "Don't blame him. You were out by a mile. You should be on the bench instead of out here." Shoo-Shoo turned on the manager and the fans turned with her, and boos cascaded down on Grant. The pilot concluded, "Shoo-Shoo's run-scoring single in the [12th] inning could have saved me from being lynched!" Also, Chet observed, the male managers were destined to be blamed for the players' mistakes as well as the team's losses by fans and often by the players. Years later, Grant reflected on Wirth: "Short, dark, vivacious Shoo-Shoo, darting to and fro at shortstop like a waterbug — was Rookie of the Year: our People's Choice."[82]

Several women wrote to the *South Bend Tribune* and blasted Grant — and ripped Costin for defending Grant. The sports editor, however, argued the obvious: players like Wirth were professionals. They were paid to play every game to the best of their ability, and that included running the bases until the third out was called. Wirth failed to do so. She was wrong, and Grant was correct to chastise her. Still, given the standards and values for the treatment of the "fairer sex" in the 1940s, the manager needed to correct her in gentlemanly fashion. In any event, Grant's difficulties were hardly unusual for male pilots in the All-American League.[83]

Following games on July 31, the top three teams finished with these results for the month:

- Muskegon beat Grand Rapids, 1–0, but the Chicks won 22 out of 34 games.
- Racine whipped Kenosha, 11–0, and the Belles won 26 of 35 games.
- South Bend lost to Rockford, 4–2, making the Sox winners of 18 out of 32 games.

At that time, the Chicks led the league with a 50–25 ledger, the Belles were second at 49–26, and the 44–32 Blue Sox ranked third.[84]

Faut, Sidearming, and Winning in August

On Friday, August 2, at Playland, two fan favorites, Koehn and Jochum, gave clutch performances to lift the Blue Sox over the Peaches, 3–2, a victory that started South Bend on a seven-game winning streak. Koehn spaced two hits and deserved a shutout, but she earned the victory when the Sox rallied in the ninth, starting with Wirth's triple to the flag pole in center. After two intentional passes, Jochum singled to win the exciting contest.[85] On Saturday, the fifth-place Daisies arrived for four games, and the local heroines swept the series. Afterward, the South Benders made the late-night trip to Rockford, hoping to continue their five-game streak.

By that time, sidearm pitching had appeared around the league. In June, Rockford's Rose Gacioch and Millie Deegan and Fort Wayne's Faye Dancer used a sidearm delivery. On July 29, Grant tried Jean Faut in relief. On Tuesday, August 6, in the first of two games at Beyer Stadium, Jean, who made "lightning throws" from third base,[86] started her first game and hurled a two-hitter to win, 1–0. Relying on sharp control and her moving sidearm fastball, she was tough to hit. In the nightcap, Koehn gave up seven hits but prevailed, 6–5.[87]

Rockford, however, came back to beat the visitors three straight, starting with Carolyn Morris' 4–2 victory over Luna on Wednesday night.[88] In a Thursday twin bill, the Peaches won both easily, 5–1 and 6–0. In the opener, the sidearming Deegan won a three-hitter, 6–1. In the late game, Marge Holgerson, Deegan's sub at second base, debuted with a one-hit shutout. Faut started slowly, yielding three runs on four hits in the first. Afterward, the Sox, now 51–35, ranked third, four games behind first place Racine (54–30), and Grand Rapids (54–31) was a close second.[89]

Equally important, Hutchison, Gacioch, Dancer, Faut, Deegan, Holgerson, and others reflected the new All-American trend: position players with strong arms taking the mound, hurling sidearm, and providing teams with new pitchers. Sidearming moved the league closer to overhand pitching, and to baseball. Except for distances on the diamond, the big difference between the All-American game and baseball was overhand pitching, which the league adopted in 1948. Since few underhand pitchers could adjust their delivery to sidearm, the shift meant that underhanders were facing the day they could no longer pitch in the Girls' Pro League.[90]

Chasing the Chicks and the Belles

On Friday, August 23, South Bend began the team's final stand at Playland Park with a four-game sweep of the Lassies. More than 4,000 fans saw the games, raising the season attendance to 99,124, but the Blue Sox (64–39) remained six and a half games off the pace of the red-hot Belles (70–32).[91] Dottie Kamenshek was leading the hitters with a .310 mark, and Baker, the previous leader, had slipped to .303. The top hurler by percentage was Faut with a 4–1 mark, but Connie Wisniewski was 29–8, and Jo Winter, enjoying her best season, was 28–9. Thompson paced South Bend's regular pitchers with a 13–6 ledger, Luna was 21–13, and Koehn 19–12.[92]

The following Tuesday at Playland, Faut, after pitching out of a jam in the seventh inning with runners on first and third, broke Racine's eight-game streak by beating Anna Hutchison, 2–0.[93] The next day, Winter, the Phoenix brunette, outdueled Koehn, racking up her sixth shutout in a row, 2–0. In a typical maneuver to counter wet grounds, the dirt infield was covered with sawdust, gasoline was poured over it and burned, and sand sprinkled around, thus baking the ground and making it rougher for sliding.[94]

On Thursday, the home team defeated Racine in a ten-inning nail-biter, 3–2. Luna, who missed ten days with a sore arm, returned and scattered eight hits, outlasting Hutchison, who fired a two-hitter. On a night better suited to football, 2,654 fans watched a variety of good plays. In the ninth, Brookynite Betty Trezza walked, stole second on a disputed call, moved to third on an infield hit, and tied the score at 2–2 on Ellie Dapkus' squeeze. In the tenth, Mahon walked and stole twice. Voyce hit a liner near second, Sophie Kurys knocked it down and threw to first base, but Marnie Danhauser dropped the throw, giving South Bend the triumph in what Jim Costin called "one of the most thrilling games of the season."[95]

In their final home game of 1946, before an often-roaring crowd of 4,038 that set a new team season attendance record of more than 110,000, the Blue Sox scored twice in the ninth inning to defeat the Belles, 4–3. In the ninth, Jochum singled and stole second, and Mahon singled to score the tying run. When Danhauser threw wildly to home trying to nip Jochum, Mahon took third. Manager Leo Murphy walked the bases full in hopes of getting a forceout at home. Instead, Chet Grant used Luna to pinch-hit for the weak-hitting Junor, and the California star "socked Winter's first pitch for a mile to center for the longest single she'll likely ever make," wrote Costin, "Mahon scoring the winning run to the hysterical delight of the big crowd."[96]

Anticlimax in Racine

Unloading their bags at the Hotel Racine, the Blue Sox knew they were playing well, thanks in part to the hurling of Jean Faut, their third baseman. Beginning with the last game of the Rockford series on August 2, improving South Bend won 23 and lost eight in August. At Racine on Saturday night, Koehn twirled a two-hitter and won, 3–0. When Grand Rapids (68–41) lost two to seventh-place Kenosha, the 68–40 Sox moved into second place.[97]

In a doubleheader on Sunday, September 1, playing before Racine's third largest audience, 4,453 fans, the Belles clinched the pennant for the second time in four seasons by winning, 7–4. Winter yielded four runs in three innings of the opener, but Hutchison won her 27th game with scoreless relief. However, Faut, who cracked a two-run homer in the second frame, got off to a shaky start, allowing five runs in the first, and her team could not recover. In the late game, Luna won for the Blue Sox, 4–3, as little-used Betty Emry gave up seven hits and five walks. The bad news, however, came when Jochum injured her right ankle sliding into third base in the third inning, leaving the Sox without their best outfielder for the playoffs.[98]

On Monday, the two teams split another twin bill, Racine winning the opener, 3–2, and South Bend taking the late game, 6–3. The final standings showed Racine first with a 74–38 record. Grand Rapids clinched second place by one game with a 71–41 ledger, South Bend was a close third at 70–42, and Rockford finished a distant fourth at 60–52.[99]

Tuesday was an off day, and while several players passed time waiting for the team's first postseason game by writing letters from the hotel,[100] Jim Costin praised Grant, observing that he welded the team together, kept the players hustling, encouraged them to play up to their ability, and turned Jean Faut from a third sacker into a pitcher. With Faut anchoring a four-pitcher rotation, South Bend played the league's best ball, winning 26 of the last 38 games, and the Pennsylvania rookie earned eight of those victories.[101]

In the first playoff game on Wednesday at Horlick Field, a crowd of 2,788 cheered all night as the Belles edged the Blue Sox in 17 innings, 3–2, in an All-American classic. The visitors managed five hits off Hutchison, but the Belles took a 2–0 lead off Faut in the sixth on Pirok's error. In the eighth, Wirth beat out a grounder to third, advanced on a bad throw and a sacrifice, and Dottie Naum, the catcher from Dearborn, Michigan, who was playing right field, scored the run with a long fly. Stefani, up with one out in the ninth, bounced to Hutchison, but Anna threw it away, and Marge cruised to second. Mahon singled to center for a 2–2 tie. In extra innings, the Blue Sox lost their best chance in the 14th when Baker singled, stole second, and reached third on a groundout, but Pirok fouled out and Mahon lined out, both to left field. Finally, Racine won when, with one out in the 17th, Pirok threw away Dapkus' grounder and Ellie took second, and Maddy English doubled to left-center to end the marathon. As a sign of the league's popularity, two dozen South Bend fans flew to Milwaukee, and the team's bus carried them to Racine for the game. (In the playoff at Grand Rapids, the Peaches beat the Chicks, 4–2.)[102]

Shaughnessy Playoffs in 1946—The Blue Sox pose before South Bend's first-ever Shaughnessy Playoff game at Racine's Horlick Field on September 4, 1946. That evening Jean Faut pitched against Racine's Anna May Hutchison, and the Belles prevailed in a 17-inning thriller, 3–2. The Blue Sox pictured in front of Racine's grandstand are (back row, left to right) Pinky Pirok, Daisy Junor, Jean Faut, Lib Mahon, Phyllis "Sugar" Koehn, Betsy Jochum, Mona Denton, Lucille Moore, chaperone, Betty Luna, Inez Voyce, Dottie Naum, and Lillian Luckey. Kneeling in front are (left to right) Marge Stefani, Marie Kruckel, Jenny Romatowski, Bonnie Baker, Senaida "Shoo Shoo" Wirth, and Viola "Tommie" Thompson (courtesy of the Louise Pettus Archives and Special Collections, Winthrop University).

On Thursday night, after a rain delay of 15 minutes, the second Belles-Blue Sox postseason contest got underway, but was called after a downpour in the fourth inning. In the meantime, Rockford beat Grand Rapids, 2–0, taking a two-game lead in the two teams' playoff series.[103]

South Bend and Racine faced each other again at Horlick on Friday night. Luna held the Belles to four hits, and the blue-uniformed visitors raked three pitchers, notably Winter, for 14 hits and won, 13–2. The Blue Sox took a 5–2 lead into the fourth when, following hits by Junor and Baker, Stefani singled for two runs, and Winter departed. Betty Emry and Dodie Barr fared no better, the rout continued, and Pirok and Naum led the Sox with three hits each.[104]

Back at Playland on Saturday night, September 7, the series was tied at one game apiece. More than 4,000 spectators were sharing the fun, but a storm ended the game in the second inning with the Blue Sox ahead, 2–0.[105] Returning on a pleasant Sunday evening, Hutchison pitched a two-hitter and the Belles won their second game, 7–1, before a record South Bend audience of 7,413. Unlike the two rained-out games when the Blue Sox grabbed early leads, the Belles opened with three runs in the first, two on Perlick's homer. Hometown excitement ebbed when the yellow-clad visitors batted Koehn out of the box in the second with another three-run burst for a 6–0 lead. Faut pitched tough in relief, but the damage was done. Hutchison made a bad throw to give the Sox one run, but only Baker and Junor singled as the Racine star dominated.[106]

On Monday night, the fourth playoff tilt turned into the season's anticlimax as the Belles, riding a three-hitter by Winter, jumped to a 3–0 lead in the first inning and jolted Luna, 10–2. Late afternoon rain and threatening clouds held South Bend's turnout to 3,212, but the two-night total was still 10,625 paid. After the early lead, Racine scored error-marred runs in the fourth (two), the fifth, the sixth, and the seventh. Baker opened the Sox first with a single (she had two of the team's five hits in South Bend), stole second, moved up on Wirth's sacrifice, and scored on Stefani's fly ball. The Sox scored again in the fifth when English made a two-base error on Wirth's grounder, and Shoo-Shoo scored on Stefani's groundout. The crowd was disappointed, but many fans talked about how well their heroines played all season. Elsewhere, Rockford beat Grand Rapids, 2–0, moving the Peaches into the championship playoff against the Belles.[107]

When it was over, Racine, led by Sophie Kurys, voted Player of the Year, won the Shaughnessy Playoff Championship in five games over Rockford,[108] but in South Bend, another season came to a disappointing finish. Looking at the bright spots, Jim Costin commented that Chet Grant turned in a fine managerial job. The Blue Sox made the playoffs for the first time in four seasons, and they smashed their own attendance record by more than 60,000, making the once-struggling franchise stable.[109]

In retrospect, South Bend's and the league's future looked bright. The Blue Sox defeated Racine in six of the team's last nine regular season games, before losing three out of four playoff contests,[110] Jean Faut gave the team one of the circuit's finest new pitchers, Betty Luna (23–13) and Sugar Koehn (22–15) were 20-game winners, Shoo-Shoo Wirth and Bonnie Baker made the postseason All-Star team, and their stellar teammates included Betsy Jochum, Marge Stefani, and Lib Mahon, the loop's RBI leader. Blue Sox players, packing to depart for their offseason homes, were already envisioning a better season in 1947.

The nation was facing political, social, and economic problems in the fall of 1946.[111] Nevertheless, girls' baseball, including the Bobby Sox League in South Bend, was booming in the eight medium-sized Midwestern league cities that hosted All-American teams.

• 5 •

Havana Adventure, Sidearm Pitching, and the Playoffs Again: 1947

"Undermanned on the firing line, the Sox fought valiantly with all they had [in the Shaughnessy Playoffs]. Jean Faut gave yeoman service in four of the five games, winning one and saving another for her team."[1]

Spring Training and National Publicity

Returning for his second season, Chet Grant, manager of the South Bend Blue Sox, believed his ball club would finish higher in the standings of the ever-changing All-American Girls Baseball League. "Bigger and better than ever before," declared Max Carey, the circuit's president, who said that more than 700,000 fans saw games in 1946. The war-born circuit was well established in eight medium-sized cities that operated women's teams on a non-profit basis, and the ball clubs subsidized youth and recreation activities. In addition, the league was planning its greatest spring camp: a two-week jaunt to Havana, Cuba, followed by exhibition tours with four pairs of teams playing their way back to the Midwest.

According to the *Official Girls' Baseball Rules*, the game on the diamond was unchanged, featuring the same 11-inch ball, 43-foot pitching distance, and 70-foot base paths used in 1946.[2] Fort Wayne's *1947 Year Book* reprinted the diagram from the Official Rules to illustrate those diamond dimensions.[3] The league did expand on the delivery used the previous season by hurlers such as Racine's Anna Hutchison and South Bend's Jean Faut, both of whom threw with a below-the-shoulder motion,[4] even though the loop's rules required the pitcher's hand must pass the body "not higher than the belt line."[5] For 1947, the league fully authorized sidearm hurling, baseball umpires were again lenient in observing rules about the hurler's delivery, and the game moved further toward overhand pitching—baseball's trademark.[6]

For batters, adjusting to more sidearming pitchers was a big change. In 1946, led by South Bend's team mark of .220, six of the eight teams batted .200 or more, but Fort Wayne at .184 and Peoria at .181 ranked seventh and eighth, respectively. In 1947, Muskegon averaged .223 and Peoria batted .217, but the other six teams hit less than .200, and Fort Wayne's .176 was eighth. The Howe News Bureau, the league's statistical service, kept no team records for pitching, but in 1946, Connie Wisniewski, the tireless fastballing underhander, led all hurlers with a 33–9 record and a 0.96 ERA, and eight of the loop's 37 regular pitchers (those who worked more than 45 innings), posted an ERA below 2.00. In 1947, Grand Rapids' Millie Earp, who went 20–8 with a 0.68 ERA, and Muskegon's Doris Sams, who

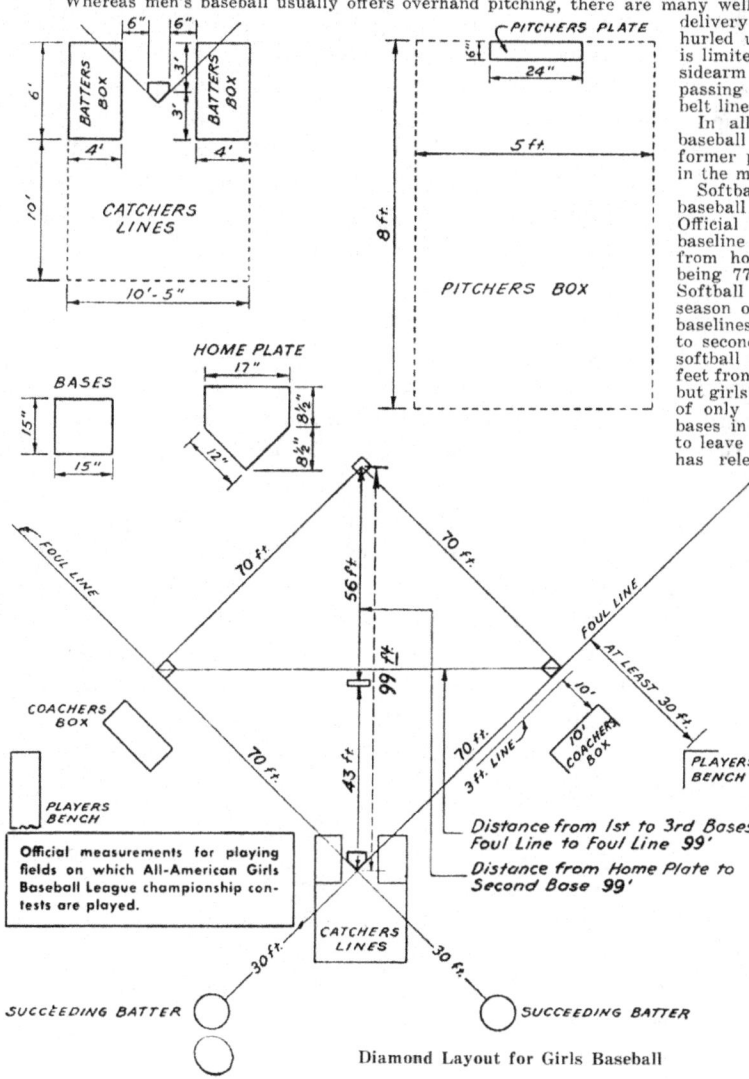

THE GREAT AMERICAN PASTIME

Just how does baseball as played in the All-American Girls' League differ from men's baseball or men's softball? That's a question often posed by AAGBBL fans, new or old, and we would like to explain briefly the few differences in the three so similar games.

With only a few exceptions, girls' baseball is almost exactly the game being played in the Major Leagues of men's baseball. Principal differences lie in the size of diamond and pitching styles. Men's baseball calls for 90-foot baselines, setting up a distance of 127 feet, three and three-eighths inches from home plate to second base or first base to third base. In girls' baseball the baselines are 70 feet long, setting up a distance of 99 feet from home plate to second or from first to third.

It is 60 feet, six inches from pitcher's box to home plate in men's baseball, whereas the girls' pitching distance is 43 feet.

The balls are very similar. Men's baseball rules call for a ball "not less than five ounces nor more than 5¼ ounces and from 9 to 9¼ inches in circumference."

The girls' baseball rules call for a ball "of 5⅛ ounces, with a tolerance of an eighth of an ounce and 11 inches in circumference, with a tolerance of an eighth of an inch." So the weight is almost exactly the same, with that used by the girls being slightly larger in size, giving them a little bigger target to hit and field.

Whereas men's baseball usually offers overhand pitching, there are many well-known twirlers with a sidearm delivery and there have been pitchers who hurled underhanded. The girls' pitching is limited to "a underhand or underhand sidearm delivery, with the pitching hand passing the body no higher than the belt line."

In all other rules, girls' and men's baseball are exactly the same, with the former permitting a leadoff of bases as in the men's game.

Softball differs from both of the baseball setups in several respects. Official softball rules now call for a baseline of only 55 feet, the distance from home to second or first to third being 77 feet, 9½ inches. The National Softball League, however, is playing this season on a diamond calling for 60-foot baselines, with the distance from home to second being 84 feet, 9 inches. Men's softball rules call for a pitcher's box 43 feet from home plate, as in girls' baseball, but girls' softball twirlers pitch a distance of only 35 feet. There is no leadoff of bases in softball, runners being allowed to leave the bases only after the pitcher has released his pitch. Softball, both men's and women's, calls for a strictly underhand pitch, with hand and arm coming through parallel to the body.

The softball is limited from 6 to 6¾ ounces in weight and a circumference of from 11⅞ to 12⅛ inches. It is, therefore, considerably heavier and larger than the balls used in men's and girls' baseball.

Bats are limited to 34 inches in length in softball, whereas they can be up to 42 inches and slightly rounder and heavier in both baseball games. The girl baseball tossers, however, use a bat slightly lighter, on the average, than most men players would swing.

Well, those are the differences between baseball and softball. All in all, the rules, strategy and general play are very similar. But AAGBBL fans will tell you they believe the girls have a game that is a happy medium between the two, producing the lightning-like plays of softball with more of the general aspect of baseball. No matter how you look at it. It's still *The Great American Pastime*—the most popular game in the world.

Diamond Dimensions—The Fort Wayne Daisies' *1947 Year Book* included an article called "The Great American Pastime," comparing men's baseball, women's baseball, and regulation softball, along with a diagram illustrating the league's field dimensions (courtesy of the Louise Pettus Archives and Special Collections, Winthrop University).

was 11–4 with an ERA of 0.98, topped the circuit, but 17 of the 40 regular hurlers compiled an ERA below 2.00.[7] Thanks to the large near-softball (a regulation baseball measured 9.25 inches around) and the new motion, it was still a pitchers' league. Or, as Jean Faut reflected, "I was a better pitcher than they were batters."[8]

Men's professional baseball was also changing. The 1946 major league season featured the big stars back from military service, including Ted Williams, Joe DiMaggio, Stan Musial, and dozens more. In 1947, however, Branch Rickey's Brooklyn Dodgers broke baseball's "color barrier" when Jackie Robinson became the first black athlete to play in the majors since the 1880s. That racial barrier, however, was first broken in the minors in March 1946, when Robinson's courage kept him training with the Montreal Royals, Brooklyn's Triple-A ball club, in Daytona Beach, Florida, despite threats, insults, and harassment.[9] Breaking the color line was so controversial that the Dodgers began their 1947 training camp in Cuba with the Royals,[10] rather than in Florida, where life was segregated.[11] Before 1947, African Americans played their highest level of baseball in the Negro Leagues. Robinson signed a Brooklyn contract on April 10, 1947, and he played his first National League game five days later.[12] A player strike against Robinson's presence by certain players on the St. Louis club on May 6, the Cardinals' first game in Brooklyn, was averted only when NL President Ford Frick threatened to suspend any player who struck.[13] Indeed, many of Robinson's teammates at first resented his presence.[14]

Americans lived in a largely segregated society, including the U.S. military services during and after World War II. On February 2, 1948, President Harry Truman ordered the Secretary of Defense to eliminate remaining instances of segregation in the armed forces, and on July 26, Truman signed Executive Order 9981, setting up a federal committee to oversee equal treatment and opportunity in the military. However, the last all-black unit was not abolished until 1954, and unfair treatment of blacks in the military persisted beyond the 1950s.[15]

The All-American League was largely a baseball circuit, except for the larger ball, the shorter diamond distances, and the lack of overhand pitching. The women were playing a predominantly men's game and, consequently, they were breaking a societal norm breached by females who worked at nontraditional jobs during wartime, a trend idealized by "Rosie the Riveter." Also, the league's feminine image and the reality of living in a "man's world" on and off the diamond were so different that the contrast seemed like a split personality. Regardless, the players accepted their lives, as author Susan Johnson observed: "To them it was simple: they were tomboys who had to look like girls, and sometimes like women, so they could play baseball like men."[16]

The league broke no social barriers in 1947. "Fan appeal," author Merrie Fidler observed, "was more important than defying the era's social conventions."[17] In the circuit's ten-team 1948 season, 11 Latinas played,[18] but no black woman was ever signed by an All-American team. Sue Macy found that two African Americans worked out with the Blue Sox in May 1951, but they did not make the team. After that season, the league's board of directors debated the issue. The minutes noted, "The consensus of the group seemed to be against the idea of colored players, unless they would show promise of exceptional ability."[19]

The Havana Adventure

The historic league offered even greater excitement in 1947. On April 20, the players, managers, chaperones, and circuit personnel were scheduled to fly from Miami to Havana

5. Havana Adventure, Sidearm Pitching, and the Playoffs Again

Cuban Adventure—In April 1947 the All-American League flew all eight teams to Havana, Cuba, where team personnel and players lodged at the Seville-Biltmore Hotel and worked out, practiced, and played games at Gran Stadium. These players are waiting to board one of eight Pan American Airlines' clippers for the fight. For many of them, it would be their first airplane trip (courtesy of the Louise Pettus Archives and Special Collections, Winthrop University).

on eight Pan American Clippers.[20] The players, both veterans and recruits, had been briefed by the league's newsletter, *A-A-G's Mail Bag*. First, they needed a visa. In keeping with the loop's guidelines for feminine deportment (which Lib Mahon called "lots of 'rubbish' about femininity"),[21] the newsletter said to bring: "A light weight coat, a good basic suit with several blouses and light weight sweaters (it's chilly up north till mid–June), several non-crushable dresses, a couple of 'nice' dresses, a pair of heeled shoes, a pair or two of sneakers, a pair of rubber bands for sox, sunglasses, several pair of white cotton sox, a sweat shirt, your own glove and spikes." Baseball spikes, incidentally, were made for men, and rookies who had no spikes needed to order a pair (spikes cost $10 to $12). Like previous years, "mannish" haircuts or clothes were banned.[22]

Players who returned their signed contracts and intent-to-go forms to the league's Chicago office received a coach train ticket to Miami. Once they arrived in south Florida, the league provided a plane ticket (return air fare to Havana cost $34.50, including taxes). However, those who failed to sign by March 15 had to pay their own transportation. Incidentally, the league suggested bringing at least $25 for spending money, warning that no more than $100 worth of goods could be brought out of Cuba without paying duties. Illustrating the loop's concern for the proper image, Max Carey reminded the women to behave as *professionals,* saying a pro player "knows how to deport herself in any company — being unselfish, modest, humble, without braggadocio, cooperative, non-primadonnish, winning graciously, losing sportingly — taking hard knocks as a matter of course and blaming none for her mistakes or her shortcomings."[23]

The Havana adventure has been described by several women who made the trek, and many took pictures as a memento of Havana and baseball. Doris Sams, Muskegon's pitcher-outfielder, recalled, "It was hotter than Hades for one thing! It must have been 110 over there. But it was interesting. I'd never been anywhere, really. Havana was really good. Golly, the people were bug-eyed. They just couldn't believe that women were playing ball like that! We drew thousands of fans."[24] Betsy Jochum called it one of her favorite memories: "I took my first airplane flight, we stayed at the Seville-Biltmore Hotel, and we played our games at the 'Gran Stadium.' All the teams were filmed for Fox News going down the steps at the University of Havana."[25]

Players remembered many aspects of life in Havana, notably the food. The most popular eatery was Sloppy Joe's, but some girls found the food difficult to eat. Also, the plan called for players and league personnel to lodge at the two-storey Seville-Biltmore Hotel, ride buses to the Gran Stadium each morning, work out doing calisthenics and baseball drills, take the afternoon off and go sight-seeing or sun-bathe in shorts and halter-tops on the hotel roof, or perhaps swim in the Gulf of Mexico. Later, players, joined by chaperones, could enjoy an evening meal.

Like Jochum, most players had never flown in a plane, and like Sams, before she joined the league, many had never been outside their home state. After a week of workouts, the teams spent another week playing in a round-robin tournament. The Havana odyssey became a national publicity highlight for the league, and it was reported that one Cuban native, Eulalia Gonzales, or Viyalla (the "Smart One"), returned as the first of several Cubans to join the All-Americans.[26]

On Friday, May 2, after two weeks of spring camp, Chet Grant, enjoying his stay at the Seville-Biltmore, received South Bend's roster from the league's allocation board. The ten returning players were Marge Stefani, second base; Shoo-Shoo Wirth, shortstop; Pinky Pirok, third base; Daisy Junor, left field; Betsy Jochum, center field; Lib Mahon, right field; Bonnie Baker, catcher; and pitchers Jean Faut, Sugar Koehn, and Tommie Thompson. At that point, Blue Sox rookies included Theda "Tee" Marshall, Marie "Red" Mahoney, Jacquelyn "Jackie" Kelley, Evelyn Keppel (released before the regular season began), Fredda (Thompson) Acker (the Mrs. America runner-up and sister of Viola), Delores "Dolly" Brumfield, Jaynne Bittner, and Liz Nahtyk (also soon released).[27] Mahoney came from Rockford in a deal for Betty Luna, who was traded after refusing to pitch. Inez Voyce was traded to Grand Rapids for Marshall, because Tee, although untested, was considered a better first sacker, and Dottie Naum was allocated to Kenosha.[28]

On Saturday, the players and league personnel flew back to Miami and boarded buses to begin the four exhibition tours through a number of southern cities. On Sunday, by the time South Bend played the first exhibition with Kenosha in Greensboro, North Carolina, Ruby Stephens had rejoined the team. A right-hander from Clearwater who loved to play the guitar and sing on bus trips, she posted a 2–1 record for the Belles in 1946. Against the Comets, Stephens shared mound duties with Koehn, Thompson, and Faut. Led by the hitting of Baker and Marshall's play at first base, the Blue Sox won, 5–2, as the two teams entertained 2,000 fans.[29]

5. *Havana Adventure, Sidearm Pitching, and the Playoffs Again*

Spring Training in Havana, Cuba 1947

Spring in the Hot Cuban Sun—Players work out with conditioning drills in the hot sun at Gran Stadium in Havana in April of 1947. Jean Faut (right center) is seen closest to the camera. At Jean's right, also running in place, are Betsy Jochum, Lil Faralla, Shoo Shoo Wirth, and Pinky Pirok. Behind Faut is Lib Mahon (courtesy of the Louise Pettus Archives and Special Collections, Winthrop University).

The Blue Sox and Comets toured the Southeast, attracting new fans and making one or two-day stops for games at Savannah, Raleigh and Charlotte, Charleston (South Carolina), Roanoke (Virginia), and, finally at Dayton (Ohio). Altogether, the league scheduled 60 games in 31 cities. Typical of newspaper coverage, the story in the *Charlotte Observer* pictured four smiling, uniformed "Glamour Gals" standing beside a ballpark fence: South Bend outfielder Daisy Junor, Kenosha flychaser Mary Wood, Blue Sox stalwart Betsy Jochum, and Kenosha's Mona Denton, the former South Bender. The picture's tag line added, "The girls combine skill and action with beauty and play a fast, exciting brand of baseball."[30]

Newspaper and magazine stories often portrayed the All-Americans as "ordinary girls," but they were extraordinarily talented women who were living their baseball dream. For example, Dayton sportswriter Harold Boian concluded that the game on Sunday, May 18, showed 2,091 fans that their city could host an All-American team. "In a game that was complete with stellar hitting," Boian wrote, "classy fielding, plenty of spark and smart baseball," the Comets beat the Blue Sox, 5–4, in 11 innings. Faut and Koehn hurled for the visiting team, and Helen Fox and Janice "Jerry" O'Hara pitched for the Comets. Faut, winding

Blue Sox in Havana — In 1947 the league flew about 200 people from Miami to Havana to hold spring training and promote the league internationally. The Blue Sox are posed on the roof of the Seville Biltmore Hotel, where all the teams stayed during their two-week spring camp. Pictured standing in the back row (left to right) are Chet Grant, manager, Daisy Junor, Pauline "Pinky" Pirok, Phyllis "Sugar" Koehn, Theda "Tee" Marshall, Lib Mahon, Jaynne Bittner, Betsy Jochum, Jackie Kelley, Delores "Dolly" Brumfield, Liz Nahtyk, and Lucille Moore, chaperone. Seated in the front row are Evelyn Keppel, Fredda Acker, Viola "Tommie" Thompson, Marie "Red" Mahoney, Jean Faut, Ruby Stephens, Senaida "Shoo Shoo" Wirth, Marge Stefani, and Bonnie Baker (courtesy of the Louise Pettus Archives and Special Collections, Winthrop University).

up and firing a "speed ball from a sidearm delivery," held Kenosha to a pair of hits in five innings. At the end, the crowd was asked if they would like to see future league games, and "fans applauded rousing approval."[31]

The First Sidearm Season

On the day before the season opened, Jim Costin interviewed Chet Grant, and the manager said the league was stronger in 1947. All four second-division teams from 1946, Muskegon, Fort Wayne, Peoria, and Kenosha, were improved: "They've added power hitters and they have new pitching strength which certainly will level off the league as it has never been evened up before." Grant called Muskegon "the team for everybody to beat." Indeed, the Lassies later won the regular season title, but Grand Rapids won the Shaughnessy Playoff Championship.[32]

Grant chose not to say so, but the Blue Sox lacked enough first-rate pitchers to improve over their 1946 performance. A good baseball team needs a four-pitcher rotation to excel. The underarm motion is less strenuous on the athlete's arm, but sidearm or overhand hurling means that most athletes need to rest at least three days between turns on the mound. In other words, a pitcher can work every fourth or fifth day. Therefore, a good team needs four starters and one or two spot starters. Later, it was clear the Sox did not have enough hurlers for a first-rate rotation.

With South Bend prepared to open the new season in Fort Wayne on Wednesday, May 21, most pitchers had adopted the delivery (several still threw underhand). Grant worked on teaching the motion to hurlers like Koehn and Stephens, but they needed game experience. At that time, the Blue Sox lineup featured Baker, a spray hitter, catching and leading off. Wirth, who often got on base, hit second and played shortstop. Stefani, a solid hitter who ran the infield from second base, was slated third. Jochum, with her quick bat and good speed, played center field and batted clean-up. Mahon, back in right field, hit fifth. The speedy Junor, in left field, followed Mahon. Marshall, an erratic-fielding and free-swinging first baseman, batted seventh. Brumfield, the 15-year-old rookie, could play third base and hit eighth, but Pirok would replace her later, and the pitcher batted last.[33] On Wednesday, the Blue Sox left on their special bus, but rain all night and throughout the morning forced cancellation of the opener at Fort Wayne's Memorial Park.[34]

On Thursday night (again the league played all night games), the Blue Sox, with Pirok at third base and Mahoney in right, began the season by defeating the Daisies, 3–1, thanks to the hurling of Koehn. She was called the "blond submarine pitcher;" the motion of the Chicago righty — who grew up in Wisconsin — led to 22 assists by the infield, five hits, and, in the ninth, one run.[35]

At Memorial Park on Friday, South Bend split a twin bill as Faut won the seven-inning opener, 5–3, and Stephens lost the late game, 4–3. Faut's mixture of fastballs and curves had the opposing batters hitting the ball mostly at the fielders, and her teammates played errorless ball, but the Daisies bounced three hits through the infield in the third to score twice. The white-uniformed home team — the loop's standard format starting in 1946 — notched a final run in the seventh. The visitors, sporting their light blue uniforms with royal blue caps and trim, totaled eight hits, two each by Wirth and Stefani. The Blue Sox scored twice in the third and won with three runs in the seventh, partly due to several bad throws. In the late game, Stephens allowed five hits, and Fort Wayne's Irene Kotowicz spaced four safeties. Afterward, South Bend had a 2–1 mark and a tie for third place with 2–1 Muskegon, but Racine and Rockford led the league with 2–0 records.[36] The series finale was rained out on Saturday, and the Blue Sox rode the bus home on Sunday.

In South Bend, fans learned the team's "new faces" included Tee Marshall at first base and perhaps Red Mahoney in right field, because Mahon, who was still favoring the left knee she twisted before the Cuban trip (and had first injured in 1945), had yet to play. The veteran Koehn would pitch, and other starters included the team's three fifth-year standouts, Baker, Stefani, and Jochum.

Again Playland Park used the Ushers Club, now headed by George Van Der Heyden. The ushers helped in selling tickets, greeting and seating fans, and boosting the team.[37]

On Sunday, May 25, South Bend launched a four-game win streak before 4,700 shivering folks at Playland when Faut blanked Muskegon, 7–0. Backed by errorless defense, the fastballing right-hander with the exceptional control permitted five hits, none after the fifth frame, but right-hander Nancy "Hank" Warren threw away a double-play ball in the first inning that, combined with two more Lassie errors, led to five unearned runs.[38] In the lid-lifter of Monday night's doubleheader, Koehn threw a five-hitter to top Erma Bergmann, 5–2, and Stefani paced the seven-hit attack with three blows. In the late game, the 5'4"

Stephens made her South Bend debut by spinning a one-hitter, retiring the first 13 Lassies, and winning, 4–0. RBI singles by Stefani in the third and Marshall in the fourth led to lefty Amy Applegren's loss. The wins lifted South Bend into the league lead with a 5–1 record.[39] Tuesday's finale with Muskegon was rained out, but Rockford won, moving the 5–1 Peaches into a first-place tie with South Bend.[40]

Later that night, the Blue Sox, packed and ready for another fling at living out of suitcases in hotels away from home, made the four-hour journey by bus to Grand Rapids and the Hotel Rowe. Rain and cold weather, however, forced cancellation of two straight games.

On Friday, May 30, despite "chilly weather highly unsuitable for baseball," 3,553 fans saw the Chicks split a Memorial Day doubleheader. Faut won the opener, 2–0, allowing two hits, both by youthful Arkansas right-hander Millie Earp, and the Blue Sox scored both runs in the fifth. In the nine-inning nightcap, tall Connie Wisniewski, Player of the Year in 1945, scattered seven hits and won, 7–1. Grand Rapids solved Koehn in the fifth for five singles, two stolen bases, and a hit batter to take a 4–1 lead, and Stefani's error on an infield roller cost two runs in the seventh. Also, Marge twisted her weak knee on the play, and Grant tried Wirth at second base and Brumfield, the high schooler, at third, moving the veteran Pirok to shortstop. Jochum was out with a muscle pull, and a limping Mahon played center field.[41]

Injuries, Errors, and Losses

South Bend's momentum turned with Stefani's injury (she was leading the league with a .426 mark) and Jochum's absence, and Friday's defeat started a five-game skid. On Saturday night at Grand Rapids, Stephens gave up six hits in an 8–3 loss, but she added five walks, two balks, and a hit batter, and the makeshift Blue Sox lineup kicked in five errors.[42] Returning home, the Blue Sox saw Sunday's scheduled twin bill with the Daisies rained out. Playland's infield had been covered by a tarpaulin since the previous Friday, but soaking rains caused team officials to borrow a military flame thrower from Notre Dame to dry the field on Monday.[43] More rain forced cancellation of Monday night's games, but the delay helped. Stefani was expected to miss a week, and Jochum was sidelined with a cramped leg muscle. Grant figured to use Wirth at second, Pirok at shortstop, Brumfield at third, Kelley in right, and Mahon in center.[44]

At home on Tuesday, June 3, the same day that 4,500 employees at Bendix Aviation postponed a costly strike, South Bend dropped a twin bill to Fort Wayne by scores of 2–1 and 3–0. Although Koehn yielded only four hits, she walked the bases full in the sixth, and two sacrifice flies scored the tying and winning runs. In the nightcap, Faut pitched a four-hitter and deserved a better fate, but four throwing errors gave the game away. Daisy ace Dottie Collins gave up three scratch hits, and she won when shortstop Marge Pieper made a one-handed grab of Wirth's two-on, two-out liner in the eighth to rob the local favorites of two runs.[45]

South Bend hosted Rockford at Playland, but each team won just once in four scheduled tilts. Stephens lost on Wednesday, and Koehn broke the slump with a victory on Thursday, but rain wiped out the league's games on Friday. However, the Blue Sox received help in the form of rookie right-hander Ruth Williams, from Nescopeck, Pennsylvania, who arrived on Thursday.[46] On Saturday, a big crowd of 2,538 watched Rockford's Lois Florreich, converted to pitching, battle Stephens to a scoreless tie, until rain stopped play in the seventh inning. Team personnel put a tarp on the infield and burned it with gasoline, but after waiting over an hour, the umpires called the game. South Bend's 7–6 ledger left the club tied for third place with 7–6 Fort Wayne.[47]

Following the bus trip to Wisconsin and registration at the Hotel Racine early on Sunday morning, June 8, the Blue Sox lost three straight to the defending champion Belles—and only a rainout on the last night saved them from a possible sweep. Boasting the loop's most experienced team, Racine also featured good pitching, including second-year ace Anna Hutchison and fifth-year star Jo Winter. For example, on Monday night, Stephens lost, 6–4, marking the visitors' third straight defeat at the hands of the Belles, but the Florida native contributed to her own demise by walking seven and giving away two runs with wild throws on pickoff attempts.[48]

Heavy rains washed out Tuesday night's contest, so the 7–9 Blue Sox returned home in sixth place. Chet Grant hoped Stefani, who had hurt her knee on Memorial Day, could play. After the veteran suffered the injury, South Bend dropped seven of eight and fell four games off the pace set by Racine (11–5) and Muskegon (14–8). Further, Mahoney, who suffered a charley horse on the spring tour, had yet to play, but Jochum returned to the lineup after missing ten days.[49]

Kenosha arrived at Playland Park on June 11, a chilly Wednesday, and the tail-end Comets dropped three out of four to the Blue Sox. Faut won the first contest, 1–0, hurling a four-hitter that kept 2,740 fans on the edge of their seats, notably when she fanned slugger Audrey Wagner with two outs and the bases loaded in the eighth.[50] On Thursday, South Bend won another thriller when Koehn hurled a five-hitter, overcoming four errors to beat teenaged lefty Jean Cione, 2–1. Jochum collected three of her team's six hits, batting in the first run and scoring the second marker.[51] On Friday, rain wiped out South Bend's seventh home game. The teams split a twin bill on Saturday evening as the home team, before a shivering crowd of 2,003, rode Stephens' two-hitter to a 5–1 victory, reaching Helen Fox for ten hits. In the late contest, the Comets won, 10–2, totaling 12 hits off the combination of Ruth Williams, who left with two outs in the seventh, Tommie Thompson, who gave up five runs in the eighth (her final game for South Bend), and rookie Jaynne Bittner, who worked a scoreless ninth. The loss left South Bend in fourth with a 10–10 ledger, three and a half games behind first-place Racine.[52]

Hoping to gain ground, South Bend traveled to Peoria to face the sixth-place Redwings.[53] In a cold Sunday night twin bill that received little press coverage (typical of Peoria), an audience of 2,573 saw Faut win the best game of the series, 7–3. She yielded four hits and two walks, but Jo Kabick gave up six hits, three off the bat of Jochum, who also knocked in three runs, and the Redwings committed five errors. In the nightcap, Koehn pitched well until the seventh, when the Redwings started a "bunting game," and the Blue Sox made three errors, allowing all five runs in Peoria's 5–1 victory.[54] The blue-uniformed visitors won for the second time in three tries on Tuesday, and after the next game was rained out, they departed by bus for Wisconsin.

The Blue Sox struggled during the last two weeks of June, losing more than they won. On a four-game trip to Kenosha and Lakefront Stadium, South Bend lost three of the four games. Returning to Playland to host Peoria, the Blue Sox lost three out of four again, the finale by a 4–3 margin on Tuesday, June 24. In that heart-breaking defeat, Stephens, who could display erratic control or lose her stuff, was relieved by Faut in the third with her team trailing, 1–0. Faut gave up Mary Wisham's two-run triple in the fifth. Despite Tee Marshall's two-run three-bagger in the seventh and another run in the ninth, Stephens took the loss after Dottie Mueller moved from catcher to pitcher and preserved the Redwings' 4–3 lead.[55] Hitting the road for Muskegon, the Blue Sox were frustrated again, losing all four contests to the second-place Lassies. The finale was a tough 4–3 loss in 15 innings, when Koehn, who relieved Williams in the sixth, gave up the game-winner on singles by Charlene "Shorty" Pryer, Sara Reeser, and Dottie Stolze. The loss was South Bend's fifth straight and tenth in 12 games, leaving the unhappy travelers holding fifth place with a 14–21 mark, a full ten games behind league-leading Racine (24–11).[56]

Hot Weather, Cool Sox

The Midwest weather warmed up in July, but the Blue Sox launched just two good win streaks. They won four straight (not counting two rainouts) against Fort Wayne beginning in the second half of a twin bill at Playland on Thursday, July 10, and nearly three weeks later, the home team's 7–0 success against Rockford on July 29 started a five-game streak and revived playoff hopes. During the last two days of June, South Bend hosted Racine and won the first three of a four-game set, but on Tuesday, July 1, the local favorites fell to the Belles in the tenth, 4–3, after the usually reliable Baker had a mental lapse in the ninth. The score was tied 1–1 when Baker singled. Anna Hutchison made several throws to first and finally, as Jim Costin observed, "nailed Bonnie sound asleep off the bag." Wirth singled, Stefani bunted safely, and Jochum hit a long fly that would have scored Baker, but Koehn flied out to end the threat. In the tenth, Pepper Paire doubled, Edie Perlick singled her home, and Hutchison held the lead. South Bend fell to 17–22 and prepared to face Grand Rapids (26–15), with the chicks locked in a three-way tie for first.[57]

Too often in July, South Bend performed inconsistently. One night the team lost on bad base running, another night on shoddy fielding and errors of omission and commission, but in most cases, the Sox failed to hit in clutch situations during many tense, low-scoring games.

The South Benders also experienced uneven pitching performances, due partly to underhanders learning the sidearm motion. Chet Grant was relying on a four-person rotation, notably Faut, the team's star, who started out as a third baseman in 1946 and, after mid-season, used her strong sidearm motion to fashion an 8–3 record and a 1.32 ERA, third best in the circuit. In 1947, Faut, never a softball pitcher, worked in 44 games, hurled a league-high 298 innings, struck out 97 hitters and walked 67, fashioning a 19–13 record with a 1.15 ERA, the loop's fifth best. Her control kept improving. Jean, virtually unique among pitchers, could throw hard and move the ball around the plate—in and out as well as up and down—but still fire strikes. She also learned opposing batters' weaknesses, and when she lost, errors almost always contributed.

However, South Bend's other pitchers depended mainly on breaking balls and displayed less control, and none threw a hard fastball. Ruth Williams, the teacher from Pennsylvania, joined the team after the school year ended, showing promise with her 12–8 ledger and 1.70 ERA. However, the 5'4" rookie threw mainly slow curves in 180 innings spread over 25 games, and Faut's relief preserved Williams' victories at least twice. Sugar Koehn, who learned the delivery in late 1945, posted a 16–16 record with a 2.17 ERA in 1947. Koehn, a veteran right-hander, now relied on a submarine motion, but when her control was off (she issued 76 walks and fanned 73 batters), she gave up too many hits and free passes. Ruby Stephens, 22, who began with a 2–1 mark in seven games with Racine in 1946, worked to control her fastball and slow curves in 1947. Finishing with a 9–15 mark and a 2.88 ERA, 32nd among 40 pitchers, the pleasant but strong Clearwater gal walked 70 batters but fanned only 25. Finally, rookie Jaynne Bittner appeared in eight games, but helped little with her 1–2 record.

South Bend's bumpy ride continued with a split of four games with Grand Rapids at Playland, capped by a twin bill on Friday, July 4. Performing on the holiday, the Blue Sox won the opener, 3–2, in two extra innings. In the ninth frame of a 2–2 tie, Pirok and Faut, who relieved in the fifth, both walked, and Baker singled for the win, thrilling 6,010 fans, the second largest Playland crowd ever. The home team fell in the nightcap, 8–3, when Koehn yielded nine hits and seven runs in five innings. South Bend (19–24) slipped to sixth place, and Grand Rapids (28–17) trailed league-leading Racine (28–15) by one game.[58]

Saturday, July 5, was a day off, and on Sunday, the Blue Sox, having won five out of eight against pennant-contending Racine and Grand Rapids, made their first visit of 1947 to Rockford and the Hotel Faust. The series would finish the first half of the season's schedule, and Blue Sox would then return home for a Thursday makeup of a rained out doubleheader against Fort Wayne.

At Rockford's Beyer Stadium on Sunday night, amid reports of "flying saucers" in almost 40 states,[59] the Blue Sox defeated the Peaches, 7–3, with a six-run sixth inning against Marge Holgerson, nicknamed "Mobile" after her hometown in Alabama. The Peaches got to Williams and her curveballs for two runs in the second and one in the seventh, but with Faut's relief, the recruit notched the win.[60] On Monday, Faut, aided by Rockford's league-record nine errors, hurled a 5–2 triumph, added two hits, and helped the visitors retake fourth place.[61] On Tuesday, the Peaches tried to throw the game away, committing seven errors on top of Betty Luna's five walks, but the Blue Sox tossed in two errors and collected just three hits. Koehn relieved Stephens in the seventh with a 5–5 tie, but Luna's two-run single in the eighth gave her a 7–6 victory.[62] South Bend won number three in Wednesday's finale, 6–5, on a ninth-inning error by Snookie Harrell. Koehn, hurt by Dottie Kamenshek's three-run homer in the fifth, won when her teammates reached Luna for eight hits, two each by Stefani, Pirok, and Kelley. Afterward, South Bend (22–25) rose to fourth, eight and a half games behind first-place Racine (31–17).[63]

On July 10, back at Playland Park on a pleasant Thursday, the Blue Sox divided a makeup twin bill with Fort Wayne. A crowd of 2,923 saw Dottie Collins, the "strikeout queen," pitch a three-hit shutout and fan six to beat Faut in the opener, 2–0. In the late tilt, Williams blanked the Daisies, 4–0, on two hits. The home team was boosted by heads-up base running, for example, when Pirok walked in the third inning, stole, advanced on a bunt, and scored on a passed ball.[64]

However, fans reacted angrily in the fifth when Wirth tripled and Stefani lined a shot to right-center that Tiby Eisen speared, whirled, and fired one-hop to the plate, where Shoo-Shoo was tagged out on a "fielding masterpiece." Several fans booed Grant for sending her. Jim Costin concluded Wirth would have scored 99 percent of the time. Most folks applauded Eisen's great effort, but Costin called it unfair to fault the pilot for his coaching on the play.[65]

As the league's eight teams approached mid–July, South Bend was improving and Grant was meshing his players together. After losing three of four to Kenosha and to Peoria, both weak sisters in 1947, and losing four straight to tough Muskegon, the Blue Sox then won three of four games from contending Racine, divided four with contending Grand Rapids, won three of four from sixth-place Rockford, and split a twin bill with seventh-place Fort Wayne. Full of hope, the All-Americans riding the bus to Fort Wayne believed they were finally on the right track.[66]

The Blue Sox in Mid-1947

The Blue Sox boosted fielded several fine players in 1947, still featuring Bonnie Baker. Despite slipping from her all-star form of 1946, Baker, now 29, generated good publicity for South Bend. Writing for *Sport*, William Fay reported an anecdote that highlighted an essential part of the women's game as well as a bemused masculine perspective on females playing a game formerly reserved for males. The Blue Sox were slumping, partly because too many bases were being stolen on the catcher. One day at batting practice, Chet Grant spoke about it to Baker. Afterward, he trotted to the first base coaching box to watch her wag signals under her mitt.

"Elementary, my dear Bonnie," quipped Grant. "You'll have to tone down your nail polish." The manager noticed her bright mahogany polish glistened in the sun against the background of her white thighs. Baker indicated she made a good living in Regina as a fashion model, so she knew beauty tips. Chet called for a lighter nail polish. Bonnie reluctantly tossed out her current polish, but several hours later in that night's game, she threw out three runners at second base.

Sport's writer used the apocryphal incident to emphasize two major points. First, the women who played in the All-American League were "thoroughly feminine." Their muscles all "curved," but they would rather be out at the *plate* than out of *fashion* with their hair styles. Equally important, Fay observed, "they play a running, stealing game that's an exciting facsimile of the baseball their daddies enjoyed — 'way back when Ty Cobb was honing his spikes on infielders' shins." In fact, the scribe concluded, baseball was the world's fastest growing sport for women.[67]

Baker played 106 games, but her hitting fell from .286 in 1946 to .217 in 1947. Adding five doubles and a triple, she contributed 40 walks, 58 stolen bases, and 20 RBI. Hitting to all fields, she epitomized the loop's "small ball" style — singles, bunts, steals, hit-and-run, and hustle. The Canadian brunette had a strong presence with the players, due to her status as a fifth-year regular and her charismatic personality. After hours, she enjoyed playing poker, usually with a Coke in one hand and a cigarette in the other. The Regina star also had her favorites. For example, Jean Faut recalled that Baker tried more than once in 1946 to get her "sent home," because Bonnie wanted her friend Moe Trezza at third base. Grant, however, wisely ignored the requests.[68]

Baker, who was married, was also the highest-paid South Bender, earning $100 a week, although the loop's stated maximum was $85. The extra amount was an illegal payment, but a bonus that one or two stars likely received on each team.[69] Two months before spring camp in 1948, Baker wrote to Harold Dailey, the new team president, agreeing to play, but only for the "same deal" as she enjoyed in 1947. "I am quite certain that you know that I was getting a hundred a week," she wrote. "The extra 15 to be paid in a lump sum or weekly."[70]

The other half of the team's best battery was Jean Faut, a multi-talented athlete who took her baseball career very seriously. Paid $65 a week in 1947,[71] the Pennsylvania right-hander with the strong arm, sharp curve, and excellent pitch location was a fine pitcher, but she was also a good hitter. Playing in 56 games, she batted 123 times and averaged .236, almost 60 points above her rookie mark of .177. For perspective, Faut's average ranked 14th in the league among regulars who played 50 or more games. Rockford's Kamenshek set the bar with a .306 average, Kenosha's Audrey Wagner was next at .305, and Muskegon's Doris Sams, voted Player of the Year, hit .280. For South Bend, only Marge Stefani, hitting .237, averaged more than Faut.

Mainly a pitcher, Faut's talent, increasing value, and growing popularity were incalculable to South Bend. Despite an unsettled home life, Jean later enjoyed greater achievements, setting the unique league record of hurling two perfect games as well as two no-hitters, and partly as a result, she was voted the league's Player of the Year in 1951 and 1953.[72] Only Doris Sams, who excelled as an underhand pitcher and long-ball hitter, was also twice voted Player of the Year. Married after the 1947 season, Faut would be a mother and a pitcher starting in 1948.[73]

Ranking closely behind Baker and Faut was Betsy Jochum, the quiet star who kept producing big games in the field, big nights at the plate, and big RBI figures. The Cincinnati star averaged .211 in 105 games, slugging 11 doubles and five triples. She also scored 36 runs, drew 17 walks, stole 44 bases, and produced 42 RBI, tops for the Blue Sox. Friendly and sociable, she enjoyed her teammates, friends on other teams, and the fans. Like many players, she tolerated the boredom of travel and living out of suitcases in hotels, but she avoided late-night card games and did not drink with those who did. Like most girls, she enjoyed occasionally sun-bathing on a hotel roof in shorts and halter-top on nice days.[74] The consummate team player, Betsy was dedicated to the Blue Sox, and she made her home in South Bend after her baseball career ended in 1948.

Marge Stefani anchored the infield. A solid hitter, she ran on an unstable knee that was first injured in mid–1945. Marge could play any infield spot, but Chet Grant often used her at third base in 1947. The Detroiter batted .237 in 99 games, clouting seven doubles, one triple, and a pair of home runs. She also scored 34 runs, drew 33 bases on balls, stole 27 times, and produced 38 RBI, second only to Jochum's 42. Stefani, 29, was a fifth-year veteran, a tough competitor, and a buddy of Baker since 1943. Also, she served as a secret liaison with the club's directors as well as shepherd of the rookie flock. Allocated in 1948 to Rockford, she returned to South Bend as chaperone in 1949 and 1950, often advising on team personnel.[75]

At first base, the Blue Sox played tall, strong Tee Marshall. At spring camp, Grant and the team's directors ranked the 22-year-old Marshall above Inez Voyce, the dependable run-producer who played the initial sack for the Blue Sox in 1946. Neither player had good speed, but the position usually features a slugger who can drive in runs. Marshall, from Denver, proved to be an erratic fielder who made a loop-high 42 errors, nearly triple the miscues of any first baseman except Kenosha's Alice Hohlmayer, who made 20. Marshall started strong at the plate, but leveled off. The hard-swinging right-handed hitter played every game but averaged only .141. She did belt 10 doubles and five triples, and she contributed 24 walks, 27 stolen bases, and 31 RBI, the third-best Sox total. However, after facing Marshall a few times, pitchers learned her hitting habits, and her average declined. Still, Tee was a likeable athlete who was cheerful, ready to play ball, and, as she later remarked, "always gave 110 percent."

Shoo-Shoo Wirth, who often found herself at second base after an all-star performance as a rookie shortstop in 1946, produced another good season. After twisting an ankle midway through her recruit year, she did not display quite the same zip in 1947. Wirth, often a slick fielder, lacked the rifle arm needed for shortstop. Also, she suffered more than one injury, and as a result, played 73 games. Still, she hit .227, the team's third highest mark. A spray hitter, the curly-haired brunette from Tampa, who spoke Spanish fluently, swiped 32 bases, drew a team-high 42 walks, and scored 35 runs. Often batting second, she could move up the runner, but she drove in only five runs. A versatile fielder, Wirth was fourth among second sackers (27 games) with a .971 percentage and third among shortstops (47 games) at .920.

Pinky Pirok, like Wirth, split time between positions. She played shortstop but, depending on the team's needs, also handled third base, because Dolly Brumfield, besides Stefani, was the other option at the "hot corner." Pirok played all 113 games and hit .193, although she did clout six doubles and four triples. She racked up 24 walks, 53 stolen bases (second on the team to Baker), and 17 RBI. Pinky, a spirited athlete, fielded best at shortstop. In 68 games, she averaged .931, second only to Grand Rapids' Teeny Petras. At third base, Pirok played 47 games and also fielded .931. Pirok, like Wirth, was a team player with the determination to win every game.

Besides Jochum, who normally played center because of her fielding ability and speed, the outfield featured Lib Mahon in right, when her problematic left knee was in good shape. Mahon, who missed 30 games, averaged .234 in 83 contests, belting five doubles and a team-high eight triples. Lacking her usual mobility, the South Carolina flychaser drew 15 walks, stole 22 bases, and added 23 RBI. Even during an off year, she was adept at driving in runs in the clutch. A dependable outfielder but with a suspect arm, Lib was an important team member, helping rookies and providing stability in the dugout. After hours, she liked to socialize and drink with the club's core of poker players.

Attractive, popular, and friendly, Daisy Junor, the left fielder (unless Jochum was out of the lineup, and then Daisy shifted to center) had the speed associated with fine ballhawks and sometimes made the difficult catch. Statistics showed the slender brunette ranked fourth in the league for outfielders playing 50 or more games, finishing at .982 with three errors and nine assists. However, Jochum, who averaged .956 with eight errors and 11 assists, was more likely to make the big play after a long run. Also, Daisy was a light hitter. In 1947, Brumfield, only 15, recorded the team's lowest mark, but Junor, the Regina native, played 90 games and hit .133, including two doubles and a triple. The Saskatchewan outfielder also drew 16 walks, stole 17 bases, and scored 17 runs, figures consistent with her low on-base percentage.

The Blue Sox had several rookies. Jackie Kelley was a good catcher and utility player, getting into 44 games and batting .178, hitting three doubles and two triples. An eager hitter, she drew just nine walks and fanned 28 times in 107 at-bats, but she still produced 13 RBI. Formerly a softball star in Lansing, Michigan, she tried out at catcher in 1947, but during her career she handled all nine positions, even recording a 12–11 record as a right-hander in 1952. A moody, introverted, good-hearted person who smoked three or four packs of cigarettes per day, Kelley later played for perennially strong Rockford, and, therefore, she was never a regular.[76]

South Bend also acquired Dolly Brumfield, the Prichard, Alabama, high school student, who played in 39 games, batted 103 times, and hit 12 singles for a .117 average. She played 32 games at third base, making three errors and fielding .861, ranking her 16th among players at the position. But she was young, and by 1953 she hit more than .300. Red Mahoney, a utility player, averaged .204 in 47 games, slugging three doubles, seven triples, one home run, and producing 13 RBI. Mahoney, the Houston speedster, was an accomplished athlete with good quickness and all-around ability. Her softball experience in Texas brought her an invitation for the spring trip to Havana. Like so many of her teammates, Red reflected the "We're all for one, we're one for all" spirit made famous by the league's Victory Song.[77] Last, Jaynne Bittner, 21, a right-handed pitcher and utility player from

Lebanon, Pennsylvania, best known in high school as a star in basketball, tennis, and table tennis, made the Cuban trip, the exhibition tour, and South Bend's *1947 Year Book*. A first-rate starter in later seasons, she pitched 35 innings and posted a 1–2 record in eight games. Bittner played nine games total and batted .188, going 3-for-16.[78]

Fighting for Fourth Place

Two of South Bend's best highlights occurred six days apart. On Thursday, July 31, the Blue Sox set a new record for long games as Faut, yielding just three hits, outlasted Racine's Ellie Dapkus, the star center fielder who was making her first pitching start, to win a 22-inning marathon, 4–3. On a misty evening near Lake Michigan, both pitchers worked the distance, both teams made one error, both teams scored two runs in the first six innings, and both scored a run in the 14th. In the top of the 22nd, Stefani scratched a single, one of four Sox hits, and Mahoney doubled her home. In the bottom of the inning, Maddy English was safe on Stefani's error, and she reached third on a pair of outs. Faut fanned Dodie Barr, batting for rookie Sarah Lonetto, to end the game and break a record set six weeks earlier when Grand Rapids defeated Racine, 3–2, in 19 innings. If South Bend had not scored in the 22nd, the tense battle would have ended in a tie, because the league did not allow an inning to start after 11:30 pm, and Barr whiffed at 11:35. The night's second contest was moved to Friday.[79]

At Playland on Tuesday, August 5, for the finale of a four-game set against Kenosha, South Bend sponsored "Jean Faut Night" to honor the second-year star. The events included free admission for 500 fellow employees at the Ball-Band plant, where she worked in the off-season. Almost 2,700 fans cheered as Jean received a vast array of gifts, including a cedar chest, pillow slips, sheets, blankets, towels, and more, presented by announcer Joe Boland in a pregame ceremony. Afterward, Faut hurled a two-hitter and won her eighth shutout, 7–0. Her teammates, appreciating the likeable, talented blond, racked up 15 hits off Millie Deegan, starting with a four-run first inning. Baker, Stefani, and Brumfield each rapped three hits, and the Sox, now at 42–38, led the fifth-place Redwings (40–43) by three and a half games as they boarded the bus for Peoria.[80]

Against Peoria at Playland eight days later, on Wednesday, August 13, a crowd of 2,117 saw Faut relieve Stephens in the top of the seventh inning, stop a rally after the Redwings moved ahead, 3–2, and win, 5–3. In South Bend's seventh, Junor walked, Faut sacrificed, and Baker legged out a bunt, with Junor taking third on the play. Pirok bunted down the first base line, using a fadeaway slide to avoid second baseman Alice DeCambra, who fielded the ball and tried to tag the runner. The visitors protested that Pirok was out, but umpire Barney Zoss ruled otherwise, and Junor had scored to tie the game at 3–3. After Stefani flew out, Baker and Pirok worked a double steal, and Bonnie scored when catcher Joyce Hill's throw to third base bounced away. Jochum singled home Pirok for the 5–3 margin, and Faut's sterling relief sealed the success.[81]

Buoyed by the comeback victory, the Blue Sox and Chet Grant knew that if they could sweep Peoria, they would have a virtual lock on fourth place and the playoffs. By mid–August, the league had five contenders for the four spots in the Shaughnessy Playoffs:

- Muskegon, in a circuit still dominated by good pitching, featured the solid rotation of Amy Applegren (16–10 in 1947), Hank Warren (17–11), Erma Bergmann

JEAN FAUT Night

AUG. 5
Tuesday — 8:00 P.M.
PLAYLAND PARK

Special BALL-BAND Night Honoring the BLUE SOX STAR PITCHER, JEAN FAUT, Who Works at BALL-BAND Off-Seasons.

Special Ceremonies Begin At 8:00 P.M.
JOE BOLAND, Announcer

She Works in our Foam Division . . .

Special Section of Reserved Seats

Hundreds of tickets available in special BALL-BAND Section for Employees, their families, and friends.

Price, $1.00
Includes Admission and Donation for Gift

Tickets On Sale By The Committee:

G. A. Peachey (Phone 384)	Ray Ritchey (Phone 391)	Dorothy Troiola (Phone 580)
J. Dentino (Phone 489)	George Baughman (Phone 317)	Peggy Pozorski (Phone 203)
B. W. Button (Phone 348)	Lud Hanson (Phones 258-508)	Toots Burrows (Phone 510)
B. F. Broaddus (Phone 404)	E. L. Campbell (Phone 310)	Dorothy Hungerford (Phone 217)
G. D. Tobey (Phone 218)	Fred Cecchi (Phone 528)	Irene Kepler (Phone 325)
L McDaniels (Phone 303)	Doc Nierle (Phone 537)	Olive Lebo (Phone 329)
Ed Singleton (Phone 367)	A. C. DeCraene (Phone 537)	Rachel Coffing (Phone 543)
Roy Hobbs (Phone 208)	F. H. Christoph (Phone 445)	June Coffing (Phone 234)
Bill Hosler (Phone 241)	F. C. Thayer (Phone 230)	Mary Hollos (Phone 489)

Jean Faut Night — South Bend held the first "night" to honor Jean Faut on August 5, 1947. The team sponsored a second special night for her near the end of the 1953 season, her final year in the league. On her first night, after receiving a wide assortment of gifts, Faut pitched a two-hitter and defeated Kenosha, 7–0 (courtesy of the Louise Pettus Archives and Special Collections, Winthrop University).

(11–10), and Sammye Sams (11–4). As a result, the Lassies were pacing the league with a 57–35 record.
- Racine, with the mound duo of Anna Hutchison (27–13) and Jo Winter (22–13) and a playoff-tested lineup, remained a close second at 56–37, one and a half games behind the Lassies.
- Grand Rapids, paced by the pitching of Millie Earp (20–8), Al Haylett (19–11), Annabelle "Lefty" Lee (9–11), who was later traded to Peoria, and Connie Wisniewski (16–14), who also helped her team by hitting .291, ranked third at 54–38 behind the Belles.
- South Bend was fourth at 48–42, trailing the leaders by eight games. If the Blue Sox could avoid further injuries, the pitching of Jean Faut (19–13), rookie Ruth Williams (12–8), veteran Sugar Koehn (16–16), and recruit Ruby Stephens (9–15) could lift them to the playoffs.
- Peoria, after playing well until mid-season, owned a losing mark of 45–48. Still, thanks to the hurling of Dottie Mueller (21–13), Jo Kabick (13–16), and Audrey Haine (13–12), who came to Peoria in the trade sending Lefty Lee to Grand Rapids, the Redwings had high hopes.

South Bend did sweep the four-game home stand with Peoria. Typically, besides timely hitting, the series was highlighted by spectacular plays, as Jim Costin pointed out, "which would have done credit to even the best of the major league baseball stars." No player made catches greater than Jackie Kelley, subbing in right field. Kelley's first "robbery" came on Thursday when Eleanor "Ellie" Callow hit an apparent triple to the right field screen, but Kelley made a leaping circus catch after a long run. On Friday, however, she topped that gem by making a backhanded running catch of another would-be triple by Faye Dancer, after which Jackie "drew one of the greatest rounds of applause accorded to an individual player in the girls' league in this city." Also, Dodie Crigler, the team's new third baseman, Betsy Jochum, and Daisy Junor all made spectacular defensive plays.[82] The hitting and fielding in the South Bend–Peoria series showed again why folks who saw the All-Americans perform became fans of the Girls' Pro League.

However, in baseball, like other sports, a team's momentum can turn in a hurry, and on Sunday, August 17, Grand Rapids arrived, practiced, and won the first game of a twin bill at Playland. Haylett stifled South Bend on one hit to win the short opener, 4–0. Her teammates notched all four runs on six hits, two each by Inez Voyce and Haylett. The tense nightcap was tied at 1–1 after 12 innings with Faut battling Lefty Lee on equal terms. In the bottom of the 13th, at 11:27 pm (the last possible inning), Faut, who scattered six hits, slugged a triple to right center. Lee walked Baker and Pirok to get at Stefani, who was hitless in 24 at-bats. Marge responded by tripling to deep left-center, and when the ball hopped through a hole in the fence, her blast became a grand slam home run, producing a 5–1 victory, a split, and, as Jim Costin remarked, "sending 3,375 cash customers home in a happy frame of mind."[83] Still, the Chicks came back to win single games the next two nights, taking three of the series' four contests.

At the same time, Peoria (48–52) was fading from the playoff picture, and manager Johnny Gottselig, ejected from a game with South Bend for arguing heatedly about a call at first base, was fired. The Redwings' directors hired Leo Schrall, a onetime Notre Dame gridder who had played baseball for Peoria of the Three-Eye League before starting a business career in Peoria.[84]

Also, South Bend, after traveling to Rockford, lost three out of four. In the opener on Wednesday, Mobile Holgerson, the little Alabama right-hander, walked four but no-hit the blue-uniformed visitors, 6–0.[85] The next night, Williams started and, after three innings, left with a 2–1 lead. Ruth was credited with the win, but Faut, who relieved, blanked the Peaches and preserved the final margin of 3–1. A clutch player, Jean's quick thinking led to the final run in the ninth. She drew a walk and, with Junor on second base via a single and an error, let herself get caught in a rundown between first and second so that Daisy could score.[86] Finally, losing on Friday and Saturday, the Blue Sox, now 53–48, rode home for the season's final stand at Playland.[87]

Despite a boisterous crowd of 3,347 on Sunday, August 24, Racine won, 1–0, marking the home team's seventh loss in nine games. Faut, who usually faced the other team's best hurler, dueled Hutchison, and the Sox star allowed six hits, but the stingy Hutchison permitted just two. In the seventh, Perlick lined a shot into center that Junor tried to shoestring, but the ball escaped her for a double, and Dapkus singled for the game's only run.[88] On Monday, Koehn rose to the occasion with a two-hitter, and the South Benders, providing errorless support and timely hitting, ended the losing string, 5–1. The local favorites rapped six hits, highlighted by Junor's two RBI singles and Mahon's two-run single.[89]

On Tuesday, South Bend's attendance passed the 100,000 mark, and the Sox celebrated by thumping the Belles, 7–3. Williams spaced two hits, both by Perlick, and the home team scored four times in the fourth to go ahead for good, 5–2.[90]

In Wednesday night's season finale at Playland, 3,732 of South Bend's faithful paid tribute to their heroines. "The girls' pro league ended its fifth year in South Bend last night," stated Jim Costin, "in what was perhaps the greatest exhibition of the game ever seen in this city." Performing in a playoff atmosphere, the aces, Hutchison and Faut, produced a marathon contest that the Belles won in 16 innings, 1–0. The Blue Sox had their best chance to win in the ninth, but Baker had twisted her ankle and was limping. Bonnie opened the inning with a single, Stefani sacrificed her to second, and Jochum popped out. Faut lined a single past third base, but Grant held Baker at third, touching off a "terrific chorus of boos." Marshall scorched a shot off Hutchison's glove, but Pepper Paire fielded it at short, and her throw nipped Marshall for the third out, preventing a South Bend victory. The Belles rallied in the 16th, starting when Faut hit Irene Hickson with a pitch. Marnie Danhauser bunted her to second, and Faut fanned Hutchison. Sophie Kurys bounced one past the pitcher and Stefani fielded it, but Hickson rounded third and kept on running. Stefani saw Kurys would be safe at first, but her throw home was wide of the plate, allowing Hickson to score.[91] In the bottom of the inning, the Sox tried to rally. Baker walked, and Williams ran for her. Ruth moved to third on a sacrifice and an out, but Mahon ended the battle by flying out to Betty Trezza in deep center.

The night's results left Racine in third with a 64–45 record, one and a half games behind Grand Rapids (64–43) and three games behind first-place Muskegon (66–42). The Sox kept their grip on the last playoff spot with a 55–50 mark, but Peoria (53–55) was still in the race.[92]

On the Road Again

The remainder of South Bend's regular season was spent on the road. On Thursday, August 28, the Blue Sox traveled to Fort Wayne, practiced, rested, and made up a rained-

Playoff Scorecard — The *Tribune's* scorecard for South Bend's second-ever Shaughnessy Playoff victory in 1947. The Blue Sox won their first playoff game on September 6, 1946, when they defeated the Belles, 13–2, but Racine won the semifinal playoff, three games to one. On Friday evening, September 5, 1947, Jean Faut preserved an 8–7 win for starter Ruth Williams at Grand Rapids (courtesy of the Louise Pettus Archives and Special Collections, Winthrop University).

out game at Zollner Piston Stadium, home of the city's world softball champions. The Daisies, lifted by a three-hitter twirled by Dottie Collins, who fanned ten, won, 5–0. The home team, holding down seventh place, ripped Stephens, who lasted just one inning, and Bittner for 11 hits, with Kellogg's three safeties and two apiece by Schroeder and Rountree setting the pace.[93]

On Friday at Grand Rapids, South Bend won, 5–1, over the second-place Chicks. Koehn tossed a two-hitter, one being Petras' RBI single in the fifth, but the visitors reached Haylett for six hits, starting with Mahon's two-run double in the third. Haylett was hurt by five errors, while Koehn pitched shutout ball after the fifth inning. Savoring the victory, the Blue Sox laughed, joked, sang the Victory Song, and played cards on the bus to Muskegon for the final four games.[94]

On Saturday at Muskegon's Marsh Field, South Bend lost a ten-inning battle, 1–0, but made the playoffs when Racine eliminated Peoria at Horlick Field, 3–2. Williams and Applegren both yielded three hits, but both were tough with runners on base. In the tenth, the visitors had Williams at the plate with one out, Marshall, hit by a pitch, standing at third base, and Junor, who singled, at second. Williams bunted, but she tossed her bat in such a way that it hit the ball, and she was called out for interference. Marshall, who scored, was sent back to third, and Pirok grounded out to end the inning. In the Lassies' tenth, Dottie Stolze drew a walk, and the dangerous Sams was passed. After a groundout, Mickey Maguire singled to win the contest.[95]

South Bend, with the playoff pressure gone, lost two of its three remaining contests. On Sunday, Muskegon manager Bill Wambsganss, eager to clinch the pennant, started the dependable Sams, and, with good offensive support, she pitched well enough to win, 8–2.[96] The two teams divided an evening twin bill on Labor Day. Faut lost the short opener, 2–0, when a first inning single, an error, and a two-run double by Jo Lenard provided all the scoring. In the nightcap, Bittner won her only game of the year, 3–2, as both teams played substitutes. The Blue Sox scored all three runs in the second inning, the Lassies scored both of their runs in the eighth, and Bittner pitched a scoreless ninth. However, the playoff teams were not yet decided because Grand Rapids, tied for second with Racine, was rained out of a twin bill with Fort Wayne.[97]

The Chicks and the Daisies split their two games on Tuesday, September 2. Afterward, Grand Rapids won Max Carey's coin toss to host the best-of-five round of the Shaughnessy Playoffs against South Bend, beginning on Thursday. Racine would play at Muskegon, also on Thursday. Chet Grant announced his ace, Jean Faut, would pitch, and Bonnie Baker, with her swollen ankle taped, would catch. The lineup also featured Marshall at first, Stefani at second, Pirok at short, Crigler at third, Jochum in left, Junor in center, and Mahon in right field.[98] Although none of the South Benders knew it, Faut was almost three months pregnant with her first child.[99]

Yet Another Anticlimax

After a day away from baseball, the Blue Sox made the bus trip to Grand Rapids, registered at the familiar Hotel Rowe, and prepared to play at South Field on Thursday, September 4. The *Tribune* reported that a throng of 4,380 saw Faut "blow up completely in her fielding in the second inning to give the Chicks three unearned runs and the ball game." In the fateful frame, Inez Voyce singled to center and took second on a sacrifice. Twi Shively walked, and when Faut made a wild pickoff throw, Voyce raced to third. Jane "Jeep" Stoll bunted in front of the plate, but Faut's throw was too late to catch Voyce sliding home. Doris Tetzlaff bunted to Faut, and she threw it so far over first base that Shively scored. Millie Earp tested Faut with another bunt, and Jean's bad throw allowed the third run to score. The visitors scored in the third on Pirok's run-scoring single and in the fifth on Junor's fielder's choice, but Earp held the 3–2 lead.[100]

Faut, however, redeemed herself on Friday night, saving an 8–7 victory by striking out Stoll with two out in the ninth and runners at second and third base. The Blue Sox jumped to a 6–0 lead in the second frame as Al Haylett gave up three singles, issued two free passes, and made two bad throws. The visitors added two more in the fourth for an 8–0 edge. Williams yielded single runs in the sixth, seventh, and eighth, after which Grant called on Koehn. In the ninth, Sugar hit a wild streak, walking three, allowing two singles, and, along with an error, coughing up five more runs. But Faut, after warming up, fanned Stoll and saved the victory.[101]

Following another bus odyssey, the Blue Sox hosted Grand Rapids at Playland on Saturday night, and the game attracted 4,341 fans, making 13,221 paid for the teams' three Shaughnessy contests. Koehn, with spotty control, started badly, and the home team fell, 6–1. In the first inning, 11 Chicks batted. Sugar walked three, including Gabby Ziegler twice, allowed four hits, and the Blue Sox added an error, handing Grand Rapids a 5–0 lead. The visitors scored in the second for a 6–0 lead, and for all practical purposes, the game was over. Connie Wisniewski did permit nine hits, three to Baker, and a solo run in the fifth on Koehn's RBI single.[102]

With his team facing elimination on Sunday, Grant sent Faut to the mound, and South Bend's biggest star pitched a brilliant 1–0 shutout, her tenth in 1947, to outshine Earp, the Chicks' ace. Baker collected three of South Bend's four hits (Bonnie batted over .300 in the playoffs), and stole home in the fourth for the game's only run — after her walk, a steal, and a sacrifice. On the play, Earp broke her windup to throw home, umpire Gadget Ward ruled it a balk, and Baker's run counted. Johnny Rawlings played the game under protest, but Max Carey upheld the call. Elsewhere, Racine topped Muskegon, 2–1, and advanced to the Shaughnessy Finals.[103]

The Blue Sox hoped to advance to the finals, but on Monday night, September 8, South Bend wasted several chances to score and lost, 6–1. Both teams notched one run in the second, the visitors on Stoll's bunt and the Blue Sox on Crigler's infield hit. Williams battled Haylett evenly for seven innings, but in the eighth, she yielded singles to Teeny Petras and to Wisniewski, playing right field. Grant called on Faut, but it wasn't her night. Voyce bunted, and Crigler threw it away, allowing Petras to score and Wisniewski to reach third. After a walk, an infield hit, and two forceouts at home, Haylett won it with a three-run double.

The night's action ended with a skirmish, when Grant chided a heckling fan, "We both like to watch girls play baseball like men. You pay. I'm paid. Who's the knothead?" Writing in 1972, Grant said he socked the nose of "a badgering Blue Sox director affectionately known as Doc [Dailey]. My cup ran over."[104] Later, at the police station, the fan's charge of assault was dropped and the two men shook hands.[105]

The All-American League was booming, and the Chicks won the Shaughnessy title over the Belles in seven games,[106] but South Bend's 1947 season ended in yet another anticlimax. Grant managed the Blue Sox into the Shaughnessy Playoffs two years in a row, but after punching a director, he resigned. Following yet another "almost" season, the ball club needed a new manager for 1948. In other team-related changes, Lib Mahon moved her residence from Greenville, South Carolina, to South Bend, taught physical education at Jefferson Elementary, and underwent surgery on her left knee.[107] Three of the team's stars, Betsy Jochum, Marge Stefani, and Jean Faut, who lived in South Bend during the offseason and worked at Ball-Band, prepared to join an exhibition tour in South America,[108] but for reasons that are unclear, Jochum and Faut never made the trip.[109] Also, Faut, the team's inspirational leader, gave birth to her first child before the 1948 season began.[110] Although the league featured few mothers playing baseball, Jean, now her team's mainstay, had no intention of leaving the game she loved.

• 6 •

Overhand Pitching and the Ten-Team League: 1948

"The year 1948 was a season of still further expansion and growth for the All-American Girls Baseball League, with over-all attendance in ten Midwestern cities approaching the 1,000,000 mark and several of the clubs showing important attendance gains."— Dell's *Major League Baseball: 1949*[1]

All-Americans Pitch Overhand

Fifteen years later, when Bob Dylan sang his famous song, "The Times They Are a-Changing," he could have been referring to the All-American League in 1948, because change was the order of the day in the nation's top women's pro baseball circuit. In a history prepared for Dell's 1949 edition of *Major League Baseball*, the author, likely president Max Carey, wrote, "The season saw the further opening up of the game by the adoption of full overhand pitching regulations, a 50-foot pitching distance, an increase of the distances between bases to 72 feet and the adoption of a still smaller ball, ten and three-eighths inches in circumference." He added, "The original under-hand pitch disappeared entirely from the game and the season was memorable for its development of fine overhand pitchers, with curves, drops, change of pace and other scientific wizardry."[2]

Changes in the ball's size, the dimensions of the diamond, and the pitching actually began with the All-American's second season in 1944. Pitching changes, however, accelerated when the loop first permitted a sidearm delivery in 1946 and then authorized the sidearm motion in 1947, meaning that baseball-style pitching was in effect. In 1948, overhand hurling, the signature of baseball, dealt a death knell to many of the underhand pitchers who populated the league during the war years, because few could adjust to the new motion. Sugar Koehn, for example, recalled her downfall occurred with the switch to sidearming: "I did have a few good years, but the unorthodox throw took its toll."[3] On the other hand, Jean Faut, who never played fast-pitch softball but often threw sidearm from her position at third base, recalled, "When the league went to overhand pitching in 1948, I was home free."[4]

The adoption of overhand pitching meant the league needed to develop more new pitchers, because softball hurlers could not learn the delivery, the pitches, and the control needed in two weeks of spring camp.[5] Further, the overhand motion is harder on a pitcher's arm, due partly to the frequent throwing of breaking balls — pitches that require using different grips and twisting, or snapping, the wrist during delivery. Koehn's sore arm after 1947 illustrated that point. As a result, few baseball pitchers can work more often than every fourth day. Therefore, a good team needs a rotation with at least three strong hurlers as well as "spot" starters to win consistently.

The circuit not only expanded to ten teams in 1948 but also, under Max Carey's guidance and supervised by Lenny Zintak, formed a four-team junior league for younger girls in Chicago modeled after the "big" league.[6] The expanded All-American League, Carey said from his office in the Windy City on February 17, had ten teams split into Eastern and Western Divisions. Each team was scheduled to play 126 games, meeting the other nine clubs at home and away 14 times and visiting each league city twice. Each division's top four teams would square off in a best-of-five Shaughnessy Playoff, and the division winners would meet for the title in a best-of-seven series. The Chicago Colleens would compete in the East against South Bend, Fort Wayne, Muskegon, and Grand Rapids. The Springfield, Illinois, Sallies would play in the West against Peoria, Rockford, Racine, and Kenosha. The new teams had former big leaguers for managers. Dave Bancroft was set to lead the Colleens. A stellar shortstop with the New York Giants and the Philadelphia Phillies and a four-time World Series veteran starting with the Phillies of 1915, Bancroft would be inducted into the National Baseball Hall of Fame in 1971. Carson Bigbee would pilot the Sallies. A star outfielder for the Pittsburgh Pirates who peaked with a .350 average in 1922, Bigbee was currently working in the auto business in his native state of Oregon.[7]

The league's history summarizing the 1948 season commented on the changes, including the fact that Springfield and Chicago clubs failed. Springfield lasted five weeks before becoming a "traveling team" on June 16, much like the Millerettes of Minneapolis in 1944. The Sallies played the rest of the schedule under league management, but finished in last place in the Western Division with a record of 41–85. The Colleens completed the season, but ranked last in the Eastern Division with a 47–76 ledger, and Chicago resigned from the loop on September 27, 1948.[8]

Also, an important social issue resulted from the Havana spring camp in 1947 and the first postseason Latin American tour. Several Cuban players made the league in 1948: "For the first time in the six year history of the league, a bevy of senoritas from the Republic of Cuba made the grade in spring training and several of them performed throughout the season with AAGBL clubs, including Mirta Marrero with Chicago, Gloria Ruiz with Peoria, Luisa 'Chi-Chi' Gallegos with Peoria–South Bend and Migdalia 'Mickey' Perez with Chicago."[9]

Harold "Doc" Dailey, dentist, sports fan, and president of the Blue Sox, saw himself as the team's expert on women's baseball. He kept his hand in all club matters, even provoking Chet Grant to fisticuffs at the end of the 1947 playoffs. Writing on November 18, 1947, Dailey criticized Arthur Meyerhoff, who was voted league commissioner a month earlier, for expanding to ten teams in 1948 and thus increasing costs while diluting the talent and fan base. By Dailey's convoluted reasoning, ten teams meant attendance would be cut by 20 percent and the salaries increased by 20 percent. "You birds never learn," Dailey complained, "that the club stands all the losses and Management gains in the three cents on attendance [the fee returned to the league for each paying customer], but suffers no losses." Dailey failed to appreciate the value of publicizing women's baseball, but the loop's expansion to ten teams did prove to be a mistake.[10]

Marty McManus Again

Also, Dailey and South Bend's directors rehired Marty McManus. A Chicago native and former big leaguer, McManus led the Comets into the 1944 Scholarship Playoffs and the Blue Sox of 1945 into fifth place, half a game short of the Shaughnessy Playoffs. On January 13, 1948, after analyzing the team's statistics for the previous season, McManus warned Dailey to "be careful on Jochum, for she was the leading hitter in the runs batted in department." The point was not lost on Dailey: Jochum, who held out in 1945, later asked for a raise (which Dailey refused). McManus figured the team needed a new first baseman, since Tee Marshall made 42 errors, "and that must be a record for a professional." Also, the team needed a "strikeout pitcher." Catchers Irene Hickson of Racine and Grand Rapids' Ruth Lessing both had 100 putouts more than Baker (the catcher gets a putout when the pitcher fans a batter), and better pitching allowed the Belles and the Chicks to meet in the finals of the 1947 playoffs.[11]

In South Bend's board meeting of January 7, 1948, the ten-team league, the Eastern and Western Divisions, and the 126-game schedule — the circuit's longest ever — were confirmed, but the directors voted 4–4 on whether to hold the spring camp in Cuba or the United States. Later, the league picked Opa-Locka, Florida, as a compromise.[12]

A city chartered in the mid–1920s and designed on an "Arabian Nights" theme, Opa-Locka was located 15 miles northwest of Miami. The city featured several air fields, and the founders gave a small air strip to the Navy in 1931. Seven years later the field was enlarged to serve as a Naval Reserve Station. Converted into a Naval Air Station at the onset of World War II, the facilities were expanded to include acres of wooden barracks and several ball fields. The war brought a major stimulus to Opa-Locka, a city now covering four square miles. After the war, local leaders kept one air field open, converted the base's facilities to peacetime use, and turned some of the barracks into hotels.[13]

Spring in Opa-Locka

The postwar spring camps at Pascagoula in 1946 and Havana in 1947 offered players the usual mixture of hope and fear, because rookies and veterans alike dreamed of making or keeping their position in the All-American League. But in 1948, with two new teams added and each existing team allowed to keep a core of eight players (no more than two could be pitchers), the usual springtime feeling of optimism was tempered by greater fears of being uprooted, if the player was a veteran, or not making it, if she was a rookie. In other words, allocation day promised more reshuffling of players, and veterans especially disliked being relocated. Also, Lois Browne, in her book *Girls of Summer*, called 1948 the "Last Ascending Season," partly because attendance reached an all-time high of roughly 910,000, and partly because new teams in Springfield and Chicago did not last, but instead became rookie touring teams in 1949 and 1950.[14]

During the postwar era, the nation's recreation culture was changing. The number of families owning television sets leaped, and TV was becoming the main medium of communication. Also, individual sports like golf, tennis, and badminton became more popular.[15] As a result, fewer fans attended major league baseball games. Like the All-American League, baseball's postwar attendance peaked in 1948. The two leagues' 16 teams drew 20,920,000 fans, but the majors did not see attendance surpass the 1948 mark until 1962, the second expansion season.[16]

Regardless, Opa-Locka, part of the sprawl of Miami, Florida's largest city, was an ideal location for spring training. The league's site included several recreational ball fields and several private hotels that served good food and offered swimming pools, but nothing for players to do after workouts ended — except sit around and chat with each other or write letters home.[17] Most players arrived during the first week of April, notably pitchers and catchers, and many rode trains that departed from Chicago's Union Station in a snowstorm. The sunny atmosphere of Miami was a great change-of-pace from the Midwest, and soon many of the girls were wearing white zinc paste or suntan lotion on their noses and faces to protect them from sunburn.[18] The exercises and drills for 40 rookies, supervised by Grand Rapids' manager Johnny Rawlings, began on April 5, and pilots from the other seven established teams helped run the camp.

Due to the introduction of overhand pitching, the 50-foot pitching distance, and a smaller ball, the league's spring drills posed greater challenges to new players. During the winter, when Rawlings supervised tryouts in Los Angeles, Denver, New York City, and Allentown, Pennsylvania, scouts selected thirty-two out of four hundred candidates to attend Opa-Locka. But new prospects had little time to make the adjustments needed. "Our game is so different than anything they've played before," explained McManus, who managed Denver of the Class A Western League in 1947, "that the star softball player may still be a good two years away from baseball. Naturally we watch first to see how a girl throws the smaller ball and we're mighty anxious to see how she handles herself at the plate."[19] Longtime players helped coach the recruits. South Bend's returning veterans were Marge Stefani and Betsy Jochum, who, along with Bonnie Baker, were the only players left from the original Blue Sox of 1943.[20] As usual with spring camp, the league generated maximum publicity, photographers set up cameras around the fields, and reporters took detailed notes.[21]

Cuban Newcomers

An interesting highlight at Opa-Locka revolved around the seven recruits from Cuba. According to official league statistics, no Cuban played in a regular season game prior to 1948. However, after the circuit's excursion to Havana in 1947, Ralph Leon, a wealthy distillery owner, provided the backing for Cuban girls to play in a Havana-based professional circuit under the rules used in the All-American League, and seven candidates were sent to Opa-Locka. The Sallies drew two, Georgiana Rios, a third baseman, and Vialat Zonia, a catcher. The Colleens received five Cubans: second baseman Maria Hernandas; third baseman and pitcher Mickey Perez; infielder-pitcher Luisa Gallegos; outfielder Gloria Ruiz; and right-hander Mirta Marrero. The *South Bend Tribune* enthused, "The Cubans are all attractive young ladies, well schooled in the discipline and abilities required by the All-American League." South Bend's Shoo-Shoo Wirth, raised by her Cuban-born mother in Tampa, grew up speaking Spanish and English. She functioned as an interpreter for the Cubans, since she was one of the few Americans who could speak Spanish.[22]

Those newcomers broke a social barrier as the first Cubans to play in the All-American League. The major leagues saw the first two Cubans, Rafael Almeida and Armando Marsans, debut with the Cincinnati Reds in 1911, but the first Cuban star, Adolfo "Dolf" Luque, began his career in 1914 with the Boston Braves. The Havana-born right-hander rose to fame with Cincinnati and, in 1923, led the majors with a 27–8 mark and a 1.93 ERA. Luque, however, was light-skinned and could pass the majors' unofficial "color" line. The same was true of most other players from the Caribbean before 1947. Rob Ruck concluded in *Total Baseball*, "And while Negro Leaguers went south [of the border] to adulation and greater pay, dark-skinned Latinos who came north encountered prejudice based on both skin color and nationality."[23]

Cubans in the All-American League had better experiences because they were welcomed by most American and Canadian players. For example, Dolly Brumfield, who was 15 and studying Spanish in high school when she trained at Opa-Locka, received help with Spanish from more than one Cuban. Dolly recalled, "Mickey Perez was a big help and was a good friend over all those years."[24]

Still, the Cubans were separated from their families, and if Mirta Marrero's experience was typical, the language barrier caused problems. Mirta, who was 17 and a talented pitcher in 1948, did not know any English, and communicating with her Chicago teammates was difficult. "I cried a lot because the American girls couldn't understand me and I couldn't understand them," Marrero recounted in 2003. "I had a hard time." When it came to chatter, players learned different phrases. Mirta remembered yelling "Oye, fulana!" (Hey, you!) to her American teammates, and "Dale, chica!" (Go, girl!) to Latinas.[25] Indeed, most fans in South Bend treated Shoo-Shoo Wirth, who spoke broken English, as a heroine, and even little kids admired her.[26]

The New Sox Roster

The Opa-Locka camp continued two-a-day drills for almost two weeks and, after a week of practice games, the league's allocation meeting was held on Wednesday, April 21. Ten members, including one from each team — South Bend's representative was Dailey, advised by McManus — met all day and late that night assigning players to teams. The Blue Sox kept three pitchers, Faut, Ruth Williams, and Sugar Koehn; Bonnie Baker behind the plate; Jochum, Lib Mahon, and Red Mahoney in the outfield; and Pirok, Marshall, and Wirth in the infield. South Bend added fourth-year veteran Helen Filarski, a right-handed batting infielder from Harper Woods, Michigan. Also, the Sox acquired two catchers: Lake Worth, Florida, native Norma Metrolis, a backup for Muskegon in 1946 and Racine in 1947, and rookie Dorothy Whalen from Kew Gardens, New York. In addition, the team received three more rookies: flychaser Jean Smith, from Kalamazoo (soon switched to Kenosha), and two utility players, Jaynie Krick, of Fort Wayne, and Kalamazoo's Marjean Smith, who had a brief trial with Grand Rapids in 1947.

Rounding out the Blue Sox' roster were California right-hander Lil Faralla and three recruit right-handers, Louise "Lou" Arnold from Pawtucket, Rhode Island, Bernice Metesh from Joliet, Illinois, and Shirley Kleinhans of Sheboygan Falls, Wisconsin. The major losses were stellar infielder Marge Stefani, who was reallocated to Rockford, and light-hitting Daisy Junor, who was sent to Kenosha, until Audrey Wagner finished the college semester.[27] Finally, Dolly Brumfield was named in an earlier story about rookies, but she was not allocated to the Sox.[28]

South Bend played several exhibitions in Tampa against Kenosha and Muskegon, but with so many missing regulars, nobody could gauge the team's quality. Stefani, a fixture at second base for five seasons, was reduced to tears when she was shifted to Rockford. Junor, who refused to play when told she was traded to Kenosha, was returned to South Bend when McManus and Comet pilot Chet Grant, the former South Bender, made a deal for Kenosha to receive rookie Jean Smith. For pitching, until Faut and Williams were ready, South Bend would rely on Koehn and three rookies, Bernice Metesh, Lou Arnold, and Shirley Kleinhans (who was soon released), as well as Lil Faralla, who played infield for Peoria in 1946 and pitched for Fort Wayne in 1947, posting a 3–12 record and hitting .279.

Baker would catch, with Metrolis in reserve. The infield looked solid with Filarski at third base, Pirok at second, Wirth at short, and Marshall at first. Jochum was slated for left field, Junor for center, and Mahon for right. McManus, however, figured the Blue Sox were unlikely to rise above their fourth-place finish in 1947, because the top three teams, Grand Rapids, Muskegon, and Racine, were not hurt by allocation.[29]

Launching the New Season — Slowly

Amid the usual fanfare from the *Tribune*, Bonnie Baker arrived from Regina on Wednesday, May 5, expressed regret at the loss of her friend Marge Stefani to Rockford, said the Blue Sox should perform well in 1948, and called McManus the team's second best pilot.[30] The team celebrated the new season with a banquet dinner at Dan Clark's restaurant on Thursday, and guests included Jean Faut, Lib Mahon, Pinky Pirok, Marie Kruckel, who was not yet under contract, and chaperone Lucille Moore.[31] McManus called off a Friday morning practice at Playland Park after "frigid" winds blew on Thursday, but the full team worked out on Saturday. Mahon's left knee "popped out" while throwing, so she was doubtful for Sunday's opener. Also, Dorothy Whalen was sent to the Springfield Sallies when Shirley Stovroff, the team's rookie catcher, underwent an emergency appendectomy. McManus named his battery as Koehn and Baker, and club officials expected a big crowd of 6,000 on Sunday.[32]

Instead, South Bend's hopes were dashed by three days of cold and rainy weather, hardly an unusual circumstance in the Midwest during springtime. In fact, the league was hurt more in 1948 by chilly or wet conditions than any previous season. All the openers were rained out, except at Fitzpatrick Memorial Stadium in Springfield, where the Daisies, fighting cold temperatures and threatening rain, beat the Sallies, 5–1. South Bend's pregame ceremonies, featuring the American Legion's color guard raising the flag in center field while playing the national anthem, were rescheduled.[33] The Blue Sox, ready to don their white uniforms for home contests and their colored — in their case, light blue — outfits for away games, saw the Playland opener reset for May 19 against the Belles. Also, the South Benders stayed home on Wednesday after Racine's management reported that rain and cold weather prevented play.[34]

After a fifth rainout on Thursday, May 13, the Blue Sox and the Belles each played their first game in a chilly rain on Friday night at Racine's Horlick Field. The visitors' spirits were dampened, 10–3, as Racine rapped seven hits and knocked the sidearming Koehn out of the box after four innings. The loss left South Bend (0–1) fourth out of five teams in the Eastern Division. Muskegon topped the East with a 3–0 record, followed by Grand Rapids at 1–0 and Fort Wayne at 3–1, while 0–2 Chicago was last, a position the Colleens maintained all summer.[35]

On a chilly Saturday night (the league still played night games), Lil Faralla, a strong-armed natural sidearmer with a good fastball and slider, began her stellar Blue Sox career by no-hitting Racine to win the seven-inning lid-lifter, 1–0. The visitors scored in the first inning off Jo Winter, combining Baker's single and steal, Pirok's walk, Jochum's forceout, and a double steal by Jochum and Baker. Faralla would have notched a perfect game, but with two outs in the seventh, Marshall dropped Pirok's throw to first base. Racine won the nightcap, 13–5, belting Lou Arnold with a five-run sixth for a 12–2 lead, and Jaynie Krick mopped up.

Afterward, the Blue Sox rode the team bus to Peoria. The players typically spent their time on such trips chatting, singing, sleeping fitfully, or playing card games like poker at the vehicle's built-in poker table. Cards or not, the women soon grew used to the rigors of late-night bus travel from one city to another.[36]

The Illinois trip was a disaster for the South Benders. On Sunday evening at Peoria Stadium, the Redwings defeated the Blue Sox twice, 5–2 and 7–1. In the short opener, hard-throwing Cuban rookie Chi-Chi Gallegos won a two-hitter. The Peoria right-hander was wild, but she was hurt only by Wirth's two-run single, and Koehn walked five and allowed five hits, the big blow being Rita Meyer's two-run double in the fifth for a 4–2 lead. The Redwings might have scored more, but Filarski snagged a bases-loaded liner, stepped on third, and fired to first for a triple play, the second in team history — after the first game against the Daisies on May 23, 1946.

In the nightcap, Daisy Junor beat out a bunt to end Dottie Mueller's no-hit bid, and Faralla lost by walking seven and yielding eight hits.[37] On Monday, with Arnold scattering six hits, the blue-uniformed visitors' big fourth inning, featuring Marshall's two-run triple, gave them a 3–1 victory over Peoria's Audrey Haine.[38] On Tuesday, the 5'11" Krick made her first start, but she was wild and ineffective, allowing six runs on four hits and 12 walks. With her club behind, Koehn took over, and though South Bend outhit Peoria, 13–7, Elaine Roth won for the home team, 7–5. Afterward, the "quite-blue Sox" (said Costin), having lost five of seven on the road trip, embarked on the long bus ride to South Bend for a home stand.[39]

Struggling in May

The Blue Sox often performed better at home, typical for a professional team, but Racine won two out of three at Playland. On May 19, a chilly Wednesday, 2,645 fans, enduring another in a seemingly endless string of cold nights, saw Faralla space five hits and help the Blue Sox to a 6–3 lead with two outs left in the game, even though Racine stole 11 bases against Baker's weak arm on the longer 72-foot base paths. In the ninth, Filarski threw away a grounder, opening the door to three runs and a 6–6 tie. In the tenth, Georgette "Jette" Vincent's RBI single won it for the Belles, 7–6.[40] On a cold Thursday before 4,546 customers, Racine's Jo Winter (with her back taped to support a bad vertebra[41]) won a two-hitter, 5–1, firing sharp-breaking curves and "smoky" fastballs and fanning 12. Koehn walked five and allowed seven hits, but Racine's two runs in the first proved enough to win.[42] On Friday, the Blue Sox won for the first time in 1948 at Playland, 7–4, taking a 6–4 lead on Faralla's two-out, bases-loaded pinch double in the seventh, and Lil, relieving Arnold, preserved the win with two innings of hitless pitching.[43]

The Daisies proved equally tough. On May 22, after traveling to Fort Wayne for a Saturday night tilt, the Blue Sox dropped a heartbreaker, 3–2, despite Faralla's four-hitter.[44] On Sunday, Faut, coming back from her pregnancy, made her first appearance of the season, but the home team won, 4–2. Jean gave up four runs on four hits and three walks in five and two-thirds innings, Norma Metrolis left the game when she twisted her knee sliding into third base in the fifth, and Baker, despite her "dead" arm, switched from second base to catcher.[45] On Monday, the Blue Sox salvaged a win, 8–7, by scoring three times in the ninth.[46]

South Bend, now fourth in the East with a 4–9 record, packed and left for a four-game series against Springfield, but at Fitzpatrick Memorial Stadium on Tuesday, May 25, temperatures in the upper 30s again forced a postponement.⁴⁷ On Wednesday, the 5–10 Sallies, tail-enders in the West all year long, handed the struggling Blue Sox — minus Pirok, Mahon, and Williams — a pair of defeats, the first when Ruby Stephens threw a no-hitter

Yes, Mom Plays *Baseball* — Jean Faut, getting ready to go to Playland Park, leaves her son Larry with Mrs. Singleton, the neighbor and friend who took care of him while Faut was at the ballpark or on a road trip (courtesy of the Louise Pettus Archives and Special Collections, Winthrop University).

and won the opener, 4–0. In the late game, Arnold started but, after surrendering eight runs in three innings, the visitors lost to the Sallies and Erma Bergmann, 11–6. McManus tried Jochum, who gave up one run in the fifth, and Krick, who yielded two in the eighth.[48] On Thursday, South Bend won, 6–2, in 14th innings as Faut allowed nine hits, whiffed nine, and walked four. Against Dodie Barr in the 14, Jochum and Krick singled and Pirok walked. Pinch-hitting for Marshall, Faralla singled for a 4–2 lead, and Filarski and Wirth added RBI singles, giving South Bend the win and a 5–11 mark.[49]

Off on Friday, May 28, the Blue Sox were finally at full strength, with the academic year nearly over for teachers like outfielder Lib Mahon and second-year right-hander Ruth Williams, who relied on good control and pitch location for her slow breaking stuff, and the versatile Pinky Pirok, a college student. South Bend needed pitching, so McManus converted Jochum to mound duty.[50]

Calling Saturday night's 6–0 victory over Fort Wayne "one of the best pitched games the Playland Park diamond has ever seen," Jim Costin reported that Jochum permitted two singles, walked none, and struck out five, displaying a hard fastball, a sharp-breaking curve, and good control, and her teammates rapped eight hits, including three singles by Pirok. An enthusiastic crowd of 1,697 cheered the popular Jochum all night.[51] On Sunday, the Blue Sox dumped the Daisies, 6–3, on Faut's three-hitter, and Jochum, back in left field, led the attack with two hits.[52]

Any euphoria South Bend was enjoying evaporated on Memorial Day, Monday, May 31, when Fort Wayne won twice. A crowd of 3,550, the largest of 1948 to date, saw the Sox kick away Faut's first home start, 6–2, thanks to six errors as well as a bases-loaded double in the fourth by Lee (Surkowski) Delmonico, the former South Bend star. In the nightcap, Williams spaced seven hits but lost to Dottie Collins, 2–0, as Helen Callaghan rapped a pair of RBI singles. After the holiday, the standings showed Grand Rapids first in the East with a 16–6 record, Fort Wayne second at 11–10, and Muskegon third at 8–12. South Bend, with a 7–13 ledger, was fourth, and Chicago, at 4–14, remained in last place.[53]

Chicago, meanwhile, was failing after a 1–12 start. Effective on June 1, in a deal the league announced five days earlier, Tee Marshall was one of eight regulars transferred from other teams to the Colleens to strengthen the loop's weakest team, and Betty Whiting, Chicago's versatile first sacker, was sent to South Bend to replace Marshall.[54] By late May, Max Carey and Arthur Meyerhoff realized that Chicago, where they really wanted an All-American team to succeed, had received a weak allocation. Unless they acted, the Colleens might collapse, blasting hopes of profiting off the huge Chicago market and leaving the loop with an oddball nine-team schedule.

Therefore, the league reallocated eight regulars from the eight established teams (but not weak Springfield), and in return, Chicago sent a player to each team that lost a regular. In addition to South Bend's Marshall for Chicago's Whiting, the following switches were made:

- Fort Wayne sent catcher Mary Rountree and received catcher Kate Vonderau.
- Muskegon sent lefty Amy Applegren and received southpaw Donna Cook.
- Peoria sent third baseman Mary Reynolds and received Doris Tetzlaff, also a third sacker.
- Grand Rapids sent shortstop Teeny Petras and received rookie shortstop Marilyn Olinger.
- Racine lost Ellie Dapkus but added flychaser Twi Shively and right-hander Betty Tucker.

- Rockford sent catcher-outfielder Rita Briggs and received outfielder Ellie Callow.
- Kenosha sent outfielder Marge Pieper and received, from the league's pool of players that were unallocated after spring training, former South Bend infielder Dolly Brumfield.

Optimistic, Carey told team officials that these changes would allow the Colleens to "compete with the rest of the league and more or less approximate an even and fair allocation." Instead, the Colleens finished last in the West, and the team's failure hurt the credibility of Meyerhoff and Carey as well as the league's finances. The Sallies, already "orphans," and the Colleens both failed, showing that expansion to ten teams was a mistake. The league was no longer ascending.[55]

Playing .500 Ball

Beginning on June 1, the Blue Sox won nearly half of their games over the rest of the season, but the slow start contributed to a losing record (57–69) for the second time in six campaigns. South Bend's other losing ledger (49–60) came in 1945, when McManus first managed the team, but that season was injury-marred. Before the summer of 1948 ended, Marty again demonstrated his teaching and coaching skills. The positive results showed interested observers why standouts like Betsy Jochum called McManus the team's best manager.[56]

By the time the Blue Sox traveled to Chicago in the early hours of Saturday, June 12, McManus made another change. The players registered at the Hotel Southmoor, caught some sleep, and prepared to play the rebuilt Colleens at Shewbridge Field, but torrential rains gave the teams an unwanted day off. South Bend announced "bombshell" news: Friday's trade of two sore-armed pitchers, Sugar Koehn and Bernice Metesh for Peoria's Cuban fastballer, Chi-Chi Gallegos (who never won for South Bend). McManus said Koehn could only throw a "slow ball" sidearm, and batters hit her so freely that he decided not to pitch her. The former Comet, who came to South Bend with Pirok in a 1945 trade, also failed in the outfield. Sugar's weak arm limited her throws, and her hitting fell to .160. Later, Peoria sent Koehn to Racine, and she posted an overall 6–8 record and a 3.02 ERA in 128 innings. Ironically, Gallegos also experienced arm trouble and control problems, and she finished with a 2–6 mark and a league-high 5.79 ERA in 73 innings.[57]

On Sunday, Chicago's lanky Hank Warren, the former Chick, scattered singles by Mahon, Jochum, Krick, and Whiting, and the home team notched victory number seven, 2–1. Faralla pitched well, except in the seventh, when the Colleens bunched three of their eight hits with an error by Gallegos, playing third base, to score twice.[58] On Monday, the Blue Sox split a doubleheader as Jochum hurled a two-hit shutout to win the opener, 2–0, and Faralla, playing the outfield, singled in the first inning to score both runs. In the nightcap, Krick, showing good control, dueled right-hander Mickey Perez evenly until the ninth, when Chicago's Charlene Barnett doubled to left field, and Arnold, replacing Krick, took a 2–1 loss on Teeny Petras' RBI single. Afterward, the Sox, having lost two of three to the Colleens, traveled home for a series against Muskegon.[59]

South Bend, now with a 12–20 record, was still struggling. According to league statistics through mid–June, the Blue Sox ranked seventh in team batting and fourth in team fielding. Before their Monday twin bill, Chicago's mark was 7–21; the loop's worst team was first in fielding but last in hitting. Audrey Wagner, Kenosha's slugging outfielder, was leading the league with a mark of .443 in 15 games. Wagner was followed by Chicago right-hander Betty Tucker, a Detroiter who was hitting .409 (9-for-22), and Lil Faralla, the best Blue Sox hitter to date, at .388 (12-for 36). Faralla's teammates and their averages were Lib Mahon at .241; Shoo-Shoo Wirth, .235; Jaynie Krick, .224; Helen Filarski, .214; and Bonnie Baker at .193. Other South Benders ranged from Pinky Pirok, hitting .176, to a team low of .121 for the slow-starting Betsy Jochum, who was working hard learning to pitch.[60]

South Bend's best news was the hitting of the versatile Faralla, who was playing the outfield and pitching. Lil did a good job of both, although her current record of 2–6 did not show it. Three of her four losses came by one run. When Faralla lost a 3–0 decision to Springfield on May 27, she gave up three hits, but curveballing Ruby Stephens hurled a seven-inning no-hitter. Faralla took time to get accustomed to South Bend and her new teammates, but she was a stellar performer. Reflecting on her career, Lil said, "I got assigned to South Bend [in 1948] and was not popular after refusing to go there the year before." She added, "Besides, they always put the mike in front of me and asked how come I refused to go to South Bend."[61]

Wins, Losses, and Expansion

Shaking off the bad baseball played in Chicago, South Bend, welcomed by a crowd of 1,529 at Playland on June 15, a chilly Tuesday evening, opened four games against Muskegon by hitting well enough to win, 5–4. Faut, still pitching herself into condition after her son Larry was born in March, gave up eight hits and struck out eight, and the home team made six errors.[62] On an even colder Wednesday, 1,521 unhappy folks saw the Lassies trounce their favorites, 12–1. Arnold did not display enough control over her slow curves in her five-inning stint, but sloppy fielding hurt the Blue Sox. Doris Sams scattered six hits, and she twice fanned rookie outfielder Nancy DeShone, as the Elkhart native made her All-American debut. Fifteen players took the field for the Sox, and recruit right fielder Alice Meyer went 1-for-1, tripling home Mahon in the second.[63]

Despite more cold weather on Thursday, a crowd of 1,500 saw Faralla no-hit Muskegon, 4–0, boosting Lil's record to 3–6. Metrolis returned to catching duties, Baker played second, and Pirok played third. In the ninth, Pinky's fine play on Sams' smash and Whiting's one-handed pickup at first of the throw saved the no-hitter. The Blue Sox won with four runs in the seventh, fueled by Krick's walk, Whiting's triple, Metrolis' squeeze, Junor's double, Baker's single, Wirth's infield hit, and Pirok's single. Afterward, fans learned that Betty Wagoner had been acquired from Muskegon, and South Bend officials asked waivers on two or three current (unnamed) players.[64] On Friday, behind the five-hit pitching of Jochum, the Sox won their third out of four games, climbing past Muskegon (14–22) into third place with a 15–21 record. The crowd of 1,369 boosted the total for the "overcast series" to an impressive 4,998 fans. The home team totaled seven hits and clinched the outcome in the eighth on Mahon's two-run double. In a related note, Costin reported Marie Kruckel, who pitched for South Bend on Wednesday, was claimed by Muskegon and appeared in a Lassie uniform — but did not play — on Friday.[65]

South Bend was improving, but expansion was failing. The *Tribune* reported that Springfield's franchise lacked the funds to continue, and the league would operate the Sallies as a "traveling team" for the rest of 1948, much the same as Minneapolis in 1944. The problems included a lack of hometown press coverage for the Sallies and competition with Springfield's popular Browns, members of the Class B Three-I League. Further, many baseball fans disliked seeing a pro team use Fitzpatrick Memorial Stadium, a facility specifically built for youth recreation, and attendance lagged. On May 26–27, when South Bend played three games in Springfield, the visitors' share of the gate was $44.50, meaning that on two nights a total of 450 customers paid for admission.

Jim Costin pointed out that league officials proposed the idea of adding franchises in Springfield and Chicago when, first, Rockford lost support of the businessmen who created the franchise in 1943, and second, Kenosha, weak in attendance, considered withdrawing from the league after the 1947 season. However, when the Peaches and Comets decided to return, the loop was stuck with ten teams. Moreover, since the Sallies and the Colleens had little chance of rising out of last place, the pennant race, based on each division having the top four teams play off, was no race at all. The eight established teams were virtually guaranteed to make the Shaughnessy Playoffs. Later, the circuit reorganized for 1949, and the Sallies and Colleens became traveling "minor league" teams. By 1948, in an omen for the future, there were not enough female athletes of "big league ability" to staff more than eight teams, notably with overhand pitchers.[66]

Winning in July

By late June, after the Soviet Union launched the Berlin Blockade, and a United Auto Workers' strike at Bendix Aviation in South Bend kept more than 3,000 engineering and office employees out of work, the Blue Sox watched as heavy rain washed away the first game of the Rockford series at Playland. Meanwhile, the team received good news: Helen Filarski was back in uniform after being injured for two weeks, and Eddie Deslauriers, the team's business manager, announced the purchase of a set of new white and blue-trimmed uniform outfits for home games.[67] At the same time, McManus commented on the obvious: his team's pitching and fielding was good, but recent losses came because Sox hitters had produced just three runs in 52 innings.[68]

On Tuesday night, June 29, the make-up twin bill with Rockford began after a two-hour wait, but heavy rain returned, soaking Playland's diamond and forcing another cancellation with Rockford leading, 1–0, in the fourth inning.[69] On Wednesday, the home team opened another twin bill by shelling Rockford, 12–0. Williams, cushioned by a big lead, hurled a two-hit shutout. The Blue Sox, led by Mahon's two doubles, raked the versatile Mobile Holgerson, who failed to last one inning, and Metesh, the recent South Bender, for 12 hits, scoring five times in the first inning. In the nightcap, Helen Fox revived the Peaches' spirits by winning a two-hitter, 6–1, over Jochum, who yielded eight hits and five runs. After the rain-shortened series, Rockford, with a 30–21 ledger, was second in the West, and South Bend, now 20–27, was third in the East.[70]

The schedule seemed to give South Bend a break with the Comets and the Sallies on deck at Playland. On Thursday, July 1, Faralla delivered a three-hit performance and helped her club squeak out a 3–2 victory over Kenosha. Due to injuries to both Comet catchers, Dottie Naum and Marge "Poncho" Villa, Chet Grant, the former Sox pilot, used a volunteer behind the plate, Marilyn Jones, a rookie pitcher who caught for the second time in her career. Jones was charged with four passed balls, two of which allowed runners to score—including Pirok with the winning run in the sixth.

The *Tribune* reported that Daisy Junor was swapped to Springfield for Alice Meyer, who was on loan from the Sallies.[71] On Friday, Faut hurled a two-hit shutout to beat Kenosha, 4–0,[72] and on Saturday, the Blue Sox, now 23–27, won again, 4–0, on Williams' three-hitter.[73]

On Sunday, South Bend hosted Springfield and won for the fourth straight time, 3–0.[74] In a holiday doubleheader on Monday night, South Bend's largest crowd of the season, 4,576 fans, watched their favorites split two scheduled seven-inning games that were followed by a large fireworks display. The local heroines took the opener in the ninth, 5–4, when hustling Betty Whiting, who caught both games with a taped finger, doubled, the speedy Mahoney ran for her, and Faralla, the pitcher, singled to win it. In the late tilt, Springfield's Jean Marlowe hurled a three-hit shutout and won, 1–0, breaking the home team's win string at five. Faut gave up four hits, but the Sallies won in the sixth when Junor walked and Wirth's error let Daisy score.[75] In the finale on Tuesday, Krick blanked the Sallies for six innings, and the home team led, 2–0, but lost, 6–2, after committing a record ten errors in the last three frames. When the night was over, the Sox owned a hometown mark of 18–9, plus a tie, but they were a miserable 7–20 on the road.[76]

The Blue Sox at Mid-Season

By the time Blue Sox players and fans heard the starting lineup announced at Playland shortly after eight o'clock on Tuesday evening, July 13, McManus had settled on a lineup that differed greatly from Grant's 1947 playoff team. Marty, a good baseball strategist, was deft at shifting his players to the positions where he needed their hitting or fielding skills during a game:

- 1B — Whiting (97 Games), from Ida, Michigan, a light-hitting but hard-charging veteran of four seasons who could handle many positions, mostly played first base. A good fielder, Betty played 120 games, including 29 as catcher, and averaged .183 with six doubles, five triples, and one home run, scoring 33 times and producing 20 RBI. Marshall played the initial sack before being traded to Chicago on June 1, and Baker, on a few occasions, filled in at first base.
- 2B — Filarski, another good-fielding but light-hitting athlete, was living her dream by playing pro ball. The Detroit native played 49 games at second, more than anyone except Baker, who also played 49 games, but Mahon and Wirth filled in at the position when needed. Helen played 101 games, including 32 as a flychaser and 23 at third. Averaging .179, she scored 29 times and also drove home 29 runners, illustrating her all-around value.
- SS — The energetic and popular Wirth continued to sparkle in the field, playing 102 of her 113 games at shortstop and the remaining 11 at second base. A slap hitter, the five-foot speedster averaged .241, third highest on the team behind Wagoner (.278) and Mahon (.258). Shoo-Shoo's hustle helped her record six doubles and four triples. She drew 26 walks, scored 60 runs — second behind Baker's 62 — and the dark-haired Tampa native contributed 26 RBI.
- 3B — Peppery and sure-handed, Pirok played 99 games at third base and 12 games at short, while Filarski played 23 games at third. Usually dependable in the field and always an aggressive base runner, Pinky played 119 games and hit .218,

including five doubles and four triples, walked 32 times, scored 37 runs, and added 19 RBI.
- LF — Jochum typically played left (72 games), where she had been making great plays since the inaugural season of 1943. Showing her versatility, she also played ten games at first base. Because of her speed and range, she usually played center field in 1944 and 1945. In 1948, the all-around fan favorite from Cincinnati played 107 games, hitting .195, producing two doubles, four triples, one homer, and 24 RBI. Equally important, Betsy pitched 29 games and had a 14–13 mark. Her ERA of 1.51 was tenth best in the loop, and several of her losses were due to errors.
- CF — Wagoner, the 18-year-old rising star who grew up playing baseball and basketball, graduated from high school in Bolivar, Missouri, in June 1948. She spent four games with Muskegon before being shifted to South Bend. Altogether, the rookie played 84 games, 82 in center, and replaced the weak-hitting Daisy Junor (.125), who was traded to Springfield on July 2. A singles hitter with little power, Betty topped the Sox by averaging .278, adding two doubles, one triple, and 11 RBI. Oddly, she walked, struck out, and scored 42 times each.
- RF — Mahon covered right field, when she was not filling in at second base (14 games). She batted .258, second on the Sox behind Wagoner. Playing 117 games and again showing good power, Lib slugged 12 doubles, four triples, and two home runs. She also scored 59 runs and led the club with 65 RBI, more than twice the run production of any teammate.
- C — The receiver's position was the Achilles heel of South Bend early in the season when Baker, despite her erratic throwing arm, still caught 49 games, primarily due to her batting prowess. Playing all 126 regular season games, 49 as catcher, 49 at second, and a few at first, the photogenic Bonnie ranked fourth

Senaida "Shoo Shoo" Wirth — South Bend's most popular shortstop, circa 1948 (courtesy of the Louise Pettus Archives and Special Collections, Winthrop University).

on the team at .233, adding three doubles, four triples, and 29 RBI, and led the team in runs scored with 62. Metrolis, expected to succeed Baker because of her defensive skills, suffered knee injuries and caught only 12 games. Stovroff, 17 years old, was an excellent defensive player who arrived from Springfield on July 16. Shirley hit .158 in 100 games (half for the Sallies), but she solidified the position of catcher and became Faut's preferred receiver. Janet Jamieson, a rookie from Minneapolis who mainly coached first base, caught one game on September 1, going hitless in one trip for the season.

For pitching, the Blue Sox relied mainly on four starters, but Faut was again the team's brightest star. Pleasant but often reserved while also talented and determined, she had to overcome physical changes from having her first child, Larry, at the end of March. Though her control was sometimes off during games through July, Jean, who also hit .231, played herself into game condition and became the equal of any All-American hurler in August and September. The Pennsylvania right-hander, who quietly endured a difficult personal life that included being a wife and a mother in her "spare" time,[77] fashioned a 16–11 record with an ERA of 1.44, seventh best in the circuit.

Indeed, the manager relied on his "Big Three," meaning Faut, Jochum, and Faralla. Second to Faut, Jochum won 14 games, but South Bend's biggest pitching surprise was Faralla, the pretty sidearmer who was allocated to South Bend at Opa-Locka after pitching for Fort Wayne in 1947. The Daisies did not want her, but McManus worked to improve her pitching, and she posted a 10–20 record with a 1.99 ERA. Faralla, who hurled two no-hitters among her ten wins, was too often hurt — like Jochum — by errors or by too little offensive support. Remarkably, 13 of Lil's 20 losses came by one run, and she won twice by the no-hit route. Faralla pitched every third or fourth day she also helped the Sox by playing the outfield 18 times and by pinch-hitting. In 66 games, she hit .225 with three doubles and 23 RBI.

McManus used four other pitchers, notably Ruth Williams. After completing her teaching duties, the curveballer posted a modest record of 10–10 and an ERA of 2.25. Spot starter Lou Arnold, another slowballing right-hander, pitched 20 games and posted a 4–4 mark with a 4.06 ERA. Chi-Chi Gallegos, the hard-throwing right-hander who stood barely five feet tall, was often limited by a sore arm, and she had a 2–6 record with a fat 5.79 ERA. Jaynie Krick, an 18-year-old rookie who also played as a reserve in the outfield (31 games), appeared in 52 games, batted .191, and pitched 13 times, mostly in mop-up work, finishing with a 2–6 mark and a 4.12 ERA.

McManus deserved more credit from team officials. After Faut shut out Racine, 4–0, on July 17, Jim Costin explained that Marty's "long and patient coaching of the Blue Sox is at last bearing fruit." Despite having few good pitchers to start the season, the pilot "has his pitching staff in form now, his fielding has been little less than brilliant, and his direction of the base runners has been smart and tricky, as last night's big turnout of 2,506 fans saw to their great delight."[78]

Behind the scenes, however, Harold Dailey meddled in managing the Blue Sox. After the season ended, McManus resigned. In a long letter to Dailey, he accused the club president of interference as well as breaking his promise of a $250 bonus to the pilot. On one occasion, McManus wrote that Dailey went so far as to come down into the dugout and call the players "bitches," thus insulting the team.[79] Dailey, for his part, countered in his notes for the season that McManus was "Drunk 9/10th of the time," a phony claim that four players, notably Jochum, Koehn, and Mahon, later stated in writing was false.[80]

Still, South Bend fielded one of the better lineups as the league made baseball history. Writing about the circuit in a Sunday newspaper story published in July, sportswriter Robert Sullivan summarized the loop since 1943, explaining that 200 players on ten teams were playing *baseball*, not softball. "The AAGBL game is fast, tight and highly professional. The girls play hard and for keeps," Sullivan observed. All of the players, from the U.S., Canada, and Cuba, "have at least one thing in common — devotion to baseball that is almost religious."

Further, the women played with emotion. Sullivan, a male writing about females playing a man's game, explained that men mainly played ball with "their muscles and sometimes their brains." Thus, if a conflict developed, the result would be a few profane insults, and if blows seemed imminent, the manager would separate the contestants, and afterward, the two would play ball together. "But if two of the girls get on the outs," Sullivan said, "and comes a tight place like a possible double play, one may refuse to throw the ball to the other because she's mad at her." The story featured several pictures, and one illustrated the league's glamour image. The photo showed Betty Whiting putting bobby pins into the hair of Marie Kruckel, and the caption read, "By the Rules: Boyish bobs are banned by AAGBL and grooming must be as perfect as possible."[81]

The photo made for great publicity, but most players had abandoned applying makeup and lipstick before games. Instead, the league faced a crossroads in 1948 with overhand pitching, the expensive burden of two failing teams, and a shortage of quality players. Partly as a result, there was a decline in the number of first-rate newspaper or magazine articles such as Sullivan's that once provided the Girls' Pro Circuit with essential national exposure.

Win Some, Lose Some

After two losses on Memorial Day left the team with a 7–13 mark, South Bend fashioned a 49–51 record for the rest of the regular season. The longest winning streak was seven games, but the longest losing skein was eight games. Most of the streaks were two or three games. Beginning on Saturday, July 24, at Playland, the Blue Sox lost the first three out of four tilts to Kenosha. Following a 3–0 loss and a rained-out nightcap on Sunday, the teams played twice on Monday. In the opener, Faralla hurled a four-hitter but still lost to Ruby Stephens, 1–0, when, in the fourth frame, Regina native Christine Jewett singled, stole second, and scored when Alice Hohlmayer doubled. Finally, after losing seven of eight games, the Sox tasted victory in the nightcap, 7–1, as Jochum fired a three-hitter while Wirth and Meyer led an eight-hit assault with two each.[82]

Enjoying the season's longest stretch of Playland appearances as well as their home-away-from-home families and surroundings, the Blue Sox hosted the orchid-clad Daisies for three games, and won them all. On Tuesday, July 27, a crowd of 1,684, including a number of "boo birds," saw Faut's 5–3 victory. The Blue Sox moved ahead with three runs in the second, capped by Baker's two-run single. But in the fifth, when McManus removed Wagoner — who had legged out two bunts — for Jochum, several fans booed the manager. Wagoner had a charley horse, and most spectators understood the manager was trying to prevent a worse injury. Still, after Jochum was tagged out at home on a squeeze play gone awry, the fans vented their displeasure with McManus. Another double play in the sixth brought forth more boos, while many of the "faithful" seemed to take Faut's five-hitter for granted.[83]

Following two more wins over Fort Wayne, Springfield came to the LaSalle Hotel and Playland on Friday, July 30, and the traveling Sallies broke the home team's four-game win streak, 5–4. However, Sallies manager Carson Bigbee was stricken with a heart attack before leaving the hotel, and center fielder Jeep Stoll managed the team, the first time in All-American history that a team was piloted by either a female or a player. Faralla took the loss, after Stoll turned Lil's shot at a two-run triple to deep right-center into a fine catch and an inning-ending double play at second base. The fielding gem earned Stoll an ovation. The Blue Sox rapped nine hits, drew four walks, and received help from four errors, but in the tenth with runners at second and third, Mildred Meacham bunted to Faralla, who threw wildly to home plate, and Springfield (31–55) won.[84]

Resilient, the Blue Sox won on Saturday, 6–1, led by the big bat of Mahon, who singled twice and tripled. Lib's long drive was a home run that stuck in the wire fence, according to umpire Al Chapman, who reaped a chorus of boos when he ruled it a three-bagger. Jochum hurled a four-hitter and improved to 11–6, best for the Blue Sox.[85] The win started the South Benders on a string of seven straight victories, including two home successes against Springfield on Sunday.

The skein ended in a twin bill on Thursday, August 5, when South Bend split with lowly Chicago (31–59). Williams hurled a 3–0 shutout in the lid-lifter, but Gallegos, displaying what Jim Costin called her "wild-as-a-March-hare" form, lost the late tilt, 10–3. Wirth, during the midday practice, suffered a badly bruised knee sliding into third base for the benefit of photographer Hy Peshkin, who was taking photos for a *Collier's* story to be published early in 1949. Later, Shirley Stovroff left the game with a bruised knee, and Betty Whiting, who replaced her as catcher, departed after being grazed in the head by a bat.[86] On Friday night, playing another twin bill without Wirth, South Bend deflated a warm crowd of 2,062 by losing twice to Peoria, 3–0 and 3–2. The downcast Sox sported a 45–46 record as they rode through the night to Muskegon.[87]

Closing Out the Regular Season

As the season wound down, South Bend opened the trip at Muskegon on Saturday, August 7, with another fine performance by Faut, who fired a seven-hitter to win, 4–2. As a result, the Blue Sox improved to 46–46, tying Muskegon (47–47) for second place.[88] On Sunday, Williams twirled a four-hitter for a 5–1 victory, boosted by a three-run fifth inning sparked by Mahon's two-run single, and Whiting, who also belted a triple and a single, added a run-scoring base hit.[89]

However, during the next 16 days, the South Benders' streaky performances were shown again. They lost the last two games at Muskegon, won only the opener of a four-game stand at Chicago, returned to Playland and fell twice to Muskegon, traveled to Grand Rapids and captured only the finale of a four-game series, and rode the bus with the built-in poker table to Rockford, where the Peaches won three out of four games. The fourth loss to the Peaches, a 3–0 defeat despite Faralla's five-hitter, marked the club's 11th loss in 13 games.[90]

South Bend returned to Playland on Wednesday, August 25, and defeated division-leading Grand Rapids, 6–3, to launch the final nine-game home stand on a winning note. Williams, saved by Faralla's two and one-third innings of scoreless relief, won the game thanks to her teammates' 12 hits and a four-run burst in the first frame — helping the struggling Sox improve to a 51–59 record.[91]

In an exciting follow-up on Thursday, Faut, no stranger to the pressure of extra-inning games during her eight-year career, lost a titanic duel to Al Haylett, who won her 23rd game in the 14th inning, 1–0, when Pepper Paire squeezed home a run.[92] In the late game, South Bend led, 5–3, when the loop's curfew ended the game after four innings of a seven-frame contest. The umpires called it no contest, but the next day, Max Carey ruled the game could be completed. Jochum finished her game and won, 6–4, in the first game of two played on Friday. In the regulation game, the Chicks won behind Earp, 4–1, as Faralla was backed by only five hits.[93]

On Saturday, August 28, the Blue Sox hosted the high-flying Peaches and split another doubleheader, as Alabama star Mobile Holgerson tossed a one-hitter to defeat Williams in the opener, 7–1. In the nightcap, the local favorites again showed their competitive fire and thrilled 1,702 sweltering spectators by rallying for three runs in the eighth to help Krick win, 4–3. Prospects for success looked dim with two outs in the eighth, but Filarski tripled to right, Pirok was hit by a pitch, and Whiting walked. Wagoner drew a bases-loaded walk for one run, and Baker lined a two-run single for the winning margin.[94] Still, on Sunday night, playing a third straight twin bill at Playland, the Blue Sox lost a pair of shutouts. Faut hurled a sterling two-hitter but lost, 2–0, when two unearned runs—aided by Filarski's miss of a bunt and Baker's wild throw to third—scored in the seventh. The nightcap was all Rockford as Jochum and Gallegos both suffered off nights, and the Peaches racked up 11 hits to win, 2–0.[95]

On Monday night at Playland, the Blue Sox, professionals to the end, rode Faralla's five-hitter to a 2–0 victory.[96] On Tuesday, making up a game postponed from August 14, the Blue Sox hosted the Lassies and won, 5–3, when Faut retired the final batter with two runs already home and the tying runs aboard. The Sox scored five times in the first three frames, and Williams, aided by Faut, held the lead.[97]

Traveling to Kenosha for a three-game stand, the Blue Sox lost all three, the finale being a 16-inning tilt on Friday, September 3, when Faralla walked in the winning run to lose, 7–6.[98] The trip's brightest highlight came in a game at Racine on Saturday when Faut pitched her first no-hitter to win, 7–0. The Blue Sox scored enough to win in the first inning on Mahon's two-run double, but they raked three Belles pitchers for nine hits.[99] The Blue Sox dropped the next two games to the Sallies, the first by a 5–1 score in Michigan City, Indiana,[100] and the second at Playland as part of the season-ending Labor Day twin bill. Barr won a one-hitter, 1–0, as South Bend was shut out for the 23rd time. In the nightcap, Arnold gave her best performance, winning a two-hitter, 12–2. The Sox pounded out 12 safeties, two each by Baker, Wirth, and Mahon. Still, the Blue Sox finished with a 57–69 mark, the team's worst season to date.[101]

South Bend's Anticlimax and the League's Zenith

South Bend, playing in a ten-team loop with one non-competitive team in each division, finished third in the East and moved into the best-of-five semifinal playoff against Grand Rapids, the 1947 Shaughnessy Champion and winner of the Eastern Division in 1948 with a 77–47 ledger. Tuesday, September 7, was an off day, and the Chicks arrived in South Bend for Wednesday evening's 8:15 opener. The winner of the series between Grand Rapids and South Bend would meet the winner of the matchup between second-place Muskegon and fourth-place Fort Wayne. Also, the West had first-place Racine meeting third-place Peoria, and second-place Rockford facing fourth-place Kenosha. McManus announced that Jean Faut, awarded a classy wrist watch for being named the club's most valuable pitcher, would face Al Haylett, the league's top hurler with a 25–5 record and a remarkable ERA of 0.77.[102] Instead, rain and wet grounds postponed the opener.

Thursday's contest was an All-American classic, one of the many great performances the hard-throwing Faut made in her storied career, and Haylett very nearly matched it. The teams battled for 20 innings, until South Bend won, 3–2, at 12:34 am (the league suspended the 11:30 curfew for playoffs). Haylett surrendered 11 hits, walked four, and struck out 16, and Faut yielded eight hits, issued ten walks, and fanned 13, but in the end, an error and a wild pitch beat Grand Rapids. In the 20th, Whiting opened with a popout to rookie shortstop Marilyn Olinger. Up next, Shirley Stovroff reached base on an error. Baker singled and Filarski beat out a roller to load the sacks. Haylett, perhaps tired, uncorked a wild pitch, and Stovroff raced home with the winning run to the cheers of a crowd that once numbered 1,821.[103]

On Friday night before 1,239 fans, the year's smallest turnout in South Bend, Millie Earp outdueled Betsy Jochum as Grand Rapids won in 11 innings, 3–2. After the Blue Sox took a 2–1 lead in the fifth, the Chicks tied the score in the seventh on Earp's RBI single, and in the 11th, after a pair of singles, Millie's clutch base hit scored the eventual game-winner.[104]

Traveling to Grand Rapids for Saturday night's contest, the blue-clad visitors won just one game. Entertaining an excited crowd of 3,719, the Chicks matched the Blue Sox inning for inning with strong defense and heads-up baseball, but the likeable Faralla, a tough-luck hurler all year, smiled as she walked off the field with a 2–1 victory over Gabby Ziegler, normally a second sacker. Grand Rapids took the lead in the fourth frame on Satterfield's run-scoring single. The visitors tied the score in the sixth when Stovroff singled, Baker singled her to third, and Shirley scored on Wagoner's ground ball. In the seventh, Faralla walked and Pirok hit a triple to center that scored the winning run, thanks to Lil's stellar hurling.[105]

Despite another fine performance by Faut on Sunday, South Bend's elusive third playoff victory failed to materialize. Instead, the Chicks won a 15-inning contest, 1–0, the fourth straight extra-inning battle of the year between Haylett and Faut. In the visitors' 15th, with the bases loaded and one out, Faut lined a shot over second base, but center fielder Lorraine Fisher speared the ball at her shoe tops — and her quick throw held the runners. Filarski drove the next pitch to deep left-center, but Fisher made a fine running catch to end the inning. In the Chicks' 15th, a tired Faut walked the first two batters and hit the third, and Pepper Paire's long fly gave the home team the hard-fought victory.[106] On Monday night, the disappointed South Benders fell to Earp's one-hitter, 3–0. Baker notched the visitors' only hit, a double in the seventh, Jochum worked five innings and surrendered a pair of runs, and Faralla finished up. The Blue Sox had a number of highlights, including five sensational plays by Wirth, but their longest season was over.[107]

In the end, Fort Wayne surprised Grand Rapids in three games, but Rockford, winner of the Western Division playoffs, won the Shaughnessy title by defeating the Daisies in five games.[108]

In South Bend, however, the loss in Grand Rapids marked one more disappointing end to a once-promising season. Marty McManus resigned, supposedly due to poor health, but mainly because of Harold Dailey's interference with his managing.[109] Also, chaperone Lucille Moore resigned after four seasons, and Dailey announced that the club would bring back Marge Stefani, who spent 1948 as Rockford's player-chaperone. "It is practically certain that a housecleaning job is in sight for the new manager," observed Jim Costin, "as several of the players depended upon to come through this year failed to live up to expectations, causing the team to have the worst year in its six-year existence, despite the presence of one of the best pitching staffs in the league."[110] Nevertheless, the Blue Sox players were already hoping the year 1949 would finally produce a championship in South Bend.

In a footnote to the season, Betsy Jochum — who again displayed her all-around talent, this year adding her hard fastball, sharp curve, and good control to her stellar outfielding and solid hitting — took McManus' advice and asked Dailey for a raise. Instead, the club's president, whose mistreatment pushed the manager to resign, traded one of the loop's all-time standouts to Peoria. When Betsy learned of the deal from another player, she quit baseball, but remained in South Bend to live and work.[111] The stark contrast of Jochum's treatment compared to Baker's rumored signing bonus of $2,500, both approved by Dailey, again showed that the league's teams were willing to pay for an All American-type girl who had a "showbiz" personality as well as a good bat.[112]

In retrospect, the All-American Girls Baseball League's expansion to ten teams was doomed from the start. As it developed, the Springfield Sallies became a traveling team by mid–June, and the Chicago Colleens lasted the entire season, but left the circuit in late September. Neither the Sallies nor the Colleens, however, had any real hope of rising above last place in their respective divisions. The larger question was whether the glamour circuit would continue to prosper, as the lyrics to Sarah Vaughan's current hit song promised, "It's summertime, and living is easy." Instead, while the women's teams were finally playing baseball, but with a larger ball and smaller diamond distances, several team officials, including those with South Bend, feared the Girls' Pro League had reached its glorious zenith.[113]

• 7 •

The Blue Sox and the Peaches Win the Pennant: 1949

"Well, the South Bend Blue Sox and the Rockford Peaches after battling through 114 games since last May have finished way ahead of the All American Girls Baseball League pack without accomplishing anything decisive"—Paul Neville, *South Bend Tribune*, September 6, 1949[1]

Mid-Season Changes

Baseball played by women was rather different from the game played by men, and if the problems encountered by Dick Bass, manager of the Fort Wayne Daisies, were any example, piloting a girls' team was easier said than done. Sportswriter Bill Fay, writing for *Collier's*, explained that the Daisies were leading the All-American League in the middle of 1948 when two of the married regulars became "acutely pregnant." As it developed, Bass lost his job, but the Daisies rebounded and advanced to the finals of the Shaughnessy Playoffs, losing in five games to Rockford.

Altogether, the league, composed of ten teams, attracted 910,000 fans in 1948, but two teams, the Springfield Sallies and the Chicago Colleens, folded after the season. Still, the league was prospering, even if 28 managers had resigned or been fired since the circuit began in 1943. For the record, players earned from $85 to $125 per week. On the diamond, they took orders from men. Off the field, reported Fay, they were counseled by women, "vigilant team chaperones who knew how to discourage bleacher wolves and dugout-door Johnnies."

The women looked like they ran and threw a baseball as well as men, but that was an "optical illusion" created by the loop's president, Max Carey. As Carey explained it, "by putting our bases 72 feet apart, fixing our pitching distance at 50 feet and using a ball that's not quite as lively as that big-league jack-rabbit, our girls play baseball that looks as fast as a major-league game on a 90-foot [base path] diamond." The league combined femininity with skills, good looks with talent, grace with hustle. Bill Fay illustrated those points with a story about former Grand Rapids manager Benny Meyer, who was photographed with his Chicks, a team full of "ballet-skirted, bare-thighed, pretty girls." Several days later, Meyer received a letter from his wife in Arkansas. She sent the clipping and marked an X on her husband. Benny wired home, "Dear Ma. It ain't the femininity that gets me. It's the skill."[2] The story, perhaps apocryphal, suggested the perils for the men who tried to run a women's game in what was traditionally a masculine milieu.

A glimpse into that long-ago season was recorded by the management of the Rockford

Peaches. The team filmed part of pregame practice and an afternoon game at Peoria Stadium against the Redwings. The film allowed the viewer to see all the usual events of a trip to ballpark, including the Peaches taking batting and infield practice. For example, the manager hit grounders to the fielders, who caught the ball, flipped it to second base to begin a double play, or threw to first to practice getting a runner out. Overall, the rhythm of the practice, including the girl catching the infielder's return throw and flipping the ball to the manager, who hit another grounder, and the flow of the game, the pitching, the hard swings of the batters, the runners hustling around the bases, the adept defensive plays, and the throws by the fielders, all looked like any other professional game — except that the players were girls wearing short-skirted uniforms.[3]

In addition, the league evolved almost every season, adjusting from modified fast-pitch softball with an underhand delivery in 1943 to baseball with a much smaller ball and overhand pitching in 1948. In mid–1949, the league made further changes to appeal to fans who loved baseball, but couldn't watch major or minor league games in Midwestern cities such as South Bend, Grand Rapids, or Rockford. The DeBeer Company's red-seamed, livelier ball that was ten inches in circumference, down from the ten and three-eighths inches ball, came into play, and to balance the hoped-for harder hitting, the pitching distance was lengthened from 50 to 55 feet.[4]

The league was a historic work in progress, and the players had to adapt their pitching, batting, and fielding skills almost every season. As early as January 5, 1949, circuit officials considered introducing the new ball, but the decision was deferred until the ball could first be tested in practices.[5] "Finally, league management, always concerned with what the public wanted," Barbara Gregorich explained in *Women at Play*, "concluded that what fans liked most of all was a live ball — one that traveled far and fast and resonated with a resounding crack when the bat met it squarely."[6] That goal was finally achieved in mid–1949.

On Friday, July 22, in the first game at South Bend's Playland Park with the livelier ball in play, the Blue Sox topped the Chicks, 7–3, as pitchers, hitters, and fielders alike got used to the new horsehide. Blue Sox starter Ruth Williams, relying on slow curves and good control, won, giving up five hits and four walks. Grand Rapids' Earlene "Beans" Risinger lasted four innings, but manager Johnny Rawlings yanked her in the fifth after the tall right-hander gave up a single and two walks, making five free passes for the game. On a pleasant evening before a big crowd of 2,579, the home team pounded 11 hits off Risinger and Jayne Bittner. Shortstop Shoo-Shoo Wirth rapped three singles, and Lib Mahon, the Sox's slugging left fielder, connected for three hits, including two run-scoring doubles. Reported the *South Bend Tribune*, "The outfielders on both sides chased down some of the longest balls hit in Playland Park this year."[7]

The All-American game as played on often inadequately-lit diamonds in eight Midwestern cities was now quite similar to regulation baseball, but perhaps that wasn't enough for the league to survive. The circuit already found it harder to attract talented new players, and South Bend made the only profit in 1948, a mere $236.16. In fact, the pioneering loop was beginning a slow decline.[8]

Let's Play Ball

By springtime, most of the Blue Sox' veterans from 1948 were ready to play ball again, but the league had made important changes. First, under pressure to cut expenses from local boards of directors, including South Bend chief Harold Dailey, Max Carey and league officials decided teams could hold individual spring camps, dropping the circuit's tradition of group training camps dating to the tryouts and drills at Wrigley Field in 1943.[9] South Bend's workouts for pitchers and catchers were set to begin on Wednesday, April 27, at Playland.[10]

For the city's team, an important change was the new manager, silver-haired Dave Bancroft. A slick-fielding shortstop with good hands who spent 16 seasons in the National League, Bancroft enjoyed his best years as the Giants' field leader from 1921 through 1923. After the shortstop turned 32, John McGraw dealt the aging veteran to the Boston Braves, where Bancroft served as player-manager from 1924 through 1927. A Baseball Hall of Famer who would be inducted in 1971, the Sioux City, Iowa, native had no experience managing women, but he was a good strategist, so he was respected in the Girls' Pro League.[11]

Bancroft, starting strong, ran 21 players through twice-a-day workouts at Playland for two weeks. The roster included right-hander Ruth Williams, still teaching at Nescopeck, near Philadelphia, and stellar flychaser Lib Mahon, teaching at South Bend's Jefferson Elementary. Neither could attend the camp nor play full-time until school was out. Other pitchers drilling in the cool April breezes were Jean Faut, Lil Faralla, Jaynie Krick, and Lou Arnold. Two rookies were still attending high school, Dolores Mueller and Theresa McKinley, and they trained on weekends. The team's three experienced catchers were Norma Metrolis, who missed most of 1948 with a knee injury; Shirley Stovroff, who caught most of the games after arriving in a mid-season trade; and Rita Briggs, the onetime Massachusetts high school star who was a catcher on her school's boys' varsity team and spent most of 1947 and 1948 with the Peaches. The infielders were Betty Whiting, Bonnie Baker, Shoo-Shoo Wirth, Marge Callaghan (acquired from the Daisies), Norma Whitney, and Dolores "Dolly" Niemiec, a Chicago high school girl who played with the Colleens in 1948. Besides Mahon, the Sox had two outfielders: good-hitting Betty Wagoner and Jeep Stoll, who starred for the Sallies in 1948. Further, southpaw Jo Hasham, who posted an 0–6 record for Muskegon and Peoria, was working out. Exhibitions would soon begin, and South Bend was slated to host Rockford in the season's opener on Sunday, May 22.[12]

When the USSR's Berlin Blockade was about to end and perhaps lessen East-West tensions in the Cold War,[13] Jim Costin, 55 years old and one of South Bend's greatest sports fans, passed away on Sunday, May 8. Costin died of a coronary thrombosis while his wife and youngest daughter, Mina, were attending church. Jim began his long journalistic career in his hometown of Peru, Indiana, in 1909, served in the Navy during World War I, and returned to practice his craft with several newspapers. He became sports editor of the *Tribune* in 1942.[14] He quickly became an astute Blue Sox fan and critic, and he chronicled the ball team's successes and failures until his last day. Costin was replaced by Paul Neville, the new Sox expert.[15]

Three days later, South Bend and Fort Wayne kicked off an eight-game exhibition tour in the tri-state region, and the Blue Sox rode hurling by Faut and Arnold to a 7–4 win in Van Wert, Ohio.[16] South Bend won every exhibition but the finale, including games at Lansing, Michigan (two); Milford, Indiana; Jackson, Michigan; and Lima, Ohio (two). For the Friday twin bill at Lima, Marge Stefani, the chaperone, replaced Bancroft for a night and managed the Sox to a split.[17] Back in their adopted home town on Saturday, the Blue Sox practiced at mid-day and then settled into the private homes where they roomed.

The *Tribune* touted the opening day doubleheader against Rockford, last year's All-American champions. On Sunday evening, May 22, the South Benders prepared to launch the 1949 campaign at Playland Park in a festival-type atmosphere, including a fireworks display. Local officials expected a big crowd, but rain and wet grounds caused a postponement.[18] The two teams returned on Monday night, and Faut started strong, yielding one hit until the ninth, when she tired and gave up three runs on four hits, but hung on to win, 9–3. Right-hander Mobile (Holgerson) Silvestri, married in the offseason, pitched well for Rockford, but seven errors killed the Peaches. Faut singled twice in five trips and Stovroff doubled to left, marking three of the home team's six safe blows. Afterward, the audience of 2,107 enjoyed the big fireworks display. South Bend's 1–0 start tied the Sox for first place with Grand Rapids and Fort Wayne.[19]

The first Blue Sox triumph was followed by two more. Peoria arrived at Playland for a single game on Tuesday night, and Faralla's five-hitter led the home team to a 5–2 victory. Wirth singled to lead off the first, and after a series of Peoria miscues, Shoo-Shoo scored the first run. The Blue Sox tallied twice in the third, thanks to hits by second sacker Bonnie Baker (who went 2-for-3) and center fielder Rita Briggs, and some fancy baserunning.[20] Traveling to Peoria on Wednesday, the teams lost a day when wet grounds caused a cancellation. On Thursday at Peoria Stadium, 1,638 fans braved a chilly evening to see Peoria's Dottie Mueller scatter three hits, but Jo Hasham, the former Redwing, departed with the bases loaded in the eighth. Faut relieved, escaped the jam, and pitched shutout ball until the visitors scored a run in the 12th to win, 1–0.[21]

Batter Up — Posing for the annual team picture, South Bend's 1949 players appear ready to hit. Standing in the back row (left to right) are Bonnie Baker, Jeep Stoll, Jean Faut, Shoo-Shoo Wirth, Rita Briggs, Shirley Stovroff, Helen Filarski, Betty Whiting, and Betty Wagoner. Kneeling in front are Marge Stefani, chaperone, Lil Faralla, Norma Metrolis, Josephine Hasham, Marge Callaghan, Dolly Niemiec, Jaynie Krick, Dolores Mueller, Lou Arnold, and Dave Bancroft, manager (courtesy of the Louise Pettus Archives and Special Collections, Winthrop University).

The Blue Sox, however, lost three one-run games on the first trip of the year to Rockford. On Friday, Mobile Silvestri, who hurled two no-hitters in 1948, just missed another one, as Wirth led off with a single in the ninth, but the Peaches eked out a 1–0 victory, managing three hits off Faralla.[22] On Saturday, South Bend, in one of the team's all-too-frequent marathon contests, lost in 16 innings, 1–0, when Wirth muffed two grounders around a walk. Faut, suffering the loss, took over for Arnold in the ninth, worked seven frames, and deserved a better fate.[23] On Sunday evening, the Blue Sox lost another heartbreaker, 2–1, this time in 12 stanzas. Hasham hooked up with Lois Florreich, the former South Bender, in a tense pitchers' battle. The blue-uniformed visitors scored in the fifth, the home team tied the game in the seventh, and the Peaches won in the 12th on Ruth Richard's bases-loaded bunt. The night's action left Rockford in first place with a 6–1 record, Kenosha and Muskegon were tied for second with 5–4 marks, and South Bend was fourth at 3–3. In the second division, Racine and Grand Rapids were tied for sixth with 3–4 ledgers, Peoria ranked seventh (2–4), and Fort Wayne was last (2–5).[24]

Keep On Winning

Continuing the week-long trip to Fort Wayne on Memorial Day, Monday, May 30, the Blue Sox split a holiday doubleheader with the Daisies. In the opener, which lasted nine frames instead of the scheduled seven, Faut outdueled Kay Blumetta, and each right-hander whitewashed the opposition for eight innings. Finally, the Blue Sox won, 4–0, scoring four unearned runs in the ninth on three errors and singles by Stoll, Filarski, and Whiting. In the nightcap, Jaynie Krick's wildness and six team errors cost the Blue Sox a 6–3 defeat, as the Daisies scored one run in the first, three runs in the fourth and two more in the fifth — all with one hit, while former South Bender Betty Luna tossed a four-hitter.[25] On Tuesday, despite third baseman Betty (Petryna) Allen's record-breaking 12 assists, the sidearming Faralla hurled a four-hitter and the Sox beat Millie Deegan, 4–0.[26]

Returning to Playland Park on Wednesday, June 1, the Blue Sox won three out of four tilts against Kenosha. Arnold started the opener, but later tired. In the seventh, four Comet hits and two infield errors gave the lime green-uniformed visitors four runs and a 7–5 lead. Faut relieved and stopped the rally, and in the home seventh, Rita Briggs' two-run single tied the game. In the eighth, Faut won her own game, 8–7, with a looping RBI single to left-center.[27] On Thursday, the Blue Sox swept a twin bill by scores of 10–4 and 7–4. Hasham won for the first time in the opener, scattering eight hits, and Krick, the rookie, notched her first victory in the nightcap, even though surrendering nine hits.[28] But on Friday, Kenosha broke the home team's four-game streak, rallying from a 4–0 deficit in the ninth to win, 5–4. The results left South Bend in second place with an 8–5 record, but red-hot Rockford paced the league with a 12–1 ledger.[29]

The local heroines bounced back by bopping seventh-place Racine four straight times, starting with a 14–3 rout on Saturday. Faut counted her fifth win, but she tired in the seventh, yielding the last two runs. The Blue Sox clinched the game with three runs in the eighth, and Faralla held the big lead, while Racine's Ellie Dapkus and Sugar Koehn together surrendered 14 hits.[30]

Racine, however, was no longer a formidable foe. The play of the veteran Belles showed one of the league's problems — what Lois Browne termed "aging in place."[31] The eight All-American teams were led by experienced players, but none more so than the Belles, who now lacked a formidable pitching staff. In Sunday's doubleheader, South Bend won twice, 3–0 and 15–10. Hasham hurled a one-hitter in the opener to defeat onetime ace Jo Winter (she was 11–13 in 1949), and Baker singled home the first run in the second inning. In the two hour and 20-minute late game, the Sox won with a 12-run second frame, as Erma Bergmann (11–14 for the season) and Irene Kotowicz (8–15) coughed up a combined 13 hits. Krick, often wild, earned credit for her second win. However, the 19-year-old from Auburn, Indiana, walked eleven and left during the Belles' four-run rally in the eighth, and Arnold closed out the victory.[32]

After sweeping the Belles, the Blue Sox left on a road trip to Michigan to visit Muskegon and Grand Rapids for three games each. On the same night that Paul Neville was named the *South Bend Tribune's* sports editor, Faralla, permitting five hits, snuffed rallies in the seventh and eighth to beat the Lassies, 2–1. Faut, playing left field, hit an RBI single in the first, and Whiting beat out a bunt in the fourth to score Wagoner, who walked and stole second.[33] On Tuesday in near 40-degree weather, Faut, no stranger to extra-inning battles, waged a 16-inning duel with Dodie Barr that ended in a 1–1 tie, after the league's curfew stopped the three-hour contest.[34] On Wednesday, the Indiana visitors resumed their winning ways as Arnold, pitching tough, outlasted former Belle Anna Hutchison, hitting a run-scoring double in the ninth to win her own game, 3–2. When Rockford (13–6) fell to Racine, the excited South Benders owned first place with a 13–5 mark.[35]

The Blue Sox, after winning nine of ten games and tying another, made the one-hour bus ride to Grand Rapids, but lost two out of three. On Thursday at South High Field, South Bend raked former nemesis Millie Earp for 12 hits. Hasham, who pitched seven frames, recorded a 5–3 triumph when the visitors rallied for three runs in the eighth, and Faut, relieving her, protected the lead.[36] On Friday, Tex Fischer won a two-hitter, 5–1, outlasting Faralla and Krick,[37] and the Chicks won on Saturday when Al Haylett tossed a two-hitter to top third-year right-hander Jette Vincent, 6–2. After Rockford beat Racine, the Peaches (15–7) moved ahead of the Sox (14–7).[38]

Battling for First Place

On Sunday, June 12, when the Blue Sox returned to Playland's familiar diamond, where the home plate area sat on racetrack cinders, Faut, the ace, lifted her team back on the winning track by hurling a 3–0 victory over visiting Muskegon. Jean, who went on to win a new personal best 20 games in 1949, including 13 shutouts, gave up a pair of singles.[39] Rain washed out the league's schedule on Monday, but the local favorites moved back into a tie for first place on Tuesday by dropping Grand Rapids, 5–2. Hasham, the lefty, was doing her part as the club's third pitcher behind Faut and Faralla by winning her fourth game. Jo scattered nine hits, three apiece by Connie Wisniewski and Doris Satterfield, but the Sox collected nine safeties, two each by Wirth and Mahon, and rode a three-run fifth and three double plays to the triumph.[40]

South Bend and Grand Rapids split a twin bill at Playland on Wednesday evening. In the lid-lifter, an audience of 2,005 saw the home team squander a four-run lead when the Chicks rallied for five runs in the sixth. Four of the ten visitors wearing gray uniforms who batted in the inning drew a walk. Faut, who relieved Williams, gave up two of the passes and a pair of hits, and took the 5–4 loss. In the nightcap, Faralla, who permitted three hits, won, 2–0, against Risinger, the 6'2" fastballer from Hess, Oklahoma, who deserved a better result from her two-hitter.[41] Thursday's finale with Grand Rapids was rained out, and the Sox departed by bus on Friday for Fort Wayne.[42]

South Bend's winning pattern, consisting of two or three victories followed by a loss and then more successes, was repeated in Fort Wayne. The diamond at Memorial Park was too soggy on Friday night, but the game was shifted to nearby Zollner Stadium, where the Blue Sox, behind Faut's stellar three-hitter, topped the Daisies, 4–1.[43] On Saturday, Hasham, her control and breaking ball steadily improving, won a five-hit shutout, 4–0. Mahon and Wagoner each contributed two hits, and the first two runs scored in the fourth on Donna Cook's wild pickoff throw.[44] Shifting back to Playland for two more games with the Daisies, the Blue Sox split a pair of squeakers, losing on Sunday as Millie Deegan hurled a 1–0 shutout,[45] and winning on Monday when Faut laid down a pinch run-scoring bunt in the tenth to win a 2–1 thriller for Williams. Elsewhere, Rockford also continued to win, edging Peoria, and the 22–7 Peaches led the 20–9 Blue Sox by two games.[46]

At Racine's Horlick Field starting on Tuesday, June 21, the blue-clad visitors won two out of three games. The fastballing Faut won a seven-hitter, 2–1, thanks to two unearned runs scored by her teammates. For the once-popular Belles, the paid attendance of 538 was an ill omen.[47]

On Wednesday, South Bend lost for the first time in 1949 to Racine, 6–2, as Hasham surrendered seven hits in five innings, and Vincent finished the game. Two Sox players were injured: Whiting was shaken up in a collision with Moe Trezza, and Filarski suffered a spike wound when tagging out the sliding Edie Perlick.[48] South Bend won on Thursday, 5–3, in a poorly-played game attended by 653 hardy fans. The Belles committed seven errors while the Blue Sox made three, making just one run earned of the eight runs scored, but Faralla's five-hitter showed what good pitching can do, even when the fielders make miscues.[49]

After splitting two games at Kenosha and returning to South Bend to defeat visiting Peoria two out of three times, the Blue Sox traveled to Rockford. On Wednesday, June 29, at the so-called "Peach Orchard," the league's best two teams staged a 15-inning battle with Faut prevailing over Nicky Fox, 3–1, when the Blue Sox scored twice in the 15th. The visitors scored in the tenth when Wagoner reached second on Alice "Al" Pollitt's error, Mahon popped out, Stoll singled the runner to third, Filarski fouled out, and Wirth singled for a 1–0 lead. In Rockford's half of the tenth, Ellie Callow singled, stole second, and Pollitt doubled to tie the score. In the 15th, Stoll singled for her fourth hit, Filarski walked, and Wirth sacrificed them along. Stoll scored on pinch-hitter Hasham's grounder, Faut and Baker singled for the second run, and Faut retired the Peaches, leaving first-place Rockford, now 26–9, one and a half games ahead of 26–12 South Bend.[50]

Rockford, always tough at home, won the next two tilts. On Thursday night, the day when a strike lasting more than ten weeks at Bendix ended and 2,800 employees returned to work,[51] an audience of 3,260, the biggest Beyer Stadium crowd so far, saw the Peaches reach Williams for seven hits and win, 5–0. Left-handed batting Dottie Kamenshek totaled four hits, but the highlight came on Ellie Callow's two-run homer in the seventh — for which she won $25. Florreich, firing her fastball with more control than usual, gave up four hits, including Baker's single and three more by Mahon.[52] On Friday, the visitors slipped as the Peaches grabbed a 2–1 verdict in a drizzle, thanks to fine hurling by Lou Erickson, who notched her seventh victory. Faralla, who was nursing a 1–0 lead until rain fell harder in the eighth, walked Kamenshek and Snookie (Harrell) Doyle. After a forceout, Rose Gacioch singled over shortstop to score the game-winning runs.

Afterward, the All-American standings showed Rockford leading the pack with a 28–

9 record, and South Bend in second place, now three and a half games back, with a 26–14 ledger. Grand Rapids ranked third with a 25–15 mark, and Kenosha was fourth at 22–20. The second-division clubs all had losing records: Fort Wayne was fifth at 17–21, Racine sixth at 16–25, Muskegon seventh at 14–25, and Peoria, the league's weakest club, had a 9–28 mark.[53]

The Livelier Baseball

When the new baseball, smaller and livelier with red seams, was introduced at Playland Park on Friday, July 22, South Bend defeated visiting Grand Rapids, 7–3, and tied Rockford for first place. South Bend and Rockford owned identical 42–20 marks,[54] and both finished the season tied for the league lead with records of 75–36. After losing two out of three at Rockford near the end of June, the Blue Sox closed the gap against the Peaches by fashioning a pair of six-game winning streaks (including one tie) separated by a 1–0 loss at Kenosha on July 8. Against the Comets, Faralla pitched well, but in the ninth, Marge Villa lined a two-out single to center, and the fleet Helen (Callaghan) Candaele, who walked and stole second, scored on a close play at the plate — barely beating Stoll's fine peg from center field to Briggs.[55]

Returning home, South Bend launched another six-game streak, defeating Racine twice, Kenosha twice, and Muskegon twice. The Lassies broke the string on Thursday, July 14, when Doris Sams, backed by two double plays, twirled a one-hitter to win, 3–1, while Williams and Vincent were hurt by three errors and a pair of unearned runs.[56] The Sox bounced back on Friday and rode Faralla's three-hitter to a 3–0 victory over the Lassies. The home team managed just three hits off the stingy Silvestri, but Baker bunted home a run in the first, Mahon doubled home a run in the fourth, and Filarski's sacrifice fly added a third score in the sixth.[57]

The league introduced the new baseball on Saturday, July 16, with startling results. The South Benders made the four-hour bus ride to Grand Rapids, followed by their customary registering at the Hotel Rowe, unpacking of bags, and practicing at midday. That evening, Faut, pitching the new ball for the first time, lost in unusual fashion, 8–7, when the Chicks rallied for three runs in the ninth. Faut, issuing a surprising 12 bases on balls, walked twice as many as Beans Risinger. Indeed, during four league games that night, the teams committed a total of 18 errors. The Blue Sox profited from the Chicks' handling of the livelier ball, as they scored four runs in the third frame on three walks, two hits, an error, a sacrifice, and Baker's two-out steal of home. The visitors added two runs in the fourth on two walks, an error, and Mahon's two-run single to left. In the end, Faut scattered six hits, and Risinger yielded eight, two apiece to Baker and Wagoner. After the night's action, South Bend fell to second place with a 39–17 record, and Rockford, victors over Racine, took the top spot by a few percentage points with a 38–16 mark.[58]

On Sunday, South Bend booted the ball five times and lost to the Chicks, 11–5, making a total of 19 runs scored by Grand Rapids in two games with the new ball. The Blue Sox outhit the home team, 10–8, but Hasham fell on errors. After Rockford lost a twin bill to Racine, South Bend's 39–18 mark lifted the visitors into first place by half a game over the 38–18 Peaches.[59]

Play with the new baseball proceeded, and teams were still adjusting to the ball and the new pitching distance when Grand Rapids faced South Bend at Playland on July 22.

The day before, manager Dave Bancroft agreed that the ball was "definitely jumpier." Bancroft and other pilots believed hurlers would reduce the number of walks allowed once they got used to the 55-foot pitching distance, but fielders needed to adjust to handling the livelier ball. "Throughout the league," reported the *South Bend Tribune*, "nearly as many errors were committed the first week the new ball was in play as were made during the first half of the season."[60]

The Blue Sox by Mid-Season

Based on All-American statistics through the games of July 11, South Bend, enjoying the franchise's best season to date, was leading the loop in hitting with a team mark of .208 and tied with Kenosha for first in fielding with a .961 average. Grand Rapids ranked second in hitting at .202, Kenosha was third at .194, Rockford fourth at .191, and Peoria last at .170. In fielding, Rockford's figure of .960 was one point behind South Bend and Kenosha. Grand Rapids was fourth at .958, while Peoria and Fort Wayne tied for seventh (last) with .940 marks.

For individual batting, Fort Wayne's Melba Alspaugh, an outfielder from Wichita, ranked first with her .328 average in 26 games, but she had only 64 at-bats and did not qualify for the league lead. Jean Faut ranked second, hitting .304 in 23 games, but her 56 trips to the plate also left her short of qualifying. Among the regulars, Connie Wisniewski paced the league with a .288 mark in 52 games. She also contributed 14 RBI, but Faut already had 13 RBI. The Chicks' Doris Satterfield ranked second with her .280 average in 53 games, but she racked up 31 RBI. Other top hitters included Racine's Edie Perlick, third at .265 and 21 RBI; Ellie Callow of Rockford, fourth at .262 and 21 RBI; Fort Wayne's Vivian Kellogg, fifth at .246 with 13 RBI; and sixth, Lib Mahon, who was averaging .244 with 18 RBI. Other South Benders included Jeep Stoll, .231 and 12 RBI; Betty Whiting, .224 and 18 RBI; Lil Faralla, .220 (for 17 games) and three RBI; Shoo-Shoo Wirth, .219 and 13 RBI; and Rita Briggs, .200 and eight RBI.

South Bend's pitching staff, the main reason for the club's success, featured Faut currently with a 12–3 record. To date, she had worked a remarkable 133 innings. The stellar Blue Sox staff also included Jo Hasham at 9–2 (97 innings), Lil Faralla at 6–6 (110 innings), Ruth Williams at 5–1 (57 innings), Lou Arnold at 1–1 (33 innings), and Jette Vincent, who was 0–1 in 9 innings.[61]

Faut was enjoying her finest season to date. Twenty-four in 1949, Jean was maturing as an athlete. Later, she reflected, "You get better, your control gets better. You work on new pitches." Faut, unlike Lois Florreich, did not have intimidating speed, but Dottie Kamenshek ranked Jean the best pitcher in the league because, regardless of speed, she got batters out. Faut recalled that her greatest asset was good control. She had strong wrists and could throw different pitches: "I had a good curveball and could throw it overhand, three-quarters, or sidearm. If overhand, it went straight down. I threw a screwball, like a slider, but not often. And a fastball. I could throw them with different speeds." Jean knew that a big part of the game was mental. She varied the pitches and the rotation she put on the ball for each batter. "They'd never know what was coming, so they'd start guessing." She added, "When batters start guessing, they're never right."[62]

Various All-Americans later recalled Faut's pitching. When asked why Jean was better than other pitchers, Lib Mahon, her longtime teammate, remarked, "Hell, she threw a curveball like a man!"[63] Wilma Briggs, the hard-hitting Fort Wayne outfielder who was dealt to South Bend in 1954, recalled that Faut threw mostly strikes: "Jean moved the ball all around the plate, but you could count on her throwing strikes. If she threw inside, she was telling you to back away."[64]

Next to Faut, Faralla, the strong-armed sidearmer, did not get the recognition she deserved. Twenty-five when the season started, Lil was a first-rate pitcher and also a solid

Lillian "Lil" Faralla — One of South Bend's top pitchers during the overhand years, starting in 1948, Faralla is pictured circa 1949 (courtesy of the Louise Pettus Archives and Special Collections, Winthrop University).

right-handed hitter who could play the infield or the outfield. A 5'6" brunette who grew up in San Pedro, California, she entered the league in 1946. Sent to Peoria, Faralla was given a tryout behind the backstop, signed a contract, watched the first game of a twin bill, and played the second game at third base. In high school in California, she had played shortstop, the position she handled later for the Woolworth team in Long Beach. Lil graduated from San Pedro High in 1942. World War II led to blackouts on the West Coast, thus ending softball games at night, so she found a job working in the JJ Newberry dime store as a window-trimmer. Later, she worked in an airplane plant, as California became the nation's leading producer of military aircraft and plane parts. In 1944, Faralla joined the Coast Guard, served for two years, and played service softball. A scout for the All-American League saw her play a game in Long Beach and, after the war, she received a telegram asking her to join the league. Dropping her plan to attend Santa Barbara State College in 1946, she rode the train to Chicago and ended up with Peoria.

Faralla played 55 games for the Redwings as a rookie and batted .181. Sent to Fort Wayne in 1947, she averaged .279 in 32 games. The Daisies also used her as a pitcher, but her record was 3–12 with a 1.98 ERA. The Californian refused a trade to South Bend in mid–1947, because she was told the team needed another player—but the Blue Sox really wanted to dump slowballing Tommie Thompson. When the two women chatted, Faralla did not understand the deception, so she refused the trade. Later, the Daisies saw the independent-minded Faralla as expendable, and the league allocated her to South Bend in 1948. At first she met resistance from teammates and fans, but her stellar hitting, solid pitching, and winning personality soon made her many friends. She finished the year with a 10–20 mark and a 1.99 ERA, but she lost several games by one run.

In 1949, Faralla enjoyed her greatest year, improving her control and fashioning a 19–9 ledger with a 1.36 ERA, but seven of her nine losses came by one run. Always second to Faut, Lil called her a super person: "Jean Faut is tops. She was a wonderful ballplayer. She was our ace. She was always number one, but I was proud to be number two on her team."[65]

South Bend's surprise of the year was left-hander Jo Hasham, who lost all six games she hurled for Muskegon and Peoria in 1948. Improving her control in 1949, Hasham, who grew up in Waltham, Massachusetts, fashioned a 12–8 record and a 2.02 ERA, but she won nine of those contests by mid–July, and she did not adjust well to the new 55-foot pitching distance. As a hitter, she compiled a .159 mark in 35 games. Hasham's early-season hurling was illustrated by her seventh victory, 5–2, over visiting Fort Wayne on Saturday, July 2. On a pleasant evening at Playland, the teams entertained an audience of 1,510, typical for a weekend game in South Bend that summer. Hasham faced Donna "Cookie" Cook, a right-hander who grew up in Muskegon. The Blue Sox lineup featured Baker, playing second base and leading off; Wagoner, playing right field and hitting second; Wirth, the shortstop, batting third; Mahon, playing left field and hitting cleanup; Stoll, the center fielder, as the fifth hitter; Filarski, at third base, batting sixth; Whiting, at first base, in the seventh slot; Stovroff, batting eighth and catching; and Hasham.

Jack Wright, a *Tribune* scribe, reported that Hasham made a "wobbly start," permitting three hits in the first two innings, but no runs. The southpaw settled down and allowed only three more hits, blanking the Daisies until the ninth, when she yielded Betty Allen's two-run double to left. South Bend's batters bunched five safeties in the fourth, scoring once on Stoll's bunt, again on a grounder, and a third run on Whiting's single. The Blue Sox scored twice in the fifth on singles by Baker, Wirth, and Stoll, and Hasham continued her steady pace. Afterward, Jo's record improved to 7–2, but the story contained few details about her, and she remained out of the spotlight.[66] Still, Hasham's best season helped her team tie the Peaches for first place.

Ruth Williams rounded out South Bend's starting rotation. Twenty-three, the 5'5" right-hander from Pennsylvania who relied on curveballs and good control, ranked ninth in the league with her record of 10–6 and ERA of 1.64. A graduate of East Stroudsburg State Teachers College, she majored in physical education and worked as a teacher in Amber, near Philadelphia. Williams, one of the girls who loved passing time on trips by playing poker on the bus, was enjoying her third year with the Blue Sox. After a rookie season when she fashioned a 12–8 record, Ruth slipped to 10–10 in 1948.[67] Altogether, she pitched seven seasons but never again won more than ten games—a mark she reached four times. Also, like Hasham, Williams had difficulty with the longer pitching distance, and she posted a 5–5 ledger after mid-season.

Still, Williams, when backed by good fielding and hitting, pitched well enough to win, as she did in the first game of a twin bill against Fort Wayne on Monday, July 4. Ruth faced the Daisies' Millie Deegan, a hard-throwing right-hander who compiled a 16–11 record and a 1.77 ERA, ranking her 12th in the loop—three notches below Williams. In this game, Ruth allowed six hits and coasted to an 8–2 win, after the Blue Sox grabbed a 4–0 lead in the first inning. But the *Tribune*, similar to the story about Hasham's win, gave few details about Williams' pitching.[68]

South Bend had talented, experienced players at every position, and Dave Bancroft, a quiet but knowledgeable leader who was liked by most of the players, came up with a regular lineup and, like most pilots, stayed with it. Bancroft, however, ran a loose ship and did not believe in daily mandatory practices, unlike the regimen of Chet Grant and Marty McManus before him.[69] Still, Bancroft's style worked with the players. Indeed, a team's camaraderie is boosted when players know their positions, know how others play their positions, and mesh well together on, and hopefully off, the diamond. As Kenosha's Ruby Stephens, the former South Bender, wrote about the Comets early in the 1949 season, "They seem to click—You know how it is, one player knows what the other is going to do."[70]

At first base, Bancroft started the 24-year-old Whiting, the amiable, talented, hard-playing southern Michigan girl who starred on several town softball clubs before joining the league in 1944 with Milwaukee. In 1945, the Chicks, now in Grand Rapids, switched her from the outfield to first base.[71] In 1949, the 5'7" all-around athlete played 93 games (all at first) and averaged .193, her second best mark to date. Also, she walked 48 times, got hit by the pitcher 20 times, and scored 25 runs. Short on speed, the right-handed hitter was a big run-producer, belting seven doubles and three triples and contributing 40 RBI.

At second base, the manager used Baker for 88 games (she played another 26 games at first). Bonnie, who turned 31 in mid-season, no longer had the arm for catcher, but she was a timely hitter who got on base—and she ran the sacks with abandon. Her fielding was erratic at times, as indicated by the 33 errors she committed playing second and first base. Off to a slow start at the plate, the good-looking model from Regina was hitting .190 by mid-season, but she improved to .216. She also drew 50 walks, stole a team-best 68 bases, scored 58 runs, and added 25 RBI. Indeed, Baker's hitting prowess continued to be a valuable asset for the Sox.

At shortstop, Bancroft depended on Wirth, who was 23 and a fourth-year Blue Sox stalwart. Talented, agile, quick-thinking, and a real crowd pleaser, the vivacious Shoo-Shoo sparkled on the diamond, perhaps because her petite five-foot stature made her seem the essence of an All-American when she made a sensational play. Overall, she played 113 games, and her .229 average ranked fifth on the team. Shoo-Shoo was valuable in many ways, walking 55 times, stealing 66 bases, sacrificing 29 times, and tying Mahon with a team-high 62 runs scored.

Bancroft liked Filarski at third base. The fifth-year infielder was a standout athlete from Detroit, where she grew up playing ball, competing with other girls in Detroit's Catholic League. She graduated from Saint Josephat's High in 1942, played amateur ball for the Hudson Motor Company, and worked as a riveter on airplanes manufactured by the Briggs Company. The 5'2" Filarski had joined Rockford in 1945. Now in her second year with South Bend, Helen, a slick fielder, liked the city and her teammates, including roommate Shirley Stovroff. "The people," Filarski recalled in 2010, "they were very, very nice to us." A serious player dedicated to improving her game, the right-handed batter played in 92 contests, averaging .207, hitting three doubles and three triples, walking 30 times, scoring 31 runs, and contributing 26 RBI.[72]

In left field, Bancroft preferred Mahon, the longtime star from Greenville, South Carolina. Playing with a weakened left knee that she often wrapped with an Ace bandage, Lib, as everyone called her, watched opposing hitters carefully and learned where to play each one. At the plate, the 5'7" right-handed batter hit with power and drove in runners, slugging 16 doubles and three triples and leading the loop with 60 RBI. Mahon had also paced the circuit with 72 RBI in 1946, her only All-Star season. An all-around contributor, she and Wirth tied for the most runs scored with 62. Aggressive base runners, Lib and Shoo-Shoo both stole 66 bases.

Bancroft usually played the hustling Stoll in center. A sure fielder who knew where to play the hitters, she had the speed to run down long fly balls. Jeep, a nickname based on her rugged style, joined the league in 1946 as a 17-year-old rookie from West Point, Pennsylvania. She started playing ball at age eight, learning from her father, an umpire and semi-pro player. As a teenager, she played industrial league softball, and her high school coach secured her a tryout with the league. After coming off the bench as a reserve for Peoria in 1946 and Grand Rapids in 1947, the 5'0" Stoll became a regular for Springfield in 1948, hitting .191. For the Sox in 1949, she turned into one of the league's top defensive outfielders.[73] She also improved at the plate, batting .232, the third highest mark on the team. A good all-around ballplayer, Jeep hit three doubles and one triple, walked 49 times, stole 42 bases, scored 50 runs, and produced 28 RBI.

In right field, Betty Wagoner was a mainstay, playing 113 games and hitting .230. An all-around athlete with good speed, the 5'2" flychaser from Lebanon, Missouri, was in her second season with the Blue Sox, and she led the team in 1948 with a .278 average. A fine fielder, the left-hander also hit plenty of line drives, but she showed little power. In 1949, Betty hit four doubles and a triple, but she never hit a regular-season home run. Still, the 19-year-old helped the Sox in many ways, drawing a team-high 87 bases on balls, stealing 64 bases, scoring 58 runs, and adding 26 RBI.

At catcher and for reserves, Bancroft had several options, since most All-Americans could play more than one position. Shirley Stovroff caught the majority of games (75), and due to her good receiving and defensive skills, she was Faut's preferred catcher.[74] A 5'6" brunette from Madison, Illinois, the hard-nosed, aggressive Stovroff, who often threw out runners going to second, played 77 games and averaged .191. Rita Briggs, a 5'3" catcher and outfielder from Ayers, Massachusetts, spent 1947 with Rockford and split the 1948 season between Rockford and Chicago. Joining the Blue Sox in 1949, Briggs played 64 games, 45 behind the plate, and hit .209, but she also helped her team in the outer gardens. Marge

Betty "Old Reliable" Wagoner — South Bend's speedy outfielder, circa 1949, wearing her large five-finger baseball glove (courtesy of the Louise Pettus Archives and Special Collections, Winthrop University).

Callaghan, 28, the older of two speedy sisters from Vancouver, British Columbia, began in 1944 with Minneapolis and moved with the team to Fort Wayne in 1945. A right-handed batter who loved to bunt, she spent four more seasons playing mainly the infield. With the Sox, her average slipped to .169, but the Canadian's bright personality, useful experience, and versatility (26 games at third and 20 at second) made her a valuable reserve.

Two-Team Pennant Race

The Blue Sox slipped twice against Grand Rapids when the new ball was introduced, but the players adjusted and resumed their winning ways, fashioning a 24–10 mark (plus one tie) in July. At the end of the summer's hottest month, they set a torrid pace with a seven-game winning streak. The seventh victory came in the finale of a three-game set at seventh-place Racine on Thursday, August 4. Winning for the 12th time in 13 games, the visitors capitalized on spot starter Lou Arnold's four-hitter to record a 3–1 success. Arnold, the second-year right-hander from Rhode Island who won five games in 1949, was hurt in the fourth by Edie Perlick's home run down the left field line, a blast that cut the deficit to 2–1. Facing Erma Bergmann, the Blue Sox jumped to a 2–0 lead in the first when Wirth, showing rare power, homered to left after Baker walked, and they added an insurance tally in the eighth when Baker bunted home Wagoner, who tripled. After Rockford (52–24) lost to Grand Rapids, South Bend (53–23) took over first place by one game. The see-saw race for the All-American pennant continued, with the Chicks (41–39) a distant third, 14 games behind the leaders.[75]

Surprisingly, after traveling to Kenosha on August 6, the Blue Sox lost four straight, allowing the Comets to climb into third place. Kenosha won the first two tilts easily, thanks to errors and the stellar pitching of southpaw Jean Cione on Friday and rookie right-hander Beth Goldsmith on Saturday. In Sunday's twin bill at Lakefront Stadium, South Bend suffered a pair of one-run defeats, mainly due to the batwork of former South Bender Dolly Brumfield, Kenosha's first sacker. In the opener, Brumfield singled home Helen Candaele in the sixth, after Helen walked, stole, and advanced on a bunt. Jean Marlowe earned the 1–0 victory with a three-hitter, two by Wirth, and Williams lost, although yielding just two safeties. In the late game, Faralla nursed a 2–0 lead until the eighth, when she walked three straight Comets. Audrey Wagner fanned, but Faralla uncorked a wild pitch, scoring one run, Brumfield hit a two-run single, and right-hander Barbara Rotvig saved the lead. Elsewhere, Lois Florreich fired a no-hitter to lift Rockford (54–25) over Muskegon, and South Bend (53–27) slipped to one and a half games behind the Peaches.[76]

Undaunted, the Blue Sox returned to Playland Park and continued the heated pennant battle by winning four straight, two against Racine (a third game was rained out) and two against Kenosha. The second game against the Comets hinged on Faut's one-out, bases-loaded, pinch-hit single in the eighth, giving the Blue Sox a 4–2 lead that Faralla protected.[77] However, the string ended when Muskegon, in town for one game on Saturday, August 13, pulled out a 3–2 victory in 12 innings. Doris Sams battled Williams on even terms, until Ruth walked bespectacled Doris Tetzlaff to open the fateful 12th. June Schofield sacrificed the runner to second, and Sally Meier singled to send Tetzlaff to third. Williams passed Sams intentionally to load the bases, but Marie Wegman singled to score one run, and the Lassies took a 3–1 lead on Marie Kruckel's groundout. In the bottom of the 12th, Filarski singled to center, took second on Meier's bobble, and Briggs looped a single to right.

Hasham, batting for Williams, struck out, but Wagoner sacrificed, scoring one run. However, Baker ended the thriller by lining a shot to Sams. Rockford beat Kenosha, so the Peaches tied the Blue Sox. Both owned 57–28 ledgers.[78]

South Bend and Rockford were doing what officials like Max Carey and Arthur Meyerhoff always hoped All-American teams would do — stage an exciting race for the pennant and attract more fans. On the other hand, six of the teams could not compete with the talented, experienced Blue Sox and Peaches, and that did not bode well for the league's future.

Fighting to the Finish

Whenever the Blue Sox lost a game or two (or more) in 1949, they came back with two or more consecutive wins, but the victory streaks got shorter near the season's end. True to form, South Bend traveled to Muskegon for a doubleheader on Sunday, August 14, and took over first place by winning twice. The visitors wearing pastel blue capped the series on Monday, when Wirth's hit-and-run single scored Baker from second base for a 5–4 lead. Relieving Arnold, Williams, though giving up a single and two walks to load the bases in the ninth, saved the win.[79]

Returning home for a two-game set against Grand Rapids, South Bend won both, the second being a 4–3 11-inning triumph on "Dave Bancroft Night." Watched by 3,136 fans, Williams started, but showed little stuff on the ball, retiring in favor of Faut after loading the bases with one out in the fifth. Faut walked home one run, but she pitched well until the ninth, when the Chicks rallied for two runs and a 3–3 tie. Tex Fischer gave up solo runs in the first, fourth, and seventh innings, but she lost in the 11th when Wagoner singled and Baker slugged a two-out triple to win yet another tense contest. Elsewhere, Rockford (59–31) defeated Kenosha, but South Bend (62–28) held a three-game lead as the pennant race moved toward a close.[80]

Before the game, Bancroft was honored with a special night that included an array of gifts from local merchants, sponsors, and his "kids," as he called the Sox. Sportswriter Bob Towner observed that the manager was always encouraging his players, clapping about a good play as he ran back from the third base coaching slot to the bench. In the dugout, Bancroft kept up a humorous banter to lighten the tension. In practice sessions, he taught the "small ball" tactics of the squeeze play, the hit-and-run, and running hard on the base paths. Bancroft, combining toughness with gentleness, often waved from the coaching box to fans in the stands, notably to crippled children who were brought to games. Afterward, he usually asked the writer to credit his kids for good plays in the field and at bat, and to "thank all the fans for me — I can't reach them personally."[81] Bancroft was a very successful and well-liked pilot in 1949.

A few days later, the struggle with Rockford — and perhaps the season — was highlighted when the Peaches came to Playland and divided a four-game series starting on Monday, August 29. With her team holding a one-game edge over Rockford, Faut, who usually pitched the biggest games, notched her 23rd win with a four-hit 4–0 shutout, boosting South Bend's lead to two games over the peach-uniformed travelers. Jean allowed runners to reach second and third base in the third inning, but after that, not another Peach advanced as far as second base. Also, Mahon made feature plays twice. Lib snagged a liner off her shoe tops to bring the crowd of 3,263 to its feet in the first inning, and in the second, she ran down Pollitt's drive to the left field fence, and her throw and a relay caught Al sliding into third base. In the home team's second, Stovroff squeezed in Stoll, who singled and advanced on an error and a fielder's choice. Taking advantage of errors, the Sox beat the stellar Nicky Fox with three runs in the fifth.[82]

The up-and-down series continued with Tuesday's doubleheader when Rockford won the seven-inning opener in the ninth, 4–1, scoring three runs off Hasham, who surrendered nine hits. In the nightcap, shortened to six innings by the 11:30 curfew, the Blue Sox won, 4–0, as Faralla twirled a two-hitter. The local heroines reached Lou Erickson for two runs in the fourth and two in the fifth, bunching all four hits with a pair of walks in the two innings. When the clock-watching and the game ended, South Bend, now 71–33, remained two games ahead of 69–35 Rockford.[83]

On Wednesday, with the temperature at fifty-five degrees, the field wet from an earlier downpour, and the Playland crowd down to 1,584, Faut, pitching for the second time in three nights, lost a tough one, 4–3, despite fanning seven and allowing only four hits. Afterward, South Bend (71–34) led Rockford (70–35) by one game with six games remaining. The Peaches, however, would face last-place Peoria (then 35–68) six times, and the Sox would play six contests against fifth-place Fort Wayne (50–53).[84]

In the end, South Bend took two of three at Playland against Fort Wayne, winning the first game and losing the second. On Saturday, September 3, in the year's final home contest for the Blue Sox, Faut hurled a nine-inning no-hitter, her second—the first came at Racine on September 4, 1948.[85] Easily disposing of the Daisies, 2–0, Jean won number 24 but missed a perfect game by walking Dottie Schroeder in the eighth. Schroeder, however, was erased on a double play, and Faut, with her assortment of fastballs and curves finding the corners, faced only 27 hitters. Receiving flawless support, Faut also scored the first run in the third when she singled, stole a base, and scored on Wagoner's single off Donna Cook, who gave up six hits. In the sixth, after singles by Stoll and Whiting, Faut drove in the game's last run with a long sacrifice fly. The victory was a fitting climax at home for the Sox (now at 73–35), and the win kept them one game ahead of the Peaches (72–36), after Rockford defeated Peoria.[86]

Who Wants a Tie?

Traveling to Fort Wayne, the Blue Sox also won two out of three. The crucial loss came in the first game at Memorial Park on Sunday, September 4, when Millie Deegan, pitching a steady game, spun a three-hitter to outduel Faralla, 6–2. Lil surrendered four runs in the first inning on three hits, a walk, and an error, Arnold, in relief, worked four scoreless innings, and Hasham, who pinch-hit for her in the eighth, gave up two runs in the ninth. The Blue Sox scored once in the third when the Daisies made an error on a double play, and once in the sixth when Wirth singled home a run, cutting the deficit to 4–2. Elsewhere, Rockford defeated Racine, leaving the Blue Sox and the Peaches tied for first place.[87]

Facing a Labor Day twin bill on Monday, South Bend won both, posting scores of 2–1 and 10–5. Williams, who spaced seven hits, outlasted Blumetta in the opener, although Kay only allowed three hits. The visitors scored the winning run in one extra inning, the eighth, when Wirth walked, stole second, and rode home on Mahon's clutch double. In the nightcap, the Blue Sox raked Sugar Koehn for 13 hits, three by Mahon, and led, 10–4, in the eighth, when Bancroft, hearing about Rockford's twin victories, yanked Faralla.

In Illinois, Rockford squeaked by Peoria in the opener, 2–1, and the Peaches were leading, 2–0, in the fifth inning of the second game when a dispute broke out that led to a forfeit. Peoria's Mary Reynolds doubled. When Twi Shively grounded to short, Snookie Doyle threw to second to trap the runner, but the new base umpire, watching the play at first, called Reynolds safe. After manager Bill Allington protested, Ray Schalk, the home plate umpire, called Reynolds out. Redwing pilot Leo Schrall disputed the call and refused to play, and Schalk, after a time limit expired, called the game a forfeit — despite its critical importance in the penance race.[88]

At the same time, South Bend officials appealed to the league to set up a one-game playoff to decide the pennant. However, Max Carey refused, deciding the winner of the Sox-Peaches playoff also won the pennant.[89]

The story of the Carey Cup Playoff was short but not sweet. After a travel day for the Peaches, the Blue Sox hosted the opener of the best-of-seven series at Playland on Thursday, September 8, but a turnout of 2,279, dressed for temperatures in the mid–50s, was unhappy with the result. On a soggy, sand-covered diamond, Bancroft started his ace, Jean Faut, but she received too little support. In the critical third inning, Nicky Fox's dribbler rolled through Whiting's legs for an error. Melba Alspaugh, on loan to Rockford, bunted to Faut, who threw to second, but Fox slid in ahead of the throw. Kamenshek sacrificed the runners along, and Dottie Key bunted in front of the plate. Stovroff retrieved the ball and tried to tag Fox, but missed. Doyle walked to load the bases, and Callow hit a grounder to Baker at second base. Bonnie chased down Doyle, who was heading for second, but Alspaugh scored. Spotting Key heading for home, Baker cut loose a wild throw, and her error made the score 3–0. Rockford linked two hits and a walk for one run in the fourth, and in the fifth, when Mahon fell down going after a fly ball, Pollitt had a run-scoring double. Arnold took over in the sixth and pitched shutout ball, but it was too late. The Sox, totaling five hits, two by Wagoner, scored once in the sixth, but otherwise failed to hit with runners in scoring position.[90]

On Friday evening, Rockford, behind Florreich's two-hitter, won the second game, 2–0, even though Williams pitched a three-hitter and Arnold hurled a scoreless ninth inning. The Peaches rapped two hits in the fourth, and Callow scored from third as Whiting fielded Charlene Barnett's dribbler toward first base and tagged her. The Peaches scored again in the eighth when Florreich drew a walk, moved up on a bunt, and took third on a passed ball. Kamenshek grounded to Baker, who, faking a throw to third to hold the runner, tossed out Rockford's first baseman. Whiting, however, "fell asleep" at first and did not see Florreich racing in to score. In the lower bracket of the Carey Playoffs, Grand Rapids beat Fort Wayne and Muskegon defeated Kenosha as the four teams opened two best-of-five quarterfinal series. The winners would play off and the victor would meet the Rockford-South Bend winner for the title.[91]

Embarking on one more late-night bus trip to Illinois, South Bend lost a pair of heartbreakers at Beyer Stadium. On Saturday night, the Peaches rode the combined three-hitter of their aces, Gacioch and Fox, to a narrow 2–1 victory. In the fifth, Pollitt and Barnett singled off Faralla, and Ruth Richard tripled for a 2–0 lead, but on an attempted pickoff, Lil caught Richard trying to score. In the seventh, after missing opportunities in the fifth and sixth, the Blue Sox scored to cut the gap to 2–1. Stoll walked and stole second. Fox replaced Gacioch, and Faralla greeted Nicky with the second of her two singles to bring home Stoll, but neither team scored again.[92]

On Sunday, Faut pitched stellar ball for eight innings, but South Bend lost, 1–0. Jean issued her only free pass to Kamenshek leading off the ninth. When Faut fired to first to pick off the runner, Whiting, who made a critical error in game one and a mental mistake in game two, let the throw get by her, and Kamenshek advanced. Wirth turned Doyle's grounder into the first out, but the runner took third. Callow lifted a high fly to left center, and Stoll, because Mahon lost the ball in the dim light, apparently made the catch after a long run, but the umpires, unsure of what happened, delayed the call. In one of those moments that seem timeless, the two fielders stood motionless, until Mahon reached down and picked up the ball Stoll had dropped, and Kamenshek, half way home, trotted in to score the season's biggest run.[93] The blue-clad visitors, managing just two hits off Lou Erickson, missed four scoring opportunities. In the end, South Bend's lack of clutch hitting was the culprit in all four losses.[94]

Maybe Next Year

Later, Rockford, winning the club's second playoff championship in a row, captured the Carey Cup by defeating Grand Rapids in four games,[95] but that mattered little to South Bend. After producing the most wins of any season in franchise history, 76, the Blue Sox, who battled the Peaches on even terms all season, led the league in hitting with an average of .216, and Rockford ranked fifth with a .196 mark. South Bend also matched Rockford in fielding,[96] but the Sox failed to hit well in must-win games. Overall, Rockford totaled 18 hits and scored 10 runs in four playoff games, and South Bend collected 12 hits while scoring only twice.

Regardless, the Blue Sox had entertained fans with their finest year to date. One day before the playoffs opened, the *Tribune's* Paul Neville, looking at the season "nobody won," observed that other teams claimed South Bend did not have the individual talent to win so many games. Neville cited an important intangible factor: "The answer almost always is, 'Dave Bancroft. He has them hustling and playing ball.'"[97] In addition, South Bend also featured the most tangible strength of any team: Jean Faut. An all-around performer and the circuit's best player in 1949, Faut pitched a league-high 24 regular season victories and also averaged a league-best .291 at the plate.

Looking at women playing the fast-paced game on the field, observers believed the league was on the rise. In a story inspired by the league's office, Adie Suehsdorf, writing for the *Los Angeles Times*, pointed out differences in the All-American game, including how a star like Dottie Collins of Fort Wayne could get pregnant and depart in mid-season, or how others could get married and leave the diamond. Regardless, the league was not "softball, or vaudeville, or a leg show," but rather, the girls were playing *professional baseball*. They threw overhand, used "man-sized" gloves, wore spiked shoes, hit a slightly larger baseball with Louisville Slugger bats, and they executed drag bunts, squeeze plays, and delayed steals. To top it off, Suehsdorf wrote, these were nice girls with good athletic ability, or "sluggers in skirts."[98]

Still, to paraphrase Jim Bouton's comment from his 1970 book *Ball Four*, you spend a good part your life gripping a baseball, and in the end, it turns out to be the other way around. In addition, baseball, as commentators like to say, is a game of inches, and South Bend, at important moments near the end of the 1949 season, watched the livelier baseball take a few bad hops. Perhaps more important, baseball, regardless of gender, is also a game of hopes and dreams. Given the talented team that South Bend fielded and the solid managing provided by Dave Bancroft, the players and fans were already looking forward to a great season in 1950.

Rookie Touring Teams in 1949 — After the Springfield Sallies and the Chicago Colleens failed following the 1948 season, the league created two teams of rookies and sent them on a nationwide tour in 1949. In this picture, the teams posed before playing two games at Oklahoma City, Oklahoma, on July 3–4, 1949. Several players later made the "big" league, and four played for South Bend. Those with the Colleens (top row) who later played for the Blue Sox are Betty Francis (1954), seventh from left, and Arlene Kotil (1950), tenth from left. Two posed with the Sallies who later played for South Bend are Wimp Baumgarter (1950–1954), eighth from left, and Sue Kidd (1950–1954), ninth from left (courtesy of Betty Francis).

Indeed, many All-Americans, notably the younger girls, could hardly wait for the next season. They didn't know or didn't care about intricacies like the league's finances. They just loved playing the game. Pitcher Sue Kidd, from Choctaw, Arkansas, who later starred for the Blue Sox, received a tryout and made the rookie tour in 1949 when the Colleens and the Sallies met in a pair of contests in Little Rock. Her entire life changed when the touring teams came to Arkansas, and she joined the Sallies. "I hated to see the season end," Kidd recalled, "and I just hoped and prayed I'd get to play the next summer."[99]

• 8 •

The League Crisis and Fifth Place: 1950

"So many crises have been survived by the All American Girls Baseball League this year that the patient is gradually losing strength"—Paul Neville, *South Bend Tribune*, July 19, 1950[1]

Perils of the 1950 Season

Dave Bancroft's first season as South Bend's manager in 1949 almost resulted in a dream finish, because his "kids" tied Rockford for first place. But in the 1950 season, after some unsettling personnel changes in the first half of June and a controversy surrounding the league's elimination of players' meal money near the end of July, the Blue Sox, lacking good reserves, dropped from first place to fifth, compiling a 55–55 record. Still, South Bend started strong. The magazine *Girls Baseball*, in its issue of July 1, said the All-American League was off to a "rip-snotin' [sic] knock down race," and the top six teams were separated by only six games following one month of play. After one month, Fort Wayne, combining good hitting and fielding, ranked second in both categories with a club batting mark of .248, paced by Evie Wawryshyn at .343, and a team fielding average of .951. "So.[outh] Bend, the other Indiana entry," *Girls Baseball* reported, "got away well and has been one of the leaders continuously, currently running second to the state rivals."[2] The article, typical of league-inspired promotional stories, omitted mention of any off-the-field problems, giving fans the impression the loop was in great shape.

By late 1949, the Management Corporation, created in 1945 after Phil Wrigley sold his interests in the league to Arthur Meyerhoff, was making less profit annually. Under the Management Corporation, the league's board of directors consisted of President Max Carey, serving his fifth year, and the team presidents, or their representatives. This decentralized setup allowed Management to develop, supervise, and regulate play by the teams, while the board maintained control of circuit government by majority vote. In other words, the teams' boards of directors essentially controlled the oversight of the league without having to deal with administrative responsibilities. Those responsibilities, Merrie Fidler explained, included approving or dismissing member teams; approving the budgets, annual and supplementary; approving the loop's president; disciplining club members; determining admission charges for games; calculating visiting teams' share of the gate receipts; creating procedures for contracts, releases, and waivers; establishing rules and procedures, and more.[3]

The Management Corporation had strengths and weaknesses. The advantages included allowing the franchises to run their own operations without being concerned with publicity, scouting, and evaluating new personnel. Also, the teams benefited from a major regional advertiser, the Meyerhoff Agency, which publicized the circuit across the country and beyond American borders. The main disadvantage was the split between Management's expenses and the perception by team directors, such as South Bend president Doc Dailey, that the league was profiting at the expense of the teams. As Dailey noted in 1949, the league's board had more than one discussion about the clubs buying out Management's contract for $10,000. Most directors hated paying Management the annual assessment plus three cents per paid admission. The idea was to "get rid of it" and save money, since attendance in every league city was declining. Six of the eight teams together suffered losses that totaled more than $90,000 in 1949.

The 1950 season was a financial disaster. Rockford and Peoria survived by conducting public drives to sell stock at $100 per share. Grand Rapids held a drive but raised only $4,000, when $20,000 was needed. The Chicks were able to complete the season partly because team members and the manager agreed to play with no guarantee of earning their salaries. Also, Jim Williams, owner of the Jets, a local semipro team, allowed the Chicks to use his ballpark. In addition, Muskegon shifted to Kalamazoo, Michigan, because the Lassies' board ran out of funds. For perspective, the entertainment life of consumers was changing. Most people spent less on local amusement, including baseball, staying home to watch programs like "sitcoms" and big league baseball on television, the technological change that revolutioned American culture in the 1950s. Regardless, no financial changes could solve the league's greatest problem: the more the game evolved toward baseball, the lesser the talent pool from which to select new players.[4]

The late 1940s was a time of growth, change, and apprehension in America. First, the booming U.S. economy accounted for half of the world's gross annual product. However, economic expansion and technological changes, including improvements in health, safety, and convenience, were accompanied by population growth, social change, and personal fears. Rampant inflation marked the first postwar baseball season. Prices across the nation rose much faster than wages and, as a result, unions struck in record numbers for better pay and working conditions. In 1947, when the league flew the players to Cuba for spring training, Americans were concerned about the Cold War, fueled by the USSR's apparent intention to expand its control beyond Eastern Europe. President Truman responded with the Truman Doctrine, the "containment" policy, and the Marshall Plan to rebuild war-torn European nations. In 1948, when the league switched to overhand pitching, Americans watched the Truman administration thwart the Soviet Union's military blockade of Berlin with the Berlin Airlift, the flying of supplies into the Western-controlled city for a year. In 1949, the Communists won the long-running civil war in China in January, and about the time All-American League's playoffs began, the USSR exploded an atomic device, a pair of seemingly sinister events threatening peace in the free world.

Finally, when the league eliminated meal money in late July of 1950, the Korean War had just begun. Thousands of families were directly affected as United Nations troops, the majority of whom were Americans, intervened to stabilize the conflict at the 38th parallel, the boundary between North and South Korea. The Korean War was blamed on the Soviet and Chinese Communist specter. The fighting in faraway Korea turned into an ugly stalemate that Americans not only did not want to know about but also soon forgot. The Cold War heightened fears of Communist subversion at home, a conspiratorial belief shrewdly exploited by Wisconsin Republican Senator Joe McCarthy's phony charges of spies at home. So great were the public's fears of Communists that author Mickey Spillane used his tough-guy detective Mike Hammer to root out "Commie" subversives, rather than chase gangsters, crooks, or corrupt politicos.[5]

Within that cultural milieu, one major message of the media, now featuring TV, was that a "woman's place" was in the home taking care of her family, preferably in the growing suburbs.[6] At the same time, attendance for major league baseball peaked in 1948 when close to 21 million fans entered turnstiles, and fell to 17,400,000 in 1950. The majors reversed the decline in 1957, but the 21 million mark was not reached again until the expansion season of 1961.[7] Minor league baseball boomed through the 1949 season, peaking at 59 circuits. Only one league failed in 1950, but the Korean conflict helped reduce attendance in the minors to 34,700,000, a drop of seven million.[8]

Indeed, the women of the Girls' Pro League were talented, independent-minded, determined pioneers who were moving ahead on a sports frontier, but doing so largely against the era's male-dominated social forces.

The "Balanced" Blue Sox

As usual, the All-American League was changing. Max Carey resigned as president at the board meeting in November 1949, and he managed Fort Wayne in 1950 and 1951. Publicity director Fred K. Leo was voted into the top office. Leo began with the circuit in 1946 by helping to organize his hometown Peoria Redwings, and he worked as the league's chief publicist in 1947. Later, Leo became Carey's assistant, so he was familiar with the structure and operation of the league. By 1950, the team presidents as well as Leo realized that they needed more spending cuts and, as a result, the teams again trained on local fields. Leo promoted a "rookie rule," requiring that a player with less than 50 games played must be in the lineup, offensively and defensively. In 1949 and again in 1950, the league fielded two touring teams with younger players, the Sallies and the Colleens, providing, in effect, minor leaguers so that All-American managers could comply with the rookie rule. In fact, the circuit's stars were almost all veterans who were aging each season, even though the number of players and, later, the number of teams were decreasing.[9]

The league's bright idea for the 1950 season was to convene a Balancing Committee to make the eight teams as competitive as possible. The committee consisted of two managers: Bill Allington of Rockford, and John Rawlings of Grand Rapids; two presidents, Don Black of Racine, and South Bend's Doc Dailey; Fred Leo; and an alternate, Judge Edward Ruetz of Kenosha. A good deal of back-room maneuvering took place, but Dailey liked this "balancing" plan better than the previous allocation process. After the committee met on March 12, South Bend emerged with 14 veterans, most of last year's players. They were Betty Whiting, first base; Bonnie Baker, second base; Shoo-Shoo Wirth, shortstop; Lib Mahon, left field; Jeep Stoll, center field; Betty Wagoner, right field; and 19-year-old Shirley Stovroff and 22-year-old Jenny Romatowski, at catcher. The pitchers were Jean Faut, Lil Faralla, Ruth Williams, and three-year Redwing star Dottie Mueller. The team received two utility players, Jette Vincent, a second-year right-hander, and Helen Filarski, the previous season's third sacker. That left third base "open," supposedly to be filled by a rookie, but Filarski was the real choice.[10]

The circuit's other bright idea was to hold a two-week rookie camp in South Bend and invite more than 100 selected players for tryouts. Starting on Thursday, April 13, Dave Bancroft and the other managers conducted the camp in the rain and cold of springtime

Indiana. By April 19, 60 recruits, including all the girls who staffed the Colleens and the Sallies in 1949, were still contending for roster spots at the "finishing school." The league wanted five rookies on each team. Once the school's two-a-day workouts ended, the eight teams would train at four locations, beginning April 24: South Bend; Peoria; West Baden, a resort town in Indiana; and Cape Girardeau, Missouri, where the St. Louis Browns practiced during World War II. The preseason schedule began on May 7, and the 112-game regular season opened on May 18. The Blue Sox would join the Muskegon Lassies for a regional tour, and the other six teams would pair off for their exhibitions. Bancroft expected one local recruit to make the roster, Janet Wiley, a former Sox bat girl and Riley High grad who had tossed several sandlot no-hitters.[11]

On Saturday, April 22, 54 hopefuls who tried out were offered contracts and living arrangements. For the Blue Sox, Baker and Williams received rooms with the Cattrell family in nearby Mishawaka, and, in the same town, Marge Stefani, the chaperone, roomed with the Montgomerys. In South Bend, Mahon and Wirth moved in with Warner family, Stovroff and Vincent bunked with the Larsons, and Faralla and Stoll took rooms with the Kendalls. All six players lived on Caroline Street, within walking distance of Playland Park. Rookies Anna Kunkel and Helen Waddell (who was soon shifted to Rockford) also lived on Caroline with the Marsh family. Dottie Mueller, the former Redwing, and Ruth Middleton, a recruit who was later sent to the Colleens, lived with the Garmicans on 24th Street. Filarski and Romatowski, who spent 1949 with Peoria, stayed with the Davis family on 23rd Street. Rookies Jackie Mattson, a catcher from Waukegan, Illinois, and infielder Audrey Bleiler lived with the Lindstroms on Pleasant Street. Across the street, Whiting and pitcher Elaine Roth, the former Redwing, roomed in the Patty household. Finally, Faut, the only married player, lived at home on Strathmore Street, rookie Janet "Pee Wee" Wiley lived at home on Marine Street, Mary Dailey, another rookie, lived in the Bowers' home on Leer Street, and Dave Bancroft took a room in Mishawaka. In addition, four major newsreel companies were set to film the rookie school and the spring camp at South Bend, and the footage would be released in movie theaters nationwide during the last week of April.[12]

Facing unusually cold and wet weather, Bancroft and the Blue Sox forged ahead. The preseason exhibitions began with two in Muncie on Sunday and Monday, May 7–8. The Lassies won on Sunday night, 5–3, and the Blue Sox won the Monday matchup, 10–3. Jackie Mattson and Mary Dailey collected two hits each in the second game. Mattson split receiving duties with Stovroff, and Elaine Roth and Jette Vincent shared the mound work.[13] In the remaining exhibitions, Bancroft used three or more rookies each night, hoping to decide which players to keep. His starting infield was Whiting at first, Baker at second, Wirth at short, and Filarski at third, and those four usually played the first four or five innings. Before it was over, the Blue Sox and the Lassies staged exhibitions at Dayton, Ohio, and Jackson, Michigan, while two others were rained out. On Monday night, Faut and Vincent, hurt by four errors, fell to the Lassies at Battle Creek. After the final game was washed out on Tuesday, Bancroft released Mattson, and the Sox acquired catcher Mary "Wimp" Baumgartner, who finished the 1949 season with Peoria.[14]

Fred Leo announced the league's back-to-the-old approach for 1950, notably regarding rules of conduct, dress, and behavior — rules widely ignored by most veterans. "This league has only two things to sell the public," Leo said on May 11, "baseball and femininity. Girls that wear anything that appears masculine don't look like girls and we want and insist on femininity at all times." Leo said most girls were proud of playing in the league, but others needed to "feel the sting of a shortened pay check if they don't comply with our rules." For example, umpires would check the stands and enforce the anti-fraternization rule. The loop already prohibited players wearing slacks and shorts and having short haircuts. Now the wearing of wind breaker jackets outside of dugouts was banned, and public bars were out of bounds, but beer was allowed with meals.[15] Lest anyone forget, the league wanted players and fans to know that it was a man's world.

Finally, the game on the diamond was stable. Using overhand pitching, adopted in 1948, 72-foot base paths, also started in 1948,[16] a 55-foot distance from the mound to home plate, and the 10-inch red-seamed baseball, both introduced in mid–1949, the All-Americans, except for the smaller field, were virtually playing regulation baseball.

Another Fine Season

On Wednesday, May 17, an evening full of good dining, laughter, and fun amid the vision of another fine season, the Blue Sox enjoyed the camaraderie of a banquet open to the public. The audience, congregating downtown at the Oliver Hotel, the current overnight

Baseball in the Fifties — After finishing in a first-place tie with Rockford in 1949, the Blue Sox pose in the bleachers at Playland Park for their 1950 team picture. Seated in the back row are (left to right) Dottie Mueller, Ruth Williams, Jean Faut, Georgette "Jette" Vincent, Elaine Roth, Shirley Stovroff, and Jenny Romatowski. In the middle row are Arlene Kotil, Janet "Pee Wee" Wiley, Charlene "Shorty" Pryer, Senaida "Shoo Shoo" Wirth, Helen Filarski, and Audrey Bleiler. Seated in the front row are Dave Bancroft, manager, Lib Mahon, Jane "Jeep" Stoll, Betty Wagoner, and Marge Stefani, coach-chaperone (courtesy of the Louise Pettus Archives and Special Collections, Winthrop University).

lodgings for visiting teams, heard remarks from master of ceremonies Paul M. Butler, a Blue Sox board member. Following up, Dave Bancroft praised his team, promised another good season, and introduced his veterans and rookies. Mahon and Stefani, again the chaperone, spoke for the players, and Harold Dailey as well as Bill Sheehan, the vice president, discussed the team's prospects. Bancroft named Faut, his ace, as the starting hurler, and Anna Kunkel, a left-handed hitting rookie from Wescosville, Pennsylvania, as his right fielder for Thursday's opener against Grand Rapids. Stovroff was the catcher, and rest of the lineup featured last year's starters: Whiting at first base, Baker at second, Wirth at short, Filarski at third, Mahon in left, and Stoll in center field. Besides the highly-touted Kunkel, the rookies were Audrey Bleiler of Philadelphia; Helen Waddell from Lemoyne, Pennsylvania; Mary Dailey of Lexington, Massachusetts; and Ruth Middleton of Winnipeg, Manitoba. Finally, the roster included Elaine Roth, a right-hander from Michigan City, Indiana, who spent the previous two seasons with Peoria, and two more catchers, fifth-year reserve Jenny Romatowksi from Wyandotte, Michigan, and Wimp Baumgartner.[17]

On Thursday, performing in the chill of the low 50s, the Blue Sox lost to the visiting Chicks, 13–5. Faut showed that she was not yet in good form, surrendering seven hits and eight runs, before giving way to Faralla in the eighth. The local heroines made five errors, four while Jean was pitching, but they reached Beans Risinger for three runs in the first, boosted by Mahon's first of four hits. But Risinger, who gave up ten hits, settled down and afterward allowed just a solo run in the seventh and another in the ninth. More than 2,000 folks, many of them wrapped in blankets, left when the Chicks led, 8–3, after six frames, and only a handful saw the end of the loosely-played contest.[18]

The Blue Sox bounced back at Playland Park on Friday night (again the league's games were all scheduled at night) and won, 4–3, riding the five-hit pitching of Mueller, the tall sidearming curveballer from Cheviot, Ohio, and the hot bat of Mahon, the cleanup hitter, as she went 3-for-4 and drove in three runs. The Chicks bunched four hits in the sixth to score all three runs, but in the seventh, Kunkel led off with one of her two singles. Bancroft signaled Wirth and Baker to sacrifice the runner to third, Mahon hit an RBI single for a 4–3 edge, and Mueller preserved the lead.[19] The victory jump-started the local favorites on a six-game win streak. They rode the team's special bus to Grand Rapids and won on Saturday, 11–5. Roth, with Romatowski catching, lasted until the seventh when Bancroft, needing an 8–3 margin protected, called for Faut. Anna Kunkel, however, was carried from the field when she broke her ankle chasing a fly ball in the eighth. Afterward, South Bend was tied for first place with Kenosha, Fort Wayne, and Racine, all at 2–1. The other four clubs, Rockford, Grand Rapids, Muskegon, and Peoria, had 1–2 records.[20]

Leading the League

The Blue Sox made a winning start, and many of the players, "counting their chicks before they were hatched," as the saying went, figured they would continue to repeat the success enjoyed in 1949. Chasing the first-place dream, they traveled to Muskegon and, following a rainout, won their sixth straight game on Saturday night, May 27, beating the Lassies, 6–2. The blue uniformed visitors racked up four runs in the second on Wagoner's double, an error, a wild throw, a bunt, and four walks. Faut, in left field for Mahon, who had an eye ailment, tripled home two more runs in the sixth, and Mueller hurled a complete game.[21] On Sunday, however, the Lassies broke their seven-game losing streak by winning,

5–1. Roth gave up ten hits, and Arlene Kotil, the 16-year-old who had played for the Blue Island Stars, one of four teams in the All-American's Chicago minor league (which lasted through the 1950 season),[22] hit two doubles. Afterward, the first-place Sox (6–2) returned home to face the second-place Daisies.[23]

At home at Playland on Monday, Faut pitched a five-hitter to top Fort Wayne, 8–1, helping her own cause by driving in three runs. Ace right-hander Maxine Kline gave up ten hits, and South Bend won with a four-run fifth, keyed by an infield single, an error at second base, a safe bunt, singles by Baker, Wirth, and Faut, and Whiting's run-scoring fielder's choice.[24] On Tuesday, Memorial Day, 3,040 fans, the second largest Playland audience in 1950, saw the teams split the holiday twin bill. The Daisies won the shorter first game, 9–5, and the Blue Sox took the nightcap, 4–3. Roth, hurling her submarine slants, took the loss in the seven-inning opener when she surrendered nine hits and her teammates made seven errors. In the late game, Mueller outdueled Kay Blumetta, and Wagoner's bases-loaded single in the ninth, with Mahon pinch-running at third base (Lib missed several games with her eye problem), scored the game-winning run.[25]

The league had no games on Wednesday, May 31, and on Thursday, Faut notched her third triumph over visiting Peoria, 5–2. Filarski led the win with a 3-for-3 night, scoring one run and batting in another as the home team took a 5–1 lead in the three-run fourth. Former South Bend southpaw Jo Hasham lost, and Faut picked up an infield single to continue her mark of hitting in every game she played.[26] Friday's contest with Peoria was called due to wet grounds.

On a chilly Saturday, Rockford arrived and won the first two games of a three-game set, beating Roth and South Bend, 2–1. The peach-clad visitors scored twice in the first inning, and Lois Florreich won her fifth straight game, thanks to a break. Facing Roth in the first inning, Jackie Kelley hit a fly ball down the right field line, but Wagoner, making a diving try, evidently crossed into foul territory before missing the ball. However, the base umpire ruled the hit fair, Kelley ended up at second base, and, after Charlene Barnett singled, Snookie Doyle lifted a two-run double over Dailey's head in left. In the eighth, after a walk and a single, Faut belted a drive to right-center that was limited to a run-scoring fly after Kelley's great running catch.[27]

The evenly-matched teams split two more exciting contests. On Sunday, the Peaches, led by Dottie Kamenshek, squeaked out a 3–2 triumph and dropped the Blue Sox into second place behind 12–6 Fort Wayne. Mueller, a submarine curveballer like Roth, hurled hitless ball until the fifth when Kamenshek sparked a two-run rally with a double to right, and the Peaches' star, playing only her second game of the season (Dottie was also a college student), won it with an RBI double in the sixth. Baker and Dailey each rapped two of the Sox' eight hits, and Baker's RBI single in the second capped a two-run rally, but lefty Amy Applegren pitched tough in the clutch.[28] On Monday, Faut's stellar performance helped the home team regain the league lead with a 6–1 victory. Permitting five hits, Faut, batting cleanup, also singled home one run in the first and doubled home another in a three-run third. Leading 4–1 in the eighth, the Sox, racking up 13 hits off Lou Erickson, sealed the outcome with two insurance tallies.[29]

Shaking Up the League

Not knowing about an impending shakeup of the league, South Bend traveled to Peoria for a two-game set beginning on Tuesday, June 6. In the opener at Peoria Stadium, Elaine

Roth and Mary Dailey led the visitors to a 3–1 win. Roth, the underarmer, was effective in the clutches, spacing four hits and yielding one run in the sixth, and Dailey, off to a good start as a rookie, hit a two-run single and later scored on an error in South Bend's three-run fifth.[30] On Wednesday, the Redwings started the Blue Sox on a three-game skid by winning 5–4. Mueller took the loss in ten innings, despite the heroics of Wagoner, who tied the game at 4–4 in the ninth with a single to score pinch-runner Jette Vincent. In the tenth, Mary Reynolds singled, Faye Dancer sacrificed, and Mary Carey singled to center. The loss dropped the Sox to third place with an 11–6 ledger.[31]

Also on June 6, South Bend's longtime and popular but now aging and highly-paid star,[32] Bonnie Baker, the second baseman, was suddenly traded to Muskegon in return for infielder Charlene "Shorty" Pryer. Even more surprising, Baker was named temporary manager of the Lassies. The trade came after a meeting by the league's board that mainly resulted in the suspension of Muskegon's franchise. "Discouraging attendance and inadequate local financing," noted Fred Leo, "have combined to make necessary the suspension of the Muskegon franchise." After the vote, manager Lenny Zintak, who had wanted the Baker-Pryer trade, resigned, and the deal was approved. Baker took over the Lassies that night in Kenosha, and Leo indicated the Lassies might move to Kalamazoo, Michigan, where "important interests" wanted the franchise.[33]

Leo, facing the collapse of Muskegon (4–11) and Grand Rapids (4–12), wanted to boost the Lassies by trading to them 31-year-old Baker and her baseball expertise, good bat, and star power. The loop's president persuaded Zintak to give up Pryer, a fifth-year second sacker who turned 29 in August. Leo wanted Marge Stefani for manager, but Harold Dailey refused. He agreed to the trade, he noted, because Baker was "about done anyhow."[34] Later, when South Bend went downhill in August, Dailey concluded the real loss involving Baker was "less brains in the infield."[35] The tight-fisted Dailey was happy to see Baker's salary, likely the league's largest because of "under the table" supplements that he first approved in 1947,[36] paid by another team.

At a board meeting in Chicago on June 11, the league agreed to shift Muskegon's franchise to Kalamazoo. Dailey was asked to lend Lil Faralla to Kalamazoo in return for rookie Irene Kotil, and he agreed.[37] The Faralla-for-Kotil deal made it evident the success of the Lassie franchise was crucial to the league's survival. Also, Baker moved the Lassies from last place to fourth, after she received several new players. At season's end, however, the loop's directors, all men, voted to ban female managers, except in emergency circumstances. When asked years later about her acceptance as a pilot, Baker said, "They didn't want me beating former big-league stars."[38]

South Bend kept playing good ball, finally reaching the elusive goal of first place on Thursday, June 22. Faut, backed by a 13-hit attack, improved her record to 7–3 by stifling the Daisies at Playland on Wednesday, 8–1.[39] Mueller's stellar four-hitter on Thursday knocked Fort Wayne (21–13) out of the top spot with a 5–1 win, a success helped by Mahon, who hit three singles in four trips and knocked in three of her team's five runs.[40] Having won three straight, the Blue Sox traveled to Fort Wayne on Friday and beat the second-place Daisies again, 7–4. Ruth Williams, coughing up 11 hits and four runs, pitched tough with runners aboard, stranding 12. Bancroft closed the game by using Faut, his ace, who hurled hitless ball for the final inning and two-thirds. The visitors collected ten hits, three by Wagoner and two by Mary Dailey, boosting their ledger to 21–14 and their loop lead to one and a half games.[41]

On Saturday night, rain washed out the second Daisy-Blue Sox tilt, but South Bend slipped to 20–11 after the league's president ruled that a forfeit at Racine on June 20 must be played from the spot the game was halted. South Bend was trailing a riotous affair in the ninth, 10–6, with the bases loaded and nobody out, when umpire Al Zingone ejected Racine's catcher, Irene Hickson, for arguing. When the Belles failed to produce another catcher within a "reasonable time," the arbiter declared a forfeit. When the Sox traveled back home to meet Grand Rapids in a Sunday evening doubleheader, they held a one-game lead over 21–14 Fort Wayne.[42]

Winning in Streaks

After splitting a twin bill with Grand Rapids at Playland on Sunday, June 25, South Bend stood on top of the standings with a 21–14 record, followed by Fort Wayne (22–14), Rockford (22–17), Kenosha (20–16), and Racine (19–16). Grand Rapids and Peoria were tied for sixth place with losing marks of 16–20, and Kalamazoo was still last with a dismal 8–20 ledger.[43]

Traveling by bus to Grand Rapids for another two games, the Blue Sox split again. On Monday at Bigelow Field, a crowd of 1,324 saw Alma Ziegler, better known as Gabby and also a second baseman, hurl a three-hitter for her third straight shutout to pace the Chicks' 6–0 win.[44] On Tuesday, South Bend won, 2–1, with a two-run second inning. Mahon reached on an infield error, Stoll singled, Filarski sacrificed, Kotil hit a run-scoring single over third, and Stovroff was safe on a grounder to pitcher Mobile Silvestri, who hesitated and threw too late. Ruth Williams' grounder to third was bobbled, Stoll scored, and Williams protected the lead. The narrow victory left the Sox in first place with a 22–13 mark, just ahead of 24–15 Fort Wayne.[45]

Returning home to Playland, South Bend met Baker's struggling Kalamazoo team in a twin bill on Wednesday, June 28, and rain allowed the Lassies to escape with just one defeat. Faut, winning her ninth game, outdueled Lassie star Doris Sams in the short opener, firing a three-hitter. The Blue Sox rapped six hits and won with a three-run sixth that boosted the lead to 6–0. Thanks partly to four errors, the local favorites were leading 4–0 in the nightcap against Eilaine Roth, the twin sister of South Bend's Elaine, when rain ended the contest.[46]

In a make-up twin bill on Thursday, the Blue Sox defeated Lil Faralla, 2–1, just over two weeks following the loan of their former teammate to Kalamazoo. Faralla and Dottie Mueller each permitted four hits and pitched shutout ball after the first frame. The Lassies scored once in the first when Eilaine Roth, playing left field, singled and later scored on a groundout, but the Blue Sox tallied twice in the bottom of the inning, when Stoll hit a two-run single following two walks and a groundout. In the nightcap, Vincent, who added two hits, won, 9–2, behind a 12-hit barrage featuring three by Mahon and two each by Wagoner and Kotil. Elsewhere, Grand Rapids and Fort Wayne split two contests, so the Sox (25–13) led the Daisies by two games.[47]

South Bend continued to hold the loop's top spot in early July, winning and losing in streaks. At Grand Rapids, the Blue Sox lost twice, the second being a 2–1 defeat when Wagoner made her pitching debut and gave up nine hits. At the same time, Fred Leo's Balancing Committee ordered South Bend to send first baseman Arlene Kotil to Fort Wayne, and the Daisies had to send the Sox either first sacker Vivian Kellogg or outfielder Betty Luna, a pair of veterans near the end of their careers. Instead, Harold Dailey refused the order, and

Dave Bancroft defied the league by playing Kotil in both games. The South Benders, ignoring the league's "balancing" act, made matters worse by playing all of their games after July 1 under threat of forfeit.[48]

At Playland on Sunday, July 2, the Blue Sox battled the Daisies three times in three days, but won just once — taking the Sunday contest by riding Faut's four-hitter to a 5–3 victory.[49] Monday's tilt between the league's two top teams was rained out. Entertaining a festive audience of 4,276 on Tuesday, the home team lost the Fourth of July twin bill by scores of 4–3 and 5–2 to Fort Wayne. The late defeat, occuring because Mueller gave up three runs in the eighth, dropped South Bend (26–17) into second place behind Rockford (29–18), after the Peaches split their holiday set with the Redwings.[50]

Starting on Wednesday in Kalamazoo, the Blue Sox met the last-place Lassies in a four-game set. The visitors won the opener, regaining first place when Faut relieved and quashed a one-out, ninth-inning rally. Baker's Lassies had scored twice and the bases were still loaded. The first tally came home on Faralla's pinch-hit single, following Jean Lovell's base hit and Marge Wenzell's pass, and the second run scored when Vincent walked two more batters. Faut preserved the win, inducing Baker to pop out and walking in one run, but ending the game on Betty Francis' groundout. At the same time, the league's Balancing Committee, again trying to save Kalamazoo, ordered another switch: South Bend was told to lend Betty Whiting to the Lassies, Fort Wayne had to send Betty Luna to Kalamazoo, the Daisies would obtain Sally Meier, and the Sox could keep Arlene Kotil. Also, the forfeit threat would be dropped when all teams completed the trades.[51]

The Blue Sox lost two of their remaining three games in Kalamazoo, but they bounced back by returning home and knocking off Peoria four straight times. After the local favorites swept a twin bill from the Redwings on Sunday, July 9, Paul Neville, sports editor of the *Tribune*, observed that South Bend and Fort Wayne successfully "embarrassed" the league by refusing to move rookies to Kalamazoo, despite the circuit's threat of forfeiture. When each team sent a player to Kalamazoo (the Sox loaned Whiting and the Daisies gave up Luna), Neville called it another example of politicking and personal feuding that would end up hurting the league. "The girls' league might well declare a moratorium on further trades so that the players and fans," Neville pointed out, "can settle down for the remainder of the season."[52]

The Lineup at Mid-Season

Settling down was necessary, and by mid–July, the Blue Sox fielded an experienced lineup. Aside from Faut and Mueller, however, the pitching was erratic. Faut, the fastballing right-hander who also threw three types of curveballs as well as a slider, usually displayed pinpoint control. Jean upped her record to 12–3 by defeating Peoria in 11 innings, 3–2, when Filarski hammered a two-out, two-run double for the victory in the first game of a Sunday pair on July 9. By July 13, when she lost the first game in what became South Bend's season-turning eight-game skid, Faut had saved three games in relief. The stout-hearted blond again finished the season as the best pitcher, completing 29 of 36 games, working a league-high 290 innings, and fashioning a 21–9 record with a circuit-best 1.12 ERA.[53] Jean was an exceptional performer, and her teammates knew they could win every time she pitched. Few outside South Bend realized that she handled "double duty," also raising her son Larry, two years old, and caring for her home.[54]

Next to Faut, South Bend's second-best pitcher was sidearm-underhander Dottie Mueller, 24, who won 16 games. A 5'11" curveballer with good control, Mueller was coming off three stellar seasons with Peoria, where she was the team's ace. Called "Sporty" by her buddies, she made the All-Star team as a rookie in the sidearm season of 1947, finishing with a 21–13 mark and producing a 1.41 ERA for fifth-place Peoria. In 1948, Dottie enjoyed another fine year, going 21–9 with a 1.31 ERA and leading her team to third place in the Western Division. In 1949, the Redwings, with less punch in the lineup, fell to last (eighth) place at 36–73, and Mueller slipped to a 7–16 ledger. In 1950, the tall Ohio native with the good repertoire of pitches was a steadying influence on the Sox mound, completing 22 of 27 games, working 221 innings, walking 53 batters, striking out 90, and posting a 16–9 record with a 2.48 ERA.

However, once Dave Bancroft got past the experienced one-two punch of Faut and Mueller, he was out of stellar pitchers. For example, Faralla, who had pitched so well in 1949, made only one appearance for South Bend — in relief of Faut in the opening game — before she was loaned to Kalamazoo on June 12. Lil finished the season with an 8–10 mark and a 3.12 ERA. Bancroft decided not to pitch the Californian, for reasons that remain unclear. His decision left him with three other right-handers: Elaine Roth, Ruth Williams, and Jette Vincent. Roth, an underhander who relied on her curveball and good control, had a 7–13 record with a 3.28 ERA in 1950, but she was 6–5 by mid–July. Williams, a right-handed slowballer who worked as a teacher in Pennsylvania and could not join the team until mid–June, finished with a 5–10 record and a 3.57 ERA, but she was 2–4 by mid–July. Later, Ruth was traded to Peoria because, as Dailey noted, she lost six games in July and refused to play apart from Bonnie Baker, her friend who was now managing Kalamazoo.[55] Vincent, from Fall River, Massachusetts, appeared as a spot starter for South Bend in 1949. She compiled a 3–2 record, after going 5–2 as a hurler and infielder in her second year for Racine in 1948. In 1950, Jette lost her first two decisions, but she won five times by mid–July, finishing with an 8–12 mark and a 3.12 ERA. Indeed, the dearth of

Ace of Diamonds — Enjoying a happy moment at Playland Park in 1950 after one of her many victories, Jean Faut fashioned an eight-year won-lost record of 140–64 with a sterling ERA of 1.23. Starting out as a third baseman with a rifle arm in 1946, she was a good fielder and a timely hitter who batted .243 lifetime. In addition, Jean led the league in ERA in 1950, 1952, and 1953, hurled no-hitters in 1948 and 1949, and pitched perfect games in 1951 and 1953, the two years she was voted the Player of the Year (courtesy of the Louise Pettus Archives and Special Collections, Winthrop University).

quality pitchers like Faut and Mueller caused Bancroft to try Betty Wagoner on the mound, but she was 0–3 in four starts.

By July, Bancroft's lineup, barring injuries, usually featured the following players:

- 2B — Shorty Pryer was a feisty, aggressive, fifth-year player from Watsonville, California, who was a good fielder and a solid hitter. The 5'1½" Pryer averaged .269, third best for the Blue Sox. In 112 games, the right-handed hitting speedster, who spent two years in the female branch of the Marine Corps toward the end of World War II, scored a team-high 75 runs, stole 75 bases, and added 25 RBI. Excitement seemed to follow the pretty Californian's presence. Shorty, who once saved a teammate from drowning, made a strong contribution to South Bend's fortunes.
- RF/CF — Betty Wagoner, 20, a Missourian and a college student in the off-season, was starring in her third season for South Bend. She led her team in hitting with a .296 mark, the ninth-best average in the league, and she was still hitting above .300 in mid–August. Betty loved movies as well as golf, bowling, and baseball. The southpaw, who also batted left, put her heart and soul into the game. A fast runner with a good arm and the ability to track down balls hit deep into the outer gardens, Wagoner, who spoke with a southern drawl, said little and blushed easily. On the diamond, she displayed excellent skills, making more than one game-saving catch.[56] In 106 contests, mostly in right field, the 5'2" curly-haired brunette connected for 11 doubles and three triples, also scoring 61 runs and producing 39 RBI from the second slot in the order.
- SS — Shoo-Shoo Wirth, returning for her fifth season, was a first-rate defensive shortstop with a quick release, but her arm was better suited to second base. Smart, agile, and exciting to watch, the five-foot Tampa speedster was a community favorite who often signed autographs with a drawing of two shoes. Hustling and smiling, her dark locks flying, she excited Sox fans as well as her teammates. Shoo-Shoo played 105 games and averaged .268, fourth best on the team, rapping nine doubles and two triples, drawing 49 walks, and stealing 67 bases. A good clutch hitter, the right-handed batter drove in 49 runs, second to a career-high 54 RBI in 1951, her final season.
- LF — Lib Mahon, now in her seventh season, played less in 1950, partly because she suffered a vision problem, first sitting out of South Bend's victory over Grand Rapids on May 24. Mahon appeared in 69 games and hit .246, slugging 11 doubles, one triple, and one homer, but fewer games cut her RBI figure to 37. After a home game in late July, the South Carolina native was the target of a verbal "dressing down" from board member Al McGann, who blamed her for the meal money protest. Two weeks later, on August 11, Lib, still upset, resigned from the league, supposedly due to an inflammation of her eye.[57] She returned in 1951, but Lib remained unhappy with management. Doc Dailey, who disliked Mahon, saw her as a clubhouse problem, but friends saw her as a fine athlete and a good teammate who spoke up on behalf of the girls.
- CF — Jeep Stoll, now 21, enjoyed her best All-American season yet, posting the second highest average — behind Wagoner — for South Bend. Like Wagoner, Jeep had good defensive skills, and she studied the opposing hitters in order to play each one correctly. At the plate, the sturdy five-footer, a right-handed batter,

showed a good eye. In 99 games, the Pennsylvania native hit .271, belting 14 doubles, two triples, and one homer. She drew 44 walks but whiffed only 13 times, scoring 40 runs while driving home a team-high 50 runners. Jeep gave her team a good at-bat in a clutch situation, and she became one of South Bend's most popular players.

- 3B — Helen Filarski usually covered the "hot corner" for Bancroft. A steady fielder and a versatile performer who batted .209 in 93 games, she contributed six doubles and six triples. She also walked 44 times, scored 25 runs, and produced 26 RBI. Helen worked hard to improve. She liked to practice, as did most of the league's more serious players. Bancroft, however, made practices optional in 1949, and he continued his loose rein in 1950. During a home stand, players like Filarski, Faut, and others would walk to Playland Park in the middle of the day and take batting and fielding practice, but the entire team should have been practicing together.[58]
- 1B — Bancroft had no first-rate choice for the initial sack. Betty Whiting started the season at first base, but after 28 games, she was loaned to Kalamazoo, where she played 64 games, averaging a combined .207. Arlene "Riley" Kotil, loaned for Faralla on June 11, came to South Bend after playing 16 games for Muskegon. She got into 67 contests for the Blue Sox, hitting a combined .205 in her only All-American season. A 5'6" brunette from Chicago with good fielding skills who batted and threw left-handed, she played first base after Whiting moved to the Lassies on July 6. In addition to 50 hits, including five doubles and a triple, Kotil drew 30 walks, scored 21 times, and drove home 21 runners, but the experienced pitchers struck out the rookie 64 times — tying her for the league high with Peoria infielder Twi Shively, who averaged .192. Later, when the Sox fell to fifth place, the *Racine Journal-Times*, analyzing the playoff picture, observed that South Bend, occasionally missing players like Wagoner, Mahon, or Stoll due to injuries, was hampered by "serious weaknesses at first base and third base."[59]
- C — Bancroft had two first-rate defensive backstops, but neither added punch to the lineup. Shirley Stovroff, the strong-armed receiver favored by Faut, and Jenny Romatowski split the catching duties. Stovroff, a 5'4" 145-pounder from Madison, Illinois, may have been the league's top defensive catcher, but she was far from the top hitter. In 1950, the first full season in which batting marks began rising because of the smaller, livelier ball introduced in mid–1949, South Bend averaged .230, the team's highest mark to date. In 85 games, Stovroff hit just .197, walking 25 times, scoring 20 runs, and adding 18 RBI. Romatowski, a career back-up from Wyandotte, Michigan, matched Stovroff exactly in height and weight. In 46 games, Jenny batted .209, walking 12 times, scoring 11 runs, and contributing nine RBI.

Next to Kotil, South Bend's best rookie after Anna Kunkel was injured, Bancroft had three choices. Mary Dailey hit the ball well in spring games, but she tapered off against experienced hurlers in the regular season. The 5'7" outfielder from Massachusetts, a right-handed batter who excelled at golf, tennis, and bowling, was loaned to Peoria for two games. Returning to South Bend, Dailey played a total of 54 games, averaged a combined .138, hitting two doubles and a triple, scoring 20 times, and contributing 14 RBI. The new local favorite was 5'4" Janet "Pee Wee" Wiley, the South Bender who served as bat girl in 1947 and 1948. Wiley played 40 games but hit only .134, with a double, a triple, five runs scored, and seven RBI. Finally, Audrey Bleiler, the 5'7" Philadelphia native, filled in at third base on occasion. Lanky Audrey received six free passes, rapped four hits, scored four times, and knocked in three runs, but she hit just .093. In retrospect, Bancroft had a weak bench, and one or two injuries could hurt the Sox.

Trouble in July

While Fred Leo and the teams' directors debated further cuts in expenses and additional moves to "save" teams like Kalamazoo, Peoria, and Grand Rapids, the Blue Sox, after leading the loop for most of the first two months, hit several bumps in the playoff road. At Playland on Monday, July 10, the home team completed a four-game sweep of Peoria before a paid crowd of 1,422, not counting 500 free guests on Ladies Night. Roth hurled a classy, two-hit, 4–1 victory, boosted by Mahon, who excited folks with a three-hit, two-RBI night. At that point, South Bend was leading the league with a 32–19 record, and Peoria was struggling in seventh place at 21–31. The game story included a special box stating that Shoo-Shoo Wirth was leaving the team for a brief visit with her husband, Robert Malott, a soldier stationed at Fort Lewis, near Tacoma, Washington. Malott was alerted for overseas duty (the Korean conflict would soon erupt, as U.S. officials realized), and Wirth, who went 2-for-4, planned to fly to the West Coast.[60]

Following a split of two home games against Rockford, the Blue Sox boarded their bus for a fateful road trip. The blue-uniformed visitors lost three straight to the Redwings, and the league's games were rained out on Sunday. Journeying to Rockford, the Blue Sox lost a Monday night doubleheader to the Peaches, falling in the nightcap, 1–0, when Vincent pitched well but gave up a bases-loaded single to pitcher Nicky Fox in the last of the eighth. For all but one road game, Wiley replaced Wirth and played adequately, but the Sox were not getting clutch hits.[61]

By the time the team returned to Playland on Tuesday, July 18, South Bend was in trouble and so was the league. The local favorites lost their sixth straight, falling to the Comets, 4–1, thanks partly to shoddy defense. Wirth was still missing, and Bancroft shifted Wiley to first base in place of the slumping Kotil, and at short he tried Vincent, the third-year hurler. The remainder of Bancroft's lineup included Wagoner in right, leading off; Pryer at second base; Stoll in center; Mahon in left; Faut pitching; Filarski at third; Stovroff behind the plate; and Wiley. In the sixth inning, Bancroft's strategy failed when Vincent, new to the shortstop position, fielded a grounder with runners on first and second and hesitated so long that her throw missed the batter racing for first, allowing the lead run to score from second base. Faut (now 12–5) took the loss, even though she retired the first 14 batters, allowed just four hits, and led her team with two of five Sox safeties. As a result, South Bend slipped to third place with a 33–26 record.

At the same time, league officials were meeting on Wednesday night in Chicago to resolve the latest emergency. Peoria was given one week to raise enough money to keep the club going, and Grand Rapids, $20,000 in debt, had not met the team's payroll for two weeks. Paul Neville compared the loop's problems to financial crises suffered by various minor leagues, citing the recent collapse of the Class B Colonial League of New York and Connecticut. Declining attendance was hurting baseball everywhere, but Neville concluded that the league's fans hoped "the directors tonight may discover a transfusion that will resolve their plight."[62]

Harold Dailey, at the meeting in Chicago, asked for the return of Betty Whiting, who was loaned to Kalamazoo on the basis of a 48-hour recall. Bancroft wanted to bolster his team's hitting, but nothing came of the request.[63] On Wednesday, the second game with Kenosha was rained out, and South Bend, with Wirth returning, rode to Racine. However, Thursday's contest was also washed away, and the players spent the day hanging around the Hotel Racine.

The ups and downs continued. On Friday, the Blue Sox lost a twin bill at Horlick Field, despite having Wirth at shortstop (she was 0-for-6 for the night), and the loss made eight in a row. For the opener, a small but excited crowd of 736 saw Ellie Dapkus win a two-hit shutout, 3–0. In the late tilt, the Belles defeated Vincent, 4–3, with a two-run seventh-inning rally based on two hits and two Sox errors.[64] In another doubleheader on Saturday, Faut, who often broke her team's losing streaks, allowed six hits and South Bend won, 6–3, boosted by a two-run rally in the seventh for a 4–3 lead. The nightcap was a replay of the ninth inning of the game forfeited on June 10. Racine, ahead 10–6 at the time, won by the same score, and the Sox slipped to fourth place at 34–29.[65]

South Bend's inconsistent hitting was again displayed at Kenosha in Sunday's doubleheader, as the Comets won the opener when Williams, still unhappy with her team, surrendered two runs in the sixth on a walk and three hits for the final margin of 4–2. South Bend won the nightcap, 4–1, on Roth's stellar effort, and her teammates put the victory away with a two-run fifth, featuring an RBI single by Wirth, who also scored on an error.[66] In Monday's game at Simmons Field, South Bend triumphed when Mahon's two-out double in the 12th scored Pryer, who had singled, to give the visitors a 7–6 victory. Mueller pitched well until the eighth, when two Sox errors and three Comet hits led to four runs and a 6–6 tie. Vincent relieved and stifled Kenosha's bats, yielding no further runs. The *Tribune*'s story, however, headlined how thousands of fans in Peoria and Grand Rapids raised money, $12,500 by the Redwings' backers, to keep both teams in the league.[67] All the while, South Bend launched a new success streak, winning seven of eight.

Meal Money and Controversy

The league's turmoil in the summer of 1950 was recorded in some detail by Doc Dailey, partly to justify the positions he took as team president. At the circuit meeting on July 5, the board discussed several main issues, notably stopping the Balancing Committee from making player shifts to help weaker clubs. Speaking for Fort Wayne, hotel magnate Harold Van Orman argued it was unfair to use a player like Vivian Kellogg to help Kalamazoo, indicating that Rockford would not give up a star such as Dottie Kamenshek. That was also Dailey's position. After the group discussed financial issues, Leo offered to resign but instead won a vote of confidence.[68]

On July 12, after receiving Leo's letter explaining that he did not move players due to personal interests, Dailey said league officials had no idea of how much money and support were needed to build a good local club. When Sox fans saw their team lose two key players while the Peaches lost none (actually, Rose Gacioch was loaned to the Lassies), they resented the league. Further, Dailey wanted to trade Ruth Williams for Lil Faralla because, he said, Williams and Baker, Kalamazoo's manager, lived together for three years, and Williams would "not pitch away from Baker." Also, Faralla and Stoll purchased a car together, and the trade would help both. In other words, personal issues were always involved in player deals. Later on July 12, Dailey agreed to take Lassie right-hander Mobile Silvestri for Williams, whom he wanted to dump.[69]

Still concerned about budget matters, the league's board met on Wednesday, July 19, and decided to cut out meal money paid on road trips beginning the next Monday. Dailey opposed the cut, unless South Bend's board approved, but the board agreed, concluding that for players to lose meal money was better than losing salary. When the girls heard about the impending slash, they discussed it and informed Marge Stefani they would not make the next road trip to Grand Rapids, scheduled for Sunday, July 30. Bancroft learned of the refusal and told Dailey on Saturday morning, and Dailey informed Leo. At 11:53 A.M., Leo wired Dailey that any player "threatening revolt" and not appearing at the scheduled game in Grand Rapids on Sunday would be suspended indefinitely. Bancroft so informed the players before Saturday night's game.

On Saturday, South Bend blanked visiting Grand Rapids, 4–0, as Faut (now 15–5) missed a no-hitter when Inez Voyce lined a seventh-inning single off Kotil's glove. Afterward, believing she called the wrong pitch, Stovroff cried on the bench, but Faut consoled her. Still, the local favorites scored the runs they needed in the fourth when Stoll walked, Faut, who had two of her team's eight hits, tripled to the right field corner for one run, and Filarski singled for a 2–0 lead. The win left South Bend in fourth place at 41–31, four and a half games behind Fort Wayne.

More important, the meal money dispute spilled over onto the diamond. In front of the stands after the game, Sox director Al McGann "really took Mahon apart and in no uncertain terms." Dailey figured Mahon was one of the "ring leaders" in the threat not to travel to Grand Rapids, where the Chicks, because of the team's financial crisis, had not been paid for three weeks.[70]

Instead of a revolt, the players showed up at Playland on Sunday morning ready to board the bus, but first they wanted to talk to Dailey. The president found Mahon "pretty well cooled off," and at Faut's request, he explained to the team why the league as well as South Bend eliminated the meal money. Dailey recorded that he left everyone in a "pretty good frame of mind," and he hoped all went well because "Marge and Dave are pretty well beat by now."[71]

Instead, the Blue Sox were coming unglued. As of July 31, when they held fourth place with a 41–32 record, four and a half games behind league-leading Fort Wayne (44–26), the South Benders ranked third in hitting with a .239 mark, and they were tied for third in fielding with Peoria, both averaging .950. The top Blue Sox hitter was Wagoner at .325, making her third in the circuit behind Fort Wayne's Betty (Weaver) Foss, at .379, and Rockford's Dottie Kamenshek, at .327. Other South Benders and their marks included Stoll, .287; Wirth, .279; Pryer, .260; Mahon, .249; Kotil, .227; Stovroff, .221; Filarski, .217; and Faut, .216. The league's top pitcher was Rockford's Lois Florreich with a 14–4 ledger, and the Sox pitchers and records were Faut, 15–5; Mueller, 9–6; Vincent, 8–6; Roth, 7–7; Williams, 2–6; and Wagoner, 0–2.[72]

At Grand Rapids, South Bend continued to skid, dropping two out of three. On Tuesday, August 1, the Blue Sox finally grabbed a win, 4–3, in the late tilt of a doubleheader. Mueller got credit for the success, but Faut shut down a sixth-inning rally, allowed a run in the seventh, and saved the game by pitching two shutout innings. The visitors collected seven hits, two by Stoll, and reached Rose Gacioch (on loan from Rockford) for four runs in the first frame on four hits and four walks. Later, Bancroft announced the release of Mary Dailey and the trade of Ruth Williams to Peoria for Sue Kidd, a 5'8" right-hander who played with the Sallies on the rookie tour in 1949.[73]

After traveling through the night to Rockford and the Peach Orchard, South Bend lost four straight. Saturday, August 5, was a league day off, and the Blue Sox rode their special bus home to meet Peoria for three games, beginning with two Sunday evening contests at Playland. The Redwings, however, won all three, ending the series by beating South Bend on Monday, 7–2. Vincent gave a poor performance, allowing seven walks and seven runs before being relieved by Kidd with the bases loaded in the sixth. The recruit from Arkansas gave up one run on Stovroff's passed ball, but Peoria, leading 6–1, scored no more, and Hank Warren earned the victory. Afterward, South Bend still held fourth place with a 42–40 mark, but Rockford, now 51–31, topped the circuit and led the Sox by nine games.[74]

At Playland on Tuesday and Wednesday, Mueller and Faut, South Bend's one-two punch, beat the Peaches. On August 8, Mueller ended her team's seven-game slide with a 3–1 victory, as Wiley played first and handled 18 putouts, and Audrey Bleiler, covering third base for Filarski, who was out with an injured hand, scooped up a low peg from Stovroff in the fourth and tagged Jackie Kelley, trying to steal. The Blue Sox scored twice in the first off Florreich when Wagoner doubled to left, advanced on Wirth's bunt single, scored on Mahon's single to right, and Shoo-Shoo tallied on Stoll's sacrifice.[75] On August 9, Faut won her 16th game with a three-hitter, 5–1. In the first frame, the Blue Sox scored four times off Nicky Fox when Pryer reached second on a two-base error, Wagoner singled to score one run, Wirth sacrificed, and, after Mahon flew out, Faut, Stoll, and Stovroff singled for a 4–0 lead. Fort Wayne (48–31) split with seventh-place Peoria, lifting the Daises into first place by a few percentage points over Rockford (51–33).[76]

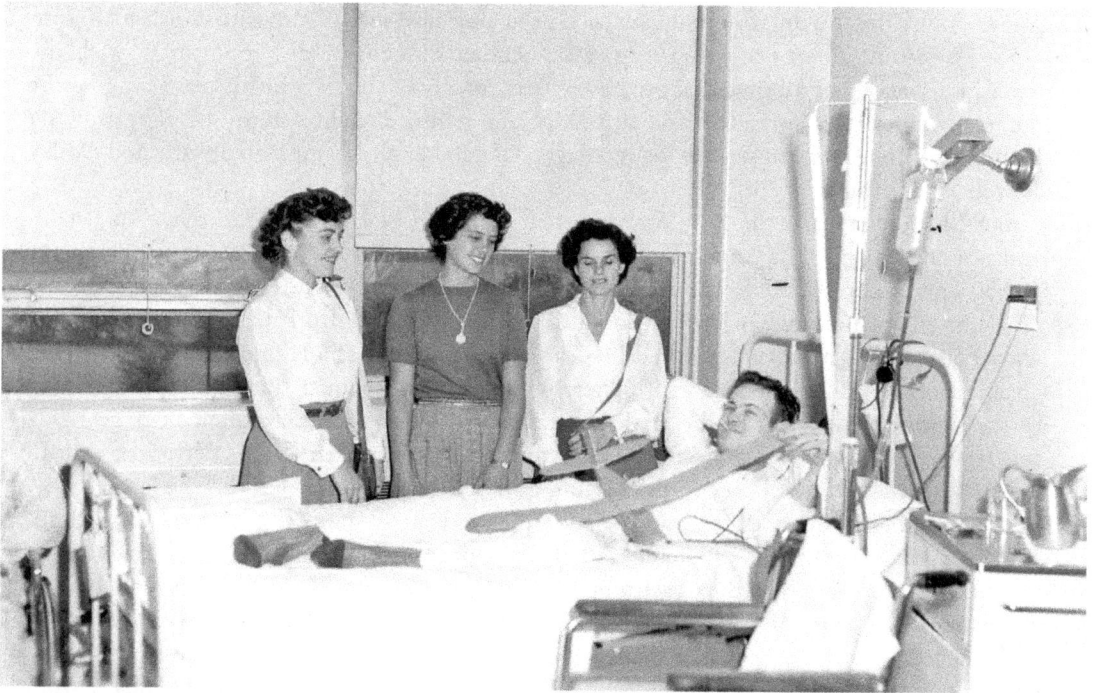

Boosting Morale — In an off day event not unusual for the league's players, three Blue Sox visit a patient in the hospital during the summer of 1950. The man in the bed is unidentified, but the cheery South Benders are (left to right) Lou Arnold, Shirley Stovroff, and "Shorty" Pryer (courtesy of the Louise Pettus Archives and Special Collections, Winthrop University).

On Thursday, August 10, Rockford's Amy Applegren, with relief help from the veteran Gacioch (back from Kalamazoo), defeated the Blue Sox and Roth, 6–3.[77] On Friday at Peoria, the Redwings blanked the Blue Sox, 1–0. Ruth Williams, not satisfied with her trade to the Redwings, nevertheless hurled a four-hitter in perhaps her best performance of the year. The Pennsylvania teacher outdueled Vincent, who spaced five hits, and won when Peoria scored in the ninth off Joyce Hill's single, Vincent's wild throw, and a run-scoring grounder by Rita Briggs.

However, the big news came after the game when Mahon announced her retirement from baseball due to "neuritis of the optic nerve," a condition that had bothered her all year long.[78] Lib, however, was upset by a team director having embarrassed her in front of the crowd two weeks earlier. Dailey spoke with the Sox' star. Later, failing to understand the girls' commitment to professionalism, including playing hard every night and being involved in community activities in their spare time, Dailey instead concluded that they "dogged" games after the meal money issue arose.[79] Although Mahon later changed her mind, Dailey noted she's "sore at McGann and says that the crowd is against her and some more guff about such a bad deal she has gotten."[80]

Struggling in the End

Little did South Bend's president realize it, but the issues surrounding Lib Mahon's retirement sank the Sox for the remainder of 1950. Faut and Mueller won eight of the nine games South Bend won after August 11, but the club also lost 14 times to finish fifth with a 55–55 record. The once-promising season ended in a major disappointment with the team in disarray. For all practical purposes, Bancroft lost control over his team long before the meal money issue surfaced and before McGann rebuked Mahon in public. The growing frustration in the clubhouse over losing players like Baker and Faralla finally affected Dailey as well as the team.

Still professionals, the Blue Sox returned to Peoria Stadium on Saturday, August 12, and pounded out 12 hits, three each by Pryer and Wagoner, off Hank Warren and reliever Jo Hasham to clip the Redwings, 8–5. Vincent played left field and went 2-for-5, Mueller yielded nine hits, and when Peoria scored three runs in the ninth, Faut came in to save the win. The *Tribune*, however, featured Dailey's announcement of a 12-man committee to sell an additional 7,500 tickets in 1950, thereby ensuring that South Bend would finish the season without a deficit.[81] In the finale at Peoria on Sunday, Faut played left field, going 2-for 3, while Kidd pitched and yielded eight hits. Peoria bunched three safeties in the fifth for a 3–2 lead, and Mary Reynolds' hurling gave her team a 4–2 victory.[82]

Struggling in the end, the South Benders played the remainder of the season without Mahon's potent bat, with a depleted bench, and without the team's usual camaraderie, an intangible factor eroded by the unsettling events of June and July. At Fort Wayne on Monday, August 14, Faut and Millie Deegan battled to a 2–2 tie that lasted 17 innings and ended with the league's 11:30 pm curfew. Faut yielded 11 hits, and Bancroft used Stoll in left, Wagoner in center, and Vincent in right field.[83] In a ragged game on Tuesday, the Daisies won, 9–7, as Max Carey employed four pitchers to defeat Vincent, while South Bend committed four errors and Fort Wayne made five. Faut played right field, but the Sox, rapping nine safeties, could not overcome the Daisies' 6–0 lead after three innings.

In positive news, Dailey called the response to South Bend's ticket-selling campaign "highly gratifying." The Blue Sox needed about $84,000 for the 1950 season: salaries, uniforms, travel, medical needs, and insurance totaled $47,850; league and management costs were $18,261; the operation of Playland Park cost $5,889; and administrative expenses were $12,500. Those figures meant the Sox would end up $7,500 in the red, and thus the sales campaign.[84]

At Fort Wayne's Memorial Field on Wednesday, August 16, South Bend (46–44) moved back into fourth place ahead of Grand Rapids (44–44), winning on Mueller's three-hitter, 4–2, but the Daisies made ten errors to hurt Kay Blumetta's efforts.[85] Back home on Thursday, the South Benders split a twin bill with third-place Kenosha, winning the short opener, 7–1, behind Faut's stellar pitching. The Blue Sox batted around in the first frame against Jean Marlowe, scoring four runs on three hits, three walks, and a sacrifice, and Faut did the rest. But Kenosha won a 9–2 slugfest against Roth in the nightcap, outhitting the home team, 13–12. Even so, the fans enjoyed Wirth's inside-the-park homer in the third and her sparkling play at shortstop.[86] Kenosha also won on Friday, 6–3, as Vincent lost a 3–1 lead after the first inning, and Ruby Stephens, another former South Bender, scattered nine hits for the win.[87]

On Saturday, Mueller took a 3–2 loss as her team stranded 13 runners against the Comets' Beth Goldsmith and Dottie Naum, normally a catcher, as they combined on a four-hitter. Wagoner twisted her knee sliding into third base, adding to Bancroft's injured list that included Filarski, Bleiler, and the departed Mahon. Faut played third base, Vincent played right, and Wiley, at first base, was the rookie in the lineup. The loss dropped the Sox into fifth place with a 47–47 mark, and they finished the season in fifth.[88]

Baseball Is Alive and Well

South Bend was disappointed, but All-American baseball was alive and well, according to newspaper and magazine articles inspired by the league's office. When Paul Neville discussed the team's financial problems in mid–August, he also argued that the Blue Sox provided an essential ingredient to South Bend's summer entertainment. "The game as played by the girls is the best of its kind in the country," the sports editor wrote, even though it was played in only eight cities. Neville called the All-Americans "marvelous" athletes and compared them to Patty Berg in golf, Louise Brough in tennis, and Eleanor Holm Jarrett in swimming. A general "tightening of the belt" was in the league's future, but he quoted Dailey's words about the Sox being a community asset, providing "good, clean, healthy entertainment as well as top-quality baseball."[89]

A typical story inspired by the league appeared in *McCall's* in September 1950. Morris Markey praised the All-American game, indicating nearly a million spectators (an exaggeration) bought tickets to contests in 1949, with more than half of them women. Many men were fans, but after gawking at the players' bare knees and legs for an inning, they watched in "wonderment at the skill of the fielders, the lusty swings of the batters, the assortment of 'stuff' the pitchers display." Citing Faut along with Merle Keagle and Dottie Collins as mothers as well as first-rate ballplayers, and offering Mahon, a teacher in the off-season, as an example of a star who was preparing for the future by using baseball earnings to pay for a Master's degree, the scribe said that the game was great for players and fans, but especially for the athletes. "The opportunity to show that you are good at something," Markey observed, "to have people yell their approval of you, injects powerful ingredients into the soul."[90]

Harold Dailey, less idealistic and more chauvinistic, figured he had the solution for 1951: more discipline for South Bend's ballplayers. After seeing the Blue Sox lose what the president called a "badly played" game in Kalamazoo, 6–3, he said most of the players were "taking the game as a play day for a summer vacation." At the same time, he had a "long talk with Carl Wench [sic] and I am sure he could run the ball team and Jean could be the chaperone. He knows the players and all the dirt that his wife knows." To Dailey, hardly a baseball expert, South Bend's downfall needed scapegoats. In particular, he blamed Dave Bancroft and chaperone Marge Stefani, saying they "caused a lot of trouble on themselves and that Dave has been drinking a great deal."[91]

The team president, who saw the game from a businessman's perspective, agreed to trade Bonnie Baker and loan Lil Faralla (who earned $100 per week[92]) partly to cut salaries.[93] In searching for answers, Dailey had no idea that his star pitcher on the field endured a troubled marriage away from the ballpark.[94] As Jean Faut later said, "Karl and I never talked baseball. We lived in two separate worlds."[95] Furthermore, Dailey failed to realize that players sided with players and, therefore, a player married to the manager would be placed in an impossible position. Perhaps if the team's president had looked closely at the featured picture in Morris Markey's article showing Faut standing next to Playland's concrete grandstand with Karl Winsch, son Larry, and two other men sitting on the benches,[96] he might have noticed that Jean's smile was forced.

• 9 •

South Bend Wins the Shaughnessy Championship: 1951

"Jean Faut, a sturdy gal with a lot of heart, a fast ball that hops, and a curve that breaks off like a country road, pitched a perfect no-hit, no-run game to subdue the Rockford Peaches, 2–0, at Playland Park Saturday night"— Paul Neville, July 22, 1951[1]

League Changes for 1951

For the first time in the nine-year history of the All-American Girls Baseball League, South Bend won the Shaughnessy Playoff Championship — thanks to excellent pitching, timely hitting, good fielding, and better camaraderie. Ironically, the team survived a series of changes in the front office, in players, and in league management. The Blue Sox prospered against long odds, clinching a playoff spot in the split season with a remarkable 16-game winning streak in late August. One difference between the city's ball club in 1951 compared to the 1950 season was the improved pitching staff, once again led by Jean Faut, who won 15 games and posted a 1.33 ERA, third best in the circuit. Voted the league's Player of the Year in a postseason poll of sportswriters, Faut, who pitched a no-hitter in 1948 and another in 1949, hurled her first-ever perfect game against Rockford on July 21, 1951. Furthermore, the league, desperate to attract more fans, adopted a split-season format (first used in 1943 and 1944), and South Bend earned a trip to the playoffs by winning first place with a second-half record of 38–14. Karl Winsch, the new manager, attributed the victorious season to the "superb team spirit" of the players.[2]

Long before South Bend won the title, however, the league was changed for the 1951 season. The teams' directors decided collectively to buy out the contract with Arthur Meyerhoff's Management Corporation for $1,000 per team, or $8,000 total,[3] and operate each team on an independent basis with a commissioner to supervise the league. The circuit's eight teams were community owned, although none had a wealthy backer that could supply $10,000 to $15,000 per year to offset the revenue lost from declining ticket sales. As indicated about the 1950 season, the teams' directors resented the league's Balancing Committee shifting, or "loaning," players from the stronger teams with better attendance, such as South Bend, Rockford, and Fort Wayne, to weaker teams, such as Muskegon-Kalamazoo, Peoria, and Grand Rapids. Fans wanted to see their favorite players, notably the veterans (who earned the highest salaries), play good baseball and compete for the pennant, so the Management Corporation often took a black eye.

The league's structure was basic. Fred Leo, president during the 1950 season, was selected as commissioner for 1951. Leo replaced the Management Corporation by functioning as the circuit's business manager. Edward J. Ruetz, judge of the Kenosha Municipal Court, the Comets' president and a participant in league affairs since All-American ball began in 1943, became the circuit's powerless president. Previously, the front office consisted of the president, a secretary, and a publicity agent. In 1951, the league switched to decentralized management and the budget was cut further, eliminating scouting expenses, touring teams, tickets costs and a secretary's salary.[4]

For all practical purposes, the circuit supervised, without regulating, the affairs of individual teams. The commissioner was a figurehead. As of November 1950, the eight teams told players that the clubs owned their contracts.[5] Also, each team handled its own personnel problems, scouting, recruitment, contracts, and training, but the league created the schedule. Leo explained the changes, saying the circuit attracted a total of 481,981 fans in 1950, a loss of almost 100,000 in paid attendance from 1949.[6]

South Bend needed a new manager because Dave Bancroft stepped aside, supposedly to help the team "ease its economic problems." Frank Helvie announced the opening on

Guys Running Girls' Baseball — Pictured are members of the all-male board of directors of the Blue Sox, who enjoy a laugh while smoking and drinking and talking baseball. Manager Karl Winsch is seated in the center and president Harold Dailey is on the far right. The picture was taken shortly after Winsch was hired in January 1951 (courtesy of the Louise Pettus Archives and Special Collections, Winthrop University).

Tuesday, November 14, 1950, one day after the directors elected him as the team's new president. Helvie, self-described as a former college and pro baseball and football player, succeeded Harold Dailey, who remained on the board and handled contracts and salaries. Bill Sheehan was retained as vice president, and Harold Condit and W.R. Schmeider were elected as treasurer and secretary, respectively.[7] On January 6, 1951, the club hired Karl Winsch — who had been talking to Dailey since early 1950 about the job.[8] The husband of Jean Faut, Winsch, according to Paul Neville, the *Tribune's* sports editor, was "one of the closest observers of the girls' game and [he] is well acquainted with the abilities of the league's athletes and the style of play required of consistent winners."[9] Faut, however, recalled not knowing Winsch was a candidate. Also, she disliked being placed in the difficult position of player-chaperone as well as manager's wife.[10]

Winsch grew up, like Faut, in East Greenville, Pennsylvania. After high school, the 5'10" right-hander pitched for the town's semipro team, the East Greenville Cubs, until 1942, when he was signed by the Philadelphia Phillies. The parent club sent him to Class C Rome, New York, where he posted a 1–3 mark with a fat 7.24 ERA. The minor leagues, like the majors, needed manpower during the World War, and Winsch, 28 years old, was exempt from the draft because he was married with a family to support. He finished 1942 with last-place Trenton of the Class B Interstate League, but lost all four decisions. Bothered by a sore arm, Winsch returned to Trenton in 1943 and produced a 10–9 ledger with a 4.58 ERA, and the Packers finished fifth in a six-team circuit. In 1944, he was one of Philadelphia's six rookie hurlers in mid–March,[11] but he never appeared in a regular season game. On May 8, the Phillies optioned him to Utica of the Class A Eastern League, and he went 4–4 with a 4.07 ERA. On August 24, 1944, the Phillies cancelled the option and ended his pro career. Interviewed in 1996, Karl, reflecting on his baseball memories, recalled, "I had coffee and doughnuts with the Phillies."[12]

At the All-American League's board meeting in Chicago on December 18, 1950, the new organizational structure was officially adopted and, accordingly, the circuit's name was changed to the American Girls Baseball League.[13] By late February, new rules were completed for the 1951 season. In addition to teams now owning player contracts, the more important changes included the following: teams were limited to a maximum of $5,400 in salary per month, excluding the pay of managers and chaperones; clubs could have a minimum of 14 and a maximum of 16 active players on the roster as of July 1, thus allowing teams to keep rookies longer and give them more time

Blue Sox Baseball — South Bend's new insignia appeared on the front of Blue Sox uniforms starting in 1951, after the teams voted to end the league's Management Corporation following the 1950 season. The insignia, representing a baseball, was white with a blue circle and blue stitched letters, and the "seams," representing a baseball, were red (courtesy of the Louise Pettus Archives and Special Collections, Winthrop University).

to develop; a team's list of players would be forwarded to the league office at the end of each season so those players could be reserved for that team in the future; and no team could employ a "feminine manager,"[14] the loop's male backlash against Bonnie Baker managing the Lassies in 1950. Also, teams such as South Bend and Fort Wayne adopted new uniform insignias to help with promotional efforts.[15]

For 1951, the league scheduled each team for 56 home and 56 away games. South Bend was slated to be in town for all three holidays, and the schedule's only "disconcerting" feature was that the team had to travel for eight days in late August, when they hoped to be locked in a pennant race.[16] Also, by April 15, the Blue Sox had signed most of the returning players. Helen Filarski, however, planned to get married, and she notified the team that she was leaving the loop.[17]

When the first group of players, rookies and veterans alike, reported to South Bend for two-a-day spring drills on Tuesday, May 1, they walked onto Playland Park's revamped diamond. The fences in left and right field, set at 250 feet in 1946 when the Blue Sox first occupied Playland, were shortened to 225 feet, but the center field wall at the flagpole remained at 290 feet. The changes allowed the team to move the bleachers closer to the infield, and it was hoped the games would feature more home runs. The exhibition schedule opened at St. Joseph, Michigan, on May 12, and South Bend opened the regular season by hosting Grand Rapids on May 20.[18]

After a week of drills, the *Tribune*'s Paul Neville praised Faut as an all-around great player. In 1950, she not only appeared in 76 games and averaged .217, fifth highest for the Sox, but she also hurled 36 games and completed 29, fashioning a 21–9 record with a league-best 1.12 ERA. Further, she pitched a circuit-high 290 innings, 24 frames more than Fort Wayne's Maxine Kline, who finished with a 23–9 record and a 2.44 ERA. Indeed, Faut also played third base and a few games in the outfield. "Watching Jean, you'd wonder how the Sox can afford this season to use her only as a pitcher," Neville wrote. "She's far and away the strongest hitter on a club that needs batting power if it's to move up from the fifth place finish of last season."

South Bend was improved. The local heroines had the league's best outfield with Lib Mahon, who had decided to return after retiring, in left, Jeep Stoll in center, and Betty Wagoner in right field. Faut led the "seasoned mound corps," Neville observed, but other stellar hurlers were Dotty Mueller, Elaine Roth, Sue Kidd, Jette Vincent, and Lou Arnold, who returned after a year's absence. Kidd had lost weight and was "really firing that fast one," and Roth gave up her "underhand slants" and was developing as an overhander. At this stage, the pennant race shaped up as a battle between South Bend, Fort Wayne, and Rockford.[19] As it turned out, Grand Rapids also finished among the top four teams in a season later divided into first and second halves.

Baseball Is Here Again

The players reporting to South Bend by May 1 featured a strong contingent of longtime veterans who figured this would be their best year. The pitchers were Faut, Mueller, Roth, Vincent, Kidd, and Arnold, and the position players included Shirley Stovroff, Shoo-Shoo Wirth, Lib Mahon, Jeep Stoll, Betty Wagoner, and little-used Mary Dailey, with Shorty Pryer and Arlene Kotil expected on May 5. Winsch also looked at as many as 18 rookies, including Janet Wiley, Barbara Hoffman, Anna Kunkel, Gertrude "Gertie" Dunn, and Audrey Bleiler.[20]

After working out for several days, the Blue Sox played a handful of exhibitions, including a blanking of Kalamazoo, 5–0, at the Catholic Athletic Association Field, the new home of the Lassies, on Tuesday, May 15. The visitors won in the first frame with a three-run burst fueled by Dottie Mueller's two-run double. In the ninth, Wimp Baumgartner singled to score Barbara Hoffman. Mary Dailey and Jean Faut followed with singles, and Rose Montalbano, who played on the rookie tour in 1950, grounded out to score the final run.[21] Wednesday's game was rained out, and the Blue Sox held a workout open to the public at Playland on Thursday night.[22] The final exhibition was a 7–6 loss at Fort Wayne, and injuries sidelined rookie catcher Loretta Janowsky (broken finger) and first sacker Janet Wiley (pulled knee muscle).[23]

On Saturday, May 19, South Bend hosted a tryout for hopefuls who had failed to make any team. They would play a nine-inning regulation game at Playland, and the managers would have a final chance to scout the rookies. Afterward, the *Tribune* did not report on the event, but a picture was taken showing the managers and nearly 40 girls, including one African American, who tried out.[24]

On a damp Sunday at Playland Park, Mayor George Schock was slated to toss out the first ball for the 8:15 game against Grand Rapids. Winsch named recruit Barbara Hoffman, in accordance with the league's rookie rule, to start at third base. The manager also listed

Rookie Tryout — Nearly 40 candidates hoping to make the renamed American Girls Baseball League pose for a picture before a game staged at Playland Park on Saturday afternoon, May 19, 1951. The event was planned to give the league's managers a final chance to scout rookies who might help their teams. The candidates include one African American, standing in the back row. Two chaperones and six managers are also standing in the last row. South Bend's new pilot, Karl Winsch, is second from the right (courtesy of the Louise Pettus Archives and Special Collections, Winthrop University).

Mueller, the tall right-hander who could hit a long ball, at first base, the talented Stovroff as the catcher, the speedy Pryer at second base, the flashy Wirth at shortstop, and the veterans Mahon in left, Stoll in center, and Wagoner in right field. The Sox roster also included Wimp Baumgartner and Beatrice Kemmerer as utility players; Rose Montalbano, Arlene Kotil, Janet Wiley, and Audrey Bleiler as infielders; and Mary Dailey and Anna Kunkel as reserve outfielders.[25]

Rain washed out Sunday's game, so Mitch Skupien and his veteran-dominated Chicks, again featuring hard-hitting Connie Wisniewski, had to wait for a day at the hotel.[26]

On Monday night, under Playland's high light poles (the outfield was the most weakly-lit area), the experienced Blue Sox won as Faut outdueled right-hander Mobile Silvestri, 1–0. Both hurlers scattered four hits. The gray-uniformed Chicks lost their best chance to score in the fourth inning, when Doris Satterfield led off with a double to left. Wisniewski, back after a year in the Chicago League, fanned, but Stovroff dropped the ball. As Connie hustled down the base path, Stovroff threw to first base for one out, and Mueller pegged the ball to third to nail the sliding Satterfield, but her throw got by Hoffman. Satterfield arose and headed for home, but Hoffman grabbed the ball, fired to the plate, Stovroff made the tag, and Faut shut down Grand Rapids for the last five frames. In the sixth, the Blue Sox won when Wirth singled to left and Mahon hit her second double of the night for the game's only run. Afterward, South Bend was tied for first place with Fort Wayne, Kenosha, and Rockford, all with undefeated ledgers. Grand Rapids (0–1) joined the winless teams, Peoria, Kalamazoo, and Battle Creek, the new home of the Belles, at 0–2.[27]

A crowd of 1,715 watched the two closely-matched teams play ball, but mulling those figures, Paul Neville observed that attendance was off in the major leagues as well. Recently the Boston Braves, who tried a variety of attractions, hosted two night games with the Cincinnati Reds and one Ladies' Day afternoon game, but just 13,617 total paid to see the three contests. Many critics blamed television for the majors' slump in attendance. In 1950, however, the Chicago Cubs, in addition to the standard daily radio coverage, televised more games than any other major league club, and the Cubs were one of only two teams boosting attendance over 1949. There was no need to panic, stated *The Sporting News*, but "there is a need for a wide, intense selling campaign — something that many people in baseball either seem to know little about, or about which they care less."[28]

It was too early to be concerned about attendance at American Girls Baseball League games, but a better comparison was with the minor leagues, not the majors. In 1951, the minors saw a big drop in spectators, from the 34.7 million mark in 1950 to 27 million, a loss of more than seven million in paid admissions for the second straight year. In fact, the minors had begun "a 25 year downward spiral that many believed would end minor league baseball in most U.S. cities."[29]

Rain forced cancellation of the games on Tuesday, May 22, including South Bend's second with Grand Rapids.[30] On a chilly 50-degree Wednesday evening at Playland that saw most fans sporting coats or blankets, Vincent surrendered seven hits and walked six, but her teammates rapped 13 hits to win, 5–3. The Blue Sox, trailing after the visitors in mustard yellow uniforms scored in the first, responded with four runs to put the game away.[31] On Thursday, Lil Faralla, who missed spring drills, won her first game, fueling the home team's three-run fourth with a two-run double. In the fifth, Mahon provided the final margin of 5–2 by driving a 235-foot home run to left field off Elaine Roth, the little curveballer who was recently sent to Kalamazoo. Faralla left with a twisted ankle in the sixth, and Arnold, a junkballer, finished the victory.[32]

On Friday, May 25, the Blue Sox rode their chartered bus to Peoria on the first road trip, but rain wiped out Friday night's game (again the league mainly played contests at night). On Saturday evening, Faut worked three innings before rain halted the game. Sunday's contest was called off, and, as a result, the team spent most of the weekend lounging at Peoria's Hotel Jefferson.[33]

Laughing, joking, playing cards, and napping, the South Benders made the three-hour bus trip north to Rockford on Monday. At Beyer Stadium, also known as the Peach Orchard, the Blue Sox split two games with the league's 1950 Shaughnessy Champions, losing the first game, 8–5, when Jackie Kelley cracked a bases-loaded double in the eighth inning off Vincent for the final margin.[34] On Tuesday, Faut lost to Amy Applegren in a tight ten-inning duel, 1–0. Rockford's lefty, an eight-year league veteran, hurled a three-hitter, and Faut, who allowed three hits before tiring in the tenth, gave up three more hits, capped by Ellie Callow's bounder off Pryer's glove.[35] Back at Playland on Wednesday, a night highlighted by a Memorial Day fireworks display, the Blue Sox rocked three Peaches' hurlers for a 15–1 rout. Pryer, Wagoner, Mahon, and Kidd, who coasted to her first win, picked up three hits apiece. Afterward, South Bend was third with a 4–2 ledger, following Fort Wayne (8–0) and Grand Rapids (6–2), while 4–3 Rockford slipped to fourth place.[36]

Good Hitting, Good Pitching

The Blue Sox fielded a good-hitting lineup as well as a good pitching staff, and the 4–2 start was promising. Peoria arrived at Playland Park on Thursday, May 31, and Arnold started, surrendering nine hits and walking seven. The South Benders, bunching most of their nine hits off lefty Jo Hasham and fastballing rookie Lenora Mandella, who took over in the five-run fourth frame, led after the sixth by the winning margin of 11–2, allowing Winsch to play an all-rookie infield.[37] Friday's tilt was rained out, but the two teams met in a Saturday doubleheader, and Peoria won both. In the opener, Faralla was cruising with a 5–3 lead in the seventh when she walked the first two hitters and gave up Mary Carey's base hit for one run. Winsch summoned Kidd, but the tall, bashful Arkansan gave up one run. Kidd pitched a solid eighth, but gave up three runs in the ninth and lost, 8–5. In the nightcap, Janet "Jan" Rumsey, making her first start, showed a variety of stuff but allowed seven hits. The Redwings, bunching their safe blows for a four-run lead in five frames, rode Alice Hohlmayer's five-hitter to the 4–0 success.[38]

At that point, South Bend made the short trip to meet league-leading Fort Wayne at Memorial Field, and Max Carey's unbeaten Daisies racked up their 11th win by defeating Faut, 1–0, in the afternoon game of a Sunday day-night twin bill. Under threatening weather, Faut battled right-hander Mirta Marrero, giving up six hits. In the ninth, Wagoner, playing right field, lost Wilma Briggs' fly ball in the sun, but Hoffman snared Evie Wawryshyn's grounder at third base and forced Briggs at second. After a single and a walk, Sally Meier's shot between shortstop and third won it. In the night game, Vincent had a poor outing, and Arnold took over in the sixth, but the Daisies already led, 10–2. Winsch used rookies in the last three innings, including Montalbano at second base, Bleiler at shortstop, Dailey in right field, Wiley at first base, and Baumgartner at catcher, and the Daisies won easily, 13–3.[39] On a chilly Monday, 741 fans saw the Daisies reach Kidd and Rumsey, both nervous, for 11 hits and score all of their runs in the first five frames of an 11–3 cakewalk. South Bend dropped

Promoting the Blue Sox — The first Sox team managed by Karl Winsch (back row, far right) is featured in this 1951 advertising poster showing the players and, below the picture, their signatures — including Shoo Shoo Wirth's distinctive "signature" of two shoes (bottom row, third from right).

to sixth place with a 5–7 ledger. The bright spot, concluded Paul Neville, was Mahon's hot bat; at that point, Lib had driven home half the team's runs.[40]

The schedule gave the Blue Sox a break, and the players talked over their plight on the three-hour bus ride to Battle Creek, Michigan. Facing the hapless Belles at Bailey Field, first on Tuesday, June 5, the Blue Sox swept three games. Faralla won the first contest, Arnold took the second, and Rumsey won her first game on Thursday, 7–1. Rumsey matched Mickey Perez and her breaking balls for five innings, but the Belles were leading 1–0 when the Blue Sox tallied five runs in the sixth on singles by Wagoner, Wirth, Mahon, and Hoffman, plus two errors. Mahon, who went 1-for-4, was leading the loop in hitting at .395, and Fort Wayne's Betty Foss was next at .388.[41]

Back at Playland on Friday, Faut, allowing ten safeties, lost, 5–2, because of three unearned runs in the sixth that gave a 4–2 lead to the light brown-uniformed Daisies (they switched from their pink, or orchid, uniforms with red accessories for the 1951 season). Evie Wawryshyn and Betty Foss started the rally with singles, and Dottie Schroeder bounced one to Hoffman at third, but the ball went through her legs into left field. Mahon, taking her time, spotted Wawryshyn racing for home, but she threw the ball over Stovroff's head. Faut, backing up the catcher, fired the ball into left field, where Mahon, now with her back to the infield, did not see the ball until the third run scored. When the error-marred contest ended, Fort Wayne led the circuit at 17–0 and South Bend (8–8) held fourth place.[42]

At home on Saturday, June 9, South Bend bounced back behind a solid performance by Vincent, who displayed better control and won, 3–2. Permitting five hits, Jette, who liked working the plate's corners, allowed single runs in the fifth and sixth for a 2–2 score, but she blanked the Daisies thereafter. In the ninth, facing Fran Janssen, Mahon led off with a single to left, Hoffman bunted her to second, and with the crowd of 1,500 clamoring for a victory, Mueller bounced a single up the middle to win the exciting contest.[43] The victory launched the Blue Sox on a six-game win streak, and in Sunday's twin bill, the home team beat Fort Wayne twice. The sidearming Faralla, her slants finding the mark, hurled a five-hitter to win the opener, 6–3, and in the nightcap, Kidd showed her stuff, firing her fast ball, her "drop," and an assortment of curves to win, 7–4, as the Sox reached Maxine Kline for eight hits and a big five-run first inning.[44]

Rockford (7–11), floundering in sixth place, arrived for a four-game series starting with a twin bill on Monday, June 11, and South Bend swept both games.[45] On Tuesday, Faut, reported Paul Neville, "with her fast ball booming and her curve dropping off sharply," won a sterling two-hitter, 6–0, fanning eight hitters. Al Pollitt singled in the seventh to end the no-hitter, and Nicky Fox spaced five hits, but the Blue Sox scored enough in the second on Stoll's RBI single and Stovroff's run-scoring bunt. South Bend owned six straight wins, a 14–8 mark, and third place.[46]

Perhaps more important, the Blue Sox, receiving better mound work, fielding, and hitting, were beginning to gel. Travelling to Rockford on Wednesday, June 13, the blue-clad visitors split two single games with the Peaches, falling to Rose Gacioch's four-hitter, 4–0,[47] but rapping 11 hits to help Faralla win, 8–4.[48] Moving on to Kenosha on Friday, Rumsey and her teammates lost, 3–0, to curveballer Jean Marlowe's four-hitter.[49] Undaunted, South Bend returned home on Saturday and torched the Comets in three straight games, the closest a 4–1 win on Monday when Mueller tossed a three-hitter.[50]

In such fashion did the good-hitting, good-pitching Blue Sox play in late June, splitting a pair of twin bills at Peoria on June 19–20, hosting Battle Creek and winning a doubleheader and a single game, winning two contests at Kalamazoo, and dropping the first of a three-game set at Grand Rapids, 7–3, after Pepper Paire's two-run single off Kidd ignited a five-run eighth. When the night ended, South Bend occupied third place with a 25–13 record, and Grand Rapids (26–7) and Fort Wayne 25–8) stood as the loop's top two rungs.[51]

Surprise First Half

On Thursday, June 28, following a league day off, South Bend, still in Michigan's "Furniture City," split another twin bill with the Chicks. At Bigelow Field, Faut squared off with fiery Gabby Ziegler in the opener. Both aces pitched well, but Ziegler grabbed a 1–0 squeaker when her teammates scored one run in the fifth, using a bunt single, a wild throw, a wild pitch, and Dolly Niemiec's squeeze. Faut allowed one other hit, but the Blue Sox failed to score. In the nightcap, Faralla won, 4–0, when the South Benders pounded Jayne Bittner for ten hits, two apiece by Wagoner and Faut, now playing third base. Jean, hitting in the fifth slot, led off the second frame with a long double, Wagoner beat out a bunt, and Faralla squeezed home the run. The visitors put the game away with two runs in the third on Mahon's RBI single and Faut's run-scoring bunt single. The split left South Bend in third place with a 26–14 record, three and a half games behind league leading Grand Rapids (27–8).

South Bend, carrying the league's largest roster with 24 players as of May 21,[52] placed seven players on waivers. Those affected included veterans Lil Faralla, now 6–1, and Lou Arnold, 4–0. Also, the team waived infielder Rose Montalbano, from Staten Island, New York (she was released on July 5);[53] Arlene Kotil, who had played two games at first base; infielder Audrey Bleiler; flychaser Mary Dailey; and catcher Beatty Kemmerer.[54] One day later, however, the versatile Faralla, whom Winsch was now calling a "clubhouse lawyer,"[55] and Arnold were removed from the list.[56] In the end, the Blue Sox, like other teams, cut several rookies, because the league mandated that teams could have no more than 16 active players by July 1.

July for the Blue Sox turned into a roller-coaster ride, an uneven trip best illustrated by five games with the sixth-place Comets. In a twin bill at Kenosha's Simmons Field on Monday, July 9, Faut won the eight-inning opener, 2–1, with a one-hitter. The Blue Sox, stymied by several sparkling defensive plays, collected ten hits and finally scored the go-ahead run in the eighth when Mahon singled home Wagoner. The win improved Faut's record to 7–5, a mark indicating 1951 was a subpar season for her. In the nightcap, Mueller won, 5–2, when the Sox notched five runs in the fifth, featuring a bunt single by third sacker Faut, a sacrifice, a walk, and three singles.[57]

The series showed that when the Blue Sox benefitted from a fine pitching performance, they usually played a tight game, whether they won or lost, but when the hitters broke out the heavy lumber for nine, ten, or more, hits, they often won easily.

Home at Playland on Tuesday for a doubleheader, the Blue Sox topped the Comets in a pair of squeakers, 2–0 and 2–1. Nearly 1,000 fans, a small crowd by South Bend standards, braved threatening weather and enjoyed seeing Arnold outlast Dottie Naum by spacing four hits. In the fourth frame, the Blue Sox bunched four of their six hits to score twice. During the nightcap, Vincent pitched a three-hitter and scored the first run in the fifth, walking and racing home after a two-base error on Pryer's bunt. Kenosha tied the score in the eighth on Fern Shollenberger's run-scoring single, but in the last of the eighth, Mueller won it with an RBI single.[58] Still, Kenosha slugged out a 12–8 victory in Wednesday's finale, starting in the first inning when Jean Cione cracked one of Kidd's slants for a grand slam homer into the left field seats, giving the Comets a lead they never lost. The Blue Sox rapped 12 hits, three each by Pryer and Wagoner, but the Comets reached Kidd and Rumsey for ten safeties. Afterward, South Bend, now with a 35–21 mark, remained in third place behind Grand Rapids (37–12) and Fort Wayne (33–14).[59]

Bigger issues than won-lost marks loomed, however. The league's critical matter in 1951, a carryover from economic problems suffered the previous season, was the survival of all eight teams. Even as Faralla hurled a five-hitter to win, 1–0, at Kalamazoo on Wednesday, July 12, league and club officials were pondering the latest financial crisis. Local boards met that morning in Kenosha and Battle Creek, two clubs hurt by poor attendance, and Fred Leo said that a decision on whether both teams would stay in the league was expected.[60] On Thursday, when the Blue Sox needed ten innings to beat the Lassies, 4–3, thanks to Mahon's single, two stolen bases, and Faut's bunt, Leo announced that the Belles and the Comets, thanks to well-heeled "angels" in both cities, would finish the season, although backers in Dubuque, Iowa, expressed a desire to buy Kenosha's franchise.

Also, in a last-minute development, Leo said the league was splitting the season, following the format used in 1943 and 1944. The first half ended with Sunday's games, but the remainder of the schedule was unchanged.[61]

The Blue Sox finished the "surprise" first half by splitting a pair of contests at league-leading Grand Rapids. On Saturday, July 14, the Chicks reached Mueller for nine hits, but the Blue Sox, totaling six safeties, won, 6–3, scoring twice each in the fifth, sixth, and seventh innings. Also, Faut moved to right field, although she had often played third base when not pitching, a dual role that gave her little rest between starts.[62] In Sunday's windup, the Chicks defeated the Blue Sox, 2–0, when 16-year-old right-hander Gloria Schweigerdt allowed just four hits. Faut, who slipped to 7–6, permitted three doubles, but two of the two-baggers came in the sixth, one before and one after an error by Pryer, allowing the Chicks to score the game's only runs.

Afterward, the first-half standings showed Grand Rapids in first place with a 40–13 ledger, Fort Wayne second at 34–17, South Bend third at 38–22, and Rockford fourth at 31–26. The next best team was Peoria with a 28–25 mark, followed by the three weaker clubs: Kenosha, 21–36; Kalamazoo, 19–38; and struggling Battle Creek, only 11–45.[63]

The Blue Sox at Mid-Season

South Bend fans reading the league's first half statistics could not be blamed if they figured the Blue Sox would continue to hang onto third place. The figures, prepared by the Howe News Bureau and published on July 15, showed Betty Foss, the Daisies' slugging first sacker, leading the regular hitters with a .378 mark and a league-high 18 doubles. Dottie Kamenshek, longtime Rockford heroine, ranked second at .368. The Peaches' Ellie Callow, with a .328 average and a circuit-high 53 RBI, and Alice Pollitt, averaging .314, were not far behind. The only South Benders among the top thirty hitters were Audrey Bleiler with a .308 average, though she had only 26 at-bats; Lib Mahon at .303, ninth among regulars; Shorty Pryer at .291; and Shoo-Shoo Wirth at .273. Mary Lou Studnicka, a rookie right-hander for the Chicks, paced the league with her 9–0 record, but surprising Lou Arnold ranked second at 5–0 and Dottie Mueller was third at 3–0. Lil Faralla was the only other Sox pitcher listed in the top 17, and her record was 6–3.[64]

The hitting was improving, but the circuit was going downhill. For example, Fred Leo was unable to generate much publicity. In fact, one of the few promotional stories of 1951 appeared in the *Chicago Tribune*'s Sunday Magazine. Neatly titled to debunk the now common family-oriented message of newspapers, magazines, and television, Robert Cromie's "A Woman's Place is At Home — Plate" described the eight-team AGBL operating around the Chicago media market. The article featured a large color photo of Dottie Naum, "who catches and hammers the ball for the Kenosha, Wis., Comets," and a smaller one of Naum, showing her short white skirt up, her satin shorts, and her nice legs, capped by knee-length socks. Readers could see at a glance the ever-shorter uniform dresses and the athletes' sex appeal — accounting for the often bawdy comments from males, who first looked at the legs and knees, and then saw the players' talent and skills.[65]

Cromie described a game at Kenosha's Simmons Field where the players stole bases, argued with the umpires, and, in the only concession to their sex, played on a diamond somewhat smaller than fields used for men's baseball. Also, players received four uniforms, two for home games and two for the road, but they purchased their own gloves and spikes. Their ages ranged from 15, with parental consent, to the nearly 40 of veteran Comet catcher Irene Hickson. The author lauded players such as Betty Foss, who "weighs about 184 pounds, stands close to six feet, and runs like a deer." Foss also whacked the ball, as she proved last year by leading the league with a .346 average. Furthermore, the loop's fans were as rabid as any rooting for the Brooklyn Dodgers; the players' autographs and pictures were much in demand; and players came from all over the U.S., with 20 from north of the border, notably Fort Wayne's Evelyn Wawryshyn, the "best girl hockey player in Canada." The story omitted mention of the league's money problems,[66] because the *Tribune* was more interested in promoting a positive feminine image.

By this time, Karl Winsch had an established lineup, and he often used the following batting order:

- 2B — Pryer, 29 and fast, usually led off. Enjoying her best year at the plate and in the field, the assertive California brunette, who played seven seasons, posted a career-high .312 average, adding 32 RBI, drawing 40 walks, leading the loop with 129 thefts, and making the postseason All-Star team. An outspoken, often divisive presence in the locker room, Shorty was a take-charge, in-your-face leader who was respected by strong personalities like Mahon.
- RF — Wagoner, 21, a quiet, friendly, personable player, averaged a solid .272, drawing 63 walks, stealing 50 bases, scoring 77 runs, producing 41 RBI, and making so many spectacular catches that her teammates dubbed her "Old Reliable." Skilled at bunting, the left-handed batter could throw her bat at a ball for a bunt, and, as teammates marveled, be halfway to first when the ball hit the ground.
- SS — Wirth, 24 and batting third, had married a serviceman that she adored. Returning for what became her final season, the scurrying Florida native still excited fans, still got on base often, and still made her share of slick plays in the field. Averaging a career-high .274, Shoo-Shoo posted good numbers: 95 hits, 64 walks, 69 stolen bases, 77 runs scored, and 23 RBI.
- LF — Mahon, recovered from the eye problem as well as the personal slight she suffered in 1950, batted clean-up and hit .269 in her eighth season. A dependable clutch performer at age 29, she slugged 14 doubles and five triples, but only one four-bagger. Lib also drew 60 walks, stole 53 times, scored 69 runs, and produced a team-high 68 RBI.
- C — Stovroff, in her third full season with the Blue Sox, was one of the league's best defensive catchers. Faut, who preferred Stovroff as her receiver, recalled that Shirley had a strong arm and liked fastballing pitchers, but Wimp Baumgartner was a better low-ball catcher.[67] Stovroff, 20, and a close friend of Pryer, was improving at the plate. A singles hitter, she played 100 games and, using a heavier bat, lifted her average to .266, including 37 runs scored and 54 RBI, a figure that tied her for second on the Sox with Wirth. Baumgartner, also 20, was the reserve, playing 24 games, batting 44 times, averaging .205, and driving in three runs. "Mainly what I did in 1951," recalled Wimp, who loved hamburgers as a kid and thus got her nickname from "Wimpy" of *Popeye* comics' fame, "was carry Stovroff's equipment!"[68]
- CF — Stoll, the dependable five-foot flychaser who turned 23 in August, had a strong arm and covered the outer gardens efficiently, studying the hitters and playing to their weaknesses. Also a good friend of Pryer, Jeep averaged .268, belting 15 doubles and two triples, drawing 51 bases on balls, scoring 46 runs, and producing 47 RBI, third highest on the team.
- 1B — Mueller's big bat — she averaged .236, belting nine doubles, scoring 18 runs,

Playing Catcher — In the spring of 1951, Shirley Stovroff works on throwing out of the correct stance under the watchful eye of manager Karl Winsch, as reserve catchers Mary "Wimp" Baumgartner and Beatty Kemmerer look on (courtesy of the Louise Pettus Archives and Special Collections, Winthrop University).

and producing 30 RBI — and her versatility helped fill Winsch's need for a reliable first sacker, although she was hardly a great fielder. Dottie, 25, was tall, strong, and slow at 5'11" and 160, but she was a stellar pitcher with good stuff who produced a 10–2 mark. At first base in 1950, Dave Bancroft started with veteran Betty Whiting, but she was loaned to Kalamazoo in the second week of June. Youthful Arlene Kotil, who arrived in the trade for Bonnie Baker, played well at first, but the rookie's hitting tailed off later in the season. When Kotil finally arrived in 1951, Winsch tried her at first a couple of times in late June, but she made her final appearance as a pinch-hitter for Janet Wiley on July 2.[69] Increasingly, the manager turned to the 17-year-old Wiley, who needed a knee brace after being hurt sliding. Pee Wee improved, playing 74 games and hitting .221. The South Bend teen, who liked to bunt, scored 21 times and added 13 RBI. Blessed with good hands, she often came into games in the late innings for her defense.

- 3B — The league was still using the rookie rule, so Winsch had to play a recruit. Barbara Hoffman, 20, from Belleville, Illinois, started the season strongly at third base, but she made 23 errors in 41 games, compiling the lowest mark of all but

Sliding in a Skirt — A group of Blue Sox players watch and listen as manager Karl Winsch talks about the finer points of sliding and tagging a base runner in 1951. Pictured (standing, left to right) are Rose "Monty" Montalbano (hands on knees), Barbara Hoffman, Audrey Bleiler (with pigtails), and Janet "Pee Wee" Wiley. Kneeling (from left) are Charlene "Shorty" Pryer, holding the glove, Arlene Kotil (behind Pryer), Shoo Shoo Wirth, sliding, Gertie Dunn (above Wirth), and Dottie Mueller, with hands on knees beside Winsch (courtesy of the Louise Pettus Archives and Special Collections, Winthrop University).

one player at that position. A right-handed batter, she hit .212, good for a first-year player, but she suffered a knee injury and played less, and her average tailed off. Audrey Bleiler, who was married in the first week of July, played third base often. A right-handed batter, the lanky Philadelphia native, sure-handed in the field, batted .202, but like Hoffman, her hitting tailed off after mid-season. Still, Faut, a better hitter, played 29 games at third and led all league third sackers in fielding with a mark of .956

South Bend was blessed with good pitchers, perhaps too many. Faut, 26 years old and in her prime as an athlete, was the ace, but sometimes she received too little offensive support, and sometimes the defense allowed unearned runs, or both. In fact, Jean's ERA of 1.33 was excellent. The classic example of non-support occurred on Tuesday, July 3, at Grand Rapids, when the Chicks rallied for three runs in the ninth to win, 8–7, but eight errors killed the Blue Sox.[70] Faut, who pitched, committed two miscues herself, including a bad throw that led to a pair of runs, but the visitors lost when they made three infield errors in the crucial ninth.[71] The defeat was Faut's most disappointing of the season. She was still the league's top pitcher, and her repertoire included one of the loop's best fastballs, several curves, a change, and sharp control. She was a true heroine — the ballplayer that younger girls dreamed of becoming.

After Faut, Winsch most often started Lil Faralla, Jette Vincent, Lou Arnold, and Sue Kidd, but he also used rookie Jan Rumsey and the versatile Dottie Mueller as spot starters.

Faralla, 27, had a 7–3 mark after the first half of the season. A strong sidearmer with good control who could field and hit well, the easy-going, hard-throwing Californian, back after spending most of 1950 with Kalamazoo, enjoyed a fine season. In 22 games, Lil went 15–4 with an ERA of 1.85, fifth best in the league among hurlers who worked 20 or more games.

Vincent, 23, was 7–4 at the break on July 15. Showing good speed, she tried to spot her pitches high and low, but sometimes walked hitters by working too close to the plate's edges. Often inconsistent, Jette pitched 23 games and went 13–9 with a 2.42 ERA.

Kidd, hurling her second full summer, had a 5–5 mark at midseason. Talented, determined, but painfully shy, the Choctaw, Arkansas, native, tall and strong at 5'8" and 160, grew up playing ball better than most of the boys. At age 17, she was still developing as a pitcher, but she worked 19 games and finished with an 11–7 mark and a 2.51 ERA.

Arnold, Winsch's favorite "cheerleader" on the bench, always encouraged others to keep on trucking. Friendly, hard-working, and soft-throwing at 28, she showed an assortment of "junk" balls, including a curve (recalled one catcher) that "barely wrinkled." Lou, if she had her control, could win games, but mostly she needed offensive support. The Rhode Islander worked 20 games and enjoyed a 10–2 record with a 2.62 ERA.

Rumsey, 19, from Greensburg, Indiana, was later loaned to Battle Creek, where, like Kidd, she appeared in four games. Even as a rookie, Jan helped the Blue Sox. A slender 5'8" right-hander, she had good talent and good speed. The brunette, who wore glasses, needed work on her control, her curve, and her changeup, but so did most young pitchers. Rumsey, who threw a "heavy" fastball, appeared in 19 games, going 4–8 with a 2.51 ERA.

Mueller, the former Peoria ace, pitched 13 games and fashioned a 10–2 record with a sparkling 1.36 ERA, a mark exceeded by only four of the league's pitchers — one of whom was Faut.

A New Ball Game

The second half of the season was a whole new ball game in South Bend. "We were two teams socially," recalled Wimp Baumgartner in 2010. She roomed with three younger players, Sue Kidd, Jan Rumsey, and Gertie Dunn on the top floor of the McGowans' home in nearby Mishawaka. The shy Kidd was the only second-year player in the bunch. Others who were part of the younger group — but lived elsewhere — were Jette Vincent, Pee Wee Wiley, and Lou Arnold. Still, recalled Baumgartner, "We played together on the field."[72]

Winsch did little to help younger players, and most veterans wanted no help. Karl had no prior managing experience, and no experience coaching women. Kidd recalled tough practices when the manager batted grounder after grounder to infielders and pitchers, hit fungo after fungo to the outfielders, and told pitchers to run in the outfield, circling the area time after time on the day after a start. "Karl would hit those grounders hard enough to knock you down in practice," Kidd recollected, "but I'd just stop the ball somehow. I was determined not to let him beat me."[73] "Karl didn't teach us anything," recollected Wimp Baumgartner, "but he had good players."[74]

Longtime players, usually set in their ways and more independent-minded, disliked or distrusted the rookie pilot. "The two worst managers I ever played for," recalled Lil Faralla,

Baseball in the Family — Jean Faut, son Larry, and husband Karl Winsch, manager of the Blue Sox, pose in the dugout at Playland Park in 1951. Three-year-old Larry, wearing his baseball uniform, is holding one of the league's 10-inch baseballs introduced midway through the 1949 season (courtesy of the Louise Pettus Archives and Special Collections, Winthrop University).

"were John Gottselig and Karl Winsch. They didn't know how to treat women."[75] Recalled Jean Faut, "Karl was a player's manager in 1951, but he changed in 1952."[76] But younger players were more accepting. Janet Wiley, speaking in 2007, observed, "I didn't like him personally, but I could play for him." Winsch accused Wiley, a hometown favorite, of having friends make "cat-calls" from the stands. Instead, they razzed him on their own — probably hoping that Pee Wee would play more.[77] Lou Arnold later said, "Lots of girls didn't like Karl, but he was good to me."[78]

Most players were reluctant to say so, partly because the cultural values of the times proscribed women from criticizing men, at least publicly, but Winsch had a dominating presence and often displayed a quick temper that he needed to harness. In addition, he was trying to manage a core of experienced female athletes who not only disliked second-class treatment but also had little respect for a male manager who didn't know the game better than they did. In fairness, Karl had his hands full learning his players' strengths and weaknesses, and that took time.

On Monday, July 16, eager to start strong in the second half, the Blue Sox hosted the Comets at Playland Park and won easily, 6–1, behind Vincent's five-hitter. The Massachusetts right-hander was hurling a shutout until the ninth, when Fern Shollenberger singled into short center, and Stoll, foolishly trying to throw her out at first base, heaved the ball into the dugout. Shollenberger took third, and Dolly Brumfield scored her with a fly ball to center. The local favorites took a lead they never lost in the third when Pryer popped a single behind first base, advanced on a wild pitch and a sacrifice, and scored on Wagoner's bunt. Wirth doubled to left and Mahon tripled to right for another run. The Sox counted single runs in the fifth and sixth, and clinched the game with two more in the eighth, featuring Mahon's RBI double.[79]

After a day off on Tuesday, the South Benders traveled to Kenosha and split two games. On Wednesday, Winsch, who was done experimenting with rookies, saw his team ride Arnold's five-hit hurling to a 3–1 victory over Jean Marlowe with a three-run burst in the seventh inning. Just 340 spectators paid to see the contest, and the Comets remained in dire financial straits.[80] On Thursday, Kenosha won behind lefty Jean Cione, 5–3, rallying for all five runs in the seventh and eighth off Faralla. Afterward, South Bend ranked third at 3–1, and the team's record now included credit for a 2–1 win over Kenosha,[81] scheduled in the season's second half but played as part of a twin bill on July 10, due to the conflict with a circus date at Playland.[82]

Helped by the schedule, South Bend, playing at home against mainly second division teams, won 11 straight games to climb into first place. Hosting Rockford on Friday, July 20, on a special night where fans who had never seen the Blue Sox were admitted free, Mueller picked up a 4–2 victory after working out of a bases-loaded jam in the first frame. The home team moved ahead with three runs in the second, featuring Mahon's double to right, Stovroff's run-scoring single, Stoll's RBI triple to center, and Mueller's sacrifice[83] Still, Dottie's performance was all but forgotten when, on the following night, Faut displayed her remarkable talent by pitching a perfect game.

Paul Neville neatly summarized her achievement: "Jean Faut, a sturdy gal with a lot of heart, a fast ball that hops, and a curve that breaks off like a country road, pitched a perfect no-hit, no-run game to subdue the Rockford Peaches, 2–0, at Playland on Park Saturday night." The crowd of 1,490 was aware of history in the making. So were Jean's teammates, but, fearing they might "jinx" it, nobody in the dugout mentioned the looming no-hitter, the third of her career. Backed by the lineup of Pryer at second base, Wagoner in right field, Wirth at shortstop, Mahon in left, Stovroff catching, Stoll in center, Mueller at first, and Bleiler at third base, Faut, an intense competitor with a dazzling repertoire, fanned 11 Peaches and allowed just two balls to be hit out of the infield.

The Blue Sox scored both runs in the sixth. With two gone, Bleiler walked, took second on Pryer's sacrifice, and reached third after second sacker Bobbye Payne bobbled Wagoner's grounder. Wirth bunted perfectly for one run, and when nobody covered first, Shoo-Shoo was safe. Mahon lined a shot down the first base line, but Kamenshek made the play, stepped on first for the out, and pegged to second to nab Wirth, who overran the base, but Payne let the ball get away, and Wagoner raced home for a 2–0 lead. After that, Faut was invincible, whiffing five of the last nine hitters. Jean's happy teammates carried her off the diamond as soon as she fanned Fox to wrap up the gem. Mahon quipped about Faut, who now owned an 8–6 mark, "I guess Jean figured she had to pitch a no-hitter for us to win a game for her!" Grand Rapids (7–0) maintained first place by defeating Battle Creek (2–5), but South Bend took over second with a 5–1 ledger.[84]

South Bend kept winning. Battle Creek arrived for three games, and the local heroines, the toast of the town, won all three easily, two by shutouts. On Monday, July 22, Arnold gave her career-best performance with a one-hitter to win, 7–0,[85] and one evening later, Faralla boosted the win streak with a three-hit 4–0 triumph. Afterward, the Blue Sox loaned Dunn, Dailey and Kidd, who owned a 5–5 mark, to Battle Creek to bolster the loop's weakest club. None of the trio had played much for three weeks, because Winsch had a surplus of talent.[86] The Blue Sox finished the nine-game stand by winning twice over fourth-place Fort Wayne, and the second, Faut's 9–3 victory, moved South Bend into first place, one and a half games ahead of Grand Rapids.[87]

The Blue Sox defeated sixth-place Kenosha twice before traveling to Battle Creek on Sunday, July 29, and sweeping a twin bill against the last-place Belles by a combined score of 16–1.[88] South Bend's streak came to a halt on Monday night in front of 3,200 fans, mainly guests of the Belles' management. Erma Bergmann outlasted Rumsey, 4–3, as Battle Creek scored four runs in the third inning on two singles, three bases on balls, a sacrifice, and three Sox errors. In the ninth, the Blue Sox narrowed the gap to 4–3 on Wirth's RBI single, but good-fielding Gertie Dunn, now with the Belles, ended the game by making a fine play on Mahon's bounder in front of second base. At that point, with just over a month remaining, the Blue Sox, on top of the standings with a 14–2 ledger, were getting better as the season progressed.[89]

Sixteen Straight Victories

Once the streak was snapped, South Bend lost two out of three games in an unusual series at Fort Wayne. At Memorial Field on Tuesday, July 31, Faut lost to hard-throwing Mirta Marrero, 2–1. The visitors tried to rally in the ninth, but Pryer, who singled and reached third base on a steal and a sacrifice, was caught when Wirth tried to bunt, Marrero pitched out, and Pryer was trapped. Faut's record slipped to 9–7 as she suffered her fourth one-run loss, but she did not lose again in 1951.[90] One night later, the Blue Sox won behind Faut's solo homer, Stovroff's safe run-scoring bunt, and Mueller's four-hitter, 2–0.[91]

In one of the year's strangest contests on Thursday, the Daisies thumped the Blue Sox, 11–1, but the visitors became embroiled in the biggest rhubarb ever in Fort Wayne. After two straight Daisy steals of home resulted in "safe" calls by umpire Al Ringenberg,

Winsch (from the dugout), Faut (from third base), Mueller (from the bench), and Stovroff (behind the plate), protested the blown call. Winsch called his team off the field. Reconsidering his impulsive decision, he sent the players back, but Arnold, who surrendered seven walks and four hits in the nine-run inning, was yanked in favor of Rumsey, who finished the blowout. Walking past the stands, Faut, who recalled that fans always razzed her when she played third base at Fort Wayne, where the stands were only 15 feet from the base paths, kept going when a fan dumped ice water on her. The defeat frustrated the entire team.[92]

At the same time, the league remained in turmoil. Kenosha was becoming a "road" team because of poor attendance and the "invasion of television to the saturation point."[93] The Peoria Redwings and the Battle Creek Belles were falling further into debt each day, and several umpires were resigning,[94] claiming the league failed to back their authority in games.[95]

In any event, the Blue Sox rode all night on their bus, arriving in Dubuque, Iowa, on the morning of Friday, August 3. That night the blue-clad troubadours fell to the Comets, 4–2, before an audience of 1,000 in the first American Girls Baseball League game ever played in Iowa. Jean Marlowe, her curveball working, pitched a no-hitter going until the seventh, and Vincent, who yielded seven hits, took the loss.[96] On Saturday, the Blue Sox won, 5–1, behind a five-hitter by the sidearming Faralla. The visitors collected seven hits and eight walks off Barbara Rotvig, scoring single runs in the first and second, and taking a 4–0 lead with another pair in the sixth.[97] Following the long return trip, the Blue Sox hosted the financially troubled Redwings and split a pair of games. Back on the bus, the travel-weary players, now in first place, motored to Rockford on Tuesday, August 7, and Faralla, working for the second time in three days, spun a six-hitter for a 7–1 victory.[98] But on Wednesday, the improving Peaches won in 11 innings, 3–2, thanks to Ruth Richard's RBI single off Vincent. The loss moved Rockford (18–8) back within a half game of the league-leading Blue Sox (18–7), as the tight race for the playoffs continued.[99]

Suddenly, South Bend hit one of those remarkable streaks for which all baseball teams hope and dream. After losing the opener of a two-game set at Battle Creek on Friday, August 10, and winning the second game on Saturday, the talent-heavy Blue Sox could do no wrong, reeling off 15 more victories to clinch first place in the season's second half. The Indiana team won almost every way possible, and every player made contributions. For example, back at Playland on Sunday, the South Benders blasted the Daisies, 24–0, as Faut cruised to her easiest victory ever behind a loop record 23 hits, erasing the old mark of 19 safeties set in 1943 and tied by the Sox against the Peaches on June 18, 1945. Faut, who boosted her record to 11–7, blasted a homer into the left field bleachers in the eighth and, by doing so, won a free case of Wheaties. Pryer tied Sophie Kurys' 1946 mark of five runs scored in a game, but Winsch, despite the huge lead, used only ten players, replacing Stovroff (who had a broken finger) with Baumgartner.[100]

South Bend won three 2–1 squeakers in the streak, two hurled by Mueller and another when Arnold and Vincent combined on a one-hitter. But the closest contest was one of the season's finest: Faut's 1–0 victory in a 16-inning marathon at Kalamazoo on Tuesday August 21. Jean, who fanned 11 and outlasted former teammate Ruth Williams, won her own game by leading off the 16th with a double and advancing on a sacrifice. After Stoll received an intentional pass to set up a double play, Bleiler drove a sacrifice fly to center to bring home the run. Faut retired the Lassies in the bottom of the frame, giving South Bend (29–8) 11 straight wins and a three and a half game lead over second-place Rockford (25–11).[101] Also, Faut col-

Relaxing — In a typical postgame picture of players on a road trip, several of them enjoy a beer after playing a night contest, circa 1951. The Blue Sox pictured (left to right) are Jane "Jeep" Stoll, Audrey Bleiler, Dottie Mueller, Janet Rumsey, and Barbara Hoffman (courtesy of the Louise Pettus Archives and Special Collections, Winthrop University).

lected the team's 16th win when she outlasted Grand Rapids, 7–6, at Bigelow Field on Saturday, August 25, boosted by two bases-loaded double plays that helped overcome her 12-hit outing.[102]

The 16-game string for Winsch's nine finally ended at Grand Rapids on Sunday, August 26, when Sue Kidd, recalled from Battle Creek, permitted nine hits but, hurt by three costly errors, lost, 4–2. Chicks star Mobile Silvestri allowed eight hits, three by Pryer, but the Alabama right-hander pitched tough with runners aboard, allowing solo runs in the third and the eighth frames. Afterward, South Bend's manager praised his team. Asked why the Blue Sox were the league's most feared club, Winsch replied, "Team spirit. Every play is for keeps and they never quit."

Paul Neville observed that the pilot had worked hard to improve his club, mainly in pitching and hitting, including many hours spent in batting practice. In addition, the Sox worried pitchers by stealing bases. Pryer easily led the loop in thefts with 129, but all of the players stole bases, setting the stage for hit-and-run plays and leaving the bunt, once more important, to be used in strategic situations. Winsch's work with two rookies, Janet Wiley and Audrey Bleiler, helped the team's success, and "the pitching staff of Faut, Arnold, Faralla,

Mueller, Vincent, and Kidd have been able to work in rotation, an event which brings smiles to any manager's face."[103]

Winning the Championship

As matters stood, the Blue Sox had a six and a half game lead over second-place Rockford, so the race was all but over. South Bend won three of the final seven games, clinching the pennant on September 1, a drizzly Saturday, by defeating Rockford at Playland, 5–1. Kidd, with her nasty drops and curves working, won by scattering five hits and fanning five. She issued her only free ticket to Kamenshek with two away in the first inning and, moments later, Ellie Callow drove home the Peaches' run, but the home team tied the game in the second on Bleiler's RBI single. Actually, the Blue Sox walked to the victory in the third when Marie Mansfield, who lost the plate, gave up five straight bases on balls, and Mueller drove in the third run with a long fly. Afterward, South Bend had a 37–12 record, and Rockford fell to 31–15 with three games left.[104]

The South Benders won the first of three games at Peoria, but the series did not matter, and Winsch left Faut, Vincent, Mahon, and Stovroff at home to rest. The finale with the Redwings, the nightcap of a twin bill on Labor Day, turned into a farce. The Peoria club, struggling all year for financial survival, attracted a record of 2,055, and the fans greeted South Bend's antics with "howls of laughter." Winsch, who thrived on being the center of attention, played second base in the sixth. He struck out on three pitches. Later, reentering the game as a pinch-runner, Karl stole second, but walked back to first base. Mueller started the game at catcher, and she played a different position in each inning. Each of the Sox covered at least two positions in the 11–4 loss.[105]

Winning the Shaughnessy Championship became one of the two greatest highlights in Blue Sox history. On Tuesday, September 4, Faut, later selected Player of the Year,[106] ignored the big-game pressure and fired a six-hitter to defeat visiting Fort Wayne, 2–1, in the best-of-three first round playoff. Maxine Kline, the Daisies' ace, yielded nine hits, two each to Faut and Mahon. The home team scored in the second when Stovroff singled, Stoll sacrificed, and Faut and Mahon followed with base hits. Fort Wayne tied the game at 1–1 in the sixth on a walk to Tiby Eisen, a single by Rita Briggs, a groundout, and Jo Weaver's single. In the bottom of the frame, Mahon doubled to the fence in right center, Mueller popped out, Bleiler beat out a single to shortstop, and Wagoner slashed a hit into left field to score the game-winner.[107]

Wednesday's matchup at Fort Wayne was rained out, giving the teams a day of rest. Elsewhere, Rockford won for the second time, edging first-half winner Grand Rapids in 11 innings, 7–6, lifting the Peaches to the best-of-five league championship series.[108] Playing at Fort Wayne's Memorial Field on Thursday, the blue-uniformed visitors scored in the first inning on Pryer's single, a steal, a bunt, and Stovroff's run-scoring sacrifice. Following two more walks by Hank Warren, Max Carey lifted her for Pat Scott. The Kentucky right-hander stifled the visitors' bats while the Daisies, reaching Vincent for 11 hits, won easily, 9–1. Faut started at third, but Winsch subbed Bleiler after Jean batted twice, because she was needed to pitch the next night.[109]

At Memorial Field on Friday, September 7, Faut again proved her greatness, winning a pressure-packed ten-inning thriller, 2–1, despite permitting eight hits, two each by the hard-hitting Weaver sisters, Jo (the youngest) in right field and Jean at third base, and one by Betty Foss, their older married sister. Wagoner, who went 4-for-4, and Mahon and Bleiler, with a pair of hits each, led the Blue Sox' offense, but the visitors won in a fashion common to the league. Stovroff led off the tenth with a double and took third on Stoll's sacrifice. Scott, the third Daisies' hurler, walked two clutch batters, Faut and Mahon, to set up a force play, but Mueller bunted neatly, Stovroff raced home to score, and, in the bottom of the inning, Faut retired the side to nail down the win.[110]

For the championship round, South Bend and Rockford met, also at Fort Wayne's Memorial Field, on Saturday and Sunday. The Peaches, looking like the champions they were in 1950, won twice to take a huge 2–0 series lead. In the opener, the Blue Sox, facing veteran Rose Gacioch, who had relieved starter Nicky Fox, came close to winning in the ninth. With the bases loaded, two outs, and one run home on Faut's pinch-hit single, Dottie Key raced in from center field to make a shoestring catch of Stoll's liner for the final out. South Bend outhit Rockford, nine to seven, but Gacioch stranded ten while Faralla gave up one run in the sixth and four more in the seventh for a 5–4 loss.[111] On Sunday, the Peaches won easily, 7–1, taking advantage of Kidd's nervousness. In the first frame, Sue walked Kamenshek, Pollitt singled the runner to third, and Kamenshek scored on Ruth Richard's squeeze. Callow doubled for another run, and Joan Berger singled for a 3–0 lead. Arnold, who liked chatting with fans in the bullpen, relieved and pitched one-run ball until the seventh, and Rumsey finished, allowing three runs.[112]

When their odds seemed the longest, the Blue Sox proved their fortitude by winning three straight times. At home on Monday, September 10, rain swept the region and the game was cancelled, but the *Tribune* highlighted a familiar tale: "Same Old Story! Jean Faut to Hurl Crucial Game for South Bend Blue Sox."[113] On Tuesday, Faut, full of determination, pitched a six-hitter and led her team to a 3–2 win. Rockford's Bill Allington started recruit Marie Mansfield, known for her wildness, and she issued 13 walks. The Blue Sox notched all the runs they needed in the third inning on Stovroff's single, Faut's run-scoring double, an error, two walks, and a hit batter. Faut, who walked four, bore down and, firing her fastball when necessary, struck out 11 Peaches, including the side in the sixth after Callow led off with a triple. In the ninth, Jean blew a fast one by Dottie Key to end the battle, stranding Joan Berger on third base.[114]

On Wednesday, a downpour ended the game after seven innings, giving the Blue Sox a 6–3 win. The Peaches, without catcher Ruth Richard (she had the flu), jumped to a 3–0 lead, scoring once in the first and twice in the third, but Jette Vincent persevered, hurling her finest game to date. The never-say-die home team came from behind for the 24th time in 1951 (compared to four in 1950),[115] scoring two runs in the third, adding one in the fourth, and winning with three more in the sixth on hits by Pryer, Wirth, and Mahon, two errors, a walk, and a bunt.[116]

The stage was set for an exciting showdown at Playland Park on Thursday. Instead, the Blue Sox romped over the Peaches, 10–2, winning the championship in the team's first-ever trip to the final round of playoffs. The Peaches scored once off Faralla in the top of the first frame, but Gacioch did not have her stuff. In their first, the South Benders entertained an exuberant crowd of 2,268 with Pryer's "Texas League" double, her first of three hits, Wagoner's single, her first of four hits, walks to Wirth and Stovroff, a two-base error on Faut's grounder, and Mahon's sacrifice fly for a 5–1 lead. Faut moved over from third base to relieve Faralla in the third inning, with the Sox leading, 6–2, one out, and the bases loaded. Jean won her fourth playoff contest by blanking the Peaches, while her teammates kept hitting and scoring runs. In the ninth, when Pryer tossed out Kamenshek to end the rout, the Sox reserves and many of the jubilant fans streamed onto the diamond to celebrate with their heroines on the memorable night they finally won the championship.[117]

The Bittersweet Aftermath

In retrospect, the 1951 season ended on a mixed note. Back home the following Monday night, Karl Winsch helped celebrate the title won by the Blue Sox during a banquet at the South Bend Country Club. Winsch, enjoying his role as man of the hour, praised the team spirit of all the players. The successful manager went down the lineup and told an anecdote about each player, showing her value to the team. Shirley Stovroff, he revealed, played the last month with a broken finger on her throwing hand. Also, Lib Mahon announced her retirement, saying, "When you're on top is a good time to quit."[118] Lil Faralla said nothing at the time, but later observed, "I could see the caliber of play was going down. I figured I may as well quit while I'm on top."[119]

Still, while the Blue Sox enjoyed their finest season, the American Girls Baseball League was in trouble. The Battle Creek Belles and the Kenosha Comets suffered major financial losses, and both appeared unable to raise the necessary funds to rejoin the league in 1952. Commissioner Fred Leo, who was exhausted, resigned in late August, citing, among other issues, financial losses, a lack of player and umpire compensation (arbiters earned $10 per game) commensurate with the rising cost of living, and the inability to administer the rules. Leo, an astute observer, told Harold Dailey that the girls' game was dead "unless someone pours some 'fresh' into it and it moves from the dead towns."[120] Although neither the players nor team officials wanted to think about it, Leo was warning about a time when the cheering could stop.

◆ 10 ◆

Champions Again — The Beautiful Dozen: 1952

"Out-hit, out-fielded, out-pitched, but never out-fought. That's the Blue Sox story as the defending American Girls Baseball League champions trek off to Freeport, Ill., today for the final game of 1952"—*South Bend Tribune*, September 11, 1952[1]

Planning for the 1952 Season

By the end of the 1951 season, even as the good-hitting, great-pitching Blue Sox came from behind to win the Shaughnessy Playoff Championship, the American Girls Baseball League seemed to be falling apart. The game on the diamond looked better to spectators, but attendance still declined in every city, including South Bend. No professional team of that era could succeed without stable or rising paid admissions. According to the U.S. Census of 1940, South Bend had a population of 101,268. The baseball axiom of the postwar years was that a team needed to draw the city's population annually to ensure stable finances. After playing three wartime seasons at Bendix Field and seeing the club's attendance surpass 49,000 in 1944 and 1945, the Blue Sox moved to larger Playland Park. In 1946, the first postwar season, the ball club drew an all-time peak of 112,135 in the new eight-team All-American League.

The heroic stature of the Second World War was fading into the nation's memory. The economic, social, and political problems of the postwar atomic era affected Americans in every walk of life, including pro sports. In 1947, the year of the Havana adventure, the Blue Sox drew 104,000 fans. In 1948, the year the league trained ten teams at Opa-Locka and introduced overhand pitching, South Bend's attendance slipped to 93,600. In 1949, the year of the smaller, livelier baseball and the increased pitching distance, paid admissions improved to nearly 96,000. When the fifties, the Korean War, and television arrived, the Blue Sox fell to fifth place and fan interest dropped to around 67,000. In 1951, after the eight teams voted to end the league's Management Corporation, the South Benders won the championship and drew a few more spectators — a total of 68,268, to be exact. In 1952, the club won another championship while entertaining just over 57,000 folks.[2] Indeed, the team's directors, facing a $20,000 debt by July 1952, voted to sell the franchise to Toledo,[3] but the Ohio city backed away from the deal.

In 1951, as the eight-team league and South Bend struggled with financial problems, the Blue Sox relied on a core of star players who, not understanding the club's precarious financial situation, grew more assertive about their salaries. After the team's last home game,

Fred Leo, who recently resigned as the league's commissioner, met with several Sox players. Shorty Pryer did most of the talking. Leo patiently answered their questions, including how the club's share of league profits was derived and how that share was distributed to players.[4] In December, team officials picked Karl Winsch to serve as the team's general manager as well as field boss.[5]

After winning a championship, Winsch was entrenched in South Bend, but when he served as manager, it created a dilemma for Jean Faut, his wife. Karl spent much of the 1951 season learning the ropes. He functioned as a "player's manager," being sympathetic to players' needs. Accordingly, Jean's role of player as well as the manager's wife seemed to work. In her book *Women at Play*, however, Barbara Gregorich explained that the team already experienced dissension, and that the discord became visible in 1952: "Groups of players wouldn't talk to the manager, and they wouldn't talk to Jean. Winsch wouldn't talk to Jean, either."[6]

In any event, the circuit as well as the teams made plans for the 1952 season. The league's board elected Fort Wayne hotel magnate Harold Van Orman as president and chose Earl McCammon of Kalamazoo as business manager. By December 1951, it appeared that all eight teams were returning for 1952, but later, Peoria and Kenosha withdrew, lacking the needed funds. Also, South Bend's 13-member board elected William Sheehan as president, Julius Tucker as vice president, Art Hauck as treasurer, and William Schmeider as secretary.

Once again each team would scout, recruit, and sign players. Always looking for new talent, Harold Dailey, no longer on the board, was helping with contracts. Dailey tried to line up trades and wanted to obtain Audrey Wagner from Kenosha, giving the Blue Sox "the heavy hitting outfielder we are after." On December 14, 1951, Dailey conferred with Sheehan and Winsch at the Hoffman Hotel. Fort Wayne offered several deals, apparently to cut salary. The Daisies asked to swap Tiby Eisen for South Bend's Jeep Stoll, but the team later withdrew the offer.[7]

In late March of 1952, league officials, in order to divide equally players from the disbanded Peoria and Kenosha clubs, held a drawing with representatives from the six teams. South Bend picked Joyce (Hill) Westerman, Peoria first sacker; Ruby Stephens, a right-hander who joined the league in 1946, pitched for South Bend in 1947, and spent 1950 and 1951 with Kenosha; Lenora Mandella, who pitched briefly for the Sox in 1949, the touring Sallies in 1950, and Peoria in 1951; and Jo Lenard, a ninth-year flychaser who played the last two summers for Kenosha. Stephens, from Clearwater, Florida, chose not to return, and, at first, so did Westerman.[8]

Dailey, however, was contacting other players. On March 30, he learned that Audrey Wagner declined South Bend's offer, saying she was satisfied with the salary she received from the Chicago League. Dailey kept in touch with Joyce Westerman, a seven-year catcher and first baseman who joined the league with Grand Rapids in 1945. Westerman, who was allocated to South Bend in 1946 and, later that year, loaned to Fort Wayne, played much of her career for Peoria. She had long since proven herself as a good all-around player. On April 4, Westerman, who was married after the 1950 season, indicated she would not play pro ball in 1952. Also, Lil Faralla, who was asking for more money than the team was willing to pay, left the loop and moved on with her life in California.[9]

Once more, salary was an issue with many of South Bend's stars, but club officials were in a bind. The league followed the arrangement devised in 1951: a team salary maximum of $5,400 per month for players, not including managers and chaperones — and paying monthly instead of weekly also meant a small cut. For 1952, team records showed that South Bend supported a monthly salary of $5,367.29. Therefore, in order to grant one player a raise, another player had to take a cut, or to sign a new player, another player had to go. Faut earned more than $500 per month. The team's top salary included pay as a chaperone. Later, Jean called that an excuse to pay her better, because she didn't even receive the usual first-aid kit.[10] Veteran players commanded the most pay, and Shorty Pryer, Lib Mahon, Shirley Stovroff, and Betty Wagoner earned at least $400 per month. First and second-year players made much less — between $200 and $300.[11]

In the first ten days of April, several players returned their contracts unsigned. On April 11, Pryer met with Bill Sheehan and argued for a raise, but he refused. In a classic macho reply, doubtless typical of male team officials around the league, South Bend's president told the second baseman that he was done talking salary; she could play for the contract offered, or not at all. Pryer, Stovroff, Pee Wee Wiley, and others soon signed contracts, but the resentment that surfaced as the season proceeded began in April over money. Also, the team swapped Sue Kidd to Battle Creek for outfielder Pauline Crawley, who refused to report, but Judge Edward Ruetz, chair of the loop's board, ruled that the deal stood (the Sox later paid to regain Kidd).[12]

When Faut, the league's Most Valuable Player in 1951, signed the first contract offered by the Blue Sox on April 3,[13] the six-team circuit was already organized. South Bend, thanks to business manager Eddie DesLauriers, was marketing ticket prices at Playland Park as follows: a daily box seat was $1.50, and a season upper box seat was $40. In the concrete grandstand on the hill behind home plate, lower box seats were selling for $37.50 per season; daily reserve seats for $1.25; daily non-reserve seats for $1.00; and unreserved children's seats for 25 cents.[14]

A Short Spring

Winsch's team was set to begin two-a-day workouts at Playland on Monday, April 21, and the first day was used for issuing uniforms and equipment, taking pictures, and conditioning. The team's returning veterans included Faut, Pryer, Stovroff, Wagoner, Wiley, and Jette Vincent. The manager expected more of the previous season's players to report, along with a handful of rookies. The season was slated to begin on Thursday, May 15, with South Bend opening at Battle Creek.[15] The twice-a-day workouts started at ten o'clock in the morning and lasted three hours, and following a one-hour break for lunch, the players practiced from two o'clock until 3:30. On Sundays, the team held a single workout beginning at one o'clock.[16]

The three-week spring camps of 1951 and 1952, however, were a far cry from the glory years when the All-American League flew more than 200 recruits to Havana in 1947 and transported a similar number by train to Opa-Locka in 1948. By 1952, however, the circuit had little funds for generating national publicity or paying umpires, let alone sending teams on a spring jaunt. The teams from South Bend, Battle Creek, Fort Wayne, Grand Rapids, Kalamazoo, and Rockford could only make the best of difficult circumstances.

On May 11, South Bend staged a Sunday afternoon intra-squad game at Plymouth, Indiana. The "Blues" used Pee Wee Wiley at first base, Shorty Pryer at second, Audrey Bleiler at shortstop, and Barbara Hoffman at third, with Jo Lenard, Betty Wagoner, and Sue Kidd in the outfield, Wimp Baumgartner catching, and Lenore Mandella, Jette Vincent, and Pi Sandford, a rookie, pitching. The "Whites" listed Shirley Stovroff behind the plate and Lou Arnold, Lois Sheffield, and Mary Lou Graham as pitchers. Lib Mahon, Janet Rumsey, and Jeep Stoll had the outfield slots, and Dottie Mueller, Rose Monty, Mary Froning, and Jean Faut played infield. A few were rookies or inexperienced players who did not make the team, including Sandford and Sheffield.[17]

Missing was crowd-pleasing shortstop Shoo-Shoo Wirth, a popular favorite since 1946. Wirth, married, was sitting out the season and expecting her first child. Winsch, in a typically bombastic claim, said Audrey Bleiler would make fans forget that Wirth ever played shortstop. The manager also praised Rose Monty, short for Montalbano, at third base,[18] although neither Bleiler (who was pregnant) nor Monty lasted long. Also, Harold Dailey signed Joyce Westerman. After receiving favorable terms, the Kenosha native, who hit .242 for Peoria in 1951, reported in late May.[19]

Tuning up with an exhibition in Lafayette, Indiana, on Wednesday, May 14, South Bend beat Fort Wayne, 5–4, after Faut made a shaky start and allowed four runs in the first inning. The Blue Sox received timely hitting—one safety each from Stovroff, Wagoner, Mueller, Faut, Bleiler, and Monty. However, Mueller hurt her hand sliding into second base, and the cut required half a dozen stitches. After the first frame, Faut hurled scoreless ball for six innings, and Kidd closed the game. Lenard started in the outfield, Wiley subbed at first base for the injured Mueller, Mary "Fearless" Froning pinch-ran for Mueller, and Hoffman played third base in the ninth.[20]

Defending Champions

After traveling and practicing at Battle Creek's Bailey Park on Thursday, the defending champion Blue Sox opened the season by blanking the Belles, 6–0, with a stellar effort by Kidd. Mixing her fast one with a drop and different curves, the Arkansas native, showing improved control, scattered five hits, and her teammates reached Mickey (formerly Perez) Jinright for 11 hits. Pryer, leading off, Stovroff, hitting clean-up, and Monty, batting eighth, each had two hits. The visitors scored twice in the second inning, added a run in the sixth, and put the game away with three in the seventh.[21] On Friday, Rumsey and Arnold allowed nine safeties, but Lou yielded no runs in the last three frames. Trailing 3–2 in the seventh, the Blue Sox tied the Belles when Kidd, pinch-hitting for Rumsey, doubled, Froning pinch-ran, Pryer sacrificed, and Wagoner delivered an RBI single. In the eighth, after singles by Lenard and Wiley and a walk to Faut, who was pinch-hitting for Monty, Arnold bunted in one run, and the Sox claimed a 6–3 win with two more runs in the ninth.[22]

Saturday's home opener was postponed due to wet grounds at Playland Park, but on Sunday evening, after the appropriate ceremonies, including throwing out the first ball by the wives of South Bend's and Mishawaka's mayors, the Blue Sox pounded the Belles, 11–1. A happy crowd of 1,361 saw the city's heroines reach four hurlers for 11 hits, including two each by Pryer, Mahon, Faut, and Lenard. The Blue Sox drew 16 walks, Faut and Stoll both drove in three runs, and Jean fired a three-hitter and passed five. Elsewhere, Grand Rapids beat the Peaches and stayed undefeated with a 4–0 mark, followed by South Bend at 3–0, Fort Wayne at 2–1, and Kalamazoo at 1–2, but Battle Creek (0–3) and, surprisingly, Rockford (0–4) were winless.[23]

To most observers, South Bend, currently tied for the league lead with Grand Rapids, fielded a talented, experienced, well-rounded ball club ready to challenge for another pen-

Sue Kidd reporting for spring training from Arkansaw

Country Girl — Sue Kidd, from Choctaw, Arkansas, shows her country background by posing with her suitcase and bat on a mule during spring training in 1952. The picture illustrates the publicity photos that teams often used to attract fans. Indeed, on July 8, 1953, Sue tried to ride a mule onto the diamond during "Sue Kidd Night" at Playland Park, but the stubborn beast refused to cross the foul line. The fans, as well as Sue, enjoyed lots of laughs, and she was honored with a wide array of nice gifts. Afterward, Kidd pitched a seven-hitter to defeat Kalamazoo, 6–3 (courtesy of the Louise Pettus Archives and Special Collections, Winthrop University).

nant. The Blue Sox had several strengths, including a hard-hitting outfield, a better-than-adequate infield, anchored by the speedy Pryer at second base, and a pair of good catchers, Stovroff and Baumgartner. The team also featured an experienced pilot. Karl Winsch, called by Joe Doyle, the *Tribune's* new sports editor, a "fair-to-middling semipro player," led the team to a championship pennant in 1951, after three former big leaguers failed to do so.[24] The Blue Sox also had first-rate pitching with veterans like Vincent, Mueller, and Arnold combined with younger hurlers like Kidd and Rumsey. Still, the team relied on the league's best athlete and pitcher, Jean Faut.

Indeed, Faut was embarking on the greatest single-season pitching performance in the league's history: an almost unreal 20–2 mark and a 0.93 ERA. Before she arrived there, however, her team endured a considerable amount of turmoil in one of the most unusual baseball seasons ever.[25]

Rain wiped out the scheduled tilts between South Bend and Grand Rapids on Monday and Tuesday, but at Playland on Wednesday evening (the league continued to play almost all night games), the gray-uniformed Chicks won, 5–3. Vincent yielded eight hits, but her teammates stranded 14 runners, failing to hit in the clutch against Jayne Bittner and second-year right-hander Mary Lou Studnicka. Mueller returned to the lineup while batting fifth, Hoffman played third, and Bleiler covered shortstop. Still, the versatile Faut, who took over at shortstop, batted in the ninth with two outs and two runners on base, but she took a called third strike to end the game.[26]

Leaving Thursday on an unusual road trip, South Bend arrived in Muskegon and split a twin bill with the Belles; the games were staged in Muskegon as exhibitions to test the fan base for another season.[27] Continuing on to nearby Battle Creek, the Blue Sox received a forced day off when rain cancelled Friday's contest, but when first-place Grand Rapids lost to Rockford, South Bend gained half a game.[28] On Saturday against the Belles, Faut led her team to victory with a three-hitter, 6–2. The visitors broke a 2–2 tie against Mirta Marrero with four runs in the ninth, fueled by two-run singles off the bats of Stovroff and Faut. When Rockford stopped Grand Rapids, the Blue Sox led the loop with a 4–1 record, followed by the Chicks at 6–2 and the Daisies at 4–2.[29]

A Winning Combination

Traveling by bus to Fort Wayne on Monday, May 26, for a two-game series at Memorial Park with its closer "home run fence,"[30] the Blue Sox lost a seesaw contest to the hurling of Maxine Kline, 5–4, after the Daisies scored their second run of the ninth on Vincent's base-loaded walk to Dottie Schroeder. Wagoner, Stoll, and Mueller each collected two hits, but it wasn't enough.[31] On Tuesday, Kidd pitched her team back into first place with a sterling two-hitter, 3–0, snuffing a ninth-inning rally after Jo Weaver doubled to left center and Pryer dropped a popup hit to short right field. The blue-uniformed visitors notched a pair of runs in the second on singles by Kidd and Stovroff, a sacrifice, Monty's infield hit, and an error. Returning home for two contests against the Daisies, South Bend (5–2) owned first place, followed closely by Grand Rapids (6–3) and Fort Wayne (5–3).[32]

Good pitching continued to fuel South Bend. Facing Fort Wayne at Playland on Wednesday and Thursday, the Blue Sox won both, the first a 6–2 victory paced by Rumsey's four-hitter and a 13-hit attack.[33] The second came with Faut's five-hit 6–0 shutout, her third win. Mueller rapped three of her team's 11 hits, helping lift the Sox to a 7–2 ledger.[34] Kalamazoo arrived in South Bend for the first time on Friday and outlasted the local favorites in ten innings, 7–6, capped by Jenny Romatowski's RBI single.[35]

Saturday's game was rained out, but Joyce Westerman reported, giving Winsch two good choices to play first: Mueller, who pitched and batted right-handed, and Westerman, a good fielder who batted left. Suddenly Wiley was expendable.[36] On Sunday, South Bend swept a twin bill from visiting Fort Wayne, with Kidd and Rumsey handling the pitching honors. The home team won the opener, 3–0, with Westerman (she was 0-for-2) covering the initial sack, and in the late-night 6–1 victory, Mueller (she was 2-for-4) played first base.[37]

However, the competition resulted in tension between the two players. Westerman's main problem at South Bend in 1952, she recalled, was that Mueller resented her joining the team. Dottie, not known for her friendliness, refused to speak to Joyce all season.[38]

After they traveled back to Fort Wayne and Faut won her fourth game against no losses on Monday, the 10–3 Blue Sox led the second-place Daisies (9–6) by two games. Jean's teammates made her task easy, reaching Eleanor Moore and hard-throwing Jo Weaver for 14 safeties, three by Faut and two each by Stoll, Mueller, Pryer, and Bleiler.[39] However, the Daisies bounced back and beat the Blue Sox three straight, the last two in a Wednesday doubleheader. The Daisies, as usual, hit well, showing no favor to the slants of Vincent, Rumsey, or Arnold.

Winsch, feeling the need to shake up his lineup, made changes on Thursday. First, he moved Betty Wagoner from right field to the mound, and the Missourian won a steady nine-hitter, 4–2. The manager also moved newly-arrived Gertie Dunn to shortstop (she was 1-for-2), started Faut at third base, because she could field and hit better than Hoffman, and sent Mahon to right—and Lib singled to drive in the first of three runs in the second inning. Afterward, 11–6 South Bend topped the standings, Fort Wayne was second at 12–7, and improving Rockford third at 11–9.[40]

On the bus again, the Blue Sox launched a road trip where they won two straight at Kalamazoo (game three was washed out) and split a pair at Grand Rapids. On Friday, June 6, against the Lassies at Catholic Athletic Association (CAA) Field on Mill Street, Faut, at third base, rapped three of her team's five hits, and her eighth-inning RBI double off the center field fence helped Kidd win, 4–3.[41] On Saturday in support of Mueller, the visitors reached slugger Doris Sams, who hadn't pitched recently, and Aggie Allen for 18 hits and a 13–4 victory.[42] Sunday's game was washed out. The team, asking waivers on Lenora Mandella and Janet Wiley,[43] made the 130-mile journey north to Grand Rapids. On Monday night, Vincent lost, 6–5, largely due to four errors that led to four unearned runs.[44] Faut, slated to start on Monday, took the mound on Tuesday and, as she did so often, won an important victory, 10–2. South Bend's thirteen hits made it no contest. Pryer (leading off), Mahon (playing left field and hitting second), Faut (batting clean-up), and Westerman (playing first base and batting seventh), each collected two hits, as three Chicks twirlers allowed every visiting player to hit safely.[45]

Taking the long excursion home and arriving early on Wednesday morning, the 14–7 Blue Sox, thanks to a solid and improving lineup, trailed the league-leading Daisies (16–7) by one game. The circuit's pennant race was developing into a three-team fight; Rockford (13–12) held third place, three and a half games behind Fort Wayne. The last three clubs, Grand Rapids (10–13) in fourth, Battle Creek (8–13) in fifth, and Kalamazoo (4–13) in last place, all had losing records.

South Bend, moreover, boasted the league's deepest roster. Winsch could play Mueller or Westerman at first base, and both batted and fielded well. Pryer, an attractive but assertive athlete who often criticized teammates, played as well as any second sacker. At shortstop, Gertie Dunn, who had finished her college semester, replaced Bleiler, who was pregnant (Audrey was soon released). Hoffman was performing well enough at third base, and the team's doctor did not believe she was affected by a knee injury sustained in 1951. Regardless, Faut, when not pitching, usually covered third base. Lenard, a solid all-around flyhawk in left, Stoll, who got a good jump on batted balls in center, and Wagoner, who was even faster than Stoll in right field, were enjoying good seasons. Mahon, who quit at the end of 1951, returned to action, but the manager played her only in spots. Finally, the strong-armed Stovroff handled the catching duties. Baumgartner was improving as a receiver, but she seldom had a chance to show it.

Nevertheless, team officials were looking to cut players with higher salaries as well as those they perceived to be less than adequate contributors, believing, for example, that Vincent was over-paid and that Rumsey and Arnold could not pitch well enough against heavy-hitting teams like the Daisies. Ironically, Bill Sheehan wanted to acquire Kalamazoo's Jane Moffet, figuring she would improve South Bend's catching corps. He was willing to trade Wiley, Arnold, and a rookie for Moffet. Also, Sheehan, according to Harold Dailey, contacted "a colored player, shortstop, in Cincinnati and she will report Monday."[46] The African American player was not named and never reported, and the Moffet trade fell through, but South Bend kept looking.

Inches, Breaks, and Winning Streaks

Faut's fifth victory at Grand Rapids launched South Bend on a ten-game win streak. Facing the Chicks at Playland in a doubleheader on Wednesday, June 11, and a single game on Thursday, the Blue Sox received winning efforts from Kidd, Rumsey, and Mueller, who took on more of the pitching load with Westerman playing first base. Friday's tilt against Rockford was rained out. But on a Saturday, the Blue Sox swept a twin bill against the Peaches, easily winning the first game, 11–1, behind the pitching of Jette Vincent, who had married Robert Mooney that afternoon. Faut, who worked out of a ninth-inning jam with a pickoff, won the nightcap 3–2.[47] Wagoner won on Sunday, 4–3, hitting an 11th-inning RBI single.[48] On Monday, Arnold, relieving Rumsey in the seventh, won, 3–2, when the Peaches' Jackie Kelley walked five Blue Sox in the ninth. Afterward, 21–7 South Bend had a three and a half game lead on Fort Wayne (17–10).[49]

Now the winners of eight straight games, the South Benders motored to Battle Creek for a doubleheader on Tuesday at Bailey Park. Against the improving Belles, Faut, showing her mid-season form, walked three but won a nifty one-hitter, 2–0, thanks to Lenard's two-run single in the ninth. In the nightcap, the visitors rode Mueller's eight-hit performance to a 5–4 win when Stovroff squeezed home Wagoner in the ninth. Elsewhere, Fort Wayne split with Kalamazoo, allowing the 25–7 Blue Sox to up their loop lead to four and a half games.[50]

Baseball, however, is a game of inches, breaks, and clutch performances, and the Belles came back to win on Wednesday and Thursday, boosted by good hurling

Gertie Dunn — South Bend's flashy shortstop, circa 1952 (courtesy of the Louise Pettus Archives and Special Collections, Winthrop University).

from left-handers Jo Hasham and Jean Cione, who topped Arnold and Kidd, respectively. After the split, the Blue Sox made the long trip to Rockford, but Friday's games were rained out. On Saturday, the Peaches, piloted by Bill Allington, lost to Wagoner's hurling, 9–2.[51]

Suddenly the argumentative Karl Winsch pushed his luck too far. On Sunday, June 22, Rockford won a disputed game, 4–3, after a "near-riot" that began when Winsch was ejected for arguing a balk called on Rumsey in the first inning. After the manager exchanged heated words with Ken Valentine, the plate umpire, he was ejected. Karl, refusing to leave, protested further, and, finally, the arbiter lost his temper and hit the pilot. A melee erupted, police arrived, Winsch and Valentine were escorted out of the stadium, and Rockford won, scoring twice in the seventh.

Before the game, Winsch revamped his lineup because Pryer hurt her ankle at Battle Creek, an injury that caused her to miss an entire month. At second base, Karl started Marge Wenzell, a league veteran since 1945 who was recently loaned by Battle Creek to the Sox. After Winsch's ejection, Lib Mahon, the team's senior member and a savvy baseball person who was respected by her teammates, managed the Sox.[52] Lib continued those duties until Winsch returned three days later. South Bend fell on Monday, 3–1, as Rose Gacioch spaced seven hits. Mueller suffered the loss after Faut, at third, and Wenzell, at second, booted grounders in the sixth inning with the bases loaded.[53]

The big news, however, concerned Winsch's ejection, because it was the *umpire* who swung at the *manager*, not vice versa. Earl McCammon, who functioned as the loop's chief executive in 1952, listened to players and officials at Rockford, fined Winsch $50, suspended him indefinitely (later reduced to three days), and banned Valentine from the league.[54] Winsch claimed innocence. He wrote a detailed letter to McCammon explaining that Rumsey, taking the stretch position, saw the runner going for second and backed off the pitching rubber, thus making her an infielder, so her throw to second was a valid play, not a balk. Words were exchanged, Valentine cursed Winsch and told him to get out, but, as Karl wrote, "I said, 'put me out.' As soon as I said this he hit me and I never raised a hand on him." Winsch, with his players crowding around, claimed that Valentine swung at more Sox players and actually grabbed Lenard before the police ended it. Karl said he left the park, showered, and returned, arguing that the first base umpire had been drinking and calling Valentine a "maniac" who should be banned from the loop for life.[55]

The truth of the incident was less flattering. Jim Johnston, sports editor of the Rockford paper, indicated the conflict was burned into the memory of the 1,025 paying customers. The dispute began with Rockford's Amy Applegren on third and Snookie Doyle on first base with two outs in the opening inning. Doyle took off for second, and Rumsey "made a forward motion, halted, whirled and threw the ball into the outfield," and the run scored. Ken Valentine ruled the play a balk, Winsch immediately protested, and after several minutes of heated conversation, Valentine ejected Winsch. "The Blue Sox pilot, known throughout the league for his more-than-frequent rhubarbs," observed Johnston, "decided he wouldn't be ousted." After what reporters termed Winsch's abusive language, Valentine "lost his temper and went out swinging," and several Sox players jumped on the umpire, "beating him with fists, catcher's mask or anything handy." Inspired by the fracas, the Peaches won the game.[56]

Regardless of the observer's interpretation, the umpire was out of line, but Winsch also displayed his volatile temper, a characteristic that he repeated often in 1952.

All-Stars and the Pennant Race

Returning to Playland Park on Tuesday, June 24, Mahon, managing her third (and final) game, started Faut on the mound. The Blue Sox defeated the visiting Belles, 8–1, as Jean scattered six hits, and her teammates, contributing fine glove work, nailed down the victory with three runs in the sixth inning and three more in the seventh. The success gave South Bend a two and a half game lead over Fort Wayne. Both teams hoped to be in first place on July 1, because that was the loop's new requirement for hosting the All-Star game.[57] The South Benders split with Battle Creek and lost two out of three at Fort Wayne, but beat the Daisies, 3–1, at Playland on June 29. In that decision, the Blue Sox rode Faut's neat three-hitter, her ninth win against no defeats, to a record of 28–13, clinching the top spot by July 1 with a two-game edge over Fort Wayne.[58]

The league devised a new concept for the star-spangled exhibition in 1952: press and radio representatives from the six league cities would select the players, and the All-Stars would meet the current first-place team. The stars' manager was Bill Allington of Rockford, because the Winsch-managed South Benders qualified as the host team. The Blue Sox had four players selected for All-Stars: Shorty Pryer, second base, although she was still sidelined with an injury; Jean Faut, as the number two pitcher; Shirley Stovroff, as catcher; and outfielder Betty Wagoner. The Peaches led the voting with six selections: Ruth Richard, as catcher; Joan Berger, at second base; Ellie Callow, in left field; the seemingly ageless Rose Gacioch, 37, as a pitcher; Snookie Doyle at shortstop; and Alice (Pollitt) Deschaine, as the utility player. The Daisies had four All-Stars chosen, the Lassies three, and the Chicks and the Belles two each.[59]

The two squads met at Playland on Monday, July 7, and the All-Stars triumphed, 7–6, scoring an unearned run in the ninth to win. Fort Wayne slugger Betty Foss led off the last inning with a single, stole second, took third when Stovroff's throw bounced into center field, and raced home on a high bouncer to third by Doris Sams, Kalamazoo's big hitter. Vincent, who relieved Wagoner with none out in the fifth, took the loss. Barbara Hoffman provided the home town fans with their biggest thrill by hitting a towering two-run homer into the left field seats for a 2–0 lead in the fourth. The All-Stars rallied for six runs in the fifth, and Sams, who led the league with 12 home runs in 1952, slammed Vincent's first pitch for a long two-run circuit clout. A large crowd of 3,528 saw the exciting contest, cheering as the Sox racked up ten hits off Fort Wayne's Maxine Kline, the Peaches' Rose Gacioch, and Kalamazoo's Gloria Cordes, the winning pitcher.[60]

Amid behind-scenes problems that continued to escalate, the Blue Sox returned to the diamond on Tuesday, July 8, winning at Kalamazoo, 1–0, in the opener of a three-game jaunt. Mueller tossed a four-hitter, preserving the lead her team grabbed in the fourth when Hoffman hit a run-scoring single. Later, Barbara injured her knee sliding. Afterward, South Bend, now owning a 35–15 mark, held a five-game lead over Fort Wayne (29–19).[61] In Wednesday night's doubleheader, the Blue Sox fell twice to the fifth-place Lassies (20–28). Faut lost for the first time in the seven-inning nightcap, 3–2, after Kidd and Mueller combined on a four-hitter but lost the opener, 1–0.[62]

Five weeks earlier, when South Bend wanted to trade Wiley and two others for Kalamazoo's Jane Moffet, Winsch exchanged words with Pee Wee and suspended her for supposed "insubordination."[63] Wiley, who played fewer than ten games in 1952, was riding the bench during a June 4th doubleheader at Playland against Fort Wayne. The light brown-clad Daisies won the opener, 3–1, Pryer went hitless, and Winsch, who liked to shuffle his lineup, benched her for the late game. Pryer asked why, and Winsch reportedly gave a profane reply. When Wiley said, "She's just asking a question, Karl," Winsch barked, "Go take a shower!" Pee Wee left, but was later suspended. Wiley was never told why she was suspended or why she was not invited back.[64]

Stovroff, perhaps because the events "tore at her heart," as one teammate said, later summarized the most controversial incidents during Winsch's second season as manager in a four-page typed letter to Faut. Shirley remembered that the "whole mess" started when Wiley was suspended in the second half of the twin bill against the Daisies. The players, as usual, heard the starting lineup from the loudspeaker, not the manager, before the game. Partway through the nightcap, when Pryer asked why she was not in the lineup, Winsch replied (according to Stovroff), "God dammit, I'm the manager, don't tell me what to do!"

When Shorty asked again why she was benched, the manager said, "I pulled you because you weren't hitting." When she indicated others also failed to hit, Winsch repeated his profanity, adding, "I'm the manager, don't argue with me." Wiley interjected that Pryer was just asking a question, and Karl quickly sent her to the clubhouse. She replied, "Roger Dodger," and left. "He then suspended Pee Wee," Stovroff wrote, "the reasons were as he gave them that Pee Wee cussed him out."[65] Winsch, for his part, told the directors on July 7 that Wiley "repeatedly 'talked back' to him on the field."[66] Players like Joyce Westerman, who knew her, said Wiley was not a person who disputed the manager or used profanity.[67]

Further, South Bend was in financial trouble. The ball club had a $20,000 deficit by July, and the directors voted to sell the franchise. Needing to reschedule a game at Playland on August 20 due to a conflict with the circus, the directors opted to play the game in Toledo, where financial backers indicated an interest in buying the Blue Sox. Harold Dailey, who understood the profit-loss situation, figured Toledo promoter Hank Rigney would make the arrangements, once the league learned that neither Battle Creek nor Kalamazoo wished to sell to Toledo.[68] Later, the Blue Sox played that game and lost to the Belles, 3–2, in front of 4,000 fans. In fact, so many people lined up for tickets at Swayne Field, the former home of the Triple-A Toledo Mudhens, that the game was delayed half an hour to accommodate those wanting to see the contest.[69]

Also in Toledo, an incident occurred that further hurt Pryer's status with the manager. Stovroff, as she later wrote to Faut, "popped off" to South Bend's business manager, Marty Ross, about the value of selling the team to Toledo, since investors there could afford it. However, word got back to South Bend's directors that it was Pryer who made the critical statements, so she was called to the team's office and given a "dressing down." Stovroff heard about the mistake, went to the Sox office, and admitted making the remarks, but the directors chose not to believe her. Shirley reflected, "They told me I was just sticking up for Shorty. Here I was telling the truth and they wouldn't believe me, so there was another strike against Shorty."[70]

Fighting for First Place

The Blue Sox had more than enough talent to win the 1952 championship, but after the All-Star game, the road was long and winding. The brightest spot during South Bend's two longest months continued to be Faut. Additionally, the experience Jean and her teammates gained in the long pennant fight helped the ball club in September, when the Shaughnessy Playoffs arrived and the South Benders were reduced to 12 players. In fact, the team finished second with a 64–45 record, after a long battle with the Daisies, who led the league by three games with a 67–42 mark. Before the All-Star break, South Bend had a 34–15 mark and held first place. After the break, the Sox played ball, going 30–30, with ten of those games being pitched and won by Faut.

Following the All-Star game, South Bend was hindered by injuries and inconsistency. Six days later against the Chicks, Faut was hit on the wrist by a thrown ball when, advancing from first base on Mahon's grounder to second, she raised her right hand to avoid being hit in the face by hard-nosed Gabby Ziegler, who, Jean recalled, "looked me in the eye and threw it right at me." Faut, sidelined for more than a week, had a lump on her right wrist for years.[71] Pryer, out since June 18, returned to the lineup in a 4–2 loss at Rockford on July 17.

Also, Blue Sox pitchers turned inconsistent on occasion. For example, at Grand Rapids on Sunday, July 13, the contest when Faut was injured, the resurgent Chicks, under new manager Woody English, belted Kidd for 11 hits and won, 6–0, marking South Bend's fifth loss in six games.[72] Three days later, South Bend dropped both ends of a doubleheader at Rockford, as Wagoner allowed 13 hits and lost, 12–1, and Mooney fell, 6–1, after yielding four runs in the fourth inning on two hits, two walks, and two errors. At the same time, a fire destroyed Bigelow Field in Grand Rapids and burned the team's uniforms and equipment. The Chicks had to move to another field and be reequipped to finish the season.[73] Faut, however, remained steadfast, returning to win her 11th game, 9–0, in the first of a twin bill against Rockford on July 23.[74]

Following a loss in the nightcap and another defeat the next night against Rockford as well as a nine-inning 3–3 deadlock at Battle Creek on Friday, July 25,[75] the Blue Sox bounced back to win 11 of the next 13 games. After that streak, Faut, facing the Daisies at Memorial Field on Wednesday, August 6, finally lost her second game of the season, 5–4, because of four ninth-inning errors, two by Jean herself. The Blue Sox belted the offerings of Maxine Kline, rated the loop's top pitcher in All-Star balloting, for 12 hits, three each by Wagoner and Faut. South Bend rallied in the ninth when Dunn led off with a single and stole second. Faut rapped her third single, and Dunn held up at third. Faut stole second, and Pryer popped out, but Wagoner walked to load the sacks. Mahon, pinch-hitting for Lenard, flew out to left field, but Dunn tagged up and streaked for home, sailing into catcher Kate Vonderau, who dropped the throw for a 3–3 score. Faut, who took third on the play, raced home for a 4–3 lead when Dottie Schroeder juggled a Westerman grounder. Kline worked out of the jam, and the Daisies scored twice to win. The night's results left the Sox (52–29) in first place with a two-game lead over the Daisies (50–31).[76]

South Bend's fight for first place with Fort Wayne continued through most of August, and Faut continued to win big games. Four days later, at Rockford on Sunday, August 10, Faut won a five-hitter, 3–2, to keep her team in first place.[77] At Playland against Fort Wayne on August 14, South Bend's ace, backed by a 12-hit barrage, won her 16th game, 9–6, despite giving up four hits and four runs in the first inning.[78] Following a rainout and a pair of home losses to Rockford, Faut hurled a 6–2 victory, stopping the much-improved Peaches on seven hits.[79]

Two days later, on August 20, the South Benders traveled to Toledo, partly to impress local investors. Meeting the last-place Belles at Swayne Field, the Indiana club lost, 3–2, although Rumsey and Mooney combined on a five-hitter. Rumsey, however, gave up all three runs in the second frame, starting with two walks. After a bunt, Marge Pieper stole home; Rumsey's throw caught her, but Stovroff dropped the ball. Betty Whiting singled home the second run. Following a steal and another bunt, Marilyn Jones singled for another score. When Fort Wayne (58–37) beat third-place Rockford (51–46), South Bend (58–36) led the league by half a game.[80]

The loss at Toledo was the second in a four-game skid, but in the nightcap of a twin bill at Grand Rapids on Friday, August 22, Faut came through again. She preserved a tie with Fort Wayne by stopping the Chicks, 8–0, spacing seven hits and striking out nine. Jean helped her cause with three hits, and Pryer and Westerman added two hits each to the ten-blow night.[81] In the end, however, the Blue Sox fell out of first place, losing two more to the Chicks. Regrouping at home on Monday, South Bend topped Battle Creek in 11 innings, 5–4, as Jette Mooney, after a shaky start, persevered to win in the 11th when Stoll singled home Wagoner, who walked, stole second, and took third on a wild pitch.[82] On Tuesday, in the opener of a four-game series at Kalamazoo, Faut fired a sterling three-hitter to win, 3–0. Fort Wayne also won, but Winsch was "pleased with the hustle displayed by his Sox in complimenting them after the game."[83]

Regardless, the blue-clad visitors dropped the last three games to Kalamazoo, losing a 1–0 heart-breaker in the finale to Gloria Cordes' two-hitter. Mueller scattered five hits, but Doris Sams doubled in the fifth, scoring when Mueller threw away a bunt by June Peppas. However, a critical incident occurred on South Bend's bench in the ninth, after Wagoner hit a two-out single and Winsch called on Pryer to pinch-run.[84]

Returning home to face Grand Rapids at Playland in a doubleheader on Saturday, August 30, the Blue Sox won twice, highlighted by Faut's 20th victory, a three-hit 4–0 shutout in the opener, but the *Tribune's* headline read: "Blue Sox Sweep Pair; Four Players Suspended." The team's internal dissension had boiled over and South Bend faced a "player walkout" resulting in Pryer, Stovroff, Stoll, and Mahon leaving the team for the season.[85]

The Worst Hour

The Blue Sox player walkout of August 1952 — with the total reaching six when Mueller and Hoffman left the team — was South Bend's worst hour, but it was the predictable culmination of a series of events dating to the last day of the 1950 season. At that time, several players, led by Shorty Pryer, Shirley Stovroff, and Jeep Stoll, accosted loop president Fred Leo after the game, demanding answers to questions about how the playoff money was divided among players. By mid–1951, the team was split into two groups socially, the younger players such as Wimp Baumgartner, Gertie Dunn, Sue Kidd, Jan Rumsey, and Pee Wee Wiley, along with Lou Arnold, on the one hand, and most of the team's veterans on the other. Jean Faut was caught in the middle, because she was the manager's wife. In the spring of 1952, resentment resurfaced when Pryer, Stovroff, and Stoll, among others, threatened not to sign their contracts because the team did not offer pay raises. To the smoldering embers of the core of South Benders who had lots of talent but little tolerance of second-class treatment, Karl Winsch added the match of his often quick temper — a characteristic exemplified by suspension of Janet Wiley followed by the bizarre incident of an umpire swinging at Winsch in Rockford.

Pryer was the center of the gathering storm, and the incident sparking the walkout occurred in the finale of the Kalamazoo trip on Friday, August 29. Gloria Cordes, the All-Star right-hander, was blanking the Blue Sox and leading, 1–0, with two outs in the ninth, when Wagoner singled to keep the visitors' hopes alive. Winsch, from the third base coaching box, yelled for Pryer to pinch-run. Shorty, who was watching Wenzell play in her place at second base, had replaced her spikes with moccasins, and others on the bench like Mahon also had loosened their laces or removed their spikes. Complaining, Pryer slowly donned her baseball shoes and trotted to first base.[86] The Lassies knew that Shorty led the loop in steals in 1951 (129), and was leading again in 1952 with 59, a lower figure because the fleet Californian was injured for a month. Knowing her speed, catcher Jenny Romatowski called for a pitchout, Cordes pitched outside, and Romatowski's throw caught Pryer sliding into second — ending the game and leaving Winsch furious.

Reflecting on those events in 1955, after the league went out of business, Stovroff said Winsch was "teed off" because Pryer had taken off her spikes, but so did others on the bench. Also, Shorty realized that if Winsch called for a steal on the first pitch, it would be a "red flag" to the Lassies. Winsch did just that, Cordes pitched out, Romatowski threw out Pryer, and the game was over.[87] In addition, the next batter would have been Lenard, but Winsch had called for Mahon to pinch-hit. Lib had also taken off her spikes, but the manager said nothing about her delay.[88]

Afterward, the players boarded the bus for the long ride to South Bend. According to W.C. Madden, who provided no citations but interviewed several former players for his 1997 book, *The Dutiful Dozen*, Harold Dailey pulled Winsch aside after the game and told him to suspend Pryer. That statement was inaccurate, because Dailey was no longer a director and had no such authority. Instead, Winsch acted on his own. Before the team left Kalamazoo, Madden wrote, Winsch took Pryer aside and suspended her for a week, but indicated she could return for the playoffs. Shorty was upset, and during the trip home, she told Stovroff and Mahon about it. Lib approached the manager, but he refused to reconsider his decision.[89]

On Sunday, August 31, the *South Bend Tribune* quoted Winsch as saying that trouble had been brewing for weeks, and that on Friday night at Kalamazoo, Pryer had "balked" at pinch-running. The article also indicated that before Saturday's game, Winsch "called Pryer on the carpet. She notified him of her intentions to leave the club. Winsch immediately suspended her." Stovroff was reported as saying that she would leave the team if the suspension was not lifted, and when "reinstatement was not forthcoming," Stovroff, Mahon, and Stoll started a walkout.[90]

Pryer, wrote to the league's president and to South Bend's directors protesting her suspension. When asked to pinch-run, she wrote, "I said, 'Why is he putting me in to run for her [Wagoner] when she's as fast as I am, and she's warm and I'm cold?'" Shorty said she "unconsciously started to remove my game shoes." The *Tribune* also said that Pryer denied quitting the team: "Winsch suspended me. I positively did not quit.'"[91]

In addition, a flare-up took place in Playland's smoky locker room, just before the Saturday night game with Grand Rapids. Baumgartner was warming up Faut, when Wimp tossed the ball to Jean and left for the clubhouse. A players' meeting was taking place, but Faut was not informed, and she sat in the dugout, later pitching without a good warm-up. Actually, few players were talking to Faut, because she was the manager's wife. Jean recalled that Winsch was a manager on the players' side in 1951, but in the second year, things changed. Karl "was tight with the board, and would do whatever they told him to do."[92]

During the players' meeting, when Stovroff asked the manager why Pryer was suspended, Winsch first claimed she quit, but then admitted suspending Shorty because "she was the reason we lost all of our games." That statement was hardly true. Even though Pryer led the league with her .312 average in 1951 but dropped to .245 in 1952, no single batter causes a team to lose. In fact, South Bend's batting average of .248 was second behind slugging Fort Wayne's mark of .257, but the Blue Sox were fifth in fielding with a .947 average.[93] When Stovroff and others indicated they would leave in support of Pryer, Shirley later wrote, Karl replied, "Well, manage your own team."[94]

Regardless, Pryer's suspension stood. Mahon recalled quitting the team because Pryer was treated unfairly, not because they were close friends. Later, Lib regretted the way her baseball career ended, but regarding Winsch, she observed, "Anybody who played ball won't have kind words for him. It was Winsch's way, or it was wrong."[95] On the other hand, Pryer was a difficult player to manage. Wimp Baumgartner recalled Shorty's brash comments caused many of her own problems. "She'd let you know if you did something wrong," Baumgartner said, "but she wasn't the manager."[96] Even Pryer later conceded that she had a personality conflict with Winsch.[97]

In the end, the object of the players' meeting was to persuade others to join the walkout, and maybe get rid of the manager. That goal was fruitless. Winsch was tied closely to the Blue Sox' board. He had managed South Bend to the championship in 1951, and the directors supported his actions, right or wrong.[98] Moreover, younger players were not going to throw away their baseball dreams by quitting. Women like Kidd, Rumsey, and Baumgartner loved playing pro ball, and salary was not a factor to them. Kidd refused to give her answer that evening. Later, she called her father, who advised her not to leave. Sue was too concerned about what would happen to her team and her career to join such a revolt.[99]

Also that Saturday evening, Faut hurled her 20th victory, stifling the Chicks on a three-hitter, 4–0. When Jean walked into the locker room after the game, Stoll called her a "squealer." Actually, Winsch was not speaking to his wife on or off the diamond. Regardless, Jean never passed gossip to him. Reacting furiously to Stoll's unfair accusation, Faut slugged Jeep so hard in the chin that her head banged off the lockers.[100] Stoll often had spread rumors behind Faut's back, and Jean's solid punch reflected the tension surrounding the team late in the season.

The Beautiful Dozen

As a result of Pryer's suspension and the resulting walkout (soon joined by two more players), South Bend's season hinged on 12 players. Baumgartner believed the walkout improved team morale. "When the players walked out," she commented, "I was glad. The dissension was gone, and we were determined to win."[101] Reflected Joyce Westerman, "We won, first, because we had the desire to win, and, second, we were determined to show the players who left that we could win without them."[102] Faut recalled, "You could relax and play ball and not worry about what players were saying."[103]

Indeed, the remaining South Benders quickly gelled. On Sunday, August 31, pitching for a more cohesive team, Kidd gave one of her best performances, tossing a three-hitter to blank the visiting Chicks, 2–0. After the game, Dottie Mueller and Barbara Hoffman joined the walkout. Traveling to Grand Rapids for a season-ending Labor Day twin bill, South Bend fell twice. Marge Silvestri won the seven-inning opener, 3–0, and Rumsey took the loss. In the late tilt, Mary Lou Studnicka gave up six hits and bested Arnold, as the Chicks improved to a 50–60 mark and squeezed into the Shaughnessy Playoffs, half a game ahead of 49–60 Kalamazoo. Winsch's ball club, with 12 players, scored a total of one run in both games, and that tally came in the seventh inning when Faut singled and Dunn hit an RBI double. Returning to Playland to defend their 1951 playoff title on Tuesday, the Blue Sox hosted the same improved Chicks.[104]

The semifinal playoff was a best-of-three series against Grand Rapids, and Winsch, marking his lineup card, chose from his 12 players, usually listing them as follows:

- Wagoner, CF — Betty, a left-handed Missourian who now made her home in South Bend, normally played right field. Needing a spot starter in 1952, Winsch used his southpaw — one of the few in the loop. She posted a 5–2 record, but with the league's fifth-worst ERA, 4.25. In the field, Old Reliable played fine defense, and she batted .295, the circuit's fifth-best mark.
- Mooney, 2B-P — Jette, a 5' 3" right-handed batter who got married in June, was a weak hitter who averaged .153 lifetime in six seasons. She batted .169 in 1952. A good-fielding pitcher, she had no experience at second base. Mooney provided the Sox a bigger lift on the mound, although her record for 1952 was an uninspiring 8–8 with a 2.36 ERA.
- Lenard, LF — Jo, a 5' 4" right-handed batter, was born and raised in Chicago. A ten-year league veteran, she was acquired by the Blue Sox in 1952 from the defunct Kenosha club. Lenard, who turned 31 as the playoffs began, batted .259. The team's best-fielding flychaser, she was skilled, experienced, and friendly, with a dry wit — and altogether she was a major contributor.
- Westerman, 1B — Joyce, the 5'5" Kenosha native, began her eight-year career as a catcher with Grand Rapids in 1945. Later, she played the outfield and first base. After the 1950 season, she married Ray Westerman. Joyce, a dependable fielder and a solid hitter who batted .277 with five doubles and 36 RBI in 1952, began wearing glasses after she missed a fly ball in the outfield with Racine a few years previously. Married, she lived alone in a single room and socialized little, mostly keeping to herself after games.[105]
- Faut, P-3B — Jean, the sandy blond superstar, was also raising her four-year-old son, Larry. Faut, the heart of the Blue Sox, gave an MVP performance in 1952: a 20–2 record in 23 games and the loop's best ERA, a stingy 0.93. Jean also starred in the field, playing 50 games at third base, fielding well, and hitting .291, the sixth-best average for women who played at least 70 games. Nobody in the loop played better under pressure.
- Dunn, SS — Gertie, the 18-year-old rookie from Sharon Hill, Pennsylvania, was a fine all-around athlete who also excelled at field hockey, lacrosse, and, later, golf. A sparkling personality who was full of self-confidence and fun to be around, the 5' 2" rookie with the quick hands and the accurate arm batted .236 in her first full season.
- Wenzell, OF-2B-3B — Marge, 27, was a 5'5" utility player who broke into the league with Grand Rapids in 1945. Born and raised in Detroit, the right-handed hitter handled every position, except pitcher and catcher. Usually an infielder, she started 1952 with Battle Creek (five of her ten seasons were split between two teams), but South Bend acquired her after Audrey Bleiler became pregnant. A quiet person, Marge played 57 games and averaged a combined .216.
- Baumgartner, C — Wimp, 22, the team's reserve catcher in 1951 and 1952, was the virtual equal of Stovroff as a receiver, but Shirley was faster and a better hitter. In professional ball, however, back-ups like Baumgartner — unless there are

injuries — seldom received a chance to play, so their hitting often fails to improve. Wimp, who appeared in 34 games, averaged .100 in 50 at-bats, but she added a run-scoring squeeze and a big hit against Rockford in the tying game.

- Kidd, P-OF-3B — Sue, the tall, versatile, 19-year-old right-hander, came into her own as a pitcher with South Bend in 1951, fashioning an 11–7 record with a 2.50 ERA. Improving with experience, the quiet, hard-throwing country girl with the deep southern drawl produced a 13–7 ledger in 23 contests. Kidd also finished 1952 with a 2.00 ERA, eighth best in the league, and she rose to the occasion with her pitching and hitting in the playoffs.
- Rumsey, P — Jan, 20, the third hurler behind Faut and Kidd, posted a 9–10 record and a 2.22 ERA in her second season. Wearing black plastic glasses, the tall, slender right-hander from Greensburg, Indiana, showed a variety of stuff. Still improving her control, Rumsey's best pitch was the low fastball. Quiet and hardworking, she won once against Rockford in the playoffs.
- Arnold, P — Lou, who decided not to return after the 1952 season, was reduced to a spot starter when the manager began using Mueller and Wagoner. Still, Arnold remained an eternal optimist and the team's cheerleader on the bench. In her final season, the Rhode Island slowballer posted a 4–8 record with a 3.43 ERA, but she helped her beloved team any way possible.
- Froning, OF — Mary, 18, was a right-handed batter who usually covered an outfield post. Her teammates called her "Fearless," because the speedster would run into a fence chasing the ball. A pretty brunette from Minster, Ohio, who later worked as an airline hostess, Froning played in 13 regular season games and batted .180, but she never got a chance in the playoffs.

In the opener at Playland on Tuesday, September 2, the day after the home team dropped a twin bill to the Chicks in Grand Rapids, Faut, "never in better form," fired a three-hitter to win, 2–1. Showing the versatility needed to win, Mooney played second base and Kidd, who started in right field, exchanged places with Wenzell at third base in the ninth. Gabby Ziegler scattered five hits, but in the second inning, Wagoner's RBI single, following singles by Faut and Dunn and a fielder's choice, gave the home team a 1–0 edge. In the eighth, Westerman singled and took second on a passed ball. Faut grounded to Inez Voyce, who made the out at first base but threw wildly to third, and the Sox took a 2–0 lead. In the ninth, Faut allowed an unearned run on a single and two errors — making it the first run scored against her in 35 innings.[106]

South Bend traveled to Grand Rapids, and Kidd limited the Chicks to six hits, but she left in the ninth. Faut relieved with a runner at first base and one out, retiring the side to save the 6–1 win. Eleanor Moore and Beans Risinger held the Blue Sox to two singles, but the Chicks committed four errors, the pitchers walked six, and the visitors stole nine bases, four by Lenard, who swiped third twice. South Bend counted once in the first when Lenard reached on a fielder's choice, stole second, and scored on an error. The Sox added two in the third on two walks, a double steal, a squeeze, and a sacrifice fly. Finally, Dunn's scratch single in the seventh helped score a run, and two more runs in the eighth capped the win. Also, Fort Wayne beat Rockford in ten innings, so that Winsch's happy dozen enjoyed the ride home to await the winner of that series.[107]

South Bend, as decided at a league meeting, would open the best-of-five final round of playoffs at Rockford, but only if the Peaches beat the Daisies, because the Illinois team had to vacate Beyer Stadium on Sunday. When Mickey Jinright blanked the Daisies on Friday, 6–0, the stage was set.[108]

Traveling to Rockford for the final time on Saturday, September 6, the Blue Sox suffered a major disappointment. Faut, enduring an off night, yielded seven runs and 13 hits in seven innings, topped by Ellie Callow's two-run homer in the seventh. Arnold pitched a scoreless eighth. The blue-uniformed visitors scored three unearned runs off Jackie Kelley, including one in the ninth on three walks and a wild pitch, but it was too little — and the Peaches won, 7–3.[109]

On Sunday evening at the Peach Orchard, the Blue Sox scored twice in the first inning on Faut's two-run double, but fell to Rose Gacioch's pitching, 3–2, in a game with an unusual twist. In the fifth inning with the score tied at 2–2, Ruth Richard lifted a Rumsey slant over the 190-foot right field fence. The Blue Sox loaded the bases in the seventh and the eighth, but Gacioch pitched out of both jams. Winsch protested the outcome, due to the shortened fence, a result of the field being converted for football. In return, Bill Allington protested South Bend's roster, because the visitors had 12 players, instead of a league-required 15. Until the circuit could rule on the protests, the Sox felt subdued as they made the tiring journey home. Down two games to none in the best-of-five series, South Bend's dozen faced elimination.[110]

At Playland Park on Monday night, the Blue Sox won the game, but the Peaches lost *twice*. The second loss came during the third playoff contest when Earl McCammon upheld South Bend's protest of Sunday's game, ruling the game must be replayed. The league's requirement for the minimum distance to an outfield fence was 210 feet, and McCammon decided that Rockford officials were wrong in refusing to discuss a ground rule to cover the shorter length.

In Monday's game, Kidd, with her fastball and breaking stuff working, hurled one of her finest games, until she tired and allowed two runs in the eighth and a double to Callow in the ninth. Faut relieved, surrendering two runs for a 4–4 tie, but nothing thereafter. The local favorites had scored four runs off seven hits against nemesis Mickey Jinright in the first four frames. After two outs in the twelfth, Westerman singled, Faut walked, and Kidd, having switched to right field, connected for the greatest run-scoring base hit of her life — and the Sox won, 5–4.[111]

In another nail-biter on Tuesday, the never-say-die Rockford club came back to win, 5–4, thanks largely to five double plays in seven chances. The peach-clad visitors scored unearned runs in the second and third off Mooney. Baumgartner made an error in each inning, dropping the ball during a rundown in the third that gave the Peaches a 2–0 lead, a margin they upped to 5–1 in the fifth with two hits, two steals, a wild pitch, and a squeeze. Amy Applegren spaced eight hits, but won thanks to her teammates' five twin killings — the last in the eighth to snuff a rally. The lefty preserved the win by retiring Wagoner on a popup with two runners aboard in the ninth. The result left the Peaches in the driver's seat, needing just one victory for the championship.[112]

The Finest Hour

"Out-hit, out-fielded, out-pitched, but never out-fought," declared the *Tribune*, the "dutiful dozen" topped Rockford's Gacioch, 2–1, in ten innings for the season's last game at Playland Park before 1,200 cheering fans. With her team again facing elimination, Rumsey

Beautiful Dozen — South Bend won the 1952 Shaughnessy Playoff Championship in five games over Rockford. Due to Rockford's Beyer Stadium being unavailable, the final game was played in Freeport, Illinois. The team members along with manager Karl Winsch are pictured after the game, with Earl McCammon, the league's business manager, presenting the championship trophy to Jean Faut. Accepting on behalf of her teammates, Faut, chosen the league's Player of the Year in 1951, had just pitched and batted — she slugged two triples — the Blue Sox to the clinching 6–3 victory over the Peaches (courtesy of the Louise Pettus Archives and Special Collections, Winthrop University).

came through with her greatest game, allowing nine hits — but just one run, when Westerman failed to hold Jan's pickoff attempt with runners on first and third base in the fifth. Baumgartner, who hurt the Blue Sox the previous night with two errors, squeezed home Dunn with the tying run in the seventh, after Gertie singled and advanced on an error and a sacrifice. In the tenth, the Blue Sox rallied, starting with Wimp's clutch single. Rumsey bunted her to second, and Wagoner beat out an infield hit, leaving runners on first and third. Mooney, playing second base, fouled off a bunt attempt, but drew a walk. After Lenard skied to short center, Westerman came through, smashing the game-winning single between first and second base for the series-tying victory.[113]

Traveling on Thursday to Read Park in Freeport, Illinois, 30 miles west of Rockford's unavailable stadium, the Blue Sox, fired with enthusiasm, desire, and determination, came through with a big-time effort worthy of Hollywood. Entertaining 2,200 in a ballpark set up for men's baseball, the South Benders, led by Faut, who pitched and slammed two triples as part of the 12-hit attack, captured a stirring 6–3 triumph. Mooney, batting second, was safe on an error in the first inning, and, hitting fourth, Westerman doubled her home. The visitors took a big lead with a three-run burst in the third, starting with Wagoner's base hit, an error, and Mooney's RBI single. Lenard singled, Westerman hit into a force play, and Faut, connecting for perhaps her greatest hit, slugged a long two-run triple to left center for the 4–0 lead. The Peaches replied with a run in the fourth on a single, a walk, and an error, cutting the deficit to 4–1.

In the sixth, the heroic Faut slammed another triple — a blast that could have been a home run, but she was so tired after rounding third base that she stopped, walked back, and sat down on the bag. Out of Rockford's dugout boomed Gacioch's deep voice, "My God, that girl is tired!"[114]

The memorable season was all but over. Moments later, Dunn scored Faut with a grounder, and South Bend added an insurance run in the seventh inning for a 6–1 lead. In a fitting finish, all nine of the Blue Sox hit safely, and longtime stars Wagoner, Lenard, and Faut collected two hits each. Rockford used Mickey Jinright and Marie Mansfield on the mound, but not even two runs in the ninth against an exhausted Faut could make any difference. After a local photographer captured the timeless moment of McCammon making the trophy presentation to Faut on behalf of her team, the 12 women headed for the locker room, the showers, and the happy trip home.[115]

The Blue Sox had repeated as champions. Baumgartner admired her favorite battery mate, Jean Faut, whom she later called "one of the most talented, if not the best ballplayer, in the league." Wimp added about Jean, "With her Pennsylvania Dutch voice, you could hear her all over the field. After she said what she had to say, she'd just stand there and grin. She was a people person, and her personality was truly optimistic."[116] Baumgartner also called Faut fiercely competitive, explaining that she always gave baseball her greatest effort. "The tougher the situation," Karl Winsch later wrote about his ex-wife, "the better she performed."[117]

In a fitting tribute to the heroines in pastel blue, Joe Doyle of the *South Bend Tribune* concluded that they won their second straight title "on just one basis — determination, the will to win."[118] For the Shaughnessy Playoffs of 1952, the beautiful dozen, rising above the disruptive drama of the player walkout, delivered a once-in-a-lifetime team performance. Led in their finest hour by the indomitable Jean Faut and boosted by timely contributions from almost every member of the Blue Sox nine, South Bend won an against-all-odds championship that ranks with the greatest achievements in the history of the Girls' Pro League.

• 11 •

The Blue Sox and the League Struggle: 1953

"If the Blue Sox are to stir up interest in South Bend fans [in 1954], a far better team must take the field. Box-office patrons get excited about winning baseball, but it must be good baseball as well"— Joe Doyle, September 10, 1953[1]

A Time to Leave?

The South Bend franchise and the American Girls Baseball League both struggled through the season in 1953. Even though the Blue Sox had won two straight Shaughnessy Championships on the uneven surfaces of the diamonds in the Girls' Pro League in 1951 and 1952, Joe Doyle, writing for the *South Bend Tribune*, was concerned that the city's team and the circuit would not succeed financially. Writing near the midpoint of the 1953 season, Doyle pointed out that local attendance had dropped 30 percent, but a gate of 1,000 per game would make South Bend's club profitable. The same six teams returned for the league's 11th season, but the Belles, due to poor attendance and dwindling finances, moved to Muskegon, Michigan, after the league was forced to operate Battle Creek's Belles for the last three weeks of the 1952 campaign.[2] Moreover, the total debt of the six teams by the end of 1953 was $80,000, a staggering deficit in the 1950s.[3] Further, the female baseball player, Doyle explained, was no longer "particularly feminine," but neither was the top-notch lady golfer or tennis player. To succeed, South Bend needed to sell women's baseball and to play the game well. "It's up to the fans," the sports editor concluded, "to make the team a contender at the gate and a member of the league in the future."[4]

South Bend faced a major rebuilding job, because five of the six players who left the team at the end of August 1952 were talented veterans, and four were regulars. Shorty Pryer, suspended by manager Karl Winsch after the Blue Sox lost to the Chicks on August 29, was the team's stellar second baseman. Pryer led the Blue Sox in 1951 with her average of .312, a mark that ranked fifth in the league. In 1952, however, she sat out four weeks in the middle of the season with an injured ankle. In the end, she averaged .239, eighth best on the team. Shorty, who disliked the manager, was a strong presence on the diamond, but a divisive force in the clubhouse.

In addition to Pryer, the Blue Sox lost four other mainstays: catcher Shirley Stovroff, center fielder Jeep Stoll, outfielder Lib Mahon, and Joyce Westerman, the steady first baseman who was married and gave up baseball. The strong-armed Stovroff was the team's best receiver, despite making 20 errors, the second-worst total for a catcher. However, Shirley batted .250 and contributed 39 RBI, making her a valuable run producer. Stoll, a dependable outfielder, led the club in batting with a .301 mark and paced her team with 60 RBI in 1952. Mahon, a reserve because she had retired following the 1951 season, played 59 games and hit .229, including nine doubles and 16 RBI. Lib also added her forceful presence to the team's leadership. Westerman, who hit .277 during her eighth and final season, had retired from the loop and would be missed greatly.[5]

Furthermore, the league moved a step closer to regulation baseball. The special ten-inch ball, manufactured by the DeBeer Company and adopted in mid–1949, was used again, but DeBeer was working on making it "a little harder and a little faster."[6] As a result, the pitching distance was increased one foot to 56 feet, and base paths were lengthened from 72 feet to 75.[7] Earl McCammon, the loop's business manager, was named commissioner for 1953. Again, McCammon's office lacked any real authority, because during the period of independent ownership after the 1950 season, the teams' boards of directors ran the show. Ball clubs were allowed to contract with 16 or 17 players, but the salary limit again was $5,400 per month for 16 players, or $5,700 for 17. The league continued the player draft, but thus far the draft had proven inadequate to attract enough new talent. Last but not least, the salary maximum meant no raises for veterans and, therefore, teams were signing mainly rookies or second-year players with less skill and experience. The circuit was facing a talent drain.[8] To paraphrase Pete Seeger's song, "Where have all the players gone?"

During the 1950s, the girls who left after each season sang a similar song. Kalamazoo star Doris Sams, Player of the Year in 1947 and 1949, led the loop in homers with 12 in 1952, but in 1953, "Sammye" (her favorite moniker) had to overcome an off-season illness. She returned in July and batted .312, but belted only two homers (one in the playoffs). Sams recalled retiring following the 1953 season partly because she was offered a job as a computer operator with the Knoxville Utilities Board. She added, "The league was going down by 1953. You could see it. It was getting to be the same old teams, over and over, and the same old players. It was time to leave."[9]

Hope Springs Eternal

For the Blue Sox in 1953, acquiring new talent became a top priority, but before anything else happened, the player walkout resurfaced. Earlier, the Kalamazoo Lassies contacted South Bend and wanted to acquire Jeep Stoll. Although she was one of six who walked out, her status — like that of any player in the league — was reserved by her team. Stoll, a very good but temperamental athlete who worked at Bendix in the off season, refused to sign, saying she would retire rather than play for Karl Winsch. "If he is the manager again," she told the *Tribune*, "I'm definitely not going to play." In fact, Dottie Mueller was the only player of the six to sign her 1953 contract with South Bend. Barbara Hoffman had been traded to Fort Wayne, but she never signed a contract, so her career was over.[10] Later, Stoll accepted the trade to Kalamazoo, and in doing so, she hit back at Winsch, using her bat to defeat her former team more than once.

Regardless, South Bend forged ahead on April 22 when Norwood Craighead, the team's new president, signed ace hurler Jean Faut to her eighth contract. As usual, terms were not disclosed, but Jean was the team's highest paid player with a salary exceeding $500 per month.[11] However, she remembered not receiving a raise after the 1951 season.[12] The ball club already had signed infielder Marge Wenzell, pitcher-first baseman Dottie Mueller, who was soon traded to Grand Rapids, and outfielder Mary Froning, but others were expected to sign soon.

The Blue Sox planned a joint spring camp with the Rockford Peaches beginning on Monday, May 4, at Playland Park. After a week of training, the teams would embark on a ten-day, five-state exhibition odyssey.[13]

The 110-game regular season schedule was set, and the Blue Sox would open with an away game at Grand Rapids on Thursday, May 21. Muskegon would arrive that Sunday to open South Bend's 55-game home season. Four teams would visit Playland Park three times, twice for a four-game series and once for three games, and Grand Rapids would make four trips. The format used during the eight-team days featured frequent doubleheaders, usually on Sundays and holidays, but now the loop scheduled twin bills mainly on Memorial Day and Labor Day. Rainouts, of course, were made up by doubleheaders. Since Playland featured a new lighted raceway, the first tier of box seats was raised for better viewing by fans. South Bend, facing declining attendance, also removed the bleachers from around the outfield and offered 26 spectator parking places, similar to the layout of the newly popular drive-in movie theaters.[14]

The two-team training camp was successful, despite chilly weather. Blue Sox veterans who worked on conditioning and hitting were infielders Gertie Dunn, Marge Wenzell, and Rose Monty (actually, Montalbano), catcher Wimp Baumgartner, outfielders Betty Wagoner and Mary Froning, and pitchers Jean Faut, Sue Kidd, and Jan Rumsey, the trio who became the team's hurling rotation. Three rookies reported after looking good in a "tryout school" attended by 46 hopefuls on April 24–26 in Battle Creek: Doris Reardon of Norwood, Massachusetts, Nancy Hobbs of Oxford, Massachusetts, and Ann Garman of Avilla, Indiana. Other rookies included Betty Talbott of Chicago; Joan Matuzewski from Milwaukee; Arlene Buszka of Detroit; Joanne Ogden of Rochester; Virginia Carver of New Brighton, Pennsylvania; Mary Lerner and Mildred Ferro from Elkhart; and Shirley Ann Salisbury and Mary Lou Graham, both from South Bend. Graham had served as the team's bat girl in 1952.[15]

As usual, both managers would depend largely on experienced veterans. The Peaches had a new manager, Johnny Rawlings, who piloted Peoria in 1951, sat out of the league for a season, and agreed to serve as Rockford's pilot after Bill Allington left to manage Fort Wayne. Rawlings greeted ninth-year star Rose Gacioch, the team's best pitcher, along with standouts such as catchers Ruth Richard and Carol Habben, second baseman Joan Berger, and pitcher-infielder Jackie Kelley. Winsch was pleased to see returning regulars such as Wimp Baumgartner, Jan Rumsey, and Betty Wagoner. Actually, Wagoner, pressed into mound duty in 1952, was a good contact hitter and a speedy runner who now played center field. Faut, working with the rookies, offered tips on pitching. South Bend's main problem would emerge only later: the Sox lacked the quality starters for a strong four-person rotation.[16]

Publicity for the spring tour started after the teams met at Redbirds Stadium in Columbus on the evening of Tuesday, May 12, when South Bend topped Rockford, 8–7, for the team's third win in four tries. Already the Blue Sox had defeated the Peaches twice, at Playland on Saturday night and again in Monroe, Michigan, on Sunday, but Rockford prevailed in Toledo on Monday. The managers experimented with rookies and veteran players. Winsch was using Baumgartner and Monty as catchers; Faut, Rumsey, Kidd, Wagoner, and Graham as pitchers; Garman at first base; Ogden and Wenzell at second; Dunn at short; Monty and Carver at third; and Froning, Wenzell, Buszka, and Wagoner in the outfield.[17]

The tour's second week produced mixed results as South Bend won games but lost a few players to injuries. Also, the club was negotiating with veteran Amy Applegren to play first base, hoping Jo Lenard would follow suit. The two were friends who worked in Chicago and roomed together in the off season.[18] Applegren, who hit .253 with 49 RBI for Rockford in 1952, could fill the gap at first base, and Lenard's .259 mark ranked fifth for the Sox the previous year. At Dubuque, Iowa, on Sunday, May 17, South Bend endured cold weather and injuries to defeat Rockford in 11 innings, 3–2, on Wenzell's third single. Arlene Buszka, the promising infielder from Detroit who suffered a broken left ankle in practice, would miss at least a month (she never returned). Dunn, the shortstop, sustained a bruised elbow when she was hit with a Marie Mansfield fastball during South Bend's fifth victory in six exhibitions.[19] The next night, the Blue Sox won at Rockford, 6–3, as Matuzewski, Kidd, Wagoner, and Rumsey combined on a seven-hitter, but Wenzell broke her right ankle when, chasing a pop-up, she stepped in a small hole.[20] On Tuesday in Freeport, Illinois, the Sox won, 5–1, but Monty turned her ankle and left the game.[21]

South Bend traveled to Grand Rapids, registered at the Hotel Rowe, rested, practiced, and prepared to open the regular season on Thursday, May 21. Winsch's lineup card included four veterans and five rookies. Baumgartner was the catcher, Dunn the shortstop, and Wagoner the center fielder, but Wagoner was the only starter, except Faut, with more than two years of league experience. Winsch listed Ann Garman at first base, "Jo" Ogden at second, Gertie Dunn at short, and Rose Monty at third. Mary Froning, who was on the team in 1952 but hit .080 in 13 games, took over left field and performed well, and Joan Matuzewski, who also pitched during the spring, was slated for right field. Manager Woody English and his defending regular season champion Chicks fielded more veterans, featuring a first-rate starting rotation of Alma Ziegler, Beans Risinger, Marge Silvestri, and Mary Lou Studnicka.

Joe Doyle said the Blue Sox needed to battle on the diamond to win ball games and battle off the field to win the hearts of more fans. The *Tribune's* sports editor explained that three kinds of spectators attended: those who supported the city's one constant summer sports attraction; those who were repeatedly amazed at how well women played baseball; and those who scoffed at women's baseball, regardless of the quality of the athletes. The league originated in wartime when it was feared men's baseball might be dropped for the duration, but play continued in 1946 and afterward due to the popularity of the new sport. South Bend, a team that last made a profit (less than $100) in 1948, never won a championship before Karl Winsch arrived in 1951. Ironically, the team was losing popularity with fans even as it won playoff titles in 1951 and 1952. "Winsch, back for his third season," Doyle wrote, "is in the process of rebuilding a team that was torn by rebellion and strife at the conclusion of last season." The club's advance ticket sales exceeded those of 1952, but fans were buying fewer ducats than during the late 1940s. Still, it appeared the city would support the Blue Sox again when umpires called, "Play Ball!"[22]

Hitting, Winning, and Errors

In hindsight, the opening series at Grand Rapids looked like a microcosm of South Bend's new season: win one on hitting, lose one, or more, on errors. On a Thursday night when the thermometer fell below 50 degrees and the wind howled at South High Field, South Bend won, 14–9, after Grand Rapids took an early 6–1 lead. Facing a threat of tornado warnings, the crowd still reached 1,296, but fans saw a sloppy contest highlighted by 21 hits—11 by the visitors—and a total of 30 walks, six errors, five passed balls, and 30 stranded runners, making the event look like a "baby track meet." Rumsey, the curveballer, won, despite issuing 16 free passes, thanks to her teammates' nine-run fifth inning and relief help from Kidd in the eighth.[23] Friday's league games were washed out by rain, but on Saturday, the Blue Sox lost a frustrating battle in ten innings, 5–4, on a pair of errors—an unfortunate scenario that the team repeated too often in 1953. The visitors tied the score at 4–4 in the ninth on Monty's RBI single, and in the tenth, with Kidd pitching, Ogden, playing second base, booted Joyce Ricketts' grounder for a two-base error. Following a sacrifice, an infield hit, and a walk, Faut, playing the "hot corner," bobbled Eleanor Moore's grounder, allowing the winning run to score.[24]

After the bus journey back home for their first contest at Playland Park on Sunday, May 24 (once more the league played night games), South Bend, facing a Belles squad now located in Muskegon, dropped three out of four contests. Playing the home opener before 900 chilled spectators, the Blue Sox lost, 5–3. South Bend, stacked with younger players, lacked finesse in the field and experience at the plate. Ann Garman dropped two throws at first base, the first leading to three runs in the third. In the ninth, with the score tied at 3–3, Faut walked Katie Vonderau, Barbara Sowers bunted, and Garman dropped Baumgartner's peg to first. After a sacrifice, Faut fanned pitcher Hank Warren, but left-handed batting Jo Hasham slashed a pinch two-out single to left field to cap the scoring.[25] On Monday, Rumsey, who yielded nine hits and walked four, won, 8–4, thanks to 13 hits off Hasham and a four-run fourth frame fueled by three bunt singles. Faut played third base, Dunn again looked good at shortstop, Monty replaced Ogden at second base, and the inexperienced Garman muffed another throw at first.[26]

South Bend lost the last two games to the Belles mainly due to errors. On Tuesday, the local favorites scored seven times in the first inning to lead, 7–4. Both managers started rookies, but neither Muskegon's Noella "Pinky" LeDuc nor South Bend's Mary Lou Graham retired a batter. Youthful Phyllis Baker, soon to be 16, and the Belles' Hank Warren, who relieved in the sixth, pitched well, but Kidd, hurt by eight errors, lost.[27] On Wednesday, Winsch sent Wagoner to the mound, but the Belles bunched five of their six hits in the third frame and won, 5–2. Afterward, the loss left South Bend in fifth place with a 2–4 record. Kalamazoo led the loop with a 5–1 ledger, Grand Rapids was second at 3–2, and Fort Wayne and Muskegon, both 3–3, were tied for third.[28]

Hosting the league-leading Lassies for a four-game series beginning on Thursday, South Bend rebounded and won three out of four times. In the first tilt, Faut, displaying the fastball, the wicked curves, the control, the poise, and the determination that made her the league's best pitcher, boosted her teammates' confidence with a sterling two-hitter to win, 2–0, as she fanned 13 along the way. In the first inning, Faut drove home Wagoner, who singled, and in the second, Betty scored again when Dunn deliberately got herself into a rundown.[29] There were no games scheduled on Friday, but South Bend split a Memorial Day twin bill with Kalamazoo. In the tenth inning of the scheduled seven-inning lid-lifter, Rumsey lost, 5–3, when Fern Shollenberger singled, second baseman Jo Ogden booted a bunt, and Jenny Romatowski doubled to score both runs. In the nightcap, Kidd was breezing to a shutout until the seventh, when Baumgartner dropped a throw on a play at the plate. Still, the home team won, 4–1, thanks to three runs in the fourth on doubles by Dunn, Ogden, and Baumgartner, and Garman's single.[30] On Sunday, when Wagoner spun a three-hitter and her teammates rapped ten hits for a 9–3 victory, South Bend maintained fourth place with a 5–5 record. Elsewhere, Kalamazoo, still the league leader, slipped to 6–4, and Fort Wayne and Grand Rapids were tied for second at 5–4.[31]

Hoping to move up in the standings, the Blue Sox, after a sojourn to Muskegon, the Occidental Hotel, and Marsh Field on Monday, June 1, had mixed success. In the first contest, the visitors beat Joe Cooper's nine, 4–3, behind Faut's fine performance. Entertaining a small crowd, Jean fanned 12, drove in two runs with three hits, and outlasted right-hander Phyllis Baker, who yielded six hits and all four runs in the first two innings. The win gave the Blue Sox (6–5) a brief hold on first place,[32] but the team lacked enough first-rate pitching, timely hitting, and solid fielding to win consistently. The squads battled to a 2–2 tie on Tuesday before the game was called due to the league's curfew. In the 11th, Rumsey, who tired, walked four batters to lose a 2–1 lead before Faut, playing third base, relieved her and preserved the tie.[33] On Wednesday, the Belles defeated Kidd, who allowed 11 hits and lost, 4–1, the big blow being Nancy Mudge's three-run double in a four-run fourth stanza.[34] Thursday's game was rained out.

When the South Benders returned to Playland for Friday's clash with first-place Fort Wayne, they were paced by Faut's .404 hitting. The blue-eyed, strong-armed athlete also pitched two of the team's six victories. With Kidd doubling as center fielder, armed Wagoner, who owned one victory, took a turn on the mound. She had a 1–3 record, but she pitched well enough to win more than once. Rumsey posted the other two victories, and the tie with Muskegon would be replayed later.[35]

Battling the Blues

Playland Park, an amusement center with a racetrack around the diamond, hosted auto racing on Friday, June 5, causing South Bend's game to be postponed. Although Faut was the greatest pitcher Blue Sox fans ever applauded, her best efforts sometimes fell short. But on Saturday, she opened the Fort Wayne series with an easy win, 11–4, spacing seven hits while her team collected 15 safeties, including two apiece by Matuzewski (playing right field), Dunn, Kidd (playing first base), Froning (playing left field), Monty (at third base), and Faut herself.[36]

By June 6, a knowledgeable observer of the American Girls Baseball League could not be blamed for thinking South Bend was on the verge of many more victories. Instead, the local favorites lost 11 in a row, enduring a disastrous month by winning eight times, losing 20, and tying one. It is a baseball axiom that experienced players usually can be trusted to outperform rookies or inexperienced players, because the veterans have proven themselves under pressure in previous seasons. In 1953, Blue Sox rookies often were error-prone fielders and light hitters who were especially weak in run-scoring situations.

South Bend's 11-game skid started when the team lost a doubleheader at Playland to Fort Wayne on Sunday, June 7, lost again to the Daisies on Monday, traveled to Rockford and dropped four straight, and returned to Fort Wayne and lost four more. During that stretch, Faut lost twice, once due to sloppy fielding and once due to lack of hitting. At Rockford on June 9, the Blue Sox lost their fourth straight — and fell to the league's basement — when Faut was beaten on five unearned runs, 5–4. The visitors committed eight errors, including three in the first frame — including one by Faut — when the Peaches added three hits for a 3–0 lead. Helen Nordquist won, but Rockford's John Rawlings had to use two relievers to stop the blue-uniformed visitors' four-run rally in the sixth.[37] Four days later at Fort Wayne, the Blue Sox lost for the eighth time in a row, 5–0. Faut (3–3) gave up nine hits, but her teammates collected only four off the Daisies' Pat Scott.[38]

South Bend's final loss in the skein came by a 2–1 score in a 13 inning heart-breaker on June 16 at Fort Wayne, when Kidd gave up a bases-loaded single to Wilma Briggs in the 13th. The defeat left the Blue Sox in last place with a 7–16 record, nine games behind first-place Fort Wayne (17–8). Faut, slated to pitch at Playland, was leading the team's regulars with her .344 average. South Bend rookie Joy Perkins, who was 3-for-4, owned a .750 mark as a pinch-hitter. Sixth-year veteran Marguerite "Dolly" Pearson, acquired from Fort Wayne, started out batting .429, but finished with a .185 mark for the season. In addition to Pearson, the team acquired two recruits: Lois Youngen, a catcher, and Donna Norris, an infielder.[39]

As happened often in previous summers, Faut delivered a clutch performance that followed one or more losses, defeating the third-place Peaches, 4–1, before a small crowd of 783. At Playland on Wednesday, June 17, Rockford played like losers, making four errors to bolster the home team's five hits, as Faut, off her form, surrendered 12 hits, six in the first two innings. Still, Jean was tough under pressure, stranding nine runners and finally allowing one run in the seventh on three singles. The Blue Sox won on timely fielding and hitting, scoring four solo runs, the eventual winning tally crossing home plate in the third on Dunn's triple.[40]

South Bend, however, continued to experience a rough ride, dropping two out of the next three to Rockford and losing three out of four at Kalamazoo. Facing the Lassies at South High Field on Wednesday, June 24, the Blue Sox lost, 7–6, in what might be called typical fashion for 1953, when they grabbed an early lead but could not hold it. The visitors racked up 15 hits, taking a 5–2 lead with a five-run fifth that was highlighted by Faut's two-run homer, but they stranded 15 runners, much to the dismay of Karl Winsch. The manager's nemesis, Jeep Stoll, Kalamazoo's spunky center fielder who refused to play for Winsch in 1953, drove in five runs for the Lassies. Wagoner, the starter, tired and lost her control in the ninth, yielding four runs for a 6–6 tie, and in the 11th, Stoll squeezed home the winner off Rumsey with the bases loaded.[41]

Returning home and delivering a fine performance against Grand Rapids, Faut, before 1,100 fans at Playland during "Shrine Crippled Children and Goshen Night" on Thursday, June 25, won her fifth game, 5–2, with a seven-hitter. Jean also lifted her team with a two-run homer in the first. Shirley Salisbury, a Goshen native, played two innings in left field and gave way to Doris Cook, who had just arrived from Muskegon in a swap for Rose Monty. In the fifth, Dolly Pearson doubled home Wagoner for a 3–2 lead. The local favorites won by scoring twice in the sixth on bases-loaded walks, one by erstwhile South Bender Dottie Mueller and one by Mary Lou Studnicka.[42]

No game was slated on Friday, but the Blue Sox, facing sagging attendance, announced that fans would be admitted free for Saturday night's game against the second-place-Chicks. Also, Winsch reported that Wimp Baumgartner, who broke a finger in a workout Tuesday in Kalamazoo, would be out of the lineup, and Lois Youngen, the former Daisy, would replace her. Lois, a brown-haired, green-eyed Ohio girl who learned to play ball from her father, began her league career by spending a month with Kenosha after graduating from high school in 1951. In 1952, she was a reserve for Fort Wayne.[43]

On Saturday, boosted by a subsidy from the Northern Indiana Truckers Association, a promotion team officials hoped might bring a corporate sponsorship (the effort failed), South Bend again hosted Grand Rapids. Opening Playland's gates with no charge, the Blue

Sox attracted 3,500 fans, the largest crowd of 1953. After a rain delay, the boisterous crowd, roaring during a winning four-run rally in the ninth, enjoyed the 5–4 triumph. Rumsey, the lanky slender curveballer from Greensburg, Indiana, pitched well for eight frames, but Faut, working in relief, gave up two runs in the ninth for a 4–1 deficit. In the bottom of the inning, Ogden singled, Wagoner popped out, Pearson singled, and Dunn rapped her third hit, scoring Ogden. Faut was passed to load the bases. Jo Lenard, who reported to South Bend just before the game, bounced an infield hit to the shortstop, scoring Pearson. Amy Applegren, who, like Lenard, joined the team after leaving the Chicago League, tried to squeeze home Dunn, but first sacker Inez Voyce sensed the play and hustled in to tag the runner. Baumgartner, pinch-hitting for Youngen, tapped a roller to first, but Renae Youngberg pulled her foot, and Faut scored for a 4–4 tie. Doris Cook chopped one off the pitcher's glove, driving home Lenard with the winning run. Faut got the win, and South Bend, looking improved with the addition of Lenard and Applegren, climbed into fifth place.[44]

Sox in the Summer

The Blue Sox survived a roller-coaster June, and, boosted by the experience of Amy Applegren and Jo Lenard, found a winning groove through the July All-Star break. During the later part of the summer, however, the local favorites could not overcome the lack of first-rate pitching and steady fielding to win consistently. Recalled Sue Kidd, "Team fielding could be terrible, as well as timely hitting, but we did have some injuries."[45] The Sox endured losing steaks, including five, seven, and six-game skids in August that ruined a once-promising season. In the end, Faut's perfect game at Kalamazoo on September 3 was South Bend's most glorious hour.

Faut was the heart of the Blue Sox. An exceptional athlete in any era, she played 98 of a possible 110 games, batting 316 times and hitting .275, a mark that ranked 17th in the league. She also belted 11 doubles, one triple, and four home runs, contributing 38 RBI. Remarkably, besides playing third base, where she was a reliable fielder for 60 contests, Jean started 26 games on the mound and relieved three times. Overall, she fashioned a 17–11 record with a team that tied Muskegon for fourth in fielding with a .942 mark. Faut's earned run average was a dazzling 1.51, making her the best pitcher in a league that included three other hurlers with ERAs below 2.00: Grand Rapids' Beans Risinger, at 15–10 and 1.75, Kalamazoo's Gloria Cordes, 13–11 and 1.98, and the Lassies' Kay Blumetta, 10–9 and 1.98.

Compared to the top major league pitchers for 1953, Faut's performance was the equivalent of Warren Spahn of the Milwaukee Braves or Ed Lopat of the New York Yankees, the ERA leaders in the National and American leagues, respectively, playing at a regular position and, every fourth day, pitching a complete game — a feat that Faut achieved in 24 of 26 starts. She hurled quality pitches, including a hard fastball, and she usually won big games when the pressure was greatest. "I feel like one of my greatest assets," Jean recalled, "was my good control. I could put the ball exactly where I wanted it, and I always varied the rotation of my pitches."[46]

Faut also helped her teammates improve their skills. "I learned by catching and working with Jean," Wimp Baumgartner recollected. "She did more to help me and the other pitchers than the manager. She always told you how to do it better in a nice way, but she got her point across. Jean was a terrific person."[47]

Commenting on the manager, Lois Youngen, also a catcher, recalled, "Karl was stiff, seldom smiled, and he did very little teaching." Lois wanted to learn and improve: "I'm sure he was nice, but in my mind he wasn't very approachable. I could have used some encouragement."[48]

In any event, Winsch found a settled lineup by the All-Star break. For example, on Thursday, July 9, Faut, pitching and winning her eighth game and South Bend's fourth straight during a season-longest eight-game win streak, permitted four hits and beat Kalamazoo in the finale of a four-game set, 5–1. Jean also singled once in four trips, and scored on Dunn's game-clinching two-run single in the eighth. In that tilt, the manager used nine players, as follows:

- Froning, RF, who hit a long double in the seventh to score Wenzell from first base
- Pearson, 2B, who was hitless in three at-bats but walked and scored in the two-run sixth
- Wagoner, CF, singled in three trips and sacrificed Pearson to second base in the sixth
- Lenard, LF, singled home Pearson in the sixth, and prevented a double with a fine running catch in the second
- Faut, P, yielded a run on two hits in the fourth frame, but allowed just one more single
- Applegren, 1B, singled home Lenard, who hit an RBI single and stole second in the sixth
- Dunn, SS, contributed two hits in four trips, notably her two-run single in the eighth
- Baumgartner, C, caught with a taped finger but singled once in three tries
- Wenzell, 3B, hitless in three at-bats, but reached base on an error in the seventh and later scored[49]

Besides Faut, South Bend's only reliable pitchers were Sue Kidd and Jan Rumsey. Kidd, the tall "iron-armed" Arkansas native, worked a holiday twin bill before 5,000 fans at Playland on Saturday, July 4, the day after the two teams split a twin bill at Grand Rapids. Creating the greatest highlight of her career, Kidd pitched and won *two complete games*—the only time the feat was accomplished after the league began overhand pitching in 1948. In the seven-inning opener, the Blue Sox won, 2–1, on bases-loaded squeeze bunts in the sixth by Applegren and Dunn, after a walk to Wagoner, Lenard's single, and a pass to Faut. In the seventh, Kidd gave up the game's final run on two singles and two groundouts. Following 20 minutes of rest, the usual doubleheader break, Kidd, again backed by errorless defense, twirled a four-hitter to win, 6–1. The Blue Sox scored twice in the first on singles by Froning and Pearson, Lenard's groundout, and Faut's single. The visitors took a 4–0 lead in the fifth on Froning's run-scoring double and Pearson's RBI single. Kidd finally yielded a solo run on a grounder in the ninth, but the two victories kept South Bend in fourth place with a record of 18–25.[50]

The events of the following Wednesday, July 8, designated as "Sue Kidd Night," began with a presentation to the shy right-hander who, as a publicity gag, tried to ride a mule onto the diamond. When the balky beast, stubborn as a Missouri mule, refused to cross the foul line, the tall brunette hurler, grinning, dismounted, walked to the mound, and polished off Kalamazoo, 6–3, allowing seven hits. She also rapped two of her team's 11 hits to defeat Dottie Naum, the former South Bend catcher-turned-pitcher. The home team opened with three runs in the first on Froning's single, Pearson's infield out, Wagoner's walk, Lenard's fielder's choice grounder, and Applegren's two-run double. Kidd belted an RBI double in the two-run seventh, the Blue Sox added one run in the eighth, and Choctaw's favorite daughter gave up a two-run homer to Jeep Stoll in the ninth. Typical of South Bend's promotions to boost attendance (no paid figure was given), the special night brought Kidd 30 gifts, ranging from a cash prize of almost $100 to a "Mule-Rider's License," presented by Mishawaka's chief of police.[51]

When the season was over, Kidd, who lost several close games due to errors, owned a 13–15 record and a 2.37 ERA, ranking her 12th in the league. Showing her hard fastball on occasion, she displayed good control, a wide-breaking curve, and a nasty drop ball. A strong, durable athlete, the 5'8" Kidd started 29 games and completed 25, pitching twice in relief. At bat in 66 games, she averaged .187 with four doubles and 17 RBI. In addition, like some of South Bend's other all-around performers, she filled in where needed, often in the outfield, but on occasion in the infield. Her can-do attitude, talent, and determination made Sue a valuable team player.

Rumsey, a 5'8" right-hander who wore black plastic-rimmed glasses, mixed in a few fastballs with her breaking pitches, but she was mainly a curveballer who tried to work the plate's corners. Jan, a third-year pitcher who did not play any other position, dropped a tough 3–2 decision to Muskegon at Playland on Tuesday, June 30. In the seventh, Nancy Mudge and Marge Pieper drew walks, Jo Ogden muffed Sally Meier's two-out grounder, and Betty McKenna hit a bases-loaded single giving the Belles a 3–1 lead. The home team scored once in the seventh, but in the eighth, after Lenard singled and advanced to third, The Belles' Phyllis Baker stranded her and protected the lead.[52] Rumsey, facing last-place Muskegon two weeks later, endured another control blip when she took over in the bottom of the ninth for Wagoner — who walked the first two batters — with South Bend leading, 3–1. Jan induced one batter to pop out but walked the next one, loading the bases. The South Bender uncorked a wild pitch, allowing two runs to score, and when Baumgartner retrieved the ball and threw to Rumsey at home plate, she dropped it, allowing the game-winner to score. For the fourth-place Blue Sox (26–27), the defeat ended an eight-game string, the team's longest winning streak of the season.[53]

Pleasant, friendly, and down-to-earth, Rumsey enjoyed her most memorable evening at Rockford's Beyer Stadium on Monday, July 20, when she won both ends of an unusual twin bill. The first game completed a disputed game that the Peaches won at home, 2–1, on June 10. In the earlier game, Rumsey lost, but Karl Winsch filed a protest, claiming umpire Ed Pratt's ruling of interference was wrong, and saying that Kidd was allowed to run out of the baseline going to first base. Dunn then doubled, and Kidd would have scored for a 2–1 lead. On June 16, Commissioner Earl McCammon upheld Winsch's protest, ruling the game must be played over from the eighth inning. On July 20, the Blue Sox started the replay with Kidd at first base, a 1–1 score, and no outs in the eighth. After a sacrifice, Dunn singled, Baumgartner drove in Kidd with a single, and the Blue Sox won by scoring twice in the ninth off Mickey Jinright. Rumsey, working two shutout innings, earned the 4–1 triumph. In the regulation game, she scattered eight hits and blanked Rockford, 8–0. South Bend scored three times in the first frame, capped by RBI singles from Applegren and Faut, and in the ninth, the visitors reached Jinright and reliever Helen Nordquist for five runs to seal the win. Afterward, South Bend was still fourth with a 28–31 ledger, ten and a half games behind pace-setting Fort Wayne (38–20).[54]

Perhaps Rumsey's season and the team's frustration over losing close games when they could not hold leads were best illustrated in the loss of the opener of a twin bill at Kalamazoo on Wednesday, August 5. Winsch, who was enthused when the strong-armed Kidd won two complete games against Grand Rapids on the Fourth of July, planned to use the same tactic. Rumsey delivered a heady performance, scattering nine hits over 13 innings in the opener, but Dottie Naum matched the feat and Kalamazoo finally won, 2–1. Both teams scored in the 11th of the scheduled seven-inning tilt, the Blue Sox on Applegren's run-scoring single and the Lassies on Stoll's RBI double. Stoll, enjoying another payback, singled home the game-winner in the 13th. Out of regular pitchers, Winsch tried Dolly Pearson, the second baseman, but she gave up five runs in the first inning and left trailing, 5–4. Doris Cook finished the curfew-shortened second contest, yielding one run, but Kazoo and Kay Blumetta won, 6–4. South Bend maintained fourth place with a 33–39 record, 14 games behind Fort Wayne.[55]

Next to Faut, the ace, and the durable Kidd, Rumsey offered the Blue Sox their best hope for a victory. Altogether, the likeable Hoosier fashioned a 11–19 record, and her 2.42 ERA ranked 13th in the league—one notch below Kidd's 2.37. Rumsey started 29 games, completed 18, and appeared six times in relief. She also batted .145 in 36 games, driving home five runners. Wagoner, averaging .239, played 107 games. A left-handed hitter in her sixth season, she led the team with 63 bases on balls, finished second in runs scored with 42 (Dunn scored 46), hit nine doubles, slugged two triples, and produced 32 RBI, trailing only Faut's 38 and Dunn's 36 in that department. Wagoner also posted a 4–13 record with a 3.02 ERA, making her the team's fourth pitcher. While she could break off a good curve, the Missouri southpaw often displayed inconsistent control, especially when she was tired. She did have a good pickoff move to first base, and that helped her in jams. In the end, Wagoner started all 19 games she pitched, and the manager doubtless wished he had more all-around athletes like her.

Peaking in July

Kidd's impressive doubleheader victories on July 4 launched the Blue Sox on a good run until the league's All-Star game at Fort Wayne on Tuesday, July 14. The local favorites made a one-game jaunt to Grand Rapids, where southpaw Donna Cook, a sixth-year hurler who had posted a 1–7 mark with the Battle Creek Belles in 1952, made her first Sox start and lost, 5–1, allowing nine walks and seven hits. Mary Lou Graham, the team's bat girl in 1952, relieved, issuing one pass but hurling a scoreless eighth.[56] Returning to Playland, South Bend swept a four-game set from Kalamazoo. Journeying to Muskegon for five games, the Blue Sox won four out of five.

South Bend's eight-game win streak was crowned by two shutout victories in a doubleheader at Muskegon's Marsh Field on Sunday night, July 12. Faut, chosen that day as the league's Most Valuable Player, won her tenth game by firing a three-hit 7–0 whitewash of the Belles. Pinky LeDuc, a third-year right-hander from Massachusetts, surrendered five runs in the first two innings, and Phyllis Baker finished the contest, but Faut was unbeatable. In the nightcap, Kidd matched pitches with Hank Warren for seven innings, before Applegren's double, an infield out, and Baumgartner's single gave the Blue Sox 1–0 lead. The visitors clinched their eighth straight triumph, 4–0, scoring three times in the eighth, thanks to four errors, a walk, singles by Froning and Wagoner, two stolen bases, and a passed ball. The two wins lifted 26–26 South Bend to .500, the high-water mark of the season, half a game behind third-place Kalamazoo (27–36).[57] Yet on the following night, Rumsey's ninth-inning wild pitch in relief of Wagoner followed by Baumgartner's throwing error helped the Belles rally for three runs and a 4–3 win.[58]

The league's All-Star game, hosted by first-place Fort Wayne at Memorial Field on July 14, showcased two teams with first-rate players, but the Daisies won, 4–3, when Jean Geissinger hit a towering home run over the left field wall in the 11th frame. A total of 3,462 spectators enjoyed the exciting contest, and Fort Wayne's Bill Allington, the former Rockford pilot, emptied his bench, using six pitchers. Thirty-five players saw action, including 18 All-Stars. South Bend was represented by Faut, who pitched the first three innings and gave up one hit, Dolly Pearson, who played second and third base but went hitless, and Betty Wagoner, who drew a walk when pinch-hitting in the seventh. Karl Winsch, South Bend's pilot when the Blue Sox won the 1952 Shaughnessy Playoff title, managed the All-Stars.[59]

While a meeting of the first-place team as of July 1 against the best players from the other teams attracted a large audience, South Bend, facing a "financial crisis," wasn't averaging the 1,000 fans per night needed to break even.[60]

After a day off, the South Benders made the 90-mile bus journey to Fort Wayne, but the Daisies won all four games, defeating each member of the team's rotation once—Rumsey, Kidd, Faut, and Wagoner. The only time the Blue Sox kept the losing margin less than five runs occurred on Saturday, July 18, when Kidd, who spaced two hits in the first eight innings, saw left-handed hitting slugger Betty Foss slam her first pitch of the ninth inning over the right field fence to give Fort Wayne a 1–0 victory.[61] After losing both ends of a Sunday doubleheader, the Blue Sox had a 1–11 mark against the first-place Daisies. Traveling to Rockford and the Lafayette Hotel, South Bend took the first two games when Rumsey won the Peaches' game that Winsch protested on June 10 and, in the regulation game, pitched an 8–0 shutout. After a rainout on Tuesday, July 21, the Blue Sox lost on Wednesday and Thursday. In the finale, the visitors concluded the 6–7 road trip by losing, 4–3. The Peaches built a 4–2 lead by the end of the fifth, and Rose Gacioch preserved the lead. Both teams made five errors, and Faut, going 3-for-4 and playing third base, batted in two runs, but only Pearson, Applegren, and Dunn added singles, while the Peaches collected ten hits off Wagoner. Afterward, Rockford moved into fourth place with a 28–32 ledger, and South Bend, now with a 28–33 mark, fell to fifth.[62]

Back home, the Blue Sox, relying on three dependable hurlers, kept fighting to reach a winning record. Following an off day on Saturday, July 25, the local heroines, enjoying the friendly cheers of nearly 2,000 folks on Saturday, made their five hits count in a 4–2 triumph behind "stout-armed Jeanie Faut." Using her fastball to fan eight Daisies, Faut allowed no hits until pinch batter Katie Horstman singled to center in the eighth. In the ninth, after two scratch hits and an error, All-Star Jean Geissinger bounced a two-run double over the fence in left center, before Faut retired the side. The Blue Sox took a 1–0 lead in the first and scored two more in the fourth, when Faut reached base on rookie shortstop Jean Havlish's error, Dunn singled her to third, Baumgartner squeezed home the run, Doris Cook singled, sending Dunn to third, and Froning sacrificed for a 3–0 lead. The Sox scored an insurance run in the fifth, and Faut preserved the lead. Also, the big crowd enjoyed another nightly promotion, this time the display of equipment and prizes offered by the Northern Indiana Truckers Association.[63]

South Bend, battling for the hearts of fans, lowered the cost of 800 seats on each end of the grandstand from 74 cents to half a dollar and also allowed a carload of fans to sit in the parking areas around the outfield fence for $1 per auto. After lowering the prices, the

Blue Sox divided four contests with the Daisies. Battling visiting Rockford for fourth place and a playoff spot, South Bend came through with two wins in three games (the fourth was rained out), after sloppy fielding turned Faut's three-hit performance into a frustrating 4–3 loss on Wednesday, July 29.

In the opener against Rockford, the visiting Peaches scored twice off Faut in the first frame on three errors, but the Blue Sox responded with three runs in the second on a run-scoring grounder by Donna Norris, a rookie flychaser from Culver City, California, who was acquired from Fort Wayne, and Doris Cook's two-run single. Mickey Jinright, whose pitching speed was compared to a "falling feather," benefitted from shortstop Joan Berger's flawless handling of 14 chances. The Peaches won with two runs in the third on Pearson's wild throw, a sacrifice, and Froning's misjudgment of Callow's high fly ball to center that fell for a double. Alice Deschaine drove home the fourth run with her team's only solid hit of the night, a line single to left.[64]

South Bend won the next two Rockford tilts, starting on Thursday with Kidd's five-hit 6–1 victory, as Dunn, Wagoner, and Froning accounted for the home team's six hits, rapping two each.[65] On Friday at Studebaker Park in Elkhart, Indiana, 2,000 fans saw Rumsey permit nine hits, but her clutch pitching in two jams led to another 6–1 win over "visiting" Rockford. The Blue Sox took a 3–0 lead in the third on Applegren's single, followed by an error, a walk, a sacrifice, a squeeze, and three walks. Rumsey blanked the Peaches until they scored on three hits in the ninth. The finale on August 1 was postponed by rain, but South Bend, poised for a playoff run, held the final playoff spot with a 32–36 mark, half a game ahead of 31–36 Rockford.[66]

Hopes for the Playoffs

The blue-uniformed "girls of summer" longed to make the playoffs. When South Bend reached fourth place on July 31, Fort Wayne, the winner of the regular season title in 1952, was running away with the pennant, and for good reason. The Daisies boasted three of the loop's top five hitters in the Weaver sisters: Joanne, or Jo, the youngest of the trio, led in hitting with a then-record .346. She belted 18 doubles, six triples, five home runs, and produced a loop-high 76 RBI. Betty Foss, the married elder sister, was third at .321, clouting 20 doubles, eight triples, and five homers, and contributing 65 RBI. Jean Weaver finished fifth, hitting .313 in 30 games, and posted a 7–1 mound record. In addition, Fort Wayne's Jean Geissinger batted .295, hitting 21 doubles, 10 triples, and eight homers, and the Daisies' Katie Horstman averaged .295, contributing 12 doubles, seven triples, and four circuit clouts.

The Daisies easily won the team batting title at .264, followed by Rockford at .237, Grand Rapids at .235, and Kalamazoo at .229. All four teams made the playoffs. South Bend ranked fifth at .219, followed by hapless Muskegon. The Belles finished last in the standings at 39–70 and last in hitting at .204. Further, the hard-hitting Daisies slugged 39 home runs, the Lassies and the Chicks clubbed 15 each, and the Blue Sox hit just four home runs — all by Jean Faut. In the important category of runs scored, Muskegon was last with 359 runs, ranking below South Bend's 391, but Fort Wayne scored 598 times, more than a hundred runs above Grand Rapids' 485. By any statistical measure, the 32–36 Blue Sox were fortunate to be fourth at the end of July. However, the team took a nose dive in August and finished fifth at 45–65, marking a huge drop from their Shaughnessy Championship teams of 1951 and 1952.

As manager, Winsch had little difficulty running his ball club in 1953. His roster was dotted by rookies, youthful players, and mid-season acquisitions, but except for Dolly Pearson, few of them made important contributions. The league was declining, and most of the players knew it. "The new players just weren't as good," recalled Wimp Baumgartner,[67] but they were happy to make the best women's pro circuit in the nation. Most would have played any position without questions about salary, and since teams offered no raises after 1950, it was just as well. Calling Winsch easy-going, Mary (Froning) O'Meara later commented, "I enjoyed Karl as a manager."[68]

Therefore, while the team lacked internal dissension, South Bend could not replace the talent and experience of departed stars like Lib Mahon, Shorty Pryer, Shirley Stovroff, and Jeep Stoll, who hit .308 for Kalamazoo in 1953. Overall, the Blue Sox were a weak team. "We had fun," Kidd observed. "We were more relaxed, but we did not have nearly the talent as before."[69]

All ballplayers have a daily routine. For example, Kidd, like every player, followed her own regimen. Reflecting on her third full season with the Blue Sox, she recalled, "I think most of the time by 1953, Karl would let you know the day before that you would be pitching. With less pitchers by then, you pretty well knew without being told. I liked to trim my finger nails early the day I was to pitch. I didn't like to eat a large meal, maybe a grilled cheese sandwich, or a cheeseburger with some potato chips, or French fries, and a Coke. I just tried to take things easy in the afternoon, maybe go to a good movie. I did more warming up to Wimp over the years, but it was Lois that year. I started slow, added speed as I got loose, and then threw the curves and drops. When it was hot, it didn't take me long to get loose."

Sue added, "By 1953, I didn't have to run in the outfield as much after I had pitched, as I would often be taking some infield at first base, or fly balls in the outfield, and I loved to chase fly balls, so I got the running in doing something I liked. I was also a good fungo hitter, and I often hit fly balls to outfielders when I wasn't playing somewhere, or pitching."[70]

Furthermore, the Blue Sox had Faut. "The things I remember about Jean," Jan Rumsey said later, "are that she was a great all-around athlete, a terrific third baseman, and, of course, an outstanding pitcher. We all looked to Jean for leadership and felt confident whenever she was pitching."[71]

The Bottom Drops Out

South Bend opened August by journeying to Kalamazoo for a four-game stand, but the Lassies won three of those contests, starting with a 2–0 victory on Sunday, August 2, when Wagoner yielded nine hits and four walks, and Kalamazoo's Jeep Stoll went 3-for-3 and made a fine shoestring catch in the ninth to rob Gertie Dunn of a base hit.[72] Bouncing back on Monday, the visitors won, 2–1, as Faut, improving her ledger to 11–7, hurled a two-hitter, giving up a solo run in the fifth on two singles and Wenzell's wild throw from third base. Jean, who bore down and retired the final 13 batters in a row, added a single to a one-run rally in the sixth, and Wenzell doubled home the eventual game-winner in the seventh.[73] Rain halted Tuesday's game after Kidd matched the seven hits allowed by Aggie Allen and Elaine Roth in a nine-inning 2–2 tie. Afterward, Winsch planned to start Rumsey in both ends of Wednesday's twin bill.[74] Instead, the tall right-hander lost, 2–1, in a 13-inning first game, and Winsch tried Pearson in the late tilt, but she failed as a pitcher and the Sox lost, 6–4.[75]

After taking the fifty mile-trip north to Grand Rapids, lodging at the Hotel Rowe, and preparing to play, the South Benders lost the first three games. On Thursday, August 6, a tired Wagoner was bombed in the series opener, 10–2.[76] Faut, likely tired herself, lost the opener of Friday's twin bill, 2–1, after giving up two runs on three hits in the bottom of the sixth. In the nightcap, Kidd, pitching on two days' rest, surrendered eight runs in five innings, before Pearson took over and finished what became the second rout in three days, 10–3.[77] On Saturday, however, Rumsey, also pitching on two days' rest, snapped the team's five-game loss streak by outlasting Mary Lou Studnicka, 2–0, in ten innings. Both teams totaled four hits, but the Blue Sox tallied the winning runs on Dunn's single, Lenard's sacrifice, Froning's walk, a wild throw from center by Jean Smith on Baumgartner's single, Rumsey's muffed grounder, and Pearson's RBI single. Afterward, South Bend (34–42), half a game behind Rockford, acquired two players from the Chicks: third baseman Renae Youngberg (on loan) and Barbara Gates, a rookie pitcher.[78]

In a development soon well-known to the players, the league suffered a life-threatening loss when Muskegon became an "orphan" traveling team on Thursday, August 6, after the Belles beat the visiting Lassies, 6–2. The franchise reverted to the circuit because the team could no longer pay the bills or the players' salaries. The Belles performed well enough early in the season. Joe Cooper's squad of rookies and veterans entertained 800 fans on opening night at Marsh Field, but they attracted as many as 1,000 fans only twice that summer.[79] In fact, Muskegon was slow on making all payments, including the loop's franchise fee (the club finally paid the $2,700 still owed on June 16) as well as the annual amounts — collected on a biweekly basis — of $1,050 for the umpire fund and another $350 for the "distress fund."[80] In the end, the league spent $8,600 to carry the Belles through the remainder of their schedule at away locations, because the alternative was a five-team league for the rest of 1953.[81]

Returning to Playland Park on Sunday, August 9, South Bend took three out of four games from "homeless" Muskegon. The Belles overcame turmoil off the diamond by pounding the Blue Sox, 15–0. The visitors ripped recruit Barbara Gates for four hits and two walks in the first frame, and they socked Donna Cook's slants for a dozen hits before the evening ended. So busy were the hitters — South Bend totaled six hits, one by Youngberg — that no player on either team struck out.[82] On Monday, however, Kidd (11–9) hung on to defeat the Belles, 3–2, despite five errors, two by Youngberg. Pearson's two-run single highlighted the home team's three-run second inning. Regardless, Joe Doyle pointed out that South Bend was the only team in the league with no increase in attendance.[83] On Tuesday, Faut (12–8) spaced five hits and recorded a 1–0 victory, as the Belles' Marilyn Jones, who won 14 games in 1953, permitted two hits but issued 14 walks, giving up the fatal 14th pass in the ninth to Dunn with the sacks loaded.[84]

Suddenly the bottom dropped out for South Bend. Hosting Grand Rapids, the Blue Sox dropped all four games, with Rumsey, Kidd, Wagoner, and Faut taking the losses. Faut's loss came on Saturday, August 15, when she was atypically wild, walking ten and allowing seven hits. Baumgartner hurt the cause with two passed balls, the second letting the eventual winning run score in the visitors' two-run fifth. The Chicks' Gabby Ziegler, Faut's "ancient rival," pitched more effectively in the clutch to win, 3–1.[85] Furthermore, Kalamazoo arrived and defeated the Blue Sox three straight times, two by big scores. Rumsey started Sunday's tilt, but left trailing, 4–3, and the Lassies reached Doris Cook for one run and Gates for eight tallies in the eighth inning for a 12–3 romp.[86]

The losses continued. On Monday, after a two-hour batting practice session, the Blue Sox came through with eight hits, but Kidd received sloppy fielding support and lost, 6–3. The turning point came when Froning misjudged Betty Francis' fly to left for a two-run double in a three-run fourth inning, the third run scoring on Applegren's first of three errors. Froning and Applegren tried to make up for the misplays with two hits apiece, to no avail.[87] In a poor night for pitchers on Tuesday, Doris Cook walked four in the first inning, and Donna Cook relieved, but passed ten more Lassies. The sisters gave up seven hits total, but Barbara Gates was worse, allowing seven hits, four walks, and nine runs in her closing four-inning stint. Six Sox rapped hits, the last being Kidd's pinch double during a three-run rally in the ninth that cut the final deficit to 16–8.[88]

Faut Crowns Her Career

Her team struggling, Faut, as she had so many times before, put aside her problems with a domineering husband and her duties as a mother—the family's friend and neighbor, Mrs. Singleton, took care of five-year-old Larry during home games and road trips—and turned into a heroine at the ballpark. In the final two and a half weeks of what became her last season, Jean, with her exceptional talent, solid professionalism, and winning smile, produced several fine performances, inspiring teammates and opponents alike, many of whom would later tell stories about Faut. "She was an awesome pitcher and a really complete ballplayer," recollected Dottie Schroeder, the only player who played all 12 of the league's seasons. "A top pitcher with few equals; great hitter who was so good with the bat, she played infield or outfield when not pitching." Reflecting further, Schroeder added, "I can't remember ever getting a hit off her pitching. She could literally 'freeze' you in your tracks at the plate."[89]

Facing the Belles, the Blue Sox broke their seven-game losing skid and won three out of four, featuring winning performances by the "Big Three" of Faut, Kidd, and Rumsey. In the late tilt of two games on Wednesday, August 19, after Rumsey opened with a 4–0 victory, Faut, boosting her mark to 13–9, cruised in a 17–1 laugher. Jean singled as her teammates ripped Pinky LeDuc and Mirta Marrero for a combined 15 hits.[90] On Thursday, however, only 500 fans saw Kidd hurl a four-hitter to win, 2–1, at South Bend's Lippincott Park.[91] On Friday, Wagoner gave her best effort, but the Belles salvaged a 5–4 victory with Kate Vonderau's RBI single in the eighth.[92]

Fort Wayne was tougher. Meeting the Daisies at St. Joseph, Michigan, in a Saturday contest to "test outlying sites for home Blue Sox games," Faut (14–9) displayed her big-game poise before 1,500 fans by scattering five hits and blanking the loop's hottest-hitting team, 3–0. The South Benders took a 1–0 lead in the first on Dunn's run-scoring single, added solo runs in the second and the fourth, and watched Faut stifle Fort Wayne's bats.[93] However, back at Playland on Sunday and Monday, the Sox fell twice to the Daisies, with Rumsey and Kidd both losing.

Once again, Faut followed one or more South Bend losses with a win. At Rockford on Tuesday, August 25, she topped the Peaches, 3–2, in 12 innings. The Blue Sox were still fighting for the playoffs, and Faut (15–9), no stranger to extra-inning games, allowed six hits and contributed a single in the 12th, after which Applegren squeezed home Wagoner with the game-winner. In the bottom of the frame, Faut preserved the triumph, after Dottie Kamenshek beat out a bunt, by starting a twin killing on Rose Gacioch's bouncer. The win gave South Bend an elusive grip on fourth place, one game ahead of Rockford,[94] but the Peaches won the last three games of the series. Packing, riding the bus, and staying at the Van Orman Hotel in Fort Wayne, the Blue Sox lost three straight to the Daisies. Faut (15–10), suffering an off night in the opening game, gave up 13 hits as her team lost, 10–3.[95] By the time the travel-weary Sox arrived home on Monday, August 31, they were all but eliminated from the postseason.

Gracing Playland's diamond once again, the Blue Sox needed to sweep four games with Rockford to keep their fading playoff hopes alive, and Faut won on the first night. Donna Cook hurled two scoreless innings, but in the third, she gave up three runs and had runners on second and third base with one out when Faut came off the bench, warmed up, and blew fastballs by Jackie Kelley and Mary Carey to end the threat. Jean pitched shutout ball thereafter, improving to 16–10. Against pint-sized Mickey Jinright, South Bend pounded 19 hits, including three by Faut, who sealed the outcome by slugging her fourth home run — with Dunn aboard — over the left field fence in a three-run seventh. Applegren and Youngberg contributed three hits each, and Dunn and Wagoner both added two hits to the 9–3 victory.[96] Despite Faut's heroics, the Blue Sox lost the last three games, a doubleheader on Tuesday and the finale on Wednesday, when Kidd surrendered three runs in the top of the ninth and her teammates could not rally to overcome the 4–3 deficit. The loss eliminated the Sox, seven games behind the Peaches, from the playoffs.[97]

Pride never mattered more than at Playland on Thursday, September 4, when, in the words of Joe Doyle, "Jean Faut, star South Bend Blue Sox pitcher who may retire when the season ends on Labor Day, capped a dismal season for her team last night by pitching a perfect no-hit no-run game against the Kalamazoo Lassies."

Second Perfect Game — The scorecard for Jean Faut's second perfect game, a 2–0 victory over the Kalamazoo Lassies on September 3, 1953 (courtesy of the Louise Pettus Archives and Special Collections, Winthrop University).

Hurling her second perfect game — and only the second perfect contest in the league's seven years of overhand hurling — Faut was brilliant, winning, 4–0. Focused on the task, she overpowered the Lassies with her hard fastball and darting curve, fanning eight and allowing just three balls to be hit out of the infield. Kalamazoo's Ruth Williams pitched well until the fifth, but she coughed up four runs when Applegren beat out a bunt, Froning doubled down the left field line, Pearson walked to fill the bases, and Lois Youngen, catching her fourth full game as Faut's battery mate, rolled an infield hit for one run. Froning scored on a wild throw, Pearson came home on an error at first base, and Faut drew a bases-loaded walk to score Youngen.[98]

Still, the Blue Sox only split the final two games of the set, suffering a 19–5 trouncing on Friday behind the hurling of Donna Cook and Barbara Gates,[99] and winning on Saturday, 1–0, as Rumsey threw a two-hit shutout.[100]

Disappointing Conclusion

In the season's last series against the Chicks, starting with the first game at Playland on Sunday, September 6, South Bend honored the league's Most Valuable Player of 1953 with "Jean Faut Night," the second such ceremony of her eight-year career. Jean, who received $400 in merchandise before the game, retired the first nine hitters before Youngberg, back with Grand Rapids, doubled in the third inning and later scored. Beans Risinger spun a four-hitter, and the visitors won, 3–0, with two runs in the sixth on four straight hits after two were out. It was a disappointing conclusion for Faut (17–11), but she walked away with pride in her baseball accomplishments.[101] Indeed, as Jean later said at Players Association Reunions, "I gave South Bend and the league my greatest effort every time I stepped on the field."[102] In the final twin bill at Michigan's Furniture City against the Chicks, Rumsey (11–19) finished her summer with a 7–2 loss, and Kidd (13–15) concluded the season by hurling an 8–3 victory in the nightcap.[103]

In retrospect, South Bend suffered in 1953 from the aftermath of the player walkout. Karl Winsch kept searching, but the team never found enough quality players to gel at a highly competitive level. The *Tribune's* Joe Doyle said that Jean Faut might retire, and that Amy Applegren and Jo Lenard were definitely gone. Those three, along with hurlers Sue Kidd and Janet Rumsey, shortstop Gertie Dunn, catchers Wimp Baumgartner and Lois Youngen, and Betty Wagoner and Mary Froning in the outfield, formed the team's core. Few others made consistently good contributions, and no team with eight or nine good players could compete on a winning basis over a 110-game season against strong teams like Fort Wayne, Grand Rapids, and Kalamazoo.

Looking to the future, South Bend faced difficult challenges off and on the field. "After Faut, Kidd and Rumsey pitched in order," Doyle stated, "Winsch had nothing else in the rotation, catching was horribly weak, and the infield only occasionally solid." The team's hitting was below average, 45 points behind pace-setting Fort Wayne. South Bend needed to improve greatly to reach the top of the American Girls Baseball League, provided the loop could handle major financial problems and launch another season. "From here it looks much as if the Blue Sox will have to be much busier in the off season," the sports editor told readers, "if the girls' league team is to survive. And there are fans who tell you that it won't."[104]

One way or the other, the Blue Sox would have to survive without Jean Faut. The two-time Player of the Year—and likely the most feared pitcher in the league—decided to leave baseball after the 1953 season. Jean, 28 years old and at the top of her game, was no longer willing to play on a team managed by her husband. She felt isolated. "Karl wasn't speaking to me. He shut me out," Faut recalled. "I quit playing because Karl took the fun out of it."[105]

• 12 •

The Blue Sox and the Final Innings: 1954

"Will the league operate again in '55? Most fans think it won't, but they also remember the league board voted to suspend operations in February and then decided a month later to try season number 12" — Joe Doyle, July 30, 1954[1]

Last-Ditch League

After the Muskegon franchise reverted to the league office on August 6, 1953, local and circuit officials struggled through the winter trying to find new financial resources and a sixth city to relocate the failed Belles franchise. Finally, on April 10, 1954, the leaders decided that proceeding with five teams was preferable to letting the circuit die.[2] Preparing for the ball club's 12th season, South Bend would field a women's nine composed largely of new players that few of the city's fans would recognize. By the time the league's final summer began, President Dwight Eisenhower, the Supreme Commander of Allied Forces in Europe during World War II, was serving his first term in the White House, the Korean War had been followed by a troubled armistice abroad and an economic contraction at home, television was dominating the national and local market for family entertainment, and declining attendance suggested that professional baseball was slipping in popularity.[3] Fewer women showed interest in pro baseball, and players and fans wondered if the league was dying. "By this time," observed Lois Browne, "only a handful of All-American veterans remained," including longtime stars such as Rockford's Dottie Key, Grand Rapids' Gabby Ziegler, and Fort Wayne's Dottie Schroeder. "Most of their former teammates were long gone," concluded Browne, "back to factories, farms, and families."[4]

The American Girls Baseball League mirrored the decline of minor league baseball, and the decade from 1952 to 1962 was the minors' worst era. Television was booming because many people enjoyed seeing shows such as *Milton Berle*, *I Love Lucy*, *The Lone Ranger*, and others that they could watch in their homes. Also, America's biggest social trend in the 1950s was the moving of families to the rapidly-growing suburbs, meaning the local professional ballpark was no longer a few blocks away. In addition, many minor league parks — and American Girls League fields were no exception — had been built during the Depression. Most of these facilities needed improvements. However, ball clubs lacked the funds for upgrades, and local governments set aside little money for what used to be considered civic gathering places.[5] Indeed, Playland Park lasted so long because it doubled as an amusement park and tripled as a racetrack.

For perspective, the All-American League was born as a kind of small-city entertainment in the Midwest during wartime. "Once World War II ended, however," explained Debra Shattuck, "social pressures for women to leave nontraditional jobs and return to household duties returned." By 1954, such forces, combined with the circuit's organizational and financial problems, the rise of TV, and the nation's economic downturn, spelled doom for the league.[6]

The biggest sign of decline for the circuit, called by the *South Bend Tribune* a "question mark operation" two months before opening day,[7] was that only five teams found the funds and the players to compete in 1954, and Rockford had to resort to backing by its fans' organization. The Blue Sox and the Peaches, the only two teams left from the league's inaugural four-team season of 1943, were joined by the Fort Wayne Daisies, the Grand Rapids Chicks, and the Kalamazoo Lassies. Muskegon's Belles, a traveling team without a home ballpark for the previous season's final month, finished last with a 38–67 record, and the league's expense of operating the team after August 6 was "too costly." Other teams had suffered losses, and Muskegon's backers gave up on raising funds for a team, so the league teetered on the edge of going out of business. Indeed, on January 24, 1954, the loop's board voted to suspend operations on March 1.[8]

By early 1954, the economic slump affected durable goods industries such as Studebaker,[9] and cities like South Bend and Battle Creek were termed "distress" areas. Commissioner Earl McCammon was still trying to sell the sixth franchise, notably to investors in Chicago, Battle Creek, and St. Joseph, Michigan, so suspension was delayed until March 20.[10] After no backers were found to start a ball club, Fort Wayne's Harold Van Orman, the loop's president, proposed the five-team league as a last-ditch alternative. All five teams approved the concept on April 10.[11]

Following work on scheduling, budget cuts, player allocation, and consideration of whether to use a regulation baseball made by the DeBeer Company, manufacturer of the league's balls since 1949, or one by the Wilson Brothers,[12] the circuit's most unusual season was set to open on Friday, May 28. The oddball schedule listed three games per night, the same as the six-team circuit listed, but the slate avoided a team with no game each day by having one team play *two* opponents in a single doubleheader. Also, South Bend would host 17 twin bills and 17 single games at the cinder track-surrounded ball field at of Playland Park. Doubleheaders featured two seven-inning games, and single contests were set for nine frames.

Looking for New Blue Sox

For the preseason draft, each team retained up to eight players, and former Belles were placed in a "player pool." South Bend acquired the rights to nine players. However, as another sign of the circuit's decline, only three of the nine reported. The best contributor was Betty Francis, a right-handed batting outfielder who wore glasses. The 5' 4" brunette began with one of the circuit's minor league teams in Chicago in 1946. The Windy City athlete was chosen by Muskegon in 1949, but she couldn't make the league, so she was sent to play on tour with the Colleens. Betty played left or right field for Kalamazoo starting in 1950, and she batted .226 in 78 games for the Lassies in 1953. The Blue Sox also signed two young right-handers: third-year pro Phyllis Baker, a Marshall, Michigan, high school senior who posted a 7–12 record and a 3.21 ERA with Muskegon the previous season, and

Charlotte, North Carolina, native Dolly Vanderlip, 17, a third-year hurler, who was 2–2 with a 2.88 ERA in 1953 for Fort Wayne.

However, six others, three of them former Belles, decided not to play another year: Betty Ventura, a first baseman from Garfield, New Jersey, who hit just .074 with Rockford in 1953; eight-year league veteran Katie Vonderau from Fort Wayne, a good catcher who averaged .202 with Muskegon; Sally Meier, who also grew up in Fort Wayne, a steady outfielder and another eight-year performer, who hit .229 for Muskegon; Betty McKenna, a third baseman from Lisbon, Ohio, who played her third year for Muskegon in 1953, averaging a career-best .215; and Ruth Middleton, from Winnipeg, Manitoba, a four-year outfielder and one of the few Canadians who played for the women's circuit in the 1950s. Ruth batted .125 in 36 games for the Belles.[13]

The sixth player, Janet Wiley, known as "Pee Wee," had left the league after surgery on her right knee. The South Bend native made the Blue Sox as a first baseman 1950, after serving as a bat girl in 1947 and 1948. A positive, energetic, and often outspoken athlete, the 5'4" right-handed batter loved to bunt. Pee Wee played for her hometown team until July 1952, when manager Karl Winsch suspended her because, he claimed, she "talked back." In May 1953, Wiley joined Rockford. She batted .206 in 33 games, but reinjured her knee sliding into third base on June 29. She endured a third operation,[14] and her physician told her to quit baseball. Just 20, she returned to South Bend. In 1955 she married Riley High sweetheart Don Sears, who used to ride his tomboy friend to Blue Sox games on his bicycle's handlebars. The couple raised six children.

Janet Sears was proud of her pro career. Echoing the feelings of countless All-Americans who lived their diamond dream, she recalled, "Every time they played the National Anthem, I thought, 'Where else in the world could I play professional baseball?' I felt blessed."[15]

Spring Training

The league was on life support. For example, circuit personnel again held a three-day "rookie school" before spring training, but only 27 candidates tried out, down from 46 in 1953.[16] Spring training, an important part of the adventure players enjoyed during the league's glory years of the late 1940s, all but disappeared in 1954. South Bend and the other teams conducted fielding and hitting practice, worked on bunting, hit-and-run plays, and held strategy meetings. The *South Bend Tribune*, which reported in detail on the local team during previous seasons, gave the Blue Sox camp virtually no coverage — and the paper ran no pictures. Indeed, as the season progressed, readers noticed stories about home games were shorter with fewer details, and the brief articles about away games often ran no more than three paragraphs.

Spring training also attracted less participation. When drills began at Playland Park, Karl Winsch greeted just 11 players on the first day, another indication of the decreased interest in women wanting to play pro ball. Fort Wayne, the regular season champion in 1953, and Kalamazoo were training together in Rockford. The Lassies ranked second in players arriving with ten, but the Daisies reported only seven. More players were expected, and team officials blamed late-arriving trains as well as school work, since several girls were still in high school. In addition, Betty Wagoner, preparing for her seventh season, said she would only play home games — an example set in 1953 when Rockford's Dottie Kamenshek played only at Beyer Stadium. Furthermore, the Blue Sox' star not present was Jean Faut, who retired after the 1953 season. Still, hope springs eternal in baseball. The *Tribune*'s Joe Doyle observed Wagoner's decision to play only home games might appeal to Faut,[17] and teammates like Sue Kidd kept wishing Jean would return.[18]

The Blue Sox welcomed several top-notch new players. The league, resorting again to a "balancing committee" of the type used by Management Corporation, made switches to equalize the teams. South Bend received three players: hard-hitting Wilma Briggs, a first baseman and outfielder with the Daisies for six years who led the loop in home runs with nine in 1953; speedy third sacker Betty Wanless, who batted .248 as a rookie with Grand Rapids during the previous season; and infielder Mary Carey, a tenth-year veteran who divided her 1953 season between three teams — mainly the Lassies — and averaged a combined .174. In return, the Sox lost Dolly Pearson, a good shortstop and second baseman, when the league sent her to Grand Rapids.

Thinking about exhibitions, Winsch favored a pitching staff of Sue Kidd, Jan Rumsey, and newly signed Helen Nordquist, who spent two seasons with Rockford, but was released by the financially troubled Peaches.[19] Phyllis Baker and Dolly Vanderlip, both in high school, would pitch later. For starters, Winsch named Wanless at third base, Gertie Dunn at shortstop, Carey at second, and Wagoner at first. Wilma Briggs, Betty Francis, and Mary Froning covered the outfield, and rookie Peggy Cramer, a 16-year-old from Buchanan, Michigan, caught.[20]

South Bend prepared for the regular season with an exhibition win over Fort Wayne in Lafayette, Indiana, on Tuesday, May 25. Details were sketchy, but Nordquist lasted one inning, Kidd pitched until the fifth, and Rumsey finished the contest and earned the win. The Blue Sox rallied for three runs in the eighth to erase a 4–1 deficit, sealing the outcome with a score in the ninth. Also, South Bend announced last-minute schedule changes, including having the Blue Sox begin the regular season with a home doubleheader against Fort Wayne and Kalamazoo on Friday, not Saturday, and the solo contest with Grand Rapids was switched from Friday to Saturday.[21]

In addition, the team's new business manager, Ted Doty, recently hired from the Detroit Tigers' farm system, announced a variety of promotions that would fill South Bend's schedule. Also, ticket prices were cut: reserved seats now sold for $1, and general admission seats cost 50 or 75 cents, depending on the location. The ball club was going all out to rekindle fan interest.[22]

Launching the Twelfth Season

On Friday night, May 28, the season's festivities at Playland began in typical fashion with the American Legion Post 50 band playing several numbers for a crowd of 1,200. The color guard and drill team of the VFW's Golden Hill Post provided further entertainment, and Mishawaka Mayor Spencer Walton tossed out the first pitch. Opening the season and the twin bill, Sue Kidd displayed mid-season form by hurling a seven-inning three-hitter to defeat Grand Rapids, 7–1. Struggling to solve Kidd's slants, the Chicks used two hits in the fifth to score the game's only earned run. South Bend's Wilma Briggs, the left fielder, doubled in the first, and three Chicks errors combined with two walks by Jayne Bittner gave the home team a 3–0 lead. The Blue Sox racked up four runs in the fourth on singles by Wimp Baumgartner and Kidd, a double by Betty Francis, the center fielder, and three errors. In the seven-inning nightcap, Phyllis Baker yielded a run in the second inning on two hits, a walk, and a bunt, but showers washed out the game.[23]

Last of the Blue Sox — South Bend's final American Girls Baseball League team is shown at Playland Park in 1954. Kneeling in front are (left to right) Wilma Briggs, Betty Francis, Louise Clapp, Peggy Cramer, Mary Froning, Gertie Dunn, Mary Carey, Lois Youngen, and Maxine Drinkwater. Standing in the back row are Mildred Roark, chaperone, Marion Hosbein, Sue Kidd, Janet Rumsey, Betty Wanless, Phyllis Baker, Dolly Vanderlip, Helen Nordquist, Wimp Baumgartner, and manager Karl Winsch. South Bend finished in second place in 1954, but lost to Grand Rapids in the postseason, winning once in three games during the semifinal round of the last-ever Shaughnessy Playoffs (courtesy of Betty Francis).

South Bend's easy victory on opening day launched the team on a five-game win streak. Making a one-day trip to Grand Rapids for Saturday's contest (one game sets were not unusual in 1954), the Blue Sox rode the hurling of former Peach Helen Nordquist, who despite issuing ten walks, won, 7–3, as her teammates rocked star right-hander Beans Risinger for ten hits. In what became the *Tribune's* usual format for away-game articles, readers learned that Betty Wanless, the Chicks' former third baseman, enjoyed a 3-for-5 night, and Briggs came through with two hits and drove home two runs, but the story carried few other details.[24]

Returning to Playland for Sunday's doubleheader, the Blue Sox blanked Fort Wayne twice. Baker hurled the opener, allowing a single to Jo Weaver in the sixth, and the Blue Sox won, 2–0, scoring a pair of runs in the fourth on Briggs' double, Wagoner's bunt single, Carey's run-scoring single, and Baker's grounder to right field that drove home a run though she was thrown out at first base. In the seven-frame nightcap, Rumsey, the lanky curveballer, permitted four hits and earned a 1–0 victory on Francis' run-scoring single in the sixth.[25]

Monday's Memorial Day contest was postponed due to wet grounds, and the unbeaten South Benders waited a day for a twin bill against Kalamazoo on Tuesday night (again, most games were played at night). However, rain spreading across the Midwest wiped out the circuit's games, leaving South Bend in first place with a 4–0 ledger. The standings showed Rockford in second place at 2–1, Kalamazoo and Grand Rapids tied for third with 1–2 records, and Fort Wayne occupying the basement with a 1–4 mark, after being belted by Rockford, 12–3.[26]

Taking the soggy field at Playland on Wednesday for two games against the Lassies, who had spent the previous day and night lounging at the Hoffman Hotel, the Blue Sox unwittingly previewed their season by dividing the doubleheader. Kidd started the evening's fun by twirling a five-hitter as the home team won, 3–0. In the late tilt, Kalamazoo won, 7–5, thanks mostly to errors. Nordquist, a versatile player without much hurling experience, yielded three runs in the fourth, thanks to a wild streak, and another in the fifth. With the home team leading in the seventh, 5–4, the Lassies' hurler, Kay Blumetta, walked, and "Nordie" threw away Nancy Mudge's grounder. The quiet Massachusetts right-hander gave way to Baker, but June Peppas greeted her with a single, scoring Elaine Roth, who ran for Blumetta. Former Sox star Jeep Stoll singled in another run, and the third run scored on Dunn's error. Roth retired the Blue Sox in the last of the seventh, but the split still left 5–1 South Bend in first place. Rockford, Fort Wayne, and Grand Rapids were rained out, leaving the Peaches second with 2–1 mark.[27]

For two weeks, the once hot Blue Sox, often displaying sloppy fielding, inconsistent pitching, and not enough clutch hitting, lost nine of 11 games. All games were rained out on Thursday, and on Friday, South Bend journeyed by bus to Rockford, checked in at the visiting team's usual lodgings, the Lafayette Hotel, and made its pregame preparations. That evening at Beyer Stadium, the Blue Sox won behind the team's new ace, Jan Rumsey, who, with good control and her sharp curve

Janet Rumsey — South Bend's best pitcher in 1954, Rumsey fashioned a 15–6 record and a league-best 2.18 ERA. The tall right-hander capped her season with a no-hitter against Grand Rapids, beating the Chicks, 4–0, on August 24 (courtesy of Betty Francis).

working, spaced four hits to win, 3–0. Her teammates rocked Lefty Lee for ten hits, one by every batter and two by Wanless. Rumsey, who proceeded to lead the league with an ERA of 2.18, collected her second win en route to her best season.[28] On Saturday, Baker hurled a six-hitter but lost to fastballing Marie Mansfield, 1–0, as the improving Peaches counted a run in the third on Rose Gacioch's run-scoring single.[29] Rockford won another squeaker on Saturday, 2–1, as Mickey Jinright dueled Kidd evenly, but finally won on Ruth Richard's RBI single off Nordquist in the ninth. The victory lifted the 5–2 Peaches above the 6–3 Sox into first place.[30] However, South Bend took over the lead at Grand Rapids on Sunday by outlasting the Chicks, 3–1, in the opener, thanks to Nordquist's three-hit stint over five innings and two perfect frames by Rumsey, who protected the lead built on Froning's two-run single in the third.[31]

Suddenly the momentum turned for the Blue Sox, and they lost seven in a row. At Fort Wayne on Tuesday, June 8, an odd situation arose when the Daisies insisted on playing a late game with South Bend, after wet grounds caused the twin bill's first game against Kalamazoo to be abandoned. Winsch, who loved to argue, favored postponing the nightcap, but the Daisies' management insisted on playing. After the verbal shenanigans, the blue-clad visitors fell, 8–5, as Pinky LeDuc outlasted Rumsey in nine innings, instead of the scheduled seven. The contest raised questions about the unorthodox five-team schedule, and on the bus ride home, the South Benders voiced frustration with the decision to play, as well as their inability to muster more than six hits.[32] At Playland on Wednesday, the Blue Sox lost another tough decision to visiting Fort Wayne, 3–1, as Maxine Kline, who topped the loop in wins in 1954 with her 18–7 record, fanned pinch-hitter Sue Kidd in the ninth with runners at second and third.[33]

Remaining at home, South Bend dropped both ends of a three-team doubleheader on Thursday to Kalamazoo and Rockford. After falling to Rockford on Friday and losing at Kalamazoo on Saturday, the traveling Blue Sox lost their seventh straight at Grand Rapids on Sunday. In that contest, Phyllis Baker, cruising with a 2–0 lead in the seventh inning, gave up four hits and lost, 3–2, when Barbara Sowers scored the winning run with a sacrifice fly. The South Benders, now with a 7–10 record, plunged from first place to the league's basement in one week.[34]

Juggling the Lineup

On June 14, the Blue Sox, returning to the familiar circumstances of their South Bend homes away from home, practiced, rested, and returned to Playland Park for a Monday doubleheader. There they broke the seven-game skid by dividing two contests. In the opener against Rockford, Dolly Vanderlip, the youthful 5'8" right-hander who lost to the Peaches four days earlier, made her second start and won a five-hitter, 4–0. Gertie Dunn belted a 240-foot two-run homer to left-center in the third, and the local favorites added two more runs in the fifth on Carey's double and an error. In the nightcap against Kalamazoo, Winsch and the Lassies' Mitch Skupien tried new pitchers. Karl started Mary Froning, but the outfielder gave up three hits, walked seven, and threw away two bunts. Rookie southpaw Judy McCormick took over in the third with the Sox down, 6–0, while Lassies southpaw June Peppas, also a hard-hitting first baseman, cruised to the 7–0 win.

In the Kalamazoo loss, the Blue Sox totaled just five hits, two by Dunn, two by Carey, and one by Maxine Drinkwater, a bespectacled 18-year-old infielder from Camden, Maine.

As a result, Winsch shifted his lineup, starting Wagoner in center, Wanless at third, Dunn at short, Briggs, hitting clean-up, in left, Francis in right, and Carey at second base. Drinkwater started at first, but later moved to second base, and Rumsey, a pitcher, took over at first when Carey left the game so that rookie Marion Hosbein, 17, could go to right field. Baumgartner was the catcher, but recruit Peggy Cramer finished the game. Froning lasted three innings, and Judy McCormick, the Chicago rookie, relieved, allowing a run in the seventh for the 7–0 finale.[35]

Departing for a six-game trip "around the league," the South Benders looked better, winning two out of three at Rockford, taking a solo game at Grand Rapids, but losing two of three at Fort Wayne. The Peaches' series was best illustrated in the opener on Tuesday, June 15, when Rumsey was hurt by only two hitters: Ellie Callow slugged a bases-empty home run in the first inning and a two-run blast in the seventh, and Marge Russo hit a two-run single in the fifth. The Blue Sox reached Mickey Jinright and her floating curves for four hits and, aided by two errors, notched five unearned runs in the third, keyed by Francis' two-run double. Later, Wanless helped win the game by socking a two-run homer in the 11th.[36] The two teams split the last two games, South Bend used Friday for a travel day, and on Saturday, Rumsey stopped the Chicks in Grand Rapids, 6–1, producing a nifty two-hitter.[37] Completing the road trip with three games at Fort Wayne, the Blue Sox won the second game of two against the Daisies on Monday, June 21.

For Monday's nightcap, Winsch started rookie right-hander Louise Clapp of Harrod, Ohio, and the Daisies' Bill Allington used Barbara Gates, who played a combined 11 games for Grand Rapids and South Bend in 1953. The Sox scored six runs off Gates in the first stanza, fueled by Baumgartner's two-run double. Winsch used three hurlers in the 10–6 victory, calling on Froning, the eventual winner, in the third, and Baker, who hurled two scoreless frames, in the sixth. Afterward, South Bend held fourth place with a 12–14 ledger, four games off Kalamazoo's league-leading pace of 15–9.[38]

The South Benders' victory at Fort Wayne ignited a six-game win streak, including four triumphs at Playland, three over Fort Wayne and the last one over Grand Rapids. Rumsey, Vanderlip, and Kidd all defeated the Daisies, and Baker won against the Chicks, with relief help from Rumsey. The sixth win came on Sunday, June 27, at Kalamazoo in the opener of yet another three-team twin bill. Rumsey (now 6–2) outlasted Elaine Roth as both hurled six-hitters, but the Blue Sox, using their speed, won in the seventh, 2–1, on a double steal. Froning beat out a bunt, and the Ohio flash raced to third on Carey's hit. Working the double steal, Carey broke for second, and shortstop Dottie Schroeder cut off the catcher's throw in order to nip Froning going home, but Dottie had to avoid umpire Harlow Kott, and the speedy Mary scored easily.[39]

The entire complexion of the game on the diamond was about to change, but first, South Bend lost twice at Fort Wayne, the second a one-hitter tossed by rookie Mary Weddle. Afterward, the 16–16 Blue Sox were in third place behind the Lassies (19–15) and the Daisies (20–16).[40]

The Home Run Era

By June 1954, when the schedule was causing teams to play fewer games in a series and travel more in order to play at least two three-team doubleheaders each week, league officials, desperate to draw more fans, voted for changes to go into effect on July 1.

First, the circuit discarded the 10-inch circumference ball and adopted a regulation baseball measuring between 9 and 9.25 inches. Second, adopting the smaller, livelier ball meant making on-field changes. The pitching distance was lengthened from the current 56 feet to 60 feet, half a foot short of the length from the pitching rubber to home plate in major league baseball, and the base paths were increased from the current 75 feet to 85, five feet short of the same dimensions for baseball. Also, if the league's supply of DeBeer balls was not used by July 1, the changes would begin after the All-Star game on July 11.[41] Initially a start-up league based on underhand hurling, a 12-inch softball, a 40-foot pitching distance, and 65-foot base paths, the pioneering All-American Girls Soft Ball League of 1943 had evolved by increments into the overhand hurling, near-regulation American Girls Baseball League of 1954.

However, the league's attendance had peaked in 1948, and paid admissions were declining almost yearly. By 1954, circuit and team officials, looking at growing deficits, reduced each team's salary maximum from $5,400 to $4,400 per month, with no player to earn more than $400. Lacking enough new talent, they dropped the rookie rule.[42] The circuit's leaders, overlooking the social factors working against women deciding to play pro ball, believed that technical changes to the game would resurrect fan interest.

"If it [the league] had been picked up by a smart sports promoter," recalled Arthur Meyerhoff, owner of the Management Corporation from 1945 to 1950, "it might have grown, but it got into the hands of local businessmen who didn't have Philip Wrigley's promotional know-how. They were primarily in it for civic purposes — they had fun managing local girls baseball teams, rather than looking at it from a promotional stand point and building it."[43]

Still, if South Bend was an example, the teams were trying every promotion that club officials could devise, and managers, concentrating on the game they could affect, liked the changes. Batters, like those in the majors, could pound out more extra-base hits with the livelier ball. "We need more hitting and less bunting and stealing," remarked Woody English, the Chicks' manager. "We should see more home runs and extra base hits." Also, the smaller ball might help pitchers, reasoned Karl Winsch, a former minor league hurler. "With the smaller ball, girls will be able to get a better grip on it, thus being able to put more 'stuff' on their pitches."[44]

Regardless, the latest changes overlooked the real strength of the American Girls Baseball League: the natural appeal of females playing baseball. The all-important fan sympathy was tied to the players' *sex*, as Chet Grant pointed out, not with their speed, strength, or power.[45]

On Thursday, July 1, after one night to practice with the new baseball and with Playland Park set up with the new diamond dimensions, the South Benders entered the circuit's "home run era" by splitting a twin bill. In the opener against Grand Rapids, entertaining the largest crowd since opening night, an estimated 1,200 fans, the Blue Sox rode a 12-hit barrage and Vanderlip's seven-hit hurling to a 5–2 victory. Wagoner slashed a two-run single to left in the first inning for a 2–0 lead, but the Chicks' Marilyn Jenkins tied the score in the second with a two-run blast, the first home run at Playland with the regulation baseball. The Blue Sox moved ahead for good with two runs in the fifth on Wagoner's RBI double and Dunn's sacrifice fly. In the nightcap against Fort Wayne, Rumsey could not stop Betty Foss, who slugged a two-run homer in the third, or Katie Horstman, who hit a solo shot in the fifth. Pinky Leduc allowed only five hits and the Blue Sox fell, 4–1. The new horsehide evidently led to more extra-base hits, but most who saw the games agreed the harder-hit balls gave infielders more trouble fielding grounders.[46]

Still, the long ball became a more important feature of games, and fortunately for South Bend, Wilma Briggs swung a big bat. A good defensive outfielder, Wilma, who grew up playing ball in East Greenwich, Rhode Island, threw right and batted left-handed. Strong, agile, and talented, she broke into the league with Fort Wayne in 1948 and averaged .258 over her seven-year career. She credited Max Carey, the erstwhile league president who managed the Daisies in 1950 and 1951, with teaching her to hit to the opposite field, bunt for a hit, and protect the runners on base. Briggs led the loop in home runs in 1953, slamming the 10-inch ball for nine four-baggers. In 1954, she slugged 25 homers, third behind the league's leader, Jo Weaver, who, while batting an all-time circuit high of .429, also set a new record with 29 blasts. A good clutch hitter, Briggs delivered 73 RBI, third to the Daisies' Jean Geissinger with 91 and Weaver with 87. Despite the salary cap, Wilma recalled that the Sox restored the $50 per month cut she lost at Fort Wayne.[47]

On the other hand, South Bend hurlers were victimized by more long balls than their teammates hit. The last game of the Fort Wayne series was rained out on Friday, July 2. Motoring to Grand Rapids on Saturday, the Blue Sox scored 11 times but fell, 12–11, as Kidd started but was relieved by Nordquist during a six-run fifth frame when the Chicks built an 11–1 lead. The visitors in light blue short-skirted outfits tied the score with seven runs in the eighth, capped by Briggs' grand slam, but Grand Rapids notched a run off Nordquist in the 11th for the victory.[48] Continuing her torrid slugging on Sunday as the Blue Sox won at Kalamazoo, 6–4, Briggs belted two homers, the second being a two-run shot in the ninth for the final score. Although Rumsey gave up two four-baggers, Briggs' hitting saved the triumph. However, playing the first of two games at Kalamazoo on Monday, South Bend lost a tough one, 5–4, when Baker walked two Lassies in the ninth, Vanderlip (who relieved her) walked two more, and Dunn committed a two-run error.[49]

Back home on Tuesday, the Sox were rained out of a twin bill, but All-Star selections were announced. Rumsey was named as a starter, and Briggs and Wanless were reserves.[50]

At Playland on Wednesday, July 7, in a spectacular display of how the new ball was changing the Girls' Pro League, South Bend divided a doubleheader with Fort Wayne. The two teams, seen by a "sparse turnout of fans" (no number was given, but the *Tribune* often omitted poor attendance figures in 1954), scored a remarkable 39 runs on 49 hits. In the opener, the Daisies rocked Nordquist and Baker for 12 hits, notably two homers by Jean Geissinger and one each by Betty Foss and Katie Horstman. South Bend scored on long balls off the bats of Briggs, Froning (who hit three in 1954), and Baumgartner (who hit two). Wagoner recorded the game's only double, but Fort Wayne won in a rout, 17–8. In the nightcap, Francis went deep, clubbing two three-run blasts and giving the Sox a 6–3 lead after two innings. Vanderlip held the Daisies to 11 hits — and no circuit clouts — for a 10–4 success.[51]

Homers and Lineups

When the All-Star game against the Daisies arrived on Friday, July 9, South Bend held third place with a 20–20 ledger, two and a half games behind pace-setting Fort Wayne (24–19) and a game back of second-place Kalamazoo (22–20). Woody English, manager of Grand Rapids, the Shaughnessy Champions of 1953, picked Rumsey (7–3) to start the star-spangled contest, but she had a rough outing. The slugging Daisies, who thrived on a left field fence that was 218 feet away, launched four solo homers to win, 10–8, but the *Tribune* reported all four clouts would have been outs at Playland.⁵² With the teams tied at 8–8 in the eighth, Jean Geissinger delivered a two-run single, and Marilyn Jones held the lead. Rumsey worked the first three innings, but gave up seven hits, including three home runs. She departed with a 7–3 deficit, and the All-Stars' runs came on Dottie Schroeder's three-run homer in the second. Wilma Briggs played left field in the last inning, but did not bat. The All-Star contests had drawn big crowds, notably the 3,462 who paid to see the show at Memorial Field in 1953, but the newspaper gave no attendance figure.⁵³

After the All-Star break, South Bend's games were often highlighted by a healthy dose of home runs. The Blue Sox hit 70 four-baggers after totaling four in 1953, all by Jean Faut. Although Kalamazoo finished in fourth place with a 48–49 record, the team led the circuit with 109 home runs. Playing at Catholic Athletic Association Field, or CAA Field, termed by many players a "bandbox,"⁵⁴ the Daisies were led by hitters like June Peppas, who averaged .333 with 16 home runs, and Joan Lovell, who batted .286 with 21 homers, but three other teammates clubbed at least 15 circuit clouts. Fort Wayne was second with 102 home runs, led by the likes of Jo Weaver, who recorded 29, and Jean Geissinger, who belted

Wilma Briggs — A fine outfielder for the Fort Wayne Daisies from 1948 through the 1953 season, Briggs was sent to South Bend in 1954 by the league's "balancing committee." After leading the circuit in home runs with nine in 1953, Wilma, or "Briggsie," paced the Blue Sox by hitting a team-record and career-best 25 homers, third behind the Daisies' Jo Weaver, who set the league's all-time home run record with 29. Briggs also led the Blue Sox with 73 RBI (courtesy of Wilma Briggs).

26 homers. Grand Rapids clouted 67 home runs and Rockford hit 60. By comparison, Fort Wayne led the league in 1953 with 39 home runs.

South Bend moved into second place by defeating Kalamazoo in a day-night twin bill at Playland on Sunday, July 11, and home runs provided the decisive scores in each game. Both games went the regulation nine innings, and Kidd racked up her fourth win of the season in the opener, 8–6, thanks to a seventh-inning two-run shot by Dunn, who also cracked a single and a double. The hot-hitting Briggs added a pair of four-baggers, the second one marking the game's final score, and Nancy Mudge, Dottie Schroeder, and Jenny Romatowski homered for the mustard-uniformed visitors. In the night game, Carol Habben hit a circuit clout for the Lassies, but South Bend won easily, 15–7, paced by a seven-run seventh featuring Francis' two-run double and Baumgartner's three-run homer. Kidd gave up 15 hits in the opener, and Vanderlip yielded 13 more, but the two stranded a total of 24 runners.[55]

By mid-July, Karl Winsch, as usual, had settled on a lineup — usually listed as follows:

Dunn, SS, leading off — Gertie, now 20, was usually a sure-handed fielder with a good arm. Batting at the top of the order, she averaged a career-high .299, hitting six homers. Getting on base was the youthful star's specialty. Excellent at field hockey and later greatly interested in flying, the 5'2" Pennsylvania native drew 47 walks, fanned only 10 times, scored 59 runs, and drove home 38 teammates, making her a major contributor to the team.

Briggs, LF, batting second — Wilma, or "Briggsie," 23, could also play first base. Mostly she batted second, third, or fourth, hitting .300, and driving in 73 runs, thanks in part to her team-high 25 four-baggers. A hard-hitting southpaw swinger, Briggsie drew 42 walks and fanned 33 times, but she scored 69 runs and also helped with her good glove and accurate arm.

Wanless, 3B, hitting third — Also new to South Bend, Betty, or "Duke," was a quick-handed third baseman who started as a rookie for Grand Rapids in 1953. The right-handed hitter displayed good power, once clubbing a 425-foot home run out of the Chicks' park. A mature 25, the Springfield, Illinois, brunette hit .274, slugging 13 doubles, two triples, and 15 home runs. Gifted with a strong arm at third base, the 5'5" Wanless gave the Sox an all-around boost.

Francis, CF, often the clean-up batter — Yet another new South Bender, Betty took over centerfield from Wagoner, who usually played home games in 1954, often at first base. The stellar Francis, a 5'4" all-around athlete who enjoyed track and field events in high school, began her career with the touring Colleens in 1949. Right-handed all the way, she often pulled balls foul to left field. Winsch suggested she try a heavier 35-inch bat, and "B.F" really improved, hitting more balls fair — and slugging more long balls. Indeed, in her first game with the bigger bat, she singled and hit two home runs.[56] Overall, the Chicago standout averaged a torrid .350, fifth best in the league, led the Sox in runs scored with 75, and ranked second on the team in RBIs with 58.

Wagoner, 1B, batting fifth — Betty, the fleet Missouri star who was now the team's senior member, played mainly home games, enjoying the best season of her seven-year career. In 48 games, she averaged .320, second high on the team, but she was caring for her infirm mother and preferred staying in South Bend. A spray-hitting left-handed batter who also pitched, Betty contributed 12 doubles and 15 RBI, but her only career home run came in the 1954 playoffs.

Baumgartner, C, listed sixth — Wimp was the regular receiver again in 1954. Twenty-three, she played 81 games, but, after breaking a finger, she struggled at the plate, averaging .186. Still, she drew 42 walks, scored 26 runs, and delivered 19 RBI. Typical of catchers, she helped her team most by calling a smart game. Also, Lois Youngen, the right-handed batting Ohio receiver who played for the Blue Sox in 1953, was recalled from the Daisies for the last ten games. For the season, Lois caught a combined 23 games and hit .284. The other catcher was Michigan teenager Peggy Cramer, who played fewer than ten games.

Carey, 2B, hitting seventh — Mary, a strong-armed, sure-handed, and versatile infielder who played second base, third base, and shortstop over her nine-year career, averaged .210, her second highest mark. A right-handed singles hitter who grew up playing ball in Detroit, the 29-year-old played the harmonica and liked leading sing-a-longs on bus trips. Mary understood the game well, and she co-managed Peoria for part of the 1950 season. In South Bend, she mostly covered second base, a position handled by several players in 1953.

Froning, RF, the last batter — "Fearless Froning," as teammates often dubbed Mary, because she let nothing stop her when running down a fly ball, came into her own in 1954, batting a career-high .231. Not always patient at the plate, the Minster, Ohio, outfielder did manage 26 walks, but she fanned 29 times. Winsch usually listed her in the ninth slot, because if she reached base, she was followed by the team's best hitters. Enthusiastic, happy, and talented, Froning, 19, who later began working as a stewardess for American Airlines, loved the league. Mary recalled, "I didn't care if I made four cents a game. I was just so happy to be playing!"[57]

Rookies — Maxine Drinkwater, 18, an all-around athlete who liked bowling, tennis, and golf, usually played first base in away games, when Wagoner stayed home, but Maxine also played second base. Selected first at South Bend's tryouts in 1954, the 5'5" right-handed hitter from Camden, Maine, performed better in the field than at the plate, averaging .156. Teenager Marion Hosbein, a right-handed hitter from Coloma, Michigan, played fewer than ten games, so the league had no statistics on the reserve outfielder. Two more rookies also played fewer than ten contests: Michigan high schooler Peggy Cramer, a catcher, and Chicago hurler Judy McCormick, but both gained experience as the summer progressed.

For pitchers, Winsch had three good choices. First, Jan Rumsey, the nicest surprise of the season, made the All-Star team and posted a 15–6 record with a league-best 2.18 ERA. The curveballing right-hander, gaining needed experience in 1953, improved her control and, therefore, improved her performance. Jan started and completed 21 games, and she relieved four times. Dolly Vanderlip, 17, an eager right-hander pitching her third season after two years as a spot starter with Fort Wayne, posted an 11–6 ledger with an ERA of 2.40, an average that ranked her second in the loop behind Rumsey. Dolly, who learned the rhythm of being a starter as the season moved along, provided South Bend with a needed boost. However, the manager depended more on Sue Kidd, the Arkansas right-hander who enjoyed her best season with a 9–5 record (or 9–6, according to Howe News Bureau stats),[58] and a 2.91 ERA, the fourth lowest mark in the league. Also, Winsch often used Helen Nordquist, who was a better hitter than pitcher, but Nordie, who batted .310, started 11 games, completed five, and won two, all before July 1. Finally, Betty Wagoner won four games and lost four, mostly after the All-Star game. Still, the Blue Sox featured three of the loop's top four hurlers. Fort Wayne's Katie Horstman, who also hit .328, placed third, just above Kidd, with a 10–4 ledger and an ERA of 2.85.

Kidd's experience reflected the learning curve of many younger players who fashioned their careers in the 1950s. The league was tough for rookies to make by 1945, as standouts like Connie Wisniewski and Betsy Jochum later pointed out.[59] The circuit used a different ball, different dimensions, and special rules. The more the game evolved toward baseball, the greater the adaptations required for softball or sandlot players. Still, like Kidd, the younger girls grew up playing hardball with brothers or friends, so they liked the regulation baseball. Tomboys all, they relished the game, but competing against superstars like Sophie Kurys, Doris Sams, Audrey Wagner, Rose Gacioch, Jean Faut, and Jo Weaver, to name a few of the league's all-time greatest players, was an exciting but difficult challenge. Decades later, Kidd reflected on 1954, when she started 16 games, completed 14, won nine, and enjoyed her best year by hitting .238. Quiet and shy, she was a dedicated team player who socked three doubles and five home runs.

"I was happy to hit a home run," Sue remembered, "but I knew I could from batting practice. However, I hit to all fields. I wasn't just a pull hitter, and it was easier to get homers by pulling down the lines. I tried to hit where the ball was pitched." Summing up the feeling of many young players who hated seeing the league fold, she added, "I would have had a better average, and more home runs too, with just a few more years of experience."[60]

Summer of '54

By July, the South Benders, who had grown used to the oddball three-team doubleheaders, experienced a roller-coaster ride of winning and losing in streaks. After sweeping two from Kalamazoo and moving into second place on July 11, the Blue Sox spent most of the rest of the all-too-short summer in the same slot, three or more games behind the league-leading Daisies.

Traveling to Rockford for a four-game visit to the Peach Orchard, starting on Sunday, July 18, the Blue Sox divided the series in typical fashion, losing the first two and winning the last two. Nordquist, the rangy right-hander, pitched and hit well, but lost to the Peaches, 4–2. Briggs and Nordie both slammed solo home runs, but the Peaches' Rose Gacioch hit a bases-empty shot and Marge Russo won it with a two-run circuit clout.[61] On Monday night, Baker lost by the same 4–2 score, after Briggs homered in the first to give the visitors a 1–0 lead. Rockford, taking the lead with single runs in the first and second, scored twice in the fifth, capped when Ann Gosbee, a seldom-used utility player on loan from Fort Wayne, worked Baker for a bases-loaded pass for the final 4–2 margin.[62] On Tuesday, Rumsey, improving her record to 9–3, scattered seven hits in a seven-inning game to whitewash Rockford, 2–0. In a game that was unusual because nobody hit a home run, Dunn collected three hits and Kidd, playing first base, contributed two safeties to lead an 11-blow assault.[63] On Wednesday, Vanderlip rode her team's five-run outburst in the first to a 6–1 triumph, and Wanless' two singles led the seven-hit attack. Elsewhere, Fort Wayne lost to Kalamazoo, leaving South Bend, now 28–26, two games behind the first-place Daisies.[64]

At Playland on Wednesday, July 21, in the most novel game of the swan song season, South Bend proved no match for a men's semipro team, Anderson Motors of the Northern Indiana League, losing, 7–1. To "even up" the teams, reminiscent of long-gone Bloomer Girl matches, the Anderson nine's pitcher and catcher worked for the Blue Sox, and Sue Kidd pitched for the men, with Peggy Cramer catching. Other special rules included one limiting men to ground rule doubles for any balls hit over the fence. As it developed, none of the Blue Sox homered, but Kidd, who went 2-for-2 and walked twice, socked a drive that bounced over the left field fence for an actual ground rule two-bagger. A crowd of 2,000, South Bend's largest turnout of the year, saw the uneven contest. Kidd permitted five hits: one to catcher Bill Mathias, another to pitcher Dick Peterson, a pair of singles to Betty Wagoner, and a base hit to Mary Carey. South Bend resident Stan Coveleski, the onetime star American League right-hander who would be inducted into the National Baseball Hall of Fame in 1969, helped the Sox — and the attendance — by coaching first base.[65] If South Bend's purpose was to attract fans, the exhibition worked. If the aim was to show that women could compete evenly with men, the idea was a flop.

The South Benders' memorable summer continued with three losses at Fort Wayne. After slipping to third place behind Kalamazoo, the Blue Sox regained the second slot by sweeping a doubleheader at Playland against the Chicks and the Lassies on Sunday, July 25. Kidd hurled the opener against Grand Rapids and, after yielding a three-run homer in the third frame to Dolly Pearson, the Blue Sox rallied for four runs on five hits in the bottom of the inning, with Dunn's two-run single providing the final margin of 4–3. Vanderlip picked up her eighth victory in the late game, 11–5, breezing after her teammates grabbed an 8–0 lead in the first, thanks to a pair of errors by All-Star Dottie Schroeder.[66] Following two losses to Kalamazoo, the first at Playland and the second at CAA Field, South Bend reeled off three straight wins, two at Grand Rapids and one at Kalamazoo, before losing at Fort Wayne, 9–7. At Memorial Field on August 1, the Blue Sox built a 5–0 lead in the top of the third inning, but the Daisies drove Baker to the bench with five runs. Vanderlip relieved, but she was the loser when, paced by Jo Weaver's 6-for-7 night, Fort Wayne scored three times in the fifth and once in the seventh to win, 9–7. Afterward, the Daisies, now 38–31, held a two and a half game lead over the second-place Sox (34–32).[67]

Still resilient, the South Benders journeyed to Rockford and won the first of what became a six-game string. The determined visitors in light blue uniforms beat the Peaches twice, and moving to Elkhart, they beat the Peaches and the Chicks in a twin bill, thanks to game-winning singles by Betty Francis in the seventh inning of both games. Traveling to St. Joseph, the Blue Sox outlasted the Chicks on Friday, August 6, when Francis again fueled a close triumph, this time singling to drive home the tying run in the ninth inning. In the 11th, with Briggs on third base and Wagoner on first (Wagener drove her car to the game), catcher Marilyn Jenkins tried to pick Briggs off, but threw the ball away, giving the Sox a 6–5 win. South Bend had enticed Jette (Vincent) Mooney to return, and, yielding four hits, she pitched well enough to win.[68]

Chasing the Daisies

By August, the last month of the league's last season, Winsch was tinkering with his rotation. Rumsey, the heady ace, improved her control, pitch selection, and curveball, and she regularly found the plate's corners in 1954. Kidd, a stellar all-around performer, was also pitching and hitting better than in 1953. Vanderlip was the team's best new hurler. Also, Mooney, who returned in August, replaced Nordquist as the team's fourth starter. Married in July 1952, Jette finished her season at 8–8 with a 2.36 ERA, but sat out in 1953. In the end, her presence mattered little in 1954, because she was 1–1 in three starts. Finally, the manager was pitching Betty Wagoner. The strong-armed lefty made eight spot starts, posting a 4–4 record with a bulging ERA of 4.66. Last, Froning appeared in five games, started twice, and compiled a 1–2 mark.

Hoping to move back into first place, Kidd won the opener of a three-game set at Kalamazoo on Saturday, August 7. The Lassies gave the game away, making eight errors.

After scoring once in the first inning on a walk, a single, and an error, the Blue Sox scored three in the third, capped by Kidd's two-run single for a 4–2 lead. Peppas closed the final margin to 4–3 with a homer in the seventh, but Kidd prevailed. Winsch shifted his lineup for the game, listing Wanless as the leadoff hitter, Dunn second, Briggs third, and Francis at clean-up, since Betty was swinging the team's hottest bat. Wagoner, who motored to Kazoo, played first base and batted fifth, Kidd hit sixth, and was followed by Froning, Carey, and Baumgartner. The victory left the Blue Sox in second place with a 40–32 ledger, now a game and a half behind the leaders.

Betty Francis — Sent to the Blue Sox in 1954 by the league's "balancing committee," Francis (pictured in Colleens' uniform in 1949) was a four-year regular in the outfield for Kalamazoo. With South Bend, Betty played mostly center field and batted a career-best .350, contributing personal highs in doubles (13), triples (2), home runs (8), and RBI (58) (courtesy of Betty Francis).

Regardless, the Daisies had the hitting and pitching to stay in front, and the Blue Sox were next, so the pennant race was boiling down to finishes by the other teams. After South Bend's six-game streak, Kalamazoo (36–39) was a distant third, a game and a half ahead of Grand Rapids (33–39), but Rockford (30–42) was 11 games back. Thus, if the Blue Sox finished second, what mattered was their playoff opponent — the fourth-place team.[69]

South Bend lost the last two games at Kalamazoo, traveled home, and fell to longtime nemesis Fort Wayne, 8–5, at Playland on Tuesday, August 10. Wagoner started and hurled a no-hitter through five innings, but as happened too often, she tired, after doubling home two runs for a 4–0 lead. The Daisies roared back, scoring three runs in the sixth on Jo Weaver's solo homer and Geissinger's two-run shot, two runs on Geissinger's single in the seventh, and three more runs in the ninth. Briggs hit a solo blast in the bottom of the ninth for the home team's final score.[70] After that, Vanderlip, Rumsey, and Kidd hurled wins, the first over Rockford and the others in a twin bill against the Peaches and the Lassies. The three wins were followed by three losses, the first at Playland against Rockford and the last two at Kalamazoo.

The second loss, an 11–3 whipping handed out by the Lassies on Sunday, August 15, came with 11 days remaining in the regular season — and the defeat stung because Wimp

Baumgartner, the team's most dependable receiver, suffered a season-ending elbow injury in practice before the game. Peggy Cramer caught (she was 0-for-3), and Winsch tried the strong-armed Froning on the mound, but she lacked the control and the pitches to limit the Lassies. The Ohio brunette gave up three walks and three runs in the first inning, and she walked the leadoff batter in the second. Winsch called on Nordquist, who was playing right field and received little chance to warm up. Nordie, shaky at first, allowed seven runs in the second, capped by Carol Habben's three-run homer, but the Massachusetts righty improved after warming up again. Still, Hank Warren and the Lassies had a 10–0 lead and cruised to an 11–3 rout. Afterward, South Bend reclaimed catcher Lois Youngen from Fort Wayne, where the Daisies were using her in the outfield.[71]

Youngen, 20 years old and in her fourth season, arrived on Monday, contributed two singles in four trips, and the Blue Sox won the series finale at Kalamazoo, 10–7, with a three-run rally in the ninth. Kidd, winning her ninth game, hit a wild streak in the second and coughed up five runs, including pitcher Jean Marlowe's three-run homer. Dunn, Briggs, Youngen, and Kidd each collected two hits, and in the ninth, Dunn walked, Wanless homered over the right field fence, and Briggs wrapped up the scoring with her 20th long ball of the season.[72]

In another pair of mid–August spurts, South Bend won the next two games and — still short on pitching, because most hurlers can only work every fourth or fifth day — lost five in a row. Back at Playland on Tuesday, August 17, the Blue Sox won a twin bill from Rockford and Kalamazoo. A large, noisy audience of 1,755 celebrated "Truckers Night," thanks to tickets sold by the Northern Indiana Truckers Association and Teamsters Local 364, the team's two biggest boosters in 1954. In the opener, Wagoner outlasted Rockford's Dolores Lee, and the Blue Sox won, 8–4, erupting for eight runs in the sixth fueled by Froning's three-run blast. In the late game, Rumsey, who stifled Kalamazoo, 7–0, was buoyed by two solo homers in the first inning, one by Dunn to right field, and one by Wanless to left. Wanless, who hit a three-run blast in the sixth, and Dunn both collected three hits, lots of applause, and helped to score all seven runs.[73]

Following a rainout on Wednesday, South Bend lost any chance at overtaking Fort Wayne by dropping five straight. Vanderlip pitched and lost the first two contests, one at Fort Wayne and one at Grand Rapids. In perhaps a harbinger of bad news for the postseason, the Blue Sox returned to Playland on Sunday, August 24, but the Daisies destroyed their hopes for first place with a 24–8 walloping. The local favorites hurt their cause with six errors, but the visitors, even without the shorter fence they enjoyed at Memorial Field, slugged seven home runs — three by Katie Horstman, two by Jo Weaver, and one apiece by Betty Foss and Mary Weddle. Wanless countered with a grand slam, but the game was over when Wagoner and Vanderlip, who relieved in the third, gave up nine runs in the inning.[74]

At Ames Field in Michigan City, Indiana, another nearby locale where the Blue Sox, "close" on funds, traveled in the older players' cars,[75] Fort Wayne clinched the regular season title by sending Kidd to her fifth defeat in 14 decisions, 9–4. The Arkansas star gave up 15 hits, including five straight for four runs and a 6–2 Daisy lead in the fifth. The loss was South Bend's 17th in 23 games to Fort Wayne, and only 400 fans paid to see it happen.[76]

Looking Toward the Playoffs

On Tuesday, August 24, the South Benders, playing for pride, hosted a twin bill at Playland, their home since 1946, and beat Grand Rapids twice, starting with Wagoner's fourth victory, 4–2. The Chicks bunched four of their eight hits in the fourth frame to score twice, but the Blue Sox scored two runs in the first, and Briggs hit a two-run clout in the third for a lead that Wagoner protected. In the nightcap, Rumsey, with her curve breaking sharply, delivered a seven-inning no-hit performance to win, 4–0. In her only career no-hitter, Jan faced 22 batters, one over the limit, and Mary Carey muffed Joyce Ricketts' grounder in the second inning to end any hope for a perfect game. Elsewhere, Kalamazoo thumped Rockford twice. Afterward, the Daisies (52–40) remained in first place, the Blue Sox (48–43) were two games ahead of the third-place Lassies (48–47), while the Chicks (43–45) were fourth, two games behind Kalamazoo.[77]

On Wednesday, South Bend again planned to travel by players' automobiles to a twin bill against Grand Rapids and Rockford at Warsaw, Indiana, but rain washed out the games, leaving the team with one final home game against Fort Wayne on Thursday.

After the rainout, South Bend was assured of second place, and Grand Rapids looked good for fourth. If so, the two teams would meet at Playland on Saturday night in the first round of the Shaughnessy Playoffs. At that point, the Blue Sox owned a 6–23 record against the Daisies, but against the league's other teams, South Bend had winning ledgers: 13–11 against the third-place Lassies, 15–6 against the fourth-place Chicks, and 14–9 against the last-place Peaches. At that time, Winsch's ball club had three pitchers with winning records: Rumsey, 15–6, Vanderlip, 11–6, and Kidd, 9–5. Wagoner, Nordquist, and Baker had losing ledgers, and Mooney had split two decisions.[78] But in a short playoff, three good pitchers gave the Sox reason for high hopes.

Regardless, the regular season ended with a disappointing event perhaps best characterized by the famous phrase of 19th century poet John Greenleaf Whittier, who, reflecting on sad words of tongue and pen, said the saddest were, *It might have been*. The Blue Sox, hoping to entertain a good audience at Playland on Thursday, forfeited. Calling it "weird," the *Tribune*, in a terse sentence, reported, "A balk called on Blue Sox pitcher Mary Froning in the third inning brought on a lengthy argument between manager Karl Winsch and the umpires and resulted in South Bend forfeiting."[79] Two days later, the newspaper said that Winsch refused to leave the field after arguing the call, and therefore his team had to forfeit. Furthermore, Grand Rapids (46–45) won twice from Rockford, so the Sox loss meant they faced Kalamazoo (48–49) in the playoffs.

After the season, sports editor Joe Doyle, piqued at the strange affairs of the league, wondered if events like forfeits were "business as usual" in a circuit numbering five teams, an experiment tested for the first time in the history of "(dis) organized baseball." For starters, Doyle wrote, "One manager, Karl Winsch, forfeits a game when a balk is called ten minutes after its occurrence.... The same manager refused to pay a $10 fine and places his share of the playoff loot in jeopardy."[80] In other words, Winsch failed to think about the welfare of his team.

The Cheering Stops

The playoffs remained, and whatever the players thought, they were professionals. On Saturday, August 28, with Winsch barred from managing because he refused to pay the fine levied by Earl McCammon, South Bend enjoyed a flying start by whipping the Lassies, 6–3, behind the hurling of Rumsey, who scattered eight hits. The favorite daughter of Greensburg, Indiana, who posted a 4–1 mark against the Lassies in 1954, gave a big-game performance. With Wilma Briggs managing the Sox, Kalamazoo grabbed a 2–0 lead in the fourth inning when Dunn threw away an easy double-play grounder. In the Sox fourth, Froning hit a two-run double to knot the score. After Chris Ballingall homered in the sixth, Wanless homered for a 3–3 tie, and, three batters later, Dottie Schroeder threw away Francis' grounder, allowing two more runs to score. Schroeder made another error in the eighth, giving the home team the final margin of 6–3.[81]

But in the final two games in Kalamazoo, the Lassies dominated. The first defeat occurred on Sunday night. Winsch was back after paying his fine, but at CAA Field, the home team topped Kidd and Vanderlip, who relieved, for a 6–3 victory. Kidd gave up a two-run shot to Peppas in the first frame, and when Vanderlip took over with two runners aboard in the second, Ballingall singled for a 4–0 lead that Hank Warren preserved. Wagoner, now playing every game, hit a third-inning single to score Dunn and Wanless, who both walked, and Wanless hit a solo home run in the seventh, to no avail.[82] On Monday, Kalamazoo won a slugfest, 10–7, as Elaine Roth and reliever Gloria Cordes limited the Blue Sox to seven hits, but the Lassies made the score closer with eight errors. The Blue Sox took a 3–0 lead when Wagoner, the starter, hit her only career home run, a three-run blast in the third. The Missourian had a 4–0 margin after her teammates scored once in the fifth, but in the bottom of the inning, she allowed four hits and four walks, combined with her club's only two errors, and Kalamazoo moved ahead, 5–4. In the sixth, Kidd, playing first base, singled, and after an error, Dunn hit a three-run homer to give South Bend a 7–5 edge. The see-saw evening continued in the Lassies' sixth when they rallied to lead 8–7 on a walk and homers off Rumsey by Ballingall and Jean Lovell. Cordes relieved and blanked the Blue Sox, while her teammates added single runs in the seventh and eighth to clinch the playoff verdict.[83]

Returning home, the South Benders talked about their lost opportunity for a title, because few thought the league would last. Most observers knew that money was short and new talent was thin. "The dearth of players was amply illustrated by the fact," observed Fort Wayne sports editor Bob Reed, "that pitchers and catchers were playing in the outfield and elsewhere."[84] The signs of the league's demise were evident to most players. "By 1954," recalled Wimp Baumgartner, who grounded out for Maxine Drinkwater to end the last-ever Sox inning, "the caliber of play wasn't there any more. Everyone knew it was the final season."[85]

"I suppose, even though I didn't want to believe the league would end," observed Sue Kidd, "I could see it coming."[86] In perhaps the most telling comment of all, Mary (Froning) O'Meara reflected, "We sort of knew this might be the end. The fans just weren't coming out."[87] Every season ends, and sooner or later for all ballplayers, the cheering stops. But after the glory fades, the players recount their tales of yesteryear.

In the meantime, Kalamazoo, the "underdog," won the league's last crown. During the other semifinal round, Fort Wayne defeated third-place Grand Rapids, but in unusual fashion. On Saturday night, the Chicks played the game under protest but beat the Daisies, 8–7. After that, Grand Rapids forfeited, at the insistence of manager Woody English on Sunday night (English and Fort Wayne's Bill Allington got into fisticuffs at home plate), and again on Monday. Despite winning on Saturday, English refused to let his team play again, because he objected to the league permitting the Daisies to replace their injured catcher with Rockford's star receiver, Ruth Richard.[88] In any event, Kalamazoo defeated Fort Wayne in five games, and June Peppas helped pitch and hit the Lassies to the circuit's final Shaughnessy Championship.[89]

Glory Wearing Blue

Today, due to several interesting books, the story is familiar, but when the American Girls Baseball League went out of business after the 1954 season, public memories of it faded away like yesterday's sunset. A few of the women, including Jean Faut, Betty Wagoner, Lib Mahon, and Betsy Jochum of South Bend, made their homes in league cities, but most onetime players returned to their families' homes. Some got married, and most found jobs, but all of them carried on with their lives. Because girls were not supposed to play *baseball*, it was as if the All-American League had never been born during World War II.

Much later, June Peppas and others began communicating with former teammates, and they launched a series of get-togethers with a national reunion in 1982 in Chicago, where the league originated in the mind of Philip Wrigley. The onetime athletes organized a Players Association; the National Baseball Hall of Fame recognized the women in 1988 as the highlight of a new exhibit of "Women in Baseball"; the AAGPBL Reunions became annual events; and the excellent 1992 movie, *A League of Their Own,* made millions aware that a women's baseball league once brought new excitement to the Midwest. Lo and behold, a considerable number of Americans and Canadians discovered they had mothers or grandmothers or aunts or cousins who used to play *professional baseball.*[90]

These athletic women took pride in their historic experiences. Peppas, the Lassies' heroine who pitched and won two games and batted .450 in the last Shaughnessy Championship, explained, "We were quite proud of our accomplishments and we hope the All-Americans will not be forgotten again. We were a proud lot."[91] "I wish we could turn back the clock and do it all again," remembered Betty Francis, calling it a "great time of my life."[92] "Baseball was very good to me," observed the Belles' Sophie Kurys, the league's all-time stolen base leader with 1,114 for her career, including a record 201 steals in 1946. "I'll never forget that time in my life."[93]

In fact, members of all the teams were talented, independent women who achieved feats on their fields of dreams that few would have believed possible, especially in the 1940s. For South Bend, dozens of young women, from famous stars to virtual unknowns, graced the All-American's short-skirted uniform in pastel blue. A "Who's Who" of the top Blue Sox stars over the years might feature Bonnie Baker, the photogenic catcher-turned-infielder from Regina, Saskatchewan; Betsy Jochum, the outfielder-turned-pitcher and ultimate team player from Cincinnati; Marge Stefani, the run-producing infielder from Detroit who later served as Sox chaperone; Sunny Berger, the Florida blonde who was the team's best underhand pitcher for two seasons; Dottie Schroeder, the pig-tailed, eye-catching shortstop from Sadorus, Illinois; Lois Florreich, the hard-hitting third baseman-outfielder from Webster Grove, Missouri; Pauline "Pinky" Pirok, the sparkplug infielder from Chicago; Lee Surkowski, the hard-hitting outfielder from Moose Jaw, Saskatchewan; Phyllis "Sugar" Koehn, the versatile outfielder-turned-hurler who grew up in Wisconsin; Elizabeth "Lib" Mahon, the outfielder from Greenville, South Carolina, who slugged her way to 400 career RBI; Senaida "Shoo Shoo" Wirth, the scurrying shortstop from Tampa who won the hearts of fans for years; Lillian "Lil" Faralla, the easygoing California sidearmer who was also a timely hitter; Shirley Stovroff, the strong-armed Illinois star who was the best Sox catcher of the overhand era; Betty Wagoner, the Missouri outfielder-pitcher who hit the ball all over the park; Jane "Jeep" Stoll, the clutch-hitting center fielder from Pennsylvania; Helen Filarski, the Michigan star who was one of the team's best third baseman; Charlene "Shorty" Pryer, the second baseman from California who led the loop in hitting and stolen bases in

1951; Gertie Dunn, the teenaged shortstop from Pennsylvania who grew up while the league was declining; Janet Rumsey, the curveballing Hoosier who became the best Sox pitcher in 1954; Sue Kidd, the laid-back country girl from Arkansas who became a good pitcher and a great team player; and last but hardly least, Jean Faut, the exceptional athlete who was the only South Bender ever voted Player of the Year, an honor she won twice.

Overall, Faut was the best player and one of the finest women to wear the Blue Sox uniform. She was also the greatest pitcher during the league's overhand years. South Bend's best-ever third baseman, Jean possessed one of the loop's strongest arms, but her pitch selection was second to none and her control was as good as any hurler could desire. Her lifetime won-lost record of 140–64 and ERA of 1.23 for eight seasons were outstanding figures for any professional baseball league.

Male and female ballplayers can get married, but only women can bear children — and Jean gave birth to her first son, Larry, in 1948, and her second son, Kevin, in 1957. The team's mainstay and most intense competitor, Faut became South Bend's superstar, a role model and a heroine for players and fans alike. At the same time, the sandy-haired blond with the friendly blue eyes and the winning smile endured a difficult marriage, a union that became more strained when her husband, Karl Winsch, managed the team starting in 1951. Jean left the game after the 1953 season, but not before she led the Blue Sox to Shaughnessy Championships in 1951 and 1952.

Because of her personal life as a mother, homemaker, and manager's wife, Faut's salvation came when she stepped on yesterday's ball fields. Baseball was her game. Speaking for almost every woman who received the opportunity to play in the league, Jean, with a faraway look in her eyes, reminisced, "Those were the best years of my life."[94] The 12-year run of the South Bend Blue Sox of the once-in-a-lifetime All-American Girls League gave more than 120 women, heroines all, the chance to live their baseball dreams, and years afterward, their remembered glory in blue evoked timeless moments of cherished camaraderie and fleeting fame.

Appendix:
South Bend Roster, 1943–1954

Players who appeared in one or more regular season games.

Ahrndt, Ellen: 1944
Applegren, Amy: 1953
Armstrong, Charlotte: 1944–1945
Arnold, Lou: 1948, 1950–1952
Baker, Bonnie: 1943–1950
Baker, Phyllis: 1954
Barr, Doris "Dodie": 1943–1945
Baumgartner, Mary "Wimp": 1950–1954
Bennett, Kay: 1943–1945
Berger, Margaret "Sunny": 1943–1944
Bird, Nalda: 1945
Bittner, Jaynne: 1947
Bleiler, Audrey: 1950–1952
Born, Ruth: 1943
Briggs, Rita: 1949
Briggs, Wilma: 1954
Brumfield, Delores "Dolly": 1947
Callaghan, Marge: 1949
Carey, Mary: 1954
Carver, Virginia: 1953
Chester, Bea: 1943
Christ, Dorothy: 1948
Clapp, Louise: 1954
Coben, Muriel: 1943
Cook, Donna: 1953
Cook, Doris: 1953
Cramer, Peggy: 1954
Crigler, Idona: 1947
D'Angelo, Josephine: 1943–1944
Dailey, Mary: 1950
Denton, Mona: 1946
DeShone, Nancy: 1948
Downs, Dorothea: 1945
Drinkwater, Maxine: 1954
Dunn, Gertie: 1951–1954
Dwojak, Loretta: 1944
Faralla, Lil: 1948–1951
Faut, Jean: 1946–1953
Filarski, Helen: 1948–1950

Florreich, Lois: 1943–1945
Francis, Betty: 1954
Froning, Mary: 1951–1954
Gacioch, Rose: 1944
Gallegos, Luisa: 1948
Ganote, Gertrude "Lefty": 1945
Garman, Ann: 1953
Gates, Barbara: 1953
Graham, Mary Lou: 1952–1953
Hageman, Johanna: 1943–1944
Hasham, Josephine: 1949
Headin, Irene: 1945
Hill, Betty (Westerman, 1952): 1946, 1952
Hoffman, Barbara: 1951–1952
Holda, Mary: 1943
Holle, Mabel: 1943
Hood, Marjorie: 1943
Hosbein, Marion: 1954
Jamieson, Janet: 1948
Jochum, Betsy: 1943–1948
Junor, Daisy: 1946–1948
Kelley, Jackie: 1947
Kemmerer, Beatrice Beatty: 1951
Keppel, Evelyn: 1947
Kidd, Sue: 1950–1954
Klosowski, Dolores: 1945
Koehn, Phyllis "Sugar": 1946–1948
Kotil, Arlene: 1951–1952
Krick, Jaynie: 1948–1949
Kruckel, Marie: 1948
Kunkel, Anna: 1950
Lenard, Jo: 1952–1953
Lester, Mary Lou: 1944
Luckey, Lillian: 1946
Luna, Betty: 1945–1947
MacLean, Lucella: 1943–1944
Mahon, Elizabeth "Lib": 1945–1952
Mahoney, Marie "Red": 1947–1948
Marshall, Theta "T": 1947

Matuzewski, Joan: 1953
Mayer, Alice: 1948
McCormick, Judy: 1954
McFadden, Betty: 1943
Metrolis, Norma: 1948–1949
Meyer, Alice (sometimes spelled Mayer): 1948
Mickelsen, Darlene: 1945
Montalbano, Rose: 1951–1953
Mueller, Dorothy "Dottie": 1950–1952
Naum, Dorothy "Dottie": 1946
Nordquist, Helen "Nordie": 1954
Norris, Donna: 1953
Ogden, Joanne: 1953
Panos, Vickie: 1944
Pearson, Dolly: 1953
Perkins, Joy: 1953
Pirok, Pauline "Pinky": 1945, 1947–1948
Pryer, Charlene "Shorty": 1949–1952
Romatowski, Jenny: 1946, 1949
Roth, Elaine: 1950
Rumsey, Janet: 1951–1954
Salisbury, Shirley Ann: 1953
Schroeder, Dottie: 1943–1945
Shafranis, Geraldine: 1943
Sopkovic, Catherine "Kay": 1945
Stefani, Marge: 1943–1947, Chaperone, 1949–1950

Stephens, Ruby: 1947–1948
Stoll, Jane "Jeep": 1949–1952
Stone, Lou: 1945
Stovroff, Shirley: 1948–1952
Surkowski, Anne: 1945
Surkowski, Lee: 1944–1946
Thompson, Viola: 1946–1947
Trezza, Betty "Moe": 1945–1946 (loaned from Racine, 1945, loaned from Fort Wayne, 1946)
Tronnier, Ellen: 1943
Vanderlip, Dolly: 1954
Vincent, Georgette "Jette" (Mooney, 1952, 1954): 1948–1952, 1954
Voyce, Inez: 1946
Wagoner, Betty: 1948–1954
Wanless, Betty: 1954
Wenzell, Marge: 1952–1953
Whiting, Betty: 1948–1950
Wiley, Janet "Pee Wee": 1950–1952
Williams, Ruth: 1947–1950
Wilson, Jean: 1943
Winch, Carol: 1951
Wirth, Senaida "Shoo Shoo": 1946–1951
Youngberg, Renae: 1953
Youngen, Lois: 1953–1954

Chapter Notes

Chapter 1

1. "Girls Softball Players Stir Fans' Interest," *South Bend Tribune* (hereafter cited as *SBT*), May 28, 1943.
2. William B. Mead, *Baseball Goes to War* (Washington, DC: Farragut Publishing Co., 1985), pp. 1–2, 17.
3. FDR's so-called "Green Light" letter from the front page of *The Sporting News* (hereafter cited as *TSN*), then considered "Baseball's Bible," in the issue of January 22, 1942.
4. "Pro Baseball in Favored in Gallup Poll," *SBT*, April 7, 1943.
5. *Total Baseball* (Wilmington, DE: Sports Media Publishing, 8th ed., 2004), p. 2421.
6. See Merrie Fidler, *The Origins and History of the All-American Girls Professional Baseball League* (Jefferson, NC: McFarland, 2006), p. 26, and message from Fidler, February 15, 2008.
7. "Wrigley and Rickey Buddies in Softball," *TSN*, February 25, 1943, p. 5, and "Cubs, Dodgers Act to Sponsor Girls' Softball," *Chicago Tribune*, February 18, 1943.
8. Fidler, *Origins and History of the AAGPBL*, pp. 71–72, and Adie Suehsdorf, "Sluggers in Skirts," *Los Angeles Times*, July 31, 1949.
9. Barbara Gregorich, *Women at Play: The Story of Women in Baseball* (New York: Harcourt, Brace, & Co., Harvest ed., 1993), p. 87.
10. This summary of the league's origins is based on Lois Browne, *Girls of Summer* (New York: Harper Collins, paperback ed., 1993), pp. 8–29; Fidler, *Origins and History of the AAGPBL*, pp. 30–36; Kenneth W. Sells to Harold Dailey, n.d. [circa 1949], in Dailey Notebooks, volume 1, pp. 20–20v [back of page], AAGPBL Files, Joyce Special Collections, Hesburgh Libraries of the University of Notre Dame; and Susan M. Cahn, "No Freaks, No Amazons, No Boyish Bobs," *Chicago History*, volume 21, number 1 (Spring, 1989), pp. 32–33.
11. Clipping from *Cincinnati Post*, April 22, 1943, in Jochum Scrapbook, in possession of Betsy Jochum (hereafter cited as Jochum Scrapbook), and Sheehan to Jochum, April 18, 1943, letter in Jochum's collection.
12. K.W. Sells to Jochum, April 22, 1943, letter in Jochum's collection.
13. See Fidler, *Origins and History of the AAGPBL*, p. 35, for a brief discussion of baseball's reserve clause and the All-American contracts.
14. "New Plan Up For Girls' League," *Cincinnati Enquirer*, March 8, 1943, clipping in Jochum Scrapbook.
15. Jim Sargent, "Betsy Jochum," posted on the web site for Bio-Project, sponsored by the Society for American Baseball Research (SABR): http://bioproj.sabr.org/bioproj.cfm?a=v&v=l&bid=2445&pid=19596.
16. See Fidler, *Origins and History of the AAGPBL*, p. 42, and "Racial Integration" in Gregory, *Women at Play*, p. 153.
17. Telephone interview with Betsy Jochum, November 25, 2007.
18. Browne, *Girls of Summer*, pp. 43–45, includes a discussion of the 1943 Charm School. Also see Sue Macy, *A Whole New Ball Game* (New York: Henry Holt and Co., 1993), pp. 8–16; and "A Guide for All American Girls," n.d., p. 1, copy in AAGPBL Files, Center for History (hereafter cited as CFH), South Bend, Indiana.
19. See the section about "Charm School" on the AAGPBL web site: http://www.aagpbl.org/league/charm.cfm; and see Macy, *A Whole New Ball Game*, pp. 14–18.
20. "Plan Welcome for Girls' Team," *SBT*, May 19, 1943.
21. Jim Sargent, "The Flint Flash: The Premier Base Stealer of the All-American Girls Baseball League," *Oldtyme Baseball News*, volume 8, number 4 (1997), pp. 30–31.
22. Letter from Betsy Jochum, December 18, 2007.
23. Letter from Betsy Jochum, November 14, 2007; message from Sophie Kurys, January 21, 2008; and message from Merrie Fidler, January 23, 2008.
24. William Cullen Fay, "Bonnie's the Belle of the Ball Game," *Sport*, May 1947, p. 97.
25. See Browne, *Girls of Summer*, pp. 40–41, and Macy, *A Whole New Ball Game*, pp. 18–21.
26. See "Girls Pro Softball Team Arrives" and see related stories in *SBT* on May 26–27, 1943.
27. The *SBT* for May 30, 1943, described Geraldine Shafranis as a "utility player."
28. Mina Costin, "Boys Have Gone to War; Now It's the All-American Girl," *SBT*, May 27, 1943.
29. See "Official Program," printed in red letters on a red background, showing a female pitcher hurling a ball underhanded. On the large white ball are the words, printed in blue letters, "All-American Girls Soft Ball League," and in the lower right hand corner, printed in red and blue letters, are the words, "Buy War Bonds"; Official Program for 1943, with the schedule and rosters inside, in Jochum Scrapbook, copy in author's possession.
30. "South Bend Girls Win Two Games," *SBT*, May 31, 1943.
31. "Rockford, South Bend Break Even," *SBT*, June 1, 1943.
32. Telephone interview with Betty (McFadden) Rusynyk, December 6, 2007.
33. "Pitcher Stars As Rockford Triumphs, 2–1," *SBT*, June 2, 1943.

34. "Racine Wins Pitching Duel to Take Lead," *SBT*, June 3, 1943. Geraldine Shafranis was 0-for-9 against Rockford and apparently went home.
35. "Blue Sox Still Singing the Blues," *SBT*, June 4, 1943.
36. "Blue Sox Beat Racine, 9–3, to End Slump," *SBT*, June 5, 1943.
37. John Palmer, *South Bend: Crossroads of Commerce* (Charleston, SC: Arcadia Publishing, 2003), pp. 8–9, 110–134.
38. See the movie pages in *SBT*, June 1, 1943, and "'Casablanca,' at the Earle, Topflight, Romantic Melo[drama]," *Washington Post*, February 6, 1943.
39. The posed picture of Perlick batting later appeared on the cover of *Allsports*, volume 4, number 2, June 1944.
40. See the variety of stories, including the movie section, in *SBT*, May 31-June 2, 1943.
41. Letter from Betsy Jochum, December 30, 2007.
42. "Rockford's Peaches to Meet South Bend Tonight," *Rockford Register-Republic* (hereafter cited as *RRR*), June 7, 1943.
43. "Rockford, Illinois: A Medium-Sized Manufacturing City," *Annals of the Association of American Geographers*, XLII, number 1 (March, 1952), pp. 1–2.
44. "South Bend Defeats Rockford by 5 to 2 Score," *Rockford Morning Star*, June 6, 1943.
45. "Blue Sox Hold First Place; Break Even with Rockford," *SBT*, June 8, 1943.
46. "Weather Again Stops Blue Sox," *SBT*, June 9, 1943.
47. "Players From Eight States and Canada on Racine Team," May 26, and "Racine Belles Arrive in Town; Will Practice Today," May 27, 1943, in *Racine Journal-Times* (hereafter cited as *RJT*).
48. "Belles Lose to South Bend in 12 Innings by 5–3 Score," *RJT*, June 10, 1943.
49. "Blue Sox Crush Racine, 10–3," *SBT*, June 11, 1943.
50. "Blue Sox Break Even; Hold First Place," *SBT*, June 12, 1943.
51. "Blue Sox and Rockford Break Even" and "Jim Costin Says," *SBT*, June 14, 1943.
52. Susan E. Johnson, *When Women Played Hardball* (Seattle: Seal press, 1994), pp. 152–156.
53. Howard F. Ohm and Leone G. Bryhan, eds., *The Wisconsin Blue Book, 1942* (Madison: State of Wisconsin, 1942), p. 434.
54. "Benders Score Five in First to Tip Comets, 6–5," *Kenosha Evening News* (hereafter cited as *KEN*), June 16, 1943.
55. "Comets and Blue Sox Break Even; Double-Header Sunday," *KEN*, June 19, 1943.
56. "Blue Sox Get 22 Walks; Beat Racine, 19–6," *SBT*, June 20, 1943.
57. "Blue Sox Down Racine ... Passes Playing Deciding Role in Each Game," *SBT*, June 21, 1943.
58. "Comets Unravel Blue Sox, 10–3," *KEN*, June 25, 1943.
59. Letter from Betsy Jochum, February 18, 2008.
60. Telephone interview with Lucella (MacLean) Ross, November 20, 2007.
61. See Judith A. Bellafaire, "the Women's Army Corps: A Commemoration of World War II Service," http://www.history.army.mil/brochures/wac/wac.htm.
62. "Free Tickets for Kenosha Fans Selecting All-Star Girls Teams," *KEN*, June 25, 1943.
63. "Softball Games Feature WAAC Rally Tonight," July 1, and "Wisconsin Girls Win, 16–0, on WAAC Program," July 2, 1943, in *Chicago Tribune*.
64. "Jim Costin Says" and "Blue Sox Fight to Retain Lead," *SBT*, July 2, 1943; "Nine Racine Girls on Team" includes the All-Star lineups, *RJT*, June 30, 1943; and interview with Betsy Jochum, November 10, 2007.
65. "Belles Beat South Bend, 4–3, to Regain All American Lead," *RJT*, July 3, 1943.
66. "Racine's Rally Beats Blue Sox, 13–8," *SBT*, July 4, 1943.
67. "Berger Loses to Rockford in Relief Role," *SBT*, July 8, 1943.
68. "Score Three in The Ninth After Two Are Out" and item in "Jim Costin Says," *SBT*, July 11, 1943.
69. "Blue Sox, Rockford Clash Tonight; Will Launch Second Half of Schedule," *SBT*, July 16, 1943.
70. "Comets Nip South Bend in First Tilt, 3–2; Yield in Second By 9–2," *KEN*, July 13, 1943.
71. See "All-American Girls Softball League Averages," marked "End of First Half of Season," copy in AAGPBL Files, CFH.
72. "Arrange Swaps to Aid Peaches," *RRR*, July 16, 1943.
73. Interview with Betsy Jochum, November 8, 2007.
74. Gals Catching On, in "Jim Costin Says," *SBT*, July 24, 1943.
75. Telephone interview with Betty (McFadden) Rusynyk, December 6, 2007.
76. Letter from Betsy Jochum, March 10, 2008.
77. See "Jim Costin Says" and "5,541 Fans Set Record for Attendance at Series," *SBT*, July 29, 1943, and telephone interview with Betty (McFadden) Rusynyk, December 6, 2007.
78. "Blue Sox Whip Kenosha, 10–8; Regain Lead," *SBT*, August 8, 1943.
79. "Blue Sox Win Twin Bill to Increase Lead," *SBT*, August 9, 1943.
80. Telephone interview with Lucella (MacLean) Ross, November 20, 2007.
81. Tom Hawthorn, "She was One Beauty of a Ball Player," [Canadian] *National Post*, December 22, 2003, copy in Baker File, National Baseball Hall of Fame Library, Cooperstown, New York; Browne, *Girls of Summer*, pp. 37–38.
82. "Blue Sox Beat Racine Twice," *SBT*, August 13, 1943.
83. Jenni Martin, *Safe at Home: A History of Softball in Saskatchewan* (Regina: Saskatchewan Sports Hall of Fame, 1997), pp. 37–39, 47–48; and telephone interview with Lucella (MacLean) Ross, November 20, 2007.
84. John M. Kovach, *Baseball in South Bend* (Charleston, SC: Arcadia Publishing, 2004), p. 94.
85. "Sox Handed 6–4 Victory," *SBT*, July 31, 1943.
86. "Sox Lead by Three Games," *SBT*, August 15, 1943.
87. "Blue Sox Are Home-Loving Regular Girls," *SBT*, August 13, 1943.
88. "Blue Sox Like Other Girls in Taste," *SBT*, August 16, 1943.
89. "Bauer Home Always Open to Blue Sox," *SBT*, August 17, 1943.
90. "Playing Ball Like Vacation, Sox Declare," *SBT*, August 18, 1943.
91. Letter from Mary (Holda) Elrod, December 26, 2008.
92. Telephone interview with Ruth Born, October 18, 2007.
93. See "Rome Declared Open City" and related stories, *SBT*, August 14, 1943.
94. Fidler, *Origins and History of the AAGPBL*, p. 36, and *SBT*, August 13, 1943.
95. "Jim Costin Says" and "Betsy Jochum Leads Hitters," both *SBT*, August 13, 1943.

96. "Comets Beat Blue Sox, 3–1," *SBT*, August 18, 1943.
97. "Comets Beat Blue Sox, 5–2, in 11th," *SBT*, August 19, 1943.
98. "Comets Win, 2–0, Tie Blue Sox for Lead," *SBT*, August 20, 1943.
99. "Sox Lose; Kenosha Wins; Race Tied," *SBT*, August 25, 1943.
100. "Blue Sox Trounced Twice," *SBT*, August 28, 1943.
101. "Blue Sox Divide; Trail By One Game," *SBT*, August 30, 1943.
102. "Sox Lose, 4–3; Comets Beaten, 3–1," *SBT*, August 31, 1943.
103. "Blue Sox Divide; So Does Kenosha," *SBT*, September 1, 1943.
104. "Kenosha Wins Second Half Pennant," *SBT*, September 2, 1943.
105. "Sox Players and Manager Meet Delays," *SBT*, September 5, 1943.
106. "Betsy Jochum Is Best Hitter," *SBT*, September 4, 1943.
107. "Racine Belles Get $228 Each," clipping dated September 23, 1943, in Jochum Scrapbook.
108. Telephone interview with Lucella (MacLean) Ross, November 20, 2007.

Chapter 2

1. "Schroeder's Worth," in "Jim Costin Says," *South Bend Tribune* (hereafter cited as *SBT*), July 14, 1944.
2. The league's name changed over the years, but the official schedule gave the title as All-American Girls Professional Ball League; see copy in folder for League: Schedule 1944, in AAGPBL Archives at the Center for History (hereafter cited as CFH), South Bend, Indiana; and see standings for "Girls' Pro League," in *SBT*, May 29, 1944.
3. "Jim Costin Says," *SBT*, April 9, 1944; and see Jochum Folder, AAGPBL Archives, CFH.
4. See Merrie Fidler, *The Origins and History of the All-American Girls Professional Baseball League* (Jefferson, NC: McFarland, 2006), pp. 43–46.
5. "M'Gann Named Blue Sox President," *SBT*, April 13, 1944.
6. Ken and Paula Weaver, who license and sell replica AAGPBL uniforms with the Players Association's approval, provided the uniform colors, and Carolyn Trombe also described the Millerettes' colors in *Dottie Wiltse Collins* (Jefferson, NC: McFarland, 2005), p. 59.
7. See "Jim Costin Says," April 16, "Jim Costin Says," May 5, "17-Day Home Stand to Open Blue Sox Card," May 7, "Jim Costin Says," May 10, and "Jim Costin Says," May 15, 1944, all in *SBT*.
8. "Jim Costin Says," *SBT*, May 18, 1944, and "120 Girls Open Ball League in Peru," unidentified clipping in AAGPBL Files, Baseball Hall of Fame Library, Cooperstown, NY.
9. "Blue Sox Given Five New Players," May 24, and "New Players Are Praised by Niehoff," *SBT*, May 26, 1944.
10. Pepper Paire Davis, *Dirt in the Skirt* (Bloomington, IN: AuthorHouse, 2009), p. 105.
11. The AAGPBL web site has a section summarizing the various changes in the game on the field and the rules as the league evolved from modified fast-pitch softball to baseball. See: http://www.aagpbl.org/league/rules.cfm
12. "Blue Sox Win in 10th, 5–4," *SBT*, May 28, 1944. In the end, the All-American League received too little support from local businessmen and newspapers in cities where men's minor league baseball was established. Thus, franchises in Milwaukee and Minneapolis lasted only one year. See Fidler, *Origins and History of the AAGPBL*, pp. 46–48. For Milwaukee's brief newspaper stories, see, for example, "Schnitts [Little Beers] Lose Two Contests," *Milwaukee Journal* (hereafter cited as *MJ*), May, 29, 1944.
13. "Blue Sox Win Two Games, 9–3, 13–0," *SBT*, May 29, 1944.
14. "Milwaukee Girls Win in 12th, 7–6," *MJ*, May 30, 1944.
15. Players like Betsy Jochum remembered the wartime travel on trains in day coaches, when traveling servicemen received priority seating. Interview with Jochum, November 2, 2008.
16. "Blue Sox Divide Before 2,252," *SBT*, May 31, 1944.
17. "Blue Sox Beat Racine, 3–1," *SBT*, June 2, 1944.
18. "Blue Sox Beat Chicks Twice Before 2,371," *SBT*, June 5, 1944.
19. "Minneapolis Whips Blue Sox, 7–5," *SBT*, June 6, 1944.
20. "Invaders Slash Inland," *SBT*, Evening Edition, June 6, 1944.
21. See Tom Brokaw, *The Greatest Generation* (New York: Random House, 1998), especially pages 17–99.
22. "Blue Sox Play Poorly Again to Lose, 5 to 2," *SBT*, June 13, 1944.
23. See "Schroeder Tops League Hitter and Base Thiefs," June 17, and *SBT*, June 15–17, 1944, for the war stories.
24. "New Blue Sox Lineup Whips Kenosha, 8 to 1," *SBT*, June 17, 1944.
25. "Blue Sox Trip Kenosha, 2–1, in 13 Innings," *SBT*, June 18, 1944.
26. "Blue Sox Are Rained Out of Sunday Bill," *SBT*, June 19, 1944.
27. "Blue Sox Get 7 in First to Win Easily, 7–1," *SBT*, June 20, 1944.
28. "Millerettes Give Blue Sox 2nd 7–1 Victory," *SBT*, June 21, 1944.
29. "Baker, Niehoff Are chased As Blue Sox Win," *SBT*, June 22, 1944.
30. "Blue Sox Beat Rockford, 3–0, for Six in Row," *SBT*, June 23, 1944.
31. "Blue Sox Smother Rockford, 10–1," *SBT*, June 25, 1944.
32. "Blue Sox Win Two for 10 in Row," *SBT*, June 26, 1944.
33. "Millerettes End Blue Sox Streak," *SBT*, June 27, 1944.
34. See Barbara Gregorich, *Women at Play: The Story of Women in Baseball* (New York: Harcourt Brace & Co., Harvest Books, 1993), pp. 114–116; and see "Bloomer Girls," in Leslie A. Heaphy and Mel A. May, eds., *Encyclopedia of Women and Baseball* (Jefferson, NC: McFarland, 2006), pp. 39–41.
35. Gregorich, *Women at Play*, p. 116.
36. See "Vickie Panos" on baseball-reference.com: http://www.baseball-reference.com/bullpen/Vickie_Panos
37. For the Royals, see Jenni Mortin, *Safe at Home: A History of Softball in Saskatchewan* (Regina, SA: Softball Saskatchewan, 1997), pp. 50–57.
38. Letter from Lee (Surkowski) Delmonico, October, 31, 2007.
39. Heaphy and May, *Encyclopedia of Women and Baseball*, p. 22; Angela C. Pancrazio, "Fans Still Cheer on Pitcher," *Arizona Republic*, August 11, 2005, and "Armstrong, Charlotte T.," *Arizona Republic*, December 6, 2008.

40. Interview with Ellen (Ahrndt) Proefrock, November 1, 2007, and letter from Proefrock, December 4, 2008; Heaphy and May, *Encyclopedia of Women and Baseball*, p. 9; and Herb Graffis, "Queens of Swat: Women's Softball is an Exciting Game and One of the Fastest-Growing Sports in the Country," *MJ*, August 27, 1944, copy in Proefrock's Scrapbook.
41. "Blue Sox Win at Racine," *SBT*, June 28, 1944.
42. Letter from Ellen (Ahrndt) Proefrock, December 4, 2008.
43. "Kenosha Cuts Lead of Blue Sox, *SBT*, June 29, 1944.
44. "Blue Sox Return to Meet Kenosha," *SBT*, June 30, 1944.
45. "Blue Sox Win, 5–1," *SBT*, July 1, 1944.
46. "Jim Costin Says," *SBT*, July 3, 1944.
47. "Blue Sox Break Even, Again Tied For Lead," *SBT*, July 10, 1944.
48. "Jim Costin Says," *SBT*, July 10, 1944.
49. "F.D.R. Willing to Run Again" and other war-related stories, *SBT*, July 11, 1944.
50. "Blue Sox Beat Rain to Gain on Kenosha," *SBT*, July 12, 1944.
51. "Blue Sox Win, 5–0; Tie Kenosha for Lead," *SBT*, July 13, 1944.
52. "Blue Sox Lose As Kenosha Divides," *SBT*, July 14 1944.
53. "Sox and Comets Lose," *SBT*, July 15, 1944.
54. "Blue Sox Win; Comets Retain Lead," *SBT*, July 16, 1944.
55. "Kenosha Captures First Half Title," *SBT*, July 17, 1944.
56. Judging Correctly, in "Jim Costin Says," *SBT*, July 18, 1944. For Niehoff's minor league record at Jersey City, see Lloyd Johnson and Miles Wolff, eds., *The Encyclopedia of Minor League Baseball* (2nd ed., Durham, NC: Baseball America, Inc., 1997), pp. 306, 314.
57. Letter from Betsy Jochum, October 12, 2010.
58. Letter from Ellen (Ahrndt) Proefrock, December 4, 2008.
59. "Rockford, Blue Sox Meet Here Tonight," *SBT*, July 19, 1944.
60. "All-American Girls Professional Ball League," by Howe News Bureau, July 19, 1944, copy in AAGPBL Archives, CFH.
61. "Jim Costin Says," *SBT*, July 19, 1944.
62. "Blue Sox Lose on Errors to Rockford in Opener, 6–4," *SBT*, July 20, 1944.
63. "Blue Sox, Peaches Play Two Tonight," *SBT*, July 21, 1944.
64. "Blue Sox Break Even," *SBT*, July 22, 1944.
65. "Blue Sox Take Another 1 to 0 Game," *SBT*, July 23, 1944.
66. "Blue Sox Win Two Games From Kenosha," *SBT*, July 24, 1944.
67. "Blue Sox Get Scare, But Win Again, 3–1," *SBT*, July 25, 1944.
68. "Barr and Blue Sox Defeat Kenosha, 1–0," *SBT*, July 26, 1944.
69. "Blue Sox Win Seventh 4–2," *SBT*, July 27, 1944.
70. "First Placers Are Last in Team Hitting," *SBT*, July 28, 1944.
71. "Blue Sox Beat Rockford For 8th in Row, 2–0," *SBT*, July 29, 1944.
72. "Peaches End Blue Sox Streak, 5–0." *SBT*, July 30, 1944.
73. "Blue Sox Win, 2–1; Remain in Lead," *SBT*, August 4, 1944.
74. "Blue Sox, Racine Divide Two Games," SBT, August 8, 1944.
75. "Gacioch Stars as Blue Sox Win, 1–0," *SBT*, August 11, 1944.
76. "Sox Divide," *SBT*, August 14, 1944.
77. "Comets Rally in Ninth to top Blue Sox, 2–1," *SBT*, August 20, 1943.
78. "Blue Sox, Chicks Each Win Two Games," *SBT*, August 2, 1944.
79. On the Millerettes losing their home field, see Fidler, *The Origins and History of the AAGPBL*, p. 46; and "Jim Costin Says," *SBT*, July 23, 1944.
80. "Blue Sox Lose, 2–1, in 12th to Minneapolis" and "Jim Costin Says," *SBT*, August 22, 1944.
81. "Blue Sox Win, 1–0; Chicks Beaten Twice," *SBT*, August 23, 1944.
82. "Blue Sox Win to Gain As Chicks Lose Again," *SBT*, August 24, 1944.
83. "Millerettes Lose Again to Bennett, 3 to 1," *SBT*, August 25, 1944.
84. Telephone interview with Lucella (MacLean) Ross, January 24, 2011.
85. For the league's 1944 statistics, see "All-American Girls Professional Ball League," in *Major League Baseball: 1945* (Racine, WI: Whitman Publishing, 1945), pp. 136–140.
86. Season's End, in "Jim Costin Says," *SBT*, September 7, 1944.
87. "Sox Beat Chicks," *SBT*, August 26, 1944.
88. "Chicks Win From Blue Sox, 3 to 1," and "Girls Get Rough," in "Jim Costin Says," *SBT*, August 27, 1944.
89. "Jim Costin Says," *SBT*, August 29, 1944.
90. "Chicks Win; Now Lead By Four Games," *SBT*, August 29, 1944.
91. "Chicks Blank Blue Sox Again, 2–0," *SBT*, August 30, 1944.
92. "Chicks Blank Blue Sox, 4–0, in 10 Innings," *SBT*, August 31, 1944.
93. "Comets Deal Blue Sox Fifth Straight Loss," *SBT*, September 1, 1944.
94. "Blue Sox End Home Stay By Losing, 2 to 0," *SBT*, September 2, 1944.
95. "Yanks Near Germany" and other war-related news, *SBT*, September 1, 1944.
96. "Faltering Sox Lose Seventh Straight, 2–1," *SBT*, September 3, 1944.
97. "Belles Lose Two to Kenosha Monday, *Racine Journal-Times*, September 5, 1944.
98. "Blue Sox Win Second Place in Pro League," *SBT*, September 5, 1944.
99. "Rockford Beats Blue Sox On Triple in Ninth, 2–1," *SBT*, September 6, 1944.
100. "Jim Costin Says," SBT, September 6, 1944.
101. "Morris Beats Blue Sox in No-Hitter, 9–0," *SBT*, September 7, 1944, and "80,000 Watch Peaches' Games," *Rockford Register-Republic*, September 7, 1944.
102. "Chicks Capture Pro Girls' Title," *SBT*, September 18, 1944, and see "U.S. Patrols Probe Germany" and related war stories in the same day's *Tribune*.
103. "Jim Costin Says," *SBT*, September 7, 1944.
104. See "All-American Girls Professional Ball League," by Howe News Bureau, Chicago, August 30, 1944, copy in AAGPBL Files, CFH, and "49,296 Fans Paid to See Blue Sox at Home in 1944," *SBT*, September 8, 1944.
105. Best Girls' Team, Here's the Team, and Omitting Schroeder, in "Jim Costin Says," *SBT*, September 9, 1944.
106. George Berkowitz, "Casey Is A Lady!" *MJ*, August

27, 1944. The same story appeared in the *Atlanta Constitution* and *Los Angeles Times*, among other newspapers.

Chapter 3

1. "Blue Sox and League Both Stronger, M'Manus States," *South Bend Tribune* (hereafter cited as *SBT*), May 22, 1945.
2. The league's name changed over the years, but publicity director Marie Keenan, in "All American Girls Professional Ball League," used that title for the official summary of the 1944 season, as printed in *Major League Baseball: 1945* (Racine, WI: Whitman Publishing, 1946), p. 129. However, the *Tribune* usually called it the "Girls' Pro League"; see "Jim Costin Says," *SBT*, February 8, 1945.
3. Merrie Fidler, *The Origins and History of the All-American Girls Professional Baseball League* (Jefferson, NC: McFarland, 2006), pp. 69–85.
4. See "Make Plans for Girls' League in 1945," *SBT*, November 16, 1944, and "League History" on the AAGPBL web site: http://www.aagpbl.org/league/history.cfm
5. See Schedule Folder in AAGPBL Files, Center for History (hereafter cited as CFH), South Bend, Indiana.
6. Fidler, *Origins and History of the AAGPBL*, pp. 69–76.
7. "Girls' Baseball: A feminine Midwest league opens its third professional season," *Life*, June 4, 1945, pp. 63–66.
8. "Snyder, Niehoff, Hudlin, Cooper to Pilot in South," *Syracuse Herald-Journal*, February 9, 1945.
9. "McManus Agrees to Terms as 1945 Blue Sox Manager," *SBT*, March 19, 1945. For background, see "Martin Joseph (Marty) McManus," *The Sporting News*, April 21, 1933, copy in McManus File, National Baseball Hall of Fame Library, Cooperstown, New York.
10. See "Jim Costin Says" on Carey's ideas for curbing base stealing, *SBT*, April 15, 1945.
11. "Blue Sox Get 55-Game Home Card," *SBT*, April 5, 1945.
12. "Jim Costin Says," April 29, and "Three Girls Out of 17 Win Chance in Blue Sox Trials," April 30, 1945, both *SBT*.
13. See "Jim Costin Says," May 7 and 10, 1945, both *SBT*.
14. James N. Giglio, *Musial: From Stash to Stan the Man* (Columbia: University of Missouri Press, 2001), pp. 125–132.
15. Fidler, *Origins and History of the AAGPBL*, p. 35.
16. Carey to Jochum, February 28, 1945, copy in Jochum Files.
17. Carey to Jochum, April 17, Carey to Jochum, April 30, 1945, copies in Jochum Files, and letter from Betsy Jochum, March 8, 2009.
18. Telephone interview with Jean Faut, November 8, 2008.
19. See records of Harold Dailey, "South Bend Blue Sox, Inc. / Statement Operations / Season 1944," in Dailey Notebooks, vol. 1, p. 56, in the AAGPBL Files, Joyce Sports Collection, Hesburgh Libraries of the University of Notre Dame.
20. "Peace Ratified in Berlin," *Chicago Tribune* (hereafter cited as *CT*), May 9, 1945.
21. "Girl Players Open Chicago Training Camp," May 9, "Eight New Players in Blue Sox Camp," May 10, and "Blue Sox Have 'One-Man' Hill Staff—She's Miss Barr," May 12, 1945, all *SBT*.
22. See Barbara Gregorich, *Women at Play: The Story of Women in Baseball* (New York: Harcourt, Brace & Co., Harvest Ed., 1993), pp. 117–118.
23. Kay Sopkovic to Carolyn Odell, Odell Letters, n.d. [May 1946], AAGPBL Files, Center for History, South Bend, Indiana (copy in author's possession). Sopkovic explained that she "really never was a catcher."
24. New Starting Time, in "Jim Costin Says," *SBT*, May 21, 1945.
25. Jim Costin, "Blue Sox and League Both Stronger, M'Manus States," *SBT*, May 22, 1945.
26. They're Off, in "Jim Costin Says," *SBT*, May 23, 1945.
27. "Blue Sox Open 1945 Season Tonight," May 23, and "Blue Sox Lose Opener in 10th," May 24, 1945, both *SBT*.
28. "Nalda Bird, 17, Wins in Sox Debut, 12–2," *SBT*, May 25, 1945,
29. "Blue Sox Game Is Rained Out," *SBT*, May 26, 1945.
30. "Betty Luna and Blue Sox Beat Kenosha, 8–0," *SBT*, May 27, 1945.
31. "Blue Sox and Chicks Rained Out on Sunday," *SBT*, May 28, 1945.
32. For information on Grand Rapids, see Willis F. Dunbar and George S. May, *Michigan: A History of the Wolverine State* (third rev. ed., Grand Rapids: Eerdmans Publishing Co., 1995), pp. 143, 339–401, 484, 485; and Gordon Olson, "A Short History of Grand Rapids, Michigan," at http://www.ci.grand-rapids.mi.us/index.pl?page_id=2398.
33. Lois Browne, *Girls of Summer* (New York: Harper Collins, Harper Perennial Ed., 1993), p. 92.
34. The *Tribune* did not publish on holidays, so all three games were covered in "Blue Sox, Fort Wayne Open Series Tonight," *SBT*, May 31, 1945.
35. "Blue Sox and Fort Wayne Play Tonight," *SBT*, June 1, 1945.
36. For the Chicago League, see http://www.sportsartifacts.com/otherleag.html#anchor776559. Lucella Ross remembered signing with the Chicks of the Chicago League for $85 in 1946, after she returned from two seasons in South Bend and played for the Edmonton Army and Navy Pats in 1945; telephone interview with Lucella (MacLean) Ross, November 20, 2007.
37. Charlene Pryor to Carolyn Odell, Odell Letters, April 5, 1947.
38. Pepper Paire called the uniforms "bubble-gum pink" in her memoir, *Dirt in the Skirt* (Bloomington, IN: AuthorHouse, 2009), p. 143.
39. "Blue Sox Win Two; Take Lead," *SBT*, June 2, 1945.
40. "Bad Weather Continues to 'Jinx' League," June 3, and "Cold Weather Again Keeps Blue Sox Idle," June 4, 1945, both *SBT*.
41. "Blue Sox Ask for Waivers on Doris Barr," *SBT*, June 5, 1945.
42. "Blue Sox Beat Racine, 9–3," *SBT*, June 9, 1945.
43. "Rain Halts Blue Sox at Fort Wayne," *SBT*, June 11, 1945.
44. Letter from Betsy Jochum, June 28, 2009.
45. See "Fort Wayne History," at: http://www.cityoffortwayne.org/index.php?Itemid=247&id=99&option=com_content&task=view
46. Carolyn M. Trombe, *Dottie Wiltse Collins: Strikeout Queen of the All-American League* (Jefferson, NC: McFarland, 2005), p. 76.
47. "Rain Halts Blue Sox at Fort Wayne," *SBT*, June 10, 1945.

48. "Blue Sox Lose Twice; Three Players Hurt," June 11, and Here and There, in "Jim Costin Says," June 12, 1945, both *SBT*.

49. "Daisies Capture Series Final, 8–2," *Fort Wayne Journal-Gazette*, June 12, 1945, and "Daisies Score 7 in 7th; Beat Blue Sox, 8–2," *SBT*, June 12, 1945.

50. "Blue Sox Beat Racine In Opener, 4–0," *SBT*, June 14, 1945.

51. "Blue Sox Defeat Racine, 3–1," *SBT*, June 16, 1945.

52. "Blue Sox Play Peaches in Daylight Game," *SBT*, June 17, 1945.

53. "Blue Sox Break Even; Bird Injured," *SBT*, June 18, 1945.

54. "Blue Sox Get 19 Hits to Win, 12–2," *SBT*, June 19, 1945.

55. "Poor Base Running Beats Blue Sox, 6–3," *SBT*, June 20, 1945.

56. "Blue Sox Take First Place," *SBT*, June 23, 1945.

57. "Kenosha Fans Cheer Bird's Courage," *SBT*, June 24, 1945.

58. "Blue Sox Ask for Waivers On Doris Barr," *SBT*, June 5, 1945.

59. "Season—1945," Dailey Notebooks, volume 1, p. 72.

60. "Chicks, Blue Sox Meet Here Tonight," *SBT*, June 27, 1945.

61. "Wisniewski and Chicks Beat Blue Sox, 11–1," *SBT*, June 28, 1945.

62. "Blue Sox Shade Chicks in Duel, 4–2," *SBT*, June 29, 1945.

63. "Chicks Defeat Blue Sox, 5–0," *SBT*, June 30, 1945.

64. "Swap Schroeder, Florreich," *SBT*, June 30, 1945.

65. See "Season 1945," under notes for meeting on June 30, 1945, in Dailey Notebooks, vol. 1, pp. 72, 74.

66. Browne, *Girls of Summer*, pp. 105–106.

67. Letter from Betsy Jochum, January 8, 2010.

68. "Florreich Stars As Comets Win, 2–1" *SBT*, July 1, 1945.

69. "Blue Sox Win Again, 7–2; Take Third," *SBT*, July 3, 1945.

70. "2,585 See Blue Sox, Chicks Divide," *SBT*, July 5, 1945.

71. "Chicks Beat Blue Sox, 3–0," *SBT*, July 7, 1945.

72. Jim Sargent, "Elizabeth Mahon," on SABR's Bio-Project site: http://bioproj.sabr.org/bioproj.cfm?a=v&v=l&bid=2449&pid=19600; and *South Carolina Athletic Hall of Fame: Program, 2005* (Columbia, SC: South Carolina Athletic Hall of Fame, 2005), p. 16.

73. Here and There, in "Jim Costin Says," *SBT*, May 27, 1945. Costin stated that Bird was a pianist, singer, poet, and composer, "her latest of the latter type being 'The All-American Girl,' the 'marching song' of the girls' pro league players."

74. Pepper Paire Davis, *Dirt in the Skirt*, pp. 143–145.

75. Bird's comments are on the back of her Fritsch baseball card.

76. Letter from Anne (Surkowski) Deyotte, October 7, 2007, and "Twin Bill to Even Series," n.d. [1944], "MacDonalds Recall Years of Royals," *Moose Jaw Herald-Times*, December 8, 1977, and "Moose Jaw Women Inducted into Hall," n.d. [1998], copies enclosed with Deyotte's letter, and message dated May 7, 2009, from Jane Shury, President of Saskatchewan's Baseball Hall of Fame.

77. League statistics for 1945 were published in *Major League Baseball: 1946* (Racine, WI: Whitman Publishing, 1946), pp. 141–152; also see "AAGPBL Questionnaire" and AAGPBL Personal Summary Pages, copies acquired from Lucretia Allen, Betty (Luna) Hill's niece, and letter from another niece, Faye Day, n.d. [2010].

78. See "Pirok, Pauline 'Pinky'" in Leslie A. Heaphy and Mel A. May, eds., *Encyclopedia of Women and Baseball* (Jefferson, NC: McFarland, 2006), pp. 230–231, and AAGPBL Records for 1945, CFH.

79. See "Koehn, Phyllis 'Sugar,'" in Heaphy and May, *Encyclopedia of Women and Baseball*, p. 159.

80. "Blue Sox Beat Racine Again, 6–0," and "Helping The Hitters," in "Jim Costin Says," *SBT*, July 12, 1945.

81. "Racine, Led by Carey, Beats Blue Sox, 2–1," *SBT*, July 13, 1945.

82. "First and Last," in "Jim Costin Says," *SBT*, July 15, 1945.

83. "Rockford, Blue Sox Clash Tonight," *SBT*, July 17, 1945.

84. "Blue Sox Beat Peaches, 8–4," *SBT*, July 21, 1945.

85. "Blue Sox Lose Ninth in Row, 3–1," *SBT*, July 29, 1945.

86. "Blue Sox, Fort Wayne Break Even," *SBT*, July 30, 1945.

87. "Blue Sox Face Fort Wayne Tonight," *SBT*, July 31, 1945.

88. "Blue Sox, Rained Out, Play 2 Tonight," *SBT*, August 1, 1945.

89. "Blue Sox Beat Daisies Twice, 4–2, 3–0," *SBT*, August 2, 1945.

90. "Blue Sox Drop to 5th Place; Home Tonight," *SBT*, August 6, 1945.

91. See *SBT* for August 8–11, 1945, including "Hiroshima 60 Percent Destroyed"; Pauline Maier, et.al., *Inventing America: A History of the United States* (New York: W.W. Norton, 2nd ed., 2006), pp. 785–787.

92. Max Carey, "All American Girls Baseball League," in *Major League Baseball: 1946*, pp. 138–140 [italics in original]; and "Season 1945," Dailey Notebooks, vol. 1, p. 70.

93. "Blue Sox Keep Fourth Place Losing, 13 to 0," *SBT*, August 19, 1945.

94. "Blue Sox Break Even But Gain On Racine," *SBT*, August 20, 1945.

95. "Blue Sox, Belles to Play Two Tonight," *SBT*, August 23, 1945.

96. "Blue Sox Beaten Twice By Racine," *SBT*, August 24, 1945.

97. "Blue Sox Win Two, 4–3, 7–2," *SBT*, August 25, 1945.

98. "Jim Costin Says," *SBT*, August 25, 1945, and letters from Anne (Surkowski) Deyotte, May 22, 2009, and Betsy Jochum, June 1, 2009.

99. "Blue Sox Win Two; Tie for 4th Place," *SBT*, August 31, 1945.

100. "Blue Sox Lose, 1–0, Then Tie, 1–1," *SBT*, September 1, 1945.

101. "Daisies Beat Blue Sox, 3–2," *SBT*, September 2, 1945.

102. "Applegren Blanks South Bend," *Rockford Register-Republic* (hereafter cited as *RRR*), September 3, 1945.

103. "To Meet Chicks in Playoffs," *RRR*, September 4, 1945.

104. "Blue Sox Divide; Racine in Playoffs," *SBT*, September 4, 1945.

105. "Season—1945," Dailey Notebooks, volume 1, p. 72.

106. "Belles Drew 70,357 ... Muskegon and Peoria May Join to Make 8-Team Loop in 1946," *Racine Journal-Times*, September 13, 1945.

107. Dottie Schroeder to Carolyn Odell, Odell Letters, January 6, 1946.

Chapter 4

1. "Well Done, Chet" in *South Bend Tribune* (hereafter cited as *SBT*), September 4, 1946.
2. Max Carey, "All American Girls Baseball League," in *Major League Baseball: 1947* (Racine: Whitman Publishing Co., 1947), n.p., section following p. 128.
3. John M. Kovach, *Baseball in South Bend* (Charleston, SC: Arcadia Publishing, 2004), p. 78.
4. Pauline Maier, et.al. *Inventing America: A History of the United States* (New York: W.W. Norton, 2nd ed., 2006), pp. 791–792.
5. Gertrude Ganote to Carolyn Odell, Odell Letters, February 15, 1946, indicated she was getting married on March 19 and would not return; AAGPBL Files, Center for History (hereafter cited as CFH), South Bend, Indiana.
6. Blue Sox Sign Up 7 Regulars of 1945 Team, *SBT*, April 2, 1946.
7. "Each Girl Team to Carry Five Pitchers," *SBT*, April 5, 1946.
8. The diamond dimensions were listed in the *Official Girls' Baseball Rules / Adopted By The All-American Girls Baseball League*, pp. 1–3, copy in AAGPBL Files, CFH, and noted in "Jim Costin Says," *SBT*, August 2, 1946. The men's softball distances were 55-foot base paths and the women's base paths were 70 feet. Both used the same 43-foot mound distance, but the women's baseball was 11 inches in circumference and the men's softball 12 inches.
9. "Evolution Of The Ball Size Used in All American Girls Base Ball League from 1943 to 1949, and Diamond Changes," Dailey Notebooks, volume 1, p. 32v, AAGPBL Files, Hesburgh Libraries of the University of Notre Dame.
10. See Carey, "All American Girls Baseball League" [n.p.]. Also, Carey confirmed the distances and ball size explained by Costin in note 8 (above), including the 70-foot base paths.
11. Anna May Hutchison, Information Sheet, n.d., copy in AAGPBL Files, CFH.
12. Telephone interview with Joyce (Hill) Westerman, October 18, 2010.
13. Interview with Jean Faut, October 17, 2009.
14. Telephone interview with Erma Bergmann, November 7, 2009.
15. See "Pascagoula: Profile and Trivia": http://www.cityofpascagoula.com/profiletrivia.htm.
16. See Max Carey's letter to players and girls trying out, February 1, 1946, with a copy of the "Rules of Conduct for Players" and a "Special Training Bulleting," in Jochum Scrapbook.
17. "14 Directors Due at Girls' Spring Camp," May 2, and "All-American Girls Baseball Loop Ends Spring Training," SBT, May 3, 1946; Lois Browne, *Girls of Summer* (New York: Harper Collins, Paperback ed., 1993), pp. 108–110; interview with Jean Faut, October 17, 2009; and "Baseball: Babette Ruths," *Newsweek*, July 29, 1946, p. 68.
18. See "Jim Costin Says," *SBT*, August 8, 1946, indicating Pirok was playing for the Patriarchy Bloomer Girls of Chicago's National Girls Baseball League.
19. "Blue Sox Given 12 New Players," *SBT*, May 5, 1946; and interview with Jean Faut, October 17, 2009, who recalled what happened to Shuman.
20. "New Blue Sox Team Arrives in Home Town," *SBT*, May 20, 1946.
21. See Jim Sargent, "Jean Faut: The All-American League's Greatest Overhand Pitcher," in *Ragtyme Sports* (March, 1996), pp. 30–38, and interviews with Faut, October 17, October 31, and December 4, 2009.
22. "Betty Luna Rejoins Blue Sox in 1946," *SBT*, May 21, 1946.
23. Letter from Betsy Jochum, October 6, 2009.
24. "Blue Sox Win Opener in 12th," *SBT*, May 23, 1946.
25. "Triple Play Aids Blue Sox in 6–0 Victory," *SBT*, May 24, 1946.
26. "Daisies Whip Blue Sox, 7–3," *SBT*, May 25, 1946.
27. "Blue Sox in Playland Park Tonight" and "Jim Costin Says," *SBT*, May 26, 1946.
28. "5,328 See Blue Sox Lose First [at Playland], 7–0," *SBT*, May 27, 1946.
29. "Chicks Trounce Blue Sox Again, 4–1," *SBT*, May 28, 1946.
30. "Chicks' Rally Defeats Blue Sox in 10th, 5–4," and "Jim Costin Says," *SBT*, May 29, 1946.
31. "Kabick Downs Blue Sox, 7–3," *Grand Rapids Press*, May 30, 1946.
32. "4,676 See Blue Sox Beat Kenosha Twice," *SBT*, May 31, 1946.
33. "Bases on Balls Give Blue Sox 6–5 Victory," *SBT*, June 2, 1946.
34. "Blue Sox End Chick Streak in 17–5 Rout," *SBT*, June 5, 1946.
35. "Comets Shade South Bend in Ninth Inning, 8–7," *Kenosha Evening News*, June 6, 1946.
36. "Luckey, South Bend Girl, Wins for Sox," *SBT*, June 9, 1944.
37. "Betty Luna Rejoins Blue Sox for 1946," *SBT*, May 21, 1946.
38. "Jim Costin Says," *SBT*, June 9, 1946.
39. "Blue Sox Beat Peaches Twice, 4–1, 5–2," *SBT*, June 10, 1946.
40. "Rockford Trounces Blue Sox, 10–4," *SBT*, June 11, 1946.
41. "Faye Dancer Hurls Daisies to 5–3 Victory," *SBT*, June 14, 1946.
42. In early 1947, Charlene "Shorty" Pryer complained about Fort Wayne's new "purplish-rose" uniforms; see Pryer to Carolyn Odell, Odell Letters, April 5, 1947.
43. "Whip Daisies By 8–1, 4–3 Scores," *SBT*, June 15, 1946.
44. "Stefani Stars in 3rd Straight Home Victory," *SBT*, June 16, 1946.
45. "Blue Sox Divide with Rockford," *SBT*, June 17, 1946.
46. See "Rain Keeps Blue Sox Idle; Play Double Bill Tonight," June 18, and "Peoria Girls and Blue Sox Play Tonight," *SBT*, June 19, 1946.
47. "Blue Sox Win in 9th, 4–3, on 'Luckey' Hit," *SBT*, June 23, 1946.
48. "Jim Costin Says," *SBT*, June 23, 1946.
49. See "Peoria: History": http://www.city-data.com/us-cities/The-Midwest/Peoria-History.html; and "Podcast #8, "Peoria: A Brief History": http://www.atlaspodcasts.org/podcast-peoria/.
50. "Blue Sox Get Even Break in Peoria Debut," *SBT*, June 24, 1946.
51. "Blue Sox Beat Peoria, 3–1, to Gain On Chicks," *SBT*, June 25, 1946.
52. "Blue Sox Win From Peoria Wings, 10–4," *SBT*, June 26, 1946.
53. See "History of Muskegon": http://www.muskegon-mi.gov/community/history/History_of_Muskegon.asp. Also for background, see Alice Prescott Kyes, *Romance of Muskegon* (Muskegon, MI: Muskegon Heritage Association, 1974), esp. p. 162.

54. "Muskegon Tops Blue Sox, 8 to 3," *SBT*, June 27, 1946.
55. "Blue Sox Top Lassies, 4–1, to Even Series," *SBT*, June 30, 1946.
56. "Blue Sox Capture Muskegon Series," *SBT*, July 3, 1946.
57. "6,745 See Blue Sox, Racine Break Even," *SBT*, July 5, 1946.
58. "Racine Beats Blue Sox, 7–0," *SBT*, July 6, 1946.
59. "Luna and Blue Sox Defeat Racine, 8–0," *SBT*, July 7, 1946.
60. Chet Grant, "Girls' Baseball," *South Bend Tribune Magazine*, Sunday, August 15, 1954, p. 9.
61. For example, see Inez Voyce to Carolyn Odell, in Odell Letters, November 14, 1946.
62. D.C.P. Grant, "I Was A Girls' Baseball Manager" [n.d.], pp. 1–6, copy in AAGPBL Files, Special Collections, Hesburgh Libraries.
63. "350,000 See All-American Girls' Games," *Chicago Daily Tribune*, July 21, 1946.
64. Grant, "Girls' Baseball Manager," p. 5.
65. Bonnie Baker to Carolyn Odell, Odell Letters, December 1, 1945.
66. For classic examples, see the picture of a smiling Baker wearing her chest protector and glove, with a face mask beside her on the ground, and posing in crouched position, as featured in William Cullen Fay's "Bonnie's the Belle of the Ball Game," *Sport*, May 1947, pp. 26–28, 97–98, and see the smiling Baker in Muskegon uniform, posing in a slightly bent-over position with hands on thighs, in Tom Hawthorn's "She was one beauty of a ballplayer," *National Post* [of Canada], December 22, 2003, copies of both articles in Baker File, National Baseball Hall of Fame Library, Cooperstown, New York.
67. See "Player of the Year—1946," and league statistics in *Major League Baseball: 1947*, copy in CFH.
68. See Sargent, "Elizabeth Mahon," on SABR's Bio-Project: http://bioproj.sabr.org/bioproj.cfm?a=v&v=l&bid=2449&pid=19600. The Mahon story is based in part on my 1997 interviews with Lib, various letters, and material in the AAGPBL files at the CFH.
69. See Sargent, "Betsy Jochum," on SABR's Bio-Project: http://bioproj.sabr.org/bioproj.cfm?a=v&v=l&bid=2445&pid=19596.
70. See "Luna (Hill), Betty Jean," in W.C. Madden, *The Women of the All-American Girls Professional Baseball League: A Biographical Dictionary* (Jefferson, NC: McFarland, 1997), p. 151.
71. Marge Lukes, "DG [Downers Grove, IL] woman remembers her glory days," n.d. [1992] article in Koehn File, Baseball Hall of Fame Library.
72. Telephone interview with Inez Voyce, August 28, 2009.
73. Jane Burns, "They threw balls like girls in [the] '40s, and got paid for it," newspaper clipping dated June 28, 1992, copy in Voyce File, Baseball Hall of Fame Library.
74. See "Junor, Daisy," in Leslie A. Heaphy and Mel A. May, eds., *Encyclopedia of Women and Baseball* (Jefferson, NC: McFarland, 2006), pp. 149–150.
75. Carmen Pauls, who interviewed Junor, wrote "Memories of an All-American Girl," on AAGPBL web site: http://www.aagpbl.org/articles/general.cfm?ID=4.
76. For examples, see Elden Auker with Tom Keegan, *Sleeper Cars and Flannel Uniforms: A Lifetime of Memories From Striking Out the Babe to Teeing It Up with the President* (Chicago: Triumph Books, 2001), pp. 41–47, 123–132, and Roger Kahn, *The Boys of Summer* (New York: Harper & Row, 1971), pp. 125–132.
77. Telephone interview with Jean Faut, September 16, 2009.
78. "Jim Costin Says," *SBT*, May 15, 1946, and "Senaida Wirth, Rookie of the Year," copy in Wirth File at Baseball Hall of Fame Library. Also see "Girls' Teams Will Meet for League Lead," in *SBT*, July 28, 1946, indicating Baker led the league with a .333 average, leaving her .026 above Wirth.
79. Quoted by Sue Macy, *A Whole New Ball Game: The Story of the All-American Girls Professional Baseball League* (New York: Henry Holt & Co., 1993), p. 74.
80. Telephone interview with Carolyn Odell, June 23, 2009.
81. "3,546 See Blue Sox Win Two Games," *SBT*, July 22, 1946.
82. Grant, "I Was A Girls' Baseball Manager," pp. 6–7.
83. "Jim Costin Says" discussed the topic in Letter Writers, *SBT*, July 24, 1946.
84. "Blue Sox Beaten Again By Rockford, 5–3," *SBT*, August 2, 1946.
85. "Blue Sox Beat Peaches, 3–2," *SBT*, August 3, 1946.
86. See "Jim Costin Says," *SBT*, August 5, 1946.
87. "Blue Sox Win Two; Gain On Leaders," *SBT*, August 7, 1946.
88. "Morris Beats Betty Luna in Rockford, 4–2," *SBT*, August 8, 1946.
89. "Blue Sox Lose Two to Peaches," *SBT*, August 9, 1946.
90. Connie Wisniewski, the league's Player of the Year in 1945, was one of the underhand pitchers who could not adjust to hurling sidearm or overhand; see Merrie Fidler, *The Origins and History of the All-American Girls Professional Baseball League* (Jefferson, NC: McFarland, 2006), p. 209, 212.
91. "Blue Sox Beat Muskegon Twice, 1–0, 11–5," *SBT*, August 26, 1946.
92. "Blue Sox and Racine Clash Tonight in Playland Park," *SBT*, August 27, 1946.
93. "4,127 See Blue Sox Beat Racine, 2–0," *SBT*, August 28, 1946.
94. "Racine Evens Blue Sox Series, 2–0," and "Jim Costin Says," *SBT*, August 29, 1946.
95. "Blue Sox Win; Close in On Chicks," *SBT*, August 30, 1946.
96. "Blue Sox Rally to Win, 4–3," *SBT*, August 31, 1946.
97. "Blue Sox Win and Take Second Place," *SBT*, September 1, 1946.
98. "Blue Sox End Season in third Place," *SBT*, September 4, 1946.
99. See "Belles Win Pennant," *Racine Journal-Times* (hereafter cited as *RJT*), September 3, 1946
100. Dottie Naum to Odell, Odell Letters, September 2, 1946.
101. "Blue Sox, Racine Open Playoffs Tonight" and "Jim Costin Says," *SBT*, September 4, 1946.
102. "Blue Sox Lose to Racine Belles in 17th, 3–2," and "Blue Sox Fans Fly to Racine to View Game," *SBT*, September 5, 1946.
103. "Belles Rained out; Play Again Tonight," *RJT*, September 6, 1946.
104. "Blue Sox Win; Play Here Tonight," and "Grand Rapids Tops Peaches," *SBT*, September 7, 1946.
105. "Blue Sox Rained Out; Play here Tonight," *SBT*, September 8, 1946.

106. "Record 7,413 See Blue Sox Lose, 7–1" and "Grand Rapids Wins to Square Peaches Series," *SBT*, September 9, 1946.
107. "Blue Sox Lose Playoffs to Racine" and "Rockford Tops Grand Rapids in Final Game," *SBT*, September 10, 1946.
108. "Racine Wins in 14th, 1–0, to Claim Title," *SBT*, September 17, 1946.
109. "Blue Sox Fete Set for Tuesday," *SBT*, May 4, 1947.
110. "Jim Costin Says," *SBT*, September 10, 1946.
111. Maier, et.al., *Inventing America*, pp. 791–804.

Chapter 5

1. "Shaughnessy Playoff Series—1947, All-American Girls Baseball League," (written, though not so identified, by Max Carey) in *Major League Baseball: 1948* (Racine: Whitman Publishing, 1948), section following page 128.
2. See *Official Girls' Baseball Rules / Adopted By The All-American Girls Baseball League*, pp. 1–3, copy in AAGPBL Files, Center for History (hereafter cited as CFH), South Bend, Indiana.
3. See *Fort Wayne Daisies: 1947 Year Book* (Fort Wayne, IN: Wayne Paper Box & Printing Corp., 1947), p. 5, copy in Faut Collection at Winthrop University's Dacus Library.
4. Interview with Jean Faut, October 17, 2009.
5. See *Official Girls' Baseball Rules*, p. 10, AAGPBL Files, CFH.
6. "All-American Girls Baseball League" in *Major League Baseball: 1948*, pp. 128 ff.
7. Batting and pitching records are taken from official figures provided by the Howe News Bureau, copy in AAGPBL Files, CFH.
8. Bob Gorman interview with Jean Faut, January 18, 2010.
9. Chris Lamb, *Blackout: The Untold Story of Jackie Robinson's First Spring Training* (Lincoln: University of Nebraska Press, 2004), esp. pp. 103–116.
10. "Jackie Robinson," March 15, 1947, and Pedro Charcon, "Order Jackie to Play First," March 22, 1947, both in *Chicago Defender*.
11. Lamb, *Blackout*, pp. 61–100.
12. "Brooklyn Calls Up Jackie Robinson," *South Bend Tribune* (hereafter cited as *SBT*), April 11, 1947. See The Robinson Debut in Arthur Daley's "Sports of the Times," *New York Times*, April 16, 1947.
13. See Stanley Woodward," One Strike Is Out," *New York Herald Tribune*, May 5, and 6, 1947, reprinted in *Best Sports Stories: 1948 Edition* (New York: E.P. Dutton, 1948), pp. 21–25.
14. James M. Giglio, *Musial: From Stash to Stan the Man* (Colombia: University of Missouri Press, 2001), pp. 147–156.
15. Pauline Maier, et.al. *Inventing America: A History of the United States* (New York: W.W. Norton, second ed., 2006), pp. 802–805; and see the Truman Library's documents at: http://www.trumanlibrary.org/9981.htm.
16. Susan E. Johnson, *When Women Played Hardball* (Seattle: Seal Press, 1994), p. 96.
17. Merrie Fidler, *The Origins and History of the All-American Girls Professional Baseball League* (Jefferson, NC: McFarland, 2006), pp. 71–72.
18. Dan Cobian, "Women in Baseball: Latinas in the All-American Girls Professional Baseball League," http://www.chicla.wisc.edu/publications/workingpapers/Dan Cobian.html.
19. Sue Macy, *A Whole New Ball Game: The Story of the All-American Girls Professional Baseball League* (New York: Henry Holt & Co., 1993), pp. 52–54; and interview with Jean Faut, October 17, 2009.
20. See Unique Training Camp, in "Jim Costin Says," *SBT*, April 20, 1947.
21. Mahon to Carolyn Odell, Odell Letters, February 7, 1947, AAGPBL Files, CFH.
22. Mahon to Odell, Odell Letters, March 20, 1947.
23. "Instructions For Your Trip to Cuba," *A-A-G's Mail Bag*, n.d. [February, 1947], AAGPBL Files, CFH.
24. Jim Sargent, "Doris Sams," on SABR's Bio-Project: http://bioproj.sabr.org/bioproj.cfm?a=v&v=l&bid=2452&pid=19603.
25. Sargent, "Betsy Jochum," http://bioproj.sabr.org/bioproj.cfm?a=v&v=l&bid=2445&pid=19596.
26. Lois Browne, *Girls of Summer* (New York: Harper Collins, Paperback ed., 1993), pp. 127–132; and Macy, *A Whole New Ball Game*, pp. 51–52, indicated that Gonzales left with the All-Americans, but according to Howe News Bureau statistics, she did not play in 1947.
27. "Blue Sox Team Roster Named," *SBT*, May 2, 1947.
28. "Blue Sox Fans Pledge Sale of 3,780 Advance Tickets," *SBT*, May 7, 1947.
29. "Blue Sox Win Opener From Kenosha, 5 to 2," *SBT*, May 5, 1947.
30. See Wilton Garrison, "All-American Gals Here This Week," *Charlotte Observer* (hereafter cited as CO), May 11, 1947.
31. Harold Boian, "Dayton Fans Approve Girls' Baseball As Kenosha Wins," *Dayton Daily News*, May 19, 1947.
32. Jim Costin, "All Girl Pro Nines Are Stronger–Grant," *SBT*, May 20, 1947.
33. "Blue Sox, Fort Wayne Play Tonight," *SBT*, May 21, 1947.
34. "Blue Sox and Daisies Rained out of Opener," *SBT*, May 22, 1947.
35. "Blue Sox Win Opener From Daisies, 3 to 1," *SBT*, May 23, 1947.
36. "Blue Sox Get Even Break in First Twin Bill," *SBT*, May 24, 1947.
37. "Blue Sox Rained Out; Open Here Tonight" and "Jim Costin Says," *SBT*, May 25, 1947.
38. "4,700 See Blue Sox Win Opener, 7–0," *SBT*, May 26, 1947.
39. "Blue Sox Win Two; Take League Lead," *SBT*, May 27, 1947.
40. "Rain Prevents Blue Sox Game with Lassies," *SBT*, May 28, 1947.
41. "Blue Sox Get Even Break at Grand Rapids," *SBT*, May 31, 1947.
42. "Blue Sox, Tied For Lead, at Home Tonight," *SBT*, June 1, 1947.
43. "Rained Out Blue Sox Plan Another Twin Bill Tonight," *SBT*, June 2, 1947.
44. "Idle Blue Sox and Daisies Schedule Another Twin Bill," *SBT*, June 3, 1947.
45. "Rain Cease and Blue Sox Lose Two," *SBT*, June 4, 1947.
46. "Blue Sox Play Rockford in Final Tonight," *SBT*, June 7, 1947.
47. "Rain Halts Blue Sox, Peaches in Seventh at 0–0," *SBT*, June 8, 1947.

48. "Racine Triumphs, 6–4, and Blue Sox Errors," *SBT*, June 10, 1947.
49. "Heavy Rains Cancel Final Racine Game," *SBT*, June 11, 1947.
50. "Blue Sox Beat Kenosha in 9th, 1–0," *SBT*, June 12, 1947.
51. "Blue Sox Shade Kenosha Again, 2–1," *SBT*, June 13, 1947.
52. "Blue Sox, Kenosha Divide Frigid Twin Bill," *SBT*, June 15, 1947.
53. Peoria's 1947 *Year Book* spelled the team's name as Redwings, and the Peoria newspaper spelled it Redwings. See "Muskegon Belts 17 Hits to Wallop Redwings," August 1, and "First Division Hopes Gone As Redwings Lose," *Peoria Journal Transcript*, August 31, 1947.
54. "2,573 Fans See Blue Sox, Wings Divide," *SBT*, June 16, 1947.
55. "Blue Sox Go to Muskegon After Losing," *SBT*, June 25, 1947.
56. "Sox Lose in 15th; Play Racine Tonight," *SBT*, June 29, 1947.
57. "High Flying Chicks Open with Blue Sox Here Tonight," *SBT*, July 2, 1947.
58. "6,010 Fans See Blue Sox Divide Twin Bill," *SBT*, July 5, 1947.
59. See "'Flying Saucer' Mystery Excites U.S." and related stories, *SBT*, July 5, 6, 7, 1947.
60. "Blue Sox Beat Rockford, 7–3," *SBT*, July 7, 1947.
61. "Blue Sox Again Beat Rockford," *SBT*, July 8, 1947.
62. "Rockford Beats Blue Sox, 7 to 6," *SBT*, July 9, 1947.
63. "Local Girls Take Series in Rockford," *SBT*, July 10, 1947.
64. "Blue Sox Take 4th Place Before 2,923," *SBT*, July 11, 1947.
65. "Booing the Manager" in "Jim Costin Says," *SBT*, July 13, 1947.
66. "Blue Sox Go to Ft. Wayne For 4 Games," *SBT*, July 12, 1947.
67. William Cullen Fay, "Bonnie's the Belle of the Ball Game," *Sport*, May 1947, pp. 26–28, 97–98.
68. Interview with Jean Faut, October 17, 2009.
69. For a discussion of league salaries and "under the table" tax-free payments, see Fidler, *The Origins and History of the AAGPBL*, pp. 198–202.
70. Baker to Harold Dailey, Dailey Records, February 28, 1948, AAGPBL Files, Joyce Sports Collection, Hesburgh Libraries of Notre Dame.
71. Faut's contract for 1947 came in a letter from Blue Sox president Al McGann on September 16, 1946, copy in author's possession.
72. Faut fired no-hitters in 1948 and 1949, and she pitched perfect games in 1951 and 1953; see Jim Sargent, "Jean Faut," at: http://bioproj.sabr.org/bioproj.cfm?a=v&v=l&bid=2457&pid=19609.
73. Interview with Jean Faut, October 31, 2009.
74. Letter from Betsy Jochum, November 5, 2009.
75. For example, see Marge Stefani to Dailey, November 21, 1948, January 6 and 11, 1949, Dailey Records.
76. See "Alice 'Al' Pollitt, with Memories of Jackie 'Babe' Kelley," in Johnson, *When Women Played Hardball*, pp. 91–101.
77. For the Victory Song, see the AAGPBL site: http://www.aagpbl.org/league/song.cfm.
78. See *South Bend Blue Sox: 1947 Year Book* (South Bend: Privately published, 1947), n.p. Bittner's picture and brief bio appeared on a page of four player sketches, including Faut, Baker, and Koehn.

79. "Blue Sox Play Record 22 Innings to Win," *SBT*, August 1, 1947.
80. "Blue Sox in Peoria For 5 Game Series," *SBT*, August 6, 1947.
81. "Blue Sox Lengthen Fourth Place Lead Over Wings, 5–3," *SBT*, August 14, 1947.
82. See "Blue Sox Sweep Series From Peoria" and "Superlative Playing," in "Jim Costin Says," *SBT*, August 17, 1947.
83. "Stefani's Home Run in 13th Gives Blue Sox Even Break," *SBT*, August 18, 1947.
84. "Gottselig Ousted" in "Jim Costin Says," *SBT*, August 19, 1947.
85. "Blue Sox, Held Hitless By Margie Holgerson, Lose, 6–0," *SBT*, August 21, 1947.
86. "Faut Rescues Williams to Beat Peaches," *SBT*, August 22, 1947.
87. "Blue Sox and Racine Clash Here Tonight," *SBT*, August 24, 1947.
88. "Blue Sox Playoff Berth Threatened," *SBT*, August 25, 1947.
89. "Blue Sox Increase Fourth Place Lead," *SBT*, August 26, 1947.
90. "3,672 See Blue Sox Beat Racine, 7–3," *SBT*, August 27, 1947.
91. One fan wrote to Jim Costin saying the defeat was due to Grant's poor coaching, because Racine scored the winning run from second base due to good base running by Hickson and a poor throw by Stefani, whereas Grant held up Baker at third on a base hit down the left field line — after she was fast enough to beat out a bunt. See The Other Side, in "Jim Costin Says," *SBT*, August 29, 1947.
92. "Racine Conquers Blue Sox in 16th, 1–0," *SBT*, August 28, 1947.
93. "Daisies Cut Blue Sox fourth Place Lead," *SBT*, August 29, 1947.
94. "Blue Sox Win, 6–1; Near Title Playoff," *SBT*, August 30, 1947.
95. "Blue Sox Lose, But Win 4th Place As Peoria Also Loses," *SBT*, August 31, 1947.
96. James F. Henderson, "Muskegon Lassies Clinch Season Championship of All American Girls League," *Muskegon Chronicle*, September 1, 1947.
97. "Blue Sox, Lassies Divide Before 6,639 to End Season," *SBT*, September 2, 1947.
98. "Grand Rapids and Blue Sox to Start Play" and "Faut to Pitch For Blue Sox in First Game," *SBT*, September 3 and 4, 1947.
99. Interview with Jean Faut, October 31, 2009.
100. "Blue Sox Toss Off Opener to Chicks, 3–2," *SBT*, September 5, 1947.
101. "Blue Sox Win; Play Chicks Here Tonight," *SBT*, September 6, 1947.
102. "4,341 See Blue Sox Bow to Chicks, 6–1," *SBT*, September 7, 1947.
103. "Sox Meet Chicks On Time Tonight," *SBT*, September 8, 1947.
104. See Grant, "I Was A Girls' Baseball Manager," n.d. [1972], p. 15, copy of typescript memoir in AAGPBL Collection, Hesburgh Libraries. Also see Grant, "I Managed Girl Baseball Teams," the same memoir as it appeared in the Sunday section of the *SBT*, July 2, 1972, pp. 3–6, where Grant identified Dailey as the "badgering" fan.
105. "Fan Attacks Grant As Blue Sox Lose," *SBT*, September 9, 1947.
106. "Chicks Beat Racine, 1–0, to Win Title," *SBT*, September 17, 1947.

107. South Bend Doctor George Green operated on Mahon's left knee on November 19; see "Doings of the Season 1948," in Dailey Notebooks, volume 2, p. 64.
108. Chet Grant Quits, in "Jim Costin Says," *SBT*, September 10, 1947.
109. Letter from Betsy Jochum, December 2, 2009.
110. Interview with Jean Faut, October 31, 2009.

Chapter 6

1. "All-American Girls Baseball League—1948," in *Major League Baseball: 1949* (New York: Dell Publishing Co., 1949), p. 2. The 32-page section about the All-American League, material that appeared only in Dell's earlier editions for 1949, followed the guide's 128-page summary of the 1948 major league season. See typescript in Dailey Notebooks, volume 2, p. 50, AAGPBL Files, Joyce Sports Collection, Hesburgh Libraries of the University of Notre Dame.
2. *Major League Baseball: 1949*, pp. 2–3.
3. "Phyllis Koehn—Kenosha Comets," in AAGPBL Newsletter, *Touching Bases*, May 2001, p. 35, copy in Koehn File, AAGPBL Files, National Baseball Hall of Fame Library, Cooperstown, New York.
4. Interview with Jean Faut, October 31, 2009.
5. Merrie Fidler, *The Origins and History of the All-American Girls Professional Baseball League* (Jefferson, NC: McFarland, 2006), pp. 71–73, and Lois Browne, *Girls of Summer* (New York: Harper Collins, paperback edition, 1993), pp. 152–153.
6. Fidler, *Origins and History of the AAGPBL*, pp. 87–94.
7. "Publicity Release—Regarding the two divisions of the ten (10) team league," February 17, 1948, copy in Dailey Records.
8. "Doings of the Season 1948," Dailey Notebooks, volume 2, pp. 64–65.
9. "All-American Girls Baseball League—1948," Dailey Notebooks, volume 2, pp. 50–51.
10. Dailey to Meyerhoff, November 18, 1947, typescript in Dailey Notebooks, volume 2, p. 20.
11. McManus to Dailey, Dailey Records, January 13, 1948.
12. "Doings of the Season 1948," Dailey Notebooks, volume 2, p. 64.
13. Seth H. Bramson, *The Curtiss-Wright Cities: Hialeah, Miami Springs, and Opa Locka* (Charleston, SC: History Press, 2008), pp. 115–117.
14. Browne, *Girls of Summer*, pp. 137–144.
15. Eugenia Kaledin, *Daily Life in the United State, 1940–1959: Shifting Worlds* (Westport, CT: Greenwood Press, 2000), pp. 133–137.
16. John Thorn, et.al. *Total Baseball: The Ultimate Baseball Encyclopedia* (Wilmington, DE: Sport Media Publishing, Inc., Eighth ed.), pp. 2421–22.
17. "Ideal Camp Site" in "Jim Costin Says," *South Bend Tribune* (hereafter cited as *SBT*), April 28, 1948.
18. Browne, *Girls of Summer*, pp. 137–142.
19. "New Players Start Drills in Girls' Camp," *SBT*, April 6, 1948.
20. "Rookies Look Good in Girls' Camp Drills," *SBT*, April 7, 1948.
21. See Browne, *Girls of Summer*, pp. 138–139, and see web site "Florida Memory" by the State Library and Archives of Florida, at http://www.floridamemory.com/
22. "Cuban Girls Bid for Jobs in Pro Loop," *SBT*, April 8, 1948.
23. Rob Ruck, "Baseball in the Caribbean," in *Total Baseball*, pp. 796–798.
24. Message from Dolly (Brumfield) White, January 7, 2010.
25. Mirta Marrero was interviewed for a story with the second-page title, "Language Barrier Made Playing Difficult at First," in *Palm Beach Post*, September 12, 2003.
26. Sue Macy, *A Whole New Ball Game: The Story of the All-American Girls Professional Baseball League* (New York: Henry Holt and Co., 1993), pp. 74–75.
27. "Girls to Get Team Berths in Pro League," April 21, and "Daisy Junor, Stefani Lost to Blue Sox," April 22, 1948, both in *SBT*.
28. Jim Costin, "Young Rookie [Doris Neal] with Blue Sox Gets Praise," *SBT*, April 17, 1948.
29. Blue Sox's Chances in "Jim Costin Says," *SBT*, April 28, 1948.
30. "Bonnie Baker Arrives For Season's Play," *SBT*, May 5, 1948.
31. "Blue Sox Squad Arrives in town," May 7, and "Blue Sox Set for Opener with Peoria," May 8, 1948, both *SBT*.
32. "Blue Sox Open in Playland Tonight," *SBT*, May 9, 1948.
33. "Blue Sox Rained Out of 1st Game," *SBT*, May 10, 1948.
34. "Blue Sox Home Opener Now Set For May 19," *SBT*, May 12, 1948.
35. "Rain lets Up Too Soon; Blue Sox Play and Lose," *SBT*, May 15, 1948.
36. "Faralla Wins No Hitter, 1 to 0," *SBT*, May 16, 1948, and Macy, *A Whole New Ball Game*, p. 68, quoted Williams on poker-playing and the South Bend bus with the poker table that could seat six or seven players.
37. "Wings Defeat Blue Sox in Both Games," *SBT*, May 17, 1948.
38. "Blue Sox Top Red Wings in 3 to 1 Battle," *SBT*, May 18, 1948.
39. "Blue Sox Open at Home Tonight," *SBT*, May 19, 1948.
40. "Blue Sox Lose to Racine in 10th, 6–5," *SBT*, May 20, 1948.
41. Browne, *Girls of Summer*, p. 154.
42. "Racine Trounces Blue Sox Again, 5–1," *SBT*, May 21, 1948.
43. "Faralla's Pinch Hit Wins for Blue Sox," *SBT*, May 22, 1948.
44. "Fort Wayne Wins From Blue Sox, 3–2," *SBT*, May 23, 1948.
45. "Faut, Blue Sox Lose to Daisies," *SBT*, May 24, 1948.
46. "Blue Sox Win in Ninth Over Daisies by 8–7," *SBT*, May 22, 1948.
47. "Cold Halts Blue Sox in Springfield," *SBT*, May 26, 1948.
48. "Blue Sox Get Twin Defeats in Springfield," *SBT*, May 27, 1948.
49. "Faut Pitches Blue Sox to Win in 14th," *SBT*, May 28, 1948.
50. "Daisies, Blue Sox Clash Here Tonight," *SBT*, May 29, 1948.
51. "Jochum Beats Fort Wayne, 6–0, On 2 Hits," *SBT*, May 30, 1948.
52. "Daisies Lose 6–3 Tilt to Blue Sox," *Fort Wayne Journal-Gazette*, May 31, 1948.
53. "Blue Sox Lose Two Before 3,550 Fans," *SBT*, June 1, 1948.

54. Helping Chicago in "Jim Costin Says," *SBT*, May 27, 1948.
55. "Carey makes a change in the personnel of all teams in order to strengthen Chicago," Dailey Notebooks, volume 2, p. 48v, June 1, 1948; and Browne, *Girls of Summer*, pp. 151–152.
56. Telephone interview with Betsy Jochum, May 6, 2009.
57. "Blue Sox Rained Out; Trade 'Sugar' Koehn," *SBT*, June 13, 1948, and for the official records, see "All-American Girls Baseball Batting Record —1948," and "All-American Girls Baseball League Pitching Records —1948," AAGPBL Files, Center for History (hereafter cited as CFH), South Bend, Indiana.
58. "Blue Sox, Held to Four Hits, Lost to Chicago, 2–1," *SBT*, June 14, 1948.
59. "Blue Sox Open Home Stand Tonight," *SBT*, June 15, 1948.
60. "League Statistics," in "Jim Costin Says," *SBT*, June 14, 1948.
61. Message from Lil Faralla, January 14, 2010.
62. "Blue Sox Hit Hard to Win Opener From Muskegon, 5–4," *SBT*, June 16, 1948.
63. "Blue Sox Walloped By Muskegon, 12–1," *SBT*, June 17, 1948.
64. "Faralla Wins Her Second No-Hitter, 4–0," *SBT*, June 18, 1948.
65. "Blue Sox Advance in League Standings," *SBT*, June 19, 1948.
66. "Jim Costin Says," *SBT*, June 18, 1948.
67. See Here and There, in "Jim Costin Says," *SBT*, June 27, 1948.
68. "Peaches, Blue Sox Play Two Tonight," *SBT*, June 29, 1948.
69. "Rained Out Peaches and Blue Sox Play Two Tonight," *SBT*, June 20, 1948.
70. "Blue Sox Trounce Peaches, 12–0, Then are Beaten, 6–1," *SBT*, July 1, 1948.
71. "Blue Sox Accept 3–2 Kenosha Gift," *SBT*, July 2, 1948.
72. "Faut, Mahon Star as Blue Sox Win, 4–0," *SBT*, July 3, 1948.
73. "Blue Sox Sweep Kenosha Series, 4–0," *SBT*, July 4, 1948.
74. The final scores only appeared under Sunday Night's Results in "Girls' Pro Circuit," SBT, July 6, 1948. Springfield's *Illinois State Journal* for July 5, or any other date in 1948, has no record of AAGPBL games.
75. "4,576 See Blue Sox, Sallies Divide," *SBT*, July 6, 1948.
76. "Blue Sox' 10 Errors Set League Record," *SBT*, July 7, 1948.
77. Interview with Jean Faut, October 31, 2009.
78. "Blue Sox Blank Racine Again, 5–0," *SBT*, July 19, 1948.
79. McManus to Dailey, September 23, 1948, AAGPBL Files.
80. "Season 1948," Dailey Notebooks, vol. 2, p. 47, has an arrow pointing to Dailey's note saying that McManus was "drunk" with the handwritten statement, "This was not true about Marty McManus," signed by four players, Jochum, Koehn, Mahon, and Lil Jackson.
81. Robert Sullivan, "Who Said Girls Couldn't Play Baseball? All-American League's Highly Professional Skills Building Up New Sport," *Sunday News*, July 4, 1948, pp. 6–7, copy in Kruckel File, Baseball Hall of Fame Library.
82. "Blue Sox Divide with Comets to End Losing Streak," *SBT*, July 27, 1948.

83. "Blue Sox Beat Fort Wayne in Series Opener, 5–3," *SBT*, July 28, 1948.
84. "Sallies Beat Blue Sox in Tenth, 4 to 3," *SBT*, July 31, 1948.
85. "Lib Mahon Leads Blue Sox to 6–1 Victory," *SBT*, August 1, 1948.
86. "Blue Sox, Red Wings Play Two Tonight," *SBT*, August 6, 1948.
87. "Blue Sox Skid with Wirth on Sidelines," *SBT*, August 7, 1948.
88. "Blue Sox, Faut Win From Muskegon, 4–2," *SBT*, August 8, 1948.
89. "Williams Holds Lassies As Blue Sox Win Again, 5–1," *SBT*, August 9, 1948.
90. "Blue Sox to Open Home Stand Tonight," *SBT*, August 25, 1948.
91. "Umpires 'Star' As Blue Sox Win, 6–3," *SBT*, August 26, 1948.
92. "Blue Sox Lose to Chicks in 14th, 1–0," *SBT*, August 27, 1948.
93. "Blue Sox Gain Even Break with Chicks," *SBT*, August 28, 1948.
94. "Blue Sox Rally to Get Even Break," *SBT*, August 29, 1948.
95. "Blue Sox Blanked Twice by Peaches," *SBT*, August 30, 1948.
96. "Blue Sox, Faralla Beat Peaches, 2–0," *SBT*, August 31, 1948.
97. "Faut Halts Muskegon in 9th to Save Blue Sox, 5–3," *SBT*, September 1, 1945.
98. "Blue Sox Get 9–2 Beating at Kenosha," *SBT*, September 3, 1948.
99. "Faut Pitches No-Hitter to Top Racine, 7–0," *SBT*, September 5, 1948.
100. There is no account of the game in Michigan City, Indiana, because the *Tribune* did not publish on Labor Day, but the score appeared a day later in "Blue Sox Divide Last Twin Bill," *SBT*, September 7, 1948.
101. *Ibid.*
102. "Blue Sox Face Chicks in Playoffs Here Tonight," *SBT*, September 8, 1948.
103. "Faut Defeats Chicks After 20 Innings," *SBT*, September 10, 1948.
104. "Chicks Beat Sox in 11 Innings, 3–2," *SBT*, September 11, 1948.
105. "Blue Sox Win From Chicks, Need 1 More," *SBT*, September 12, 1948.
106. "Chicks Beat Blue Sox, 1–0, in 15 Innings," *SBT*, September 13, 1948.
107. "Blue Sox Lose Playoff Final," *SBT*, September 14, 1948.
108. Browne, *Girls of Summer*, p. 170.
109. McManus to Dailey, September 23, 1948, AAGPBL Files.
110. McManus Quits in "Jim Costin Says," *SBT*, September 15, 1948.
111. Telephone interview with Betsy Jochum, May 6, 2009.
112. Browne, *Girls of Summer*, pp. 160–161, commented on Baker's signing bonus.
113. *Ibid.*, p. 171.

Chapter 7

1. Paul Neville, "On the Level," *South Bend Tribune* (hereafter cited as *SBT*), September 6, 1949.

2. Bill Fay, "Belles of the Ball Game," *Collier's*, August 13, 1949, p. 44.

3. The home movie, later converted to DVD, is marked 1949 and has three segments: the Peaches taking batting and infield practice, filmed in black and white; a color film of a 1949 Rockford-Peoria game; and color segments of Bill Allington's All-Americans on tour in 1955–1956. I received the VHS tape from Dottie Collins in 1997.

4. Merrie Fidler, *The Origins and History of the All-American Girls Professional Baseball League* (Jefferson, NC: McFarland, 2006), p. 71.

5. "Minutes of the Meeting," AAGBL Board of Directors, January 5, 1949, Dailey Notebooks, volume 9, p. 52, AAGPBL Files, Joyce Sports Collection, Hesburgh Libraries of the University of Notre Dame.

6. Barbara Gregorich, *Women at Play: The Story of Women in Baseball* (New York: Harcourt Brace & Co., 1993), pp. 84–85.

7. "Blue Sox Top Chicks, 7 to 3," *SBT*, July 22, 1949.

8. Lois Browne, *Girls of Summer* (New York: Harper Collins, 1992, paperback ed., 1993), pp. 177–182; and Fidler, *Origins and History of the AAGPBL*, pp. 77–79.

9. Statement by Fred Leo, the league's publicity director, December 21, 1948, in Dailey Notebooks, volume 2, p. 42v, AAGPBL Files.

10. "Arnold to Pitch," in "Jim Costin Says," *SBT*, April 14, 1949.

11. Trey Stecker, "Dave Bancroft," http://bioproj.sabr.org/bioproj.cfm?a=v&v=l&pid=560&bid=951.

12. "21 Blue Sox Now Working Out at Playland," *SBT*, May 3, 1949, and "Carey Meets with Heads of Blue Sox," May 4, 1949; and on Rita Briggs, see George McGuane's column "The Lookout," *Lowell Sun*, May 9, 1949.

13. "Berlin Blockade Near End" and related stories, *SBT*, May 10, 1949.

14. "James M. Costin, 55, Sports Editor, Dies," *SBT*, May 9, 1949.

15. "Messages From Far and Near Pay Tribute to Jim Costin," May 10, and "Jim Costin," *SBT*, May 11, 1949.

16. "Blue Sox Whip Fort Wayne Foe," *SBT*, May 12, 1949.

17. "Miss Stefani Sox Pilot — For a Night," May 20, and "Daisies Beat Blue Sox for First Time," *SBT*, May 21, 1949.

18. "Faut to Toss Initial Game for Bancroft," May 22, and "Blue Sox and Peaches Try Again Tonight," May 23, 1949, both in SBT.

19. "Blue Sox Beat Rockford in Opener, 9–3," *SBT*, May 24, 1949.

20. "Blue Sox Beat Peoria, 5–2, For Second Straight Victory," *SBT*, May 25, 1949.

21. "Blue Sox Win Third in Row; Beat Peoria," *SBT*, May 27, 1949.

22. "Peaches Hand First Defeat to Blue Sox," *SBT*, May 28, 1949.

23. "Faut and Blue Sox Lose in 16 Innings," *SBT*, May 29, 1949.

24. "Peaches Nip Blue Sox in 12 Innings," *SBT*, May 30, 1949.

25. "Blue Sox and Fort Wayne Daisies Split Doubleheader," *SBT*, May 31, 1949.

26. "Daisies' Allen Shatters Record But Blue Sox Win, 4–0," *SBT*, June 1, 1949.

27. "Jean Faut's Single For Blue Sox Defeats Kenosha, 8–7," *SBT*, June 2, 1949.

28. "Blue Sox Sweep Double-Header From Kenosha," *SBT*, June 3, 1949.

29. "Kenosha Halts Blue Sox Winning Streak, 5–4," *SBT*, June 4, 1949.

30. "Faut and Blue Sox Defeat Racine Belles, 14–3," *SBT*, June 5, 1949.

31. Browne, *Girls of Summer*, pp. 171–173.

32. "Blue Sox Win Two; Closing On Rockford," *SBT*, June 6, 1949.

33. "Blue Sox Now Game Out of First Place," *SBT*, June 7, 1949.

34. "Blue Sox in 16-Inning Tie with Lassies," *SBT*, June 8, 1949.

35. "Blue Sox Take Over First Place in All-American Loop," *SBT*, June 9, 1949.

36. "Blue Sox Increase League Lead to 1 Games," *SBT*, June 10, 1949.

37. "Blue Sox League Lead Cut to One Half Game," *SBT*, June 11, 1949.

38. "Blue Sox Drop Out Of Girls' Loop Lead," *SBT*, June 12, 1949.

39. "Faut Hurls Blue Sox to Victory, 3–0," *SBT*, June 13, 1949.

40. "Blue Sox Gain Tie For Lead in Girls' Baseball Loop," *SBT*, June 15, 1949.

41. "Walk Costs Blue Sox Twin Victory Over Grand Rapids," *SBT*, June 16, 1949.

42. "Blue Sox Visit Daisies Tonight," *SBT*, June 17, 1949.

43. "Faut Hurls Blue Sox to Win Over Daisies," *SBT*, June 18, 1949.

44. "Hasham Hurls 4–0 Victory For Blue Sox," *SBT*, June 19, 1949.

45. "Blue Sox Shut Out By Fort Wayne, 1–0," *SBT*, June 20, 1949.

46. "Faut's Bunt Enables Blue Sox to Win, 2–1," *SBT*, June 21, 1949.

47. "Unearned Runs Bring Sox Win," *SBT*, June 22, 1949.

48. "Two Injured As Sox Lose in Wisconsin," *SBT*, June 23, 1949.

49. "Sox Victory Moves Club Nearer Lead," *SBT*, June 24, 1949.

50. "Blue Sox Beat Rockford, 3 to 1, in 15 Inning Battle," *SBT*, June 30, 1949.

51. "Bendix Workers Returning" and related stories, *SBT*, June 30, 1949.

52. "Season's Biggest Crowd Sees Rockford Beat Blue Sox," *SBT*, July 1, 1949.

53. "Rockford Trips Sox, 2–1 in Rain to Win Series," *SBT*, July 2, 1949.

54. "Blue Sox Top Chicks, 7 to 3," *SBT*, July 22, 1949.

55. "Sox Outhit Kenosha But Comets Win," *SBT*, July 9, 1949.

56. "Sams Chills Sox Leaders with One Hit," *SBT*, July 15, 1949.

57. "Blue Sox Triumph Over Muskegon, 3–0," *SBT*, July 16, 1949.

58. "Sox Lose to Chicks in Ninth Inning, 8–7," *SBT*, July 17, 1949.

59. "Five Errors Help Chicks to Victory," *SBT*, July 18, 1949.

60. "Sox vs. Chicks at Playland with New Ball," *SBT*, June 22, 1949.

61. "Blue Sox Leading Loop in Fielding and Batting," *SBT*, July 17, 1949.

62. Gregorich, "Jean Faut" in *Women at Play*, pp. 143–144.

63. Telephone interview with Lib Mahon, June 23, 1997.

64. Telephone interview with Wilma Briggs, January 28, 1011.

65. Telephone interview with Lil Faralla, November 16, 2009.
66. "Hasham Hurls Her Seventh Win of Year," *SBT*, July 3, 1949.
67. "Sportraits of the Ladies," *Kalamazoo Gazette*, June 8, 1952, copy in Ruth Williams File, Baseball Hall of Fame Library.
68. "South Benders Top Fort Wayne," *SBT*, July 5, 1949.
69. Telephone interview with Helen (Filarski) Steffes, July 7, 2010.
70. Ruby Stephens to Carolyn Odell, Odell Letters, n.d. [May 30, 1949], copy in author's possession.
71. Heinie Martin, "Betty Whiting a Converted Outfielder," copy of 1946 clipping in Betty Whiting File, Baseball Hall of Fame Library.
72. Telephone interview with Helen (Filarski) Steffes, July 7, 2010.
73. See W.C. Madden, *The Women of the All-American Girls Professional Baseball League: A Biographical Dictionary* (Jefferson, NC: McFarland, 1997), pp. 233–234.
74. Interview with Jean Faut, October 31, 2009.
75. "South Bend Sox Leading Girls' League," *SBT*, August 5, 1949.
76. "South Bend Defeated Twice by Kenosha Comets, 1–0, 3–2," *SBT*, August 8, 1949.
77. "Jean Faut's Single Wins for Blue Sox, 4–2," *SBT*, August 13, 1949.
78. "Muskegon Defeats Blue Sox in 12th, 3–2," *SBT*, August 14, 1949.
79. "Sox Sweep Series From Lassie Nine," *SBT*, August 16, 1949.
80. "Blue Sox Celebrate Bancroft Night with 4–3 Victory," *SBT*, August 18, 1949.
81. "Kids Defeat Chicks; Pa, Ma and Everybody Very Happy," *SBT*, August 18, 1949.
82. "Blue Sox Win First Game of Crucial Rockford Series," *SBT*, August 30, 1949.
83. "Sox Split with Rockford; Maintain Lead," *SBT*, August 31, 1949.
84. "Sox Lead Cut by Rockford's Victory," *SBT*, September 1, 1949.
85. "Faut Pitches No-Hitter to Top Racine, 7–0," *SBT*, September 5, 1948.
86. "Jean Faut Hurls No-Hitter for Blue Sox," *SBT*, September 4, 1949.
87. "Daisies Win, 6–2; Play 2 Tonight," *Fort Wayne Journal Gazette*, September 5, 1949.
88. Rockford Win is Comedy Material, in "On the Level," *SBT*, September 9, 1949.
89. "Blue Sox-Peaches Tie for First in League," *SBT*, September 6, 1949.
90. "Rockford Wins First Game of Carey Playoff, 5–1," *SBT*, September 8, 1949.
91. "Rockford Takes Commanding Lead in Playoff," *SBT*, September 9, 1949.
92. "Sox Drop Third Straight Game to Rockford," *SBT*, September 10, 1949.
93. "Fourth Game at Rockford — Sept. 11, 1949," Dailey Notebooks, volume 2, p. 111, has details on the game-ending play.
94. "Sox Lose Carey Cup Playoffs to Rockford," *SBT*, September 11, 1949.
95. "Peaches Win Playoffs From Grand Rapids," *SBT*, September 20, 1949.
96. According to the league's final statistics, Rockford paced the eight teams in fielding with a .959 mark, but South Bend's .958 average was a close second; see "All-American Girls Baseball League — Official 1949 Averages," by Howe News Bureau, copy in AAGPBL Files of Center for History, South Bend, Indiana.
97. See Neville's "On the Level," *SBT*, September 6, 1949.
98. Adie Suehsdorf, "Sluggers in Skirts," *Los Angeles Times*, July 31, 1949.
99. Message from Sue Kidd, March 26, 2011.

Chapter 8

1. "Girls' League Faces Still Another Crisis," in "On the Level," *South Bend Tribune* (hereafter cited as *SBT*), July 19, 1950.
2. "All-American Girls Baseball League," n.p., *Girls Baseball*, July 1, 1950, copy in AAGPBL Files, Center for History (hereafter cited as CFH), South Bend, Indiana.
3. Merrie Fidler, *The Origins and History of the All-American Girls Professional Baseball League* (Jefferson, NC: McFarland, 2006), pp. 69–83.
4. *Ibid.*, pp. 83–85.
5. David Halberstam, *The Fifties* (New York: Fawcett Publishing, 1993), pp. 59–77.
6. For a discussion of changes in postwar America, see Pauline Maier, et. al. *Inventing America: A History of the United States* (New York: W.W. Norton, 2nd ed., 2006), pp. 790–816, and Eugenia Kaledin, *Daily Life in the United States, 1940–1959: Shifting Worlds* (Westport, CT: Greenwood Press, 2000), pp. 20–22.
7. John Thorn, et. al., *Total Baseball* (Wilmington, DE: Sports Media Publishing, 8th ed., 2004), pp. 2417–2422.
8. Lloyd Johnson and Miles Wolff, eds., *The Encyclopedia of Minor League Baseball* (Durham, NC: Baseball America, Inc., 2nd ed., 1997), p. 347.
9. Fidler, *The Origins and History of the AAGPBL*, pp. 80–83, and Lois Browne, *Girls of Summer* (New York: Harper Collins, paperback ed., 1993), pp. 171–178.
10. Work of the Balancing Committee as of Sunday, March 12, 1950, Dailey Notebooks, volume 3, p. 64, AAGPBL Files, Joyce Sports Collection, Hesburgh Libraries of Notre Dame.
11. "On the Level / with Paul Neville," April 4, 1950, and "A.A.G.B. Rookies Work Outdoors," April 16, 1950, SBT, and AAGBBL Press Release, April 19, 1950, in Dailey Notebooks, volume 3, p. 80–80v (front and back).
12. "Girls Rooms — Roommates — Addresses and Phone Numbers," and Press Release, April 24, 1950, in Dailey Notebooks, volume 3, pp. 84–84v.
13. "Rookies Star at Plate for Traveling Sox," *SBT*, May 9, 1950.
14. "Sox Prepare for Thursday League Start," *SBT*, May 17, 1950.
15. Press Release, May 11, 1950, Dailey Notebooks, volume 3, p. 9v.
16. The base paths were lengthened to 70 feet from 68 feet for the 1946 season; see Max Carey, "All American Girls Baseball League" in *Major League Baseball: 1947* (New York: Dell Publishing, Inc., 1947), pp. 128ff. The length was increased from 70 feet to 72 feet in 1948; see *Major league Baseball: 1949* (New York: Dell Publishing, 1949), p. [3] (at back of book).
17. "Sox Launch Title Race," *SBT*, May 18, 1950.
18. "Blue Sox Trounced in First Game, 13–5," *SBT*, May 19, 1950.
19. "Blue Sox Triumph Over Grand Rapids, 4–3," *SBT*, May 20, 1950.

20. "Rookie Kunkel Hurt as Sox Defeat Chicks," *SBT*, May 21, 1950.
21. "South Bend Blue Sox Defeat Muskegon for Sixth Straight," *SBT*, May 28, 1950.
22. Fidler, *Origins and History of the AAGPBL*, p. 92.
23. "Lassies Break Losing Streak," *SBT*, May 29, 170.
24. "Blue Sox Tighten Grip on First Place," *SBT*, May 30, 1950.
25. "South Bend-Fort Wayne Split Memorial Day Twin Bill," *SBT*, May 31, 1950.
26. "Blue Sox Setting Fast Pace in Girls' League," *SBT*, June 2, 1950.
27. "Blue Sox Shaded by Rockford's Peaches," *SBT*, June 4, 1950.
28. "Sox Drop to Second by 24 Percentage Points," *SBT*, June 5, 1950.
29. "So Go West; Regain Slight League Lead," *SBT*, June 6, 1950
30. "Roth, Dailey Hurl and Bat Sox to Win," *SBT*, June 7, 1950.
31. "Peoria Beats Sox in Extra Inning Game," *SBT*, June 8, 1950.
32. Kathleen Birck estimated that while other top players earned $100 per week, Baker was paid between $200-$300; see Birck's essay, "Baker (George), Mary 'Bonnie,'" in Leslie Heaphy and Mel May, eds., *Encyclopedia of Women and Baseball* (Jefferson, NC: McFarland, 2006), pp. 24–25.
33. "Bonnie Baker Manages Muskegon; Pryer to Sox," *SBT*, June 8, 1950.
34. *Ibid.*, and also Dailey journal for June 6, 1950, Dailey Notebooks, volume 3, p. 95.
35. Dailey journal, August 22, 1950, Dailey Notebooks, volume 3, p. 117.
36. Baker stated her deal in a letter to Dailey on February 28, 1948, Dailey Records, AAGPBL Files, Joyce Sports Collection, Hesburgh Libraries of Notre Dame.
37. Dailey journal, June 11, 12, 1948, Dailey Records.
38. Browne, *Girls of Summer*, pp. 181–182.
39. "Sox Approach First Place; Beat Daisies," *SBT*, June 22, 1950.
40. "Blue Sox Knock Daisies From First Place, 5–1," *SBT*, June 23, 1950.
41. "Blue Sox Beat Daisies Again," *SBT*, June 24, 1950.
42. "Rain Halts Sox, Fort Wayne; Leo Upholds Racine Protest," *SBT*, June 25, 1950.
43. "Chicks Down Sox, 3–1, After Losing First," *SBT*, June 26, 1950.
44. "Ziegler Hurls 6–0 Shutout Against Sox," *SBT*, June 27, 1950.
45. "Blue Sox Take 2–1 Tilt From Grand Rapids," *SBT*, June 28, 1950.
46. "Faut Wins From Lassies; Nightcap Called in Fourth," *SBT*, June 29, 1950.
47. "Blue Sox Take Two-Game Lead in Girls' League," *SBT*, June 30, 1950.
48. "Alma Ziegler Defeats Sox," *SBT*, July 1, and "Girls Baseball Loop Embroiled in Forfeit Ruling," *SBT*, July 2. 1950.
49. "Sox Beat Daisies; Defy Forfeit," *SBT*, July 3, 1950.
50. "Rockford Leads Girls Loop After Sox Lose Two," *SBT*, July 5, 1950.
51. "South Bend Regains Slim Lead in Girls' League," *SBT*, July 6, 1950.
52. "Filarski's 11th-Inning Double Gives Sox 3–2 Win" and "On the Level," July 10, 1950, both SBT.
53. All season statistics are derived from the Howe News Bureau's official figures, copies of which are in the AAGPBL Archives, CFH.
54. Interview with Jean Faut, October 31, 2009.
55. Dailey journal, August 22, 1950, Dailey Notebooks, volume 3, p. 114.
56. "Betty Wagoner Wins Fame as 'Old Standby' of Blue Sox," *SBT*, August 15, 1950.
57. "Peoria Blanks Blue Sox by 1–0," *SBT*, August 12, 1950. The story included a box, "Lib Mahon Retires From Sox Outfield," noting that team officials said a doctor prescribed rest for the ailing star.
58. Telephone interview with Helen (Filarski) Steffes, July 7, 2010.
59. "Belles Conclude Home Stay Against Blue Sox Tonight," *Racine Journal-Times*, August 22, 1950.
60. "Roth's Two-Hitter Gives South Bend 4–1 Triumph," *SBT*, July 11, 1950.
61. "Blue Sox Lose Double-Header to Rockford," *SBT*, July 18, 1950.
62. Poor Defense and Sox Lose Sixth Straight, and Girls' League Faces Still Another Crisis, in "On the Level," *SBT*, July 19, 1950.
63. "Betty Whiting Return Asked," *SBT*, July 20, 1950.
64. "Blue Sox Loss Streak Hits Eight in Row," *SBT*, July 22, 1950.
65. "Blue Sox Win Over Racine; Lose Replay," *SBT*, July 23, 1950.
66. "Sox Divide Two Games with Comets," *SBT*, July 24, 1950.
67. "Peoria and Grand Rapids to Remain in Girls League / Hit by Mahon Gives Blue Sox Victory in 12th," *SBT*, July 25, 1950.
68. Minutes of Board of Directors Meeting, Chicago, July 5, 1950, Dailey Notebooks, volume 3, pp. 101–103.
69. Leo's letter, evidently received on July 12, Dailey's reply, and journal entry for 12th, Dailey Notebooks, volume 3, pp. 105–105v.
70. Journal entry starting on July 24, Leo telegram to Dailey, July 29, 1950, Dailey Notebooks, volume 3, p. 111; and "Faut Hurls One-Hitter as Blue Sox Win, 4–0," *SBT*, July 30, 1950.
71. Dailey journal, July 31, 1950, Dailey Notebooks, volume 3, p. 111v.
72. Records as of Monday, July 31, 1950, *Ibid.*, p. 112.
73. "Sox and Grand Rapids Split Pair Before 2,026," *SBT*, August 2, 1950.
74. "South Bend Nine Drops Seventh Straight Game," *SBT*, August 8, 1950.
75. "Blue Sox Tumble Rockford, 3–1," *SBT*, August 9, 1950.
76. "Sox Victory Drops Rockford to Second in A.A.G.B.L.," *SBT*, August 10, 1950.
77. "Blue Sox Lose, 6–3; Peaches Back on Top," *SBT*, August 11, 1950.
78. "Peoria Blanks Blue Sox by 1–0," *SBT*, August 12, 1950.
79. Dailey journal, August 8, 1950, Dailey Notebooks, volume 3, p. 112v.
80. Dailey journal, August 11, 1950, Dailey Notebooks, volume 3, p. 114.
81. "South Bend Sox Launch Fund Raising Campaign" and "Mueller Bests Peoria," *SBT*, August 13, 1950.
82. "Wings Defeat Blue Sox, 4–2; Take Series," *SBT*, August 14, 1950.
83. "Sox Battle to 17-Inning Tie with Daisies," *SBT*, August 15, 1950.
84. "Vincent and Blue Sox Lose in Ragged Game at Fort

Wayne," and "Sox Ticket Sales Program Well Underway" in "On the Level," *SBT*, August 16, 1950.
85. "Sox Defeat Fort Wayne by 4–2 Score," *SBT*, August 17, 1950.
86. "Wirth Homers at Playland as Sox Split," *SBT*, August 18, 1950.
87. "Comets Defeat Blue Sox, 6–3," *SBT*, August 19, 1950.
88. "Wagoner Hurt as Sox Lost to Kenosha, 3–2," *SBT*, August 20, 1950.
89. They're the Best in Their Line of Sport, in "On the Level," *SBT*, August 16, 1950.
90. Morris Markey, "Hey Ma, You're Out," *McCall's*, September 1950, pp. 40, 41, 68, 74, 77, 80.
91. Dailey journal, August 29, 1950, Dailey Notebooks, volume 3, p. 118.
92. Message from Lil Faralla, August 31, 2010.
93. Dailey journal, August 22, 1950, Dailey Notebooks, volume 3, p. 117.
94. Interview with Jean Faut, October 31, 2009.
95. Letter from Jean Faut, January 31, 12011.
96. Markey, "Hey Ma, You're Out," pp. 40–41.

Chapter 9

1. "Jean Faut Hurls Perfect Game," *South Bend Tribune* (hereafter cited as *SBT*), July 22, 1951.
2. "Sox Manager Karl Winsch Credits Team Spirit" in "On the Level," *SBT*, September 18, 1951.
3. "Brief Historical Summary of the South Bend Blue Sox," Dailey Notebooks, volume 4, pp. 2–3, AAGPBL Files, Joyce Sports Collection, Hesburgh Libraries of Notre Dame.
4. See Merrie Fidler, *The Origins and History of the All-American Girls Professional Baseball League* (Jefferson, NC: McFarland, 2006), pp. 83–85, 125–129.
5. Frank Helvie to Jean Faut, November 20, 1950, original in Faut Scrapbooks for 1950–51.
6. "Immediate Release," November 21, 1950, Dailey Notebooks, volume 3, pp. 136v–137.
7. "Blue Sox Heads Seek New Manager for '51," *SBT*, November 14, 1950.
8. Journal entry, August 29, 1950, Dailey Notebooks, volume 3, p. 118.
9. "Winsch Succeeds Bancroft as Blue Sox Boss," *SBT*, January 7, 1951.
10. Interview with Jean Faut, September 7, 2010.
11. "Colley See Um of Sports," *Morning Herald*, Hagerstown, Maryland, March 23, 1944.
12. Contract assignments card and clipping, "Women's Baseball Manager is in a League of His Own," February 1996, in Winsch File, National Baseball Hall of Fame Library, Cooperstown, New York. Winsch's minor league record can be found on Baseball-Reference.com: http://www.baseball-reference.com/minors/player.cgi?id=winsch001kar
13. Journal entry, Dailey Notebooks, volume 5, p. 14.
14. "American Girls Baseball League Rules," February 22, 1951, Dailey Notebooks, volume 5, pp. 2–2v.
15. South Bend's insignia was a white circle representing a baseball with the blue letters saying "So. Bend" on the top half of the ball and "Blue Sox" on the bottom part, and a pair of red baseball "seams" to complete the design.
16. "Blue Sox Card 56 Home Games at Playland," *SBT*, March 4, 1951.
17. All Blue Sockers But One Have Signed in "On the Level," *SBT*, April 16, 1951.
18. "Blue Sox Begin Spring Practice on Playland Diamond," *SBT*, May 1, 1951.
19. See "On the Level," *SBT*, May 9, 1951.
20. "1951 Squad Reporting for Spring Training, May 1st," Dailey Notebooks, volume 5, p. 37v.
21. "Blue Sox Shut Lassies Out Before 1,500," *SBT*, May 15, 1951.
22. "Blue Sox Work Under Lights on Playland Field Tonight," *SBT*, May 17, 1951.
23. "Blue Sox Lose to Fort Wayne in Exhibition," *SBT*, May 19, 1951.
24. "Mayor Ready for Blue Sox' First Game / Rookie Tryouts Set For Playland Saturday," *SBT*, May 18, 1951.
25. "Sox Open Season Against Grand Rapids," *SBT*, May 20, 1951.
26. "Sox Opener Washed Out at Playland," *SBT*, May 21, 1951.
27. "Blue Sox Open Season with 1–0 Win Over Grand Rapids," *SBT*, May 22, 1951.
28. See "On the Level," *SBT*, May 22, 1951.
29. Lloyd Johnson and Miles Wolff, eds., *The Encyclopedia of Minor League Baseball* (Durham, NC: Baseball America, Inc., 2nd ed., 1997), p. 347.
30. "Rain Plagues Blue Sox; Kalamazoo Next Foe," *SBT*, May 23, 1951.
31. "13-Hit Attack on Kalamazoo Wins for Sox," *SBT*, May 24, 1951.
32. "Kalamazoo Becomes Blue Sox's Third Victim, 5–2," *SBT*, May 25, 1951.
33. "Rain Cancels Sox Series with Peoria," *SBT*, May 28, 1951.
34. "Sox Suffer First Defeat in Rockford," *SBT*, May 29, 1951.
35. "Peaches Best Faut and Blue Sox, 1–0," *SBT*, May 30, 1951.
36. "Sox Bash 16 Hits in Rout of Rockford," *SBT*, May 31, 1951.
37. "Blue Sox Boost Two-Day Run Production to 26," *SBT*, June 1, 1951.
38. "Blue Sox Suffer Doubleheader Loss to Peoria," *SBT*, June 3, 1951.
39. "Fort Wayne Dumps Blue Sox Twice," *SBT*, June 4, 1951.
40. "Blue Sox Lose Third Straight" and "On the Level," *SBT*, June 5, 1951.
41. "Faut to Face Fort Wayne in First Tilt," *SBT*, June 8, 1951.
42. "Daisies Boost Streak to 17; Beat Sox, 5–2," *SBT*, June 9, 1951.
43. "Blue Sox End Fort Wayne Streak at 17 Games," *SBT*, June 10, 1951.
44. "Sox Win Doubleheader From Fort Wayne, 6–3 and 7–4," *SBT*, June 11, 1951.
45. "Peaches Drop Pair to Blue Sox," *SBT*, June 12, 1951.
46. "Blue Sox Win Sixth Straight Behind Faut, 4–0," *SBT*, June 13, 1951.
47. "Gacioch Hurls Four-Hit Ball at Blue Sox," *SBT*, June 14, 1951.
48. "Blue Sox Rake Rockford for 11 Hits to Triumph, 8–4," *SBT*, June 15, 1951.
49. "Kenosha Defeats Blue Sox on Four-Hitter by Marlowe," *SBT*, June 16, 1951.
50. "Mueller Hurls Sox to 4–1 Win," *SBT*, June 19, 1951.
51. "Grand Rapids Nips Blue Sox," *SBT*, June 27, 1951.

52. "Players on South Bend Roster — May 21, 1951," Dailey Notebooks, volume 5, p. 43v.

53. Journal entry, July 5, Dailey Notebooks, volume 5, p. 40v.

54. "Waiver List Claims Seven Sox Players," *SBT*, June 29, 1951.

55. Winsch wanted to trade Faralla and Wiley to Battle Creek for left-handed first sacker June Peppas, but the deal fell through; see Journal entries, June 5 and 8, 1951, Dailey Notebooks, volume 5, pp. 39–39v.

56. See Frank Helvie's statement in "Blue Sox Bow to Kalamazoo by 8–4 Score," *SBT*, June 30, 1951.

57. "Sox Whip Kenosha Twice; Jean Faut Tosses One-Hitter," *SBT*, July 10, 1951.

58. "Sox Take Pair From Comets Again, 2–1, 2–0," *SBT*, July 11, 1951.

59. "Cione's Grand Slam Subdues Sox," *SBT*, July 12, 1951.

60. "Girls Pro League May Lose Two Teams," *SBT*, July 13, 1951.

61. "Girls League — Stay at Eight Teams; Sox Win," *SBT*, July 14, 1951.

62. "Blue Sox Win Easy Victory by 6–3 Score," *SBT*, July 15, 1951.

63. "Chicks First Half Victor in Girls League; Sox Third," *SBT*, July 16, 1951.

64. "Betty Foss Keeps Girls' Bat Margin," *Grand Rapids Herald*, July 15, 1951.

65. See Morris Markey, "Hey Ma, You're Out," *McCall's*, September 1950, pp. 40, 41, 68, 74, 77, 80.

66. Robert Cromie, "A Girl's Place is at Home — Plate," *Chicago Sunday Tribune*, July 15, 1951.

67. Bob Gorman interview with Jean Faut, September 7, 2010.

68. Telephone interview with Wimp Baumgartner, September 7, 2010.

69. "Chicks Lose League Lead After Splitting Pair with Sox," *SBT*, July 3, 1951.

70. The *Tribune* did not publish on holidays, but there is a one-paragraph game account in "Blue Sox Nip Peoria Wings By 6–2 Score," *SBT*, July 5, 1951.

71. Journal entry, July 4, 1951, Dailey Notebooks, volume 5, p. 40v.

72. Telephone interview with Wimp Baumgartner, September 7, 2010.

73. Telephone interview with Sue Kidd, September 6, 2010.

74. Telephone interview with Wimp Baumgartner, September 7, 2010.

75. Telephone interview with Lil Faralla, November 20, 2010.

76. Interview with Jean Faut, October 31, 2009.

77. Interview with Janet (Wiley) Sears, November 6, 2007.

78. Interview with Lou Arnold, November 6, 2007.

79. "Sox Win First Tilt in Loop's Second Half," *SBT*, July 17, 1951.

80. "Blue Sox Top Kenosha, 3–1," *SBT*, July 19, 1951.

81. "Comet Rally Turns Back Blue Sox, 5–3," *SBT*, July 20, 1951.

82. For the game story, see "Sox Take Pair From Comets Again, 2–1, 2–0," *SBT*, July 11, 1951.

83. "Blue Sox Stop Rockford by 4–2 Score," *SBT*, July 21, 1951.

84. "Jean Faut Hurls Perfect Game," *SBT*, July 22, 1951.

85. "Lou Arnold Shuts Out Battle Creek, 7–0, on One-Hitter," *SBT*, July 24, 1951.

86. "Sox Beat Battle Creek, 4–0; Gain on Grand Rapids," *SBT*, July 25, 1951.

87. "Sox Leading Girls League by 1 Game," *SBT*, July 27, 1951.

88. "Blue Sox Sweep Twin Bill at Battle Creek, 6–0, 10–1," *SBT*, July 30, 1951.

89. "Belles Snap Blue Sox Victory Streak," *SBT*, July 31, 1951.

90. "Marrero Bests Faut in 2–1 Duel at Fort Wayne," *SBT*, august 1, 1951.

91. "Dottie Hurls, Faut Homers Sox to Victory," *SBT*, August 2, 1951.

92. "Daisies Cuff Blue Sox Nine by 11–1 Score," *SBT*, August 3, 1951.

93. "July 26, 1951, Immediate Release," Dailey Notebooks, volume 5, pp. 49v-50.

94. "Umpires Quit, But Blue Sox Keep Winning," *SBT*, August 6, 1951.

95. Journal entry and "Immediate Release," both July 26, 1951, Dailey Notebooks, volume 5, p. 49v.

96. "Blue Sox Lose in Dubuque, 4–2," *SBT*, August 4, 1951.

97. "Comets Sink South Bend, August 5, 1951, in Dubuque, Iowa, *Telegraph-Herald*.

98. "Blue Sox Beat Rockford, 7–1," *SBT*, August 8, 1951.

99. "Peaches Trip Blue Sox, 3–2, in 11 Innings," *SBT*, August 9, 1951.

100. "Records Fall as Sox Drub Daisies, 24–0," *SBT*, August 13, 1951.

101. "Faut Hurls, Bats Blue Sox to 1–0 Win in 16th," *SBT*, August 22, 1951.

102. "Sox Win 16th Game in Row by 7–6 Score," *SBT*, August 26, 1951.

103. Chicks Beat South Bend by 4–2 Score and Team Spirit Biggest Factor in Winning Ways, in "On the Level," *SBT*, August 27, 1951.

104. "South Bend Wins Girls League Pennant," *SBT*, September 2, 1951.

105. "Jean Faut Faces Fort Wayne's Kline in Playoff Opener," *SBT*, September 4, 1951.

106. "Jean Faut of Blue Sox Named Girls' Loop 'Most Valuable,'" *SBT*, November 15, 1951.

107. "South Bend Wins Opening Playoff Game, 2–1," *SBT*, September 5, 1951.

108. "Rockford Nine Whips Chicks; Enters Finals," *SBT*, September 6, 1951.

109. "Fort Wayne Wins, Evens Series with Sox," *SBT*, September 7, 1951.

110. "Sox Advance to Playoff Finals," *SBT*, September 8, 1951.

111. "South Bend Loses Playoff Tilt to Rockford," *SBT*, September 9, 1951.

112. "Sox Lose Second Playoff Test to Rockford Peaches," *SBT*, September 10, 1951.

113. "Same Old Story! Jean Faut …," *SBT*, September 11, 1951.

114. "Sox Eke Out 3–2 Win Over Rockford Nine," *SBT*, September 12, 1951.

115. Sox Pennant Chances Looked Very Glum, in "On the Level," *SBT*, September 14, 1951.

116. "South Bend[,] Rockford Clash for Girls League Title," *SBT*, September 13, 1951.

117. "South Bend Wins Girls League Pennant," *SBT*, September 14, 1951.

118. Sox Manager Karl Winsch Credits Team Spirit, in "On the Level," *SBT*, September 18, 1951.

119. Telephone interview with Lil Faralla, November 16, 2009.
120. "Resignation of Fred K. Leo as Commissioner," August 7, and "A Letter From Leo, August 20, 1951," Dailey Notebooks, volume 5, pp. 52–52v.

Chapter 10

1. "Faut to Hurl in Final Tilt at Freeport," *South Bend Tribune* (hereafter cited as *SBT*), September 11, 1952.
2. "Attendance of the South Bend Club for Entire Nine Years: 1943 to & Including 1951," Dailey Notebooks, volume 7, pp. 3, 6, 11–11v in AAGPBL Files, Joyce Sports Collection, Hesburgh Libraries of Notre Dame.
3. Journal entry, July 18, 1952, Dailey Notebooks, volume 7, p. 140v.
4. Journal entry, August 30, 1951, Dailey Notebooks, volume 5, p. 53.
5. "Winsch Tabbed for New Role," *SBT*, December 6, 1951.
6. "Jean Faut" in Barbara Gregorich, *Women at Play: The Story of Women in Baseball* (New York: Harcourt Brace, Harvest Books, 1993), p. 147.
7. Journal entries, n.d. [November, 1951] and December 6, 14, 1951, Dailey Notebooks, volume 7, p. 95.
8. "According to Doyle," *SBT*, May 14, 1952.
9. Journal entry, April 4, 1952, Dailey Notebooks, volume 7, p. 110.
10. Bob Gorman interview with Jean Faut, February 1, 2011.
11. Journal entry showing South Bend's salaries on May 10, 1952, Dailey Notebooks, volume 7, p. 110v.
12. Journal entries for April 4, 11, 24, 1952, Dailey Notebooks, volume 7, p. 110.
13. "Sign Most Valuable First" was the caption under the picture of Faut inking her contract, *SBT*, April 3, 1952.
14. Clippings, Dailey Notebooks, volume 7, p. 103v.
15. "Blue Sox Set First Workout for Monday," *SBT*, April 20, 1952.
16. "Blue Sox Infield Quartet Working Out" was the caption of a picture showing Mueller tagging a sliding Pryer, watched by Bleiler, Hoffman, and Karl Winsch; *SBT*, April 27, 1952.
17. "Blue Sox Play in Plymouth," *SBT*, May 11, 1952.
18. "According to Doyle," *SBT*, May 14, 1952.
19. Journal entries, April 27, May 6, 20, 24, 1952, Dailey Notebooks, volume 7, pp. 110–111.
20. "Blue Sox Trim Daisies, Set for Opener," *SBT*, May 14, 1952.
21. "Blue Sox Open Title Defense with 6–0 Win," *SBT*, May 16, 1952.
22. "Wet Grounds Delay Blue Sox Opener," *SBT*, May 17, 1952.
23. "Blue Sox Pound Battle Creek, 11–1, in Home Opener," *SBT*, May 19, 1952.
24. "According to Doyle," *SBT*, May 14, 1952.
25. "Official All-American Girls Baseball League — Season 1952," Howe News Bureau, copy in AAGPBL Files at Center for History (hereafter cited as CFH), South Bend, Indiana.
26. "Chicks End Blue Sox Unbeaten String with 5–3 Victory," *SBT*, May 22, 1952.
27. "Blue Sox Win, Then Get Beat in Exhibition," *SBT*, May 24, 1952.
28. "Chicks Lose, Weather Again Halts Blue Sox," *SBT*, May 25, 1952.
29. "Blue Sox Lead League On Faut's Three-Hitter," *SBT*, May 26, 1952.
30. Letter from Wilma Briggs, n.d. [April 4, 2011], who recalled that the Daisies had the shorter fence for a year or two.
31. "Blue Sox Bow, 5–4, Drop into Third Place," *SBT*, May 27, 1952.
32. "Kidd Pitches Blue Sox Back to First Spot," *SBT*, May 28, 1952.
33. Rumsey Halts Daisies on Four-Hitter, 6–2," *SBT*, May 29, 1952.
34. "Faut Hurls Shutout; Daisies File Protest," *SBT*, May 30, 1952.
35. "Blue Sox Lose to Lassies, 7–6, in Ten Innings," *SBT*, May 31, 1952.
36. "Rained on Sox Acquire New First Sacker," *SBT*, June 1, 1952.
37. "Blue Sox Take Two From Lassies; Move to Fort Wayne," *SBT*, June 2, 1952.
38. Telephone interview with Joyce (Hill) Westerman, October 18, 2010.
39. "Blue Sox Club Fort Wayne Foe," *SBT*, June 3, 1952.
40. "Blue Sox Regain A.G.L Lead," *SBT*, June 6, 1952.
41. "Faut's Double Scores Stoll for 4–3 Win," *SBT*, June 7, 1952.
42. "Blue Sox Lace Kazoo Foe, 13–4, to Keep First," *SBT*, June 8, 1952.
43. "Faut Opposes Chicks, Seeks Fourth Win," *SBT*, June 9, 1952.
44. "Blue Sox Hand Chicks Four Runs, Drop to Second Place," *SBT*, June 10, 1952.
45. "Blue Sox Win, Face Chicks in Twin Bill," *SBT*, June 11, 1952.
46. Journal entries, June 1, 2, 3, 4, and 7, 1952, Dailey Notebooks, volume 7, pp. 111–111v.
47. "Blue Sox Win Two to Lead League by 2 ," *SBT*, June 15, 1952.
48. "Wagoner Pitches, Bats Blue Sox to Win Over Peaches," *SBT*, June 16, 1952.
49. "Blue Sox Boost Lead to 3 Games with Win No. 8 in Row," *SBT*, June 17, 1952.
50. "Blue Sox Win for 10th in Row," *SBT*, June 18, 1952.
51. "Blue Sox Grab Easy Decision at Rockford," *SBT*, June 22, 1952.
52. "Manager and Umpire Ejected as Blue Sox Lose to Peaches," *SBT*, June 23, 1952.
53. "Blue Sox Open Home Stand Without Winsch," *SBT*, June 24, 1952.
54. "Bulletin," including "Turmoil at Rockford," June 27, 1952, Dailey Notebooks, volume 7, p. 125.
55. Letter from Winsch to McCammon, June 24, 1952, Dailey Notebooks, volume 7, pp. 124–124v.
56. "Blue Sox Mob Umpire, Peaches Win," *Rockford Register-Republic*, June 23, 1952.
57. "Faut Stops Battle Creek to Boost Sox 'Star' Claims," *SBT*, June 25, 1952.
58. "Blue Sox Capture All-Star Bid; Beat Daisies, 5–1," *SBT*, June 30, 1952.
59. "Rockford Dominates Girls' Loop All-Star Nine," *SBT*, July 2, 1952.
60. "Blue Sox Bow to All-Stars in Ninth, 7–6," *SBT*, July 8, 1952.
61. "Mueller Blanks Lassies; South Bend Leads By Five," *SBT*, July 9, 1952.

62. "Blue Sox Lose Two; Lassies Here Tonight," *SBT*, July 10, 1952.
63. Journal entry, June 16, 1952, Dailey Notebooks, volume 7, p. 111v.
64. Interview with Janet (Wiley) Sears, November 6, 2007.
65. Shirley Stovroff to Jean Faut, March 21, 1955 (hereafter cited as Stovroff Letter, 1955), copy in Faut Scrapbooks.
66. Minutes of Meeting, Board of Directors, July 7, 1952, "Janet Wiley Case," Dailey Notebooks, volume 9, pp. 126v-127. The board voted to release Wiley.
67. Telephone interview with Joyce (Hill) Westerman, October 18, 2010.
68. Journal entries, July 1, 3, 6, 8, 11, 18, 1952, Dailey Notebooks, volume 7, pp. 140–140v.
69. "Blue Sox Beaten, 3–2; Lead Cut to Half Game," *SBT*, August 21, 1952.
70. Stovroff Letter, 1955.
71. Interview with Jean Faut, November 3, 2010.
72. "Blue Sox Bow to Chicks, 6–0; Daisies Lose," *SBT*, July 14, 1952.
73. "Peaches Trip Blue Sox, 12–1 and Then 6–1," *SBT*, July 17, 1952.
74. "Blue Sox Walk to Win, Then Bow to Peaches," *SBT*, July 24, 1952.
75. "Daisies Gain Share Of Lead," *SBT*, July 26, 1952.
76. "Fort Wayne Slices South Bend Lead to Two Games," *SBT*, August 7, 1952.
77. "Blue Sox Nip Rockford, 3–2, Protect Lead," *SBT*, August 11, 1952.
78. "Blue Sox Overpower Fort Wayne By 9–6," *SBT*, August 15, 1952.
79. "Faut Topples Peaches But Daisies Keep Pace," *SBT*, August 19, 1952.
80. "Blue Sox Beaten, 3–2; Lead Cut to Half Game," *SBT*, August 21, 1952.
81. "Blue Sox Split; Daisies Gain First Place Tie," *SBT*, August 23, 1952.
82. "Blue Sox Beat Belles in 11th, Drop to 1 Game Out," *SBT*, August 26, 1952.
83. "Faut Hurls 19th Victory; Daisies Still Lead," *SBT*, August 27, 1952.
84. "Blue Sox Fall Again; Trail by 3 Games," *SBT*, August 30, 1952.
85. "Blue Sox Sweep Pair; Four Players Suspended," *SBT*, August 31, 1952.
86. Telephone interview with Lib Mahon, June 23, 1997.
87. Stovroff Letter, 1955.
88. Telephone interview with Lib Mahon, June 23, 1997.
89. W.C. Madden, *The Dutiful Dozen* (Noblesville, IN: Madden Publishing Co., 1997), pp. 49–50.
90. "Blue Sox Sweep Pair; Four Players Suspended," *SBT*, August 31, 1952.
91. "According to Doyle," *SBT*, September 2, 1952.
92. Bob Gorman interview with Jean Faut, September 7, 2010.
93. "Official All-American Girls Baseball League—Season 1952," copy in AAGPBL Files, CFH.
94. Stovroff Letter, 1955.
95. Telephone interview with Lib Mahon, August 30, 1997.
96. Telephone interview with Wimp Baumgartner, September 7, 2010.
97. Madden, *Dutiful Dozen*, p. 65.
98. Interview with Jean Faut, October 31, 2009.
99. Message from Sue Kidd, October 23, 2010.
100. Interview with Jean Faut, November 3, 2010.
101. Telephone interview with Wimp Baumgartner, September 7, 2010.
102. Telephone interview with Joyce (Hill) Westerman, October 18, 2010.
103. Interview with Jean Faut, November 3, 2010.
104. "Blue Sox Open Playoffs Against Chicks," *SBT*, September 2, 1952.
105. Telephone interview with Joyce (Hill) Westerman, October 18, 2010
106. "Blue Sox One Game From Final Playoffs," *SBT*, September 3, 1952.
107. "Blue Sox Sweep Playoff Series From Grand Rapids, 6–1," *SBT*, September 4, 1952.
108. "Peaches Host Blue Sox in Final Series," *SBT*, September 6, 1952.
109. "Peaches Rock Blue Sox in Playoff Tilt," *SBT*, September 7, 1952.
110. "Rockford Nips Blue Sox, 3–2; Both Managers Protest," *SBT*, September 8, 1952.
111. "Blue Sox Triumph On Field and at Conference Table," *SBT*, September 9, 1952.
112. "South Bend Near Defeat in A.A.G.L. Playoffs," *SBT*, September 10, 1952.
113. "Blue Sox Tie Playoff Series with 2–1 Victory in 10th," *SBT*, September 11, 1952.
114. Interview with Jean Faut, August 9, 1995.
115. "Blue Sox Defeat Peaches, 6 to 3, For Title," *Freeport Journal-Standard*, September 12, 1952.
116. Letter from Wimp Baumgartner, August 21, 1995.
117. Letter from Karl Winsch, April 10, 1996.
118. "According to Doyle," *SBT*, September 12, 1952.

Chapter 11

1. "According to Doyle," *South Bend Tribune* (hereafter cited as *SBT*), September 10, 1953.
2. "American Girls Baseball League: Minutes of Meeting of Board of Directors," August 15, 1952, Dailey Notebooks, volume 9, pp. 129v–130, AAGPBL Files, Joyce Special Collections, Hesburgh Libraries of the University of Notre Dame.
3. Merrie Fidler, *The Origins and History of the All-American Girls Professional Baseball League* (Jefferson, NC: McFarland, 2006), p. 137.
4. "According to Doyle," *SBT*, July 7, 1953.
5. Batting and fielding averages are taken from the Howe New Bureau's statistics for each season; copies in the AAGPBL Files, Center for History (hereafter cited as CFH), South Bend, Indiana.
6. AGBL Minutes, February 8, 1953, Dailey Notebooks, volume 9, pp. 139–140.
7. AGBL Minutes, January 20, 1953, Dailey Notebooks, volume 9, pp. 133–138.
8. Fidler, *Origins and History of the AAGPBL*, pp. 125–131.
9. Interview with Doris Sams, July 1, 1997.
10. "Blue Sox Feud Flares Again; Stoll to Retire," *SBT*, April 3, 1953.
11. Journal entry for May 10, 1952, Dailey Notebooks, volume 7, p. 110v.
12. Interview with Jean Faut, October 31, 2009.
13. "Faut Signs Eighth Pact with Blue Sox Champs," *SBT*, April 22, 1953.

14. "Blue Sox Set 55-Game Card," *SBT*, April 27, 1953.
15. "Vets Get Call From Sox Pilot Winsch," *SBT*, May 5, 1953.
16. See "Blue Sox Open Diamond Drills," May 3, "Winsch Greets 25 at Playland," May 4, and pictures in the sports pages on May 6 and 8, 1953, all in *SBT*.
17. "Blue Sox Nip Peaches, 8–7, Rookies Star," *SBT*, May 12, 1951.
18. "According to Doyle," *SBT*, May 13, 1953.
19. "Blue Sox Lose Two Players with Injuries," *SBT*, May 18, 1953.
20. "Blue Sox Lose Wenzell, but Rap Rockford," *SBT*, May 19, 1953.
21. "Blue Sox Whip Peaches Again," *SBT*, May 20, 1953.
22. "Rookies Dominate Blue Sox' Opening Game Lineup" and "According to Doyle," both in *SBT*, May 21, 1953.
23. "Nine in Fifth Wins Opener For Blue Sox," *SBT*, May 22, 1953.
24. "Chicks Beat Kidd, 5–4, in 10th Inning," *SBT*, May 24, 1953.
25. "Blue Sox Bow, 5–3, in Home Opener to Muskegon," *SBT*, May 25, 1953.
26. "Blue Sox Use Bunt Weapon to Trip Muskegon, 8–4," *SBT*, May 26, 1953.
27. "Blue Sox Blow Early Lead, Bow to Muskegon," *SBT*, May 27, 1953.
28. "Loop Leaders Play Blue Sox," *SBT*, May 28, 1953.
29. "Faut Hurls Dazzling Two-Hit Shutout for Blue Sox," *SBT*, May 29, 1953.
30. "Blue Sox Split with Lassies," *SBT*, May 31, 1953.
31. "Patched Up Sox Top Kalamazoo," *SBT*, June 1, 1953.
32. "Faut Whiffs Twelve to Defeat Muskegon, 4–3," *SBT*, June 2, 1953.
33. "Blue Sox Tie Belles, 2–2, in 11 Innings," *SBT*, June 3, 1953.
34. "Belles Bunch Hits to Defeat Blue Sox," *SBT*, June 4, 1953.
35. "Blue Sox Clash with Top-Ranked Ft. Wayne in Week-End Series," *SBT*, June 5, 1953.
36. "Blue Sox Outlast Daisies in Opener, 11–4," *SBT*, June 7, 1953.
37. "Blue Sox Drop to Last Place," *SBT*, June 10, 1953.
38. "Blue Sox Lose Eighth in Row," *SBT*, June 14, 1953.
39. "Blue Sox Face Peaches at Playland After Long Losing Streak on Road," *SBT*, June 17, 1953.
40. "Blue Sox End Losing Streak, Topple Rockford, 4–1," *SBT*, June 18, 1953.
41. "Chicks Challenge Jean Faut As Blue Sox Open Series," *SBT*, June 25, 1953.
42. "Homer By Faut Sparks Sox Win," *SBT*, June 26, 1953.
43. "Rumsey Hurls in Free Game For Blue Sox," *SBT*, June 27, 1953.
44. "Blue Sox Win in Ninth, 5–4," *SBT*, June 28, 1953.
45. Message from Sue Kidd, December 28, 2010.
46. Letter from Jean Faut, January 31, 2011.
47. Telephone interview with Wimp Baumgartner, September 7, 2010.
48. Message from Lois Youngen, April 8, 2011.
49. "Sweep Of Series Moves Blue Sox Into Race," *SBT*, July 10, 1953.
50. "Kidd Pitches Double-Header Victory For Blue Sox," *SBT*, July 5, 1953.
51. "Kidd Celebrates 'Night,' Pitches Blue Sox to Victory Over Lassies," *SBT*, July 9, 1953.
52. "Blue Sox Bow to Belles, 3–2," *SBT*, July 1, 1953.
53. "4–3 Loss Ends Blue Sox Skein," *SBT*, July 14, 1953.
54. "Rumsey Hurls Two Victories For Blue Sox," *SBT*, July 21, 1953.
55. "Kalamazoo Spills Blue Sox Twice, First Games Goes 13," *SBT*, August 6, 1953.
56. "Blue Sox Open Home Stand After 5–1 Loss," *SBT*, July 6, 1953.
57. "Blue Sox Blank Muskegon Twice for Eight in A Row," *SBT*, July 13, 1953.
58. "4–3 Loss Ends Blue Sox Skein," *SBT*, July 14, 1953.
59. "Homer in 11th Wins All-Star Game For Ft. Wayne," *SBT*, July 15, 1953.
60. "According to Doyle," *SBT*, July 7, 1953.
61. "Fort Wayne Clips Blue Sox On Foss' Home Run," *SBT*, July 19, 1953.
62. "Blue Sox Home From Road Trip," *SBT*, July 24, 1953.
63. "Faut Allows Two [actually four] Hits; Sox Whip Daisies," *SBT*, July 26, 1953.
64. "Peaches Defeat Faut and Blue Sox in 4–3 Contest," *SBT*, July 30, 1953.
65. "Blue Sox Gain On Peaches; Play in Elkhart Tonight," *SBT*, July 31, 1953.
66. "Blue Sox Nip Peaches, Take Over Fourth Spot," *SBT*, August 1, 1953.
67. Telephone interview with Wimp Baumgartner, September 7, 2010.
68. Telephone interview with Mary (Froning) O'Meara, October 25, 2010.
69. Message from Sue Kidd, November 5, 2010.
70. Message from Sue Kidd, January 2, 2011.
71. Letter from Janet Rumsey, August 7, 1995.
72. "Lassies Gain Sixth in Row, Beat Sox, 2–0," *SBT*, August 3, 1953.
73. "Faut Defeats Lassies By 2–1," *SBT*, August 4, 1953.
74. "Blue Sox Tied 2–2 By Lassies," *SBT*, August 5, 1953.
75. "Kalamazoo Spills Blue Sox Twice, First Game Goes Thirteen," *SBT*, August 6, 1953.
76. "Chicks Lash Wagoner and Blue Sox For 10–2 Victory," *SBT*, August 7, 1953.
77. "Blue Sox Lose Two to Chicks," *SBT*, August 8, 1953.
78. "Blue Sox Get Two in 10th; Down Chicks," *SBT*, August 9, 1953.
79. "Muskegon Belles Franchise Turned Back to Girls League," *Muskegon Chronicle*, August 8, 1953.
80. "Financial Report," AGBL Minutes, April 26, 1953, Dailey Notebooks, volume 9, p. 152.
81. "Report on League Status," AGBL Minutes, September 12, 1953, Dailey Notebooks, volume 9, p. 164.
82. "Homeless Belles Cuff Blue Sox in 15–0 Rout," *SBT*, August 10, 1953.
83. "Stingy Kidd Defeats Ex-Muskegon Team On Six-Hitter" and "According to Doyle," *SBT*, August 11, 1953.
84. "Blue Sox Walk to 1–0 Victory," *SBT*, August 12, 1953.
85. "Blue Sox Drop Fourth in Row," *SBT*, August 16, 1953.
86. "Blue Sox Drop 12–3 Decision to Lassies," *SBT*, August 17, 1953.
87. "Blue Sox Lose Sixth in Row at Playland," *SBT*, August 18, 1953.
88. "31 Bases On Balls Mar Another Blue Sox Loss," *SBT*, August 19, 1953.
89. Letter from Dottie Schroeder, July 31, 1995.

90. "Blue Sox Whip Muskegon Twice to Snap Losing Streak," *SBT*, August 20, 1953.
91. "Kidd Defeats Belles, 2–1, at Lippincott," *SBT*, August 21, 1953.
92. "Blue Sox Play Loop Leader at St. Joseph," *SBT*, August 22, 1953.
93. "Faut Stifies Ft. Wayne Bats," *SBT*, August 23, 1953.
94. "Squeeze Gives Blue Sox Edge over Rockford," *SBT*, August 26, 1953.
95. "Ft. Wayne Bats Boom, Blue Sox Beaten, 10–3," *SBT*, August 29, 1953.
96. "Blue Sox Rap Peaches, 9–3, Two Tonight," *SBT*, September 1, 1953.
97. "Peaches Crush Blue Sox Playoff Hopes," *SBT*, September 3, 1953.
98. "Faut Hurls Perfect Game Against Lassies," *SBT*, September 4, 1953.
99. "Kalamazoo Trounces Blue Sox in 19–5 Tilt," *SBT*, September 5, 1953.
100. "Blue Sox End Home Season with Chicks," *SBT*, September 6, 1953.
101. "Blue Sox Bow Then Divide Over Holiday," *SBT*, September 8, 1953.
102. Interview with Jean Faut, August 7, 1995.
103. "Blue Sox Bow Then Divide Over Holiday," *SBT*, September 8, 1953.
104. "According to Doyle," *SBT*, September 10, 1953.
105. Telephone interview with Jean Faut, August 6, 2006.

Chapter 12

1. "According to Doyle," *South Bend Tribune* (hereafter cited as *SBT*), July 30, 1954.
2. Minutes of Meeting, Board of [AGBL] Directors, April 10, 1954, Dailey Notebooks, volume 9, pp. 172–173, AAGPBL Files, Joyce Sports Collection, Hesburgh Libraries of Notre Dame.
3. John Thorn, Phil Birnbaum, and Bill Deane, eds., *Total Baseball: The Ultimate Baseball Encyclopedia* (Wilmington, DE: Sports Media Publishing, 8th ed., 2004), pp. 2417–2422.
4. Lois Browne, *Girls of Summer* (New York: Harper Perennial Ed., 1993), pp. 189–190.
5. Lloyd Johnson and Miles Wolff, eds., *The Encyclopedia of Minor League Baseball* (Durham, NC: Baseball America, Inc., 2nd ed., 1997), p. 411.
6. Debra A. Shattuck, "Women in Baseball," in *Total Baseball*, p. 703.
7. See "Blue Sox Open with Twin Bill," *SBT*, May 28, 1954.
8. AGBL Minutes, January 24, 1954, Dailey Notebooks, volume 9, pp. 168–170.
9. H.D. Maloney, "Monetary Policy and the Recession of 1953–54," *Journal of Finance*, volume 14, number 4 (December 1959), pp. 569–570.
10. AGBL Minutes, February 29, 1954, Dailey Notebooks, volume 9, pp. 121–121v.
11. AGBL Minutes, April 10, 1954, Dailey Notebooks, volume 9, pp. 172–173.
12. AGBL Minutes, May 2, 1954, Dailey Notebooks, volume 9, pp. 174–174v.
13. "Blue Sox Open Training Camp Tuesday at Playland," *SBT*, May 12, 1954.
14. "Janet Wiley Undergoes Surgery for Bad Knee," *Rockford Register-Republic*, August 3, 1953, copy in Helen Nordquist's scrapbooks.
15. Interview with Janet (Wiley) Sears, November 6, 2007.
16. "Tryout School Report—Drawing of Rookies," AGBL Minutes, May 16, 1954, Dailey Notebooks, volume 9, pp. 175–175v.
17. "According to Doyle," *SBT*, May 21, 1954.
18. Message from Sue Kidd, January 13, 2011.
19. "Rockford Gives Up on Baseball League For Girls," *Chicago Daily Tribune*, November 22, 1953.
20. "League Deals Stars to Sox," *SBT*, May 25, 1954.
21. "Blue Sox Whip Ft. Wayne Nine," *SBT*, May 26, 1954.
22. "Blue Sox Add New Faces in Field, Office," *SBT*, May 27, 1954.
23. "Blue Sox Topple Grand Rapids in Opener, 7–1," *SBT*, May 29, 1954.
24. "Blue Sox Down Grand Rapids," *SBT*, May 30, 1954.
25. "Blue Sox Blank Ft. Wayne Twice, Seek No. 5 Tonight," *SBT*, May 31, 1954.
26. "Blue Sox Try Again Tonight Against Kazoo," *SBT*, June 2, 1954.
27. "Blue Sox Split Doubleheader," *SBT*, June 3, 1954.
28. "Blue Sox Belt Rockford, 3–0," *SBT*, June 5, 1954.
29. "Peaches Nip Blue Sox, 1–0, to Cut Lead," *SBT*, June 6, 1954.
30. "Blue Sox Bow Again, Drop to Second Place," *SBT*, June 7, 1954.
31. "Blue Sox Back in First Place," *SBT*, June 8, 1954.
32. "Blue Sox Host Pesky Daisies," *SBT*, June 9, 1954.
33. "Daisies Rap Blue Sox On Kline's Six-Hitter," *SBT*, June 10, 1954.
34. "Blue Sox Skid to Last, Lose Seven in Row," *SBT*, June 14, 1954.
35. "Blue Sox End Losing Ways in One Tilt," *SBT*, June 15, 1954.
36. "South Bend Beat Peaches By 7–5," *SBT*, June 16, 1954.
37. "Rumsey Stars For Blue Sox," *SBT*, June 20, 1954.
38. "Blue Sox Host Fort Wayne Nine," *SBT*, June 22, 1954.
39. "Double Steal Aids Blue Sox," *SBT*, June 28, 1952.
40. "Blue Sox Bow to 1-Hitter at Ft. Wayne," *SBT*, June 30, 1954.
41. "Girls' League Votes to Use Regulation 9-Inch Ball," *SBT*, June 11, 1954.
42. AGBL Minutes, April 10, 1954, Dailey Notebooks, volume 9, pp. 172–173.
43. See Jay Feldman, "All But Forgotten Now, A Women's Baseball League Once Flourished," *Sports Illustrated*, June 10, 1985, in SI Vault, pp. 1–3.
44. "Blue Sox Shift to Smaller Ball," *SBT*, July 1, 1954.
45. Chet Grant, "Girls' Baseball," *SBT's Sunday Magazine*, August 15, 1954, pp. 8–10.
46. "Blue Sox Split Pair as Home Run Era Dawns," *SBT*, July 2, 1954.
47. Telephone interview with Wilma Briggs, January 28, 2011.
48. "Chicks Hand South Bend 12–11 Defeat," *SBT*, July 4, 1954.
49. "Briggs, Wanless Lead Blue Sox to Victory," *SBT*, July 6, 1954.
50. "Rumsey Only South Bend Player on Girls' Star Team," *SBT*, July 7, 1954.

51. "Francis Slams Two Homers as Blue Sox, Daisies Split," *SBT*, July 8, 1954.
52. "Daisies Whip All-Star Nine," *SBT*, July 10, 1954.
53. *Ibid.*
54. Letter from Marilyn (Jones) Doxey, June 7, 1998.
55. "Blue Sox Sweep Pair; Gain Second Place," *SBT*, July 12, 1954.
56. Letter from Betty Francis, March 1, 2011.
57. Telephone interview with Mary (Froning) O'Meara, October 25, 2011.
58. A count of South Bend's game records showed that Kidd won nine games and lost five, not six.
59. Letter from Betsy Jochum, June 28, 2009.
60. Message from Sue Kidd, January 20, 2011.
61. "Rockford Tips Blue Sox, 4–2," *SBT*, July 18, 1954.
62. "Blue Sox Drop Third in Row to Rockford," *SBT*, July 19, 1954.
63. "Blue Sox Win at Rockford By 2–0 Tally," *SBT*, July 20, 1954.
64. "Blue Sox Win; Face Frankel Nine Tonight," *SBT*, July 21, 1954.
65. "Blue Sox No Match For Frankel Nine," *SBT*, July 22, 1954.
66. "Lassie Errors Help Blue Sox Into Second," *SBT*, July 26, 1954.
67. "Weaver Paces Ft. Wayne to 9–7 Win Over Blue Sox," *SBT*, August 2, 1954.
68. "Blue Sox Top Grand Rapids in 11 Innings," *SBT*, August 7, 1954.
69. "Blue Sox Gain Sixth in Row," *SBT*, August 8, 1954.
70. "Daisies Whip Blue Sox, 8–5," *SBT*, August 11, 1954.
71. "Lassies Rout South Bend By 11–3 Tally," *SBT*, August 16, 1954.
72. "Girls' Team at Playland For Twin Bill," *SBT*, August 17, 1954.
73. "Bus, Blue Sox Stall Lassies," *SBT*, August 18, 1954.
74. "Daisies Bury Blue Sox Under 24–8 Assault," *SBT*, August 23, 1954.
75. Message from Sue Kidd, January 11, 2011.
76. "Girls League Flag Is Won By Fort Wayne," *SBT*, August 24, 1954.
77. "Rumsey Pitches Near-Perfect No-Hitter," *SBT*, August 25, 1954.
78. "Blue Sox Set For Playoffs," *SBT*, August 26, 1954.
79. "Blue Sox End Season; Forfeit to Ft. Wayne," *SBT*, August 27, 1954.
80. "According to Doyle," *SBT*, August 31, 1954.
81. "Blue Sox Rap Lassies, 6–3," *SBT*, August 29, 1954.
82. "Blue Sox Lose, 6–3; Grand Rapids Forfeits," *SBT*, August 30, 1954.
83. "Blue Sox Beaten in Playoff Final," *SBT*, August 31, 1954.
84. The Girls League Situation, in Bob Reed's "Sports Roundup," *Fort Wayne Journal-Gazette*, September 1, 1954.
85. Telephone interview with Wimp Baumgartner, September 7, 2010.
86. Message from Sue Kidd, January 11, 2011.
87. Telephone interview with Mary (Froning) O'Meara, October 25, 2010.
88. "Ft. Wayne 'Wins' Again on Forfeit," *SBT*, August 31, 1954.
89. "Lassies Whip Ft. Wayne in Playoff Series," *SBT*, September 7, 1954.
90. Feldman, "All But Forgotten Now, A Women's Baseball League Once Existed," pp. 1–3, and Merrie Fidler, *The Origins and History of the All-American Girls Professional Baseball League* (Jefferson, NC: McFarland, 2006), pp. 229–262.
91. Jim Sargent, "June Peppas and the All-American League: Helping the Kalamazoo Lassies Win the 1954 AAGPBL Championship," SABR's *The National Pastime* (2002), p. 13.
92. Letter from Betty Francis, March 1, 2011.
93. "Cooperstown Skirts One Issue: Stolen-Base Record Stays in Man's World Despite Sophie's Feat" *Flint Journal*, April 12, 1991.
94. Interview with Jean Faut, October 31, 2009.

Bibliography

Books

Bramson, Seth H. *The Curtiss-Wright Cities: Hialeah, Miami Springs, and Opa Locka*. Charleston: History Press, 2008.

Brokaw, Tom. *The Greatest Generation*. New York: Random House, 1998.

Browne, Lois. *Girls of Summer: In Their Own League*. New York: Harper Collins, 1993.

Davis, Pepper Paire. *Dirt in the Skirt*. Bloomington: AuthorHouse, 2009.

Fidler, Merrie. *The Origins and History of the All-American Girls Professional Baseball League*. Jefferson, NC: McFarland, 2006.

Fort Wayne Daisies: 1947 Year Book. Fort Wayne, IN: Wayne Paper Box and Printing Corp., 1947.

Giglio, James N. *Musial: From Stash to Stan the Man*. Columbia, MO: University of Missouri Press, 2001.

Gregorich, Barbara. *Women at Play: The Story of Women in Baseball*. New York: Harcourt, 1993.

Halberstam, David. *The Fifties*. New York: Fawcett, 1993.

Heaphy, Leslie A., and Mel A. Mays, eds. *Encyclopedia of Women and Baseball*. Jefferson, NC: McFarland, 2006.

Johnson, Lloyd, and Miles Wolff, eds. *The Encyclopedia of Minor League Baseball*. 2nd ed. Durham, NC: Baseball America, 1997.

Johnson, Susan E. *When Women Played Hardball*. Seattle: Seal Press, 1994.

Kaledin, Eugenia. *Daily Life in the United States, 1940–1959: Shifting Worlds*. Westport, CT: Greenwood Press, 2000.

Kovach, John M. *Baseball in South Bend*. Charleston: Arcadia Publishing, 2004.

Lamb, Chris. *Blackout: The Untold Story of Jackie Robinson's First Spring Training*. Lincoln, NE: University of Nebraska Press, 2004.

Macy, Sue. *A Whole New Ball Game: The Story of the All-American Girls Professional Baseball League*. New York: Henry Holt, 1993.

Madden, W. C. *The Dutiful Dozen*. Noblesville, IN: Madden Publishing, 1997.

_____. *The Women of the All-American Girls Professional Baseball League: A Biographical Dictionary*. Jefferson, NC: McFarland, 1997.

Maier, Pauline. *Inventing America: A History of the United States*. 2nd ed. New York: W. W. Norton, 2006.

Major League Baseball. Racine, WI: Whitman Publishing. Editions for 1945, 1946, 1947, 1948, and 1949.

Martin, Jenni. *Safe at Home: A History of Softball in Saskatchewan*. Regina: Saskatchewan Sports Hall of Fame, 1997.

Mead, William B. *Baseball Goes to War*. Washington, DC: Farragut Publishing, 1985.

Palmer, John. *South Bend: Crossroads of Commerce*. Charleston: Arcadia Publishing, 2003.

South Bend Blue Sox: 1947 Year Book. South Bend, IN: Privately printed, 1947.

Thorn, John, et. al. *Total Baseball: The Ultimate Baseball Encyclopedia*. 8th ed. Wilmington, DE: Sport Media, 2004.

Trombe, Carolyn M. *Dottie Wiltse Collins: Strikeout Queen of the All-American Girls Professional Baseball League*. Jefferson, NC: McFarland, 2005.

Articles

"Baseball: Babette Ruths." *Newsweek*, July 29, 1946.

Fay, Bill. "Belles of the Ball Game." *Collier's*, August 13, 1949.

Fay, William Cullen. "Bonnie's the Belle of the Ball Game." *Sport*, May 1947.

Feldman, Jay. "All But Forgotten Now, a Women's Baseball League Once Flourished." *Sports Illustrated*, June 10, 1985.

"Girls' Baseball: A Feminine Midwest League Opens Its Third Professional Season." *Life*, June 4, 1945.

Grant, Chet. "Girls' Baseball." *South Bend Tribune Magazine*, August 15, 1954.

Maloney, H. D. "Monetary Policy and the Recession of 1953–54. *Journal of Finance* 14 (December 1959: 569–70.

Markey, Morris. "Hey Ma, You're Out." *McCall's*, September 1950.

Sargent, Jim. "The Flint Flash: The Premier Base

Stealer of the All-American Girls Baseball League." *Oldtyme Baseball News* 8, no. 4 (1997): 30–31.

———. "Jean Faut: The All-American League's Greatest Overhand Pitcher." *Ragtyme Sports*, March 1996.

———. "June Peppas and the All-American League: Helping the Kalamazoo Lassies Win the 1954 AAGPBL Championship." *The National Pastime* (2002): 9–13.

Newspapers

Charlotte Observer
Chicago Defender
Chicago Tribune
Dayton (OH) *Daily News*
Freeport (IL) *Journal-Standard*
Grand Rapids (MI) *Press*
Hagerstown (MD) *Herald*
Kalamazoo (MI) *Gazette*
Kenosha (WI) *Evening News*
Los Angeles Times
Lowell (MA) *Sun*
Milwaukee Journal
Moose-Jaw (SK) *Herald-Times*
Muskegon (MI) *Chronicle*
New York Herald Tribune
New York Times
Palm Beach (FL) *Post*
Peoria (IL) *Journal Transcript*
Racine (WI) *Journal-Times*
Rockford (IL) *Morning Star*
Rockford (IL) *Register-Republic*
South Bend (IN) *Tribune*
The Sporting News
Syracuse (NY) *Herald-Journal*
Telegraph-Herald (Dubuque, IA)
Washington Post

Interviews

Arnold, Lou. Interview by Jim Sargent, November 6, 2007.
Baumgartner, Mary "Wimp." Interview by Jim Sargent, September 7, 2010.
Bergmann, Erma. Interview by Jim Sargent, November 7, 2009.
Born, Ruth. Interview by Jim Sargent, October 18, 2007.
Briggs, Wilma. Interview by Jim Sargent, January 28, 1011.
Faralla, Lil. Interviews by Jim Sargent, November 16, 2009, and November 20, 2010.
Faut, Jean. Interviews by Jim Sargent and Robert Gorman, August 9, 1995, August 6, 2006, November 8, 2008, September 16, 2009, October 17, 2009, October 31, 2009, December 4, 2009, September 7, 2010, and November 3, 2010.
Jochum, Betsy. Interviews by Jim Sargent, November 10, 2007, November 2, 2008, and May 6, 2009.
Kidd, Sue. Interview by Jim Sargent, September 6, 2010.
Mahon, Lib. Interview by Jim Sargent, June 23, 1997.
Odell, Carolyn. Interview by Jim Sargent, June 23, 2009.
O'Meara (Froning), Mary. Interview by Jim Sargent, October 25, 2010.
Proefrock (Ahrndt), Ellen. Interview by Jim Sargent, November 1, 2007.
Ross (MacLean), Lucella. Interviews by Jim Sargent, November 20, 2007, and January 24, 2011.
Rusynyk (McFadden), Betty. Interview by Jim Sargent, December 6, 2007.
Sams, Doris. Interview by Jim Sargent, July 2, 1997.
Sears (Wiley), Janet. Interview by Jim Sargent, November 6, 2007.
Steffes (Filarski), Helen. Interview by Jim Sargent, July 7, 2010.
Voyce, Inez. Interview by Jim Sargent, August 28, 2009.
Westerman (Hill), Joyce. Interview by Jim Sargent, October 18, 2010.

Archival Collections

Center for History (formerly the Northern Indiana Center for History), South Bend, IN.
Joyce Special Collections, Hesburgh Libraries of the University of Notre Dame, South Bend, IN.
Louise Pettus Archives and Special Collections, Winthrop University, Rock Hill, SC.
National Baseball Hall of Fame Library, Cooperstown, NY.

Index

Page numbers in **_bold italics_** indicate illustrations

A-A-G's Mail Bag (newsletter) 97
Acker, Fredda (Thompson) 98, **_100_**
Admiral Music Maids 57
African American players *see* integration
Ahrndt, Ellen "Babe" 32, **_38_**, 39–40, 42, 48, 51
"The All-American Girl" a.k.a. "The Victory Song" (song) 63, 80, 108, 114
All-American Girls Baseball (Base Ball) League 3, 28, 72, **_77_**, 94, 117, 136, 177
All-American Girls Professional Ball League 31, 52
All-American Girls Professional Baseball League (AAGPBL) 2, 4–5, 9, 28, 52, 258
All-American Girls Soft Ball League 9, 11–12, 247
Allen, Aggie 206, 233
Allen, Betty (Petryna) 141, 147
Allerton (hotel) 54
Allington, Bill 43, 154, 159, 198, 208–209, 217, 222, 231, 246, 257
Alspaugh, Melba 145, 154
Ambassador (hotel) 33, 40
American Girls Baseball League 5, 179, 181–182, 195, 199–200, 220, 225, 237, 239, 243, 247, 258
Ames Field 255
Anderson, Janet 79
Anderson, South Carolina 74
Anthony (hotel) 58, 76
Applegren, Amy 36, 40, 43, 67, 70, 102, 109, 114, 125, 163, 174, 183, 208, 217, 223, 227–232, 235–237
Armstrong, Charlotte 32–36, **_35_**, 39–41, 43–50, **_47_**, 54, 57, 60–61, 66–70, 73
Arnold, Louise "Lou" 121–123, 125–127, 131, 134, 139–142, **_140_**, 145, 151–154, **_173_**, 180, 182–184, 186–187, 191, 193–196, 198, 203–204, 206–208, 212, 214, 216–217

Bailey Park/Field 184, 203, 207
Baker, Mary " Bonnie" 15, **_16_**, 21–28, **_25_**, 32–34, **_35_**, 36, 40–44, 46–49, 51, 53–54, 56–57, 60, 65–67, 69–70, 73–74, 79, 83–84, 86–87, 90–93, **_92_**, 98, **_100_**, 101, 104–109, 111–112, 114–115, 119–123, 127, 129–132, 134–136, 139–**_140_**, 142–144, 147–148, 151–152, 154, 159–160, 162–167, 171, 174, 176, 189, 258; manager of the Muskegon/Kalamazoo Lassies 164–167, 180
Baker, Phyllis 224–225, 229–230, 242–246, **_243_**, 248, 252–253, 256
Balancing Committee 159, 165–166, 171, 177, 242
Ballingall, Chris 257
balls used in league 12, 21, 28, 33, 52, 73, 94, 96, 117, 120, 136–138, 144–145, 151, 161, 169, **_192_**, 221, 240, 247–248, 252
Bancroft, Dave 118, 139, **_140_**, 145, 148–149, 152–155, 159–160, **_161_**, 162, 164, 166–172, 174, 176, 178, 189
Barnett, Charlene 126, 154, 163
Barr, Doris "Dodie" 15, **_16_**, 17, 20–24, 26–9, 32–34, **_35_**, 39–40, 43, 48–51, 54, 57–58, 61–62, 65, 68, 70–71, 82, 92, 109, 125, 134, 142; no-hit game 33
base path distances 10, 12, 28, 33, 47, 52–53, 66, 71, 73, 94, 123, 161, 221, 247
Bass, Dick 137
bat girls 86–**_87_**, 160, 169–170, **_218_**, 222, 230, 241
Battle Creek, Michigan 160, 182, 184, 207, 222, 240
Battle Creek Belles 182, 184–187, 191, 194–196, 199, 202–203, 205–212, 220, 230; financial difficulties 186, 195, 199; move to Muskegon 220
Bauer, Arnold 27, 37, 39
Baumgartner, Mary "Wimp" 160, 162, 181–183, 188, **_189_**, 191–192, 195, 202, 204, 206, 212–219, 222–224, 226–231, 233–234, 237, 242, **_243_**, 246, 248, 250, 254–255, 257

Beare, Kathryn 74
behavior/comportment 14, 37–38, 97–98, 160–161
Beirn, Ken 12
Belmont (hotel) 1, 13–14
Bendix Aviation 18, 26–27, 53, 55, 102, 128, 143, 221
Bendix Field 15, 17–21, 23, 26, 28, 32–34, 37, 40, 43–44, 46, 49, 53, 55–57, 60–63, 65, 67–68, 70, 86, 200
Bennett, Kay **_16_**, 23–29, 32–34, **_35_**, 36, 39–40, 42–43, 46, 48, 50; no-hit game 33
Berger, Joan 198, 209, 222, 232
Berger, Margaret "Sunny" 15, **_16_**, 17, 20–29, 32–34, **_35_**, 36, 39–41, 43–46, **_47_**, 48–51, 71, 258
Bergmann, Erma 73, 101, 109, 111, 125, 142, 151, 194
Berkowitz, George 51
Beyer Stadium 19, 36, 44, **_45_**, 80, 89, 105, 143, 154, 173, 183, 217–218, 229, 241, 244, 252
Bigbee, Carson 118, 133
Bigelow Field 165, 185, 196; fire 211
Billings, Josh 14
Bird, Nalda "Birdie" 54–57, 60–64, 66–69, 73; composer of "The All-American Girl" 63
Birmingham, Alabama 74, 79
Bittner, Jaynne 98, **_100_**, 103, 105, 108–109, 114, 138, 185, 205, 242
Black, Don 159
Bleiler, Audrey 160, **_161_**, 162, 170, 173, 175, 180, 182–183, 186–187, **_190_**, 194–198, **_196_**, 202–203, 205–206, 215
Blumetta, Kay 141, 153, 163, 175, 227, 230, 244
Bobby Sox League 72, 93
Boian, Harold 99
Boland, Joe 87, 109
Borchert Field 33, 40, 45, 49
Born, Ruth **_16_**, 23, 25–27, 29
Bosse Field 74
Bower Family 160
Boyle, Buzz 73
Briggs, Rita 126, 139, **_140_**, 141, 144–145, 149, 151, 174, 197

287

INDEX

Briggs, Wilma "Briggsie" 146, 183, 226, 234, 242–*243*, 246, 248, *249*, 250, 252–257
Browne, Lois 62, 119, 141, 239
Brumfield, Delores "Dolly" 98, *100*, 101–102, 108–109, 121, 126, 151, 193
bus travel 1, 75–*76*, 80, 98, 101, 123, 133, 148, 251
Buszka, Arlene 222–223
Butler, Paul M. 162

CAA Field *see* Catholic Athletic Association (CAA) Field
Cahn, Susan M. 12
Callaghan, Helen (Candaele) 46, 51, 67, 76, 125, 144, 151
Callaghan, Marge *77*, 139, *140*, 151
Callow, Eleanor "Ellie" 111, 126, 143, 145, 154–155, 183, 187, 197–198, 209, 217, 232, 246
Candaele, Helen *see* Callaghan, Helen (Candaele)
Cape Girardeau, Missouri 160
Carey, Mary 164, 236, 242, *243*, 245–246, 251, 253–254, 256
Carey, Max 32, 43–44, 49, 53–54, 57, 65–66, 68–69, 71–5, 94, 98, 114–115, 117–118, 125–126, 134, 137, 139, 152, 154–155, 157, 159, 248; manager of Fort Wayne Daisies 159, 174, 183, 197
Carey Cup Playoffs 154–155
Carver, Virginia 222
Catholic Athletic Association (CAA) Field 181, 206, 249, 253, 257
Cattrell Family 160
chaperones 3, 14–15, *16*, 22, 27, 31–32, *35*, 42, *45*, 64, *76*, 86, *92*, 96, 98, *100*, 107, 122, 135–137, 139, *140*, 160, *161*, 162, 176, 179, *181*, 201–202, *243*, 258
Chapman, Al 133
Charlotte, North Carolina 99
charm school 13–14, 37–38, 52
Chester, Bea 24, 27–28
Chicago, Illinois 1, 12–15, 18, 21–22, 26, 32–33, 35, 40–43, 48, 53, 57–58, 64, 74–75, 80–81, 85, 97, 101, 118, 125–127, 133, 139, 147, 163–164, 169–171, 179, 187, 215, 222–223, 240, 246, 250–251, 258
Chicago Colleens 118–122, 125–129, 133, 136–137, 139, 149, 159–160, 240, 250; financial difficulties 125, 136; rookie team 118, 136–137, *156*
Chicago League 57, 71, 74, 182, 201, 227
Choctaw, Arkansas 3, 11, 156, 191, *204*, 229
Christ, Dorothy 261
Cione, Jean 81, 103, 151, 186, 193, 208
Clapp, Louise *243*, 246
Coben, Muriel 15, 17, 19–21, 23–24, 26

Colacito, Lucille 36
Collins, Dottie (Wiltse) 36, 46, 50–51, 57, 59, 67, 70, 76, *77*, 80, 102, 105, 114, 125, 155, 175
Columbus, Illinois 222
commissioner 118, 177–178, 199, 201, 221, 229, 240, 256
Condit, Harold 179
contracts 12–13, 31, 53–54, 85–86, 97, 157, 178–179, 202, 212, 221
Cook, Clara 24
Cook, Donna "Cookie" 125, 143, 147, 153, 230, 234, 236–237
Cook, Doris 226–227, 230–232, 234–235
Cooper, Joe 225, 234
Cordes, Gloria 209, 212–213, 227, 257
Costin, Jim 15, 17, 20, 24–26, 28, 31–32, 34, 41, 43, 48–50, 55–8, 66, 69–70, 72, 76–77, 79, 83, 89–91, 93, 100, 104–105, 111–112, 123, 125, 127–128, 131, 133, 136; death 139
Costin, Mina 11, 15, 26, 28, 139
Coveleski, Stan 253
Craighead, Norwood 221
Cramer, Peggy 242, *243*, 246, 251–252, 255
Crawley, Pauline 202
Crews, Mary *see* Nesbitt, Mary (Crews)
Crigler, Idona "Dodie" 111, 114–115
Cromie, Robert 187
Cuban players 86, 96, 98, 118, 120–121, 123, 126

Dailey, Harold "Doc" 62, 73, 84, 106, 115, 118–119, 121, 131, 135–136, 139, 158–159, 164–165, 167–168, 171–172, 174–176, *178*, 179, 199, 201, 203, 207, 210, 213; fight with Chet Grant 115, 118
Dailey, Mary 160, 162–164, 169, 180–183, 186, 194
Dancer, Faye 42, 51, 54, *69*, 70, 76, 80, 89–90, 111, 164
D'Angelo, Josephine "Jo" 15, *16*, 21–22, 26–28, 32, 35–37, 40, 47–48
Danhauser, Marnie 90, 112
Dapkus, Eleanor "Ellie" 41, 66, 90–91, 109, 112, 125, 141, 171
Davis, Terrie 23, 29, 32, 43, 51
Davis Family 160
Dayton (hotel) 29, 35, 43, 61, 79
Dayton, Ohio 99, 160
DeCambra, Alice 109
decentralized management 157–158, 177–178, 221
Deegan, Millie 89–90, 109, 141, 143, 148, 153, 174
Delmonico, Lee (Surkowski) 32, 34–*35*, 37, *38*, 39, 41, *45*, *47*–49, 54, 56, 60–61, 66, 73–75, 81, 86, 125, 258
Denton, Mona 74, *76*, 79–80, *88*, *92*, 99

Deschaine, Alice (Pollitt) 143, 152, 154, 185, 187, 198, 209, 232
DeShone, Nancy 127
DesLauriers, Eddie 128, 202
Doty, Ted 242
Downs, Dorothea 53, 60
Doyle, Dorothy (Harrell) "Snookie" 50, 105, 143, 154–155, 163, 208–209
Doyle, Joe 204, 219–220, 223, 234, 236–237, 239, 242, 256
Drinkwater, Maxine *243*, 245–246, 251, 257
Dubuque, Iowa 186, 195, 223
Dunn, Gertrude "Gertie" 180, *190*, 191, 194, 206, *207*, 211–212, 214–216, 218–219, 222–237, 242, *243*, 244–248, 250, 252–255, 257, 259
Dwenger Park 76, *77*
Dwojak, Loretta *35*, 43, 48

Earp, Millie 94, 102, 111, 115, 134–135, 142
East Greenville, Pennsylvania 4, 11, 74–75, 179
East Greenville Cubs 75, 179
Edgewater Gulf (hotel) 74
Eisen, Thelma "Tiby" 33, 44, 57, 105, 197, 201
Elkhart, Indiana 232, 253
Emry, Betty 91–92
English, Madeline "Maddy" 60, 91, 93, 109
English, Woody 211, 223, 247–248, 257
Erickson, Lou 143, 153, 155, 163
Evansville, Indiana 2, 74

Fabac, Betty 56
Faralla, Lillian "Lil" *99*, 121–123, 125–129, 131–135, 139–*140*, 141–147, 151, 153–154, 159–160, 162, 164–167, 169, 171, 174, 176, 182–187, 191–196, 198–199, 201, 258; no-hit games 122, 127, 131; 16-inning game 134
Faust (hotel) 19, 23, 36, 40, 105
Faut, Jean 4–5, 11, 54, 72–*76*, *77*, 80–81, 83, 85–87, 89–93, *92*, 98, *99*, *100*, 101–107, 109, 111–112, *113*, 114–116, 121–123; *124*, 125, 127, 129, 131–135, 139–147, *140*, 149, 151–155, 159–160, *161*, 162–177, *167*, 179–188, 190–191, *192*, 194–198, 201–217, *218*, 219, 221–237, 249, 252, 258–259; 15-inning game 135, 143; Jean Faut nights 109, *110*, 237; no-hit games 107, 134, 153, 177; overhand pitching 117–118; perfect games 177, 193–194, *236*–237; player-of-the-year honors 107, *167*, 177, 197, 202, *218*, 230, 237–238, 259; post-season performance 91–93, *113*, 114–115, 134–135, 154–155, 197–199, 214–219; retirement 237–238, 241–

Index

242; 17-inning games 91, 174; sidearm pitching 94–96, 99–100; 16-inning games 112, 142, 195; 20-inning game 135; 22-inning game 109
Fay, William Cullen 15, 106, 137
Feaser, Howard 57, 61–62
Ferro, Mildred 222
Fidler, Merrie 96, 157
field dimensions 12, 28, 33, 47, 52–53, 65–67, 71, 73, 94, **95**, 117, 120, 123, 137–138, 144–145, 147–148, 161, 180, 217, 221, 247–248, 252
Filarski, Helen 121–123, 125, 127–129, 134–135, **140**, 141, 143, 147, 149, 151, 159–163, **161**, 165–166, 169–170, 172–173, 175, 180, 258
Fischer, Alva Jo "Tex" 66, 70, 142, 152
Fisher, Lorraine 135
Fitzpatrick Memorial Stadium 122, 124, 128
Florreich, Lois 15, **16**, 17, 22, 24, 26–27, 32, **35**, 37, 41, 44, 46, 50, 54, 56, 60–62, 65–66, 69, 85, 102, 141, 143, 145, 151, 154, 163, 172–173, 258; no-hit game 151
Fort Wayne, Indiana 53, 66–67, 106, 123, 141, 164, 201, 205, 231, 236, 241, 257; description 58
Fort Wayne Daisies 53, 56–63, 66–67, 70, 73–74, 76, **77**, 80–81, 89, 94, **95**, 100–106, 112, 114, 118, 121–123, 125, 131–135, 137, 139–141, 143–148, 151, 153–155, 157, 159, 162–166, 171–175, 177, 180–188, 194–195, 197–198, 201–203, 205–207, 209–212, 214–217, 221–222, 224–226, 229–232, 235–237, 239–257, **249**
Foss, Betty (Weaver) 172, 184, 187, 198, 209, 231–232, 247–248, 255
Fox, Helen (Nicol) "Nicky" 21–24, 28–29, 42, 44, 50–51, 56, 62, 99, 103, 128, 143, 153–154, 170, 173, 185, 194, 198
Francis, Betty **156**, 166, 235, 240, 242–**243**, 246, 248, 250, 253–**254**, 257–258
Freeport, Illinois 200, 218, 223
Froning, Mary "Fearless" 203, 216, 222–223, 225, 228–235, 237, 242, **243**, 245–246, 248, 251, 253–257

Gacioch, Rose "Rosie" 32–**35**, 37, 43–48, **45**, 54–55, 62, 71, 80, 89–90, 143, 154, 171–172, 174, 185, 198, 208–209, 217, 219, 222, 231, 235, 245, 252
Gadsden, Alabama 74
Gallagher, Jimmy 12
Gallegos, Luisa "Chi-Chi" 118, 120, 123, 126, 131, 133–134
Ganote, Gertrude "Lefty" 49, 55, 57, 60–61, 66, 68–70, 73

Garman, Ann 222–224
Garmican Family 160
Gates, Barbara 234–235, 237, 246
Geissinger, Jean 231–232, 248–250, 254
Gembler, Al 48
Girls Baseball (magazine) 157
Girls' Pro League 5, 28, 31, 51, 54, 57, 71–72, 83, 90, 111–112, 136, 139, 159, 219–220, 248
Goldsmith, Beth 151, 175
Gonzales, Eulalia 98
Gosbee, Ann 252
Gottselig, Johnny 14, 111, 193
Graham, Mary Lou 203, 222, 224, 230
Gran Stadium 1, 97–99
Grand Rapids, Michigan 1, 6, 68, 79, 82, 102, 135, 138, 142, 144, 158, 162, 165, 172, 211, 214, 216, 223, 234, 243, 248; description 56
Grand Rapids Chicks 53, 56–58, 60–63, 65, 67–69, 72, 74, 78–83, 85, 89–94, 98, 100, 102, 104–105, 108–109, 111–115, 118–122, 125, 133–135, 137–138, 140–145, 148–149, 151–152, 154–155, 158–159, 162, 164–165, 168, 170–172, 175, 177, 180–183, 185–187, 190, 194, 196–197, 201–207, 209, 211–216, 220, 222–228, 230, 232, 234, 237, 239–240, 242–248, 250, 253–257
Grant, D. C. "Chet" 67, 72, 74–**76**, **77**, 79, 83–84, 86–87, 89, 91, 93–94, 98, **100**–107, 109, 112, 114–115, 118, 121, 128–129, 148, 247; fight with Doc Dailey 115, 118
Green, Dorothy 22
Greensboro, North Carolina 98
Gregorich, Barbara 12, 138, 201

Habben, Carol 222, 250, 255
Hageman, Johanna "Jo" 15, **16**, 19, 22–24, 26–28, 32, **35**, 39, 47, 50, 55, 62
Haine, Audrey 36, 46, 67, 111, 123
Hamilton, Jimmy 12
Harnett, Ann 21, 40, 42, 51
Harney, Lee 21–22, 28–29, 40, 79–80
Harper, Paul 12
Harrell, Dorothy "Snookie" *see* Doyle, Dorothy (Harrell) "Snookie"
Hasham, Josephine "Jo" 139–145, **140**, 147–148, 152–153, 163, 174, 183, 208, 224
Havana, Cuba 1, 94, 96, **97**, 98, **99**–**100**, 108, 118–120, 200, 202
Havlish, Jean 231
Hawthorne, Tom 25
Haylett, Alice "Al" 74, 111, 114–115, 134–135, 142
Headin, Irene 70
Helvie, Frank 178–179

Hickson, Irene 22, 112, 119, 165, 187
Hill, Joyce *see* Westerman, Joyce (Hill)
Hobbs, Nancy 222
Hoffman (hotel) 201, 244
Hoffman, Barbara 180–185, 189–**190**, **196**, 202–203, 205–206, 209, 212, 214, 221
Hohlmayer, Alice 107, 132, 183
Holda, Mary 15, **16**, 27
Holgerson, Marge (Silvestri) "Mobile" 90, 105, 112, 128, 134, 140; no-hit games 112, 141
Holle, Mabel **16**, 24, 26–28, 32
Hood, Marjorie 23–24
Horlick Field 20, 29, **35**, 39, 41, 58, 60, 65, 91–**92**, 114, 122, 143, 171
Horstman, Katie 231–232, 247–248, 251, 255
Hosbein, Marion **243**, 246, 251
Howe News Bureau 94, 187, 251
Hunt, Mrs. Randall 27
Hutchison, Anna May 41, 72–73, 80, 90–94, 103–104, 111–112, 142; no-hit game 72

integration 96, **181**, 207

Jackson, Michigan 139, 160
Jacobs, Jane 34, 74–75, 81
Jameson, Shirley 22, 51, 56
Jamieson, Janet 131
Janowsky, Loretta 181
Janssen, Fran 185
Jefferson (hotel) 81, 183
Jenkins, Marilyn 247, 253
Jewett, Christine 132
Jinright, Magdalia (Perez) "Mickey" 118, 120–121, 126, 184, 203, 217, 219, 229, 232, 236, 245–246
Jochum, Betsy "Sockum" 1–3, 11–15, **16**, **19**–20, 22, 24, 26–29, 31–34, **35**, 36, 39–40, 42–44, **45**, 46–51, 53–58, 60, 62–63, 65–67, 69–70, 73–**76**, 77–81, 83–84, 86, 89–91, **92**, 93, 98–**99**, **100**, 101–104, 107–109, 111–112, 114, 116, 119–122, 125–128, 130–136, 251, 258; 16-inning game 57
Jochum, Frances 13
Jochum, Nick 13
Johnson, Susan 96
Johnston, Jim 208
Jones, Marguerite 34, 43
Jones, Marilyn 128, 212, 234, 249
Jonnard, Bubber 36
Junor, Daisy 74–75, **76**, 81, 83, 85–87, 91, **92**, 93, 98–99, **100**, 101, 108–109, 111–112, 114–115, 121–123, 127, 129–130
Junor, Dave 86

Kabick, Jo 48–49, 63, 74, 78–79, 87, 103, 111

Kalamazoo, Michigan 158, 164, 233
Kalamazoo Lassies 121, 158, 164–167, 169–171, 174, 176–177, 180–182, 185–187, 189, 191, 195, 201–210, 212–214, 221, 224–228, 230–237, *236*, 240–242, 244–246, 248–250, 252–258; managed by Bonnie Baker 164–167, 180
Kamenshek, Dorothy "Dottie" 13, 40, 43, 51, 66, 72, 80, 84, 90, 105, 107, 143, 145, 154–155, 163, 171–172, 187, 194, 197–198, 235, 241
Keagle, Merle "Pat" 44, 48, 51, 175
Kelley, Jackie 98, *100*, 102, 105, 108, 111, 163, 173, 183, 207, 217, 222, 236
Kellogg, Vivian 70, *77*, 114, 145, 165, 171
Kemmerer, Beatrice "Beatty" 182, 186, *189*
Kendall Family 160
Kenosha, Wisconsin 13, 23, 28, 35, 61, 134, 151; description 21
Kenosha Comets 10, 15–17, 21–26, 28–29, 31–32, 35–36, 39–45, 48–51, 53, 55–58, 60–66, 68, 74, 79, 85, 87, 89, 91, 98–100, 103, 105, 107, 109–110, 118, 121, 126–129, 132, 134–135, 141, 143–145, 148, 151–152, 154, 159, 162, 164–165, 170–171, 175, 178, 182, 185–187, 193–195, 203, 226; financial difficulties 193, 195, 199, 201, 215
Keppel, Evelyn 98, *100*
Key, Dottie 154, 198, 239
Kidd, Sue 3–4, 11, *156*, 172–174, 180, 183, 185–186, 191–192, 194, 196–198, 202–209, *204*, 211–212, 214, 216–217, 222–231, 233–237, 242, *243*, 244–246, 248, 250–257, 259; doubleheader complete-game wins 228, 230; Sue Kidd Night 228
Kleinhans, Shirley 121
Kline, Maxine 163, 180, 185, 197, 205, 209, 211, 245
Klosowski, Dolores 55, 60
Kloza, Jack 43
Knoxville, Tennessee 74
Kober, Rob 44
Kobuszewski, Theresa 87
Koehn, Phyllis "Sugar" 62, 64–70, 73–74, 76, 78–85, 87, 89–93, *92*, 98–99, *100*, 101–105, 111–112, 114–115, 117, 121–123, 126, 131, 141, 153, 258
Kotil, Arlene "Riley" *156*, *161*, 163–166, 169–170, 172, 180, 182, 186, 189, *190*
Kotowicz, Irene 101, 142
Kott, Harlow 246
Krick, Jaynie 121–123, 125–127, 129, 131, 134, 139, *140*, 141–142
Kruckel, Marie *76*, 80, 86, *92*, 122, 127, 132, 151

Kunkel, Anna 160, 162, 169, 180, 182
Kurys, Sophie 14, 22, 28, 57, 84, 90, 93, 112, 195, 252, 258; player-of-the-year honors 84, 93; stolen base leader 258

Lafayette (hotel) 231, 244
Lafayette, Indiana 203, 242
Lakefront Stadium 21, 25, 29, 44, 79, 103, 151
Landis, Kenesaw Mountain 9, 11
Lansing, Michigan 56, 139
Larson Family 160
LaSalle (hotel) 133
Latina players *see* Cuban players
A League of Their Own 2–3, 11, 258
LeDuc, Noella "Pinky" 224, 230, 235, 245, 247
Lee, Dolores 255
Lenard, Jo 114, 201–203, 206–208, 211, 213, 215–216, 218–219, 223, 227–229, 234, 237
Leo, Fred K. 159–160, 164–165, 170–172, 177–178, 186–187, 199, 201, 212
Leon, Ralph 120
Lerner, Mary 222
Lesko, Jeneane 6
Lessing, Ruth 46, 119
Lester, Mary Lou 21, 23, *35*, 40, 48
Life (magazine) 3, 53
Lima, Ohio 139
Lindstrom Family 160
Lippincott Park 235
Little, Olive 17, 20, 22, 37, 80
Livengood, Clarence 62
living conditions for players 18–19, 26–27, 86
Lonetto, Sarah 109
Lovell, Jean 166, 249, 257
Luckey, Lillian *76*, 79, 81–82, *88*, *92*
Ludwig, Harriet 26
Luna, Betty 44, 55–56, 58–61, 63–69, 75, *76*, 78–85, *88*, 90–93, *92*, 98, 105, 141, 165–166; no-hit game 85

MacLean, Lucella 15, *16*, 19, 21–23, 25–28, 30, 32, 36, 39, 42, *45*, 48, 57
Macon, Georgia 74
Macy, Sue 86, 96
Madden, W. C. 213
Maguire, Dorothy "Mickey" 48, 51, 114
Mahon, Elizabeth "Lib" 55–57, *59*, 60, 63–67, 69–70, 72–74, *76*, 79–80, 83–84, 86, 90–91, *92*, 93, 97–98, *99*, *100*, 101–102, 108, 112, 114, 116, 121–122, 124–131, 133–134, 138–139, 142–145, 147, 149, 152–155, 159–160, *161*, 162–165, 168–175, 180, 182–188, 193–194, 197–199, 202–203, 206, 208–209, 211–214, 220–221, 233, 258
Mahoney, Marie "Red" 98, *100*, 101, 103, 108–109, 121, 129
Makielski, Betty 27
Malott, Robert 170
Management Corporation (All-American League) 52, 118, 157–158, 177–179, 200, 242, 247
Mandella, Lenora 183, 201–202, 206
Mansfield, Marie 197–198, 219, 223, 245
Markey, Morris 175–176
Marks, Gloria 20, 22, 29
Marlowe, Jean 129, 151, 175, 185, 193, 195, 255
Marrero, Mirta 118, 120–121, 183, 194, 205, 235
Marsh, Doris 53
Marsh Family 160
Marsh Field 82, 114, 225, 230, 234
Marshall, Penny 2
Marshall, Theta "Tee" 98, *100*, 101–103, 107, 112, 114, 119, 121–123, 125, 129
Match Corporation Queens 57
Mathias, Bill 253
Mattson, Jackie 160
Matuzewski, Joan 222–223, 225
McAdams, Mrs. Thomas 19, 27
McCall's (magazine) 175
McCammon, Earl 201, 208, 217, *218*, 219, 221, 229, 240, 256
McCormick, Judy 245–246, 251
McCreary, Ethel 24
McCune, Frances 37
McFadden, Betty 15, *16*, 17, 20–21, 23–24
McGann, Al 31, 53, 86, 168, 172, 174
McGowan Family 191
McKenna, Betty 229, 241
McKenna, Eddie 21
McKinley, Theresa 139
McManus, Marty 52–53, 55, 58, 60–63, 65–71, 75, 83, 85, 118–122, 125–126, 128–129, 131–132, 135–136, 148
Meacham, Mildred 133
Mead, William 11
meal money revolt 157–158, 168, 172, 174
Meier, Naomi "Sally" 84, 151, 166, 183, 229, 241
Memorial Park/Field 101, 143, 153, 175, 183, 194, 197–198, 205, 211, 231, 249, 253, 255
Metesh, Bernice 121, 126, 128
Metrolis, Norma 121–123, 127, 131, 139, *140*
Meyer, Alice (sometimes reported as Alice Mayer) 127, 129, 132
Meyer, Anna 63
Meyer, Rita 123
Meyerhoff, Arthur E. 12, 14, 31, 52, 74, 118, 125–126, 152, 157–158, 177, 247

Meyers, Benny 137
Michigan City, Indiana 134, 255
Mickelsen, Darlene 55, 58, 61
Middleton, Ruth 160, 162, 241
Milford, Indiana 139
Milwaukee, Wisconsin 31, 33, 40, 91, 222; description 20
Milwaukee Chicks 31–37, 39–40, 42–46, 48–51, 53, 55, 148; financial difficulties 49; move to Grand Rapids 53, 56
Minneapolis, Minnesota 31, 131
Minneapolis Millerettes 31–34, 36, 40, 42–44, 46, 48, 50–51, 53, 55, 63, 127, 151; move to Fort Wayne 53, 151; traveling team 118, 127
Moffet, Jane 207, 209
Monroe, Michigan 222
Montalbano, Rose 181–183, 186, *190*, 203, 205, 222–26
Monty, Rose *see* Montalbano, Rose
Moon, Dottie 80
Mooney, Georgette (Vincent) "Jette" 123, 142–145, 159–160, *161*, 164–167, 170–175, 180, 182–183, 185–186, 191, 193, 195, 197–198, 202, 204–207, 209, 211–212, 215–219, 253, 256
Mooney, Robert 207
Moore, Eleanor 206, 224
Moore, Helen 32, *35*, 42, *45*
Moore, Lucille 15, *76*, 86, *92*, *100*, 122, 135
Moore, Mike *76*
Morris, Carolyn 44, 50, 60, 63, 80, 90; no-hit game 50; perfect game 63
Mudge, Nancy 225, 229, 244, 250
Mueller, Dolores 139, *140*
Mueller, Dorothy "Dottie" 104, 111, 123, 140, 159–160, *161*, 162–168, 171–175, 180–182, 185–189, *190*, 191, 193–195, *196*, 197–198, 203–209, 212, 214, 216, 221, 226
Muncie, Indiana 160
Murphy, Leo 90
Muskegon, Michigan 68, 114, 133, 147, 205, 220; description 82
Muskegon Belles 205, 220, 222, 224–227, 229–232, 234–235, 240–241; financial difficulties 234, 239; traveling team 240
Muskegon Lassies 68, 73, 82, *87*, 89–90, 94, 98, 100–105, 107, 109, 111–112, 114–115, 118, 121–122, 125–127, 130, 133–134, 139, 141–142, 144, 147, 151–152, 154, 158, 160, 162–164, 169, 171, 177; financial difficulties 158, 164; managed by Bonnie Baker 164; move to Kalamazoo 158, 164

Nahtyk, Liz 98, *100*
National Baseball Hall of Fame 2, 118, 253, 258
National Girls Baseball League *see* Chicago League
National Girls Softball League *see* Chicago League
Naum, Dorothy "Dottie" 74, *76*, 91–*92*, 98, 128, 175, 186–187, 228, 230
Nelson, Doris "Dodie" 43
Nelson, Helen 17
Nesbitt, Mary (Crews) 17, 20–21, 29, 34, 41–42, 68
Neville, Paul 137, 139, 142, 155, 157, 166, 170, 175, 177, 179–180, 182, 184–185, 193, 196
Nicol, Helen *see* Fox, Helen (Nicol)
Nicollet Park 36, 46
Niehoff, Bert 14, *16*, 23–27, 31–32, 34–*35*, 37, 39–44, 46–50, 53, 122
Niemiec, Dolores "Dolly" 139, *140*, 185
Nordquist, Helen "Nordie" 225, 229, 242–245, *243*, 248, 251–253, 255–256
Norris, Donna 226, 232
North High Field 58, 60, 66

O'Brian, Penny 70
Occidental (hotel) 225
Odell, Carolyn 86–*87*
Official Girls' Baseball Rules (1946–1947) 94
Ogden, Joanne "Jo" 222–224, 227, 229
O'Hara, Janice "Jerry" 21, 45, 99
Olinger, Marilyn 125, 135
Oliver (hotel) 82, 161
Opa-Locka, Florida 119–121, 131, 200, 202
Ortman, Dorothy "Blondie" 34
overhand pitching 6, 10, 64, 80, 90, 94, 96, 100–101, 117, 120, 128, 132, 138, 145, *146*, 155, 158, 161, 180, 200, 228, 237, 247, 258–259

Paire, Lavonne "Pepper" 33, 42, 63, 104, 112, 134–135, 185; composer of "The All-American Girl" 33
Panos, Vickie 32–34, 37, 39–40, 48
Pascagoula, Mississippi 4, 73–75, 85–86, 119
Patty Family 160
Payne, Bobbie 194
Peach Orchard *see* Beyer Stadium
Pearson, Marguerite "Dolly" 226–234, 237, 242, 253
Peoria, Illinois 68, 103, 109, 123, 140, 163, 183; description 81
Peoria Redwings 3, 74–75, 79, 81, 94, 100, 103–105, 109, 111–112, 114, 118, 121, 123, 125–126, 133, 135–136, 138–141, 143–145, 147, 149, 153–154, 158–160, 162–167, 169–174, 177, 182–183, 185, 187, 191, 195, 197, 201, 203, 222, 251; financial difficulties 170–171, 195, 197, 201
Peoria Stadium 81, 123, 138, 140, 163, 174
Peppas, June 212, 244–245, 249, 254, 257–258
Perez, Magdalia "Mickey" *see* Jinright, Magdalia (Perez) "Mickey"
Perkins, Joy 226
Perlick, Edie 18, 28, 66, 92, 104, 112, 143, 145, 151
Peru (hotel) 32
Peru, Illinois 32, 63
Peshkin, Hy 133
Peters, Marjorie "Marge" 16–17, 20, 22–23
Peterson, Dick 253
Petras, Ernestine "Teeny" 79, 108, 114–115, 125–126
Petryna, Betty *see* Allen, Betty (Petryna)
Pieper, Marge 76, 102, 126, 211, 229
Pirok, Pauline "Pinky" 22, 36, 61–67, 69–70, 74, 85, 91–*92*, 98, *99*, *100*, 101–102, 105, 108–109, 111, 114–115, 121–122, 124–129, 134–135, 258
pitching distances 13, 66, 94, *95*, 117, 120, 137–138, 144–145, 147–148, 200, 221, 247
player walkout 212–219, 221, 237
Playland Park 2, 53, 80, 82, 84, *87*, 89, 90, 92, 101–105, 109, 111–112, 115, 122–123, *124*, 125, 127–129, 132–134, 138–144, 147, 151–154, 160, *161*, 163–166, *167*, 169–170, 172–173, 175–177, 180–184, *181*, 186, *192*, 193, 195, 197–198, 200, 202–203, *204*, 205, 207, 209–212, 215–217, 222, 224–226, 228–230, 234–237, 239–250, *243*, 252–256; description 2, 77–*78*, 82, 180, 202, 222, 239, 247
Plymouth, Indiana 202
Pollitt, Alice "Al" *see* Deschaine, Alice (Pollitt)
Pratt, Ed 229
Pratt, Mary 28, 43–44, 49
Proefrock, Ellen (Ahrndt) *see* Ahrndt, Ellen
Pryer, Charlene "Shorty" 104, *161*, 164, 168, 170–174, *173*, 180, 182–183, 186–188, *190*, 193–198, 201–206, 208–214, 220, 233, 258
Pulaski Park 37

racial integration *see* integration
Racine (hotel) 39, 91, 103, 171
Racine, Wisconsin 14, 20–21, *38*, 39, 58, 60, 171; description 20
Racine Belles 10, 13–18, 20–26, 28–29, 31–36, *35*, 39, 41–46, 50, 53, 57–58, 60, 62, 65–66,

68–72, 74, 79–80, 82–84, 89–94, 98, 101, 103–105, 109, 111–115, 118–119, 121–123, 125–126, 131, 134, 141–144, 151, 153, 159, 162, 165, 167, 171, 215; move to Battle Creek 182
Raleigh, North Carolina 99
Rawlings, Johnny 74, 115, 120, 138, 159, 222, 225
Read Park 218
Reardon, Doris 222
Redbirds Stadium 222
Reed, Bob 257
Reeser, Sara 104
Reynolds, Mary 125, 154, 164, 174
Rice, Jack 48
Richard, Ruth 141, 154, 195, 198, 209, 217, 222, 245, 257
Ricketts, Joyce 224, 256
Rigney, Hank 210
Ringenberg, Al 194
Rios, Georgiana 120
Risinger, Earlene "Beans" 138, 142, 144, 162, 223, 227, 237, 243
Roanoke, Virginia 99
Rockford, Illinois 19–20, 23, 36, 40–41, 44, 50, 70, 89, 105, 143, 170, 183, 185, 195, 208, 217, 231, 244, 252–253; description 19
Rockford Peaches 10, 13, 15–17, 19–24, 26, 28–29, 31–33, 35–37, 40–41, 43–*45*, 49–51, 53–55, 57–58, 60–63, 65–67, 70–72, 79–81, 84–86, 89–93, 98, 101–102, 104–105, 107–108, 112, 118, 121–122, 126, 128, 133–145, 148–149, 151–155, 157–163, 165–166, 170–173, 177, 180, 182–183, 185, 187, 193–195, 197–198, 202–203, 205–209, 211–212, 216–219, 222–223, 225–226, 229, 231–232, 234–236, 239–242, 244–246, 250, 252–257
Rockola Chicks 57
Romatowski, Jenny *76*, 80, *92*, 159–160, *161*, 162, 169, 205, 213, 224, 250
rookies 1, 3–4, 12–13, 25–26, 39, 53–54, 119–120, *156*, 159–160, 179–*181*, 186, 189–190, 221–223, 241, 247, 251
Roosevelt, Franklin Delano 11, 22, 34, 41, 72
Ross, Lucella (MacLean) *see* MacLean, Lucella
Ross, Marty 210
Roth, Eilaine 165
Roth, Elaine 123, 160, *161*, 162–165, 167, 170–172, 174–175, 180, 182, 233, 244, 246, 257
Rotvig, Barbara 151, 195
Rountree, Mary 114, 125
Rowe (hotel) 56, 102, 114, 144, 223, 234
Ruck, Rob 120
Ruetz, Edward 159, 178, 202
Ruhnke, Irene 21, 40
Ruiz, Gloria 118, 120

rules 12–15, 17, 24, 33, 52, 73–74, 94, *95*, 120, 132, 157, 160–161, 179–180, 199, 252
Rumsey, Janet "Jan" 183–186, 191, 194–195, *196*, 198, 203–208, 211–212, 214, 216–218, 222–235, 237, 242–249, *243-244*, 251–257, 259
Russo, Marge 246, 252
Rusynyk, Betty (McFadden) *see* McFadden, Betty

St. Joseph, Michigan 180, 235, 240, 253
salaries 13, 31, 53–54, 57, 84–85, 106, 118, 136–137, 158, 164, 172, 175–176, 179, 199–202, 206–207, 221, 247–248
Salisbury, Shirley Ann 222, 226
Sams, Doris "Sammye" 74, 94, 98, 107, 111, 114, 127, 144, 151–152, 165, 206, 209, 212, 252; player-of-the-year honors 107, 221
Sandford, Pi 203
Satterfield, Doris 135, 142, 145, 182
Savannah, Georgia 99
Schalk, Ray 154
Schillace, Clara 29
Schmeider, William R. 179, 201
Schofield, June 151
Schrall, Leo 111, 154
Schroeder, Dorothy "Dottie" 15, *16*, 19, 22, 26–28, 32–33, *35*, 36, 39, 41, 44, *45*, 48, 54, 56, 60–62, 64, 71, 85, 114, 153, 184, 205, 211, 235, 239, 246, 249–250, 253, 257–258
Schweigerdt, Gloria 187
Scott, Pat 197–198, 226
Sears, Don 241
Sears, Janet (Wiley) *see* Wiley, Janet "Pee Wee"
Sells, Ken 13–14, 31
Seville-Biltmore (hotel) 97–98, *100*
Shafranis, Geraldine (sometimes reported as Geraldine Shafranas) 15, 17
Shattuck, Debra 240
Shaughnessy Playoffs 53, *92*, 93–94, 100, 109, *113*, 114–115, 118–119, 128, 134–135, 137, 177, 183, 197, 200, 210, 214, *218*, 219–220, 231–232, *243*, 248, 256–259
Sheehan, Bill 162, 179, 201–202, 207
Sheehan, Jack 13
Sheffield, Lois 203
Shewbridge Field 126
Shinen, Kay 56
Shively, Twila "Twi" 78, 114–115, 125, 154, 169
Shollenberger, Fern 186, 193, 224
Shuman, Amy 74
sidearm pitching 6, 72–74, 80, 89–90, 94, 100–101, 104, 117, 122, 126, 131, 141, 145–146, 162, 167, 185, 191, 195, 258

Silvestri, Marge *see* Holgerson, Marge (Silvestri) "Mobile"
Simmons Field 171, 186–187
Singleton, Mrs. *124*, 235
Skokan, Josephine 20
Skupien, Mitch 182, 245
Sloan, Francis 75, 80
Sloppy Joe's 1, 98
Smith, Charlotte 28
Smith, Helen "Gig" 6
Smith, Jean 121, 234
Smith, Marjean 121
Sopkovic, Catherine "Kay" 55
South Bend Tribune 5–6, 15, 17–18, 23, 26, 28–29, 31, 34, 49–50, 52–53, 55–56, 58, 61–63, 67–68, 70, 72–73, 75, 89, *113*, 114, 120, 122, 127, 129, 137–139, 142, 145, 147–148, 157, 166, 171, 174, 179, 181, 187–188, 198, 200, 204, 212–213, 217, 219–221, 223, 237, 240–243, 248–249, 256
South High Field 56, 79, 142, 223, 226
Southmoor (hotel) 126
Sowers, Barbara 224, 245
spring training 1, 32, 37–*38*, 39, 52–54, 63, 73–74, 94, 96, *97*, 98, *99-100*, 118–120, 138–139, 158–160, 180, 202–203, *204*, 222–223, 241–242
Springfield Sallies 118–119, 122, 124–131, 133, 149; financial difficulties 118, 127–128, 136; rookie team 118, 127–128, 136–137, *156*
Stefani, Margaret "Marge" 15, *16*, 20, 22–28, 32–34, *35*, 39–40, 42–43, 46, 48, 54, 56, 60, *65-67*, *69*, 73–76, 78, 80, 83, 86, 91, *92*, 93, 98, *100*, 101–105, 107–109, 111–112, 114, 116, 120–122, 258; as chaperone 136, 139, *140*, 160, *161*, 162, 164, 172, 176
Steffes, Helen (Filarski) *see* Filarski, Helen
Stephens, Ruby 98, *100*, 101–105, 109, 111, 114, 132, 148, 175, 201; no-hit game 124–125, 127
Stevenson, Emily 45
Stis, Charley 66
Stoll, Jane "Jeep" 115, 133, 139, *140*, 141, 143–145, 147, 149, 153–155, 159–160, *161*, 162, 165, 168–174, 180, 182, 185, 188, 193–195, *196*, 197–198, 201, 203, 205–206, 212–214, 220–221, 226, 229–230, 233, 244, 258
Stolze, Dottie 104, 114
Stone, Lou 66
Stovroff, Shirley 122, 131, 133, 135, 139–*140*, 147, 149, 153–154, 159–160, *161*, 162, 165, 169–170, 172–*173*, 180, 182, 184–185, 188, *189*, 193–195, 197–199, 202–207, 209–215, 220, 233, 258
Studnicka, Mary Lou 187, 205, 214, 223, 226, 234

Stumpf, Eddie 14, 20
Suehsdorf, Adie 155
Sullivan, Robert 132
Surkowski, Anne 55–56, 64, 66, 69
Surkowski, Lena "Lee" *see* Delmonico, Lena "Lee"
Swayne Field 210–211

Talbott, Betty 222
Tetzlaff, Doris 48, 63, 115, 125, 151
Thompson, Annabelle 17, 20
Thompson, Fredda *see* Acker, Fredda (Thompson)
Thompson, Viola "Tommie" 63, 74, 76, 79–81, 83, 90, *92*, 98, *100*, 103, 147
Toledo, Ohio 200, 210–212, 222
Towner, Bob 152
train travel 1, 19, *45*, 74–75
Trezza, Betty "Moe" 70, 73, 90, 106, 112, 143
Tronnier, Ellen 15
Trujillo, Nolly 72
trustee administration (All-American League) 12, 31, 52
Tucker, Betty 81, 125, 127
Tucker, Julius 201
Turkey Ridge Field 12

Ullenberg, Charley 40
umpires 9, 20–21, 40, 44, 48–49, 52, 73, 89, 94, 103, 109, 115, 133–134, 154–155, 161, 163, 165, 187, 194–195, 208, 212, 229, 246, 256; salaries 199, 202, 234
underhand pitching 6, 10, 12, 23, 28, 33, 46, 52, 57, 61, 64, 73–74, 85, 90, 94, 101, 104, 107, 117, 138, 167, 180, 247, 258
uniforms 2, *14*–15, 21, 32, 57, 80–82, 122, 128, *179*, 180, 184, 187, 211
Ushers Club 2, 78, 101

Valentine, Ken 208
Van Der Heyden, George 101
Van Orman (hotel) 236
Van Orman, Harold 171, 201, 240
Van Wert, Ohio 139
Vanderlip, Dolly 241–242, *243*, 245–248, 250–257
Ventura, Betty 241
Villa, Marge "Poncho" 128, 144
Vincent, Georgette "Jette" *see* Mooney, Georgette "Jette"
Vonderau, Kate *77*, 125, 211, 224, 235, 241
Voyce, Inez 74–75, *76*, 78–81, 83, 85, 87, 90, *92*, 98, 107, 111, 114–115, 172, 216, 227

Waddell, Helen 160, 162
Wagner, Audrey 56, 103, 107, 121, 127, 151, 201, 252
Wagoner, Betty "Old Reliable" 127, 129–130, 132, 134–135, 139, *140*, 142–144, 147, 149, *150*, 151–154, 159, *161*, 162–165, 168–170, 172–175, 180, 182–186, 188, 193–194, 197–198, 202–203, 205–209, 211–213, 215–219, 222–237, 241–243, 246–248, 250–251, 253–258
Walker, Martha 21
Wambsganss, Bill "Wamby" 53, 80, 114
Wanless, Betty 242–*243*, 245–246, 248, 250, 252, 254–255, 257
Ward, Gadget 115
Warner Family 160
Warren, Nancy "Hank" 101, 109, 126, 173–174, 197, 224, 230, 255, 257
Warsaw, Indiana 256
Washington Park 32
Waveland Park 53–54
Wawryshyn, Evelyn "Evie" 157, 183–184, 188
Way, Rose Virginia 14, *16*, 22, 27, 32, 42
Weaver, Jean 197, 232
Weaver, Joanne "Jo" 197, 205–206, 232, 243, 248–249, 252–255
Weddle, Mary 246, 255
Wegman, Marie 151
Wenzell, Marge 166, 208, 213, 215–216, 221–223, 228, 233
West Baden, Indiana 160
Westerman, Helen 22
Westerman, Joyce (Hill) 73–74, *76*, 80, 109, 174, 201, 203, 205–207, 210–212, 214–221
Western Canada Softball League 86
Whalen, Dorothy 121–122
White Star Line 75, *76*
Whiting, Betty 44–45, 125–126, 129, 132–135, 139, *140*, 141–143, 145, 147–148, 153–155, 159–160, 162–163, 166, 169, 171, 189, 211
Whitney, Norma 139
Wiley, Janet "Pee Wee" 160, *161*, 169–170, 173, 175, 180–183, 189, *190*, 191, 193, 196, 202–203, 205–207, 209–210, 212, 241
Williams, Jim 158
Williams, Ruth 102–105, 111–115, 121, 124–125, 128–129, 131, 133–134, 138–139, 142–145, 148, 151–154, 159–160, *161*, 164–165, 167, 171–172, 174, 195, 237
Wilson, Jean 17, 20
Wiltse, Dottie *see* Collins, Dottie (Wiltse)
Winch, Carol 262
Winsch, Karl 176–177, *178*, 179–*181*, 183, *184*, 186, 188, *189*, *190*, 191, *192*, 193–197, 199, 201–206, 208–210, 216–217, *218*, 219–224, 226–231, 233–234, 237, 241–242, *243*, 245–247, 250–251, 253–257, 259; player walkout 212–215
Winsch, Kevin 259
Winsch, Larry *124*, 127, 131, 166, 176, *192*, 215, 235, 259
Winter, Joanne "Jo" 23, 34, 41, 57–58, 69, 72, 83, 90–93, 103, 111, 122–123, 142
Wirth, Senaida "Shoo Shoo" 72, 74, *76*, 78–80, 83, 86–87, 89, 91, *92*, 93, 98, *99*–*100*, 101–102, 104–105, 107–108, 120–122, 125, 127, 129, *130*, 132–135, 138–143, *140*, 145, 147–149, 151–153, 155, 159–160, *161*, 162–163, 168, 170–173, 175, 180, 182, *184*, 187–188, *190*, 193–194, 198, 203, 258
Wisham, Mary (Nesbitt) *see* Nesbitt, Mary (Crews)
Wisniewski, Connie 33, 40, 44, 49–51, 57, 61, 63, 68, 72, 78, 90, 94, 102, 111, 115, 142, 145, 182, 251; player-of-the-year honors 102
Wohlwender, Marion 13
women managers in All-American League 133, 139, 164–167, 180, 208
Wood, Mary 81, 99
Wright, Jack 147
Wrigley, Philip K. 1, 9, 11–15, 23, 31, 51–52, 157, 247, 258
Wrigley Field 1, 12–14, 17, 22, 25, 85, 139

Youngberg, Renae 227, 234, 236–237
Youngen, Lois 226–228, 237, *243*, 251, 255

Ziegler, Alma "Gabby" 48–49, 51, 115, 135, 165, 185, 211, 216, 223, 234, 239
Zingone, Al 165
Zintak, Lenny 118, 164
Zollner Piston Stadium 114, 143
Zonia, Vialat 120
Zoss, Barney 109

www.ingramcontent.com/pod-product-compliance
Lightning Source LLC
Chambersburg PA
CBHW081541300426
44116CB00015B/2717